DATE DUE APR 25 '13

DEC 1 2013			
7/ JUN 0 5 2017			
JUN 0 5 2017			

Fourth Edition

CRIMINAL PROCEDURE

FROM FIRST CONTACT TO APPEAL

John L. Worrall
University of Texas at Dallas

PEARSON

Boston Columbus Indianapolis New York San Francisco Upper Saddle River
Amsterdam Cape Town Dubai London Madrid Milan Munich Paris Montreal Toronto
Delhi Mexico City Sao Paulo Sydney Hong Kong Seoul Singapore Taipei Tokyo

Editorial Director: Vernon R. Anthony
Senior Acquisitions Editor: Eric Krassow
Assistant Editor: Tiffany Bitzel
Editorial Assistant: Lynda Cramer
Director of Marketing: David Gesell
Marketing Manager: Cyndi Eller
Senior Marketing Coordinator: Alicia Wozniak
Marketing Assistant: Les Roberts
Senior Managing Editor: JoEllen Gohr
Production Manager: Susan Hannahs
Senior Art Director: Jayne Conte
Cover Designer: Suzanne Behnke
Cover Art: Fotolia
Full-Service Project Management: Abinaya Rajendran, Integra Software Services, Ltd.
Composition: Integra Software Services, Ltd.
Printer/Bindery: Edwards Brothers, Inc.
Cover Printer: Lehigh-Phoenix Color
Text Font: Palatino 10/12

Credits and acknowledgments borrowed from other sources and reproduced, with permission, in this textbook appear on the appropriate page within the text.

Many of the designations by manufacturers and seller to distinguish their products are claimed as trademarks. Where those designations appear in this book, and the publisher was aware of a trademark claim, the designations have been printed in initial caps or all caps.

Library of Congress Cataloging-in-Publication Data
Worrall, John L.
    Criminal procedure : from first contact to appeal / John L. Worrall.—4th ed.
        p. cm.
    ISBN-13: 978-0-13-270586-8 (alk. paper)
    ISBN-10: 0-13-270586-9 (alk. paper)
    1. Criminal procedure—United States.   2. Appellate procedure—United States.   I. Title.
    KF9619.W67 2012
    345.73'05—dc23
                                                                                    2011023375

10 9 8 7 6 5 4 3 2 1

ISBN 10:   0-13-270586-9
ISBN 13: 978-0-13-270586-8

To Dylan
for never letting life get boring.

CONTENTS

PREFACE

I decided to write this book, *Criminal Procedure: From First Contact to Appeal*, after I had taught criminal procedure for several years. During each course, my students typically asked a litany of "what if" questions and became curious about the rules of criminal procedure after the police arrest and book a suspect. Students also expressed frustration with the fact that many of the leading books on criminal procedure presupposed a certain degree of familiarity with the criminal process, including an understanding of basic terminology. Students came to loathe these books' excessive use of legalese and obtuse descriptions of criminal procedure topics that had no real-life applications.

In addition, students frequently pointed out, as did I, that there are often significant differences between what the courts require and what happens in the real world of criminal justice. For instance, consider the definition of a *seizure* for the purposes of the Fourth Amendment. A seizure occurs when a reasonable person would believe he or she is not free to leave. Yet many times, students find this definition wanting and ask, "If a person is not seized according to this definition, is he or she really free to leave?" This question highlights the differences between what this book calls *theory* and *reality*. It and countless other similar questions prompted me to write a criminal procedure book of my own, one that takes a comprehensive yet basic approach to criminal procedure and that connects the material to the real world with examples and exercises.

By way of preview, then, this book presents an introduction to criminal procedure, from the point at which an individual first comes into contact with the police all the way through the appeals process. Approximately half of the book is devoted to traditional criminal procedure topics—notably, search-and-seizure as well as interrogation and identification procedures. The remainder of the book moves beyond these topics and discusses the pretrial process; the roles of defense attorneys, prosecutors, and grand juries; plea bargaining and guilty pleas; rights of criminal defendants at trial; and appeals and *habeas corpus*.

PRESENTATION

The material in *Criminal Procedure* is covered, in large part, by focusing on the constitutional rights of criminal defendants, as interpreted by the U.S. Supreme Court. To this end, many leading Supreme Court decisions are discussed; however, lengthy excerpts from the actual decisions have been reduced to relevant remarks in order to avoid distracting from the many important concepts introduced. In order to maintain a real-world focus, the book also incorporates many actual legal documents and excerpts from official policy manuals of police departments and other criminal justice agencies around the United States.

Criminal procedure should not be confused with *evidence procedure* or *trial procedure*. Evidence procedure concerns the rules for presenting evidence to prove guilt (or the lack thereof); thus, evidence courses cover such topics as types of evidence, rules for presenting witness testimony, hearsay, and the like. This book touches on evidence only tangentially—by discussing witness questioning and the police actions used to secure evidence through search-and-seizure. But the focus on evidence does not move beyond these two issues. Likewise, this book is not about trial procedure. That is, it does not address the nuances of criminal trials, including the order of events at trial, what objections can be raised, instructions to the jury, and so on. Trial procedure is a topic typically covered in law school.

Instead, this book presents a comprehensive introduction to criminal procedure, thoroughly presenting basic legal concepts and issues in a conversational written style and tone. Given this content coverage and the frequent use of examples from actual legal documents and policy guides, readers who are pursuing careers in criminal justice will find this book especially useful. Individuals who are already employed in criminal justice will find the book useful as well. Moreover, because the book constitutes more than a general overview of criminal procedure, it should prove beneficial to aspiring law students. But, it should not be over the heads of students with little or no background in criminal justice.

FEATURES

Criminal Procedure has a number of pedagogical features that will benefit readers. Each chapter begins with an outline of the topics covered and learning objectives, giving readers an at-a-glance preview of the content. Lists of key terms and key cases are also included. Each term is defined in a glossary appearing at the end of the book, and each key case is then highlighted in the margins near where it is discussed in the chapter text. Each chapter ends with a set of Review Questions, which cover the basic content and also ask readers to correlate what they have learned. Bulleted summaries are also provided at the end of the chapter with each heading aligning with learning objectives. Other key features are as follows:

- Decision-Making Exercises are scattered throughout each chapter. Each exercise places the reader in the position of judge, asking him or her to decide a case based on the facts presented. The answers to the exercises are available to instructors. They explain what was decided in the actual case on which a given exercise was based or what likely would be decided given precedent in the area.
- The book makes extensive use of actual legal forms, calls attention to important rules (such as those spelled out in the *Federal Rules of Criminal Procedure*), and reprints police department policy manual excerpts. Presented as figures, these materials show how professionals working in the field of criminal justice deal with the concepts and issues covered throughout the book.
- Web links and Exercises. Each chapter concludes with a few Web links and exercises designed to elaborate on and reinforce key issues and points raised in the chapter.

In short, this book is intended to move beyond the basic introductory approach to criminal procedure that many of the competing books have taken but not to a level that presupposes any knowledge about the criminal process. Many competing texts focus overwhelmingly on search-and-seizure and on interrogation and confession procedures. This book covers these topics as well, and in great detail, but it also covers many more topics. This is because criminal procedure consists of much more than interactions between the police and criminal suspects.

NEW TO THE FOURTH EDITION

The fourth edition has been extensively revised:

- The latest Supreme Court cases, including those from the 2010 term (including some cases decided in 2011), have been added where appropriate and necessary.
- Learning objectives now appear at the start of each chapter.
- New end-of-chapter summaries are more comprehensive and are organized by chapter learning objectives.
- The latest police policy manuals are included where needed.
- Chapter 1 contains a summary of key Supreme Court cases in the war on terrorism.
- Bulleted lists have been revised and updated throughout.

- Chapter 8 contains a new section on waiver of the right to counsel in the confessions context.
- The beginning of Chapter 8 has been significantly revised and streamlined.
- Chapter 15 contains more comprehensive coverage of sentencing cases.
- Numerous changes have been made to the instructor resource materials, with improved PowerPoint slides and media.

CONTENT

Criminal Procedure continues to be divided into five parts: (1) Introduction; (2) Search and Seizure; (3) Interrogations, Confessions, and Identification Procedures; (4) The Beginnings of Formal Proceedings; and (5) Trial, Conviction, and Beyond. The latter two topics are rarely covered in conventional criminal procedure books, particularly at the level of detail found in this text. In contrast, the traditional approach to criminal procedure rarely moves beyond the material covered in the first three parts of this text.

Part 1 contains two chapters. Chapter 1 is introductory and provides readers with the information necessary to begin studying criminal procedure. In particular, it defines criminal procedure; highlights the due process/crime control dilemma, which is at the heart of all controversies in criminal procedure; discusses the relationship among the courts, including a brief section on how to do legal research; and introduces several issues and trends in criminal procedure. Chapter 1 ends with a detailed overview of the text. Chapter 2 begins by discussing the exclusionary rule, then it considers criminal, civil, and nonjudicial remedies. Remedies are presented early in the text so readers will become aware of how people's rights can be enforced in the U.S. courts.

Part 2 covers standard search-and-seizure topics. Chapter 3 provides a framework for studying the Fourth Amendment; specifically, it defines Fourth Amendment terminology and specifies when searches-and-seizures occur. This chapter also covers the doctrine of justification, focusing on the definitions of probable cause, reasonable suspicion, and what this book calls *administrative justification*. Chapters 4 and 5 go on to cover searches-and-seizures *with* warrants and *without* warrants, respectively. Chapter 6 covers actions based on reasonable suspicion, including stops-and-frisks and investigative detentions, and Chapter 7 covers actions based on administrative justification and consent, including inventories, inspections, checkpoints, school and office searches, drug and alcohol testing, and the like.

Part 3 covers interrogations, confessions, and identification procedures. To this end, Chapter 8 focuses heavily on the Fifth Amendment's self-incrimination clause and then summarizes the proper procedures for conducting interrogations and obtaining valid confessions. Further, it also examines how the Sixth and Fourteenth Amendments govern interrogations and confessions. Chapter 9 discusses identification procedures, including the guidelines for proper pretrial identifications, and also introduces identification procedures used during trial, including the proper questioning of witnesses to assist in valid in-court identifications.

The information in Part 4 is pretrial in nature. Chapter 10 begins by discussing booking, the initial appearance, the probable cause hearing, pretrial release, the preliminary hearing, and the arraignment. This chapter also introduces the rules surrounding discovery. While discovery can occur well into a trial, most often discovery is pretrial in nature; thus, it is appropriate to discuss discovery in this context. Chapter 11 covers prosecutors, grand juries, and defense attorneys, including the constitutional guidelines by which each must abide. Of course, the actions of prosecutors, defense attorneys, and even grand juries matter outside the pretrial context, but readers should be familiar with these important actors before moving into the adjudication section. Finally, Chapter 12 covers plea bargaining and guilty pleas. Again, both can occur well into a trial, but most plea bargains and guilty pleas are undertaken in an effort to avoid trial.

Part 5 is titled "Trial, Conviction, and Beyond." Chapter 13, the first of two chapters about the defendant's rights at trial, examines the right to a speedy trial and the right to an impartial judge and jury. Chapter 14 continues the focus on rights at trial, discussing openness, confrontation, compulsory process, double jeopardy, and entrapment. Lastly, Chapter 15 covers important topics in sentencing as well as appeals and *habeas corpus*.

As noted earlier, most texts on criminal procedure give only limited coverage to the topics in Parts 4 and 5, so readers should benefit by the material presented. Once again, the purpose of this book is to present a comprehensive look at criminal procedure, demonstrating that the Constitution affects much more than the actions of law enforcement personnel.

SUPPLEMENTS

Several supplements are available for this book. A test bank that has been extensively revised for the fourth edition is available. Accompanying the test bank are answers to the book's decision-making exercises. These are available for instructors. The fourth edition is also accompanied by new and improved PowerPoint slides to assist instructors with the classroom presentations.

ACKNOWLEDGMENTS

I would like to thank those individuals who reviewed the fourth edition: Scott Belshaw, University of North Texas; Brett Curry, Georgia Southern University; Mark Jones, Community College of Philadelphia; Patrick Massaro, Butler County Community College; Kathleen Nicolaides, University of North Carolina—Charlotte; and Constance St. Germain-Driscoll, American Public University System.

I would also like to thank the reviewers of the first three editions: Robert Boyer, Luzerne County Community College; Jack E. Call, Radford University; Kevin Daugherty, Albuquerque TVI Community College; Charles Dreveskracht, Northeastern State University; Russell A. Hunt, Dodge City Community College; David Kramer, Bergen Community College; Donna Nicholson, Manchester Community College; Caryl Anne Poteete, Southern Illinois University at Carbondale; Larry Salinger, Arkansas State University; Philip E. Secret, University of Nebraska at Omaha; Carol Lynn Tebben, University of Wisconsin–Parkside; Scott Belshaw, University of North Texas; Brett Curry, Georgia Southern University; Mark Jones, Community College of Philadelphia; Patrick Massaro, Butler County Community College; Kathleen Nicolaides, University of North Carolina—Charlotte; and Constance St. Germain-Driscoll, American Public University System.

Special thanks go to the following organizations (including their staff and others who responded to my many queries): San Bernardino, California, Police Department; Portland Police Bureau, Strategic Services Division; Abilene, Texas, Police Department; Alameda County (California) District Attorney's Office; Claremont, California, Police Department; Gallatin, Tennessee, Police Department; Pine Bluff, Arkansas, Police Department; Sage Publications; and the Texas Municipal Court Education Center.

I would also like to thank Craig Hemmens, Missouri State University, for fielding many of my questions. My students throughout the years deserve special thanks as well. Their "what if" questions and frustration with the traditional, heavy-on-case-law approach to teaching criminal procedure contributed in no small part to this, the fourth edition. And thanks, as always, to the wonderful people at Pearson and everyone else involved in bringing the book to press, including Eric Krassow, Tiffany Bitzel, Steve Robb, and project manager Abinaya Rajendran at Integra. Finally, special thanks go to my family, especially my wife, Sabrina, for her tolerance and understanding.

ABOUT THE AUTHOR

John L. Worrall is Professor of Criminology and Program Head at the University of Texas at Dallas. A Seattle native, he received a B.A., double majoring in psychology and law and justice, from Central Washington University in 1994. Both his M.A. (criminal justice) and Ph.D. (political science) were earned at Washington State University, where he graduated in 1999. From 1999 to 2006, he was a member of the criminal justice faculty at California State University, San Bernardino. He joined University of Texas at Dallas in fall 2006.

Dr. Worrall has published articles and book chapters on a wide range of law enforcement topics ranging from legal issues in policing to crime measurement. He is also the author of *Crime Control in America: What Works?* (2nd ed., Allyn & Bacon, 2008); coauthor of *Policing Today* (Prentice Hall, 2010), *Criminal Evidence: An Introduction* (Oxford University Press, 2005), *Introduction to Criminal Justice* (13th ed., Cengage, 2012), and *Police Administration* (3rd ed., Cengage, 2012); and coeditor of *The Changing Role of the American Prosecutor* (SUNY, 2008). Finally, he is Editor of the journal *Police Quarterly*.

Part 1

INTRODUCTION

LEARNING OBJECTIVES

When you complete this chapter, you should be able to:

- Summarize the constitutional basis for criminal procedure.
- Explain the importance of precedent.
- Compare the theory of criminal procedure to the reality.
- Describe the public order (crime control) and individual rights (due process) perspectives of criminal justice and how criminal procedure balances the two.
- Outline the structure of the court system, including the responsibilities and jurisdictions of each level.
- Summarize important issues and trends in criminal procedure.
- Provide an overview of the criminal process.

Introduction to Criminal Procedure

INTRODUCTION

What Is Criminal Procedure?

American **criminal procedure** consists of a vast set of rules and guidelines that describe how suspected and accused criminals are to be handled and processed by the justice system. Of great significance is the relationship between the police and the people suspected of criminal activity. Criminal procedure arms the police with the knowledge necessary to preserve the rights of individuals who are seized, searched, arrested, and otherwise inconvenienced by law enforcement officials. It also arms other actors—such as judges, prosecutors, and defense attorneys—with the necessary information to preserve the rights of individuals accused of criminal activity. In short, criminal procedure begins when the police first contact a person and ends well after his or her conviction.

At least three important themes run throughout criminal procedure. First, there is a concern with the constitutional rights of accused persons, as interpreted by the courts. People enjoy a number of important rights in the United States, but the bulk of criminal procedure consists of *constitutional procedure* or what the U.S. Constitution says—usually through the interpretation of the U.S. Supreme Court (i.e., the Court)—with regard to the treatment of criminal suspects.

Second, criminal procedure contains an important historical dimension, one that defers regularly to how sensitive legal issues have been approached in the past. The role of *precedent*, or past decisions by the courts, cannot be overemphasized. At the same time, though, the world continues to evolve, and it is sometimes necessary to part ways with the past and decide novel legal issues.

Third, criminal procedure creates something of a collision between two different worlds: the world of the courts versus that of law enforcement. What the courts require and what law enforcement actually deals with do not always harmonize. That is, in the real world, the influence of the courts may not always be as significant or relevant as might be expected. The following subsections will elaborate more fully on the importance of these three themes.

EMPHASIS ON CONSTITUTIONAL RIGHTS

The Preamble to the U.S. Constitution states,

> We the People of the United States, in Order to form a more perfect Union, establish Justice, insure domestic Tranquility, provide for the common defence, promote the general Welfare, and secure the Blessings of Liberty to ourselves and our Posterity, do ordain and establish this Constitution for the United States of America.

Of particular relevance to criminal procedure are the terms *justice* and *liberty*. The Constitution helps ensure these through both setting forth the various roles of government and protecting the rights of people within the nation's borders. Throughout the years, the courts have devoted a great amount of energy to interpreting the Constitution and to specifying what rights are important and when they apply.

However, the Constitution is not the only source of rights; there are others worthy of consideration. In addition, some rights are more important than others, at least as far as criminal procedure is concerned. Finally, the two-tiered system of government in the United States creates a unique relationship between the federal and state levels. Criminal procedure cannot be understood without attention to the interplay between federal and states' rights.

Sources of Rights

In addition to the Constitution, important sources of rights include court decisions, statutes, and state constitutions. Most of the court decisions discussed in this section and throughout the text are U.S. Supreme Court decisions.

Whenever the Supreme Court interprets the Constitution, it effectively makes an announcement concerning people's rights. For example, the Fourth Amendment states that unreasonable searches and seizures are impermissible. The term *unreasonable* is not self-explanatory, however, so the Court has taken steps to define it. One definition of *unreasonable* appears in the recent decision of *Wilson v. Layne* (526 U.S. 603 [1999]), in which the Court held that it is unreasonable for the police to bring reporters along when serving a warrant, unless the reporters are there to serve a legitimate law enforcement objective.

Although the Constitution and the court decisions stemming from it reign supreme in criminal procedure, statutes also play an important role. Obviously, the Constitution and the courts cannot be expected to protect all of the interests that people represent. Statutes attempt to compensate for that shortcoming by establishing that certain rights exist. An example is Title VII of the 1964 Civil Rights Act. Among other things, it prohibits discrimination in employment. Another statute of relevance in criminal procedure (one that will be considered in some depth in Chapter 2) is 42 U.S.C. Section 1983. It allows private citizens to sue local law enforcement officials for violations of federally protected rights.

In addition, each state has its own constitution, which can be considered an important source of rights. The supremacy clause of Article VI to the U.S. Constitution makes *it* the supreme law of the land and binds all states and the federal government to it. However, nothing in the U.S. Constitution precludes individual states from adopting stricter interpretations of the federal provisions. In general, if a state constitution gives *less* protection than the federal Constitution, such a limitation is unconstitutional. But a stricter interpretation of the federal Constitution is perfectly reasonable. For example, the Supreme Court has interpreted the Fifth Amendment in such a way that it requires police to advise a suspect of his or her so-called *Miranda* rights when the suspect is subjected to custodial interrogation—an action that does not necessarily rise to the level of an arrest. A *state*, however, could require that *Miranda* rights be read whenever a person is arrested, regardless of whether he or she is interrogated.

Finally, although it is not a source of rights per se, the **Federal Rules of Criminal Procedure** are worth considering.[1] Excerpts from the *Federal Rules* are reprinted throughout this book because they sometimes clarify important rulings handed down by the U.S. Supreme Court. Additionally, the *Federal Rules* set forth the criminal procedure guidelines by which federal criminal justice practitioners are required to abide.

Rights of Relevance in Criminal Procedure

Of the many rights specified in the U.S. Constitution (which, incidentally, is reprinted in the Appendix), the rights stemming from five amendments are of special importance in criminal procedure. Four of these—the Fourth, Fifth, Sixth, and Eighth Amendments—can be found in the Bill of Rights. Beyond the Bill of Rights, the Fourteenth Amendment is of special relevance in criminal procedure. Sometimes the First Amendment, which protects individual rights to assembly and speech, and the Second Amendment, which protects the right to bear arms, are relevant in criminal procedure, but only rarely.

- The **Fourth Amendment** is perhaps the most well known source of rights in criminal procedure. In fact, it is viewed to be so important that several books on criminal procedure devote the overwhelming majority of their chapters to it. The Fourth Amendment states,

---

[1] *Federal Rules of Criminal Procedure*, issued by the 107th Congress, First Session, December 1, 2001. Available online: www.house.gov/judiciary/crim2001.pdf.

The right of the people to be secure in their persons, houses, papers, and effects, against unreasonable searches and seizures, shall not be violated, and no Warrants shall issue, but upon probable cause, supported by Oath or affirmation and particularly describing the place to be searched, and the persons or things to be seized.

Several rights can be distinguished by reading the text of the Fourth Amendment. It refers to the right of people to be free from unreasonable searches and seizures, and it provides that specific requirements are to guide the warrant process. That is, a warrant must be issued by a magistrate or judge, supported by probable cause, and sufficiently specific as to what is to be searched and/or seized. Because of the complexity of the Fourth Amendment, this book devotes an entire section to its interpretation (see Part 2).

- The second constitutional amendment of special relevance to criminal procedure is the **Fifth Amendment**. It states,

No person shall be held to answer for a capital, or otherwise infamous crime, unless on a presentment or indictment of a Grand Jury, except in cases arising in the land or naval forces, or in the Militia, when in actual service in time of War or public danger; nor shall any person be subject for the same offense to be twice put in jeopardy of life or limb; nor shall be compelled in any criminal case to be a witness against himself, nor be deprived of life, liberty, or property, without due process of law; nor shall private property be taken for public use, without just compensation.

This book also examines the Fifth Amendment in detail, focusing in particular on the role of the grand jury, the statement that no person shall be "twice put in jeopardy of life or limb" (known as the *double-jeopardy* clause), the statement that no one can be compelled "to be a witness against himself" (also known as the *self-incrimination* clause), and perhaps most important of all, the requirement that an individual cannot be deprived of life, liberty, or property without due process of law.

- The **Sixth Amendment** is also of great importance in criminal procedure. It specifies,

In all criminal prosecutions, the accused shall enjoy the right to a speedy and public trial, by an impartial jury of the State and district wherein the crime shall have been committed, which district shall have been previously ascertained by law, and to be informed of the nature and cause of the accusation; to be confronted with the witnesses against him; to have compulsory process for obtaining witnesses in his favor, and to have the Assistance of Counsel for his defence.

Of relevance to criminal procedure is the Sixth Amendment's language concerning speedy and public trials, impartial juries, confrontation, and compulsory process. The Sixth Amendment also suggests that in addition to being public, trials should be open, not closed, proceedings. The Supreme Court has interpreted the Sixth Amendment as providing the right of the accused to be present at his or her trial and to be able to put on a defense.

- The **Eighth Amendment** is relevant in criminal procedure but to a limited extent. It states,

Excessive bail shall not be required, nor excessive fines imposed, nor cruel and unusual punishments inflicted.

The Eighth Amendment's language on bail and the nature of cruel and unusual punishment are addressed in Chapters 10 and 15, respectively.

- The **Fourteenth Amendment** has an important home in criminal procedure. It is a fairly long amendment, however, and only a small portion is relevant to the handling and treatment of criminal suspects. That portion states,

All persons born or naturalized in the United States, and subject to the jurisdiction thereof, are citizens of the United States and of the State wherein they reside. No State shall make or enforce any law which shall abridge the privileges or immunities of citizens of the United States, nor shall any State deprive any person of life, liberty, or property, without due process of law; nor deny to any person within its jurisdiction the equal protection of the laws.

The due process language of the Fourteenth Amendment mirrors that of the Fifth. Nonetheless, because the Fifth Amendment is part of the Bill of Rights, it is only binding on the federal government. The Fourteenth Amendment, by contrast, has been used by the Supreme Court to *incorporate*, or make applicable to the states, several of the rights provided for in the Bill of Rights. (The following subsection introduces the so-called incorporation controversy.)

The Fourteenth Amendment's due process clause has been interpreted to consist of two types of due process: (1) **substantive due process** and (2) **procedural due process**. The essence of substantive due process is protection from arbitrary and unreasonable action on the part of state officials. By contrast, a procedural due process violation is one in which a violation of a significant life, liberty, or property interest occurs (e.g., *Geddes v. Northwest Missouri State College*, 49 F.3d 426 [8th Cir. 1995]). Procedural due process is akin to procedural fairness.

Summary. Figure 1.1 lists the constitutional amendments that are of particular importance in criminal procedure. As the following section will describe, certain rights that are provided for in each amendment may not be binding on the states. Also, even though a particular amendment may provide a particular right, the Supreme Court may have interpreted that amendment to apply only in certain circumstances. Such circumstances will be discussed throughout the text.

The Incorporation Controversy

The Bill of Rights, consisting of the first 10 amendments to the U.S. Constitution, places limitations on the powers of the federal government. It does *not* limit the power of the states, however. In other words, the first 10 amendments place no limitations on state and local governments and their agencies. Government power at the state and local levels is clearly limited by state constitutions.

Even though the Bill of Rights does not limit state and local governments, the Supreme Court has found a way to do so through the Fourteenth Amendment. In particular, the Court has used the Fourteenth Amendment's due process clause,

FIGURE 1.1

Constitutional Amendments Important to Criminal Procedure and Their Relevant Provisions

- **Fourth Amendment:** Protects from unreasonable searches and seizures.
- **Fifth Amendment:** Provides protection from double jeopardy and self-incrimination and for grand jury indictment in serious crimes.
- **Sixth Amendment:** Provides for a speedy and public trial, impartial jury, confrontation, compulsory process, and assistance of counsel.
- **Eighth Amendment:** Protects from cruel and unusual punishment.
- **Fourteenth Amendment:** Includes the so-called due process clause, which has been used to incorporate various other rights described in the Bill of Rights.

which holds that no state shall "deprive any person of life, liberty, or property, without due process of law," to make certain protections specified in the Bill of Rights applicable to the states. This is known as **incorporation**.

The extent to which the Fourteenth Amendment should regulate state and local government power has been the subject of some disagreement—hence, the incorporation controversy. The basic question posed over the years has been, To what degree should the Fourteenth Amendment's due process clause incorporate the various provisions of the Bill of Rights so as to restrict state and local law enforcement in the same way federal law enforcement is restricted by the Bill of Rights?

SIGNIFICANCE OF THE DEBATE   The incorporation debate is significant because of three concerns. First, since most contact between citizens and the police occurs at the state and local levels, it is critical to determine the role of the federal Constitution at the state level. Comparatively few people have contact with federal law enforcement, so the Bill of Rights actually regulates a limited number of police/citizen contacts. Second, incorporation, according to some, threatens *federalism*. Under the doctrine of federalism, states have the authority to develop their own rules and laws of criminal procedure, but if the Fourteenth Amendment incorporates the Bill of Rights, this authority can be compromised. Third, the incorporation debate raises important concerns about the separation of powers. Namely, the Supreme Court has decided which rights should be incorporated—a decision that may better be reserved for Congress.

DECISION-MAKING EXERCISE 1.1

The First Amendment and Criminal Procedure

The First Amendment to the U.S. Constitution provides that "Congress shall make no law respecting an establishment of religion, or prohibiting the free exercise thereof; or abridging the freedom of speech, or of the press; or the right of the people peaceably to assemble, and to petition the Government for a redress of grievances." Given what you have read so far, is the First Amendment relevant to criminal procedure?

VIEWS ON INCORPORATION   There are four leading views on the incorporation debate.[2] One has won out over the others, but all of the views are important to consider, regardless.

- The *total incorporation* perspective holds that the Fourteenth Amendment's due process clause incorporates the entire Bill of Rights. In other words, all protections specified in the Bill of Rights should be binding on the states. The primary proponent of this view was Supreme Court Justice Hugo Black (e.g., *Adamson v. California*, 332 U.S. 46 [1947]; *Rochin v. California*, 342 U.S. 165 [1952]).
- The second leading view on incorporation is that of *selective incorporation*, or the *fundamental rights* perspective. It favors incorporation of certain protections enumerated in the Bill of Rights, not all of them. Further, this perspective deems certain rights as being more critical, or fundamental, than others. The Supreme Court's decision in *Snyder v. Massachusetts* (291 U.S. 97 [1934]) advocates this perspective, arguing that the due process clause prohibits state encroachment on those "principle[s] of justice so rooted in the traditions and consciences of our people as to be ranked as fundamental."
- The third view on incorporation can be termed *total incorporation plus*. This view holds that the Fourteenth Amendment's due process clause incorporates the whole Bill of Rights as well as additional rights *not* specified in the Constitution, such as the "right to privacy." This view can be found in such Supreme Court cases as *Adamson v. California* and *Poe v. Ullman* (367 U.S. 497 [1961]).
- Finally, some people believe that the topic of incorporation deserves case-by-case consideration. That is, no rights should be incorporated across the board. Rather, the facts and circumstances of each individual case should be weighed in order to determine if any protections listed in the Bill of Rights should apply at the state or local level.

OUTCOME OF THE DEBATE   So, Which perspective has won out? Arguably, the selective incorporation, or the fundamental rights, perspective is the winner. The Supreme Court has consistently held that some protections listed in the Bill of Rights are more applicable to the states than others. The Fourth Amendment, in its view, lists several *fundamental rights.* By contrast, the Fifth Amendment's grand jury clause has not been deemed fundamental and is not binding on the states (*Hurtado v. California*, 110 U.S. 516 [1884]).

To an extent, part of the total-incorporation-plus perspective has won out, as well. While not all of the Bill of Rights is binding on the states, the Supreme Court has repeatedly emphasized Americans have a fundamental right to privacy. This is despite the fact that the Constitution makes no mention of privacy. It is commonly said (as will be noted in the section on the Fourth Amendment) that people do not enjoy an *expectation of privacy* in public places. It would seem, then, that certain rights not listed in the Constitution have been identified as well as incorporated.

Figure 1.2 lists the rights that have been deemed fundamental by the Supreme Court and, as a result, incorporated to the states.[3] The Supreme Court cases responsible for these incorporation decisions are listed, as well.

---

[2] J. Dressler, *Law Outlines: Criminal Procedure* (Santa Monica, CA: Casenotes Publishing, 1997), pp. 2-3–2-4.
[3] Some scholars believe that the Ninth Amendment to the U.S. Constitution (also referred to as the *penumbra clause*) implies that all of the rights not specifically spelled out in the Constitution are automatically protected nonetheless. But to demonstrate this, a court would have to recognize a particular right as fundamental in case law. Privacy could be considered one such right.

FIGURE 1.2

Rights Incorporated to the States

Right	Deciding Case
First Amendment freedom of religion, speech, and assembly and the right to petition for redress of grievances	*Fiske v. Kansas*, 274 U.S. 380 (1927)
Fourth Amendment prohibition of unreasonable searches and seizures	*Wolf v. Colorado*, 338 U.S. 25 (1949)
Fifth Amendment protection against compelled self-incrimination	*Malloy v. Hogan*, 378 U.S. 1 (1964)
Fifth Amendment protection from double jeopardy	*Benton v. Maryland*, 395 U.S. 784 (1969)
Sixth Amendment right to counsel	*Gideon v. Wainwright*, 372 U.S. 335 (1963)
Sixth Amendment right to a speedy trial	*Klopfer v. North Carolina*, 386 U.S. 213 (1967)
Sixth Amendment right to a public trial	*In re Oliver*, 333 U.S. 257 (1948)
Sixth Amendment right to confrontation	*Pointer v. Texas*, 380 U.S. 400 (1965)
Sixth Amendment right to an impartial jury	*Duncan v. Louisiana*, 391 U.S. 145 (1968)
Sixth Amendment right to compulsory process	*Washington v. Texas*, 388 U.S. 14 (1967)
Eighth Amendment prohibition of cruel and unusual punishment	*Robinson v. California*, 370 U.S. 660 (1962)

THE IMPORTANCE OF PRECEDENT

To many students of criminal procedure, legal research is a less than desirable pursuit. Even so, it is essential in everyday practice because of the importance of precedent. A **precedent** is a rule of case law (i.e., a decision by a court) that is binding on all lower courts and the court that issued it. A past decision may not be available in each case, but when one is, the courts will defer to it. This is the doctrine of *stare decisis*.

Stare Decisis

Stare decisis is a Latin term that means to abide by or to adhere to decided cases. Most courts adhere to the principle of *stare decisis*. That is, when a court has handed down a decision on a specific set of facts or legal questions, future court decisions that involve similar facts or questions will defer to the previous decision. In short, *stare decisis* is simply the practice of adhering to a previous decision or precedent.

Why does *stare decisis* occupy such an important position in the U.S. court system? The answer is that it promotes consistency. It is well known that accused criminals enjoy the right to counsel (*Gideon v. Wainwright*, 372 U.S. 335 [1963]), but what if from one year to the next, the Supreme Court vacillated on whether this right were constitutionally guaranteed? The criminal process, not to mention the rights of the accused, would be unpredictable and vary from one point to the next.

It is important to note that the practice of deferring to precedent is not always possible or desirable. First, *stare decisis* is usually only practiced by courts in a single jurisdiction. Suppose, for example, that a federal circuit appeals court handed down a decision. All the district courts within that circuit would then abide by the appeals court decision. Courts outside that circuit would *not* be bound to adhere to the decision (although some courts often do as a matter of professional courtesy). Perhaps more important, if a case coming before a court is unique and does not resemble one decided in the past, the court may *distinguish* it.

Distinguishing Cases

When a previous decision does not apply to the current facts, a court will **distinguish** the case, saying, in effect, that this case is different and cannot be decided by looking to past rulings. Another way of understanding what it means to distinguish a case is to think of the present set of facts as unique and never before considered by an appellate court.

Since only a handful of cases make it to the appellate level, and even fewer still arrive at the Supreme Court, there is an untold number of cases waiting to be distinguished. This is a critical point. The case law in place currently addresses only a minute quantity of possible constitutional questions. Countless contacts occur between the police and citizens, and several of them may give rise to important constitutional questions. Yet they may never see the inside of a courtroom. So, while this book may appear heavy on case law, a thorough understanding of criminal procedure would require a review of the nearly infinite possible factual circumstances that could arise in the criminal process.

An example of a case that was distinguished is *Terry v. Ohio* (392 U.S. 1 [1968]). In that case, the Supreme Court held that police officers can stop and frisk suspects with reasonable suspicion, not probable cause (the latter standard appearing in the text of the Fourth Amendment). The Court felt that a stop-and-frisk is different from a search or a seizure and, as such, should be governed by a different set of standards. Had the Supreme Court *not* decided *Terry*, or any case like it, stop-and-frisk encounters would probably still be considered seizures and therefore subject to the Fourth Amendment's requirement for probable cause. *Terry* will be considered in more detail later, as will many other distinguished cases.

In nearly every class on criminal procedure, students ask, "What if . . . ?" The "what-if" question reflects a concern over possible factual circumstances not already addressed in published court decisions. In order for a "what-if" question to be answered, a court decision must result. Otherwise, the best approach to answering such a question is to look to the past and find a decision that closely resembles the hypothetical scenario. In this vein, every case discussed throughout this text should be thought of as a distinguished case. Every decision was based on a different set of factual circumstances and was deemed by the reviewing court as worthy of being distinguished. Were it not for distinguished cases, criminal procedure case law could be adequately covered in a matter of minutes, even seconds.

THEORY VERSUS REALITY

Criminal procedure consists mostly of rules and guidelines that have been handed down by the courts so as to dictate how the criminal process should play out. As already mentioned, many of these rules and guidelines have come from the U.S. Supreme Court, which has decided on thousands of occasions how the Constitution should be interpreted. However, in some circumstances, court decisions may not really have a great deal of influence. That is, some court decisions are made in the **theory world**, which is somewhat disconnected from the day-to-day operations of law enforcement. In contrast, the police occupy a position that is very definitely in the **real world**. Understandably, there can be differences, even tensions, between the worlds of theory and reality.

The fact that theory and reality may differ is a subject that receives little direct attention in criminal procedure textbooks. Indeed, that certain Supreme Court decisions may not really matter, or might even be flatly ignored, is a controversial notion, to say

DECISION-MAKING EXERCISE 1.2

Traditional Legal Doctrine Meets High-Tech Crime

In *Katz v. United States* (389 U.S. 347 [1967]), the Supreme Court decided that searches occur when a government actor infringes on a person's reasonable expectation of privacy. Assume federal agents have a trained drug dog sniff passengers' luggage on a baggage carousel in an airport. Does this constitute a search? Is *Katz* equipped to deal with a situation such as this, or is the situation such that it calls for a distinguished case?

the least. Americans are taught that the courts—and the Supreme Court, in particular—are charged with interpreting the Constitution and the laws of the United States. They are further taught that law enforcement should accept such interpretations uncritically and without much reflection. While this is mostly true, theory and reality can still differ for at least four reasons.

- First, the Supreme Court sometimes makes decisions on excruciatingly detailed matters that have almost no applicability to most law enforcement officers most of the time. A good example is the Supreme Court's recent decision in *Atwater v. City of Lago Vista* (533 U.S. 924 [2001]), a case that will be considered more fully later. (See Chapter 5 on warrantless searches and seizures.) The Court decided that the Fourth Amendment does not prohibit the police from arresting people for seat-belt violations. On one level, this decision seems significant, but how many police officers are now going to arrest people for seat-belt violations? Probably very few police will take up this cause because they usually have more important matters to address.

- Second, the Supreme Court frequently hands down restrictive decisions that would seem to have dramatic effects on the nature of law enforcement but that actually involve issues already being addressed by many police agencies. For example, the Supreme Court's decision in *Tennessee v. Garner* (471 U.S. 1 [1985]) made it a violation of the Fourth Amendment for the police to use deadly force to apprehend an unarmed and nondangerous fleeing felon. However, prior to *Garner*, many police agencies had already adopted restrictive deadly force policies—policies that, in many instances, were more restrictive than what was handed down in *Garner*. Police agency policy, therefore, can differ from, and even be more restrictive than, decisions reached by the Supreme Court. To illustrate this, several excerpts from police agency manuals and guidelines are reprinted throughout subsequent chapters.

- The third reason for the theory/reality dichotomy is that the courts sometimes hand down decisions that can be effectively circumvented or ignored by the police. Clearly, it is not in the best interest of law enforcement to ignore the courts, and it is probably quite rare that the police do so, but it can be done. For example, in *Kyllo v. United States* (533 U.S. 27 [2001]), the Supreme Court held that a search occurs when the police to scan a private residence with an infrared thermal imager without first obtaining a warrant. The consequence of conducting such a scan without a warrant is that any evidence subsequently obtained will not be admissible in court. However, in reality, what is to prevent the police from scanning someone's house if there is no intent to secure evidence?

- Finally, what the courts say and the police do can differ simply as a consequence of the U.S. legal system. It is well known, for example, that a police officer cannot stop a motorist without some level of justification. On how many occasions, though, are motorists stopped without justification? That is, how many people are pulled over every day simply because a police officer is suspicious of them? This cannot be

DECISION-MAKING EXERCISE 1.3
Theory and Reality Collide

In *Miranda v. Arizona* (384 U.S. 436 [1966]), the U.S. Supreme Court decided that the police must advise suspects who are custodially interrogated of their Fifth Amendment privilege against self-incrimination. This case will be revisited in great detail later in the book, but for now, it illustrates that (1) *custody* occurs when a reasonable person would believe the suspect is not free to leave (an arrest being a prime example of such action) and (2) *interrogation* refers to actions by the police that are reasonably likely to elicit a response from the suspect. Assume that the police arrest a man but do not interrogate him. Assume further that the man confesses to a crime. Does *Miranda* apply?

established for certain, but it does happen. It *can* happen because the legal system cannot do much to prevent it. Someone who is wrongfully stopped can file a complaint, but research shows that many such complaints are resolved in favor of the police.[4] A lawsuit can be filed, but as will be noted in Chapter 2, such suits rarely are successful. And if nothing worthy of arresting the motorist is discovered, then it is doubtful that the illegal stop will draw attention in court.

In fairness to the law enforcement community, it is not the case that the police (or other criminal justice officials) regularly trample people's constitutional rights. Most law enforcement officials are responsible, professional, and upstanding enforcers of the law, as are most judges and prosecutors. But the fact cannot be ignored that the reality of everyday law enforcement and the somewhat distant nature of certain court decisions do not always meet. It is for this reason that distinctions between theory and reality are pointed out throughout later chapters. Police department policy manual excerpts also appear throughout the book. They help bridge the gap between theory and reality by illustrating the procedures law enforcement officials must follow in addition to those laid out by the Supreme Court.

COMPETING CONCERNS IN CRIMINAL PROCEDURE

Criminal procedure is an exciting topic because of the inherent tension it creates between two competing sets of priorities. On the one hand, there is a serious interest in the United States in controlling crime, with some Americans advocating doing whatever it takes to keep criminals off the streets. On the other hand, because of their country's democratic system of government, Americans value people's rights and become angry when those rights are compromised or threatened. These two competing sets of values have been described by Herbert Packer as the *crime control* and *due process* perspectives.[5]

The values each opposing perspective subscribes to are probably familiar to many readers because the due process/crime control debate invariably pops up all throughout criminal justice. Almost without exception, whenever there is disagreement as to how best to approach the crime problem—be it through court decisions or legislative measures—the due process/crime control distinction rears its head. A delicate balance has to be achieved between the two perspectives.

The due process perspective closely resembles a liberal political orientation. Liberals often favor protection of people's rights and liberties to a higher degree than

---

[4] For an informative review, see J. L. Worrall, "If You Build It, They Will Come: Consequences of Improved Citizen Complaint Review Procedures," *Crime and Delinquency* 48 (2002): 355–379.
[5] H. L. Packer, *The Limits of the Criminal Sanction* (Palo Alto, CA: Stanford University Press, 1968).

their conservative counterparts. By contrast, the crime control perspective is the one most frequently subscribed to by conservative law-and-order types.

Of course, in reality, there can be a great deal of overlap between the two orientations. Liberals occasionally favor conservative crime control policies, and conservatives can be concerned with protecting the rights of American citizens. That is to say, although the two groups frequently stand in stark contrast to each other, they do sometimes meet in the middle. Regardless, the values espoused by each group—be it an interest in crime control, an interest in civil rights, or an interest in both—are here to stay. Given that, it is useful to consider each perspective in more detail, focusing special attention on the implications for criminal procedure.

Due Process

Packer's **due process perspective** is, first and foremost, concerned with people's rights and liberties. It also gives significant weight to human freedom. Due process advocates believe that the government's primary job is not to control crime but rather to maximize human freedom, which includes protecting citizens from undue government influence. Proponents of due process favor minimizing the potential for mistakes, as explained by Packer:

> People are notoriously poor observers of disturbing events. . . . [C]onfessions and admissions by persons in police custody may be induced by physical or psychological coercion so that the police end up hearing what the suspect thinks they want to hear rather than the truth; witnesses may be animated by a bias or interest that no one would trouble to discover except one specially charged with protecting the interests of the accused (as the police are not).[6]

Due process advocates also believe that each suspect is innocent until proven guilty, just as Americans are taught. In addition, they place greater emphasis on *legal guilt* (whether a person is guilty according to the law) rather than *factual guilt* (whether a person actually committed the crime with which he or she is charged).

Underlying the due process/crime control perspectives are four ideals: (1) The criminal process looks, or should look, something like an obstacle course; (2) Quality is better than quantity; (3) Formality is preferred over informality; and (4) A great deal of faith is put in the courts.

THE OBSTACLE COURSE   The "obstacle course" idea is rooted in a metaphor, of course. A criminal process that resembles an obstacle course is one that is complex and needs to be navigated by skilled legal professionals. Further, it is one that is somewhat difficult to operate in a predictable fashion. It is not a process that prides itself on speed and efficiency—values of great importance in the crime control perspective. In fact, the opposite could be said. The obstacle-course metaphor also stresses that each case must pass through several complicated twists and turns before a verdict can be rendered.

QUALITY OVER QUANTITY   Another way to distinguish between due process and crime control is in terms of quantity and quality. The due process view favors quality—that is, reaching a fair and accurate decision at every stage of the criminal process. It stresses that each case should be handled on an individual basis and that special attention should be paid to the facts and circumstances surrounding the event. In addition, the concern with quality is one that minimizes the potential for error. For example, due

---

[6] Ibid., p. 163.

process advocates are in favor of allowing several death penalty appeals because the possibility of executing the wrong person should be avoided at all costs.

INSISTENCE ON FORMALITY   Due process advocates do not favor informal processes. Because of the potential for human error and bias, they favor a full-blown adversarial criminal process. They also believe that early intervention by judges and other presumptively objective parties (besides, say, the police) is in the best interest of people accused of breaking the law.

FAITH IN THE COURTS   Another value inherent in the due process perspective is intense faith in the courts as opposed to law enforcement. Due process advocates correctly point out that the job of a judge is to interpret the U.S. Constitution. This, they argue, helps provide protection to people charged with crimes. Faith in the courts also corresponds with the above-mentioned insistence on formality. When guilt or innocence is determined in court, an air of fairness and objectivity must be maintained.

Crime Control

In contrast to the due process perspective, the **crime control perspective** emphasizes the importance of controlling crime, perhaps to the detriment of civil liberties. From a cost/benefit perspective, crime control advocates believe that the benefit of controlling crime to society at large outweighs the cost of infringing on some individuals' due process protections. Another way to distinguish between the due process and crime control perspectives is to consider the distinction between *means* and *ends*: Crime control is more concerned with the *ends*, with wiping out crime, or at a minimum, with mitigating its harmful effects. By contrast, due process is concerned with the *means*, with the methods by which people are treated by criminal justice officials. The result— either crime or the absence of it—is not of great concern to due process advocates.

Additional differences between the due process and crime control perspectives are illustrated in Figure 1.3.

THE ASSEMBLY LINE   The metaphor of an "assembly line" suggests that the criminal process should be automatic, predictable, and uniform. In other words, every criminal should be treated the same, with minimal variations in terms of charges and sentences. The assembly-line metaphor further suggests that the criminal process should be quick and efficient.

FIGURE 1.3

The Values of Due Process versus Crime Control

Crime Control Values	Due Process Values
• Follows "assembly line" metaphor	• Follows "obstacle course" metaphor
• Emphasizes quantity over quality	• Emphasizes quality over quantity
• Favors informality	• Prefers formality
• Has faith in the police	• Has faith in the courts
• Makes presumption of guilt	• Makes presumption of innocence
• Seeks to benefit society	• Seeks to benefit suspects
• Is concerned with ends, not means	• Is concerned with means, not ends
• Seeks to maximize police authority	• Seeks to maximize human freedom
• Seeks to control crime at all costs	• Seeks to protect people's rights at all costs
• Puts emphasis on factual guilt	• Puts emphasis on legal guilt

DECISION-MAKING EXERCISE 1.4
Due Process or Crime Control

How should the *Miranda* decision from Exercise 1.3 be charac-terized: as due process-oriented or crime control-oriented? In other words, does *Miranda* prioritize the suspect's due process rights or the interest of the police in controlling crime? What about the Supreme Court's decision in *Kyllo v. United States*, mentioned in the "Theory versus Reality" section?

The goal of the crime control perspective is to move criminals through the justice process as swiftly as possible. A full-blown adversarial criminal process, replete with hearings and other pauses in the interest of the accused, is anathema to the crime control view.

QUANTITY OVER QUALITY   As just mentioned, the due process model stresses quality over quantity. The crime control model, by contrast, favors quantity over quality, a view that is consistent with the assembly-line metaphor. The goal is to move as many offenders as possible through the criminal justice system with as little delay as possible. If mistakes are made along the way and someone is wrongfully charged or convicted, so be it. That is, the *overall* goal of ensuring that as many criminals are dealt with as possible is superior to protecting any individual's constitutional rights.

INSISTENCE ON INFORMALITY   Whereas the due process perspective favors the formality of the criminal process, with particular emphasis on the courts, the crime control perspective favors informality. The courts are to be avoided; instead, justice should be meted out beyond the walls of a courtroom. Plea bargaining, for instance, is favored because of its swift, behind-the-scenes nature (not to mention that it eliminates the need to go to trial). An insistence on informality suggests further that the law enforcement establishment should be more involved in making determinations of guilt, not the courts.

FAITH IN THE POLICE   Finally, whereas the due process perspective places a great deal of faith in the courts, the crime control perspective puts a high degree of trust in the police. All Americans are taught that each suspect is innocent until proven guilty in a court of law. Clearly, the courts are charged with making this determination. However, crime control advocates favor so-called street justice, giving the police vast discretion in deciding how to deal with people suspected of being involved in criminal activity. A fitting quote describing the crime control perspective is, therefore, "All criminals are guilty until proven innocent." In other words, all suspects should be considered guilty; if the courts determine otherwise, then so be it.

DECISION-MAKING EXERCISE 1.5
Due Process or Crime Control

In two decisions, *United States v. Leon*, 468 U.S. 897 (1984) and *Massachusetts v. Sheppard*, 468 U.S. 981 (1984), the Supreme Court created what is known as the "good faith" exception to the exclusionary rule. This exception, as well as the exclusionary rule, is discussed toward the end of Chapter 2. But for now, realize that both cases are important in that they held that violations of people's constitutional rights are permissible, under limited circumstances, when the police make honest mistakes. For example, if a police officer relies on a search warrant that was obtained on the basis of a reasonable mistake, he or she could serve the warrant, search for evidence, and seize it, even if these actions violated the rights of the person searched. The key is that the mistake must be a *reasonable* one. How, then, would you characterize both the *Leon* and *Sheppard* decisions: as prioritizing crime control or due process?

FINDING COURT CASES AND TRACING THEIR PROGRESS

Criminal procedure can be complex not only because of the many factual questions that arise in day-to-day police/citizen encounters (as well as throughout the rest of the justice process) but also because of the two-tiered structure of the U.S. court system. This two-tiered structure reflects the idea of *dual sovereignty*: that the federal and state governments are considered separate, or *sovereign*, in their own right. Each state, as well as the federal government, has its own court structure.

There is no way to succinctly describe all the variations in state court structures, but, generally, they resemble one another. Typically, the lowest-level courts in a given state are **courts of limited jurisdiction**, which have jurisdiction over relatively minor offenses and infractions. A traffic court fits in this category. Next are the trial courts, also called **courts of general jurisdiction**, which try several types of cases. Courts of general jurisdiction are often county-level courts and are frequently called **superior courts**. At the next highest level are the **intermediate appellate courts**; verdicts from courts of general jurisdiction are appealed to these courts. Finally, each state has its own **state supreme court**, the highest court in the state. Figure 1.4 shows a typical state court structure—from the state of Washington. Importantly, state courts try cases involving state laws (and, depending on the level of the court, some county, city, and other local ordinances).

The *federal* court structure can be described succinctly because, for the purposes of criminal procedure, it consists of three specific types of courts. Federal courts try cases involving federal law. The lowest courts at the federal level are the so-called **district courts**. There are 94 federal district courts in the United States (as of this writing), including 89 district courts in the 50 states and 1 each in Puerto Rico, the Virgin Islands, the District of Columbia, Guam, and the Northern Mariana Islands. At the next level are the **U.S. courts of appeals**. There are 13 of these so-called circuit courts of appeals: 12 regional courts and 1 for the federal circuit. Each is charged with hearing appeals from several of the district courts that fall within its circuit. Finally, the **U.S. Supreme Court** is the highest court in the federal system. As will be discussed, however, the Supreme Court does not only hear federal appeals.[7] Figure 1.5 shows the structure of the federal court system; the courts of relevance in criminal procedure are highlighted. Figure 1.6 presents a map of the geographic boundaries of the U.S. courts of appeals and the U.S. district courts.

The federal government and each of the 50 states are considered a sovereign entity. That is why each has a court system of its own. There is another set of sovereigns, however: the Native American tribal courts. These tribal courts will receive no further attention in this book because, in general, they do not have to follow the same constitutional requirements as state and federal courts. Rather, they come under the Indian Civil Rights Act of 1968. The U.S. military also has its own structure, in which the rules of criminal procedure differ markedly from those covered here. Because of the complexity of the Uniform Code of Military Justice, military courts and criminal procedure will not be covered in this book, either.

That said, what decides where a case will be decided? Generally, if the case involves federal law, it will be tried in federal court. If, by contrast, it involves state law, it will be heard in state court. Certain crimes—such as kidnapping, transportation of illegal narcotics across state lines, and robbing a federally insured bank—can be tried in both federal and state courts, if the prosecutors agree. As will be discussed later, such a dual prosecution does not violate the Fifth Amendment's double-jeopardy clause.

---

[7] Note that references to the federal-level Supreme Court are always capitalized (e.g., *the U.S. Supreme Court, the Supreme Court*, and even *the Court*), whereas those to state-level supreme courts are not (i.e., except in citing a particular state court, such as the *Florida Supreme Court*).

FIGURE 1.4

Structure of a State Court System (Washington)

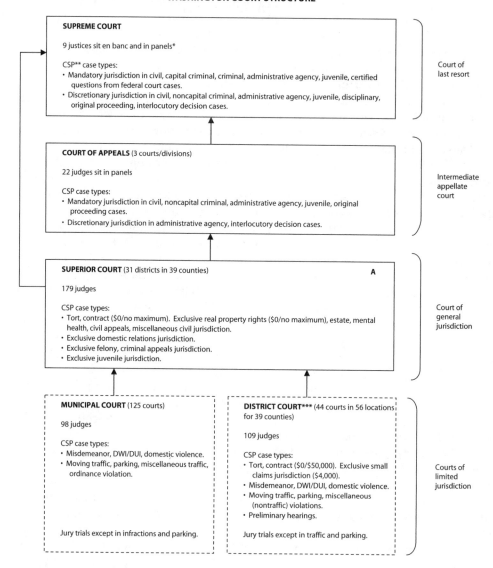

WASHINGTON COURT STRUCTURE

SUPREME COURT

9 justices sit en banc and in panels*

CSP** case types:
- Mandatory jurisdiction in civil, capital criminal, criminal, administrative agency, juvenile, certified questions from federal court cases.
- Discretionary jurisdiction in civil, noncapital criminal, administrative agency, juvenile, disciplinary, original proceeding, interlocutory decision cases.

Court of last resort

COURT OF APPEALS (3 courts/divisions)

22 judges sit in panels

CSP case types:
- Mandatory jurisdiction in civil, noncapital criminal, administrative agency, juvenile, original proceeding cases.
- Discretionary jurisdiction in administrative agency, interlocutory decision cases.

Intermediate appellate court

SUPERIOR COURT (31 districts in 39 counties)   A

179 judges

CSP case types:
- Tort, contract ($0/no maximum). Exclusive real property rights ($0/no maximum), estate, mental health, civil appeals, miscellaneous civil jurisdiction.
- Exclusive domestic relations jurisdiction.
- Exclusive felony, criminal appeals jurisdiction.
- Exclusive juvenile jurisdiction.

Court of general jurisdiction

MUNICIPAL COURT (125 courts)

98 judges

CSP case types:
- Misdemeanor, DWI/DUI, domestic violence.
- Moving traffic, parking, miscellaneous traffic, ordinance violation.

Jury trials except in infractions and parking.

DISTRICT COURT* (44 courts in 56 locations for 39 counties)

109 judges

CSP case types:
- Tort, contract ($0/$50,000). Exclusive small claims jurisdiction ($4,000).
- Misdemeanor, DWI/DUI, domestic violence.
- Moving traffic, parking, miscellaneous (nontraffic) violations.
- Preliminary hearings.

Jury trials except in traffic and parking.

Courts of limited jurisdiction

* "en banc" means all justices/judges hear the case at once. "In panels" means only some of the justices/judges hear the case.
** Court Statistics Project.
*** District court provides services to municipalities that do not have a municipal court.

Source: Bureau of Justice Statistics, *State Court Organization, 2004* (Washington, DC: U.S. Department of Justice, 2006), p. 316. Available online: http://bjs.ojp.usdoj.gov/content/pub/pdf/sco04.pdf (accessed February 16, 2011)

FIGURE 1.5

Structure of the Federal Court

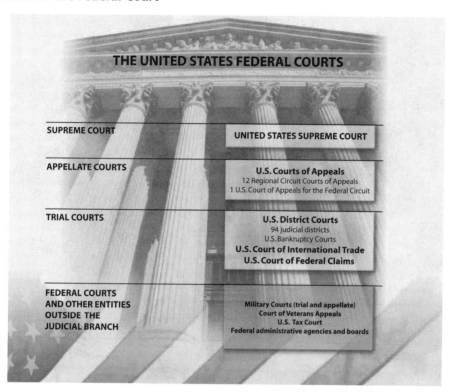

Source: Administrative Office of the U.S. Courts, *Understanding the U.S. Court* (Washington, DC: Administrative Office of the U.S. Courts, 2011). Available online: http://www.uscourts.gov/FederalCourts/ UnderstandingtheFederalCourts/FederalCourtsStructure.aspx (accessed February 16, 2011)

As indicated near the outset of this chapter, criminal procedure textbooks—this one included—focus almost exclusively on U.S. Supreme Court decisions. Why focus on *federal* Supreme Court decisions rather than *state* supreme court decisions? The answer is that many important cases move from the state supreme courts to the U.S. Supreme Court, which is the court of last resort. Decisions of the U.S. Supreme Court are, therefore, important because they represent the last word on what conduct is constitutional and what is not.

To understand the relationship between the federal and state courts, it is necessary to understand first where to find criminal cases and then how to trace the progress of criminal cases as they move from the trial to the appellate level. Following discussion of these topics, attention will turn to what types of cases are decided by the U.S. Supreme Court and how state-level court decisions arrive at the nation's highest court.

Finding Cases

Being able to find court cases requires that readers be familiar with legal citations as well as the publications in which cases can be found. Legal citations are somewhat

FIGURE 1.6

Geographic Boundaries of the U.S. Courts of Appeals and the U.S. District Courts

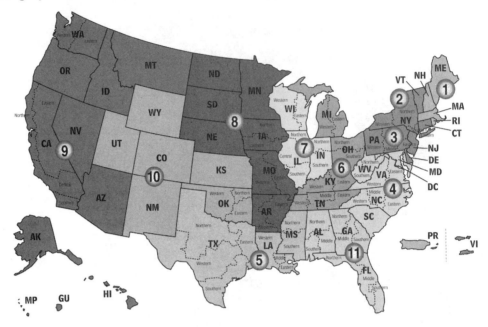

Source: Administrative Office of the U.S. Courts, *Court Locator* (Washington, DC: Administrative Office of the U.S. Courts, 2011). Available online: http://www.uscourts.gov/Court_Locator.aspx (accessed February 16, 2011)

cryptic but can be deciphered with relative ease. The following is the citation format used throughout this text:

> ### *Miranda v. Arizona (384 U.S. 436 [1966])*

Miranda and *Arizona* refer to the parties to the case. Importantly, the party listed first is the one initiating the action. In this case, *Miranda* appealed his conviction, which is why he is listed first. The legal citation format that follows the parties is interpreted as follows: The first part, *384*, is the volume; the second part, *U.S.*, is the publication in which the case can be found; the third part, *436*, is the page on which the case starts; and the fourth, *1966*, is the year the decision was published. See Figure 1.7 for a listing of publications in which court cases can be found.

After becoming familiar with case citations, it is necessary to learn where the cases can actually be found. First, most university libraries have one or several of the so-called reporters listed in Figure 1.7. They can be found in bound form on the library shelves. Online research is also an option. Cases can be found at such Web sites as www.findlaw.com. U.S. Supreme Court cases can be found at www.supremecourtus.gov. Another Web site, maintained by Cornell University, is helpful for finding Supreme Court cases: http: // www.law.cornell.edu/supct/.

Many university libraries also have access to subscription databases, such as LexisNexis, which contain cases from nearly all courts across the country. Both Lexis

FIGURE 1.7

Publications Containing Court Cases

Abbreviation	Description
U.S.	*United States Reports:* This is the official publication for U.S. Supreme Court decisions.
S.Ct.	*Supreme Court Reporter:* This Westlaw publication reports U.S. Supreme Court decisions.
CrL	*Criminal Law Reporter:* This Bureau of National Affairs publication reports U.S. Supreme Court decisions.
L.W.	*United States Law Week:* This Bureau of National Affairs publication reports U.S. Supreme Court decisions.
F.2d	*Federal Reports,* Second Series: This Westlaw publication reports decisions of the Federal Courts of Appeals.
P.2d	*Pacific Reporter,* Second Series: This Westlaw publication reports decisions from the Pacific states.
A.2d	*Atlantic Reporter,* Second Series: This Westlaw publication reports decisions from the Atlantic states.
N.E.2d	*North Eastern Reporter,* Second Series: This Westlaw publication reports decisions from the northeastern states.
N.W.2d.	*North Western Reporter,* Second Series: This Westlaw publication reports decisions from the northwestern states.
S.E.2d	*South Eastern Reporter,* Second Series: This Westlaw publication reports decisions from the southeastern states.
S.W.2d	*South Western Reporter,* Second Series: This Westlaw publication reports decisions from the southwestern states.
S.2d	*Southern Reporter,* Second Series: This Westlaw publication reports decisions from the southern states.

and West have a feature known as *Shepard's Citations.* This allows researchers to enter a case citation and retrieve every other case that has cited it. Doing a Shepard's search is useful for tracing the history and current status of an important decision.

For those who do not enjoy reading actual court decisions, other sources of legal information may be useful. For example, legal dictionaries and encyclopedias offer clarification of important legal concepts. Legal digests identify and consolidate legal issues, provide commentary on and interpret cases, and otherwise "digest" complex material. Finally, law reviews are useful places to find discussions of various aspects of the law as well as opinions on and interpretations of court cases. Databases such as LexisNexis contain full-text articles from nearly all law reviews. The Web links listed at the end of this chapter include some legal research sites with information on how to find cases, statutes, and other relevant information.

Tracing the Progress of a Criminal Case

One of the more frustrating aspects of criminal procedure, especially for those who have little familiarity with the law or legal jargon, is the sometimes laborious task of tracing the progress of a criminal case. If final decisions were reached in a single court, then criminal procedure would be vastly simplified. In reality, though, a single case can bounce back and forth between trial and appellate courts, sometimes for years. Indeed, many U.S. Supreme Court decisions concern matters that occurred a decade or more ago. Thus, it is of particular importance for students of criminal procedure to learn how to trace a criminal case.

There are several essential steps to tracing the progress of a criminal case. First, it is necessary to have a basic understanding of the nation's court structure. This requires knowing where the criminal trial in question took place. If it took place in a federal circuit court, then tracing the progress of the case will be fairly easy. There are only three possible courts—district court, circuit appellate court, and the Supreme Court—that may have handed down decisions on the matter. If the case originated in state court, however, it can be decidedly more difficult to trace the case over time. Familiarity with the state court structure is needed, as well as an understanding of how cases can jump back and forth between the state and federal courts, which will be discussed later in this section.

Second, to adequately follow the progress of a criminal case, it is also necessary to understand the legal jargon, beginning with the parties to the case. The *parties* to the case are the people involved. At the trial level, the parties of interest are the **defendant**, or the person charged with the crime in question, and the **prosecutor**, or the official representing the government. At the appellate level, these parties are no longer called *defendant* and *prosecutor* but rather **appellant** and **appellee**. The *appellant* is the party that appeals; both the prosecutor and defendant can appeal (see Chapter 15), but the defendant appeals more often than the prosecutor. The *appellee* (sometimes called the *respondent*) is the party appealed against. The term **petitioner** is also used at times, namely when a prisoner files a *habeas corpus* petition (see Chapter 15). A petitioner is one who petitions an appellate court to hear his or her case.

Next, to follow a criminal case, it is essential to have an understanding of how cases are decided and what possible decisions can be reached. At the trial level, two decisions can result: guilty and not guilty. At the appellate level, however, the picture becomes more complex. Assume, for example, that a defendant is found guilty in a federal district court and appeals to one of the circuit courts of appeals. Assuming that the court agrees to hear the case, it can hand down one of several decisions. It could **reverse** the lower court's decision, which is akin to nullifying or setting it aside. Sometimes the appellate court **vacates** the lower court's decision, which is basically the same as reversing it. A reversal does *not* always have the effect of setting the defendant free, however. The appellate court could also **remand** the case back to the lower court. When a case is remanded, it is sent back to the lower court for further action consistent with the appellate court's decision. Cases can also be reversed and remanded together. The appellate court can also **affirm** the lower court's decision, in which case it agrees with the lower court.

If there was only one appellate court, tracing the progress of a case would be fairly simple. Unfortunately, multiple appellate courts exist, which means the decisions from court to court can change. This is a very important point. Assume, for example, that a defendant is found guilty in a state trial court. He or she could appeal to the state's intermediate appellate court, which could reverse the defendant's conviction. The case could then go to the state's supreme court, which could reverse the appellate court's decision and basically uphold the defendant's conviction. Finally, the case could go to the U.S. Supreme Court, which could again reverse the defendant's conviction. Believe it or not, this is a fairly simple progression. Nothing prevents a single case from going from the trial court to the appellate court, back to the trial court, up to the appellate court again, then up to the state supreme court, back to the intermediate appellate court, and so on.

It is essential to understand what has happened with a criminal case before making any claims as to its importance or influence. In other words, doing incomplete legal research can be a recipe for disaster. If, for instance, a researcher finds a state supreme court decision that supports a point he or she wants to make but that decision was later reversed, say, by the U.S. Supreme Court, whatever argument he or she makes in reliance on that state supreme court case will be inaccurate. Thus, in tracing the progress of a criminal case, it is necessary to understand whether the issue in question has been resolved or may currently be on the docket of an appellate court, which could render an altogether different decision.

In tracing a criminal case, especially when interpreting one decided at the appellate level, it is important to understand the components of a published decision.

An appellate court often consists of a panel of judges who may not always agree with one another, even though the court reaches a single decision. For example, a 5 to 4 decision by the U.S. Supreme Court is one in which the Court reached a single decision because of a majority, but four of the justices disagreed. The **opinion** is the voice of the five justices (or the voice of the majority of the judges in a lower appellate court decision), although one or more of the five may opt to write a **concurring opinion**, which supports the majority's decision but with different legal logic. The four remaining justices will probably write a **dissent**, in which they argue why they disagree with the majority's decision. If they wanted to, each of the four minority justices could write his or her own individual dissent. Either way, it is important to distinguish between a given court's opinion and possible concurring and dissenting opinions.

There is much more to tracing the progress of a criminal case than understanding the terminology encountered along the way. How is it that certain cases are appealed and others are not? Under what circumstances may the defendant appeal but not the prosecution, and vice versa? Why do some defendants file several appeals and others do not? Answers to these questions are presented in the last chapter of this text, where special attention is given to the appellate process and other methods for challenging the verdicts of trial courts throughout the United States.

How Cases Arrive at the Supreme Court

Most criminal cases originate at the state level. This should be obvious because there are 50 state court structures and only 1 federal court system. Also, the number of state laws criminalizing certain types of conduct vastly exceeds the number of federal laws with the same objective. But just because most cases are heard in state courts does not mean they cannot be heard at the federal level. State-level cases can arrive at the U.S. Supreme Court.

Stated simply, a state-level case can arrive at the Supreme Court if it raises a federal question, which is usually a question concerning the U.S. Constitution. First, however, such a case must proceed through several steps. It must move all the way to the state supreme court. That is, a case cannot jump from a state-level intermediate appellate court to the U.S. Supreme Court.

Next, like many appellate courts, the U.S. Supreme Court must decide whether it wants to hear the case. The party seeking a decision must file documents with the Court, asking to be heard. If the Supreme Court agrees the case is worth deciding, it issues what is known as a **writ of certiorari**. This is an order by the Court, requiring the

---

DECISION-MAKING EXERCISE 1.6

Interpreting a Supreme Court Holding

Assume that John Smith was subjected to a search that was not supported by probable cause. Assume further that he was convicted in a federal district court based on evidence obtained from the search. He appealed his conviction to the U.S. court of appeals, which remanded his case back to the district court to determine if the search to which Smith was subjected required probable cause. (Some searches, as will be discussed later, do not require probable cause.) The district court concluded that the search did not require probable cause. The case was then appealed again to the U.S. court of appeals, which reversed the district court's decision, holding that the search *did* need to be supported by probable cause. The U.S. Supreme Court then granted *certiorari* and reversed the U.S. court of appeals decision, holding that the search did not need to be supported by probable cause. In plain English, what happened here? In other words, what is the practical effect of this convoluted case progression?

lower court to send the case and a record of its proceedings to the U.S. Supreme Court for review. Four of the nine U.S. Supreme Court justices must agree to hear a case before a *writ of certiorari* will be issued. This is known as the **rule of four**.

If four justices do not agree to hear the case, that is the end of the road in terms of legal options. When tracing the progress of a case, encountering a statement such as "cert. denied" will indicate this result. The case was denied a hearing by the Supreme Court. Figure 1.8 summarizes how cases arrive at the Supreme Court.

It cannot be overemphasized that only a handful of cases ever reach the U.S. Supreme Court. It is not uncommon for the Supreme Court to review thousands of petitions yet grant less than 100 *writs of certiorari.* Most cases that are appealed stop short of reaching the Supreme Court, so it is necessary to find out at what level the final decision was reached. Not tracing a case to its final decision can be fatal to a legal argument. In other words, if a researcher wants to argue a specific point with reference to a previously decided case, he or she must be sure that the decision is, if only for the time being, a final one.

FIGURE 1.8

How Cases Arrive at the U.S. Supreme Court

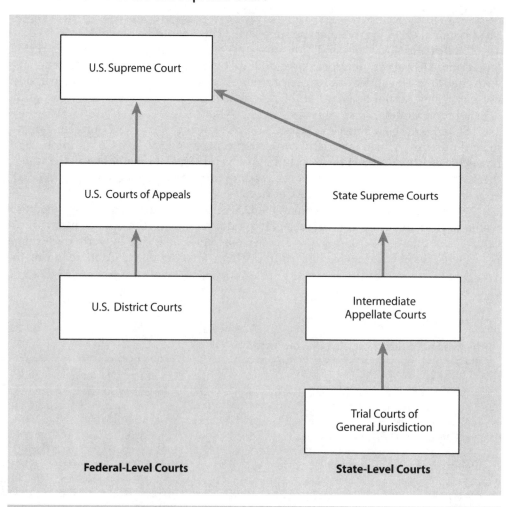

DECISION-MAKING EXERCISE 1.7

Would the Supreme Court Hear This Case?

Assume that a state supreme court heard an appeal from one of the state's intermediate appellate courts. In the appeal, the defendant argued that her conviction should be overturned, as the judge failed to declare that certain testimony provided by the government's lead witness should have been deemed inadmissible according to the state's rules of evidence. In making its decision, the appellate court sided with the government, upholding the defendant's conviction. Would the U.S. Supreme Court likely hear this case? What if, instead, the defendant argued that the original judge mistakenly permitted the prosecutor to comment to the jury concerning the defendant's refusal to take the stand and testify? Would that issue likely get a hearing from the Court?

IMPORTANT ISSUES AND TRENDS IN CRIMINAL PROCEDURE

Criminal procedure, as presented in this text, is mostly about interpreting U.S. Supreme Court decisions regarding certain constitutional rights. In interpreting those decisions, it is worth understanding some important terms, issues, and trends in the Supreme Court's decision-making practices over the years. Also, it is important to realize that criminal procedure has recently changed due to some important legislation. This section focuses on six topics: (1) bright-line decisions versus case-by-case adjudication; (2) the distinction between *subjectivity* and *objectivity*; (3) an increased faith in the police; (4) the notion of judicial restraint; (5) the issue of personal privacy; and (6) the PATRIOT Act, which was signed into law following the attacks on the Pentagon and the World Trade Center on September 11, 2001.

Bright-Line Decisions versus Case-by-Case Adjudication

There are two types of Supreme Court decisions: (1) **bright-line decisions** and (2) decisions requiring **case-by-case adjudication**. A bright-line decision is one in which the Court hands down a *specific rule*, one subject to very little interpretation. It is like the metaphorical "line drawn in the sand"; in other words, the Court emphatically communicates to the criminal justice community what it can and cannot do. An example of a bright-line decision is *Wilson v. Layne*, a case mentioned near the beginning of this chapter. In that case, the Supreme Court said that the police cannot bring the media along on the service of warrants unless its presence serves a legitimate law enforcement objective. It is easy to see that this is a clear, bright-line rule. Exactly what constitutes a "law enforcement objective" may be somewhat vague, but otherwise, this rule is quite clear. The advantage of a bright-line rule is that it promotes clarity and consistency. Also, it is easily understood by criminal justice officials.

A decision requiring case-by-case adjudication is quite different. In many cases, the Supreme Court refers to the concept of **totality of circumstances**. For example, in the case of *Manson v. Braithwaite* (432 U.S. 98 [1977]), the Supreme Court held that the totality of circumstances determines whether an identification procedure is unreliable. This means that all the facts and circumstances surrounding the case must be examined in order to determine whether a constitutional rights violation has taken place. Deciding whether the totality of circumstances supports the action in question requires looking at each case *individually*. There is no existing recipe specifying what authorities should or should not do. A case-by-case decision is preferable in some instances because it is rarely possible to know in advance all the possible twists and turns in a criminal case. That is, case-by-case decisions promote flexibility, leaving it up to the lower courts (usually, the trial court) to decide if the action in question conforms to constitutional guidelines. However, this approach can also create uncertainty for law enforcement officials.

Manson v. Braithwaite
(432 U.S. 98 [1977])

Subjectivity versus Objectivity

The terms *subjective* and *objective* are sometimes found in Supreme Court decisions. And although what these terms mean in everyday use is well understood, what they mean in the language of criminal procedure is not necessarily so well defined. Part of the confusion stems from the fact that *subjective* and *objective* are sometimes used directly before the term *reasonable*. It is not uncommon to read a Supreme Court opinion referring to *objective reasonableness* or *subjective reasonableness*. Usually, phrases such as these are considered in the context of the Fourth Amendment because of its language on reasonableness.

Police conduct that is considered subjectively reasonable, or characterized by **subjective reasonableness**, is one that would be considered reasonable by the police officer engaged in the conduct. For example, if a police officer arrests a person without probable cause but feels that probable cause was present, his or her actions can be considered subjectively reasonable. **Objective reasonableness**, by contrast, refers to what a reasonable person (usually, a reasonable police officer) would do or feel under the circumstances. A reasonable person would believe that making an arrest without probable cause is unconstitutional.

Objective and subjective language can be found in the Supreme Court's references to people's privacy interests. For example, in deciding whether a person enjoys a reasonable expectation of privacy when engaging in some sort of activity, both terms frequently appear. The Court has been forced to answer a simple question: Should individual people be trusted to identify their privacy interests, or should what a reasonable person would believe determine the expectation of privacy?

In the past few decades, the Supreme Court has moved from subjective analyses to objective analyses in many of its decisions. The reason for this should be fairly clear: A subjective analysis puts a high degree of faith in the individual police officer, citizen, or other person. Assume that a man has a marijuana field on his property, and it is observed by the police in a helicopter flyover. He will probably argue that he should be able to enjoy privacy in his backyard and that the police should not be able to spy on him. Such an argument is quite predictable in a case like this because it behooves the suspect to assert a privacy interest. However, what the suspect believes and what a reasonable person may believe could be two entirely different things. Indeed, the Supreme Court has moved to an objective analysis in many scenarios such as this for the simple reason that individuals are not entirely without bias in making such determinations. The Court now prefers to defer to what a reasonable person would believe.

In some ways, the term *objective*, as used in court decisions, mirrors its meaning in everyday use. It suggests a more or less unbiased view of a particular matter. By comparison, the term *subjective* suggests more of an individually based determination. Unfortunately, it is not always easy to identify what a reasonable person would believe. The notion of a reasonable person is, in fact, a hypothetical construct. For this reason, the Court usually decides what can be considered an objectively reasonable belief.

The distinction between objective and subjective reasonableness can be clarified with an important Supreme Court decision. In the landmark case of *Graham v. Connor* (490 U.S. 386 [1989]), the leading nondeadly force case decided to date, the Supreme Court declared emphatically that all claims involving allegations of excessive (nondeadly) force against police officers must be analyzed under the Fourth Amendment's reasonableness requirement. Namely, "[A]ll claims that law enforcement officers have used excessive force—deadly or not—in the course of an arrest, investigatory stop, or other 'seizure' of a free citizen should be analyzed under the Fourth Amendment and its 'reasonableness' standard" (p. 386).

DECISION-MAKING EXERCISE 1.8

A Bright-Line Decision or Case-by-Case Adjudication

In *Tennessee v. Garner* (471 U.S. 1 [1985]), a Memphis police officer shot and killed an unarmed 15-year-old boy who was fleeing the scene of a residential burglary. The officer called to the boy, Garner, to stop, but he did not. When Garner was about to climb a fence, the officer shot him in the back of the head, fatally wounding him. Garner's surviving family members filed a section 1983 lawsuit, claiming the level of force used was excessive. The Supreme Court agreed, ruling that deadly force may be used only when two criteria are present: (1) It is necessary to prevent the suspect's escape, and (2) the officer has probable cause to believe the suspect poses a serious threat of death or serious physical injury to other people or police officers. Can the Court's decision in *Garner* be characterized as bright line in nature?

More importantly, in *Garner*, the Court adopted a test of objective reasonableness to decide whether excessive force has been used. This requires focusing on what a *reasonable* police officer would do "without regard to [the officer's] underlying intent or motivation." In trying to decide what a reasonable police officer would do, the Court looked to three factors: (1) the severity of the crime; (2) whether the suspect posed a threat; and (3) whether the suspect was resisting and/or attempting to flee the scene. Courts must, in focusing on these three factors, allow "for the fact that police officers are often forced to make split-second judgments—about the amount of force that is necessary in a particular situation" (p. 386). Note that the Court was not concerned with what the individual officer felt with regard to these three factors. Rather, the preferred focus was on what a reasonable officer would believe.

Increased Faith in the Police

Earl Warren was appointed to the position of chief justice of the U.S. Supreme Court in 1953; thus, references to the **Warren Court** reflect the time from 1953 to 1969, during which Warren was chief justice. The Warren Court handed down a number of decisions, particularly throughout the 1960s, that provided extensive constitutional protections for criminal defendants. To use Packer's language, the Court was highly concerned with due process during this period. Others describe the Court as being extremely liberal during the Warren era. All in all, the Court did not place a great deal of trust in the police, much less other criminal justice officials. Rather, it was concerned primarily with individual rights.

Warren E. Burger held the position of chief justice from 1969 to 1986. During his tenure, the Court moved closer to the center of judicial and political thought and away from the liberal stance of the Warren Court. This movement toward conservatism gained significant momentum with the appointment of William H. Rehnquist as chief justice in 1987. The decisions handed down by the Court in the area of criminal procedure began to take on a different orientation, one that placed a great deal of faith in the police. In practice, many of the Court's decisions of late have increased the power of law enforcement as well as granted the police extensive latitude with regard to controlling crime. For example, the Court created the well-known "good faith" exception to the exclusionary rule (see Chapter 2). Also, many decisions have carved out exceptions to the Fourth Amendment's warrant requirement, suggesting that judicially authorized search and arrest warrants are not of particular use or importance much of the time.

The reader is encouraged to take note of the dates of the many Supreme Court decisions discussed throughout this text. With only a handful of exceptions, the decisions of the Warren Court in the 1960s were concerned with the rights of criminal suspects and placed significant restrictions on the authority of criminal justice officials.

DECISION-MAKING EXERCISE 1.9

Subjective or Objective

Chapter 2 will discuss civil liability against the police, but for now, realize that a police officer who is sued for violating someone's constitutional rights can assert a defense to such liability. That defense is known as *qualified immunity.* A police officer who is sued enjoys qualified immunity if he or she did not violate clearly established rights that a reasonable person would have known about (*Harlow v. Fitzgerald*, 457 U.S. 800 [1982]). Which type of *reasonableness* is considered in this context: objective or subjective?

Many of the decisions handed down since approximately the 1980s reflect something of a change in priorities, one that favors increased law enforcement authority and a concern with effective crime control, as opposed to due process.

Judicial Restraint

The term **judicial restraint** identifies the philosophy of limiting decisions to the facts of each case, deciding only the issue or issues that need to be resolved in a particular situation. The practice of judicial restraint also entails avoiding unnecessary decisions on constitutional questions that have yet to be posed. In the area of criminal procedure, a judicially restrained judge will look to the Constitution for guidance and, should the Constitution not be entirely clear, he or she will attempt to understand the framers' intent. Another way to think of judicial restraint is that it is *interpretive*, seeking only to interpret the Constitution. Yet another way to understand judicial restraint is with regard to *precedent*; the judicially restrained judge will defer to precedent as much as possible and avoid setting new guidelines and rules.

The philosophy of judicial restraint can be placed at one end of the large spectrum of judicial philosophies. At the other end is **judicial activism**. A judicially active judge is one who sees his or her role as more than interpreting the Constitution. A judicially active judge avoids precedent, preferring to hand down decisions with sweeping implications for the future. Thus, a judicially active judge looks more to the future than the past. Further, a judicially active judge favors "judge-made" law.

In *Silverman v. United States* (365 U.S. 505 [1961]), the Supreme Court elaborated on the notion of judicial restraint when it was deciding a Fourth Amendment case: "[T]he facts of the present case . . . do not require us to consider the large questions which have been argued. We need not here contemplate the Fourth Amendment implications of these and other frightening paraphernalia which the vaunted marvels of an electronic age may visit upon human society" (p. 509). The Court basically stated that large questions should not be answered, but only the specific question before the court.

Personal Privacy

The Supreme Court's landmark decision in *Katz v. United States* (389 U.S. 347 [1967]), a case that will be revisited later, reflects a high degree of respect for people's privacy. This and other Supreme Court decisions show that people should enjoy protection beyond physical intrusions into their property. In *Katz*, the Court stated that "the Fourth Amendment protects people, not places," emphasizing that the scope of the "Amendment cannot turn upon the presence or absence of physical intrusion." This has come to be known as the *privacy doctrine.*

In the past, the Court required a physical intrusion by authorities into a person's private property. This was known as the **trespass doctrine**. People did not enjoy

DECISION-MAKING EXERCISE 1.10

The Issue of Personal Privacy

In *Kyllo v. United States* (533 U.S. 27 [2001]), the Supreme Court decided that law enforcement's use of a thermal imaging (infrared) device constitutes a search. The Court stated, "Where, as here, the Government uses a device that is not in *general public use*, to explore *details of the home* that would previously have been unknowable without physical intrusion, the surveillance is a 'search' and is presumptively unreasonable without a warrant" (p. 2046). Did the Court exercise judicial restraint in its decision? Why or why not?

privacy unless the police or other government officials physically trespassed on their property. Today, fortunately, privacy has been extended to encompass more than personal property. What people say in private telephone conversations (as in *Katz*), for instance, is subject to intense constitutional protection:

> We conclude . . . that the "trespass" doctrine . . . can no longer be regarded as controlling. The Government's activities in electronically listening to and recording the petitioner's words violated the privacy upon which he justifiably relied while using the telephone booth and thus constituted a "search and seizure" within the meaning of the Fourth Amendment. The fact that the electronic device employed to achieve that end did not happen to penetrate the wall of the booth can have no constitutional significance. (p. 353)

The importance of personal privacy has been reaffirmed over the years in many court decisions and even by prominent academics. Sam Ervin's observation on the matter is illustrative:

> The oldest and deepest hunger in the human heart is for a place where one may dwell in peace and security and keep inviolate from public scrutiny one's innermost aspirations and thoughts, one's most intimate associations and communications, and one's most private activities. This truth was documented by Micah, the prophet, 2,700 years ago when he described the Mountain of the Lord as a place where "they shall sit every man under his own vine and fig tree and none shall make them afraid."[8]

The trend toward increased personal privacy is an interesting one because the Fourth Amendment (and the whole Bill of Rights, for that matter) contains no mention of privacy. In other words, there is no constitutional right to privacy. The Supreme Court has seen fit to identify a **right to privacy**, nonetheless. As such, privacy is something of a judicially created right. Another judicial creation is the *exclusionary rule* (discussed in Chapter 2). Because the exclusionary rule is a judicial creation, it has been eroded over the years. It is therefore conceivable that the right to privacy could be eroded in this way, as well. In fact, decisions such as *United States v. Dionisio* (410 U.S. 1 [1973]), in which the Court held that people cannot expect privacy in what they knowingly expose to the public, support such a possibility. Privacy in the home, however, continues to enjoy the highest level of protection.

United States v. Dionisio (410 U.S. 1 [1973])

---

[8] S. J. Ervin, "The Exclusionary Rule: An Essential Ingredient of the Fourth Amendment," *Supreme Court Review* (1983): 283, 288–289, 296–297.

Criminal Procedure and the War on Terror

Criminal procedure is sometimes altered by important changes in federal and state legislation. One example of such legislation is the Antiterrorism and Effective Death Penalty Act of 1996, passed following the 1995 bombing of the Oklahoma City federal building. It has altered federal *habeas corpus* practice (see Chapter 15). An arguably more important piece of legislation, one that has affected several aspects of criminal procedure, it was signed into law following the September 11, 2001, attacks on the Pentagon and the World Trade Center towers.

On September 14, 2001, in response to the September 11 attacks, then-President George W. Bush declared a state of emergency, which permitted him to invoke certain presidential powers. Those powers included the ability to summon reserve troops, to marshal military units, and to issue executive orders for the implementation of such things as military tribunals. Congress also took action following September 11. In order to empower the Department of Justice, Congress passed the **PATRIOT Act** on October 26, 2001.[9]

The PATRIOT Act made several important changes to past law and practice. First, it centralized federal law enforcement authority in the U.S. Department of Justice. For example, Section 808 of the act reassigned the authority for investigating several federal crimes of violence from law enforcement agencies, such as the Secret Service and the Bureau of Alcohol, Tobacco, and Firearms, to the attorney general. The act also provided

A fiery blast rocked the World Trade Center in New York City after both towers were hit by hijacked passenger planes on September 11, 2001. This attack, along with a similar attack on the Pentagon in Washington, DC, prompted passage of the Patriot Act.

---

[9] On March 9, 2006, President Bush signed a law that made the Patriot Act permanent. Certain provisions were changed and some civil liberties protections were added, but most of the original act remains intact.

for Central Intelligence Agency (CIA) oversight of all domestic intelligence gathering. Prior to the PATRIOT Act, the CIA's role was primarily concerned with foreign intelligence gathering. The act also expanded the definition of the terms *terrorism* and *domestic terrorism* to include activities that

> (A) involve acts dangerous to human life that are a violation of the criminal laws of the United States or of any state; (B) appear to be intended (i) to intimidate or coerce a civilian population; (ii) to influence the policy of a government by mass destruction, assassination, or kidnapping; or (iii) to effect the conduct of a government by mass destruction, assassination, or kidnapping; and (C) occur primarily within the territorial jurisdiction of the United States.[10]

Of particular relevance in the context of this book are the changes in criminal procedure attributable to the PATRIOT Act. First, the Supreme Court has traditionally held that the Fifth and Sixth Amendments' rights of due process and access to jury trials apply to *all persons*, not just citizens of the United States (*United States v. Verdugo-Urquidez*, 494 U.S. 259, 264–266 [1990]). In addition, the Supreme Court has held that all undocumented aliens living inside U.S. borders are entitled to the protections enunciated in the Bill of Rights (*Mathews v. Diaz*, 426 U.S. 67 [1976]). Specifically, the Court has stated that "the Fifth Amendment, as well as the Fourteenth Amendment, protects every one of these persons from deprivation of life, liberty, or property without due process of law. Even one whose presence in this country is unlawful, involuntary, or transitory is entitled to constitutional protection" (p. 77). These rights have also applied to the removal of aliens from within U.S. borders. That is, proceedings for the deportation of aliens have had to conform to constitutional requirements, especially due process (*Shaughnessy v. United States ex rel. Mezei*, 345 U.S. 206 [1953]).

In short, legal, illegal, resident, and temporary aliens have *all* historically enjoyed the same constitutional protections as ordinary U.S. citizens. But with the passage of the PATRIOT Act, that is no longer the case. In several ways, the PATRIOT Act alters and even abolishes constitutional protections historically available to legal and illegal aliens.

The war on terror has had far-reaching implications for criminal procedure. To illustrate, Figure 1.9 summarizes a number of key Supreme Court cases pertaining to terrorism and the primary holdings from each. Notice how some decisions favor the suspect and others favor the government.

Criminal Procedure and Technology

Technology continues its relentless march. New devices are constantly being invented to help law enforcement officials detect crime and catch criminals. The problem is that many technological innovations raise constitutional questions. What's more, many Supreme Court decisions were rendered years ago when many of today's technologies were not even conceived of. Is our Constitution and the resulting court decisions equipped to deal with these advances? Only time will tell. This book contains several references in upcoming chapters to technological innovations and related court cases that have implications for criminal procedure. An example is the *Kyllo v. United States* Supreme Court decision discussed in Exercise 1.10. *Kyllo* will be revisited in Chapter 3.

---

[10] USA PATRIOT ACT, Public Law 107–56, Section 802.

FIGURE 1.9

Key Supreme Court Cases in the War on Terrorism

Case	Question before the Court*	Decision
Ex Parte Milligan (1866)	Is it constitutional to try U.S. citizens before military tribunals when civilian courts are available?	No. It is unconstitutional to try U.S. citizens before military tribunals when civilian courts are available.
Hamdi v. Rumsfeld (2004)	Can U.S. citizens arrested abroad and detained on suspected involvement in terrorism challenge in court the government's justification for detaining them?	Yes. Detained U.S. citizens enjoy the right to challenge their detentions before an impartial judge.
Rumsfeld v. Padilla (2004)	Can U.S. citizens arrested domestically and detained as "enemy combatants" on suspected involvement in terrorism challenge in court the government's justification for detaining them?	Not answered. The case was remanded. The principal issue in this case remains unresolved.
Rasul v. Bush (2004)	Can noncitizen detainees at Guantanamo Bay challenge the constitutionality of their confinement?	Yes. The federal courts have jurisdiction to decide the constitutionality of detaining foreign nationals.
Hamdan v. Rumsfeld (2006)	Is it within the authority of Congress and the President to try suspected terrorists before military tribunals?	No. Bush-era military tribunals violate the Uniform Code of Military Justice and the Geneva Conventions.
Boumediene v. Bush (2008)	Are parts of the Military Commissions Act of 2006 that strip federal courts of jurisdiction to hear habeas corpus petitions from foreign citizens illegal?	Yes. Parts of the Military Commissions Act of 2006 that strip federal courts of habeas corpus jurisdiction in cases involving Guantanamo Bay detainees are unconstitutional.
Ashcroft v. al-Kidd (2011)	Does the attorney general have qualified immunity for his involvement in the arrest of a person as a material witness? Can a validly obtained warrant be challenged on the motive that the arresting authority had an improper motive?	Yes. The attorney general enjoys qualified immunity in such cases. No. Detaining al-Kidd as a material witness was constitutionally reasonable, even if the government's motive to hold him was based on a belief that he was a terrorist.

* The case may have dealt with more than one question. The key question with relevance to criminal procedure is presented here.

THE CRIMINAL PROCESS: AN OVERVIEW

There is no easy or concise way to describe the criminal process. In an attempt to do so, the 1967 President's Crime Commission described the criminal process with the flowchart reprinted in Figure 1.10, but this conceptualization is not perfect. There are countless variations, at both the federal and state levels, in how criminal cases are handled. Further, depending on the seriousness of a case, the criminal process may assume different forms.

Almost all criminal procedure texts present an overview of the criminal process, like the one that follows. But because of the variation from one jurisdiction to the next, readers should take steps to familiarize themselves with the criminal processes in the areas in which they reside. That said, think of the rest of this section as an overview of the criminal process. The rest of this book will detail the criminal process in this order.

Pretrial

A typical criminal case begins with a *complaint*. It may come in the form of a 911 call from a citizen, a report to the police that someone has been victimized, or a report from a law

FIGURE 1.10

Sequence of Events in the Criminal Justice System

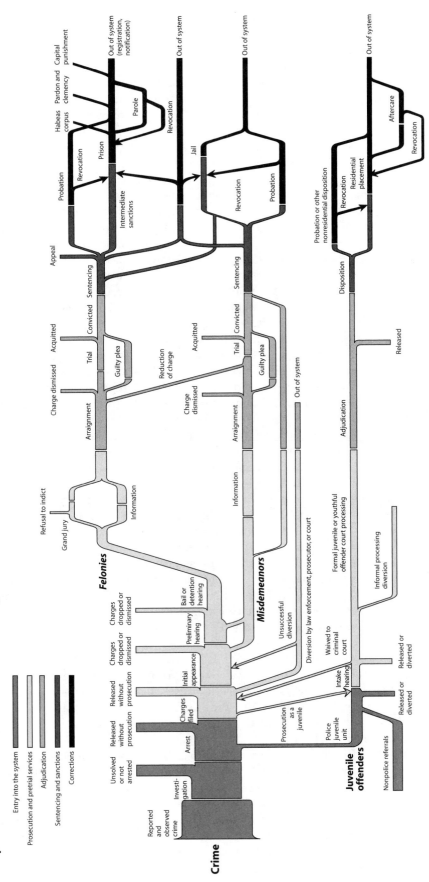

Source: President's Commission on Law Enforcement and Administration of Justice, *Task Force Report: Science and Technology* (Washington, DC: Government Printing Office, 1967), pp. 58–59.

enforcement officer who observes a crime in progress. If a citizen reports the crime, the police will usually follow up on the complaint by performing an investigation. If an officer observes the crime, not as much investigation is necessary. In the former instance, the police must take steps to confirm the observations of the citizen. A police officer's observations, by contrast, do not require as much investigative scrutiny. In fact, when an officer observes a crime in progress, he or she will probably arrest the suspect on the spot. This arrest will then be subjected to judicial scrutiny in a court hearing, in which a judge will decide if there was probable cause to arrest the suspect.

In a crime reported by a citizen, once the police have identified a suspect, they will approach a judge and seek either an arrest or a search warrant. In either case, the police must be able to show probable cause that the evidence they seek will be found in the place to be searched and/or that the suspect was the one who committed the crime. If this burden is met, an arrest, a search warrant, or both will be issued and the police will go to arrest the suspect or search the premises named in the search warrant. The burden of probable cause that is required for search and arrest warrants is not to be taken lightly and has spawned a great deal of debate in the courts. Probable cause, as well as other such standards of justification, is the focus of Part 2, Chapters 3 through 7.

The role of the police during the pretrial process cannot be overemphasized. In the period from the first contact between an officer and suspect up to the point when the suspect is arrested and detained, the police's role is complex and multifaceted. The Constitution, particularly the Fourth Amendment, places significant restrictions on what the police can and cannot do when they investigate crimes and handle suspects. This is why many criminal procedure books (this one included) devote extensive attention to the role of the police in the criminal process. *Criminal* procedure is, in many ways, *police* procedure. However, because the criminal process continues well beyond an arrest and imposing criminal charges, this book takes the additional step of considering the whole of the criminal process.

If, as indicated, a police officer arrests a suspect for a crime committed in his or her presence, no warrant is necessary. But even when arresting a suspect or searching his or her residence based on a citizen complaint, a warrant is not always required. Many situations arise in which the police are permitted to arrest or to search without a warrant. Suspects who evade authorities, seek to destroy evidence, or are likely to inflict harm on others create circumstances in which the police must act quickly. Indeed, in many other areas of law enforcement, the police may be forced to make split-second decisions, whether to arrest or search, without the protection of a warrant. These areas of law enforcement will be considered, as well.

Once a suspect is arrested—be it pursuant to an arrest warrant, a warrant to search his or her residence, or another method—he or she will be searched. This is done to protect the police and also to discover contraband that may be in the suspect's possession. Then, the suspect will be transported to the police station and booked. *Booking* is the process in which the suspect is fingerprinted, processed, photographed, and probably placed in a holding cell. The suspect may also be required to submit to testing (such as a Breathalyzer) and possibly be required to participate in a lineup for identification by a witness to the crime.

After this, the police will present their case to the prosecutor, and, assuming the prosecutor believes the evidence is persuasive enough, he or she will bring charges against the suspect, subject to certain restrictions identified by the U.S. Supreme Court. The suspect will now be considered the *defendant.* If the charges are minor, the police may release the suspect, in which case he or she will be required to appear in court at some later date.

Suspects who are booked, placed in detention, and charged with a crime face a number of different court hearings, depending on the seriousness of the crime.

Misdemeanors, because of their not-so-serious nature, tend to be fast-tracked through the courts. A misdemeanor defendant may appear at only one court hearing, in which the judge will decide guilt or innocence. Felony defendants, by contrast, face a longer legal road. If, as described already, the suspect is arrested without a warrant, he or she will be granted a probable cause hearing, in which the judge will decide whether the arresting officer had appropriate justification to make the arrest. (This hearing may, in fact, be merged with other hearings, but this book will treat it as a separate event.)

The next step in the criminal process is the *arraignment*. At the arraignment, the suspect comes before a judge and is, at a minimum, informed of the charges against him or her. The defendant will also be notified of the right to counsel, the right to remain silent, and other important rights. He or she will also be allowed to enter a *plea*. Common pleas are guilty, not guilty, and *nolo contendere* (which is akin to a plea of "no contest"). A public defender may be assigned at this stage, particularly if the defendant is unable to afford his or her own representation. Probable cause may also be determined at this stage, if a separate hearing is not required. Finally, for a misdemeanor charge, a trial may take place at the arraignment. A bail determination could be made, as well.

If the bail determination is not fused with the arraignment, a separate hearing may be warranted. (The approach taken in this book is that the bail determination is made in a separate hearing.) In deciding whether bail should be granted, the judge will take such factors into account as the seriousness of the crime as well as the defendant's prior record, likelihood of flight, and level of dangerousness. The defendant's financial status may also be considered.

It is important to note that the prosecutor's method of filing charges varies from one state to the next. Some states require that the prosecutor proceed by *information*, a document that describes the charges the prosecutor is filing. Other states require that the prosecutor proceed by a *grand jury indictment*. That is, a grand jury decides whether charges should be filed, usually with the advice and assistance of the prosecutor. Some states require or allow both methods of filing charges, depending on the nature of the case. What is important in this discussion, however, is that in jurisdictions in which the prosecutor proceeds by information, he or she is usually required to show that the charging decision is appropriate. This is accomplished in a so-called *preliminary hearing*, during which the prosecutor makes out what is known as a *prima facia case* of the defendant's guilt. A preliminary hearing can also be required in a grand jury jurisdiction, requiring the prosecutor to present his or her case before seeking a grand jury indictment.

Adjudication

Once the pretrial process has concluded and the charges have stood, a trial may or may not take place. If, at arraignment, the defendant pleads guilty, then a trial is not necessary. In such an instance, special steps must be taken to ensure that the defendant's guilty plea is valid. The defendant may also agree to a *plea bargain* agreement, in which in exchange for leniency from the prosecutor and/or the court, he or she pleads guilty to the crime with which he or she is charged. Plea bargaining of this nature can occur at any stage of the criminal process, however. That is, a suspect can reach a plea agreement with the prosecutor as early as the pretrial stage, during the trial, and, in fact, well into jury deliberations. In any case, the plea bargain, if there is one, must be accepted by the court. The judge makes this determination.

If the defendant pleads not guilty, the case is set for trial. The trial is usually scheduled for some date well after the arraignment. This allows both sides—the prosecution and the defense—to prepare their respective cases. A balance needs to be achieved between providing enough time for both sides to present effective arguments and protecting the defendant's Sixth Amendment right to a speedy trial. During this preparation process, *discovery* takes place. Discovery is the process by which each side to a criminal case learns what evidence the other side will present. Work product and legal strategy are off limits, but the identities of witnesses who will testify, the physical evidence in possession of both parties, and other items must all be made available in the discovery process.

At trial, the prosecutor bears the burden of proving that the defendant is guilty beyond a reasonable doubt. After the prosecution has presented its case, the defense steps in and presents its case. In doing so, it seeks to cast doubt on the prosecution's evidence. A criminal trial may move back and forth in this fashion until both sides rest. At this point, a verdict must be reached. Depending on the seriousness of the offense, the verdict is decided by either a judge or a jury. A judge decides the defendant's fate in a so-called bench trial but only for an offense that is likely to result in less than six months' imprisonment. A jury decides the verdict when the offense at issue is more serious. Special steps must be taken in either instance to ensure the impartiality of the judge or the jury.

Beyond Conviction

The criminal process does not necessarily end once the verdict has been read. *Sentencing* usually takes place at a separate hearing. The guilty party may be sentenced to death (for a capital crime), committed to prison, fined, placed on probation, or subjected to a host of other possible sanctions. Probation is the most common sanction; imprisonment and, of course, death are clearly much more serious. When a person is committed to prison or sentenced to death, it may seem that the criminal process has just begun, as the appeals process can drag on years beyond the criminal trial.

Appeals come in two varieties: automatic and discretionary. Most convicted criminals are entitled to at least one *automatic appeal* (also known as an *appeal of right*). An automatic appeal must be heard by an appellate court. With a discretionary appeal, however, it is up to the appellate court to decide whether the appeal will be heard. The right of a convicted criminal to file excessive discretionary appeals is deplored by supporters of the death penalty and other serious sanctions.

Making an appeal is not the only method of challenging a guilty verdict. The right of *habeas corpus*—a method of what is commonly called *collateral attack*—is guaranteed in the Constitution, providing every convicted criminal the right to petition a court to decide on the constitutionality of his or her confinement. All that is granted, however, is the right to *file* a petition, or to *request* to be heard. The decision whether to grant a prisoner's *habeas* petition is up to the reviewing court. If a prisoner exhausts all available appellate mechanisms and is denied *habeas* review, he or she will remain in prison for the full term of his or her sentence.

Summary

1. SUMMARIZE THE CONSTITUTIONAL BASIS FOR CRIMINAL PROCEDURE.

Criminal procedure is mostly about constitutional rights. What's more, it is about constitutional rights as primarily interpreted by the U.S. Supreme Court. State laws, agency policies, time-honored practices, and the like also set forth rules and guidelines, but the focus here is almost exclusively on rights spelled out in the U.S. Constitution—notably, those found in the Fourth, Fifth, Sixth, Eighth, and Fourteenth Amendments.

2. EXPLAIN THE IMPORTANCE OF PRECEDENT.

Criminal procedure and history cannot be divorced from one another because of the importance of precedent. Before making decisions, courts almost always look to the past for the purpose of determining whether a case with similar facts has already been decided. If one has not, the court will distinguish the present case and hand down a decision that may be relied on by some other court, at some other date.

3. COMPARE THE THEORY OF CRIMINAL PROCEDURE TO THE REALITY.

Even though criminal procedure, as presented in this text, is mostly about court decisions, it would be a crucial mistake to become hopelessly mired in the world of judicial decision making. In the real world, the police and other criminal justice officials must act, and what they do does not always agree with decisions handed down by the courts. That is, the theoretical world of the courts can differ in important ways from the real world of law enforcement. Understanding that these two different worlds exist and that they can be at odds with one another allows looking at court decisions with not only a critical eye but also a dose of reality.

4. DESCRIBE THE PUBLIC ORDER (CRIME CONTROL) AND INDIVIDUAL RIGHTS (DUE PROCESS) PERSPECTIVES OF CRIMINAL JUSTICE AND HOW CRIMINAL PROCEDURE BALANCES THE TWO.

Throughout criminal procedure—indeed, through-out all of criminal justice—two competing concerns can almost always be heard. The crime control perspective favors controlling crime at whatever cost, and the due process perspective is concerned with protecting people's rights. Every court decision, every crime control policy, and even every reaction by the criminal justice system to the threat of crime must balance both of these concerns. Some decisions and policies lean too far in the direction of crime control and, for that reason, become quite controversial. The same holds true for decisions and policies that cater to due process. For the justice process to flow smoothly, a balance needs to be achieved.

5. OUTLINE THE STRUCTURE OF THE COURT SYSTEM, INCLUDING THE RESPONSIBILITIES AND JURISDICTIONS OF EACH LEVEL.

The United States has a two-tiered court structure consisting of federal and state courts. At the federal level, three types of courts are relevant: district courts, circuit courts of appeals, and the U.S. Supreme Court. The district courts try cases involving violations of federal laws. The decisions of district courts are appealed to circuit courts of appeals and then to the U.S. Supreme Court. State court structures vary from one state to the next but generally consist of courts of limited jurisdiction, trial courts of general jurisdiction, intermediate appellate courts, and supreme courts.

Most criminal cases originate in trial courts of general jurisdiction; the decisions of these courts are appealed to intermediate appellate courts and then to the state supreme court. A state supreme court decision can be appealed to the U.S. Supreme Court but will only be heard if it raises a constitutional question. This is usually true for federal cases, as well.

6. SUMMARIZE IMPORTANT ISSUES AND TRENDS IN CRIMINAL PROCEDURE.

Several important topics, issues, and trends need to be understood before reading too much into court decisions. First, some decisions consist of specific bright-line rules, whereas others favor case-by-case adjudication. Next, the courts—in particular, the U.S. Supreme Court—have moved from a subjective to an objective focus, meaning that they are now more concerned with how a reasonable person would act under the circumstances. Third, Supreme Court decisions of late have reflected an increased faith in the police. Fourth, to understand why court decisions often focus on excruciating legal details, one must understand the notion of judicial restraint: the practice of deciding only the specific legal question before the court. Fifth, throughout criminal procedure there is a concern with *people's privacy*, even though the Constitution contains no mention of the term. Finally, it is important to have an appreciation for how the war on terror and technology have altered criminal procedure (these issues come up throughout the book).

7. PROVIDE AN OVERVIEW OF THE CRIMINAL PROCESS.

There is no one best way to describe the criminal process; there are simply too many variations from state to state. Even so, a more or less accurate description can be offered. The description set forth in this chapter and followed throughout the remainder of the book begins with the police/citizen encounters and then moves into arrest, booking, pretrial hearings, trial, and appeals. Along the way, special attention is given to constitutional rights stemming from several amendments to the Constitution and to the four important actors—the police, prosecutors, defense attorneys, and judges—whose decisions affect the whole of the criminal process. The reader is strongly encouraged to become familiar with the details of the criminal process in his or her area of residence.

Key Terms

affirm	22	dissent	23	judicial activism	28	state supreme courts	17
appellant	22	distinguish	11	judicial restraint	28	subjective reasonableness	26
appellee	22	district courts	17	objective reasonableness	26	substantive due process	7
bright-line decisions	25	due process perspective	14	opinion	23	superior courts	17
case-by-case adjudication	25	Eighth Amendment	7	PATRIOT Act	30	theory world	11
concurring opinion	23	Federal Rules of Criminal Procedure	5	petitioner	22	totality of circumstances	25
courts of general jurisdiction	17	Fifth Amendment	6	precedent	10	trespass doctrine	28
courts of limited jurisdiction	17	Fourteenth Amendment	7	procedural due process	7	U.S. courts of appeals	17
crime control perspective	15	Fourth Amendment	5	prosecutor	22	U.S. Supreme Court	17
criminal procedure	3	incorporation	8	real world	11	vacate	22
defendant	22	intermediate appellate courts	17	remand	22	Warren Court	27
				reverse	22	writ of certiorari	23
				right to privacy	29		
				rule of four	24		
				Sixth Amendment	6		
				stare decisis	10		

Key Cases

- *Manson v. Braithwaite*, 432 U.S. 98 (1977)
- *United States v. Dionisio*, 410 U.S. 1 (1973)

Review Questions

1. Identify several sources of rights.
2. What is the incorporation controversy? What are the leading perspectives describing it?
3. What rights have been incorporated? What rights have not?
4. In what ways can *theory* differ from *reality*?
5. Compare and contrast the due process and crime control perspectives.
6. Explain the federal court structure.
7. How does a case arrive at the U.S. Supreme Court?
8. Distinguish between a bright-line decision and case-by-case adjudication.
9. How are the terms *subjective* and *objective* used in criminal procedure?
10. In what ways have recent Supreme Court decisions shown increased faith in the police?
11. What is judicial restraint? How does it compare to judicial activism?
12. Is privacy a right? If not, why is it so important in many Supreme Court opinions?
13. What happens, briefly, during the pretrial phase?
14. What happens, briefly, during the adjudication phase?
15. What happens, briefly, beyond conviction?

Web Links and Exercises

1. Finding the law: Search the U.S. Code for "search and seizure" (put "search and seizure" in quotes in the "Search Word[s]:" box), then find and discuss a statute with implications for criminal procedure.
   Suggested URL: http://uscode.house.gov/search/criteria.shtml (accessed February 14, 2011)

2. State court organization: Compare and contrast your state court system's organization to that of another state.
   Suggested URL: http://bjs.ojp.usdoj.gov/content/pub/pdf/sco04.pdf (accessed February 14, 2011)

3. Federal court organization: Explain the relationship between the federal courts and the other branches of government.

Suggested URL: http://www.uscourts.gov/FederalCourts.aspx (accessed February 14, 2011)

4. Legal research: Find a recent U.S. Supreme Court case (one that did not make it into this edition of *Criminal Procedure*) with implications for criminal procedure.

Suggested URL: http://www.supremecourtus.gov/ (accessed February 14, 2011)

5. PATRIOT Act: Discuss the pros and cons associated with the PATRIOT Act.

Suggested URL (pro): http://www.proconservative.net/PCVol5Is293WrayTerrorism.shtml (accessed February 14, 2011)

Suggested URL (con): http://www.aclu.org/safefree/resources/17343res20031114.html (accessed February 14, 2011)

LEARNING OBJECTIVES

When you complete this chapter, you should be able to:

▸ Summarize the exclusionary rule and the issues associated with it.

▸ Summarize the "fruit of the poisonous tree" doctrine and the exceptions to it.

▸ Describe criminal prosecution and civil remedies for constitutional rights violations.

▸ Describe nonjudicial remedies for constitutional rights violations.

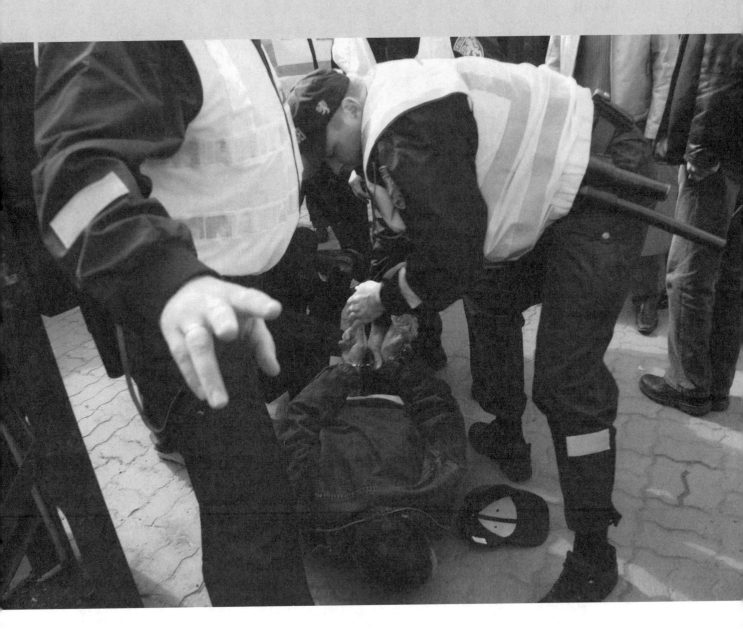

Remedies

INTRODUCTION

Remedies for Constitutional Rights Violations

Criminal procedure cannot be fully appreciated without some discussion of remedies. A **remedy** provides a method of rectifying wrongdoing. That is, when a person believes he or she has been harmed in some way, he or she may seek to ease the pain, make the person who caused the harm "pay," or both. For example, if Sandy is unjustifiably assaulted by Jim, an on-duty police officer, she may opt to remedy the wrong inflicted on her. A remedy is the enforcement mechanism for violations of people's rights.

Remedies fall into two categories: (1) legal and (2) extralegal. **Extralegal remedies** are those conducted outside the legal process. A good example of an extralegal remedy is vigilantism. For example, if one man is assaulted by another, the assaulted individual may seek revenge and opt to solve the perceived injustice with his fists. This type of remedy is not the kind discussed in this chapter or anywhere else throughout the text. Instead, this chapter focuses on **legal remedies**—that is, remedies made available by the law, by a court decision, or by a police agency policy or procedure.

The most frequently discussed remedy in criminal procedure is the *exclusionary rule*. As such, the first part of this chapter is devoted to it. It is an example of a remedy made available because of court decisions; that is, it has no statutory basis. But in order to place the exclusionary rule in context, this chapter also focuses on other types of remedies, such as those provided in law and agency practice. These remedies are important because the exclusionary rule applies only in limited contexts.

The bulk of criminal procedure concerns *constitutional* procedure. It focuses on the various forms of government action permitted and not permitted by the U.S. Constitution. Accordingly, the bulk of the discussion in this chapter is on remedies for constitutional rights violations—particularly the exclusionary rule and 42 U.S.C. Section 1983 (or, simply, Section 1983), a statute that provides people with an avenue for suing criminal justice officials. However, there are several situations in which neither the exclusionary rule nor 42 U.S.C. Section 1983 applies. Therefore, this chapter also focuses on additional remedies that are available to people whose *constitutional* rights are not violated but whose *rights* are violated, nonetheless. These include state tort litigation, disciplinary procedures, civilian review, mediation, and the criminal law.

This chapter contains four primary sections. The first section includes the exclusionary rule and the so-called "fruit of the poisonous tree" doctrine. The second section touches on criminal remedies other than the exclusionary rule, notably state and federal law. The third section looks at *civil remedies*. Civil remedies are sought by filing lawsuits. The chapter closes with a discussion of *nonjudicial remedies*, including internal review, civilian review, and mediation.

THE EXCLUSIONARY RULE

By far, the most significant remedy in criminal procedure is the **exclusionary rule**. It is, simply, a rule of exclusion. It requires that evidence obtained in violation of the Constitution cannot be used in a criminal trial to prove guilt. It is a rule, as opposed to a constitutional provision, because nowhere in the Constitution does it say that illegally obtained evidence must be excluded at trial. In other words, the Supreme Court created the exclusionary rule.

The Rule and Its History

Somewhat surprisingly, the U.S. Constitution contains no provisions for enforcing the protections enunciated in the Bill of Rights. For example, even though people enjoy the right to be free from unreasonable searches and seizures, the Constitution does not specify how this right is to be enforced.

For a time, then, the Bill of Rights was more or less a sham, especially when it came to criminal procedure. Without a means for remedying an unlawful search, improperly obtained confession, or similar violation, evidence obtained in flagrant violation of the Constitution could be admissible at trial.

Fortunately, as early as 1886, the U.S. Supreme Court suggested that improperly obtained evidence be excluded. In *Boyd v. United States* (116 U.S. 616 [1886]), the Court held that business records should have been excluded because "a compulsory production of the private books and papers of the owner of goods . . . is compelling him to be a witness against himself, within the meaning of the Fifth Amendment to the Constitution, and is the equivalent of a search-and-seizure—and an unreasonable search-and-seizure—within the meaning of the Fourth Amendment" (p. 634). This statement is interesting because the

Supreme Court argued that evidence should be excluded not only on Fourth Amendment grounds but also on Fifth Amendment grounds.

Then, in *Weeks v. United States* (232 U.S. 383 [1914]), the Court relied solely on the Fourth Amendment as a basis for exclusion. In that case, the Court held that papers seized following a search that was in violation of the Fourth Amendment should have been returned, rather than used in a criminal trial against the petitioner. Later, in *Silverthorne Lumber Co. v. United States* (251 U.S. 385 [1920]), Justice Holmes stated that without an enforcement mechanism, "the Fourth Amendment [is reduced] to a form of words" and little else (p. 392).

Weeks v. United States
(232 U.S. 383 [1914])

Silverthorne Lumber
Co. v. United States
(251 U.S. 385 [1920])

It is important to note that *Boyd, Weeks,* and *Silverthorne Lumber* were all *federal* cases. Following these decisions, the Supreme Court continued for several years to apply the exclusionary rule only in federal cases (e.g., *Agnello v. United States*, 269 U.S. 20 [1925]). Then, in 1949, the Court began to turn its attention to constitutional rights violations occurring at the *state* level. For example, in *Wolf v. Colorado* (338 U.S. 25 [1949]), the Court decided that the Fourth Amendment is applicable to the states under the due process clause of the Fourteenth Amendment, but it stopped short of mandating exclusion:

> Granting that in practice the exclusion of evidence may be an effective way to deterring unreasonable searches, it is not for this Court to condemn as falling below the minimal standards assured by the Due Process Clause a State's reliance upon other methods which, if consistently enforced, would be equally effective. . . . We cannot brush aside the experience of the States which deem the incidence of such conduct by the police too slight to call for a deterrent remedy not by way of disciplinary measure but by overriding the relevant rules of evidence. (p. 31)

Even though the Court was hesitant to mandate exclusion in state courts of improperly obtained evidence, at the time of the *Wolf* decision, many states had already adopted their own versions of the exclusionary rule. By 1960, 26 states had adopted exclusionary rules (see *Elkins v. United States*, 364 U.S. 206 [1960]).

Elkins v. United States took another step toward applying the exclusionary rule to the states. In that case, the Court denounced the so-called **"silver platter" doctrine**, which permitted the use of evidence in *federal* court that had been obtained illegally by *state* officials. For example, federal officials could not expect illegally obtained evidence to be admissible if they seized it (the decision in *Weeks*), but under the silver platter doctrine, they could ask state law enforcement officials to seize the evidence, even in violation of the Constitution, and it would be admissible in federal court. The silver platter doctrine, then, was a convenient means of circumventing the *Weeks* decision. The Court caught on to this practice and scrapped the doctrine.

A TURNING POINT: *MAPP V. OHIO*   The year 1961 marked a watershed in criminal procedure, as it was the year the Supreme Court decided the landmark case of *Mapp v. Ohio* (367 U.S. 643 [1961]). Arguably, this was, and continues to be, the most significant criminal procedure case the Supreme Court has decided. In *Mapp*, the Court decided 5 to 4 that the exclusionary rule applies to the states. It concluded that other remedies, such as reliance on the due process clause to enforce Fourth Amendment violations, had proven "worthless and futile." Justice Clark, in a related case, stated that the exclusionary rule is the "imperative of judicial integrity," noting, "The criminal goes free, if he must, but it is the law that sets him free. Nothing can destroy a government more quickly than its failure to observe its own law, or worse, its disregard of the charter of its own existence" (*Elkins v. United States*, p. 222).

Mapp v. Ohio
(367 U.S. 643 [1961])

Insofar as *Mapp* applied the exclusionary rule to the states, it did not do so fully. In the later case of *Ker v. California* (374 U.S. 23 [1963]), the Supreme Court noted that it had no "supervisory authority over state courts, . . . and, consequently, [*Mapp*] implied no *total* obliteration of state laws relating to arrests and searches in favor of federal law" (p. 31). In essence, the Court was deferring to the states to decide what made up a reasonable search or seizure, but only to the extent such decisions were "consistent with federal constitutional guarantees." Thus, whenever determining the reasonableness of a questionable Fourth Amendment action, federal standards must be applied. However, if a state adopts procedures that are *more restrictive* than federal standards, doing so follows the *Mapp* decision.

One final restriction concerning *Mapp* is that it only mandates exclusion of evidence obtained in violation of the federal Constitution. If, instead, evidence is obtained in violation of a rule or state law that is not of constitutional dimension, exclusion is not required under *Mapp* (*Cady v. Dombrowski*, 413 U.S. 433 [1973]). Such evidence may be excluded, however, under another decision.

APPLICABILITY OF THE EXCLUSIONARY RULE BEYOND THE FOURTH AMENDMENT   There is a measure of debate concerning the applicability of the exclusionary rule to violations of constitutional rights besides those stemming from the Fourth Amendment. People have asked, Should the exclusionary rule be applied to the Fifth Amendment? What about the Sixth Amendment? The short answer to both questions is that it does. As a general rule, evidence obtained in violation of either the Fifth or Sixth Amendment will be excluded at a criminal trial. The long answer, unfortunately, leaves the issue somewhat unresolved.

On the one hand, some people believe that because the Fourth Amendment contains no specific reference to what should happen when an improper search or seizure takes place, the purpose of the exclusionary rule is to enforce the Fourth Amendment. They argue, furthermore, that because the exclusionary rule operates differently outside the Fourth Amendment context, it was not meant to apply to Fifth and Sixth Amendment violations. For example, just because a confession is improperly obtained does not mean that any subsequently obtained physical evidence will be excluded.

On the other hand, some observers argue that evidence can still be excluded because of Fifth, Sixth, and even Fourteenth Amendment violations. Improperly obtained confessions are not admissible—that is, they will be excluded from a criminal trial. Coercive confessions will be excluded under the Fourteenth Amendment's due process clause, identifications stemming from Sixth Amendment violations will not be admissible, and so on. These observers' point is that evidence can technically be excluded when any constitutional provision giving rise to such evidence is violated.

The perspective adopted in this book is that the exclusionary rule applies across the board. Any constitutional provision that governs law enforcement's efforts to secure evidence that could be used in a criminal prosecution falls under the purview of the exclusionary rule. That is, whenever law enforcement violates one or more of the Fourth, Fifth, Sixth, and Fourteenth Amendments—the most common amendments in criminal procedure—the evidence resulting from such a violation will not be admissible in a court of law. It is important to note, however, that the exclusionary rule and its close cousin—the "fruit of the poisonous tree" doctrine (discussed later in this chapter)—do not always operate in the same manner outside the Fourth Amendment context.

ARGUMENTS FOR AND AGAINST THE RULE   The debate over the exclusionary rule centers on three important issues: (1) whether the rule deters police misconduct; (2) whether the rule imposes unnecessary costs on society; and (3) whether alternative remedies would be effective and should be pursued.

- With regard to deterrence, critics argue that the exclusionary rule does not deter police misconduct. They claim that most constitutional rights violations are unintentional and that such mistakes are undeterrable. And regarding police officers who act in bad faith, critics argue that such officers will commit perjury to mask a constitutional rights violation. Supporters of the deterrence argument, by contrast, state that the rule is not intended to deter individual officers (i.e., *specific deterrence*) but that it is intended to have a broader, systemic deterrent effect (i.e., *general deterrence*). This perspective is well supported because many police departments have amended their policies in the wake of the *Mapp* decision and encouraged their officers to adhere to constitutional safeguards.
- As for social costs, critics make a number of claims. First, they believe that the exclusionary rule requires throwing out some of the most reliable forms of evidence (e.g., confessions), letting suspected criminals go free. Second, critics believe that innocent people have nothing to gain from the exclusionary rule because they have nothing to be seized by law enforcement officers who would infringe on constitutional protections. Critics also believe that the exclusionary rule creates public cynicism because it allows some individuals to escape prosecution. Finally, critics believe that the exclusionary rule is too extreme, in that a relatively trivial violation by a police officer may result in the exclusion of significant evidence.

  Supporters of the exclusionary rule, by contrast, believe the benefits outweigh the costs. For example, they argue, quite persuasively, that the exclusionary rule is rarely applied. Indeed, this is true; motions to exclude evidence because of alleged constitutional rights violations are relatively rare, and they succeed even more rarely. Second, supporters believe the rule is beneficial because it *does* help innocent people. That is, since *Mapp* and other significant decisions, innocent people have been subjected to fewer unconstitutional searches, not necessarily because the police fear the exclusion of evidence but because of the potential for civil liability, citizen complaints, and the like. Supporters of the exclusionary rule also argue that public cynicism, to the extent it exists, should be directed at wayward government officials, not the exclusionary rule. Finally, supporters argue that the exclusionary rule is not disproportionate in terms of its consequences but rather is intended to serve as a general deterrent.
- Opinions about the exclusionary rule are also divided along the notion of alternative remedies. Critics of the rule claim that effective alternatives do exist and should be pursued, including civil litigation, criminal prosecution, and internal discipline. Their view is that overzealous law enforcement officers can be deterred from violating the Constitution by these enforcement mechanisms. Others do not believe that the alternatives will likely prove effective. They claim, for example, that juries are more likely to favor police officers in civil trials, that immunity is often extended to police officers in civil litigation cases, and that internal police discipline is something of a sham (i.e., disciplinary decisions tend to favor the officer, not the citizen filing the complaint).

Summary.   Needless to say, there are many divergent opinions concerning the exclusionary rule. Both sides to the debate make interesting points, and their arguments are persuasive. However, given the relatively small number of celebrated cases in which serious criminals have gone free, the exclusionary rule is probably more beneficial than it is harmful. In addition, just because evidence may be excluded because of police misconduct, this does not mean the defendant will "walk." In many cases, the prosecutor possesses other evidence. For example, suppose a defendant's confession is excluded but several witnesses are still willing to testify that the defendant committed the crime. He or she will, in all likelihood, be convicted.

WHEN THE EXCLUSIONARY RULE DOES NOT APPLY   As indicated already, the exclusionary rule applies in criminal trials. But what of other proceedings, both criminal and noncriminal? The answer is that it depends. More specifically, it depends on whether the rule's remedial objective in a given context is deterrence. In other words, if in a particular circumstance the exclusion of evidence would not in theory deter misconduct, the rule does not apply. With a handful of exceptions, the exclusionary rule does not apply in four situations: grand jury investigations, *habeas corpus* proceedings, parole revocation hearings, and civil proceedings.

- First, the exclusionary rule does not apply in the context of grand jury investigations. In *United States v. Calandra* (414 U.S. 338 [1974]), a witness called before a grand jury refused to answer questions that were based on evidence obtained from him during an unlawful search. Worried that enforcement of the exclusionary rule would impede grand jury investigations, the Court held that it did not apply in those proceedings. The Court noted that "[a]ny incremental deterrent effect which might be achieved by extending the rule to grand jury proceedings is uncertain at best" (p. 351). The reason for this is that grand juries serve investigative functions, and the evidence would still be excluded at trial.

- The rule also does not apply in *habeas corpus* proceedings. The topic of *habeas corpus* will be discussed later in this book (see Chapter 15), but it is worth defining the term here. Basically, every state or federal prisoner in the United States enjoys the constitutional right to challenge his or her conviction in federal court on the grounds that his or her constitutional rights were violated. *Habeas corpus* is not an appeal; it is known as a *collateral attack.*

   As far as the exclusionary rule goes, since a *habeas corpus* petition always *follows* a criminal trial, the Court removed Fourth Amendment issues from the list of violations that can be raised in such a petition, assuming the petitioner had a "full and fair" opportunity to challenge such violations at trial. In other words, the Court reasoned that since the exclusionary rule applies at trial, any deterrent effect is most likely served there. (Deterrence *after* the trial would essentially be pointless.) In the Court's words, "The view that the deterrence of Fourth Amendment violations would be furthered rests on the dubious assumption that law enforcement authorities would fear that federal habeas review might reveal flaws in a search or seizure that went undetected at trial and on appeal" (*Stone v. Powell,* 428 U.S. 465 [1976], p. 493).

- The third type of criminal proceeding in which the exclusionary rule does not apply is a parole revocation hearing. This was the decision reached in *Pennsylvania v. Scott* (524 U.S. 357 [1998]), in which the majority argued that application of the exclusionary rule in a parole revocation hearing "would both hinder the function of state parole systems and alter the traditionally flexible administrative nature of parole revocation proceedings" (p. 364). The Court further noted that the relationship between a *parole officer* and a *parolee* (as opposed to the relationship between a *police officer* and a *suspect*) is supervisory rather than adversarial, so it would be "unfair to assume that the parole officer bears hostility against the parolee that destroys his neutrality" (p. 368). Although this view is clearly debatable, it is one of the main reasons the Court offered for its decision not to apply the exclusionary rule in parole revocation proceedings. Finally, in line with the Court's decision in *Scott,* several lower courts have decided that the exclusionary rule is inapplicable in sentencing hearings (e.g., *United States v. Schipani,* 315 F. Supp. 253 [E.D.N.Y 1970]; *United States v. McCrory,* 930 F.2d 63 [D.C.Cir. 1991]).

- Moving into the realm of civil proceedings, the exclusionary rule does not apply in civil actions brought by the Internal Revenue Service (IRS) to collect taxes. This was the decision reached in *United States v. Janis* (428 U.S. 433 [1976]). Janis had successfully excluded evidence in his prior criminal trial, citing officer misconduct, and then moved to have the same evidence excluded in a civil action brought against him by the IRS. The Court held that the IRS case fell "outside the offending officer's zone of primary interest." Thus, excluding the evidence a second time would not deter the officer's misconduct that was remedied at the criminal trial in which the evidence was first excluded.

In another case, the Court held that the exclusionary rule does not apply in deportation hearings brought by the Immigration and Naturalization Service (INS), which are noncriminal. In *INS v. Lopez-Mendoza* (468 U.S. 1032 [1984]), the Court moved away from the "zone of interest" language expressed in *Janis* and adopted a balancing test similar to that espoused in *Calandra*. Specifically, the Court looked at the social benefits of applying the exclusionary rule versus the costs to society of excluding evidence. In support of its decision, the Court noted that since most illegal aliens do not defend themselves in deportation hearings and agree to leave voluntarily, it is doubtful that the exclusionary rule would deter border agents from committing Fourth Amendment violations. On the other hand, the Court noted that releasing illegal aliens into the United States because of constitutional rights violations would frustrate the purpose of the INS.

There are some civil proceedings in which the exclusionary rule *does* apply. In particular, if the civil proceeding is the primary focus of the investigating law enforcement officer (e.g., a civil forfeiture investigation in lieu of a criminal investigation), then the exclusionary rule may apply. The Supreme Court has not directly confronted this issue, but some lower courts have. For example, lower courts have applied the exclusionary rule in juvenile delinquency proceedings (e.g., *State in Interest of T.L.O.*, 94 N.J. 331 [1983]; *New Jersey v. T.L.O.*, 469 U.S. 325 [1985]) and in some administrative proceedings (e.g., *Donovan v. Sarasota Concrete Co.*, 693 F.2d 1061 [11th Cir. 1982]). The key in each situation was that the investigating law enforcement officer worked directly with the adjudicating body. Contrast this with, for example, *Janis*, in which the IRS's civil case was secondary to a criminal prosecution and the investigating officer was involved only with the criminal prosecution.

EXCEPTIONS TO THE RULE Critics of the exclusionary rule routinely argue that it constitutes a loophole in the criminal justice process and is responsible for otherwise guilty criminals going free. On the whole, this argument is somewhat deceptive, in part because of the exceptions allowed to the exclusionary rule. Over the years, the Supreme Court has seen fit to *allow* evidence in light of honest mistakes as well as for other purposes. There are two exceptions to the exclusionary rule: (1) the "good faith" exception and (2) the impeachment exception.

Good Faith Exception. As a general rule, when an honest mistake is made during the course of a search or seizure, any subsequently obtained evidence will be considered admissible. Two cases decided together were responsible for this **"good faith" exception**: *United States v. Leon* (468 U.S. 897 [1984]) and *Massachusetts v. Sheppard* (468 U.S. 981 [1984]). In both *Leon* and *Sheppard*, the Supreme Court concluded that evidence obtained in reasonable (good faith) reliance on a defective warrant was admissible:

United States v. Leon (468 U.S. 897 [1984])

> [W]e cannot conclude that admitting evidence obtained pursuant to a warrant while at the same time declaring that the warrant was somehow defective will in any way reduce judicial officers' professional incentives to comply with the Fourth Amendment, encourage them to repeat their mistakes, or lead to the granting of all colorable warrant requests. (*United States v. Leon*, p. 917)

The good faith exception enunciated in *Leon* and *Sheppard* is not unqualified, however. If, for example, a warrant is "so lacking in indicia of probable cause as to render official belief in its existence entirely unreasonable, then evidence obtained following its service will not be admissible" (*United States v. Hove*, 848 F.2d 137 [9th Cir. 1988], p. 139). Similarly, if a warrant is "so facially deficient—i.e., in failing to particularize the place to be searched or things to be seized—that the executing officers cannot reasonably presume it to be valid, then the exception does not apply" (*United States v. Leary*, 846 F.2d 592 [10th Cir. 1988], p. 607). Furthermore, if the judge issuing the warrant is deliberately misled by information in the affidavit, as when a police officer acts in *bad* faith, then the good faith exception will not apply (*Lo-Ji v. State of New York*, 442 U.S. 319 [1979]). Also, if the judge issues a search warrant without sufficient consideration, then good faith cannot later be asserted.

The good faith exception is not held in the highest regard by some. Critics believe that it gives police officers an incentive to "forum shop" or to find judges who will be quick to sign off on a warrant. Justice Brennan argued in opposition to the exception as follows:

> Creation of this new exception for good faith reliance upon a warrant implicitly tells magistrates that they need not take much care in reviewing warrant applications, since their mistakes will from now on have virtually no consequence: If their decision to issue a warrant is correct, the evidence will be admitted; if their decision was incorrect but [not "entirely unreasonable" and] the police rely in good faith on the warrant, the evidence will also be admitted. Inevitably, the care and attention devoted to such an inconsequential chore will dwindle. (*United States v. Leon*, p. 956)

The good faith exception has been extended to other situations besides searches and seizures based on defective warrants. For instance, if a police officer acts in reasonable reliance on a statute that is later found to be unconstitutional, then the good faith exception will not apply (see *Michigan v. DeFillippo*, 443 U.S. 31 [1979]). In addition, if evidence is obtained following a search or seizure that is conducted in reasonable reliance on computer records that turn out to be inaccurate, then, again, the exception will not apply. In *Arizona v. Evans* (514 U.S. 1 [1995]), for example, a defendant was arrested during a traffic stop because the officer's computer showed an outstanding warrant that, unknown to the officer, had been quashed 17 days earlier. Evidence obtained from a search of the vehicle was admissible because, according to the Court, "there is no basis for believing that application of the exclusionary rule in these circumstances will have a significant effect on court employees responsible for informing the police that a warrant has been quashed" (p. 15). A similar decision was reached in a more recent case where police arrested an individual and found contraband in a search incident to arrest, yet unbeknownst to the officers, the arrest warrant had been recalled months earlier (*Herring v. United States*, 555 U.S. 135 [2009]).

DECISION-MAKING EXERCISE 2.1

When Does the Exclusionary Rule Not Apply?

Two officers from the state liquor control board, acting without a warrant, stopped and searched an automobile. They found that the car contained many cases of liquor not bearing state tax seals. The driver was arrested, and his car was seized. The government sought to forfeit the automobile, but the trial judge, concluding that the officers had acted without probable cause, did not permit it on the grounds that doing so depended on the admission of evidence illegally obtained in violation of the Fourth Amendment. Should the exclusionary rule apply in a civil forfeiture case, such as that described here?

Impeachment Exception. The next leading exception to the exclusionary rule is the so-called **impeachment exception**. If one of the good faith exceptions does not apply, then the prosecution cannot use, as part of its case, evidence resulting from an illegal search or seizure. However, if the prosecution seeks to use such evidence for the purpose of impeaching (i.e., attacking the credibility of) a witness, then it will be considered admissible for that purpose. In *Walder v. United States* (347 U.S. 62 [1954]), a narcotics case, the Supreme Court permitted the introduction of heroin that had been illegally seized from the defendant two years earlier (and excluded from the trial it was supposed to be used in) in order to attack his statement that he had never purchased, used, or sold drugs. An important restriction concerning the impeachment exception is that it applies only to criminal defendants, not other witnesses (*James v. Illinois*, 493 U.S. 307 [1990]).

Walder v. United States
(347 U.S. 62 [1954])

Good faith and impeachment are, again, the only two recognized exceptions to the exclusionary rule. Three additional exclusionary rule–type exceptions (i.e., inevitable discovery, independent source, and purged taint) are sometimes blended together with these two, but they should be kept separate. They are actually exceptions to the "fruit of the poisonous tree" doctrine, to which the discussion turns now.

The "Fruit of the Poisonous Tree" Doctrine

In *Silverthorne Lumber Co. v. United States* (251 U.S. 385 [1920]), the Supreme Court created the **"fruit of the poisonous tree" doctrine**.[1] In that case, Silverthorne Lumber Company was convicted on contempt charges for failing to produce documents that were learned of during the course of an illegal search. The Court reversed the conviction, stating that forcing the company to produce documents that were learned of strictly because of an illegal search violated the Fourth Amendment. The *Silverthorne* holding was reaffirmed in the case of *Nardone v. United States* (308 U.S. 338 [1939]). In it, the Court noted that it should be left to the discretion of "experienced trial judges" to determine whether "a substantial portion of the case against [the accused] was a fruit of the poisonous tree" (p. 341).

The metaphor of the "fruit of the poisonous tree" can be traced to the biblical story of the Garden of Eden. As the story goes, Adam and Eve ate the apple, the forbidden fruit, from the tree, bringing original sin into the world. The poisonous tree,

---

DECISION-MAKING EXERCISE 2.2

An Act of Good Faith?

After learning from an informant that some businesses had been broken into during the previous night and without making any effort to corroborate the information supplied by the informant, County Deputy Smith signed a complaint naming Mark Laurel and Carl Rogers as those who had broken into the buildings. After receiving this complaint, a judge issued a warrant for the arrests of Laurel and Rogers. Deputy Smith then sent out a police radio bulletin, describing both suspects, the car they were likely to be driving, and items that had been taken from the buildings. Police Officer Wesson, who was employed by the city, stopped a car that met the description in the radio bulletin. Wesson observed that the car had two men in it and that one of the men met Laurel's description in the radio bulletin. Officer Wesson arrested both occupants and searched the car. He found items that had been taken from one of the buildings and described in the radio bulletin in the interior of the car and burglars' tools in the trunk. Assuming the warrant is invalid (which is because it lacks any corroboration), should Officer Wesson's arrest come under the good faith exception to the exclusionary rule?

---

[1] Courts often use the term *derivative evidence* in lieu of "fruit of the poisonous tree." The former refers simply to evidence *derived* from a previous unconstitutional search or seizure.

DECISION-MAKING EXERCISE 2.3

The Impeachment Exception

Dewey and Rodriguez boarded a flight from Lima, Peru, and flew to Miami, Florida. In Miami, a customs officer searched Rodriguez and found cocaine sewn into makeshift pockets in the T-shirt he was wearing under his clothing. Rodriguez was arrested and claimed that Dewey, who had cleared customs, was also carrying cocaine. Dewey was located and arrested. His luggage was then seized and searched without a warrant. The officers found no drugs but seized a T-shirt from which pieces had been cut that matched the pieces sewn to Rodriguez's T-shirt. Because Dewey's luggage had been searched without a warrant, the T-shirt and other evidence were suppressed prior to trial. At trial, Rodriguez, who had pleaded guilty, testified as a witness for the prosecution that Dewey had supplied him with altered T-shirt and had sewn the makeshift pockets shut. Dewey, the defendant, then took the stand in his own defense and denied Rodriguez's claims. On cross-examination, the prosecutor introduced the shirt into evidence. Could this be permissible for any reason?

then, is the initial unconstitutional search or seizure. Anything obtained from the tree is considered forbidden fruit. Here are some examples of how the fruit of the poisonous tree doctrine would work:

- A suspect is coerced to confess and alerts police to where evidence can be found. The evidence would be inadmissible because it is fruit of an unconstitutional confession.
- Police arrest a suspect without probable cause and he confesses. The confession would be inadmissible as fruit of the unconstitutional arrest.
- Police arrest a suspect without probable cause. The suspect rats out two co-conspirators who the police then arrest. The second set of arrests would be considered fruit of the poisonous tree, assuming the police had no other basis for arresting the co-conspirators.

In short, the exclusionary rule applies not only to evidence obtained as a direct result of a constitutional rights violation but also to evidence *indirectly* derived from a constitutional rights violation. In many ways, the fruit of the poisonous tree doctrine resembles a "but for" test, in which the courts have to ask, But for the unconstitutional police conduct, would the evidence have been obtained regardless? If the answer is no, then the evidence will be excluded. If the answer is yes, then the issue becomes more complicated. The Supreme Court has carved out three important exceptions to the fruit of the poisonous tree doctrine.

EXCEPTIONS TO FRUIT OF THE POISONOUS TREE   There are three main exceptions to the fruit of the poisonous tree doctrine. They are purged taint, independent source, and inevitable discovery.

Purged Taint.   The first exception to the fruit of the poisonous tree doctrine is known as the *attenuation*, or **"purged taint" exception**. In *Nardone*, Justice Frankfurter observed that in some cases, "sophisticated argument may prove a causal link obtained through [illegality] and the Government's proof. As a matter of good sense, however, such a connection may have become so attenuated as to dissipate the taint" (p. 341). This observation was somewhat prophetic in the sense that the Court did not actually admit evidence because of attenuation. Several years later, in the case of *Wong Sun v. United States* (371 U.S. 471 [1963]), however, the Court did admit evidence because of attenuation.

Wong Sun v. United States
(371 U.S. 471 [1963])

In making an attenuation analysis, the court must decide whether the derivative evidence was obtained by exploitation of the initial unconstitutional act or instead by other means that are purged of the primary taint. In *Wong Sun*, the Court determined that statements provided by a defendant who was illegally arrested and released but later returned to the police stationhouse on his own initiative were admissible because the statements did not result from the illegal arrest. Instead, the defendant decided to come back *later*, following his release. The Court noted that his statement had become attenuated to the extent that it dissipated the taint of the initial unconstitutional act.

In *Brown v. Illinois* (422 U.S. 590 [1975]), the Supreme Court pointed to several factors that should be considered in determining whether the purged taint exception applies: (1) whether the *Miranda* warnings were given prior to a voluntary confession; (2) the "temporal proximity" of the illegal police conduct and verbal statements made by a suspect; (3) the presence of intervening events or circumstances; and (4) the "purpose and flagrancy of the official misconduct." Several later cases focused on these four factors to varying degrees.

For example, in *Dunaway v. New York* (442 U.S. 200 [1979]), the Court chose to decide whether a confession obtained following a questionable stationhouse detention was admissible. The *Miranda* warnings had been given, but the Court still held that stationhouse detention intruded "so severely on interests protected by the Fourth Amendment as necessarily to trigger the traditional safeguards against illegal arrest" (p. 216). The Court then held that despite the *Miranda* warnings, Dunaway's statements should not be admissible. To hold differently would allow "law enforcement officers to violate the Fourth Amendment with impunity, safe in the knowledge that they could wash their hands in the 'procedural safeguards' of the Fifth" (p. 219).

In another case, *Taylor v. Alabama* (457 U.S. 687 [1982]), the Court held that the purged taint exception should not apply even under these circumstances: (1) the defendant had been advised of his *Miranda* rights; (2) six hours had elapsed between the defendant's illegal arrest and confession; and (3) the defendant had been permitted to visit with friends before making his confession.

Contrast *Taylor* with *Rawlings v. Kentucky* (448 U.S. 98 [1980]), in which the Court held that statements made 45 minutes after an illegal arrest *were* admissible because the defendant (1) had been advised of his *Miranda* rights just before making an incriminating statement; (2) had been in a house instead of a police station; and (3) had made spontaneous statements that did not result from direct questioning. Furthermore, the Court noted that the illegal arrest was not flagrant and that the defendant never argued that his admission was an involuntary product of police questioning.

Independent Source.   The second exception to the fruit of the poisonous tree doctrine is the so-called **independent source** exception. The first case to affirmatively establish this type of exception was *Segura v. United States* (468 U.S. 796 [1984]). There, the Court held that evidence found in an apartment pursuant to a valid search warrant was admissible, even though the police had entered the apartment illegally *prior* to serving the search warrant because the warrant was based on information totally disconnected with the initial illegal search. In other words, even though the police first entered the apartment illegally, the warrant they later served was based on information independent from that search.

Segura v. United States
(468 U.S. 796 [1984])

Inevitable Discovery.   The third exception to the fruit of the poisonous tree doctrine is known as the **inevitable discovery** exception. Stated simply, if evidence would be found regardless of unconstitutional police conduct, then it is admissible. This exception was first recognized by the Supreme Court in *Nix v. Williams* (467 U.S. 431 [1984]). In that case, the evidence was the body of a young girl, which was discovered after the police

Nix v. Williams
(467 U.S. 431 [1984])

DECISION-MAKING EXERCISE 2.4

The "Purged Taint" Exception

Officer Lewis was taking a break in a flower shop and conversing with an employee of the shop when she noticed an envelope with money protruding from it lying on the cash register. Lewis examined the envelope and found that it contained not only money but betting slips. She placed the envelope back on the register, and without telling the employee what she had found, she asked who it belonged to. The employee told Lewis that the envelope belonged to Steve Stevens, the store's owner. The officer reported this information to local detectives, who interviewed Stevens some four months later without referring to the incident at the flower shop. About six months after that incident, Stevens was summoned before a grand jury, where he testified that he had never taken bets at his flower shop. However, the store employee testified to the contrary. Stevens was then indicted for perjury. Should the employee's statement be ruled inadmissible at trial?

DECISION-MAKING EXERCISE 2.5

The Independent Source

Suspecting that people were storing marijuana in a warehouse, several police officers entered the building without obtaining a warrant to do so. (Later, they argued that they had suspected that evidence would be destroyed or that the people would escape if they had waited to obtain a warrant.) In fact, the search revealed bales of marijuana but no people. The police then applied for a warrant to search the building, deliberately failing to mention their previous search. The warrant was granted, the search was conducted, and the police "discovered" the marijuana. Should the marijuana be considered admissible at trial?

had illegally questioned the defendant concerning the body's whereabouts. Under ordinary circumstances, the body would not have been considered admissible, but the prosecution was able to prove that at the time of the illegal questioning, a search party looking for the girl's body had narrowed in on its target and would have "inevitably discovered" the body. The Iowa Supreme Court affirmed the lower court's decision to admit the body into evidence because "(1) the police did not act in bad faith for the purpose of hastening discovery of the evidence in question, and (2) . . . the evidence in question would have been discovered by lawful means" (*Iowa v. Williams*, 285 N.W.2d 248 [Iowa 1979], p. 260).

The inevitable discovery exception bears striking resemblance to the independent source exception. For all practical purposes, evidence that would be inevitably discovered comes from an independent source. The search that was underway in *Nix v. Williams*, for example, was totally disconnected from the questioning of the defendant. In light of the similarities between these two exceptions to the fruit of the poisonous tree doctrine, some courts have simply opted to call the inevitable discovery exception the *hypothetical independent source* exception (see *Nix*, p. 438).

CRIMINAL REMEDIES BESIDES THE EXCLUSIONARY RULE

Various statutes at the federal and local levels provide criminal remedies for police misconduct, just like the exclusionary rule does. Some states make it criminal for police officers to trespass and/or to falsely arrest people. In fact, most criminal sanctions that apply to ordinary citizens also apply to police officers. Likewise, various statutes at the federal level make it not only improper but also criminal for police officers to engage in certain types of conduct.

Federal Law

At the federal level, the most common statute for holding police officers criminally liable is **18 U.S.C. Section 242**. Section 242 is to criminal liability what Section 1983 (discussed further below) is to civil liability. It can be used to prosecute either a state or a federal law enforcement officer. Section 242 states,

> Whoever, under color of any law, statute, ordinance, regulation, or custom, willfully subjects any inhabitant of any State, Territory, or District to the deprivation of any rights, privileges, or immunities secured or protected by the Constitution or laws of the United States, or to different punishments, pains, or penalties, on account of such inhabitant being an alien, or by reason of his color, or race, than are prescribed for the punishment of citizens, shall be fined not more than $1,000 or imprisoned not more than one year, or both; and if death results shall be subject to imprisonment for any term of years or for life.

To be held liable under Section 242, a law enforcement officer must act with specific intent to deprive a person of important constitutional (or other federal) rights (*Screws v. United States*, 325 U.S. 91 [1945]). Also, for criminal liability under Section 242, a constitutional right must be clearly established (*United States v. Lanier*, 520 U.S. 259 [1997]). Together, these restrictions have resulted in the filing of relatively few Section 242 cases. In fact, criminal liability under Section 242 is reserved for the most egregious forms of police misconduct.

Screws v. United States
(325 U.S. 91 [1945])

Despite its relatively infrequent application, there is a handful of noteworthy cases invoking Section 242. For example, in *Miller v. United States* (404 F.2d 611 [5th Cir. 1968]), a police officer was held criminally liable for allowing his canine unit to bite a suspect. In *Williams v. United States* (341 U.S. 97 [1951]), a defendant had been beaten, threatened, and physically punished for several hours, so a police officer was held criminally liable. And in *Lynch v. United States* (189 F.2d 476 [5th Cir. 1951]), Section 242 was applied in the wake of the assault and battery of several criminal defendants.

Additional federal statutes make it a criminal act to unlawfully search and seize individuals (18 U.S.C. Section 2236), although applications of this statute are rare, as well. Section 2235 of 18 U.S.C. makes it criminal to maliciously procure a warrant, and Section 2234 makes it criminal to exceed the authority of a warrant. Regardless of which criminal statute applies, an important distinction needs to be made between the various criminal statutes and 42 U.S.C. Section 1983. An officer who is held *criminally* liable will receive a criminal conviction and can even go to prison. Section 1983, by contrast, is *civil*, meaning that it is used independently of the criminal process. A successful Section 1983 lawsuit will never result in imprisonment of the defendant.

State Law

The same laws that apply to ordinary citizens also apply to police officers. For example, if a police officer knowingly and intentionally kills someone and is not legally justified in doing so (e.g., to prevent injury to a third party), that officer can be held criminally liable for murder. Similarly, if a police officer trespasses on private property without appropriate justification, he or she can be held criminally liable. Criminal liability can extend to a police officer for virtually any conceivable offense.

Some crimes are committed by police officers more often than other crimes. Birzer places such offenses into three categories: (1) violent and sex crimes; (2) drug crimes; and (3) other crimes.[2] With respect to violent crimes, the so-called Miami River Cops

---

[2] M. L. Birzer, "Crimes Committed by Police Officers," in M. J. Palmiotto (Ed.), *Police Misconduct* (Upper Saddle River, NJ: Prentice Hall, 2001), pp. 171–178.

were charged with murdering drug smugglers. As for sex crimes, a police officer in Fort Myers, Florida, was charged with sexual assault against a 19-year-old female. These examples are not offered to suggest that police officers frequently engage in criminal activity but only that it happens. No one is above the law, even police officers.

Clearly, police officers also engage in many actions that would be crimes if performed by ordinary citizens. Police officers, however, enjoy immunity from criminal liability for these actions, if the actions are committed (justifiably) as part of their official duties. The so-called law enforcement or **public duty defense** to criminal liability is what shields police officers from criminal liability on most occasions. It is useful to think of this defense in terms of deadly force and nondeadly force.

As a general rule, *deadly force* cannot be used to effect an arrest for or to prevent a misdemeanor. Indeed, rarely can deadly force be applied in the felony context. A police officer can only use deadly force to prevent a felony if he or she reasonably believes that the other person is about to commit an "atrocious" or "forcible" felony (see *People v. Ceballos*, 526 P.2d 241 [Cal. 1974]). And with regard to arrest, deadly force can only be used to effect an arrest if (1) the force is necessary to prevent the suspect's flight; (2) the officer can attempt to warn the suspect of his or her intention to use deadly force (e.g., "Stop or I'll shoot!"); and (3) the officer has probable cause to believe that the suspect, if not immediately apprehended, poses a significant threat of death or serious bodily injury to the officer or others (*Tennessee v. Garner*, 471 U.S. 1 [1985]).

As for *nondeadly force*, the standard is objective reasonableness. A police officer enjoys immunity from criminal liability if when applying nondeadly force, he or she does so in an objectively reasonable fashion (*Graham v. Connor*). This requires asking whether a reasonable officer would, under the circumstances, have acted in the same way. If the answer is no, criminal liability may attach.

Beyond the realms of deadly and nondeadly force, police officers do not have much in the way of defense against criminal liability. If a police officer who committed burglary for his or her own personal gain attempted to assert a public duty defense, he or she would almost certainly fail. Similarly, if a police officer shoots and kills a person not for the purpose of preventing a crime or effecting an arrest but, say, for vengeance, that officer will almost certainly be convicted of some degree of homicide and probably sentenced to prison.

New York City Police Officer Sean Carroll becomes emotional during testimony about his suspected involvement in the Amadou Diallo shooting, one of the most infamous cases of criminal behavior by police.

DECISION-MAKING EXERCISE 2.6

Use of Deadly Force

Officers responded to a call that a woman in an isolated cabin was shooting at people who were camped out on her property. On arriving at the scene, officers heard loud music coming from inside the cabin. They knocked on the door and said they wanted the woman to identify herself and to ask her some questions about what happened earlier that night. After hearing nothing, one of the officers shined his flashlight into a window and observed the woman lying on her bed with a rifle next to her. Shortly thereafter, the woman left her room, apparently without the rifle, and knelt on her couch with her hands behind it. Still not receiving a response from the woman, the officers kicked in the locked front door and entered. Once inside, the woman pointed a rifle at one of the officers. They ordered her to put down the gun, but when she did not do so, she was fatally shot. Was deadly force justified?

CIVIL REMEDIES FOR CONSTITUTIONAL RIGHTS VIOLATIONS

When a person's constitutional or other federal civil rights are violated, he or she can sue. Even if a person merely *believes* his or her rights have been violated, litigation is still an option. The worst (or best) that can happen is that the lawsuit will be dismissed. In this section, we look at one particular type of civil liability (casually referred to as "Section 1983"), but there are others, such as state tort liability, that are beyond the scope of this book. Before we continue, know that while civil liability may be an effective remedy for people whose rights are violated, litigation may come with a high price tag.

What is the purpose of **civil litigation**? Aside from sometimes being the only remedy available, civil lawsuits are attractive because money can be awarded. A lawsuit in which one or more parties seeks monetary compensation is called a **damage suit**. The *plaintiff*, or the person filing the lawsuit, seeks payment for injuries or perceived injuries suffered. In addition to damages, the plaintiff can also seek **injunctive relief**, which basically means he or she wants the court to bring the injurious or offensive action to a halt. Figure 2.1 provides an overview of the stages of a typical civil lawsuit.

Why should we care about civil remedies in a book about criminal procedure? One answer is that criminal remedies do not always apply. The exclusionary rule does not apply if there are no criminal charges. Likewise, criminal remedies made available by state and federal law generally apply in cases of the most egregious police misconduct. Another answer is that several important criminal procedure decisions (e.g., *Tennessee v. Garner*) began as civil lawsuits.

42 U.S.C. Section 1983: Liability of State Officials

42 U.S.C. Section 1983 provides a remedy in federal court for the "deprivation of any rights . . . secured by the Constitution and laws" of the United States. Specifically, Section 1983 states,

> Every person who, under color of any statute, ordinance, regulation, custom, or usage, of any State or Territory, subjects, or causes to be subjected, any citizen of the United States or other persons within the jurisdiction thereof to the deprivation of any rights, privileges, or immunities secured by the Constitution and laws, shall be liable to the party injured in an action at law, suit in equity, or other proper proceeding for redress.

FIGURE 2.1

Stages of a Civil Lawsuit

1. *Citizen complaint*: The first step in filing a lawsuit normally involves a citizen complaint. In a citizen complaint, the aggrieved party can do one of two things: call attention to inappropriate police conduct *or* demand some form of remedial action (e.g., injunctive relief or monetary damages). This latter form of citizen complaint is considered a *demand.*

2. *Demand*: If the complaint filed with the police by a citizen (the *complainant*) requests some action on the part of the police, then the complainant will make a more or less informal demand of the police, who will then send a *response*. This may lead to informal discussions between the two sides. The complainant may retain the services of an attorney, but the procedure remains largely informal at this early juncture.

3. *Citizen complaint board*: In some jurisdictions (e.g., Spokane, WA), the complainant can further file a complaint with a local citizen complaint board if the police agency in question fails to take satisfactory action. Citizen complaint boards vary considerably in use, authority, and terminology, so they are only mentioned here in passing as one mechanism for dispute resolution. Other avenues of dispute resolution may well be in place.

4. *Lawyer's letter*: If the complainant and the police cannot work things out informally, the complainant usually brings in an attorney. The attorney will send a so-called lawyer's letter to the police agency, the officer(s) in question, and/or the city or county. While this letter may not have any legal significance, it usually gets a serious response.

5. *Prelitigation settlement discussion*: An informal prelitigation settlement discussion is often held, in which the police and/or their representatives and the complainant and/or his or her representatives work together to try to reach a settlement. If no settlement is reached, the complaint/demand will likely evolve into a full-blown lawsuit.

6. *Claim with city/county clerk*: Before being able to proceed with a lawsuit, the citizens in some states and counties are first required to file a claim with the city or county against which the complaint is made or to give the police agency a chance to respond to a formal complaint or a request for damages. This *claim* should be distinguished from a *citizen complaint*, discussed above. This claim is an explicit prerequisite that must be completed before a lawsuit can move forward; it is mandated by law. The purpose of such a claim is primarily to inform officials of what is about to transpire. Often, a lawsuit cannot be filed until the parties in question are given the opportunity to respond to a claim.

7. *Lawsuit*: A citizen complaint/demand evolves into a full-blown lawsuit when none of the informal proceedings discussed satisfy the complainant. To reach the stage of a lawsuit, two actions must occur: First, a *complaint* must be filed with the clerk of the court in which the lawsuit will be heard. (This complaint is a legal requirement and differs from the citizen complaint already filed.) Second, the court or an attorney must issue a *summons* to be *served* on the agencies or people named in the complaint. Sometimes, the summons is personally delivered; other times, it is sent by registered or certified mail. The parties named in the complaint (e.g., the police, their agencies, municipalities) are now known as the *defendants,* and the aggrieved party or parties filing the lawsuit are now known as the *plaintiffs.*

8. *Answer*: Once the defendants have been served with the summons, they must provide their formal answer within a prescribed timeframe. For obvious reasons, defendants in police civil liability cases rarely fail to acknowledge the summons.

9. *Discovery*: A lawsuit may involve pretrial discovery, in which one or both parties attempt to get evidence as to what happened in the alleged incident, perhaps by taking the testimony of witnesses or examining documents or physical evidence.

10. *Motions*: In a lawsuit, either side may make motions to try to narrow the issues, to compel the other side to do something, or even to have the court decide the matter without actually conducting a trial. In police civil liability cases, two motions are commonly raised by the defendants: The first is the motion to *dismiss*, in which the defendants attempt to have the case thrown out on the grounds that it does not raise a question of law or other legitimate legal issue. Motions to dismiss are rarely granted. The second common type of motion calls for a *summary judgment*, in which the defendants ask the court to find in favor of the police without going to trial. The majority of these motions succeed, leaving only a few lawsuits that actually progress to the trial stage.

11. *Pretrial conference*: Before the start of the trial, the court will typically order a pretrial conference to narrow the issues still further and perhaps to get the parties to agree to a settlement. Again, the aim is to avoid a lengthy trial proceeding.

12. *Trial, judgment, and post-trial motions and appeals*: If a lawsuit progresses all the way to trial, it will be decided either by a judge alone or by a jury that decides the facts and a judge who decides the law. After the trial, the court will enter a judgment, in which the plaintiff, for example, might be entitled to a fixed amount of money. Post-trial motions might also be raised, in which the losing party tries to convince the judge that some other judgment would be more appropriate (e.g., perhaps more money, added relief, or none at all). Finally, the losing party might appeal to a higher court.

13. *Collecting the judgment*: The party who wins the lawsuit may have received a judgment stating what he or she is entitled to recover. It is then his or her job to collect the judgment. This can be a difficult and time-consuming process, so it is typically put on hold until all relevant appeals have been exhausted.

Section 1983 was originally enacted as part of the Ku Klux Klan Act of April 20, 1871 (also known as Section 1 of the Civil Rights Act of 1871). The act was designed to address atrocities being committed by Klan members in the wake of the Civil War, but it did not target Klan members as such. Instead, Section 1983 imposed liability on state representatives who failed to enforce state laws against illegal Klan activities. The statute was rarely used, however, and remained effectively dormant for some 90 years after it was signed into law.

Section 1983 enjoyed a resurgence in *Monroe v. Pape* (365 U.S. 167 [1961]). In that case, a group of police officers allegedly entered the home of James Monroe without warning and then forced the occupants to stand naked in the living room while the house was searched and ransacked. Monroe brought a Section 1983 action against the police officers and the city of Chicago. The case eventually reached the U.S. Supreme Court, where eight justices held that the alleged misuse of authority could support a Section 1983 action against the police officers. That is, the Supreme Court held that Section 1983 could be used as a vehicle to sue the police.

Monroe v. Pape
(365 U.S. 167 [1961])

Since *Monroe*, Section 1983 litigation has become quite popular. The reasons for this increase are many, but the Supreme Court's decision in *Monroe* almost certainly had a strong influence. For example, as cited in Lieberman, Chief Justice Rehnquist has referred to *Monroe* as "the fountainhead of the torrent of civil rights litigation of the last 17 years."[3] In a similar reference to Section 1983 as the "cornerstone of police federal liability litigation," Kappeler and his colleagues have observed that "[t]he increased use of the 1871 Civil Rights Act may be attributable to expanded interpretation of the legislation by the Supreme Court."[4] And Vaughn and Coomes have noted that "Section 1983 is extremely controversial because of its widespread impact on criminal justice personnel, particularly police officers."[5]

The next four subsections focus carefully on Section 1983. The first discusses the concept of *color of law*, a requirement for any successful Section 1983 claim. Second, the types of actions that amount to constitutional rights violations are considered. Third, theories of liability under Section 1983 are reviewed. Finally, qualified immunity, the main defense available to defendants in Section 1983 actions, is introduced.

COLOR OF LAW One of the requirements for a successful Section 1983 lawsuit is that the *defendant*, the person being sued, acted under color of law. The Supreme Court has stated that someone acts under **color of law** when he or she acts in an official capacity (*Lugar v. Edmondson Oil Co.*, 457 U.S. 922 [1982]). For example, a police officer who is on duty acts under color of law. By contrast, someone acting in a private capacity, such as an ordinary citizen, cannot be said to have acted under color of law.

Offering further clarification, Vaughn and Coomes have shown that police officers act under color of law when one or more of the following conditions are satisfied:

- They have identified themselves as officers.
- They are performing a criminal investigation.
- They have filed official police documents.
- They are making an arrest.
- They are invoking police powers in or outside their jurisdiction.
- They are settling a personal vendetta with police power.
- They are displaying weapons or police equipment.[6]

Interestingly, plaintiffs *can* sue private parties under Section 1983 when private parties conspire with state officers. With regard to this point, the Supreme Court has held that "a state normally can be held responsible for a private decision only when it has exercised coercive power or has provided such significant encouragement, either overt or covert, that the choice must in law be deemed to be that of the state" (*Blum v. Yaretsky*, 457 U.S. 991 [1982], p. 1004).

CONSTITUTIONAL VIOLATION The second requirement for a successful Section 1983 lawsuit is that a constitutional rights violation has taken place. In determining whether

---

[3] J. K. Lieberman, *The Litigious Society* (New York: Basic Books, 1983), p. 152.

[4] V. E. Kappeler, S. F. Kappeler, and R. V. del Carmen, "A Content Analysis of Police Civil Liability Cases: Decisions of the Federal District Courts, 1978–1990," *Journal of Criminal Justice* 21 (1993): 325–337, p. 327.

[5] M. S. Vaughn and L. F. Coomes, "Police Civil Liability under Section 1983: When Do Police Officers Act under Color of Law?" *Journal of Criminal Justice* 23 (1995): 395–415, p. 396.

[6] Ibid., p. 409.

DECISION-MAKING EXERCISE 2.7
Color of Law

Officer Webster regularly patronized a bar. One night, while off duty, he got into a fight, drew his gun, and shot and killed James Ramos. Ramos's heirs filed a Section 1983 lawsuit against the city for which Webster worked, alleging that it failed to adequately train him as to whether and how to react during off-duty altercations. Furthermore, Ramos's heirs alleged that this failure caused Webster, acting under color of law, to deprive Ramos of his constitutional rights. Will this lawsuit succeed?

a **constitutional rights violation** has taken place, the plaintiff must establish that the defendant's conduct violated a specific constitutional provision, such as the Fourth Amendment. As noted in *Daniels v. Williams* (474 U.S. 327 [1986]), "[I]n any given Section 1983 suit, the plaintiff must still prove a violation of the underlying constitutional right" (p. 330).

Recently, the courts have mandated that constitutional rights violations alleged under Section 1983 be committed with a certain level of **culpability**. That is, the plaintiff generally has to prove that the defendant officer intended for the violation to occur. There is a very clear reason for this: Not all constitutional rights violations are (or should be) actionable under Section 1983. In other words, Section 1983 is generally reserved for the most egregious of civil rights violations. The level of culpability required for a constitutional rights violation varies, depending on the type of unconstitutional conduct alleged by the plaintiff.[7] Some of the specifics of this issue will be addressed in the following section on individual liability.

THEORIES OF LIABILITY   The term **theory of liability** is the logic offered for who should be held accountable—and why. Typically, in Section 1983 cases, the plaintiff's lawsuit will target an individual officer, that officer's supervisor, the city or municipality for which the officer works, or any combination of each. While the individual officer responsible for inflicting harm should arguably be held liable, it is often attractive to plaintiffs to go after the "bigger fish" because that is likely where the greatest rewards will be. Governmental entities, in particular, are attractive targets for civil litigation. Following is a discussion of the three most common theories of liability under Section 1983.

Supervisory Liability.   The only Supreme Court case concerning **supervisory liability** in the Section 1983 context was *Rizzo v. Goode* (423 U.S. 362 [1976]). In *Rizzo*, the plaintiffs sued the mayor of Philadelphia, the city's managing director, the police commissioner, and two other police department supervisors, alleging a "pervasive pattern of illegal and unconstitutional mistreatment by police officers . . . directed against minority citizens in particular and against all Philadelphia residents in general" (pp. 366–367). The plaintiffs further charged supervisors with "conduct ranging from express authorization or encouragement of this mistreatment to failure to act in a manner so as to assure that it would not recur in the future" (p. 367). The lower federal courts found in favor of the plaintiffs, but the Supreme Court stated, disapprovingly, that "there was no *affirmative link* between the occurrence of the various incidents of police misconduct and the adoption of any plan or policy by [the supervisors]—express or otherwise—showing

Rizzo v. Goode
(423 U.S. 362 [1976])

---

[7] J. L. Worrall, "Culpability Standards in Section 1983 Litigation against Criminal Justice Officials: When and Why Mental State Matters," *Crime and Delinquency* 47 (2001): 28–59.

their authorization or approval of such misconduct" (p. 371, emphasis added). In other words, for a Section 1983 lawsuit to succeed against a supervisor, there must be a clear link between the supervisor and the constitutional violation committed by a subordinate.

Monell v. Department of Social Services
(436 U.S. 658 [1978])

Municipal/County Liability.   Cities and counties can be held liable under Section 1983 if they adopt and implement policies or adopt customs that become responsible for constitutional rights violations (see *Monell v. Department of Social Services*, 436 U.S. 658 [1978]). In general, a plaintiff will not succeed with a Section 1983 **municipal/county liability** claim if a common practice is engaged in by lower-ranking officials who have no authority to make policy in the traditional sense of the term. For example, if a group of police officers regularly use excessive force but do so on their own, with no authorization from the city or county, then the city or county cannot be held liable for these officers' actions.

City of Canton v. Harris
(489 U.S. 378 [1989])

In another city/county liability case, *City of Canton v. Harris* (489 U.S. 378 [1989]), the Supreme Court held that counties (and, by extension, cities) can be held liable for inadequately training their law enforcement officers. The facts of the case in *Canton* were that Harris was arrested and brought to the police station in a patrol wagon. On arrival, the officers found Harris lying on the floor of the wagon. She was asked if she needed medical attention, but she responded incoherently. After she was brought into the station, she slumped to the floor on two occasions. Eventually, she was left lying on the floor; no medical attention was summoned for her. Harris later sued, seeking to hold the city liable for a violation of her Fourteenth Amendment right, under the due process clause, to receive medical attention while in police custody. However, the Court held that "only where a municipality's failure to train its employees in a relevant respect evidences a 'deliberate indifference' to the rights of its inhabitants can such a shortcoming be properly thought of as a city 'policy or custom' that is actionable under [Section] 1983" (p. 389).

In *Board of Commissioners of Bryan County v. Brown* (520 U.S. 397 [1997]), the Supreme Court revisited the city/county liability issue. In particular, the question before the Court was whether a single hiring decision by a municipality's policy-maker could give rise to an inadequate hiring claim under Section 1983. In that case, Brown's claim was fueled by the injuries she suffered at the hands of Bryan County Reserve Deputy Stacy Burns during a high-speed pursuit and by the fact that Burns had two previous misdemeanor convictions for assault and battery (both of which were overlooked during the pre-employment screening process). Brown seemed to have a good case, but the Court felt otherwise, finding for Bryan County and setting a high standard for claims against a municipality for inadequate hiring. Specifically, the Court held that "[e]ven assuming without deciding that proof of a single instance of inadequate screening could ever trigger municipal liability, [the county commissioners'] failure to scrutinize Burns's record cannot constitute 'deliberate indifference' to [the] respondent's federally protected right to be free from the use of excessive force" (p. 412).

Individual Liability.   For a finding of **individual liability**, Section 1983 requires a plaintiff to demonstrate that his or her constitutional rights were violated by someone acting under color of state law. Accordingly, numerous constitutional amendments have been implicated in Section 1983 cases, including the First Amendment (e.g., *Pickering v. Board of Education*, 391 U.S. 563 [1968]), the Fourth Amendment (e.g., *Tennessee v. Garner*, 471 U.S. 1 [1985]), the Fifth Amendment (e.g., *Veilleux v. Perschau*, 94 F.3d 732 [1st Cir. 1996]), the Sixth Amendment (e.g., *Weatherford v. Bursey*,

429 U.S. 545 [1977]), the Eighth Amendment (e.g., *Estelle v. Gamble*, 429 U.S. 97 [1976]), the Fourteenth Amendment (e.g., *County of Sacramento v. Lewis*, 118 S. Ct. 1708 [1998]), and others. The amendments most commonly invoked, however, have been the Fourth, Eighth, and Fourteenth.

BIVENS CLAIMS AGAINST FEDERAL OFFICIALS   Prior to 1971, it was not clear whether federal officials could be sued under Section 1983. In *Bivens v. Six Unknown Named Agents* (403 U.S. 388 [1971]), however, the Supreme Court held that federal law enforcement officers can be sued for Fourth Amendment violations. *Bivens* claims must meet two essential requirements, which are effectively the same requirements as for a Section 1983 lawsuit: namely, (1) the official acted under color of state law and (2) the official deprived someone of his or her constitutional rights. *Bivens* claims are not limited to the Fourth Amendment, however. Since the *Bivens* decision, many other constitutional rights violations have been recognized. For example, *Davis v. Passman* (442 U.S. 228 [1979]) and *Sonntag v. Dooley* (650 F.2d 904 [7th Cir. 1981]) both dealt with the Fifth Amendment, and *Carlson v. Green* (446 U.S. 14 [1980]) was an Eighth Amendment case.

Bivens v. Six Unknown Named Agents (403 U.S. 388 [1971])

A *Bivens* **claim** is primarily limited to law enforcement officers, as other federal officials enjoy absolute immunity. **Absolute immunity** means the official cannot be sued under any circumstances—at least as far as their official duties are concerned. Federal officials who enjoy absolute immunity include federal judges (*Bradley v. Fisher*, 80 U.S. 335 [1871]) and federal prosecutors (*Yaselli v. Goff*, 275 U.S. 503 [1927]).

DECISION-MAKING EXERCISE 2.8
Municipal Liability

Danny Koller, 17 years old, stole a van from a car lot by driving it through the showroom window. Almost immediately, members of the local police department began to pursue him. After a dangerous, lengthy, high-speed chase, the van was forced to stop. Danny emerged from the van unarmed. When the pursuing officers approached him, they hit him and pulled his hair. In the scuffle, one of the officer's pistol discharged. The bullet struck Danny in the head and he died as a result of the wound. Danny's parents brought suit under 42 U.S.C. Section 1983, seeking damages from the city. They argued that the city maintained a formal policy of using excessive police force that caused Danny's death. Assuming this tragedy is an isolated event, will the plaintiffs succeed with their lawsuit?

DECISION-MAKING EXERCISE 2.9
Individual Liability

A police officer was in pursuit of a motorcycle carrying a passenger. During the pursuit, the motorcycle crashed in the road, directly in front of the officer. Despite his attempt to stop his cruiser in time, it slid into the back of the motorcycle, killing the passenger. The passenger's family members brought a Section 1983 lawsuit against the officer, alleging that the passenger's substantive due process rights were violated. The case worked its way up to a federal circuit court, where it was decided that the appropriate standard for Section 1983 civil liability for a substantive due process violation is deliberate indifference and that the officer acted in a deliberately indifferent fashion. Finally, the case reached the U.S. Supreme Court. As a Justice of that Court, would you affirm or reverse?

By contrast, heads of federal agencies (*Butz v. Economou*, 438 U.S. 478 [1978]), presidential aides (*Harlow v. Fitzgerald*, 457 U.S. 800 [1982]), and federal law enforcement officers *can* be sued. However, these and other federal officials enjoy *qualified immunity*, the same defense that applies to state officials in the Section 1983 context. Also, *Bivens* claims cannot be brought against federal agencies (*FDIC v. Meyer*, 510 U.S. 471 [1994]) or private corporations performing federal functions (*Correctional Svcs. Corp. v. Malesko*, 534 U.S. 61 [2001]).

THE QUALIFIED IMMUNITY DEFENSE   Officials who are sued under Section 1983 can assert a **qualified immunity** defense. Qualified immunity is a judicially created defense, just like the exclusionary rule is a court creation. In some cases, qualified immunity is more than a defense; it may afford immunity from suit.

Qualified immunity was developed to accommodate two conflicting policy concerns: effective crime control vis-à-vis the protection of people's civil liberties. While the Supreme Court has clearly intimated that Section 1983 should serve as a deterrent to official misconduct, the Court has also recognized that it is not fair to hold officials liable for lapses in judgment and honest mistakes. These issues were addressed in the seminal cases of *Harlow v. Fitzgerald* and *Wood v. Strickland* (420 U.S. 308 [1975]).

Similar to the Fourth Amendment's test for reasonableness, an objective reasonableness standard has been applied in order to determine if qualified immunity should be extended to criminal justice officials who are defendants. For the purposes of qualified immunity, a defendant is said to have acted in an objectively reasonable fashion if he or she does not violate clearly established rights about which a reasonable person would have known (*Harlow v. Fitzgerald*). In some Section 1983 cases, defendants have benefited from qualified immunity even for violating clearly established constitutional rights, provided that the defendants' mistaken belief was objectively reasonable (see *Anderson v. Creighton*, 483 U.S. 635 [1987]; *Malley v. Briggs*, 475 U.S. 335 [1988]). Qualified immunity thus affords protection to defendant criminal justice officials for reasonably mistaken beliefs. In essence, it offers a defense for ignorance, provided that the ignorance in question is reasonable.

Malley v. Briggs
(475 U.S. 335 [1988])

Malley v. Briggs sheds light on the qualified immunity issue. In that case, the plaintiffs filed a Section 1983 suit alleging that a police officer applied for and obtained a warrant that failed to establish probable cause. Rather than focus on the probable cause issue, the Supreme Court stated that the "question in this case is whether a reasonably well-trained officer in petitioner's position would have known that his affidavit failed to establish probable cause and that he should not have applied for the warrant" (p. 345). It went on to note that "[o]nly where the warrant application is so lacking in indicia of probable cause as to render official belief in its existence unreasonable will the shield of immunity be lost" (pp. 344–345).

In summary, qualified immunity poses the last (or one of the first) questions in the Section 1983 process. If a criminal justice official acts on a reasonably mistaken belief, as gauged from the standpoint of a reasonable officer, then qualified immunity can be granted. Figure 2.2 provides an overview of the Section 1983 process for lawsuits against individual police officers. Note that individual officers can enjoy qualified immunity if they act in an objectively reasonable fashion.

NONJUDICIAL REMEDIES

Three nonjudicial remedies for police misconduct can be identified. First, an *internal review* refers to a police department investigating complaints against its own officers.

FIGURE 2.2

Individual Liability under Section 1983

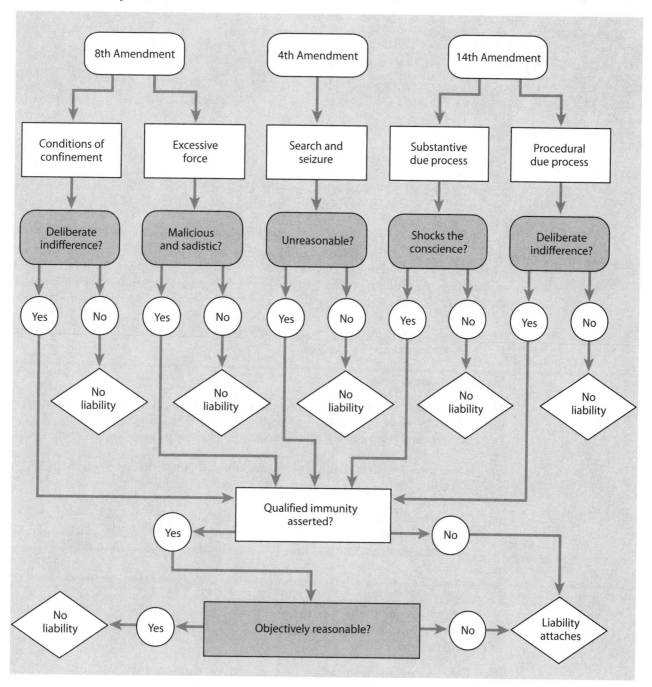

DECISION-MAKING EXERCISE 2.10

The Fourth Amendment and Qualified Immunity

In a recent case, *Wilson v. Layne* (526 U.S. 603 [1999]), the Supreme Court considered (1) whether law enforcement officers violated the Fourth Amendment by allowing members of the media to accompany them on the service of warrants and (2) whether the officers were nonetheless entitled to qualified immunity if such activity violates the Fourth Amendment. The Court decided that "a media 'ride-along' in a home violates the Fourth Amendment, but because the state of the law was not clearly established at the time the entry in this case took place, respondent officers are entitled to qualified immunity" (p. 603). Do you see any problems with this decision?

Typically, an internal affairs division takes up this task. The second *civilian review* refers to mechanisms by which private citizens serve in some capacity to review complaints of police misconduct. Not to be confused with civilian review, *mediation* asks an objective third party, such as an ombudsman, to resolve a grievance between a police officer and a citizen who complains of wrongdoing.

Why should we care about nonjudicial remedies? These remedies are available for situations where neither the exclusionary rule nor civil liability are viable options. Consider the hypothetical case of a motorist who is stopped without proper justification. Assume the motorist is released. To be sure, he or she has suffered an inconvenience, but if no contraband was found and there was no egregious misconduct on the officer's part, what can this person do? About the only choice available is to file a written complaint. A Complaint/Commendation Form from the Abilene, Texas, Police Department appears in Figure 2.3.

Internal Review

Many police agencies have developed innovative and highly respected **internal review** mechanisms. In its model police misconduct policy, the Police Executive Research Forum listed three ways that the police themselves can implement effective complaint procedures:

> (1) [T]hrough the provision of meaningful and effective complaint procedures, citizen confidence in the integrity of police increases and this engenders community support and confidence in the police department; (2) through disciplinary procedures that permit police officials to monitor officers' compliance with departmental procedures; and (3) by clarifying rights and ensuring due process protection to citizens and officers alike.[8]

Figure 2.4 shows the Claremont, California, Police Department's internal complaint review process, depicting one agency's approach to internal discipline.

Geller is a defender of internal review. In particular, he has argued that civilian input into the process of investigating complaints against the police suffers from a number of drawbacks:

- They ignore existing legal resources at citizens' disposal.
- It is difficult for people disconnected from the police department to have an adequate understanding of the internal operations of a civilian review board.

---

[8] Police Executive Research Forum, *Police Agency Handling of Officer Misconduct: A Model Policy Statement* (Washington, DC: Author, 1981), p. 1.

FIGURE 2.3

Citizens' Complaint Form

Abilene Police Department
Citizen Complaint/Commendation Form

CITY OF ABILENE

File complaints or commendations about Police Department employees on this form. Return the completed form to the desk duty officer, 1st floor at the Police Department, 450 Pecan or hand deliver to the City Manager's Office, 555 Walnut, Room 203 or by mail to P.O. Box 60 Abilene, Texas 79604. Complaints will not be investigated until a Police Supervisor has contacted the Complaining Party.

Involved Officer/Employee(s) Information:			
Name:			
Name:			

Person Making the Complaint/Commendation:			
Name:		**Phone:**	
Address:		**Phone:**	

Information:
Please provide as much information about the reason you were contacted by the officer/employee. Specific information about the date, time and location will help in locating computer-based information if you do not know the officer/employee's name.

Date of Contact:		Approximate Time:		AM/PM
Location Contacted:				

Reason For The Complaint/Commendation: (attach additional pages if needed)

Witness Information:			
Name:		**Phone:**	
Address:		**Phone:**	

Name:		**Phone:**	
Address:		**Phone:**	

Submitted by_____Date_____

Source: Abilene (Texas) Police Department. Reprinted by Permission. Available online: http://www.abilenetx .com/index/doc/APDcomplaintcommentform.pdf (accessed February 16, 2011)

FIGURE 2.4

Citizen Complaint Process (Claremont, CA, Police Department)

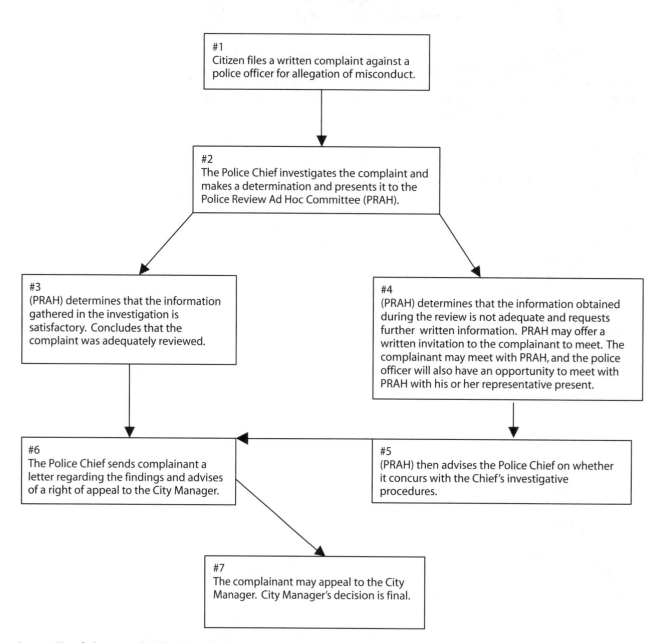

Citizen Complaint Process

#1
Citizen files a written complaint against a police officer for allegation of misconduct.

#2
The Police Chief investigates the complaint and makes a determination and presents it to the Police Review Ad Hoc Committee (PRAH).

#3
(PRAH) determines that the information gathered in the investigation is satisfactory. Concludes that the complaint was adequately reviewed.

#4
(PRAH) determines that the information obtained during the review is not adequate and requests further written information. PRAH may offer a written invitation to the complainant to meet. The complainant may meet with PRAH, and the police officer will also have an opportunity to meet with PRAH with his or her representative present.

#6
The Police Chief sends complainant a letter regarding the findings and advises of a right of appeal to the City Manager.

#5
(PRAH) then advises the Police Chief on whether it concurs with the Chief's investigative procedures.

#7
The complainant may appeal to the City Manager. City Manager's decision is final.

Source: City of Claremont (California) Police Department. Reprinted by Permission. Available online: http://www.ci.claremont.ca.us/download.cfm?ID=18112 (accessed February 16, 2011)

- Citizen review damages morale.
- Civilian review invites abdication of authority by line supervisors.
- Such boards weaken the ability of top management to achieve conformity through discipline.
- They are tantamount to admitting that the police are incapable of policing themselves.[9]

Civilian Review

There has been a marked increase in the number of cities involving citizens at some stage of the complaint review process.[10] This has occurred because of the demand for some form of external input in the investigation process. It has also occurred due to some sentiments that citizens can investigate the police better than the police themselves:

> Citizen involvement in the complaint process will produce (1) more objective and more thorough investigations; (2) a higher rate of sustained complaints and more disciplinary actions against guilty officers; (3) greater deterrence of police misconduct (through both general and specific deterrence); and (4) higher levels of satisfaction on the part of both individual complainants and the general public.[11]

West has identified three distinct forms of citizen review: (1) civilian review; (2) civilian input; and (3) civilian monitor.[12] Pure **civilian review** is the strongest form; a civilian panel investigates, adjudicates, and recommends punishment to the police chief. The second strongest form is **civilian input;** in this form, a civilian panel receives and investigates a complaint, leaving adjudication and discipline with the department itself. Finally, the **civilian monitor** form, the weakest of the three, leaves investigation, adjudication, and discipline inside the department; a civilian is allowed to review the adequacy and impartiality of the process. The research reported by West focused only on the first two forms: civilian review and civilian input. Both place investigative authority with an independent body and are arguably more satisfactory to disgruntled citizens than the third form, civilian monitor.

Mediation

Some have argued that **mediation**, or relying on a neutral third party to render decisions, is a desirable approach to address the problem of police misconduct. In it, the decision of a neutral third party, or **ombudsman** (sometimes called a "mediator" or "arbitrator"), is sought.[13] As Whitebread and Slobogin observe,

> [Another] remedial system which, like the civilian review board, operates outside the judicial and internal police spheres, is the Scand[i]navian ombudsman system. The ombudsman is, most simply, an external critic of

---

[9] W. A. Geller, *Police Leadership in America* (New York: Praeger, 1985), pp. 157–198.

[10] S. Walker and V. W. Bumphus, *Civilian Review of the Police: A National Survey of the 50 Largest Cities* (Omaha, NE: University of Nebraska at Omaha, 1992).

[11] S. Walker and B. Wright, "Varieties of Citizen Review: The Relationship of Mission, Structure, and Procedures to Police Accountability," in R. G. Dunham and G. P. Alpert (Eds.), *Critical Issues in Policing: Contemporary Readings*, 3rd ed. (Prospect Heights, IL: Waveland, 1997), pp. 319–336, p. 322.

[12] P. West, *Investigations of Complaints against the Police: Summary Findings* (Washington, DC: Police Executive Research Forum, 1987).

[13] Technically, there is a difference between the terms *arbitration* and *mediation*, but for our purposes it is safe to treat them as more or less identical.

administration. His goal is improvement of administration rather than punishment of administrators or redress of individual grievances. Thus, instead of conducting formal hearings associated with adjudicating individual complaints, he relies primarily on his own investigations to gather information. On the basis of his findings, he may recommend corrective measure to the department, although he cannot compel an official to do anything.[14]

A key characteristic of the ombudsman system is that it is independent of the complainant and the person being complained against. The ombudsman should be a person to whom people may come with grievances connected with the government. The ombudsman stands between the citizen and the government, acting as something of an intermediary.

As another alternative, Chief Justice Burger suggested in *Bivens* that a quasi-judicial body be appointed for the purpose of recovering damages against the government. Under his plan, if damages are awarded, the record of what transpired will become part of the offending officer's permanent file. Neither of these systems has gained widespread acceptance, much less adoption.

Summary

1. SUMMARIZE THE EXCLUSIONARY RULE AND THE EXCEPTIONS TO IT.

A number of legal remedies are available for addressing violations of people's rights, including those provided by the law, court decisions, and police policy and procedures. The most common remedies in criminal procedure are (1) the exclusionary rule; (2) criminal liability; (3) civil litigation; and (4) nonjudicial remedies.

The exclusionary rule is the main remedy that will be focused on throughout the remainder of this book. It requires that evidence obtained in violation of certain constitutional amendments (notably the Fourth, Fifth, Sixth, and Fourteenth) be excluded from criminal trial. Exceptions to the exclusionary rule have been recognized in cases in which (1) the police acted in good faith but nonetheless violated the Constitution and (2) the prosecutor sought to impeach a witness at trial by pointing to contradictions in his or her out-of-court statements, even if such statements were obtained in an unconstitutional manner.

2. SUMMARIZE THE "FRUIT OF THE POISONOUS TREE" DOCTRINE AND THE EXCEPTIONS TO IT.

The exclusionary rule has been extended to require that derivative evidence obtained from a constitu-

tional rights violation also be excluded. This is known as the "fruit of the poisonous tree" doctrine. Exceptions to this doctrine include inevitable discovery, independent source, and purged taint. That is, if evidence would have been discovered inevitably, if it was arrived at by means of an independent source, or if the taint of an initial unconstitutional act has been purged, then derivative evidence will be considered admissible at trial.

3. DESCRIBE CRIMINAL PROSECUTION AND CIVIL REMEDIES FOR CONSTITUTIONAL RIGHTS VIOLATIONS.

Police can be held *criminally* liable, as well. For instance, both state and federal law enforcement officers can be held criminally liable for violating certain federal laws. Officers are also bound by the criminal law at the state level. They can, of course, engage in certain authorized public duties (e.g., to use deadly force in appropriate circumstances) that would be crimes if committed by regular citizens.

Civil lawsuits against government officials—the police, mainly—can be filed when neither the exclusionary rule nor other criminal remedies apply. Section 1983 litigation requires the plaintiff to show that a constitutional rights violation was committed by

---

[14] C. H. Whitebread and C. Slobogin, *Criminal Procedure*, 4th ed. (New York: Foundation Press, 2000), p. 65.

an official acting under color of state law. Section 1983 lawsuits can be filed against individual police officers, supervisors, and municipalities/counties. *Bivens* claims are virtually identical to Section 1983 claims but are intended to target federal, instead of state, officials.

4. DESCRIBE NONJUDICIAL REMEDIES FOR CONSTITUTIONAL RIGHTS VIOLATIONS.

Nonjudicial remedies include internal review, civilian review, and mediation. Internal review, the most common of these remedies, refers to a police agency investigating its own for allegations of misconduct. Internal affairs divisions engage in this sort of activity. Civilian review occurs when citizens get involved in the investigation process; numerous varieties of citizen review are in place around the United States. Finally, a less common method of rectifying constitutional rights violations is mediation, in which a neutral third party decides on issues in dispute.

Key Terms

18 U.S.C. Section 242	53	constitutional rights violation	59
42 U.S.C. Section 1983	55	culpability	59
absolute immunity	62	damage suit	55
		exclusionary rule	42
Bivens claim	62	extralegal remedies	41
civil litigation	55	"fruit of the poisonous tree" doctrine	49
civilian input	67		
civilian monitor	67	"good faith" exception	47
civilian review	67		
color of law	58		

impeachment exception	49	ombudsman	68
independent source	51	public duty defense	54
individual liability	60	"purged taint" exception	50
inevitable discovery	51	qualified immunity	62
injunctive relief	55	remedy	41
internal review	64	"silver platter" doctrine	43
legal remedies	42		
mediation	67	supervisory liability	59
municipal/county liability	60	theory of liability	59

Key Cases

Exclusionary Rule

- *Weeks v. United States*, 232 U.S. 383 (1914)
- *Mapp v. Ohio*, 367 U.S. 643 (1961)
- *United States v. Leon*, 468 U.S. 897 (1984)
- *Walder v. United States*, 347 U.S. 62 (1954)
- *Silverthorne Lumber Co. v. United States*, 251 U.S. 385 (1920)
- *Wong Sun v. United States*, 371 U.S. 471 (1963)
- *Segura v. United States*, 468 U.S. 796 (1984)
- *Nix v. Williams*, 467 U.S. 431 (1984)

Civil Remedies

- *Monroe v. Pape*, 365 U.S. 167 (1961)
- *Rizzo v. Goode*, 423 U.S. 362 (1976)
- *Monell v. Department of Social Services*, 436 U.S. 658 (1978)
- *City of Canton v. Harris*, 489 U.S. 378 (1989)
- *Bivens v. Six Unknown Agents*, 403 U.S. 388 (1971)
- *Malley v. Briggs*, 475 U.S. 335 (1988)

Criminal Remedies

- *Screws v. United States*, 325 U.S. 91 (1945)

Review Questions

1. Define the term *remedy*, and distinguish between two types of remedies.
2. What is the exclusionary rule? Is it applicable beyond the Fourth Amendment?
3. Explain the arguments for and against the exclusionary rule.
4. When does the exclusionary rule *not* apply?
5. What are the two exceptions to the exclusionary rule?

6. Define the "fruit of the poisonous tree" doctrine, and explain the three exceptions to it.
7. How does the criminal law operate as a remedy?
8. How does civil litigation act as a remedy?
9. What are the requirements of a successful Section 1983 lawsuit against an individual police officer? A supervisor? A city or county?
10. What is a *Bivens* claim?
11. What defense is available to a law enforcement officer charged in a Section 1983 lawsuit?
12. Distinguish among three types of nonjudicial remedies.
13. What are the varieties of civilian review? How do they differ from one another?

Web Links and Exercises

1. Taking sides on the exclusionary rule, weigh the pros and cons of the exclusionary rule.
Suggested URL: http://www.wadsworth.com/criminaljustice_d/templates/student_resources/0534616232_gaines/debates/ex_rules.html (accessed June 1, 2011).
2. Police criminal liability: Discuss the incidents surrounding the shooting of Sean Bell. How does the case fit with this chapter's section on "Criminal Remedies Besides the Exclusionary Rule"?
Suggested URL: http://www.msnbc.msn.com/id/24305660 (accessed June 1, 2011).
3. Find a case: Go to the Web site of Americans for Effective Law Enforcement and browse back issues of the Law Enforcement Liability Reporter. You can find them under the "Free Law Library and Publications" link on the main page. Find and write about the facts/decisions of five civil liability cases.
URL: http://www.aele.org (accessed June 1, 2011).
4. Ask an officer: Register at the forums section of officer.com. Post a message in the "Ask a cop" section—asking a legitimate legal question.
URL: http://forums.officer.com/ (accessed June 1, 2011).
5. Alternative dispute resolution: Read about mediation and other forms of alternative dispute resolution. How does mediation differ from arbitration?
Suggested URL: http://www.adr.org/ (accessed June 1, 2011).

Part 2

SEARCH AND SEIZURE

LEARNING OBJECTIVES

When you complete this chapter, you should be able to:

▸ Define terms related to the Fourth Amendment.

▸ Explain the concept of probable cause and its implications.

▸ Compare reasonable suspicion and administrative justification to probable cause.

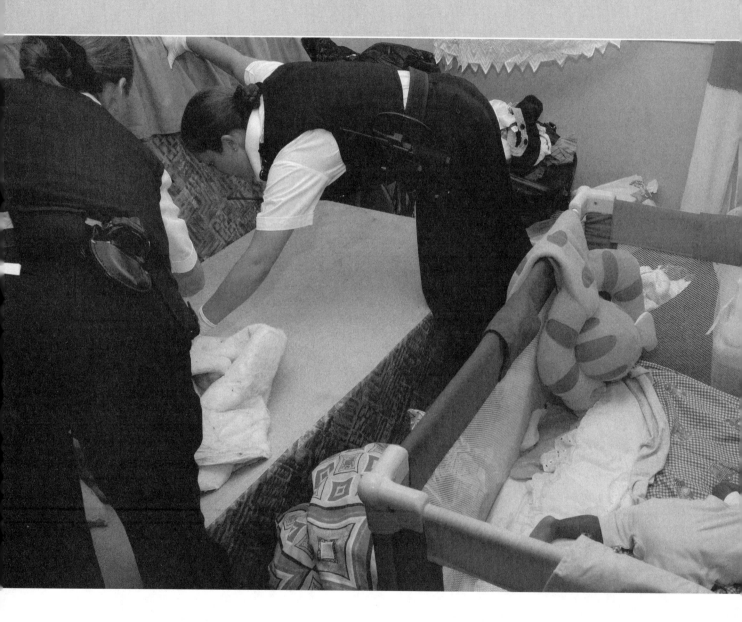

Introduction to Search and Seizure

INTRODUCTION

The Core Purpose and Elements of the Fourth Amendment

The Fourth Amendment to the U.S. Constitution reflects one of the primary grievances early American colonists had toward the Crown. The British parliament, intent on rooting out smuggling activities taking place in the American colonies, issued writs of assistance, which permitted unlimited searches. Officials needed no justification to obtain writs of assistance, and there was no judicial supervision designed to limit the scope of the searches authorized by the writs. The practice was not well received in the American colonies. By adopting the Fourth Amendment, the framers of the Constitution placed significant restrictions on searches conducted by government officials.

Despite the Fourth Amendment's seemingly simple language, the 54 words that make up its text (see Chapter 1 for its full text) have been subjected to incredible amounts of scrutiny and interpretation. There are literally millions of pages of text—in the forms of case opinions, law review articles, and legal treatises—devoted to interpreting the language of the Fourth Amendment. The Supreme Court alone has added several layers of interpretation to the Fourth Amendment through hundreds of significant decisions. As a result, a complete understanding of Fourth Amendment rules and procedures comes with considerable difficulty. In fact, it is probably impossible to fully understand the scope, reach, and language of the Fourth Amendment because of its continued evolution. Almost without exception, the Supreme Court will decide a Fourth Amendment case during every term.

Nevertheless, the Fourth Amendment contains two basic clauses: The **reasonableness clause**, which proscribes unreasonable searches and seizures, is followed by the **warrant clause**, which says that "no Warrants shall issue, but upon probable cause, supported by Oath or affirmation, and particularly describing the place to be searched, and the persons or things to be seized."

A fundamental question has been raised about these two clauses. They are joined in the text of the Fourth Amendment by the conjunction *and*, which has led to a great deal of debate over whether the two clauses are related or separate. Some people have argued that the warrant clause gives meaning to the reasonableness clause, in that it automatically renders unreasonable a search that is not conducted with a warrant. Justice Frankfurter took this position in *United States v. Rabinowitz* (339 U.S. 56 [1950]): "What is the test of reason which makes a search reasonable? . . . There must be a warrant to permit search, barring only inherent limitations upon that requirement when there is a good excuse for not getting a search warrant" (p. 83). This is the *warrant requirement* interpretation, requiring that a neutral magistrate come between the officer conducting the search and the citizen being the target of the search.

Others have argued that the search-and-seizure clause and the warrant clause should be read separately. Their position is that the reasonableness of a search should not depend on whether a warrant was obtained or on whether there was a good excuse for not obtaining a warrant. Instead, they argue that the courts should focus on the factual circumstances justifying the search. They argue, specifically, that the courts should consider the manner in which the search was executed, not whether a warrant was secured. The main protection offered by the Fourth Amendment should lie, then, not with a judge *prior* to the search but with the courts *after* the search. In this view, the courts should reflect on what occurred and seek to determine whether the search was reasonable at the time it was actually conducted.

A third view, known as the *warrant preference view*, has come to the forefront in recent years. As a result, much of the confusion surrounding the nexus of the search-and-seizure clause and the warrant clause has been cleared up. As the Supreme Court stated in *Mincey v. Arizona* (437 U.S. 385 [1978]), "The Fourth Amendment proscribes all unreasonable searches and seizures, and it is a cardinal principle that searches conducted outside the judicial process, without prior approval by judge or magistrate, are per se unreasonable under the Fourth Amendment, subject to a few specifically established and well delineated exceptions" (p. 390) (see also *Vale v. Louisiana*, 399 U.S. 30 [1970]). Basically, the rule of thumb is that a search warrant (or an arrest warrant, in the case of a seizure of a person) should be procured whenever practical. If, however, there is an emergency or other such exception, such as a significant risk to public safety, a warrant may not be necessary. This third view is most common today.

BASIC TERMINOLOGY

The Fourth Amendment protects *persons, houses, papers,* and *effects* from unreasonable searches and seizures. Few court cases have turned on the meanings of these terms, but it is still important to define them.

The term **person** encompasses the individual as a whole, both internally and externally. An arrest, for example, is a seizure of a person. If a police officer pulls up the sleeves of a suspected drug user to look for needle tracks, this is a search of a *person* within the meaning of the Fourth Amendment.

In the early twentieth century, the Supreme Court ruled that the Fourth Amendment applied only to searches and seizures of tangible items (*Olmstead v. United States*, 277 U.S. 438 [1928]). Oral communications fell outside the scope of the Fourth Amendment, so surveillance of conversations, regardless of how it was pursued, did not trigger constitutional protections. Today, however, in the wake of *Katz v. United States* (389 U.S. 347 [1967]), the Supreme Court has stated emphatically that oral communications trigger the protections of the Fourth Amendment. Thus, the definition of *person* for purposes of the Fourth Amendment not only includes the person's internal and external physical body but also (most) oral communications made by people.

House is a term that is broadly construed to mean any structure that a person uses as a residence (and frequently a business) on either a temporary or long-term basis. A hotel room is a prime example of a short-term house. Also, a garage or other structure not connected to a house can also fall within the meaning of the Fourth Amendment. Whether a garage is actually a house, though, depends on the notion of *curtilage*. An open field, by contrast, does not trigger the protection of the Fourth Amendment because it is not a house. (Open fields and curtilage are defined later on in this chapter.)

Next, **papers and effects** include nearly all personal items. Business records, letters, diaries, memos, and countless other forms of tangible evidence can be defined as *papers*. *Effects* is the catch-all category. Anything that is not a person, house, or paper is probably an effect. Effects can include cars, luggage, clothing, weapons, contraband, and the fruits of criminal activity. Given these broad definitions, then, it is easy to understand why few court cases have turned on the meanings of *persons*, *houses*, *papers*, and *effects.*

If the police activity in question does not involve a person, house, paper, or effect, no Fourth Amendment protections exist. In reality, though, almost any conceivable tangible item or form of communication falls within the protection of the Fourth Amendment. What becomes important, then, is determining precisely when the Fourth Amendment applies and when a search or seizure can be considered reasonable.

A FRAMEWORK FOR ANALYZING THE FOURTH AMENDMENT

For the sake of clarifying a fairly complex body of law, this book approaches the Fourth Amendment in a specific format. This chapter introduces basic Fourth Amendment terminology, focusing in particular on (1) which police activities trigger the protections of the Fourth Amendment and (2) what justification is required for the police to engage in certain types of activities. Later chapters focus on the types of law enforcement activity authorized (and not authorized) by the Fourth Amendment as well as on relevant procedures.

In determining when the Fourth Amendment is triggered, it is important to draw a distinction between a **search** and a **seizure**. Each action triggers the protections of the Fourth Amendment, but each is distinctly different. In addition, the law that governs searches is not the same as the law that governs seizures.

A search is, as the term suggests, an activity geared toward finding evidence to be used in a criminal prosecution. To define when a search takes place, two important factors need to be considered: (1) whether the presumed search is a product of **government action** and (2) whether the intrusion violates a person's **reasonable expectation of privacy**.

The term *seizure*, on the other hand, has a dual meaning in criminal procedure. First, *property* can be seized. Often, the result of a search is a seizure of evidence. For example, if the police successfully serve a search warrant to look for illegal weapons at 345 Oak

Street, the weapons they find will be seized. Second, *people* can also be seized. Seizures of people can occur almost anywhere and at any time. An arrest, for example, is considered a seizure within the meaning of the Fourth Amendment.

The second stage in the Fourth Amendment analysis requires focusing on the **reasonableness** of the search or seizure. In other words, once the protections of the Fourth Amendment are triggered, did the police act in line with Fourth Amendment requirements? For example, if a person is arrested, did the police have adequate reason to believe the person arrested in fact committed the crime? When the courts focus on the reasonableness of a search or seizure, they speak in terms of *justification*. If the police (or other government actors) engage in a search or seizure without justification, they violate the Fourth Amendment.

The only justification mentioned in the Fourth Amendment is *probable cause*. The untrained observer may be inclined to think that any search or seizure based on a lesser degree of certainty than probable cause would violate the Fourth Amendment. For a time, this was the case. In recent decades, however, the Supreme Court has carved out exceptions to the Fourth Amendment's probable cause requirement. Basically, the Court has ruled that there are certain situations in which the police can seize people and/or look for evidence with a lesser degree of certainty than probable cause.

Think of this chapter as being almost pre-Fourth Amendment in its orientation. It is designed to supply the reader with the tools for approaching any situation resembling a search or a seizure. Without an understanding of (1) when the Fourth Amendment applies and (2) what justification is required for the police to act, it will be impossible to judge the constitutionality of the police conduct under examination.

WHEN A SEARCH OCCURS

Again, generally speaking, a *search* can be defined as the act of looking for evidence. However, not every act of looking for evidence can be considered a search *within the meaning of the Fourth Amendment*. For example, a private citizen may look for evidence, but because private citizens are not government actors, their actions are not bound by the Fourth Amendment. The Fourth Amendment protects citizens from *government* action. Thus, one requirement in determining when a search occurs is to ascertain *who* is looking for evidence.

Even though the Fourth Amendment restricts government action, it is not the case that government actors always engage in searches when looking for evidence. The police can do many things to look for evidence, such as looking in open fields, without being bound by the strictures of the Fourth Amendment. To draw a distinction between a search and a nonsearch, then, the courts will focus on *where* the police look for evidence. This requires that attention be given to the notion of *reasonable expectation of privacy*.

Government Action, Not Private Action

The Fourth Amendment's protection against unreasonable searches and seizures has been limited by the courts to conduct that is governmental in nature. Thus, when a private individual seizes evidence or otherwise conducts a search, the protections of the Fourth Amendment are not triggered. For example, if Angela knows that her neighbor Larry has a large supply of stolen stereo equipment in the garage behind his house, she could conceivably enter his garage, seize the evidence, and turn it over to the police. They, in turn, could use the evidence, and other information provided by Angela, to arrest Larry. Of course, Angela could be found guilty of criminal trespass, but as far as the Fourth Amendment is concerned, she committed no constitutional violations. Assuming that Angela acted independent of the police, she acted in a private capacity.

The inapplicability of the Fourth Amendment to searches or seizures carried out by private individuals was first recognized by the Supreme Court in *Burdeau v. McDowell* (256 U.S. 465 [1921]). In that case, some individuals illegally entered McDowell's business office and seized records. The records were later turned over to the attorney general of the United States, who planned to use them against McDowell in court. McDowell sought return of the records, and the district court granted his petition. But the Supreme Court eventually stated that the Fourth Amendment's "origin and history clearly show that it was intended as a restraint upon the activities of sovereign authority, and was not intended to be a limitation upon other than governmental agencies" (p. 475).

Burdeau v. McDowell *(256 U.S. 465 [1921])*

The Court's decision in *Burdeau* has survived through several subsequent landmark cases. For example, in *Coolidge v. New Hampshire* (403 U.S. 443 [1971]), the Court stated that if a private person "wholly on [his] own initiative" turns over evidence to authorities, "[t]here can be no doubt under existing law that the articles would later [be] admissible in evidence" (p. 487). Similarly, in *Walter v. United States* (447 U.S. 649 [1980]), the Court ruled that "a wrongful search and seizure conducted by a private party does not violate the Fourth Amendment and . . . does not deprive the government of the right to use evidence that it has acquired [from the third party] lawfully" (p. 656) (see also *State v. Oldaker*, 172 W.Va. 258 [W.Va.1983]).

The government action prong of the Fourth Amendment actually hinges on three important questions: (1) Who is a government actor? (2) When is a private person *not* acting wholly on his or her own initiative considered a government actor for the purposes of the Fourth Amendment?, and (3) Once it is clear that a search is private in nature, what later government action does the private search authorize? These three questions are addressed in the following subsections.

WHAT ARE GOVERNMENT OFFICIALS?   Clearly, a uniformed police officer acting in his or her official capacity is a *government official* within the meaning of the Fourth Amendment. However, the police represent a comparatively small percentage of one branch of government: the executive branch. Numerous other officials are also responsible for enforcing the law.

Even those individuals whose actions will never result in a criminal prosecution are bound by Fourth Amendment restrictions. For example, in the case of *Camara v. Municipal Court* (387 U.S. 523 [1967]), the Court held that regulatory officials conducting health and safety inspections can be considered government actors for purposes of the Fourth Amendment. This ruling has been expanded, in fact, to apply to numerous other government officials, including fire inspectors (*Michigan v. Tyler*, 436 U.S. 499 [1978]); Occupational Safety and Health Administration (OSHA) inspectors (*Marshall v. Barlow's, Inc.*, 436 U.S. 307 [1978]); federal mine inspectors (*Donovan v. Dewey*, 452 U.S. 594 [1981]); and even public school teachers (*New Jersey v. T.L.O.*, 469 U.S. 325 [1985]).

The situation is decidedly less clear, however, for individuals who perform clear law enforcement functions but are not employed by the government per se. This includes

DECISION-MAKING EXERCISE 3.1

A "Moonlighting" Scenario

Officer Clark is a sworn policeman by day and a private security guard by night. One night, while on duty in the parking lot outside a major retail store, Clark witnessed Lenore Rand, a patron whom he suspected of shoplifting, leaving the store. Clark confronted Rand, seized her bag, and discovered several items that she had not paid for. The incident was reported and the evidence was turned over to the police. May Rand mount a Fourth Amendment challenge to Clark's actions?

store detectives (e.g., *Gillett v. State*, 588 S.W.2d 361, Tex.Crim.App. [1979]); security guards (*Stanfield v. State*, 666 P.2d 1294 [Okl.Crim. 1983]); and insurance inspectors (*Lester v. State*, 145 Ga.App. 847 [1978]). At the risk of simplification, the rule is this: When a private source is used deliberately in place of the police, Fourth Amendment protections are triggered. That is, the officials are said to be acting in a government capacity (e.g., *People v. Mangiefico*, 25 Cal.App.3d 1041 [1972]).

WHEN DO PRIVATE INDIVIDUALS BECOME GOVERNMENT AGENTS?   An otherwise private person can become a government official if he or she acts at the behest of a government official. In *Coolidge v. New Hampshire* (403 U.S. 443 [1971]), the Supreme Court stated that "[t]he test . . . is whether [the private person] in light of all the circumstances of the case, must be regarded as having acted as an 'instrument' or agent of the state" (p. 487). Simply put, when government officials join in on a private search or instruct a private individual to conduct a search, the private individual can be viewed as a government actor within the meaning of the Fourth Amendment.

A variation on this line of cases is one in which a government official does not actively participate in or order a search or seizure but instead merely provides information that leads to a private search or seizure. For example, in *People v. Boettner* (80 Misc.2d 3 [1974]), the court upheld a search conducted by private university officials based on information supplied to them by the police. In support of its decision, the court noted that the private search was carried out without the knowledge of the police, who, at the time, were proceeding with their own investigation of the incident.

In a slightly more controversial case, *United States v. Lamar* (545 F.2d 488 [5th Cir. 1977]), the Fifth Circuit ruled that a search conducted by an airline official of an unclaimed bag suspected of containing narcotics was private, even though a police officer expressed interest in learning of the bag's contents. The court found that the Fourth Amendment did not apply because the officer neither requested nor participated in the search. This decision would seem to suggest that law enforcement officials have at their disposal a means to evade the strictures of the Fourth Amendment by encouraging, although not expressly requesting or engaging in, private searches and seizures.

WHEN A PRIVATE SEARCH BECOMES GOVERNMENTAL   An otherwise private search may also be turned into a government search when the government recipient of the items seized by the private party subjects the evidence to additional scrutiny. An illustrative case is *Walter v. United States* (447 U.S. 649 [1980]). In that case, sealed film canisters were mistakenly sent to a company whose employees, noting the suggestive labels on the canisters, opened them but were unable to ascertain what was on the film. They turned the canisters over to the Federal Bureau of Investigation (FBI), who subsequently opened the canisters and viewed what turned out to be pornographic images. The Court ruled that

DECISION-MAKING EXERCISE 3.2

A Private or Government Search?

A meter reader for the local electric company was making her usual rounds and approached the house of Michael Cramer. While reading the meter, she looked through the window just above the meter and observed a significant number of marijuana plants growing under several rows of bright lights. The meter reader returned to her vehicle and reported her observations to the police. Armed with this new information, as well as information from an ongoing investigation, the police obtained a warrant, searched Cramer's house, and seized the plants. The plants were then entered as evidence against Cramer at trial. May Cramer move to have the plants excluded on the grounds that the meter reader was a government actor, whose actions triggered the protections of the Fourth Amendment?

this activity turned the private search into a government search. Because the Fourth Amendment came into play, the Court declared that the FBI agents should have obtained a warrant before viewing the contents of the film canisters.

In *United States v. Jacobsen* (466 U.S. 109 [1984]), however, the Supreme Court modified its earlier opinion in *Walter* and instead noted that the subsequent government search must be *substantially more intrusive* in order for the Fourth Amendment to be triggered. In *Jacobsen*, Federal Express employees opened a damaged package and found several packages containing a suspicious white powder. They closed the package and then summoned federal agents, who reopened the packages and conducted a field test on the substances. The Court held, "The agent's viewing of what a private party had freely made available for his inspection did not violate the Fourth Amendment" (p. 119), and the field test had nothing more than a "de minimus [minimal] impact on any protected property interest."

United States v. Jacobsen
(466 U.S. 109 [1984])

Infringement on a Reasonable Expectation of Privacy

Government action alone is not enough to implicate the Fourth Amendment. Coupled with government action, the Fourth Amendment is triggered only when the law enforcement activity in question infringes on a person's reasonable expectation of privacy. In other words, there are times when police officers and other government officials look for evidence (as in an open field, for instance) but do not act intrusively enough so as to trigger the Fourth Amendment.

Prior to 1967, the definition of a *search* was closely tied to property interests. Police action would only be deemed a search if it physically infringed on an individual's property. The activity basically had to amount to common-law trespassing for it to be onsidered a search. Any police activity that was not trespassory in nature was not considered a search. This definition became outdated in the landmark decision of *Katz v. United States* (389 U.S. 347 [1967]).

In *Katz*, federal agents placed a listening device outside a phone booth in which Katz was having a conversation. Katz made incriminating statements during the course of his conversation, and the FBI sought to use the statements against him at trial. The lower court ruled that the FBI's activities did not amount to a search because there was no physical entry into the phone booth. The Supreme Court reversed that decision, holding that the Fourth Amendment "protects people, not places," and so its reach "cannot turn upon the presence or absence of a physical intrusion into any given enclosure" (p. 353). Instead, the Fourth Amendment definition of a *search* turns on the concept of privacy. In the Court's words, "The Government's activities in electronically listening to and recording words violated the privacy upon which [Katz] justifiably relied while using the telephone booth and thus constituted a 'search and seizure' within the meaning of the Fourth Amendment" (p. 353).

Katz v. United States
(389 U.S. 347 [1967])

DECISION-MAKING EXERCISE 3.3
The Scope of a Private Search

Glen Olson stands accused of poisoning dogs in his neighborhood by means of feeding them dog biscuits lined with a harmful chemical. Olson's girlfriend, in a desperate attempt to bring her boyfriend's cruelty to a halt, turned a bag of dog biscuits over to the police that presumably contained the chemical used to poison the helpless animals. Since the police were not sure what the substance in the biscuits was, they took the biscuits to a laboratory and subjected them to a chemical analysis. Laboratory technicians found that the substance was a chemical known to bring about violent illness. May Olson move to suppress the evidence on the grounds that the laboratory analysis triggered the protections of the Fourth Amendment?

California v. Greenwood
(486 U.S. 35 [1988])

Despite the seemingly profound change in the search-and-seizure definition following *Katz*, several subsequent decisions have interpreted the *Katz* ruling rather narrowly. For instance, in *California v. Greenwood* (486 U.S. 35 [1988]), the Supreme Court ruled that a Fourth Amendment search or seizure occurs only when (1) the citizen has a manifested subjective expectation of privacy and (2) the expectation of privacy is one that society (through the eyes of a court) is willing to accept as objectively reasonable.

Recall from the discussion in Chapter 1 that a *subjective* interest focuses on what one individual thinks (in this case, the person presumably being subjected to a search) and that an *objective* interest focuses either on what society thinks or on what a reasonable person would think. With regard to *Greenwood*, then, this means that just because someone *feels* he or she should enjoy privacy in a particular activity is not enough to trigger the Fourth Amendment. His or her activity needs to be one that society perceives as reasonable, also. In other words, it is not enough for someone to believe his or her rights have been infringed upon; his or her belief must also be an objectively reasonable one.

Today, the courts scarcely look toward the *subjective* issue and focus almost exclusively on the *objective* expectation of privacy. The reason for this is that it is pointless to dwell on an individual's expectation of privacy because if the seizure is questionable at all, the defendant will almost certainly proclaim he or she expected privacy. Focusing on an objective (instead of a subjective) expectation of privacy seems eminently more sensible.

One important observation in *Katz* deserves further mention: The Court stated that "[w]hat a person knowingly exposes to the public, even in his own home or office, is not subject to Fourth Amendment protection" (p. 351). Protection is only afforded for "what he seeks to preserve as private" (p. 351).

Defining the vague notions of *reasonableness* and *knowing exposure* has been the focus of a number of Supreme Court cases. These cases can be placed into at least five categories: (1) the undercover agent/false friend cases; (2) the abandoned property cases; (3) the physical characteristics cases; (4) the open fields and curtilage cases; and (5) the enhancement device cases.

Hoffa v. United States
(385 U.S. 293 [1966])

UNDERCOVER AGENTS AND FALSE FRIENDS   What happens when a person privately conveys information to another individual who is, in fact, an undercover agent, or as some people describe them, a "false friend"? In *Hoffa v. United States* (385 U.S. 293 [1966]), the Supreme Court sought to answer this question. The defendant Hoffa had a conversation with a union official who was in Hoffa's private suite by invitation but who was, in fact, a government informant. The informant reported what Hoffa said to government officials, and Hoffa sought to have the evidence excluded on the grounds that it was an illegal search. The Supreme Court disagreed with this decision, noting that the informant "was not a surreptitious eavesdropper" (p. 302) but a person who "was in the suite by invitation and every conversation which he heard was either directed to him or knowingly carried on in his presence" (p. 302).

United States v. On Lee
(343 U.S. 747 [1952])

A more difficult question arose in *United States v. On Lee* (343 U.S. 747 [1952]). *On Lee* addressed the issue of whether an undercover agent could wear a recording device during a conversation with a suspected criminal. The majority ruled that this activity did not constitute a search, again, because the informant was invited into the area where the conversation took place. Justice Burton dissented, however, noting that the recorder "amount[s] to [the agent] surreptitiously bringing [the police] with him" (p. 766). The majority countered by arguing that the listening device was simply designed to improve the accuracy of the evidence obtained by the informant. Other cases have been decided in a similar fashion (e.g., *United States v. White*, 401 U.S. 745 [1971]; *Lopez v. United States*, 373 U.S. 427 [1963]).

At a glance, it may seem that *On Lee* and *Katz* are at odds with one another. After all, both involved surreptitious recordings. How do we draw a distinction? In *On Lee*, the information was conveyed voluntarily to a false friend. In *Katz*, the information was *not* voluntarily surrendered to the authorities who were listening in on the conversation. Also, in *On Lee* the recording was just that. It was not an intercepted communication, as was the case in *Katz*. Generally speaking, then, when people voluntarily convey information or provide material to third parties, they cannot have a reasonable expectation of privacy (even if those third parties are best friends) because the third parties could easily turn the information over to authorities.

ABANDONED PROPERTY   What if an individual abandons his or her property, such as by leaving it in a public place or discarding it in the trash? This question came up in the case of *California v. Greenwood.* In that case, the Court reached the following decision:

> [G]arbage bags left on or at the side of a public street are readily accessible to animals, children, scavengers, snoops, and other members of the public. Moreover, respondents placed their refuse at the curb for the express purpose of conveying it to a third party, the trash collector, who might himself have sorted through respondents' trash or permitted others, such as the police, to do so. Accordingly, having deposited their garbage in an area particularly suited for public inspection and, in a manner of speaking, public consumption, for the express purpose of having strangers take it, respondents could have no reasonable expectation of privacy in the inculpatory items they discarded. (p. 40)

While *Greenwood* dealt exclusively with discarded trash, it extends to other types of abandonment. For example, if a murder suspect discarded a gun on public property, it would be considered abandoned. Why? A person cannot have a reasonable expectation of privacy in a public place or an "open field" (see below).

PRIVACY IN ONE'S PHYSICAL CHARACTERISTICS   The courts have also held that people's external physical characteristics are knowingly exposed to the public and are thus outside the scope of the Fourth Amendment. As noted in *United States v. Dionisio* (410 U.S. 1 [1973]), for example, "No person can have a reasonable expectation that others will not know the sound of his voice, any more than he can reasonably expect that his face will be a mystery to the world" (p. 13). To this end, the government can require handwriting samples (as in *Dionisio*) and other forms of physical evidence, such as locks of hair, voice exemplars, and fingerprints (e.g., *Davis v. Mississippi*, 394 U.S. 721 [1969]).

Physical attributes not on public display, however, generally fall within the protection of the Fourth Amendment. For example, in *Skinner v. Railway Labor Executives' Association* (489 U.S. 602 [1989]), the Court ruled that blood, urine, and breath analysis all amount to searches because "they intrude upon expectations of privacy as to medical information" (p. 616) (see also *Schmerber v. California*, 384 U.S. 757 [1966]; *Winston v. Lee*, 470 U.S. 753 [1985]; and *Cupp v. Murphy*, 412 U.S. 291 [1973]).

Finally, just because external physical characteristics are knowingly exposed does not mean that the police are not restricted in other ways by the Fourth Amendment. For example, if a suspect is at home in his or her private residence and the police wish to obtain his or her fingerprints, in almost all circumstances, they will need appropriate justification to do so. This could be accomplished by demonstrating probable cause and obtaining a warrant. Think of it this way: A person may not enjoy a reasonable expectation of privacy with regard to his or her physical characteristics that are on public display, but he or she will *always* enjoy a reasonable expectation of privacy in his or her residence, provided the police attempt to find him or her at that location.

DECISION-MAKING EXERCISE 3.4

A "False Friend" Scenario

John Quinn was put in jail after being arrested as a homicide suspect. The prosecutor did not think she had enough evidence to proceed to trial, so she asked a police officer to dress in street clothes, pose as a jail inmate, and strike up a conversation with Quinn. The officer was placed in the same cell with Quinn and began to make small talk with him. Eventually, Quinn mentioned that he was involved in the murder of Valerie Hutton but that he was not the "trigger man." The police officer reported this conversation to the prosecutor, who then sought to use Quinn's incriminating statements against him at trial. Quinn's attorney moved to have the statements suppressed on the grounds that a Fourth Amendment violation took place. In particular, the defense attorney argued that Quinn had a reasonable expectation of privacy that his conversation would not be shared with or repeated to other individuals. Does Quinn have a reasonable expectation of privacy in this regard?

OPEN FIELDS AND CURTILAGE   The physical setting in which police activity takes place is also important in determining whether the Fourth Amendment applies. Clearly, the inside of a residence is protected by the Fourth Amendment, but what about the outside? And if the outside is protected, how far beyond the residence can the strictures of the Fourth Amendment be expected to apply?

In providing answers to these questions, the courts refer to the term *curtilage*. According to the Supreme Court (*Oliver v. United States*, 466 U.S. 170 [1984]), **curtilage** is the "area to which extends the intimate activity associated with the sanctity of a man's home and the privacies of life" (p. 225). This definition should be contrasted with the definition of an **open field**, which is any unoccupied or undeveloped real property falling outside the curtilage of a home (p. 170). Figure 3.1 distinguishes among a house, curtilage, and open field.

Oliver v. United States (466 U.S. 170 [1984])

Open fields do not enjoy Fourth Amendment protection but homes and curtilage do. Note, however, that open fields need not be *open* or *fields* to fall beyond the reach of the Fourth Amendment. If a barn that is located 50 yards from a house is not used for

FIGURE 3.1

Relationship between a House, Curtilage, and Open Field

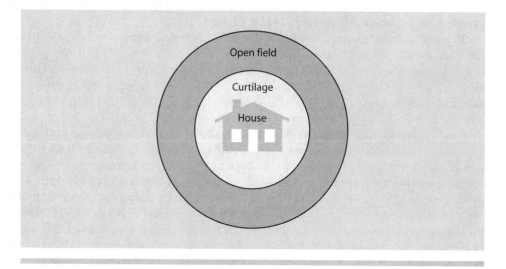

"intimate activities," it *can* be considered an open field, even though it is located on private property (see *United States v. Dunn*, 480 U.S. 294 [1987]). This is because "[o]pen fields do not provide the setting for those intimate activities that the [Fourth] Amendment is intended to shelter from government interference or surveillance" (*Oliver v. United States*, p. 179).

In *Oliver*, the Court went on to observe that

> [t]here is no societal interest in protecting the privacy of those activities, such as the cultivation of crops, that occur in open fields. Moreover, as a practical matter, these lands usually are accessible to the public and the police in ways that a home, office or commercial structure would not be. It is not generally true that fences or [No Trespassing] signs effectively bar the public from viewing open fields in rural areas. (p. 179)

The courts consider four factors when distinguishing between an open field and curtilage:

- the proximity of the area to the house;
- whether the area is included within a fence or another enclosure surrounding the house;
- the nature of the use to which the land/property is being put; and
- the steps taken by the resident to protect the area from observation (*United States v. Dunn*).

These four issues were considered by the Court in *United States v. Dunn*. In that case, police entered the defendant's property without a warrant, climbed over several fences, and peered inside his barn. They eventually obtained a warrant to search the barn, but the Court ruled that their earlier activity was a search within the meaning of the Fourth Amendment. See Figure 3.2 for a summary of these factors.

A twist in the aforementioned scenarios occurs when the police perform so-called flyovers, or aerial surveillance from a fixed-wing aircraft and/or helicopter. In *California v. Ciraolo* (476 U.S. 207 [1986]), the Supreme Court ruled that naked-eye observation of a fenced-in backyard from a height of 1,000 feet did not constitute a search. The logic offered by the Court was that in "an age where private and commercial flight in the public airways is routine, it is unreasonable for respondent to expect that his marijuana plants were constitutionally protected" from such observation (p. 215).

Similarly, in *Florida v. Riley* (488 U.S. 445 [1989]), the Court held that the Fourth Amendment was not implicated when the police flew a helicopter at an altitude of 400 feet over the defendant's partially covered greenhouse, which was found to contain marijuana. "Riley no doubt intended and expected that his greenhouse would not be open to public inspection, and the precautions he took [including placing a wire fence around the greenhouse and a Do Not Enter sign] protected against ground-level

FIGURE 3.2

Factors Used to Distinguish between a Curtilage and Open Field

1. Is the area close to a house or residence?
2. Is the area contained by a fence or similar enclosure?
3. To what use is the area being put?
4. What steps have been taken to protect the area from observation?

observation" (p. 450). The fact that any person could position himself or herself over the greenhouse in a helicopter was not enough to amount to a Fourth Amendment violation. The Court supported its position in this matter by noting that the helicopter's altitude was within legal parameters and Federal Aviation Administration (FAA) guidelines.

A similar decision was reached in *Dow Chemical Co. v. United States* (476 U.S. 227 [1986]), a case in which the Environmental Protection Agency (EPA) hired an aerial photographer to take pictures of the defendant's plant. Despite the photographer's use of a camera to take pictures (as opposed to simple, naked-eye observation), the Supreme Court ruled that aerial photography of the type used in *Dow Chemical* did not amount to a search, thereby triggering Fourth Amendment protections (see also *Air Pollution Variance Bd. v. Western Alfalfa Corp.*, 416 U.S. 861 [1974]).

ENHANCEMENT DEVICES   The rules become significantly more complicated when law enforcement officials use so-called *enhancement devices* to look for evidence. Enhancement devices can include flashlights, drug dogs, satellite photography, thermal imagery, and so on. Whatever their form, the devices are designed to enhance or replace the ability of the police to identify and discern criminal evidence or crime itself.

In determining what level of sensory enhancement is appropriate, the courts generally give consideration to six specific factors:

- the nature of the place surveilled,
- the nature of the activity surveilled,
- the care taken to ensure privacy,
- the lawfulness of the vantage point,
- the availability of sophisticated technology, and
- the extent to which the technology used enhances or replaces the natural senses.[1]

United States v. Knotts
(460 U.S. 276 [1983])

Illustrating the first consideration, the Court in *United States v. Knotts* (460 U.S. 276 [1983]) decided on the constitutionality of federal agents' actions of placing a "beeper" (a tracking device) in a container and tracking the container to the defendant's cabin. The Court concluded that "[a] person travelling in an automobile on public thoroughfares has no reasonable expectation of privacy in his movements from one place to another" (p. 281) (see also *United States v. Karo*, 468 U.S. 705 [1984]). The determinative factor in *Knotts* (and *Karo*) was that the nonsearch was conducted outside a residence. Had the beeper entered the residence, the outcome would have almost certainly been different.

With regard to the lawfulness of the police's vantage point, one thing is clear: If the police are not in a lawful vantage point but continue to look for evidence, a search occurs. Examples of lawful vantage points include sidewalks, streets, and, of course, public airways. As the Court ruled in *United States v. Dunn*, the police can take up positions

DECISION-MAKING EXERCISE 3.5

Is a Public Street an Open Field?

Officer Perez suspects that a local man is growing marijuana in his backyard but cannot tell for certain because of the large fence surrounding the house. To find out, Perez places a stepladder on a nearby public sidewalk, climbs up to the top, peers over the fence, and observes several dozen marijuana plants growing in the man's garden. Has a search occurred in this situation?

---

[1] C. H. Whitebread and C. Slobogin, *Criminal Procedure*, 4th ed. (New York: Foundation Press, 2000), pp. 120–125.

anywhere outside the home or the curtilage of the home and still be in a lawful vantage point. In fact, even if the police find themselves in curtilage that is open to the public, they may still find themselves in a lawful vantage point (see *Minnesota v. Carter*, 525 U.S. 83 [1998]).

The availability of sophisticated technology is also determinative in deciding which sensory enhancement devices the police can use. The previous discussion of *Dow Chemical* showed that the use of a camera from a publicly navigable airspace does not necessarily amount to a search. The Court deemed this activity beyond the scope of the Fourth Amendment because the camera equipment was available on the open market. However, the Court also pointed out that "using highly sophisticated surveillance equipment *not* generally available to the public, such as satellite technology, might be constitutionally proscribed absent a warrant" (p. 238, emphasis added). Moreover, the use of "an electronic device to penetrate walls or windows so as to hear and record confidential discussions of chemical formulae or other trade secrets would raise very different and far more serious questions" (p. 238).

The Supreme Court case *Kyllo v. United States* (533 U.S. 27 [2001]) fits clearly into a discussion of law enforcement's use of technology. In that case, law enforcement officials were suspicious that marijuana was being grown in Kyllo's home. Agents scanned his home using a thermal imaging device (also known as FLIR, for Forward Looking Infrared). The scan revealed that Kyllo's garage roof and side wall were relatively hot compared to the rest of his home. Based in part on the results from the thermal imager, a federal magistrate issued a warrant to search Kyllo's home. However, the Supreme Court declared that "[w]here . . . the Government uses a device that is not in general public use, to explore details of a private home that would previously have been unknowable without physical intrusion, the surveillance is a Fourth Amendment 'search,' and is presumptively unreasonable without a warrant" (p. 40).

One company, Millivision, has developed a gun detector that can be used to identify weapons and other opaque objects hidden beneath an individual's clothing.[2] While it is unclear how much or whether gun detectors are being used by police, the technology nevertheless raises Fourth Amendment concerns. If thermal imaging is a search, then wouldn't the same apply for gun detectors? Gun detectors, like thermal imagers, are devices that are "not in general public use." Time will tell whether these devices take hold in law enforcement.

The courts will also consider the extent to which a sensory enhancement device actually enhances the natural senses. In doing this, several courts have distinguished between devices that *enhance* the senses versus those that *replace* the senses. Generally, an enhancement device that is used to assist the senses (as binoculars do, for instance) is less likely to implicate the Fourth Amendment than a device that replaces the senses (as some satellites do). The permissibility of the use of binoculars can be attributed to the argument that police officers sometimes wish to avoid detection during the course of observation. Flashlights are clearly devices that enhance the natural senses, and courts have ruled that, when used, they do not trigger the Fourth Amendment (*Texas v. Brown*, 460 U.S. 730 [1983]; *United States v. Dunn*).

A slightly more controversial device is a drug dog. Some courts have ruled that their use does not trigger the Fourth Amendment under certain circumstances (e.g., *United States v. Place*, 462 U.S. 696 [1983]), but the issue is unresolved because one could argue that a drug dog's senses are used to *replace* an officer's senses. In fact, in *Commonwealth v. Johnston* (515 Pa. 454 [1987]), the court ruled that law enforcement officers' use of drug

United States v. Place
(462 U.S. 696 [1983])

---

[2] D. A. Harris, "Superman's X-Ray Vision and the Fourth Amendment: The New Gun Detection Technology," *Temple Law Review* 69 (1996): 1–60.

DECISION-MAKING EXERCISE 3.6

Drug Dogs as Sensory Enhancement Devices

A female traveler paid for a plane ticket to Miami. When she checked in at the airport, the ticket agent took her luggage and placed it on a conveyor belt so it could be loaded onto the plane. As the luggage was traveling along the conveyor, it passed a narcotics agent, whose dog sniffs every bag in an attempt to find drugs. The dog was alerted to the woman's bag, so the narcotics officer grabbed it and opened it. Several kilogram packages of cocaine were inside. Before the woman could board her flight, she was arrested. Has a search occurred?

---

dogs violated the state constitution because "a free society will not remain free if police may use this, or any other crime detection device, at random and without reason" (p. 465). The courts also need to consider *where* drug-sniffing dogs are used. For example, the Second Circuit held that the use of a drug dog adjacent to the defendant's apartment to determine the presence of narcotics *within* was a search, triggering the amendment's protection (see *United States v. Thomas*, 757 F.2d 1359 [2nd Cir. 1985]).

WHEN A SEIZURE OCCURS

The Fourth Amendment is clearly implicated when a search occurs. The same applies to a seizure. That is, whenever a person or piece of property is seized, the Fourth Amendment applies.

The definition of *seizure* has a very specific meaning in criminal procedure. It is not the case that something must be physically grasped for a seizure to take place. Indeed, the police can stop short of actually touching a person, but their actions can still constitute a seizure. At the other extreme, though, there are certain things the police can do to inconvenience people without triggering the Fourth Amendment. It is important to distinguish between two types of seizures: (1) seizures of property and (2) seizures of persons.

Seizures of Property

As the Supreme Court declared in *United States v. Jacobsen*, a **seizure of property** occurs "when there is some meaningful interference with an individual's possessory interest in that property."

In determining if a piece of property is seized, courts often refer to people's *actual* and *constructive* possessions. A piece of property is in a person's actual possession if he or she is physically holding or grasping the property. Constructive possession, by comparison, refers to possession of property without physical contact (e.g., a bag that is next to a person on the ground but not in his or her hands). A piece of property is seized, therefore, if the police remove it from a person's actual or constructive possession, such as when they take a person's luggage at an airport and move it into another room to be searched (see *United States v. Place*).

Relatively few cases are encountered concerning seizures of property. Usually, property is seized *after* a search occurs. When a search is declared unlawful, the seizure of the property that follows is generally unconstitutional because of the exclusionary rule (see Chapter 2). However, there are certain cases in which seizure occurs apart from a search. For example, in *Soldal v. Cook County* (506 U.S. 56 [1992]), the question before the Supreme Court was whether the Fourth Amendment applied when a family's trailer was removed from a trailer park. The Court held that the Fourth Amendment applied, meaning a seizure occurred.

Soldal v. Cook County
(506 U.S. 56 [1992])

Seizures of Persons

Subject to significant clarification in later chapters, a **seizure of a person** occurs when a police officer—by means of physical force or show of authority—intentionally restrains an individual's liberty in such a manner that a reasonable person would believe that he or she is not free to leave (*Terry v. Ohio*, 392 U.S. 1 [1968]; *United States v. Mendenhall*, 446 U.S. 544 [1980]). Another way of understanding what a Fourth Amendment seizure involves is to ask this question: Would a reasonable person believe that he or she is free to decline the officer's requests or otherwise terminate the encounter? (*Florida v. Bostick*, 501 U.S. 429 [1991]). A yes answer means a seizure has occurred.

The seizure of a person can take place in a number of ways. For example, a person is seized when he or she is arrested and taken to the police station for questioning (*Dunaway v. New York*, 442 U.S. 200 [1979]). A person is also seized if he or she is physically restrained or frisked (e.g., *Terry v. Ohio*) or pulled over by the police in his or her car.

The seizure of a person does not have to be *physical* for the Fourth Amendment to be implicated. For example, a seizure can occur when a police officer simply questions a person. The Supreme Court stated in *Terry v. Ohio* that "not all personal intercourse between policemen and citizens involves 'seizures' of persons" (p. 20, n. 16). Even so, a seizure *does* occur when the officer's conduct in conjunction with the questioning would convince a reasonable person that he or she is not free to leave.

Another way a seizure can occur is by *pursuit*, even if the person sought by the police is never caught. However, it is not always clear whether a pursuit constitutes a seizure. This is important because if the pursuit of a suspect is *not* a seizure, then the police may lawfully chase people without justification. Moreover, if the person discards anything during the chase, the police may lawfully seize the item because the Fourth Amendment does not apply. In fact, as the Supreme Court noted in *California v. Hodari D.* (499 U.S. 621 [1991]), when an officer chases a suspect but does not lay hands on him or her, a seizure does not occur until which point the suspect submits to police authority.

California v. Hodari D.
(499 U.S. 621 [1991])

In *Hodari D.*, a police officer chased a suspect on foot. The officer did not have justification to stop or arrest the suspect. The suspect discarded an item during the chase, which the officer stopped to pick up. The Supreme Court upheld the officer's action because the suspect was still in flight at the time the officer picked up the object. The Supreme Court did state in *Hodari D.*, however, that a seizure *does* occur the instant a police officer lays hands on a suspect during a chase, even if the suspect is able to break away from the officer's grasp.

The definitions of seizure offered in this section are general. The cases on which they are based will be encountered in the next three chapters as the topics of stop-and-frisk and arrest are considered. For now, remember that there are different types of seizures. An arrest, for example, is a type of seizure, but a seizure does not have to rise to the level of an arrest for the Fourth Amendment to be implicated. The following chapters will take care to ensure that the reader will be able to distinguish among different types of seizures.

JUSTIFICATION

To this point, only the threshold question of whether the Fourth Amendment applies has been addressed—that is, Has a search or seizure occurred? If the answer is no, then the issue will go no further, and justification will not matter because a search or seizure did not occur. However, if the government's action constitutes a search or seizure, the next issue involves deciding whether the police acted within the limits of the Fourth Amendment. If they did not, then any evidence obtained during the course of such an illegal search or seizure cannot be used in a criminal proceeding to determine guilt.

Once it has been determined *whether* the Fourth Amendment applies, it is then necessary to consider *what* the Fourth Amendment requires. The warrant requirement will be considered later, but the first and most fundamental inquiry in terms of Fourth Amendment requirements concerns the doctrine of justification. Put simply, the police need to have **justification**, or cause, before they can conduct a search or a seizure. Justification needs to be in place *a priori*—that is, before a person or evidence is sought in an area protected by the Fourth Amendment. The police cannot conduct an illegal search to obtain evidence and then argue *after the fact* that what they did was appropriate.

Although the language of the Fourth Amendment suggests that probable cause is the only important standard of justification, the Supreme Court has also focused on the amendment's reasonableness clause to carve out exceptions to the probable cause requirement. So-called *Terry* stops, for instance, do not require probable cause, but they are still required to be reasonable. (*Terry* stops are discussed in the next chapter.) At the other extreme, a quick reading of the Fourth Amendment would lead one to believe that the probable cause requirement is only necessary when a warrant is used. In actuality, however, the Supreme Court has held that the probable cause requirement applies in *warrantless* search-and-seizure situations, as well (see *Wong Sun v. United States*, 371 U.S. 471 [1963]).

Justification can be viewed as something of a sliding scale that hinges on the type of intrusion the police make. Generally, the more intrusive the police action, the higher the level of justification required. Conversely, the lower the level of intrusion, the lower the justification needed. Three primary levels of justification recognized by the courts will be considered throughout the remainder of this chapter: (1) probable cause, the standard for searches and seizures; (2) reasonable suspicion, the standard for stop-and-frisk; and (3) administrative justification, the standard for administrative searches.

Probable Cause

In principle, the definition of **probable cause** does not vary, regardless of the conduct in which the police engage. It was defined by the Supreme Court in *Beck v. Ohio* (379 U.S. 89 [1964]) as more than bare suspicion; it exists when "the facts and circumstances within [the officers'] knowledge and of which they [have] reasonably trustworthy information [are] sufficient to warrant a prudent man in believing that the [suspect] had committed or was committing an offense" (p. 91). In *Brinegar v. UnitedStates* (338 U.S. 160 [1949]), the Court added, "The substance of all the definitions of probable cause is a reasonable ground for belief of guilt" (p. 175).

*Beck v. Ohio
(379 U.S. 89 [1964])*

*Brinegar v. United States
(338 U.S. 160 [1949])*

Unfortunately, these legal definitions are of little use to those on the frontlines of law enforcement. A more practical definition of probable cause is *more than 50 percent certainty*. As such, it lies somewhere below absolute certainty and proof beyond a reasonable doubt (the latter of which is necessary to obtain a criminal conviction) and somewhere above a hunch or reasonable suspicion (the latter of which is required to conduct a stop-and-frisk).

The notion of a *prudent man* is akin to the idea of objective reasonableness already discussed. Basically, it means that courts consider what the average person on the street would believe, not what a person who has received special training in the identification and apprehension of lawbreakers (police officer, judge, etc.) would believe. This is not to say, however, that the experience of a police officer is not relevant to a probable cause determination. On the contrary, in *United States v. Ortiz* (422 U.S. 891 [1975]), the Court ruled that "officers are entitled to draw reasonable inferences from these facts in light of their knowledge of the area and their prior experience with aliens and smugglers" (p. 897) and, by extension, other people suspected of criminal activity.

Figure 3.3 lists a number of ingredients in the "recipe" for probable cause as well as examples of each ingredient. Each in isolation is rarely, if ever, enough. Rather, a combination of the factors listed in Figure 3.3 is necessary for probable cause to be established.

FIGURE 3.3

Ingredients in the Probable Cause Recipe

1. Prior record
   Examples
   - prior conviction for same activity
   - offender known to have committed similar offense in the past

2. Flight from the scene
   Examples
   - suspect sees police and runs away
   - flight from an apartment known for drug dealing

3. Suspicious conduct
   Examples
   - failure to make eye contact with officers
   - extreme inattention to police
   - suspect appears startled by police and turns quickly away
   - "casing" a jewelry store

4. Admissions
   Examples
   - *suspect tells informant that he committed a crime*
   - *officer overhears two men talking about their involvement in a crime*
   - *officer hears one suspect tell another, "I told you not to do it"*

5. Incriminating evidence
   Examples
   - *suspect found in possession of drug paraphernalia*
   - *burglary suspect found with pillowcase full of loot*
   - *sack of cash and ski mask in robbery suspect's car*

6. Unusual hour
   Examples
   - At 2:30 a.m., an officer sees a man depart a darkened property where valuables were kept
   - At 3:30 a.m., an officer observed two men walking in a business area who then fled at the sight of the officer

7. Suspect resembles the perpetrator
   Examples
   - *suspect wears clothes similar to the perpetrator of a crime*
   - suspect is an occupant of the same car thought to flee the scene of a robbery
   - the number of suspects in the car is the same as the number of suspects reportedly involved in the crime

8. Evasive and untruthful responses to questions
   Examples
   - suspect caught in a lie about where she was coming from
   - suspect gives false name and/or identification
   - use of an alias
   - suspect denies owning a car that is registered to him
   - suspect gives vague and confusing answers to an officer's questions

9. Obvious attempt to hide something
   Examples
   - officers hear a toilet flush when arriving to serve a search warrant
   - officer observes a suspect push something under the seat of his car

Figure 3.3 continued

- suspect is looking into the trunk of a vehicle but slams it quickly on seeing a police officer

10. Presence in a high-crime area and/or near a crime scene

    Examples

    - officer observes a vehicle leave the scene of a burglary at which no other people or vehicles were located
    - the suspect is the only pedestrian near the scene of a burglary
    - officers observe an apparent drug transaction in an area known for narcotics activity

11. Furtive gestures

    Examples

    - officers observe the passenger in a vehicle duck from view
    - suspect makes a quick hand-to-mouth movement
    - suspect turns away from the officers when they announce their presence
    - the driver of a vehicle reaches under the seat

12. Knowing too much

    Example

    - suspect volunteers information that only the perpetrator could possibly know

Probable cause is always required in the following scenarios:

- arrests with warrants;
- arrests without warrants;
- searches and seizures of property with warrants; and
- searches and seizures of property without warrants.

When a warrant is required, the probable cause determination is made by the magistrate charged with issuing the warrant; when a warrant is not used, the police officer makes the probable cause determination. In general,

> Probable cause can be obtained from police radio bulletins, tips from "good citizen" informers who have happened by chance to see criminal activity, reports from victims, anonymous tips, and tips from "habitual" informers who mingle with people in the underworld and who themselves may [even] be criminals. Probable cause can be based on various combinations of these sources.[3]

When the police make an *arrest*, the probable cause determination concerns whether an offense has been committed and whether the suspect did, in fact, commit the offense. In the case of a search, however, the probable cause issue concerns whether the items to be seized are connected with criminal activity and whether they can be found in the place to be searched. This means, then, that the courts sometimes treat the probable cause requirement differently, depending on the conduct in which the police engage.

One point needs to be underscored: Probable cause to search does not necessarily create probable cause to arrest, and, alternatively, probable cause to arrest does not necessarily create probable cause to search. With regard to the latter point, consider this hypothetical situation: Police officers pursue a drug suspect into her residence and, based on a hot-pursuit exigency, arrest her in her living room. Assuming probable cause was in place to pursue the suspect, the police do not possess unfettered latitude once in

---

[3] J. G. Miles, Jr., D. B. Richardson, and A. E. Scudellari, *The Law Officer's Pocket Manual* (Washington, DC: Bureau of National Affairs, 1988–1989), p. 6:4.

the house to search the place up and down. The courts have placed restrictions on what can be done in a situation such as this—that is, on how far the police can go with a search following (i.e., incident) to arrest. Searches incident to arrest will be covered in a later chapter, but this example illustrates that the ingredients in the probable cause recipe are not always the same for arrests as they are for searches.

In several arrest cases, the courts have had the opportunity to decide what sources of information meet the probable cause burden. Three sources of information can be identified: (1) informants and other third parties; (2) firsthand knowledge; and (3) information that turns out, after the fact, to be mistaken but is reasonably relied on.[4] Other information may help establish probable cause to arrest, but the courts have been most vocal about these three sources.

INFORMANTS AND OTHER THIRD PARTIES   The police routinely rely on information supplied to them by a sophisticated network of *informants*. Informants are not necessarily shady characters connected to the criminal lifestyle; they can also be victims of crime, witnesses of crime, and other police officers.

As to the first type of informant, the courts have attempted to create tests to ensure that information supplied by informants is credible. In *Aguilar v. Texas* (378 U.S. 108 [1964]), the Supreme Court ruled that an affidavit based on a tip from an informant must show (1) sufficient information to demonstrate how the informant reached his or her conclusion and (2) sufficient information to establish the reliability of the informant. Stated differently, the first prong asks, Why should the police believe this person? and the second prong asks, How does the informant know what he or she claims to know?

Aguilar v. Texas
(378 U.S. 108 [1964])

For both prongs of the *Aguilar* test to be satisfied, the police need to supply specific information in their affidavit. A statement to the effect that "this informant has provided reliable information in the past" is not enough. More appropriate is a statement such as "This informant has supplied information in the past that led to the conviction of John Doe" (see also *United States v. Freitas*, 716 F.2d 1216 [9th Cir. 1983]).

In *Spinelli v. United States* (393 U.S. 410 [1969]), the Supreme Court clarified the meaning of the first prong. It concluded that insufficient knowledge about the details of the reported criminal activity can be overcome if "the tip describe[s] the accused's criminal activity in sufficient detail that the magistrate knows that he is relying on something more substantial than a casual rumor . . . or an accusation based merely on an individual's general reputation" (p. 416). Similarly, in *Draper v. United States* (358 U.S. 307 [1959]), the Court ruled that the first prong—the credibility prong—may also be satisfied when the informant implicates himself or herself in criminal activity, provided that such a statement is against self-interest. An example of a self-interested admission of criminal activity would be one in which the informant seeks to curry favor with the police and/or prosecutors in exchange for supplying information (see *United States v. Harris*, 403 U.S. 573 [1971]; *United States v. Jackson*, 818 F.2d 345 [5th Cir. 1987]).

Spinelli v. United States
(393 U.S. 410 [1969])

The *Aguilar* and *Spinelli* tests were heavily modified in *Illinois v. Gates* (462 U.S. 213 [1983]), when the Supreme Court basically abandoned the two-pronged probable cause analysis and replaced it with a *totality of circumstances* test. Thus, if "a particular informant is known for the unusual reliability of his predictions of certain types of criminal activities in a locality, his failure, in a particular case, to thoroughly set forth the basis of his knowledge surely should not serve as an absolute bar to a finding of probable cause based on his tip" (p. 233). In other words, a deficiency in one prong can be compensated for with an abundant supply of information in the other.

Illinois v. Gates
(462 U.S. 213 [1983])

Interestingly, *Aguilar*, *Spinelli*, and *Gates* were all search cases, which would seem to limit their applicability in the arrest context. Actually, the *Illinois v. Gates* totality of

---

[4] Whitebread and Slobogin, pp. 120–125.

circumstances test is now used for determining probable cause based on information from informants in both the arrest and search/seizure contexts. However, relying on *Draper v. United States*, the courts will still give consideration to five factors in determining whether the totality of circumstances creates probable cause: (1) when the informant describes how he or she found out about the criminal activity; (2) when the informant gives a detailed description of that activity; (3) when evidence for the informant's reliability exists; (4) when the informant predicts criminal activity that is later corroborated by the police; and (5) when the informant implicates himself or herself in criminal activity.

What happens when the informant is a victim or an eyewitness? In both situations, the Supreme Court has relaxed the *Aguilar/Spinelli/Gates* tests. For example, in *Jaben v. United States* (381 U.S. 214 [1965]), the Court held that "whereas some supporting information concerning the credibility of informants in narcotics cases or other common garden varieties of crime may be required, such information is not so necessary in the context of the case before us" (p. 224). Similar rulings have been applied when the informants have been other police officers. For example, in *United States v. Ventresca* (380 U.S. 102 [1965]), the Supreme Court ruled that "[o]bservations of fellow officers of the Government engaged in a common investigation are plainly a reliable basis for a warrant applied for by one of their number" (p. 111). Of course, probable cause is still required. When probable cause is found lacking, the arrest will most likely be deemed unconstitutional (see *Whiteley v. Warden*, 401 U.S. 560 [1971]).

FIRSTHAND KNOWLEDGE   The second major category of probable cause to arrest cases hinges on information that results from *firsthand knowledge.* That is, when is probable cause established by someone other than a third party—namely, the arresting officer? The courts usually do not worry about the truthfulness or accuracy of the arresting officer's observations but, instead, whether probable cause to arrest was in place. In particular, the courts have required that probable cause *to* arrest must be determined independently from the arrest itself, meaning that probable cause to arrest must be required *before* the arrest. In *Sibron v. New York* (392 U.S. 40 [1968]), the Supreme Court stated, "It is axiomatic that an incident search may not precede an arrest and serve as part of its justification" (p. 63). In simple terms, this means that police cannot search people and illegally seize evidence simply for the purpose of establishing probable cause to arrest. Stated differently, probable cause cannot be established in hindsight. It should be pointed out, though, that evidence encountered during law enforcement activity that does not constitute an arrest or a search (a patdown, for instance) can create or be used to establish probable cause to arrest or conduct a further search, depending on the circumstances. (Patdown searches are discussed in the following section.)

In another case, *United States v. Di Re* (332 U.S. 581 [1948]), the Supreme Court held that a suspect's proximity to criminal activity is not enough to establish probable cause to arrest. In that case, officers arrested Di Re from the front seat of a car on the grounds that there were two other men in the car passing counterfeit ration coupons between one another. The Court noted that had Di Re even seen the activity, "it would not follow that he knew they were ration coupons, and if he saw that they were ration coupons, it would not follow that he would know them to be counterfeit" (p. 593). Simply put, then, proximity to criminal activity does not create probable cause to arrest (see also *Johnson v. United States*, 333 U.S. 10 [1948]).

In another case, one in which the police had a valid warrant authorizing them to search a tavern, the Court held that the search warrant did not give them permission to search the patrons of the bar, including the petitioner, because they were not named in the warrant (*Ybarra v. Illinois*, 444 U.S. 85 [1979]). If, however, the arresting officer were armed with additional information (from a third-party informant, for example), then probable cause would be easier to establish (see *Ker v. California*, 374 U.S. 23 [1963]).

DECISION-MAKING EXERCISE 3.7

Informants and Probable Cause

Here are some facts from an actual case:

> . . . a Gulf service station in North Braddock, Pennsylvania, was robbed by two men, each of whom carried and displayed a gun. The robbers took the currency from the cash register; the service station attendant, one Stephen Kovacich, was directed to place the coins in his right-hand glove, which was then taken by the robbers. Two teenagers, who had earlier noticed a blue compact station wagon circling the block in the vicinity of the Gulf station, then saw the station wagon speed away from a parking lot close to the Gulf station. About the same time, they

learned that the Gulf station had been robbed. They reported to police, who arrived immediately, that four men were in the station wagon and one was wearing a green sweater. Kovacich told the police that one of the men who robbed him was wearing a green sweater and the other was wearing a trench coat. A description of the car and the two robbers was broadcast over the police radio (*Chambers v. Maroney*, 399 U.S. 42 [1970]).

A vehicle fitting the description was stopped. The occupants were arrested and the car was driven to the police station and searched. Was the stop justified? In other words, did the officers have probable cause to arrest the occupants of the car?

What is more, courts regularly defer to officers' judgments as to whether probable cause was in place (see *Maryland v. Pringle*, 540 U.S. 366 [2003]).

REASONABLE RELIANCE ON MISTAKEN INFORMATION Interestingly, if information supplied by an informant or by an officer's firsthand observations later proves to be false, the courts will uphold the earlier action (see *Henry v. United States*, 361 U.S. 98 [1959]; *United States v. Garofalo*, 496 F.2d 510 [8th Cir. 1974]), so long as the mistake was a reasonable one (*Franks v. Delaware*, 438 U.S. 154 [1978]). When such a mistake is deemed *unreasonable*, however, the courts will almost always reach a different conclusion. An unreasonable mistake can be found in *Albright v. Oliver* (510 U.S. 266 [1994]), in which the Supreme Court implied that it was unreasonable (and a violation of the Fourth Amendment) for a police officer to rely on an informant who had provided false information on 50 previous occasions.

Reasonable Suspicion

To recap, the justification required to conduct a search or a seizure within the meaning of the Fourth Amendment is probable cause. But much police activity does not reach the level of intrusion that occurs when a search or seizure is carried out. For example, the police routinely have to confront people on the street in order to question them and to pull over automobiles to enforce traffic laws. If probable cause were required under such circumstances, the police could do little in terms of investigating suspicious activity.

DECISION-MAKING EXERCISE 3.8

Having Probable Cause to Arrest

An observant police officer was on foot patrol and noticed a suspicious person standing at the counter in a convenience store. The person, who had one hand in his coat pocket, appeared to be carrying on a conversation with the clerk, who was reaching into the cash register and appeared to be very nervous. On a hunch that she was witnessing a robbery in progress, the officer quickly entered the store, surprised the person talking to the clerk, arrested him, and upon searching him incident to the arrest, found a handgun in his coat pocket. His attorney moved to suppress the handgun on the grounds that the police officer did not have probable cause to arrest. What should the courts decide?

While police must have probable cause to make an arrest or conduct a search, a patdown is permissible with reasonable suspicion that criminal activity is afoot, a lower standard than probable cause.

Terry v. Ohio *(392 U.S. 1 [1968])*

Recognizing how essential these *lesser intrusions* are to the police mission, the Supreme Court established in *Terry v. Ohio* (392 U.S. 1 [1968]) a different level of justification for such activities. The Court created the standard of **reasonable suspicion**—something below probable cause but above a hunch. *Terry* dealt with so-called stop-and-frisk activities (the topic of Chapter 6), but reasonable suspicion as a standard of justification permeates other arenas of criminal procedure (e.g., traffic stops).

In *Terry*, an officer's attention was drawn to two men on a street corner who appeared to the officer to be "casing" a store for a robbery. The officer approached the men and asked them to identify themselves. The officer then proceeded to pat down the men and found a gun on each one. The men were placed under arrest. They tried to suppress the guns, but the Supreme Court eventually held the officer's actions valid in the interest of "effective crime prevention and detection" (p. 22). Balancing an intrusion that was arguably less serious than a search with the interests of society in apprehending lawbreakers, the Court held that a lower standard than probable cause was required because "street encounters between citizens and police officers are incredibly rich in diversity" (p. 13).

There is no clear definition of *reasonable suspicion*, just as there is no clear definition of *probable cause*. As stated in *United States v. Cortez* (449 U.S. 411 [1981]),

> Courts have used a variety of terms to capture the elusive concept of what cause is sufficient to authorize police to stop a person. Terms like "articulable reasons" and "founded suspicion" are not self-defining; they fall short of providing clear guidance dispositive of the myriad factual situations that arise. But the essence of all that has been written is that the totality of circumstances—the whole picture—must be taken into account. Based upon that whole picture the detaining officers must have a particularized and objective basis for suspecting the particular person stopped of criminal activity. (p. 417)

As a level of justification lying below probable cause, then, reasonable suspicion is "considerably less than proof of wrongdoing by a preponderance of evidence" (*United States v. Sokolow*, 490 U.S. 1 [1989], p. 7) but more than an unparticularized hunch. Figure 3.4 contains a list of specific factors that can contribute to reasonable suspicion—and some information that *cannot* give rise to reasonable suspicion.

Like probable cause, reasonable suspicion can be based on a number of different sources, including informants. But because the reasonable suspicion standard falls below that for probable cause, less information is required. In *Adams v. Williams* (407 U.S. 143 [1972]), for example, the Supreme Court held that reasonable suspicion may be based on an anonymous telephone tip, so long as the police can corroborate certain details from the informant. In a similar case, *Alabama v. White* (496 U.S. 325 [1990]), the Supreme Court observed, "Reasonable suspicion is a less demanding standard than probable cause not only in the sense that reasonable suspicion can be established with information that is different but also in the sense that reasonable suspicion can arise from information that is less reliable than that required to show probable cause" (p. 330).

Alabama v. White (496 U.S. 325 [1990])

In *United States v. Hensley* (469 U.S. 221 [1985]), the Supreme Court unanimously held that the reasonable suspicion standard is satisfied when the police rely on "wanted" flyers, even those from other jurisdictions. A restriction on this ruling was that the flyer, regardless of its place of origin, must be based on articulable facts that connect the suspect to criminal activity. The key here is **articulable facts**.

FIGURE 3.4

Factors That May and Do Not Give Rise to Reasonable Suspicion

Factors That *May* Give Rise to Reasonable Suspicion	Factors That *Will* Not Give Rise to Reasonable Suspicion
Suspect in high-crime area at unusual hour	Hunch
Suspect flees from officers	Rumor
Suspect appears to receive cash in exchange for two small envelopes	Intuition
Suspect puts television in the trunk of a car in an area where most businesses are closed	Instinct
Suspect appears to be "casing" a convenience store	Curiosity

Articulable facts are events that are witnessed and can be explained. The opposite of articulable facts would be a gut reaction or a mere hunch.

The Court in *Hensley* also had to decide if a stop based on reasonable suspicion of *prior* criminal activity was permissible under the Fourth Amendment's reasonableness standard. All decisions up to that point had dealt with suspected criminal activity immediately before the officer's arrival or criminal activity likely to have occurred but for the officer's arrival. In *Hensley,* the police stopped a man 12 days after the commission of a robbery for which he was suspected. The Court upheld the police's action and stated that it "would not only hinder the investigation, but might also enable the suspect to flee in the interim and to remain at large" (p. 229).

To further illustrate the meaning of reasonable suspicion, consider the case of *Sibron v. New York.* In that case, the Court held that talking to known addicts and reaching into their pockets does not produce reasonable suspicion that criminal activity is afoot. In yet another case, *Brown v. Texas* (443 U.S. 47 [1979]), two police officers observed Brown and another man walking away from one another. One of the officers later testified that he thought the officers' arrival broke up some suspicious activity. Officer Venegas approached Brown and asked him to identify himself. Brown refused and was later convicted under a statute that made it illegal to refuse to give an officer one's name and address. According to the Court,

> There is no indication in the record that it was unusual for people to be in the alley. The fact that the appellant was in a neighborhood frequented by drug users, standing alone, is not a basis for concluding that the appellant himself was engaged in criminal conduct. In short, the appellant's activity was no different from the activity of other pedestrians in that neighborhood. (p. 52)

Contrast *Brown v. Texas* with the Supreme Court's decision in *Illinois v. Wardlow* (528 U.S. 119 [2000]). In that case, Chicago police officers were patrolling an area known for narcotics traffic. Upon seeing the officers, Wardlow ran and was chased down by the police. When he was patted down, the officers found a Colt .38 pistol and arrested him. Wardlow appealed his conviction, arguing that the stop-and-frisk was illegal because the officers did not have reasonable suspicion. The Court disagreed noting that "a location's characteristics are relevant in determining whether the circumstances are sufficiently suspicious to warrant further investigation" (p. 119). In addition, the Court noted that "it was Wardlow's unprovoked flight that aroused the officers' suspicion" and that "nervous, evasive behavior is another pertinent factor in determining reasonable suspicion, and headlong flight is the consummate act of evasion" (p. 124). Thus, in the Court's view, the officers *did* have reasonable suspicion to stop and frisk Wardlow.

Recently, in *United States v. Arvizu* (534 U.S. 266 [2002]), the Supreme Court highlighted the importance of the totality of circumstances as well as officers' experience in making a determination of reasonable suspicion. In that case, a border patrol agent in a remote part of Arizona became suspicious of a van that slowed upon seeing him. Also, the driver failed to acknowledge the agent. The agent stopped the van, and the Supreme Court upheld this decision. The Court stated the agent was "entitled to make an assessment of the situation in light of his specialized training and familiarity with the customs of the area's inhabitants" (p. 276).

Because reasonable suspicion is of fundamental importance in criminal procedure, this text will devote an entire chapter to the role it plays in law enforcement activities. In particular, Chapter 4 will cover *Terry* stops in detail, focusing carefully on the definitions of *stop* and the scope of the *frisk*. Before continuing with that, though, it is necessary to turn attention to yet another level of justification of importance in Fourth Amendment jurisprudence. Actually, it could more appropriately be labeled a form of *nonjustification*.

DECISION-MAKING EXERCISE 3.9

Is There Reasonable Suspicion?

Officer Hopper was on patrol in a high-crime area at 3:00 a.m. and was waved over to the curb by a woman on the sidewalk. She told Hopper that there was a person sitting in a car nearby who had illegal narcotics and a gun on his lap. Officer Hopper approached the car and asked the driver to open the door. Instead, the driver started to roll down the window. Hopper quickly reached into the window and grabbed the gun from the driver's lap. Was the officer's conduct justified?

Either way, *administrative justification* is something of a fallback—a lower standard that permits fairly significant intrusions with little or no justification.

Administrative Justification

A third level of justification has arisen by virtue of the fact that government entities occasionally conduct searches in circumstances other than criminal investigations. As noted earlier, a search-and-seizure aimed at obtaining evidence for use in a criminal proceeding cannot occur without appropriate justification. Noncriminal searches also occur, however, so the Supreme Court has created a different level of justification. Instead of being based on reasonableness, the **administrative justification** adopts a balancing approach, weighing the privacy interests of individuals with the interests of society in preserving public safety.

The first case creating an administrative form of justification was *Camara v. Municipal Court* (387 U.S. 523 [1967]), which involved a health code inspection of residential dwelling units. The Supreme Court held that such inspections were subject to Fourth Amendment restrictions but rejected the argument that the appropriate level of justification was probable cause (or reasonable suspicion, for that matter). Invoking the Fourth Amendment's reasonableness clause, the Court balanced the public interest in enforcing safety codes with the "relatively limited invasion of the urban citizen's privacy," given that "the inspections are neither personal in nature nor aimed at the discovery of evidence of crime" (p. 537). The Court further noted that such searches are permissible, so long as "reasonable legislative or administrative standards for conducting an area inspection are satisfied with respect to a particular dwelling" (p. 538). In other words, administrative searches should not be conducted arbitrarily or with selective enforcement.

More recently, in *Colorado v. Bertine* (479 U.S. 367 [1987]), the Court stated that the "standard of probable cause is peculiarly related to criminal investigations, not routine, noncriminal procedures. . . . The probable-cause approach is unhelpful when analysis centers upon the reasonableness of routine administrative caretaking functions, particularly when no claim is made that the protective procedures are a subterfuge for criminal investigations" (p. 317). Accordingly, the courts have required that administrative searches be conducted according to objective, standardized procedures. Also important, authorities cannot use an administrative search as a pretext for a full-blown search.

An informative example of the balancing approach taken in justifying administrative searches can be found in *Vernonia School District v. Acton* (115 S. Ct. 2386 [1995]). In that case, the Court decided the fate of a school policy that required athletes to submit to random urinalysis for drugs. The Court allowed the search because it was not geared toward any particular individual. Further, the Court reasoned that athletes in public schools enjoy a lesser expectation of privacy because they must participate in other examinations, they dress together in the locker room, and they participate in the sports *voluntarily.* The government interest cited by the Court was preventing "drug use by our Nation's school children" (p. 2395). This was a controversial decision, indeed, as it seemed to reduce the need for justification set forth explicitly in the Fourth Amendment.

The administrative search rationale has been applied in a number of related situations. For example, the courts have been rather liberal in terms of upholding questionable searches of highly regulated business establishments. In *New York v. Burger* (482 U.S. 691 [1987]), for instance, the Supreme Court authorized a warrantless search of an automobile junkyard. In *Donovan v. Dewey* (452 U.S. 594 [1981]), the Court upheld the warrantless inspection of mines. The same logic carried over to a case involving the inspection of a gun dealership (*United States v. Biswell*, 406 U.S. 311 [1972]). In support of its decisions, the Court argued that people who choose to conduct business in highly regulated environments enjoy a reduced expectation of privacy.

Other decisions have involved such varied enterprises as arson investigations (*Michigan v. Clifford*, 464 U.S. 286 [1984]; *Michigan v. Tyler*, 436 U.S. 499 [1978]); border checkpoints to stop vehicles in an effort to detect illegal aliens (e.g., *United States v. Martinez-Fuerte*, 428 U.S. 543 [1976]); searches of impounded vehicles (*Colorado v. Bertine*) and other personal items in need of inventorying (*Illinois v. Lafayette*, 462 U.S. 640 [1983]); and mandatory drug testing of public and private employees (e.g., *National Treasury Employees Union v. Von Raah*, 489 U.S. 656 [1989]; *Skinner v. Railway Labor Executives' Association*). In *Skinner*, the Court observed,

> In light of the limited discretion exercised by the railroad employers under the [drug testing] regulations, the surpassing safety interest served by toxicological tests in this context, and the diminished expectation of privacy that attaches to information pertaining to the fitness of covered employees, we believe it is reasonable to conduct such tests in the absence of a warrant or reasonable suspicion that any particular employee may be impaired. (p. 602)

It should be noted that the courts have placed significant restrictions on the scope of so-called administrative searches. For example, in *Marshall v. Barlow's, Inc.*, the Court ruled as unconstitutional searches based on the Occupational Safety and Health Act of businesses that had not been heavily regulated in the past. At the same time, however, administrative searches can give great latitude in terms of seizing contraband and evidence of a crime to whomever conducts the search. As stated in *New York v. Burger*, "The discovery of evidence of crimes in the course of an otherwise proper administrative inspection does not render that search illegal or the administrative scheme suspect" (p. 716).

Further, if the purpose of an administrative search is to detect evidence of criminal activity, probable cause is required. This was the decision reached in the recent Supreme Court case *City of Indianapolis v. Edmond* (531 U.S. 32 [2000]). In it, the Court decided whether a city's suspicionless checkpoints for detecting illegal drugs were constitutional. The court held that stops such as those conducted during checkpoint operations require individualized suspicion. In addition, "because the checkpoint program's primary purpose [was] indistinguishable from the general interest in crime control" (p. 32), it was deemed violative of the Fourth Amendment.

Moving on, the administrative search justification that has been applied to regulatory inspections has also been applied to situations involving "special needs beyond the normal need for law enforcement" (*Skinner v. Railway Labor Executives' Association*, p. 619). In *New Jersey v. TLO* (469 U.S. 325 [1985]), a student's purse was searched by an assistant principal, who suspected that the student was violating the school's policy against smoking. The search turned up marijuana, but according to the Supreme Court, "the schoolchild's legitimate expectation of privacy and the school's equally legitimate need to maintain an environment in which learning can take place" (p. 340) did not need a warrant or even probable cause. Similarly, in *O'Connor v. Ortega* (480 U.S. 709 [1987]), a case involving the warrantless search of a government employee's office, and in *Griffin v. Wisconsin* (483 U.S. 868 [1987]), a case in which a probation

---

DECISION-MAKING EXERCISE 3.10

Adventure on the Seas

U.S. Customs and Border Protection agents used a drug dog to search the staterooms of 10 passengers aboard the *Adventure of the Seas* cruise ship while it was in port in St. Thomas, a U.S. territory. One of the staterooms searched was that of James Whitted, a man to whom authorities were alerted because he purchased his ticket at the last minute, had traveled in and through various "source cities," and had a criminal record. During the stateroom search, the drug dog alerted to a bag. Nothing suspicious was found in the bag, so it was X-rayed. At that point, the agents noticed pebbles inside a shaving cream can. On further examination, the pebbles field-tested positive for heroin. Whitted was arrested and charged with possession with intent to distribute a controlled substance. He now moves to have the drugs excluded from his trial due to an alleged Fourth Amendment violation. Will he succeed?

---

officer searched the home of a probationer under the officer's supervision, the Court invoked the logic of special needs beyond normal law enforcement to dispense with the warrant requirement.

STANDING

Standing is a topic closely tied to the Fourth Amendment. Basically, it means that a person cannot object to a wrongful search or seizure unless he or she can show standing to bring the issue to the court's attention. A person who does not have standing will not even be able to have his or her argument heard by a judge.

A person has *standing* if he or she is the victim of a Fourth Amendment violation. This means that person A cannot complain about an infringement on person B's rights. According to the Supreme Court decision in *Jones v. United States* (362 U.S. 257 [1960]), the victim of a Fourth Amendment violation should be distinguished from one "who claims prejudice only through the use of evidence gathered as a consequence of a search or seizure directed at someone else" (p. 261). Or as stated in *Rakas v. Illinois* (439 U.S. 128 [1978]), "A person who is aggrieved by an illegal search and seizure only through the introduction of damaging evidence secured by a search of a third person's premises or property has not had any of his Fourth Amendment rights infringed" (p. 134).

Originally, standing was tied to property interests. Only if one had a *possessory interest* in the thing to be seized or the place to be searched was he or she considered to have standing. However, in *Jones v. United States*, the Supreme Court declared that "it is unnecessary and ill-advised to import into the law surrounding the constitutional right to be free from unreasonable searches and seizures subtle distinctions, developed and refined by the common law in evolving the body of private property law" (p. 266). The Court conferred standing, instead, on anyone legitimately on the premises. Also in *Jones*, the Court declared that when defendants are charged with possessory offenses (e.g., possession of an illegal firearm), they automatically enjoy standing. The reason for this was that certain defendants had to admit the contraband was theirs and incriminate themselves in order to show standing.

The automatic-standing doctrine was overturned in *United States v. Salvucci* (448 U.S. 83 [1980]), and the legitimately on-the-premises-standard has been replaced with a new standard based on a person's expectation of privacy (*Katz v. United States*). The courts now focus on the *totality of circumstances* to determine whether a person has a reasonable expectation of privacy.

The courts have referred to at least three specific situations in which a person can be said to have standing. First, if a person has the right to exclude others from the premises, he or she has standing (e.g., *Rawlings v. Kentucky*, 448 U.S. 98 [1980]). Second, if a person has continuing access plus possessory interest, he or she can be said to have standing. For example, in *United States v. Jeffers* (342 U.S. 48 [1951]), the Court declared that a man who had a key to his aunt's apartment, even though it was rented, had standing, even though he could not technically exclude others from the premises. Third, in *Minnesota v. Olson* (495 U.S. 91 [1990]), the Supreme Court ruled that a person who is legitimately on the premises and has a possessory interest in the item seized can also have standing. An example of such a person is a woman who visits a friend in her friend's house. Although as the guest she cannot exclude anyone from the house and does not have continuing access, she can still have standing if an item in her possession is seized unlawfully.

The Link between Standing and the Definition of a Search

In *Rakas v. Illinois*, the Supreme Court recognized the similarity between the *standing* analysis and the definition of a *search*. Both focus on a person's reasonable expectation of privacy. In essence, the standing and search analyses collapse into one when there is a questionable search on the part of the police.

Why discuss standing separately from the definition of a search? There are three reasons. First, it is important to realize that while a search may occur, the person targeted by that search does not always have a reasonable expectation of privacy. In other words, a search may occur, but if evidence is not seized and used against that person at trial, the person cannot claim any Fourth Amendment protection. Second, there may be situations in which a search is legal but a seizure is illegal, thus requiring that the search and the seizure be analyzed separately. Finally, as Justice Blackmun observed in *Rawlings v. Kentucky*, it is possible for a defendant to demonstrate standing to challenge a search but fail to prove that the search was unlawful (p. 112). Alternatively, a defendant may show that a Fourth Amendment violation took place but not have the standing to contest it.

For all practical purposes, the standing analysis is regularly merged into the Fourth Amendment search analysis and rarely requires discussion in and of itself. Indeed, rare are the situations in which standing and the Fourth Amendment receive individual attention. As such, standing will not be revisited elsewhere in this book. Readers should understand that it is an important threshold issue, however.

Summary

1. DEFINE TERMS RELATED TO THE FOURTH AMENDMENT.

The Fourth Amendment protects *persons*, *houses*, *papers*, and *effects* from unreasonable searches and seizures. The term *person* encompasses the individual as a whole, both internally and externally. *House* is a term that is broadly construed to mean any structure that a person uses as a residence (and frequently a business) on either a temporary or long-term basis. A hotel room is a prime example of a short-term house. Papers and effects include nearly all personal items. Business records, letters, diaries, memos, and countless other forms of tangible evidence can be defined as *papers*. *Effects* is the catch-all category.

The Fourth Amendment also protects against unreasonable searches and seizures. A search occurs when government actors infringe on a legitimate expectation of privacy while looking for evidence. Seizures of property occur when a meaningful possessory interest is interfered with. Seizures of persons occur when a reasonable person would believe he or she is not free to leave. A search or seizure is unreasonable when it is not supported by proper justification (e.g., probable cause).

2. EXPLAIN THE CONCEPT OF PROBABLE CAUSE AND ITS IMPLICATIONS.

Justification requires that police must have cause before they can conduct a search or a seizure. There are three standards of justification necessary for searches in seizures. Only one of them, probable cause, is spelled out in the Fourth Amendment. Probable cause falls between 51 and 100 percent certainty, which is required for arrests and searches with and without warrants.

3. COMPARE REASONABLE SUSPICION AND ADMINISTRATIVE JUSTIFICATION TO PROBABLE CAUSE.

Reasonable suspicion, which falls below 51 percent certainty but above a hunch, is required for stops and investigative detentions that fall short of arrests. Administrative justification is required in administrative and "special needs beyond law enforcement" searches. The constitutionality of a search based on administrative justification is determined by balancing the interests of society with the privacy interests of the individual. Both reasonable suspicion and administrative justification are lower standards than probable cause. Finally, a person must also have standing in order to raise a Fourth Amendment challenge.

Figure 3.5 summarizes this chapter's Fourth Amendment introduction in question-and-answer form. Figure 3.6 summarizes the levels of proof discussed in this chapter and situates them within other popular levels of proof, such as proof beyond a reasonable doubt (note that most of the probabilities listed in Figure 3.6 are the author's approximations).

FIGURE 3.5

Fourth Amendment Checklist

1. Did a search or seizure take place?
   a. For a search, did a government actor violate a reasonable expectation of privacy?
   b. For a seizure, would a reasonable person have believed that he or she was not free to leave?

   If either of these questions can be answered no, then the Fourth Amendment does not apply.
   If either can be answered yes, continue with item 2.

2. Was the search or seizure justified?
   a. Identify the level of the intrusion: seizure, stop, nonstop, and so on.
   b. Identify the level of justification appropriate to the intrusion.

   If the justification was not appropriate, the search or seizure was not reasonable.

3. Was the search or seizure conducted in accordance with constitutional guidelines?

   See Chapters 4–7 to answer this question.

FIGURE 3.6

Levels of Proof and their Approximate Degrees of Certainty

Proof beyond a reasonable doubt	around 95 percent certainty
Probable cause	more than 50 percent certainty
Preponderance of the evidence	civil equivalent of probable cause
Reasonable suspicion	between 1 and 50 percent certainty
Administrative justification	balancing approach
Hunch	no justification at all

Key Terms

administrative justification	97	open field	82	reasonable suspicion	94
articulable facts	95	papers and effects	75	reasonableness	76
curtilage	82	person	75	reasonableness clause	74
government action	75	probable cause	88	search	75
house	75	reasonable expectation of privacy	75	
justification	88			

administrative
  justification   97
articulable facts   95
curtilage   82
government action   75
house   75
justification   88

open field   82
papers and effects   75
person   75
probable cause   88
reasonable expectation
  of privacy   75

reasonable
  suspicion   94
reasonableness   76
reasonableness
  clause   74
search   75

seizure   75
seizure of a
  person   87
seizure of property   86
standing   99
warrant clause   74

Key Cases

Searches

- *Burdeau v. McDowell*, 256 U.S. 465 (1921)
- *United States v. Jacobsen*, 466 U.S. 109 (1984)
- *Katz v. United States*, 389 U.S. 347 (1967)
- *Hoffa v. United States*, 385 U.S. 293 (1966)
- *United States v. On Lee*, 343 U.S. 747 (1952)
- *California v. Greenwood*, 486 U.S. 35 (1988)
- *Oliver v. United States*, 466 U.S. 170 (1984)
- *United States v. Knotts*, 460 U.S. 276 (1983)
- *United States v. Place*, 462 U.S. 696 (1983)

Seizures

- *Soldal v. Cook County* 506 U.S. 56 (1992)
- *California v. Hodari D.* 499 U.S. 621 (1991)

Justification

- *Beck v. Ohio*, 379 U.S. 89 (1964)
- *Brinegar v. United States*, 338 U.S. 160 (1949)
- *Aguilar v. Texas*, 378 U.S. 108 (1964)
- *Spinelli v. United States*, 393 U.S. 410 (1969)
- *Illinois v. Gates*, 462 U.S. 213 (1983)
- *Terry v. Ohio*, 392 U.S. 1 (1968)
- *Alabama v. White*, 496 U.S. 325 (1990)

Review Questions

1. Explain the various perspectives on the relationship between the warrant and reasonableness clauses of the Fourth Amendment.
2. Define *person*, *house*, *paper*, and *effect*, each for Fourth Amendment purposes.
3. When does the Fourth Amendment apply?
4. When does a search take place? Explain both elements of a search, and discuss pertinent cases.
5. When can private parties be considered government actors?
6. What can authorities *not* do following a private-party search?
7. Explain the notion of reasonable expectation of privacy. When does a person *not* enjoy an expectation of privacy? Cite relevant cases.
8. What is a seizure? Distinguish between seizures of persons and seizures of property.
9. What is the doctrine of justification? Why is it important?
10. Explain probable cause as well as acceptable sources of information for the establishment of probable cause.
11. How can a mistake serve as a source of information in the probable cause determination?
12. What is the procedure for challenging a probable cause determination?
13. What is reasonable suspicion? How does it differ from probable cause and other standards of justification?
14. What is administrative justification? How does it differ from reasonable suspicion and probable cause?
15. Explain the balancing of interests associated with administrative justification.

Web Links and Exercises

1. High-tech searches: Browse recent issues of *Law Enforcement Technology* and discuss the Fourth Amendment implications of one or more of the technologies you identify.

URL: http://www.officer.com/magazines/let (accessed February 16, 2011).

2. Confidential informants: Read about the requirements for the use of confidential informants in federal law enforcement investigations. To what extent can confidential informants participate in criminal activity?

Suggested URL: http://www.fas.org/irp/agency/doj/fbi/dojguidelines.pdf (accessed February 16, 2011).

3. Anonymous tips: Visit the site of Cornell University Law Schools' Legal Information Institute. Enter "anonymous tip" in the sitewide search box and discuss the facts and decisions of at least two cases decided in the lower courts (i.e., other than the U.S. Supreme Court).

URL: http://www.law.cornell.edu (accessed February 16, 2011).

LEARNING OBJECTIVES

When you complete this chapter, you should be able to:

▸ Outline the components of search and arrest warrants.

▸ Describe how search and arrest warrants are executed.

▸ Explain how bodily intrusions, the use of tracking devices, and electronic surveillance create "special circumstances" for Fourth Amendment purposes.

Searches and Arrests with Warrants

INTRODUCTION

Provisions of the Fourth Amendment

Five types of activities are governed by the Fourth Amendment:

- arrests with warrants,
- arrests without warrants,
- searches with warrants,
- searches without warrants, and
- the seizure of evidence.

This chapter's primary focus is on arrests and searches *with warrants*. Warrantless actions are discussed in the next three chapters.

The seizure of evidence is often a consequence of arrests and searches with and without warrants. However, if a search or arrest with or without a warrant violates the Fourth Amendment, any evidence seized will be inadmissible in court due to the *exclusionary rule*. Because of the exclusionary rule, little attention is given here (or in the next three chapters) to the seizure of evidence independent of an arrest or search. While it is possible for a seizure to take place in the absence of a search or arrest (e.g., *Soldal v. Cook County*, 506 U.S. 56 [1992]), rare is the occasion in which the police (or a private individual acting in a governmental capacity) can seize evidence without a search or an arrest.

The Fourth Amendment seems fairly clear with respect to warrants: "and no Warrants shall issue, but upon probable cause, supported by Oath or affirmation, and particularly describing the place to be searched, and the persons or things to be seized." Despite this seemingly simple language, however, the Fourth Amendment's warrant requirement has been litigated extensively in the courts. As indicated in Chapter 3, the courts have focused on the meaning of *probable cause* as well as acceptable sources of information used to determine the presence of probable cause. Many decisions have also focused on the Fourth Amendment's requirement that warrants be supported by "Oath or affirmation" and on the particularity requirement. This chapter gives special attention to these latter issues.

Even though there are many cases involving searches and arrests with warrants, the law is actually very clear with respect to *when* a warrant is required. Generally, a search warrant is required for *any* type of search, regardless of where it is conducted, provided that (1) there are no exigent (i.e., emergency) circumstances and (2) the search is not one justified on so-called administrative grounds. Even searches pursuant to arrest and searches under the automobile exception are justified in terms of exigencies. Arrest warrants, by contrast, are required for arrests in private places, provided exigent circumstances are absent.

COMPONENTS OF WARRANTS

An **arrest warrant** or a **search warrant** (see Figures 4.1 and 4.2 for examples) each has three essential components. First, it must be issued by a neutral and detached magistrate. Second, a showing of probable cause is required. Finally, it must conform to the Fourth Amendment's particularity requirement. The first requirement—a neutral and detached magistrate—is the same regardless of the type of warrant. However, the probable cause and particularity requirements differ, depending on the type of warrant in question. These requirements are considered in the following subsections.

A Neutral and Detached Magistrate

The logic for requiring a **neutral and detached magistrate** in the issuance of an arrest or a search warrant was described by the Supreme Court over 50 years ago in *Johnson v. United States* (333 U.S. 10 [1948]):

> The point of the Fourth Amendment . . . is not that it denies law enforcement the support of the usual inferences reasonable men draw from evidence. Its protection consists in requiring that those inferences be drawn by a neutral and detached magistrate instead of being judged by the officer engaged in the often competitive enterprise of ferreting out crime. (pp. 13–14)

Most judges are considered neutral and detached. Even so, the Supreme Court has focused, in a number of cases, on this first critical warrant requirement. For example, in

FIGURE 4.1

Sample Arrest Warrant

WARRANT OF ARREST ON COMPLAINT

(RCr 2.04,2.06)
(Caption)

TO ALL PEACE OFFICERS

You are hereby commanded to arrest _____

(Name of defendant)

and bring him forthwith before judge of the District Court (or, if he be absent or unable to act, before the nearest available magistrate) to answer a complaint made by _____ charging him with the offense of reckless driving.

Issued this _____ day of _____, 19_____.

_____
Judge

(Indorsement as to bail)

The defendant may give bail in the amount of $_____.

_____
Judge

(Amended October 14, 20__, effective January 1, 20__.)

Coolidge v. New Hampshire (403 U.S. 443 [1971]), the Court declared that a state attorney general cannot issue a search warrant. State attorneys general are chief prosecutors and thus inclined to side with law enforcement officers. Similarly, in *United States v. United States District Court* (407 U.S. 297 [1972]), the Court decided that the president, acting through the attorney general of the United States, cannot authorize electronic surveillance without judicial approval. Justice Powell observed,

Coolidge v. New Hampshire (403 U.S. 443 [1971])

> The Fourth Amendment does not contemplate the executive officers of Government as neutral and detached magistrates. Their duty and responsibility is to enforce the laws, to investigate and to prosecute. . . . [T]hose charged with this investigative and prosecutorial duty should not be the sole judges of when to utilize constitutionally sensitive means in pursuing their tasks. The historical judgment, which the Fourth Amendment accepts, is that unreviewed executive discretion may yield too readily to pressures to obtain incriminating evidence and overlook potential invasions of privacy and protected speech. (p. 317)

There have also been some cases in which the Court has focused on the extent to which judges can be viewed as neutral and detached. For example, in *Lo-Ji Sales, Inc. v. New York* (442 U.S. 319 [1979]), a magistrate issued a warrant for two obscene items, but

Lo-Ji Sales, Inc. v. New York (442 U.S. 319 [1979])

he also authorized the police to seize any other items that he might find obscene upon examination of the location to be searched. The magistrate then accompanied the officers on the search, discovered items that he deemed to be obscene, and added them to the initial warrant. The items were then admitted into evidence against the defendants. The Supreme Court declared that the magistrate was not acting in a neutral and detached capacity: "[H]e was not acting as a judicial officer but as an adjunct law-enforcement officer" (p. 327).

Finally, if a magistrate has a financial interest in the issuance of warrants, he or she cannot be considered neutral and detached. This issue was presented to the Supreme Court in *Connally v. Georgia* (429 U.S. 245 [1977]). A Georgia statute authorized unsalaried magistrates to receive five dollars for each warrant issued but no money for warrant applications that were denied. The Court unanimously held that the statute violated the Constitution, citing that "judicial action by an officer of a court who has 'a direct, personal, substantial, pecuniary interest' in his conclusion to issue or to deny the warrant" (p. 250) cannot possibly be considered neutral and detached.

A Showing of Probable Cause

"Probable cause" was defined in Chapter 3; as such, there is no need to revisit the definition here. However, it is important to point out that probable cause is required as a component of a valid warrant. Also, the meaning of probable cause—as opposed to the sources of information that give rise to it—differs, depending on whether an arrest or a search warrant is issued.

SHOWING OF PROBABLE CAUSE IN AN ARREST WARRANT   The showing of probable cause in an arrest warrant is not particularly complex. The officer applying for the warrant must simply show probable cause that the person to be arrested committed the crime. Acceptable sources of information for a probable cause showing were described in Chapter 3. When applying for an *arrest* warrant, the officer is not required to show probable cause that the suspect will be found at a particular location. In *Payton v. New York* (445 U.S. 573 [1980]), the majority stated, "If there is sufficient evidence of a citizen's participation in a felony to persuade a judicial officer that his arrest is justified, it is constitutionally reasonable to require him to open his doors to the officers of the law" (pp. 602–603).

SHOWING OF PROBABLE CAUSE IN A SEARCH WARRANT   The showing of probable cause in a search warrant is twofold. First, the officer applying for the search warrant must show probable cause that the items to be seized are connected with criminal activity. Second, the officer must show probable cause that the items to be seized are in the location to be searched. Note that this second requirement does not apply to an arrest warrant.

Particularity

The Fourth Amendment expressly provides that warrants particularly describe the "place to be searched, and the persons or things to be seized." Not surprisingly, the **particularity** requirement differs, depending on the type of warrant issued. For an arrest warrant, the particularity requirement is easily satisfied. The particularity requirement for a search warrant, however, is far more complex.

PARTICULARITY IN AN ARREST WARRANT   There are two ways to satisfy the Fourth Amendment's particularity requirement with regard to an arrest warrant. First, if the suspect's name is known, then simply supplying his or her name is enough to meet the particularity requirement. In some situations, however, the suspect's name is *not* known. Then, a specific description of the suspect is sufficient and a "John Doe" warrant will be issued. As long as other officers may locate the suspect with reasonable effort, the suspect's name is not required.

Even so, an arrest warrant is rarely issued without the suspect's name. This is not to suggest, however, that the police almost always know the suspect's name. Remember, there are many occasions involving warrantless arrests (e.g., after a suspect is caught fleeing the bank he or she just robbed) in which an arrest can be made without knowledge of the suspect's name. As long as probable cause is in place, the name of the suspect is not essential (regardless of whether a warrant is issued).

FIGURE 4.2

Example of a Search Warrant That Meets the Particularity Requirement

IN THE SUPERIOR COURT DISTRICT, EAST DESERT DIVISION
COUNTY OF SAN BERNARDINO, STATE OF CALIFORNIA

SEARCH WARRANT
(PENAL CODE 1529)

THE PEOPLE OF THE STATE OF CALIFORNIA: To any Sheriff, Constable, Peace Officer or Policeman in the County of San Bernardino:

Proof, by Affidavit, having been this day made before me by:

ROGER PEREZ
Deputy Sheriff
San Bernardino County Sheriff's Department
Morongo Basin Station

THAT THERE IS PROBABLE CAUSE FOR BELIEVING THAT:

There are narcotics, controlled substances and restricted substances records and documents which tend to show that a felony to wit, Transportation of Controlled Substances, in violation of Health and Safety Code Section 11379, Possession for Sales of Controlled Substances, in violation of Health and Safety Code Section 11378, Sales of Controlled Substances, in violation of Health and Safety Code Section 11379, is being committed in the County of San Bernardino, State of California.

YOU ARE THEREFORE COMMANDED at any time of the day or night _____ to make a search of:

PREMISES TO BE SEARCHED:

The premises located at:

2400 MAIN STREET, #12
TOWN OF PLEASANTVILLE
COUNTY OF SAN BERNARDINO
STATE OF CALIFORNIA

Figure 4.2 continued

The location is further described as a multi-unit apartment complex located on the east side of Main Street south of Oak Dr. The complex consists of numerous two-story buildings with each building having multiple apartments. Apartment 12 is located in building "C", which is located at the northwest corner of the complex. The exterior is tan stucco with grayish/blue trim and a gray composite shingle roof. Apartment 12 has the numbers "12" which are black and approximately 4 inches tall, affixed to the wood trim to the right of the front door, which faces north.

And all rooms, attics, basements, cellars, safes, vaults, closed or locked containers, trash receptacles and other parts therein, surrounding grounds, garages, sheds, storage rooms, vehicles, campers, trailers and outbuildings of any kind located thereon.

And all persons located on or at the premises. And all vehicles belonging to or in the control of said persons.

And you are hereby authorized to answer all incoming telephone calls received at the premises and the vehicles to be searched and to further seize and record all the incoming telephonic pager numbers and messages received at the premises and the vehicles to be searched and to seize all telephonic "fax" messages received at the premises and the vehicles to be searched. And to determine if the aforementioned telephone calls, telephonic messages, or "faxed" messages are related to illegal activities.

FOR THE FOLLOWING PROPERTY:

Methamphetamine and paraphernalia commonly associated with the possession, packaging, and sale of methamphetamine such as scales, weighing devices and measuring devices; packaging materials including paper bindles, glass vials, plastic baggies, foil; processing materials including sifters, filters, screens and cutting agents; recordation of the purchase and/or sales of methamphetamine including ledgers, notebooks, pay/owe sheets, customer lists, video tapes and phone answering machine tape recordings, personal phone books; personal photographs which document the possession, sales and/or possession for sales of methamphetamine; and proceeds from the sales of methamphetamine consisting of currency.

Financial records including expenses incurred in obtaining chemicals and apparatus and income derived from sales of narcotics and other controlled substances as well as records showing legitimate income or the lack thereof and general living expenses.

Serial numbers, model numbers, identifying marks and descriptions of all personal property including, but not limited to, televisions, radios, stereo equipment, and other electrical devices, appliances, hand and power tools, firearms, bicycles, items of jewelry, silver, gold and coins which can be identified as stolen and/or evidence of the crime of Burglary and/or Possession of Stolen Property or property which is readily traded for narcotics in lieu of cash.

All articles of personal property which will identify persons in control of the premises, storage areas or containers where controlled substances may be found, including keys to those areas that may be locked, rental agreements and receipts, deeds of trust, documents or papers bearing names, canceled mail, paycheck stubs and other employment records, tax documents and personal identification.

AND IF YOU FIND THE SAME OR ANY PART THEREOF, to bring it forthwith before me at my courtroom

GIVEN UNDER MY HAND, and dated this 17th day of September 2002.

James D. Franklin

Judge of the Superior Court
East Desert Division
County of San Bernardino
State of California

Source: Used courtesy of the San Bernardino County Sheriff's Department.

PARTICULARITY IN A SEARCH WARRANT   The particularity requirement for a search warrant is twofold. First, the warrant must specify the *place* to be searched. Next, the warrant must specify the *items* to be seized. The reason for this particularity requirement stems from the framers' concerns with so-called general warrants. *General warrants*, which were issued by the English Crown, permitted basically limitless searches for evidence of treason.

Contrary to popular belief, a search warrant does not need to state with absolute precision the place to be searched. It "is enough if the description is such that the officer with a search warrant can, with reasonable effort, ascertain and identify the place intended" (*Steele v. United States*, 267 U.S. 498 [1925], p. 503). However, the items mentioned in the warrant should be described with sufficient specificity that a reasonable officer would know where to look for them.

In situations where the warrant incorrectly specifies the place to be searched, the courts will focus on the reasonableness of the officers' mistake. For example, in *Maryland v. Garrison* (480 U.S. 79 [1987]), police officers obtained a warrant to search the person of Lawrence McWebb and the premises known as "2036 Park Avenue, third-floor apartment." They believed that McWebb's apartment occupied the entire third floor when, in fact, there were two apartments on that floor—one of which belonged to Garrison. The Court held that the warrant was valid for several reasons: It was based on information by a trusted informant, and the police had inquired with the local utility company and were given the impression that there was only one apartment on the third floor.

Maryland v. Garrison
(480 U.S. 79 [1987])

As for the items to be seized, the warrant must clearly specify what the police wish to seize. The case of *Lo-Ji Sales, Inc. v. New York* is again illustrative. Recall from the discussion about the neutral and detached magistrate requirement that the magistrate in *Lo-Ji Sales* issued a warrant that named two specific items but also permitted the police to seize anything the magistrate considered obscene. The Court unanimously held that the warrant failed to "particularly describe . . . the things to be seized" (p. 319).

DECISION-MAKING EXERCISE 4.1

Who Was That Bald Man?

The police have in their possession the video from a security camera at a bank that was recently robbed. The suspect is a white male, six feet tall, and has a mustache, a bald head, a scar on his left cheek, and a tattoo of a skull and crossbones on his neck. May the police apply for an arrest warrant based on this information, even if they never learned of the suspect's name prior to applying for the warrant?

Andresen v. Maryland
(427 U.S. 463 [1976])

Contrast *Lo-Ji Sales* with *Andresen v. Maryland* (427 U.S. 463 [1976]), in which the Court upheld a warrant that authorized the seizure of several items "together with other fruits, instrumentalities and evidence of crime at this [time] known" (p. 479). The Court noted that the crime in question was particularly complex and "could be proved only by piecing together many bits of evidence" (p. 482). This is a controversial decision, indeed, because it suggests that, under certain circumstances, the police can circumvent the Fourth Amendment's particularity requirement.

If the police have a hunch that an item is in a place to be searched but do not include the item in the application for a warrant, the item can be seized under the doctrine of plain view as long as the police are legally authorized (by obtaining a warrant) to be on the premises. *Plain view* is discussed in the next chapter. Also, if a warrant does not particularly describe the items to be seized (or the place to be searched), then it is not automatically deemed in violation of the Fourth Amendment. If there is an objectively reasonable basis for the officers' mistaken belief, then the warrant will most likely be upheld (see *Massachusetts v. Sheppard*, 468 U.S. 981 [1981]). Also, just because an item is not listed in a warrant does not mean that it cannot be seized. As will be considered in the next chapter, items in plain view can be seized, provided certain conditions are met.

ARRESTS WITH WARRANTS

Justice Powell once stated that "a search may cause only an annoyance and temporary inconvenience to the law-abiding citizen, assuming more serious dimensions only when it turns up evidence of criminality [but an] arrest . . . is a serious personal intrusion regardless of whether the person seized is guilty or innocent" (*United States v. Watson*, 423 U.S. 411 [1976], p. 428). Even so, an unconstitutional arrest has little significance by itself in criminal procedure. The reason for this is that the remedy for an illegal arrest is simply a release from custody. It is possible that a person unlawfully arrested may sue, but little recourse is generally available to a person who is unlawfully arrested. Why, then, focus attention on the constitutionality of arrests? The answer is that the constitutionality of an arrest is frequently critical in determining whether seized evidence is admissible in court.

Consider this example: Assume that a police officer arrests a defendant without probable cause. Such an arrest is automatically unconstitutional. Assume also that the officer finds an illegal firearm on the defendant and turns it over to the prosecutor, who decides to use it against the defendant at his trial on firearm charges. The defendant will almost certainly seek to have the firearm excluded as evidence on the grounds that it resulted from an unlawful arrest. In other words, the defendant will argue that the firearm is "fruit of the poisonous tree," as discussed in Chapter 2.

This hypothetical situation is the main reason it is important to study the law of arrest. It is not that the legality of an arrest matters by itself. What is important is that an unconstitutional arrest can lead to the exclusion of evidence. Virtually all arrest cases that make it to the Supreme Court have something in common: A convicted defendant is seeking to have his or her *arrest* declared unconstitutional so the evidence that led to his or her conviction will be suppressed and/or the conviction reversed.

The Definition of *Arrest*

Invariably, students of criminal procedure become confused when books and course instructors use terms like *seizure, stop,* and *arrest* with little attention to the fact that each term has a very distinct meaning. Think of **stops** and **arrests** as being different types of seizures. Additionally, think of each type of seizure as falling along a scale of seriousness: An arrest is the most intrusive type of seizure, and a stop is the next most intrusive. Apart from those simple distinctions, though, it should become clear that there is no easy, ready-made definition of a stop or an arrest (the glossary offers definitions, but even they are imperfect).

Why distinguish between stops and arrests? Arrests require probable cause; stops (the focus of Chapter 6) only require reasonable suspicion. If the circumstances surrounding a stop are such that it evolves into an arrest, then the arrest will be declared unconstitutional and the evidence will be thrown out, assuming the officer did not have probable cause.

RESTRICTED LIBERTY OF MOVEMENT AND BEYOND   Prior to the civil rights era, the Supreme Court suggested that anything the police do to restrict a person's movement constitutes an arrest. For example, in *Henry v. United States* (361 U.S. 98 [1959]), the Court found that an arrest occurred when the police stopped a car whose occupants were suspected of transporting illegal alcohol. According to the Court, "When the officers interrupted the two men and restricted their liberty of movement, the arrest, for purposes of this case, was complete" (p. 103). Since the police in *Henry* did not have probable cause to stop the men, the so-called arrest was deemed unconstitutional.

Recently, though, the Supreme Court has held that the police must do more than restrict a person's movement for an arrest to occur. In *Terry v. Ohio* (392 U.S. 1 [1968]), the case that essentially altered the definition of arrest for all time, the Court ruled that a suspect's movements can be restricted without such activity being considered an arrest. The Court distinguished between arrests that "eventuate in a trip to the station house and prosecution for crime" and lesser intrusions that can occur "whenever a police officer accosts an individual and restrains his freedom to walk away" (p. 16).

DISTINGUISHING BETWEEN A STOP AND AN ARREST   In one sense, distinguishing between an arrest and a lesser type of intrusion, such as a stop, is easy. For example, when a suspect is handcuffed, placed in the back of a patrol car, and driven to the police station for booking, an arrest has clearly occurred. Alternatively, if a person is accosted by a single police officer and asked general questions about his or her suspected involvement in a crime, an arrest has not occurred. However, there are many police/citizen encounters that fall between these two extremes. A stop can evolve into an arrest if the circumstances are just so. A seizure that falls short of a formal arrest may be so intrusive as to constitute a *de facto* arrest, in which case probable cause, rather than reasonable suspicion, would be required to make the encounter constitutional.

Generally, the courts will weigh (1) the duration of a stop and (2) the degree of the intrusion in assessing whether a stop evolved into an arrest. Sometimes, the courts also refer to the officers' intentions and the manner in which the stop took place. The importance of these issues—particularly, degree and duration—is evidenced by the Supreme Court's opinion in *Florida v. Royer* (460 U.S. 491 [1983]):

The predicate permitting seizures on suspicion short of probable cause is that law enforcement interests warrant a limited intrusion on the personal security of the suspect. The scope of the intrusion permitted will vary to some extent with the particular facts and circumstances of each case. *This much, however, is clear: an investigative detention must be temporary and last no longer than is necessary to effectuate the purpose of the stop. Similarly, the investigative methods employed should be the least intrusive means reasonably available to verify or dispel the officer's suspicion in a short period of time.* (p. 500, emphasis added)

Several Supreme Court cases are illustrative. Four categories of such cases can be identified: (1) cases involving detention in a stationhouse or similar structure, such as the investigation room in an airport; (2) cases involving an encounter between police and citizens on the street; (3) cases involving a border detention; and (4) cases involving detention in the home. Each category is briefly considered in the paragraphs that follow.

Davis v. Mississippi
(394 U.S. 721 [1969])

With regard to stationhouse detentions, in *Davis v. Mississippi* (394 U.S. 721 [1969]), several youths, including Davis, were taken into custody and fingerprinted as part of a rape investigation. The officers did not have probable cause, and Davis was held for two days and interrogated throughout his detention. On the basis of his fingerprints and confession, Davis was charged, convicted, and sentenced to death. The Supreme Court reversed Davis's conviction on the grounds that detention was too long, too intrusive, and unsupported by probable cause. The Court did not explicitly address the distinction between a stop and an arrest, but it intimated that because probable cause was required to detain Davis, the police officers had effectively arrested him.

In a similar case, *Dunaway v. New York* (442 U.S. 200 [1979]), the Supreme Court ruled that stationhouse detentions require probable cause. In that case, police officers took a man into custody during the course of a robbery/murder investigation. They read the man the *Miranda* warnings and subjected him to questioning—without probable cause. The Supreme Court reversed the man's subsequent conviction. Again, the Court did not decide on the arrest issue, but it did declare that custodial interrogation, such as that in *Dunaway*, must be supported by probable cause. The Court further declared that *Terry* was inapplicable because it permits only a "limited violation of individual privacy" while ensuring "interests in both crime prevention and detection and in the police officer's safety" (p. 209).

In *Florida v. Royer*, mentioned earlier, the Court ruled again that certain forms of detention can require probable cause, rather than reasonable suspicion. In that case, officers in an airport asked a man to accompany them into a room because he was suspected of carrying narcotics. The officers found drugs in the man's luggage, and he was arrested. The Court declared that the detention, which lasted 15 minutes, constituted an arrest, which required probable cause. As Justice White stated, "What had begun as a consensual inquiry in a public place had escalated into an investigatory procedure in a police interrogation room, where the police, unsatisfied with previous explanations, sought to confirm their suspicions" (p. 503). What is important in this case, as well as the preceding two, was that the detention was not consensual. If a person consents to the detention, he or she is not considered under arrest.

It is important to note, also, that not all *nonconsensual* encounters between police and citizens amount to arrests. As will be addressed later, detentions at the national borders and in other locations are permissible under certain circumstances. In addition, there are situations in which the courts have declared that holding a person for investigative purposes may not arise to the level of an arrest, requiring probable cause. For example, even though the Court reversed a defendant's conviction in *Davis v. Mississippi*, it did state that "because of the unique nature of the fingerprinting process, [detentions for the purpose of obtaining fingerprints] might, under narrowly defined circumstances, be found to comply with the Fourth Amendment even though there is no probable cause in the traditional sense" (p. 727).

There are also situations in which encounters on the street (as opposed to questioning in a stationhouse or its equivalent) can evolve into arrests. In *Terry*, the Supreme Court noted that a stop must be *brief*, suggesting that any stop that is not brief may require probable cause. While the Supreme Court has been hesitant to put a precise time limit on the length of a stop, it made this statement in *United States v. Sharpe* (470 U.S. 675 [1985]):

> While it is clear that "the brevity of the invasion of the individual's Fourth Amendment interests is an important factor in determining whether the seizure is so minimally intrusive as to be justifiable on reasonable suspicion," we have emphasized the need to consider the law enforcement purposes to be served by the stop as well as the time reasonably needed to effectuate these purposes. . . . Much as a "bright line" rule would be desirable in evaluating whether an investigative detention is unreasonable, common sense and ordinary human experience must govern over rigid criteria. (p. 685)

As already noted, Fourth Amendment requirements are significantly relaxed at the nation's borders. Recall that in *United States v. Montoya de Hernandez* (473 U.S. 531 [1985]), the Supreme Court upheld law enforcement officials' 16-hour detention of a suspected drug "balloon swallower" while they waited for nature to take its course, so to speak. The majority approved of the delay because the defendant's detention "resulted solely from the method by which she chose to smuggle illicit drugs into the country" (p. 559). Justices Brennan and Marshall strongly dissented, however, pointing out that the detention in this case—"indefinite confinement in a squalid back room cut off from the outside world, the absence of basic amenities that would have been provided to even the vilest of hardened criminals, repeated strip searches" (p. 556)—was effectively an arrest, thus requiring probable cause.

Finally, a handful of cases have involved detentions in the home, focusing, in particular, on the extent to which detention of a person (e.g., owner, renter, or guest) in a home can evolve into a full-blown arrest. Somewhat surprisingly, nonconsensual encounters in the home between residents and the police do not always rise to the level of an arrest. For example, in *Beckwith v. United States* (425 U.S. 341 [1976]), the Supreme Court ruled that questioning by IRS agents of a defendant in his living room was not an arrest or even custodial in nature. Contrast this decision with that of *Rawlings v. Kentucky* (448 U.S. 98 [1980]), in which several individuals were detained at a house where officers had served an arrest warrant but had failed to find the person named in the warrant. The Court declared that this type of detention amounted to an arrest because there was no probable cause to detain the individuals not named in the warrant. In addition, the detention lasted 45 minutes, which was unnecessarily long, under the circumstances (though not as long as some detentions that the Supreme Court has upheld).

DECISION-MAKING EXERCISE 4.3

What Type of Seizure?

The police concluded that a man who was suspected of rape was also responsible for a recent burglary/rape. Without a warrant and without probable cause, the police went to the suspect's home to obtain fingerprints. Arriving at the home, the police spoke to the suspect on his front porch, and when he expressed reluctance to accompany them to the stationhouse, one officer said that they would arrest him. The suspect then replied that he would rather go to the station than be arrested. He was then taken to the station and fingerprinted. Does the police action constitute an arrest?

Michigan v. Summers
(452 U.S. 692 [1981])

The Supreme Court seemed to backpedal on the *Rawlings* decision in *Michigan v. Summers* (452 U.S. 692 [1981]), decided a year later. In *Summers*, the Court held that an individual *can* be detained during a search of his or her house, without such activity rising to the level of an arrest, as long as the police have a search warrant and even if there is no probable cause to arrest him or her. In support, the Court noted that (1) such detentions are not as embarrassing or stigmatizing as public detentions and (2) when there is probable cause to search for evidence of criminal activity, it is reasonable to assume that the person who lives on the premises is involved. See Figure 4.3 for a summary of this discussion.

DISTINGUISHING BETWEEN A STOP AND A NONSTOP   Remember that it is important to distinguish not just between a stop and an arrest but between a stop and a **nonstop**. If a stop occurs when a reasonable person *would not* believe that he or she is free to leave, then a nonstop occurs when a reasonable person *would* believe that he or she is free to leave. A nonstop requires no justification at all because it is not considered a seizure within the meaning of the Fourth Amendment. As will be discussed in Chapter 6, police officers are free to confront people and ask questions of them, as long as the people are free to leave. If the people are stopped, however, then reasonable suspicion is required. And again, if an arrest is made, the requisite standard of justification is probable cause.

Summary.   Clearly, distinguishing between arrests and lesser intrusions, such as investigative stops, can be confusing. At one extreme, a seizure that is accompanied by handcuffs, or words to the effect that the person is "under arrest," is always considered an arrest. At the other extreme, when a person is confronted by a police officer and is not free to leave, but nevertheless briefly detained and not interrogated, an arrest has not occurred. Where the distinction is confusing is in the gray area between a stop and an arrest. A stop can evolve into a *de facto* arrest in a number of circumstances. The courts will give weight to four factors in making their decision: (1) the purpose of

---

FIGURE 4.3

Factors Used to Distinguish between a Stop and an Arrest

All four of these criteria should be considered together. For example, if a police/citizen encounter occurs at the stationhouse, the encounter may not be considered an arrest. However, if the encounter is overly lengthy and the citizen is not free to leave, then an arrest has taken place.

1. Purpose
   a. Intent to arrest = Arrest
   b. No intent to arrest = *Terry* stop or nonstop
2. Manner
   a. Person not free to leave = Arrest or *Terry* stop
   b. Person free to leave = Nonstop
3. Location
   a. At police station or in private = Arrest or *Terry* stop
   b. Public = Arrest, *Terry* stop, or nonstop
4. Duration
   a. Lengthy = Arrest
   b. Short = *Terry* stop or nonstop

the stop (e.g., to question or interrogate a person); (2) the manner in which the stop takes place (e.g., stopped by one officer or several); (3) the location in which the stop takes place (e.g., stationhouse, street, or home); and (4) the duration of the stop. No single factor is necessarily determinative. If, however, a person is detained by several officers in a stationhouse for several days so as to be interrogated, then the court will almost certainly consider such police activity tantamount to an arrest.

In conclusion, this section has endeavored to provide a definition of *arrest*, but in fact, no clear definition really exists. The courts must weigh each case individually. Fortunately, most people know an arrest when they see it.

When an Arrest Warrant Is Required

Under common law, if an arresting officer had probable cause to believe that (1) a person was committing or had committed a felony or (2) a person was committing a certain misdemeanor in the officer's presence, then an arrest warrant was not required. This held true regardless of where the arrest took place, even if it was effected in someone's private home (e.g., *Trupiano v. United States*, 334 U.S. 699 [1948]). The only real situation in which an arrest warrant *was* required was for a misdemeanor committed out of view of the arresting officer. The logic for this was set forth by the Supreme Court in *Carroll v. United States* (267 U.S. 132 [1925]):

> The reason for arrest for misdemeanors without warrant at common law was to promptly suppress breaches of the peace . . . while the reason for arrest without a warrant on a reliable report of a felony was because the public safety and the due apprehension of criminals charged with heinous offenses required that such arrests should be made at once without warrant. (p. 157)

Since 1925, the Supreme Court has stuck to the rule set forth in *Carroll*, subject to two exceptions. First, an arrest in someone's private home cannot be made without a warrant, unless exigent circumstances are present. Second, an arrest in the home of a third party is impermissible without a warrant, again providing no exigent circumstances are in place. An example of a third-party situation is one in which the police seek to arrest a person who is visiting a friend's house. One additional restriction was recognized in *Gerstein v. Pugh* (420 U.S. 103 [1975])—namely, a judicial determination of probable cause is required when an arrest is made without a warrant (see Chapter 9).

The remainder of this section considers two types of arrest: (1) arrests in the home and (2) arrests in third-party homes. With rare exceptions, a warrant is required for each.

ARRESTS IN THE HOME   In the landmark decision of *Payton v. New York* (445 U.S. 573 [1980]), the Supreme Court held that the Fourth Amendment prohibits a warrantless, nonconsensual entry into a private home for the purpose of making an arrest. In that case, police officers, after two days of investigation, had assembled enough evidence to establish probable cause to believe that Payton had murdered the manager of a gas station. The officers went to Payton's apartment to arrest him. When no one answered the door, they used a crowbar to open the door and entered the apartment. They did not find Payton, but they did find, in plain view, a .30 caliber shell casing lying on the floor. They seized it and admitted it into evidence at Payton's trial. Payton ultimately surrendered to the police and was indicted for murder. The lower court admitted the shell casing into evidence, but the Supreme Court reversed, stating, "In terms that apply equally to seizures of property and to seizures of

Payton v. New York
(445 U.S. 573 [1980])

persons, the Fourth Amendment has drawn a firm line at the entrance to the house. Absent exigent circumstances, that threshold may not reasonably be crossed without a warrant" (p. 590). Justice Stevens also stated, citing an earlier case (*United States v. United States District Court*), that "physical entry of the home is the chief evil against which the wording of the Fourth Amendment is directed" (p. 585). In *Payton*, then, the Court handed down a bright-line rule: An arrest in the home must be accompanied by a warrant in the absence of exigent circumstances. The decision in *Kirk v. Louisiana* (536 U.S. 635 [2002]) reaffirmed this.

ARRESTS IN THIRD-PARTY HOMES   Not long after *Payton*, the Supreme Court decided *Steagald v. United States* (451 U.S. 204 [1981]). Justice Marshall expressed concern that although an arrest warrant may protect a person "from an unreasonable seizure, it [does] absolutely nothing to protect [a third party's] privacy interest in being free from an unreasonable invasion and search of his home" (p. 213). Accordingly, the Court decided that in such situations, the police must obtain not only an arrest warrant for the person they seek but also a *separate* warrant to search the third-party residence for the arrestee.

*Steagald v. United States
(451 U.S. 204 [1981])*

The facts in *Steagald* were as follows: Acting on an arrest warrant issued for a person by the name of Lyons, Drug Enforcement Administration (DEA) agents entered the home of Steagald. This entry was made without a warrant. While searching Steagald's home for Lyons, the agents found cocaine and other incriminating evidence, but they did not find Lyons. Steagald was arrested and convicted on federal drug charges. He appealed, and the Supreme Court eventually reversed Steagald's conviction. The Court offered the following in support of its position:

> Two distinct interests were implicated by the search in this case—Ricky Lyons' interest in being free from an unreasonable seizure and petitioner's [Steagald's] interest in being free from an unreasonable search of his home. Because the arrest warrant for Lyons addressed only the former interest, the search of petitioner's home was no more reasonable from petitioner's perspective that it would have been if conducted in the absence of any warrant. (p. 216)

The Court's decision in *Steagald* was not without opposition. Justices Rehnquist and White dissented, arguing that the police and judges "will, in their various capacities, have to weigh the time during which a suspect for whom there is an outstanding arrest warrant has been in the building, whether the dwelling is the suspect's home, how long he has lived there, whether he is likely to leave immediately, and a number of related

---

DECISION-MAKING EXERCISE 4.4

A Public or Private Arrest?

Federal drug agents had probable cause to arrest John Crook. They knew he was staying at the local motel, but they did not know what room he was in. The agents asked hotel personnel to supply the room number, which they did, and then the agents went to that room. Standing in the hall, one of the agents identified himself to a housekeeping employee and asked him to knock on the door of the room and check whether anyone was in it. The employee knocked and called out, "Housekeeping." Crook opened the door. The agents recognized him immediately, at which point one of the agents drew his weapon, pointed it at Crook, and ordered him to raise his hands. Crook immediately raised his hands and said to the agents, "I won't give you guys any trouble. I've got a gun in my right pocket." Both agents, with their weapons drawn, entered the room. Crook's gun was removed, and he was advised that he was under arrest. Was a warrant required in this situation? Or, in other words, could this be considered a public arrest? Note that based on the facts supplied, there are no exigent circumstances in place.

and equally imponderable questions" (p. 213). The majority countered by pointing out that if the police did not need warrants to enter third-party residences, "[a]rmed solely with an arrest warrant for a single person, [the police] . . . could search all the homes of that individual's friends and acquaintances" (p. 215). Such a possibility would be controversial, indeed.

Thus, having an arrest warrant does *not* allow authorities to enter a third-party residence. A warrantless entry into a third-party residence violates the third party's rights. There are two exceptions to this rule, however. First, if the third party consents to a request by police, a search warrant won't be necessary (but the arrest warrant will still be necessary). Second, if there is an emergency, or "exigent circumstances," a warrant may not be required. See Figure 4.4 for a summary of situations in which an arrest warrant is required/not required.

Executing an Arrest Warrant

Assuming a valid warrant is in place, the police cannot use any means available to effect the arrest. For example, they cannot kick in a door without having any reason to do so. Similarly, they cannot use deadly force unless absolutely necessary and for the most dangerous of criminal offenders. In almost all cases, the procedures for executing an arrest warrant are laid out in police department policy manuals. One such policy from the Portland (Oregon) Police Bureau is reprinted in Figure 4.5.

The following subsections focus on four important issues with regard to the service of arrest warrants:

- when the police are required to "knock and announce" their presence,
- whether property damage is acceptable,
- when deadly force can be used, and
- the consequences of arresting the wrong person.

THE "KNOCK-AND-ANNOUNCE" RULE   Under common law, the police were entitled to break into a house to make an arrest after announcing their presence and their reason for being there. Today, the method of entry the police can use to serve warrants (arrest and search) is usually set forth in legislation. With regard to federal law enforcement, for example, 18 U.S.C. Section 3109 states that an officer "may break open any outer or inner door or window of a house . . . to execute a search warrant, if, after notice of his authority and purpose, he is refused admittance."

The law also generally requires that police officers announce their presence and state their authority (e.g., "Police officers! Search warrant!"). Doing so is important for several reasons: (1) it helps avoid needless destruction of property; (2) it helps prevent

FIGURE 4.4

Summary of Arrest Warrant Requirements

1. When an arrest warrant is required:
   a. In a home/residence absent exigent circumstances
   b. In a third-party home; a separate search warrant is also required
2. When an arrest warrant is not required:
   a. The arrest is made in public (see Chapter 5)
   b. Exigent circumstances exist (see Chapter 5)
   c. Consent is given (see Chapter 7)

FIGURE 4.5

Arrest Warrant Policy (Portland, OR, Police Bureau)

840.00 ARREST WITH WARRANT

An arrest warrant: An order in writing, in the name of the state, signed by a magistrate with his/her name of office, commanding the arrest of the defendant.

An arrest warrant must specify the name of the defendant. If unknown, the defendant may be designated by a fictitious name with a statement therein that his true name is unknown. An arrest warrant must also state a crime in respect to which the magistrate has authority to issue the warrant.

Obtaining an Arrest Warrant

A complainant or an investigator will appear before a deputy district attorney and justify the complaint.

a. All felony complaints will be handled either by the Detective Division, or by the complainant.
b. On a felony complaint, an investigator may accompany the complainant to the District Attorney's office and assist if necessary.
c. The investigator may, with the concurrence of a deputy district attorney, justify a felony complaint without the complainant being present.

If justified, an affidavit will be:

a. Prepared by a deputy district attorney or investigator.
b. Signed by the complainant or investigator.
c. Notarized.
d. Sent to a magistrate.

In felony cases, complainants or investigators will accompany the affidavit and swear an oath before the magistrate. The magistrate will examine the affidavit and, if justified, will issue an arrest warrant. On a felony complaint, the district attorney will have the option of bypassing the magistrate and submitting the complaint directly to the Grand Jury.

Arrest Warrant Processing Responsibilities

The Multnomah County Sheriff's Office (MCSO) is responsible for the physical maintenance of all warrants within Multnomah County. They will ensure the entry, modification and clearance of warrants into the computer, publish a computer printout of Warrants on File by Precinct and also a Notice of Warrant on File record card. The record card will be used to record the attempt or service of a warrant.

The Bureau restricts warrant service to the following guidelines:

a. Major Warrants (felony, Class A misdemeanor, and major traffic offense warrants) can be served on any day, at any hour, when the defendant can be found.
b. Minor Warrants (Class B and C misdemeanor, violations, traffic infractions, warrants, etc.) will generally be served during hours that will minimize the inconvenience to the defendant.
c. Exceptions, caused by unusual circumstances, require approval by an immediate supervisor.

The Bureau will actively undertake the service of arrest warrants issued within the City. The MCSO will deliver daily to the Bureau's Records Division, Mail Distribution Section, envelopes addressed to the appropriate precincts. The envelopes will contain computer-produced listings of Warrants on File Notices issued the previous day and a Warrant on File Record card for each entry.

a. Precinct commanders will be responsible for the maintenance of the Warrant File Notices computer listing. The computer listings will be retained by each Precinct for thirty (30) days and will reflect the following information:

   1. The assignment of the Notice of Warrant on File card to a relief officer and the date of assignment.

   2. The final disposition, whether served or an attempt of service is made, and the date.

   3. The date the warrant card is sent back to MCSO (must be ten (10) days of date assigned).

b. Assigned district officers will make at least one documented attempt to serve the assigned warrant. The attempt will be noted in the space provided at the bottom of the Notice of Warrant on File card.

   1. Members attempting service of a warrant will verify its status, prior to making an arrest, by MDC, radio or telephone to MCSO warrants base. Verification can be made by members directly or through precinct/unit members.

c. After the warrant has been confirmed and the member feels confident the checked subject is the person named on the warrant, the requesting member will complete the arrest procedure and transport the arrested subject to the appropriate booking facility.

   1. There is no need for the arresting member to physically serve the verified warrant on the arrested subject. The warrant will be served by MCSO staff during the booking process.

   2. Unless exceptional circumstances dictate otherwise, members will not pick up warrants from MCSO.

   3. Arresting members will not accept bail money or issue receipts to persons attempting to post bail. The arrested subject will be transported to MCDC for purposes of either posting bail or booking. Where specified on the warrant, a citation in lieu of custody may be issued.

   4. If the county warrant stipulates that a citation-in-lieu-of-custody can be written, and there are no other bookable charges, the arresting member may issue a citation-in-lieu-of-custody. The member must advise MCSO warrants base of the issuance of such as soon as possible.

d. Members will complete the Notice of Warrant on File Card by noting the served date, time, the name of the serving member and the DPSST number. It will be routed directly to MCSO Detention and Warrant Records by precinct/division members.

In those instances where a member determines a subject has moved to a new address within the city, a supervisor's approval may be requested for travel to another precinct to continue the apprehension effort. The Notice of Warrant on File Card may be transferred to another precinct if the precinct's computer produced Warrant Notice List is updated to reflect the transfer. In all cases, the cards must be returned within ten (10) days to the MCSO.

Source: Portland Police Bureau, *Manual of Policy and Procedure* (January 2007). Reprinted with permission of the Portland Police Bureau.

violence resulting from unnecessary surprise; and (3) it helps preserve people's dignity and privacy. Of course, in certain situations, these reasons for a "knock-and-announce" requirement do not serve their intended purposes. In fact, the second reason can work opposite from what is intended: If the police are required to announce their presence for all manner of suspects, such an announcement could *result* in violence, rather than reduce the possibility for it. What, then, are the criteria for determining when a "knock and announce" is not required? It is useful to turn to Supreme Court precedent to answer this question.

The first case in which the Court addressed the constitutionality of the common-law knock-and-announce rule was *Wilson v. Arkansas* (514 U.S. 927 [1995]). In that case, Wilson had conducted several narcotics transactions with an informant over a period of several months. Based on the informant's information about those transactions, police officers obtained an arrest warrant for Wilson as well as a search warrant for her home. When the officers arrived at Wilson's residence, they identified themselves and declared that they had a warrant *as they entered the home through an unlocked door*. They did not knock and wait for an answer. In addition to finding evidence, the officers found Wilson in the bathroom, flushing marijuana down the toilet. At her trial, Wilson moved to suppress the evidence collected by the officers on the grounds that the search was invalid because the officers did not follow the common-law knock-and-announce rule before entering her home to serve the warrants. The Supreme Court ruled that the officers *were* required to follow the knock-and-announce rule. According to the Court, "An examination of the common law of search and seizure . . . leaves no doubt that the reasonableness of a search of a dwelling may depend in part on whether law enforcement officers announce their presence and authority prior to entering" (p. 931).

The Supreme Court later clarified its position in the case of *Richards v. Wisconsin* (520 U.S. 385 [1997]). There, the Court held that police can dispense with the knock-and-announce rule if they have *reasonable suspicion* that such a requirement "would be dangerous or futile, or that it would inhibit the effective investigation of the crime by, for example, allowing the destruction of evidence" (p. 394). Basically, then, if the police have reasonable suspicion to believe that exigent circumstances are present, they do not necessarily have to knock on the door and announce their presence.

It is critical that when an announcement is required, police officers announce their authority *and* their intentions. This came to light in *Miller v. United States* (357 U.S. 301 [1958]). In that case, police officers arrived at Miller's apartment at 3:45 a.m. without a warrant but for the purpose of arresting Miller. One of the officers knocked on Miller's door. When Miller asked who it was, the officers did nothing more than answer "Police." Miller then opened the door slightly, as it was secured by a chain, and inquired as to the officers' intentions. At that point, Miller attempted to close the door, but one of the officers reached through the opening and disconnected the chain. The officers then entered the apartment and arrested Miller. The Supreme Court ultimately reversed Miller's conviction on the grounds that the officers never adequately announced their intention to arrest Miller.

DECISION-MAKING EXERCISE 4.5

Serving a Search Warrant in a Third-Party Residence

Sue Lyons leases an apartment and lives by herself. However, when she found out that her old boyfriend, Fred Taber, had been on the run from authorities for several months, she offered to let him stay at her apartment. She gave him a key so he could come and go at will. After eight weeks, during which time Fred continued to live with Sue, the police were alerted as to his presence by a vigilant neighbor. Officers then entered Sue's apartment without a warrant and arrested Fred. Will the arrest hold up?

In *United States v. Banks* (540 U.S. 31 [2003]), the Supreme Court considered how long the police should wait after announcing their presence and intentions. In that case, police served a warrant by first knocking on the door and then calling out "Police, search warrant." They waited 15–20 seconds and, after getting no response, broke down the door with a battering ram. The Supreme Court upheld this action, arguing that the 15–20-second wait—coupled with the announcement—was sufficient. The Court did *not*, however, require that police always wait 15–20 seconds before entering.

Most recently, in *Hudson v. Michigan* (547 U.S. 586 [2006]), the Supreme Court decided that a violation of the knock-and-announce rule need not lead to exclusion of evidence. In that case, officers had a search warrant but failed to follow the knock-and-announce rule. Evidence was seized and a trial court judge ruled that it could not be used. A Michigan appeals court reversed and the Supreme Court affirmed. In a 5 to 4 decision, the Court held that evidence need not be excluded simply because the police violated the knock-and-announce rule. The Court offered the following in support of its decision:

Hudson v. Michigan
(547 U.S. 586 [2006])

> The interests protected by the knock-and-announce rule include human life and limb (because an unannounced entry may provoke violence from a surprised resident), property (because citizens presumably would open the door upon an announcement, whereas a forcible entry may destroy it), and privacy and dignity of the sort that can be offended by a sudden entrance. But the rule has never protected one's interest in preventing the government from seeing or taking evidence described in a warrant. Since the interests violated here have nothing to do with the seizure of the evidence, the exclusionary rule is inapplicable. (p. 585)

PROPERTY DAMAGE   In *Sabbath v. United States* (391 U.S. 585 [1968]), the Supreme Court focused on the extent to which police officers can *break and enter* for the purpose of serving a warrant. In particular, the Court focused on the part of 18 U.S.C. Section 3109 that permits officers to "break open an outer door or window." In *Sabbath*, police officers enlisted the help of a man named Jones, whom they had caught trying to smuggle drugs into the country, to apprehend Sabbath, the man who was to receive the shipment of drugs. Jones agreed to deliver the drugs to Sabbath while the police looked on. After Jones entered the apartment, the officers knocked on the door. Not hearing a response, the officers opened the unlocked door, entered the apartment with guns drawn, and arrested Sabbath. The court of appeals affirmed Sabbath's conviction on the grounds that because the officers did not enter by force, the knock-and-announce rule of Section 3109 was not triggered.

Sabbath v. United States
(391 U.S. 585 [1968])

DECISION-MAKING EXERCISE 4.6

A Properly Served Arrest Warrant?

DEA agents and county police officers executed a search warrant at a drug dealer's house. In executing the warrant, the agents and officers gathered on the back porch of the house, knocked on the back door, yelled "Police, arrest warrant!" several times, and then broke down the door. During the search that followed, the officers seized a fully loaded revolver, 150 vials of cocaine, and cash in excess of $27,000. Did this action comport with the federal knock-and-announce rule enunciated in 18 U.S.C. Section 3109, which states that officers "may break open any outer or inner door or window of a house . . . to execute a search warrant, if, after notice of his authority and purpose, he is refused admittance"?

The Supreme Court disagreed with this reasoning, however, and reversed Sabbath's conviction. According to the Court, "An unannounced intrusion into a dwelling—what Section 3109 basically proscribes—is no less an unannounced intrusion whether officers break down a door, force open a chain lock on a partially open door, open a locked door by use of a passkey, or, as here, open a closed but unlocked door" (p. 590). This case seems to suggest that whether physical damage inflicted to the premises is immaterial. Instead, what is important is merely that officers knock and announce their presence.

In cases in which physical damage to the premises *is* significant, even excessive, the Fourteenth Amendment enters in. As this chapter indicates, the service of arrests warrants (and, by extension, search warrants) is governed by the Fourth Amendment. However, some *attempts* to seize people are governed by the Fourteenth Amendment's due process clause. This was the unanimous holding in *County of Sacramento v. Lewis* (523 U.S. 833 [1998]). In that case, a police officer ran over the passenger on a motorcycle, killing her, while pursuing the driver. This was another case that arrived at the Supreme Court by way of a civil lawsuit.

The Court held that since a stop had not occurred (see the discussion of *California v. Hodari D.* in the previous chapter), the Fourth Amendment was not implicated. Instead, the Court held that the Fourteenth Amendment's due process clause was relevant because it protects citizens from arbitrary government action. The Court went on to note that had the police conduct in *Lewis* "shocked the conscience," then the police would have been liable. The Court observed that "[w]hile prudence would have repressed the [officer's] reaction, the officer's instinct was to do his job as a law enforcement officer, not to induce [the driver of the motorcycle's] lawlessness, or to terrorize, cause harm, or kill" (p. 855).

Applying *Lewis* to the service of warrants, complaints about excessively destructive police conduct during the service of warrants are also governed by the Fourteenth Amendment. If the police's conduct shocks the conscience, then they may be liable under the due process clause. But there is no easy way to define what conduct shocks the conscience. At least one case has suggested that when police officers show "deliberate or reckless indifference," their conduct can be seen as conscience shocking (see *Estelle v. Gamble*, 429 U.S. 97 [1976]).

PERMISSIBLE DEGREE OF FORCE   It is appropriate at this juncture to consider what level of force is permitted against people who are the targets of arrest warrants. Almost every state has a law or regulation concerning police use of force. The American Law Institute adopted just one such regulation, which resembles many others in place around the United States. Section 120.7 states that a police officer "may use such force as is reasonably necessary to effect the arrest, to enter premises to effect the arrest, or to prevent the escape from custody of an arrested person." Further, **deadly force** is authorized when the crime in question is a felony and when such force "creates no substantial risk to innocent persons," and the officer reasonably believes that there is a substantial risk that the fleeing felon will inflict harm on other people or police officers.

Tennessee v. Garner
(471 U.S. 1 [1985])

In *Tennessee v. Garner* (471 U.S. 1 [1985])—which involved the shooting death of a young, unarmed, fleeing felon—the Supreme Court adopted a rule similar to the American Law Institute's formulation. The result was the leading Supreme Court precedent concerning the use of deadly force to apprehend fleeing felons. The *Garner* decision declared unconstitutional a Tennessee statute that authorized police officers who give notice of the intent to arrest to "use all the necessary means to effect the arrest" if the suspect flees or resists.

The Court ruled that deadly force may be used when (1) it is necessary to prevent the suspect's escape and (2) the officer has probable cause to believe the suspect poses a serious threat of death or causes serious physical injury to other people or police officers. One would think that the Supreme Court would be unanimous in a decision such as this, but three justices dissented, noting that the statute struck down by the majority "assist[s] the police in apprehending suspected perpetrators of serious crimes and provide[s] notice that a lawful police order to stop and submit to arrest may not be ignored with impunity" (p. 28).

Four years after *Garner*, the Supreme Court decided the landmark case of *Graham v. Connor* 490 U.S. 386 [1989]), which set the standard for **nondeadly force**. The Court declared emphatically that *all* claims involving allegations of excessive force against police officers must be analyzed under the Fourth Amendment's reasonableness requirement. Further, the Court adopted a test of objective reasonableness to decide when excessive force is used. This requires focusing on what a *reasonable* police officer would do "without regard to [the officer's] underlying intent or motivation." In determining what a reasonable police officer would do, the Court looked to three factors: (1) the severity of the crime; (2) whether the suspect posed a threat; and (3) whether the suspect was resisting and/or attempting to flee the scene. Courts must, in focusing on these three factors, allow "for the fact that police officers are often forced to make split-second judgments—about the amount of force that is necessary in a particular situation" (p. 386). Generally, then, if the crime in question is a serious one and the suspect is dangerous and resists arrest, then he or she will have difficulty succeeding with an excessive force claim.

Incidentally, both the *Garner* and *Graham* decisions resulted from Section 1983 lawsuits (see Chapter 2). Garner's surviving family members and Graham himself both sued on the grounds that their constitutional rights were violated. Whereas many of the cases examined in this book focus on the evidence of crimes (e.g., weapons, drugs, confessions), *Garner* and *Graham* do not. How evidence was obtained was not at issue because there was none. Thus, the only remedy available to Garner's family and Graham was *civil litigation*.

Garner and *Graham* both are necessarily general. States, cities, and counties around the country have adopted more restrictive guidelines for their officers concerning the use of force. To illustrate, the use of force policy from the San Bernardino, California, Police Department is reprinted in Figure 4.6.

ARRESTING THE WRONG PERSON On occasion, the police have a warrant to arrest someone but end up arresting the wrong person. The most obvious consequence of arresting the wrong person is that he or she must be let go (and will possibly file a lawsuit). What the courts have focused on, though, is the admissibility of *evidence* resulting from a wrongful arrest. An example of such a situation would be one in which the

*Graham v. Connor
490 U.S. 386 [1989])*

DECISION-MAKING EXERCISE 4.7
Deadly Force beyond Present Dangerousness

Garner seems to be concerned with *present dangerousness*. That is, police officers contemplating the use of deadly force have to consider, among other factors, how dangerous the suspect is before resorting to deadly force. But what if the suspect committed the crime days or even months earlier? Can the police use deadly force to apprehend, say, an unarmed, fleeing individual who is the suspect in a weeks-old robbery?

FIGURE 4.6

Use of Force Policy (San Bernardino, CA, Police Department)

STANDARD OPERATING PROCEDURE   CHAPTER #35   PROCEDURE #1

USE OF FORCE   Revised   12-22-04

PURPOSE

To provide guidelines and parameters for police personnel concerning their use of force to accomplish their lawful duties and objectives.

POLICY

Police personnel have the legal authority to use the appropriate amount of force to protect themselves and the public from assaultive criminal behavior. However, the amount of force used must be both necessary and reasonable. Personnel shall use only that amount of force that reasonably appears necessary based upon articulable facts and the totality of circumstances known to the officer at the time of the event. Personnel should choose the appropriate force response to overcome active resistance or aggressive behavior. Therefore, personnel should be reasonable in their actions and demonstrate common sense when employing force.

The primary objective in the application of force is to ensure control of resistant or combative suspect(s) with the minimal amount of force necessary. No specific guidelines or policies can apply to all situations; therefore, personnel should constantly evaluate all use of force applications or options. The use of force will either escalate or de-escalate based upon the totality of circumstances during the course of an arrest or detention.

This policy will also include the use of force on combative subject(s) who do not rise to the level of being criminal suspects, such as W&I 5150.

The scale of force options in order of increasing severity are: verbal persuasion, compliance control techniques, intermediate force (chemical agents, lateral vascular neck restraint, or electronic disabling devices), and impact weapons. It is not necessary for personnel to exercise each option before escalating to the next level of force but flexibility is essential to maintain control during the dynamics of a physical confrontation.

When choosing a particular force option, these factors should be taken into consideration:

1. The severity of the crime(s) involved or subjected.
2. The conduct/behavior of the suspect(s).
3. Whether the suspect(s) poses an immediate threat to the officer(s) or others.
4. Whether the suspect(s) has, used, or displayed a weapon.
5. The proximity of weapons.
6. Officer/suspect factors (age, physical size, relative strength, skill level, injury/exhaustion, number of officer(s) versus number of suspect(s)).
7. Influence of drugs or alcohol.
8. Potential for injury to bystanders.
9. Availability of other options.
10. Other exigent circumstances.

PROCEDURE

Personnel shall only possess that equipment authorized or issued by the department. Only those defensive tactics or arrest control techniques authorized by or instructed by department personnel or other authorized persons are permitted excluding exigent circumstances. The level of force utilized should be that level which would quickly, safely, and humanely bring resisting subject under physical control. Personnel should employ escalating scale of force options in order of increasing severity to overcome the suspect(s) resistance.

1. Scale of Force

   A. Persuasion

   The presence of a confident uniformed police officer displaying professional demeanor coupled with good verbal communication will generally convince a resistant subject to submit to your authority without the necessity of an escalation in force. Good verbalization may be advising, admonishing, warning, or persuading a subject to submit to your authority without the use of profanity or derogatory language. Officers should use their verbal techniques to de-escalate confrontations.

   B. Compliance Control Techniques

   Compliance techniques consist of the physical application of force in the form of joint manipulations, blocks, pain compliance, and takedowns. These empty handed techniques should be coupled with a police officer's verbal commands.

   C. Intermediate Force
      1. Chemical Agents

      Police personnel may use chemical agents as an intermediate level of force for controlling or subduing combative persons. Chemical agents are defensive control weapons used to control or subdue subjects who are physically resisting arrest. Chemical agents should not be used indiscriminately and shall not be used against non-combative persons. It should not be used against a subject who is under restraint unless that subject is physically assaulting officers or others.

      2. Lateral Vascular Neck Restraint

      The lateral vascular neck restraint (LVNR) is a means of subduing physically combative persons. This technique is a method which permits personnel to apprehend violent subjects who cannot be controlled or restrained with compliance or control holds.

      3. Taser

      The electronic disabling device (taser) is a device, which may be used to subdue physically combative person/s in violent or potentially violent situations lessening the injury to the subject/s or officers involved. The taser may be used if other apprehension methods or restraints have failed or are deemed impractical and there is a reasonable expectation that it would be hazardous for personnel to approach and physically contact the subject/s.

   D. Impact Weapons

   Impact weapons are methods of subduing physically combative persons or immediately impeding the threatening actions of a violently resistant subject with physical strikes to the subject's body. These physical strikes shall be directed to those areas which are easily accessible, effective for quickly subduing the subject/s, and unlikely to cause serious injury. Other self defense techniques, kicks or arm strikes, can be used if the officer's baton is unavailable. Other authorized police equipment may be used as an impact weapon in exigent circumstances.

Figure 4.6 continued

2. Reporting the Use of Force

Any physical use of force by personnel of this department shall be documented in an appropriate report depending upon the nature of the incident. When a use of force greater than a compliance control technique occurs, personnel shall promptly make an oral report to the watch commander or a supervisor. If the application of any force **including a compliance control hold** (See Procedure, Section 1, subsection B for definition) has caused physical injury or complaint of pain, personnel shall make their oral report immediately. Personnel shall document the name of the notified supervisor in their report. Any injury suffered by a suspect in our custody, whether caused by an officer or other person (including self-inflicted wounds) shall be immediately reported to a supervisor. Medical assistance shall be obtained for suspects who have been rendered unconscious, sustained injury, or complain of pain.

Any supervisor notified of a use of force including compliance control holds that result in a complaint of pain requiring examination by a medical provider or obvious physical injury, shall complete a department approved Use of Force form. The documentation of suspect's injuries, or claimed injuries, is a valuable part of the use of force process for two reasons: 1) documentation of visible injuries and, 2) prevention of false or inflated allegations of injuries that did not occur during police contact. The reporting supervisor shall ensure photographs are taken of the specific area of the body on which force was used, whether or not the suspect initially claims any injuries.

When a suspect is treated at a hospital after the use of force, the reporting supervisor shall document the name of the treating medical provider along with medical provider's brief statement (when available) as to the extent of the injuries. If a suspect is hospitalized or receives a serious injury due to a use of force incident, the watch commander shall notify the officer's division commander.

If the officer using force is a supervisor, he/she shall promptly make an oral report to the watch commander who will designate another supervisor to respond to the scene and complete the use of force report. The involved supervisor will write a follow up to the crime report describing the circumstances and the force used.

The reporting supervisor shall complete a Use of Force report. The completed Use of Force report along with a copy of the corresponding police report will be forwarded to the appropriate district or unit manager for review. The supervisor will request that the photographs be developed and forwarded to the district/unit manager. The district/unit manager will complete his/her review of the facts. If the manager determines there is a need for a more in-depth assessment, he/she will prepare a staff report before forwarding to the division commander.

3. Report Filing

Use of Force reports shall be issued a "UF" number. After final review, Use of Force reports shall be kept in a secure file located in the Internal Affairs Office. Use of Force reports in need of further review will be forwarded to the Assistant Chief of Police for further action.

Any use of force report that is referred by the Assistant Chief of Police to Internal Affairs for further review or investigation, will be provided to the officer through the administrative investigation process.

Source: Chapter 35, Procedure I, "Use of Force," from *Standard Operating Procedure*, San Bernardino, California, Police Department (rev. December 22, 2004). Reprinted with permission.

police serve an arrest warrant at the wrong house and, during the course of arresting the wrong person, discover evidence of another crime. To what extent would such evidence be admissible? It depends on the reasonableness of the police action.

In *Hill v. California* (401 U.S. 797 [1971]), the Supreme Court focused on an arrest of the wrong person. In that case, the police arrived at Hill's apartment to arrest him, but Miller answered the door. Since Miller fit Hill's description, the police arrested Miller. Miller even provided identification to prove that he was not Hill, but the Court stated that "aliases and false identifications are not uncommon" (p. 803). A pistol and ammunition clip were in plain view. These were admitted into evidence, and the Supreme Court focused on their admissibility. The Court ruled that the police could have reasonably believed that Miller was Hill. Furthermore, the Court pointed out that "sufficient probability, not certainty, is the touchstone of reasonableness under the Fourth Amendment and on the record before us the officers' mistake was understandable and the arrest a reasonable response to the situation facing them at the time" (p. 803).

SEARCHES WITH WARRANTS

Searches with warrants are subjected to many of the same restrictions that arrests with warrants are. However, because the purpose of obtaining a search warrant is to search for something, as opposed to seizing a person, the courts have placed significant restrictions on what the police can do when searching for evidence with warrants. Just because a warrant is obtained does not mean that the police can look anywhere and take unlimited time to search for the item(s) named in the warrant.

Executing a Search Warrant

The knock-and-announce rules discussed earlier carry over to the service of search warrants. As indicated before, the police do not have to announce their presence if they have reasonable suspicion that exigent circumstances are present. Likewise, even if police do not "knock and announce," evidence seized cannot be excluded per *Hudson v. Michigan*.

Use of force is rarely an issue that arises during the service of a search warrant because, strictly speaking, a search warrant authorizes the police to look for evidence. If a person gets in the way during the service of a search warrant, however, he or she may be arrested and force may be applied, if need be (i.e., subject to the restrictions discussed earlier).

If the police mistakenly search the wrong residence, the search will not automatically be declared invalid. As pointed out earlier, as long as the mistake is a reasonable one, any evidence seized during a search of the wrong residence will be admissible in a criminal trial. The key, however, is that the mistake must be an *objectively reasonable* one, gauged from the standpoint of a reasonable officer.

Four other issues are relevant to the service of a search warrant. These do not necessarily apply in the case of arrest warrants. They are: (1) time restrictions, both for when the warrant can be served and for how long the police can look for evidence; (2) the scope and manner of the search; (3) the procedure after the service of the search warrant; and (4) the presence of the media during the service of a search warrant. To illustrate the complexity inherent in search warrant procedure, the Portland (Oregon) Police Bureau's search warrant policy is reprinted in Figure 4.7.

It is important to note that the police can sometimes request a search warrant with special instructions, which can include night service, no-knock authorization,

FIGURE 4.7

Search Warrant Policy (Portland, OR, Police Bureau)

652.00 SEARCH WARRANTS

POLICY (652.00)

A search warrant should be obtained for all searches whenever there is time to do so and when there is any doubt about the necessity of obtaining a warrant.

PROCEDURE (652.00)

Any magistrate authorized to issue a warrant of arrest may issue a search warrant for:

   a. Evidence of, or information concerning, the commission of a criminal offense.
   b. Property that constitutes contraband or items otherwise criminally possessed.
   c. Fruits of a crime (see ORS 133.535).
   d. Property that has been used, or is possessed for the purpose of being used, to commit or conceal the commission of an offense.
   e. A person for whose arrest there is probable cause or who is unlawfully held in concealment.

Search Warrant Issuance (652.00)

   a. Application for a search warrant may be made by a district attorney or by any police officer. Search warrants and affidavits will normally be written by the member requesting the warrant. Warrant preparation will be coordinated with the appropriate investigative unit.
   b. Search warrants are only issued upon a finding of probable cause to believe that an offense has or will be committed. The probable cause is based upon the member's personal knowledge and/or hearsay information from another member, a named citizen or undisclosed informant. The probable cause is relayed to the magistrate through use of an affidavit. The affidavit should:
      1. Contain a clear and distinct description of the place(s) to be searched and the item(s) to be seized.
      2. Provide facts and circumstances which provide probable cause for the search. This includes:
         a) Information justifying the search; and
         b) Information leading to the belief that the object(s) of the search are in the places or the possession of the subject(s) to be searched.
   c. Before issuing the warrant, the magistrate will need to be satisfied that probable cause exists. The magistrate may examine the affiant or any witnesses under oath.
   d. Prior to the issuance of a search warrant, a magistrate may request that a meeting be arranged at a time and place convenient for all parties involved, so the magistrate can interview any informant(s) contributing information towards the probable cause.
   e. When hearsay information of an undisclosed confidential informant is relied upon to establish probable cause, that information must be independently corroborated (e.g., information demonstrating past reliability of the informant or by personal observation and corroboration).
   f. An ongoing chronological record will be maintained of each informant's activities and reliability by those divisions issuing evidence/informant funds. This file is to be reviewed by a supervisor prior to requesting a search warrant based on an informant's reliability. Members will comply with DIRs 660.00 and 660.32.

Search Warrant Checklist (652.00)

A search warrant checklist has been adopted by the Bureau, the Multnomah County District Attorney's Office and Multnomah County court magistrates.

This checklist is available on the Bureau's Intranet. Included on the checklist is a section indicating the investigator has conducted a check through Oregon State Intelligence Network (OSIN) to ensure that the warrant address is not currently the subject of an investigation by another agency and/or division.

The check is mandatory, and will be done prior to the issuance of any search warrant. This form will be used for all Multnomah County search warrants obtained by the Bureau. Members should follow warrant application and return procedures for other counties as instructed by local magistrates.

A supervisor should review the probable cause, informant reliability, and the search warrant affidavit prior to its submission to the DA's office. A deputy district attorney (DDA), from the appropriate county, will review every search warrant affidavit in person or by telephone.

A copy of the search warrant and the original affidavit will be left with the issuing magistrate. Search warrants will be served as soon as possible. Extended delay of service is to be avoided.

Threat Assessment and Planning (652.00)

All search warrant executions involving a potential threat to members or citizens require a Planned Operations Risk Assessment form be completed prior to execution. This form is available on the Bureau's Intranet.

Examples of a threat might include, but not be limited to, violent suspects, animals, obstacles causing a delay to securing the search location, or even a lack of information about the location to be searched.

The supervisor responsible for the search warrant execution is responsible for the proper completion of the risk assessment form and any other necessary planning to ensure the safe and effective service of the warrant. The supervisor will ensure that the SERT commander, or designee, will be consulted, as required by the completed Planned Operations Risk Assessment form. This will assist the evaluation for need of SERT and/or HNT in the execution of the warrant.

If SERT/HNT are needed or requested, the SERT commander, or designee, will coordinate with HNT and the originating division/unit commander or designee, to ensure all tactical considerations have been discussed. The original completed risk assessment form, if not forwarded to SERT as a request for their services, will be retained in the investigator's case file.

Execution of the Warrant (652.00)

a. Only a police officer may serve a search warrant. Generally, execution of a search warrant is restricted to between 0700 and 2200 hours unless it is otherwise endorsed on the warrant by the issuing magistrate.

b. A warrant is generally valid for five days after the date of its issuance. If the warrant is not executed within this period, it is void. A new affidavit must be filed and new search warrant issued. The issuing magistrate may, however, authorize execution of the warrant for up to ten days after its issuance. This authorization must be specified on the face of the warrant. Before entering any premises, the executing member will knock and give appropriate notice of identity, authority and purpose to the person to be searched or to the person in apparent control of the premises to be searched. If the member is not admitted after such notification,

Figure 4.7 continued

force may be used to enter the premises. In emergency situations, a no-knock entry may be performed (e.g., where members or others are at risk of bodily harm or where evidence may be destroyed). If such entry occurs, the circumstances leading to the entry will be clearly articulated in the incident report form. If it is determined that no one is at the residence, members have the authority to forcibly enter (see DIR 631.60). Before undertaking any search or seizure pursuant to the warrant, the executing member will:

1. Read and give a copy of the warrant (not the affidavit) to the person to be searched, or to the person in apparent control of the premises to be searched.
2. Affix a copy of the warrant to the premises if the premises are unoccupied, or there is no one in apparent control.

c. In the course of executing a search warrant, the member may take reasonable precautions to ensure that property will not be removed while the search is being conducted and to prevent interference with the search. Members have the same power and authority in all respects to break open any door or window and to use all necessary and proper means to overcome any forcible resistance as they do in executing or serving a warrant of arrest. In securing the premises to be searched, the member may seek out all persons on the premises and bring them to a central location for observation during the search.

d. Members of the media will not be allowed to enter private property without the consent of the property owner or individual in charge of the involved property.

Limitations of Warrants (652.00)

a. The scope of searches pursuant to search warrants is limited to the premises specified in the warrant and only for those items specified in the warrant to be seized.

1. The search must be terminated once all items specified in the warrant are discovered.
2. If during execution of a warrant, there is inadvertent discovery of evidence not specified in the warrant (even when the evidence is of an unrelated crime), it may be seized under the plain view exception.
3. Unless the warrant(s) authorize the search of a named person(s), a search warrant for a residence or other premises does not permit a search of all the persons present during the time of the search. if there is probable cause to believe that persons on the premises are carrying or concealing items which reasonably could be the objects of the search warrant, those persons may be detained and searched to the extent necessary to determine whether they are concealing items covered by the warrant.

b. A member may remain on the premises in a search warrant only during the time reasonably necessary to conduct the search for the property described in the warrant.

Post Execution Responsibilities (652.00)

Upon execution of the search warrant, the member will:

a. Leave a copy of the warrant and property receipt(s) specifying, in detail, the property taken. This copy will be left with the person from whom the property was taken, or in whose possession the property is found. In the absence of any person, the copy of the warrant/receipt(s) will be left in the place where the property was found.

b. Secure the location if the owner or other responsible party is unavailable.

c. File all affidavits, search warrants and returns, regardless of any associated cases, with the Circuit Court issuing judge. Members will file the search warrant return and receipts as soon as reasonably possible, but no later than five days, after the execution or expiration of the warrant.

d. Following execution of a search warrant which involves the distribution or manufacture of controlled substances, prostitution and/or gambling, members will complete a Drugs and Vice Division (DVD) Completed Activity Report and forward the form to DVD. The information may be used to take action against the property owner under the specified crime property ordinance.

Telephonic Search Warrant Guide (652.00)

a. Preparation:
   1. Assemble notes, outline or handwritten affidavit (for dictation).
   2. Type or hand write the search warrant.
   3. Discuss with the DDA, if appropriate.
   4. Locate the judge.
   5. Discuss briefly with the judge to resolve any questions.

b. Turn on recorder; remember, what you told the judge before the recording starts does not count, so start over at the very beginning.

c. Preface phrase:
   1. Affiant's name.
   2. Date and time.
   3. Telephonic warrant.
   4. Judge's name and authority.
   5. Note that this is a recording.
   6. Example: This is Officer (Name) presenting a telephonic affidavit for a search warrant on (Date) at (Time). This request is being made to Judge (Name), of the Circuit Court, Multnomah County, State of Oregon, and is being tape recorded for later transcription.

d. Affiant identification phrase:
   1. Name.
   2. Oath (Upon my oath, I (Name), do hereby depose and say . . .).
   3. Employer, assignment, length of service.

e. Factual information – body of affidavit; organize your dictation to cover all critical areas including:
   1. Informant credibility and reliability.
   2. Observations of informant.
   3. Location of place to be searched, property to be seized, identity of resident.
   4. Corroboration, if available.
   5. Venue (judge must be from court where search is to be done).

f. Request permission to search (Standard Request for Warrant).

g. Have judge administer oath.

h. Read typed or handwritten search warrant to judge. Judge must hand write or type original warrant.

i. Obtain permission to search.

j. Obtain permission to sign judge's name to duplicate warrant.

k. Have judge declare that the judge is signing the original search warrant.

l. Note time and date of authorization; end tape. Make sure the judge writes the time and date on the original warrant.

Figure 4.7 continued

Return of a Telephonic Search Warrant (652.00)

a. Search warrant:

1. Present to the issuing judge the duplicate warrant that was prepared and signed by you within the date specified on the warrant (normally five days from the date of issue). Remember this should be the actual duplicate of the original warrant that the judge authorized you to sign over the phone, even if handwritten.
2. Make sure the judge has the original warrant that the judge prepared and signed.
3. Both should be filed with the court. Normally the judge will handle this.

b. Tape and transcription:

1. Present both the tape and transcription to the judge at the same time and duplicate warrant is returned.
2. After the judge listens to the tape and reviews the transcription for accuracy, have the judge certify both the tape and the transcription.
3. Both the tape and the transcription should be filed with the court.

Normally the judge will handle this.

Source: Portland Police Bureau, *Manual of Policy and Procedure* (January 2007). Reprinted with permission of the Portland Police Bureau.

and the like. An example of the face sheet for a special instructions warrant from the state of California is reprinted in Figure 4.8.

TIME CONSTRAINTS There are three means by which the courts impose time constraints on the police when it comes to the service of search warrants. First, the service of a search warrant should take place promptly after its issuance. Clearly, probable cause could dissipate if an excessive amount of time elapses between the time the warrant is issued and the time it is served. To avoid this potential problem, a warrant will sometimes specify that the search be conducted within a certain period of time.

Gooding v. United States
(416 U.S. 430 [1974])

A second time restriction that is occasionally imposed pertains to the time of day. Judges commonly restrict the service of warrants to the daytime hours or at least favor daytime service (see *Gooding v. United States*, 416 U.S. 430 [1974]). The *Federal Rules of Criminal Procedure*, for example, restrict the service of warrants to daytime hours, unless the issuing judge specifically authorizes execution at another time. *Daytime hours*, according to the *Federal Rules*, are between the hours of 6:00 a.m. and 10:00 p.m.

The third time restriction concerns how long the police can search for evidence. The general rule is that a search cannot last indefinitely. Once the item in the warrant has been discovered, the search must be terminated. If the police have difficulty finding the item or items named in the warrant, they can take as long as necessary to find them. If the police do not succeed in finding the evidence named in the warrant and then leave and come back later, they will be required to obtain another warrant. Steps should always be taken to avoid the appearance of arbitrariness, and people's Fourth Amendment privacy interests should always be respected.

SCOPE AND MANNER OF THE SEARCH Two additional restrictions with regard to the service of a search warrant concern the scope and manner of the search. *Scope* refers to where the police can look for evidence. *Manner* refers to the physical steps the

FIGURE 4.8

Example of a Special Instructions Warrant

SUPERIOR COURT OF CALIFORNIA
County of _____

SEARCH WARRANT
◆ Special Instructions ◆

THE PEOPLE OF THE STATE OF CALIFORNIA to: Warrant No. _____

Any peace officer in _____ **County**

The affidavit filed herewith by _____, sworn to and subscribed before me, has established probable cause for this warrant which you are ordered to execute as follows:

Place(s) to be searched: Described in Exhibit 1A, *attached* hereto and incorporated by reference.

Property to be seized: Described in Exhibit 1B, attached hereto and incorporated by reference.

Disposition of property: All property seized pursuant to this search warrant shall be retained in the affiant's custody pending further court order pursuant to Penal Code §§ 1528(a), 1536.

◆ SPECIAL INSTRUCTIONS ◆

The Statement of Probable Cause, filed herewith, has demonstrated legal justification for the following special procedures which are authorized if checked:

☐ **Night Service:** This warrant may be served at any hour of the day or night.

☐ **No Knock Authorization:** Compliance with Penal Code § 1531 is excused *unless* a change in circumstances negates the need for non-compliance.

☐ **Special Master:** The search shall be conducted by a Special Master pursuant to Penal Code §§ 1524(c)-(g). The Special Master shall be _____.

☐ **Sealing Order:** The following documents shall be sealed and delivered into the custody of the Clerk of the Superior Court pending further court order: ☐ All documents filed herewith. ☐ Documents listed in Exhibit 2. Grounds for sealing: ☐ Informant protection (Evid. Code § 1041)   ☐ Official information (Evid. Code § 1040)

☐ **Nondisclosure Order:** The financial institution served with this warrant, including its employees and agents, shall not disclose any information regarding its content, existence, or execution pending further court order.

☐ **Blood draw:** (Not for HIV testing per Penal Code § 1524.1): A blood sample shall be drawn from the person described in Exhibit 1A by trained medical personnel in accordance with accepted medical practices.

☐ **Anticipatory Warrant**: Having determined that probable cause for this search will exist upon the occurrence of the triggering event(s) described in Exhibit 3, and that there is probable cause said triggering event(s) will occur, this warrant shall be executed promptly after said triggering event(s) occur. Exhibit 3 is *attached* hereto and incorporated by reference.

☐ **Covert Warrant:** The property described in Exhibit 1B shall not be removed from the premises. An inventory shall be prepared showing the location of all such property discovered on the premises. Said property shall be photographed or videotaped to show its location when discovered. Compliance with the receipt requirements of Penal Code § 1535 is excused until _____ unless an extension is granted by this court. [Initial compliance date must not be more than 7 days following execution of the warrant.] Within two days after executing this warrant, the following shall be filed with this court: (1) the inventory, and (2) the original or copy of all photographs and/or videotape recordings made during the execution of this warrant.

☐ **Additional instructions:** Additional instructions pertaining to this search warrant are contained in Exhibit 4, *attached* hereto and incorporated by reference.

_____   _____
Date and time warrant issued   Judge of the Superior Court

Source: Reprinted with permission of the District Attorney's Office of Alameda County, California. Available online: http://le.alcoda.org/publications/files/sw_multi.pdf (accessed February 16, 2011).

police can take to find the evidence in question, including breaking down doors, forcibly opening locked cabinets, and so on.

The scope of the search must be reasonable, based on the object of the search. In other words, the police are restricted in looking for evidence insofar as they can only look where the item could reasonably be found. For example, assume the evidence in question is a stolen diamond ring. Such an item is relatively small, so the police will be authorized to look almost anywhere for the ring. However, if the evidence in question is large in size—for example, a stolen big-screen television set—then the police cannot look in small places, where such an item could not possibly be found. The Supreme Court's statement in *Harris v. United States* (331 U.S. 145 [1947]) provides further clarification: "[T]he same meticulous investigation which would be appropriate in a search for two small canceled checks could not be considered reasonable where agents are seeking a stolen automobile or an illegal still" (p. 152).

Harris v. United States (331 U.S. 145 [1947])

The police may also detain people as needed while serving a search warrant. According to the Court in *Michigan v. Summers* (452 U.S. 692 [1981]), "[A] warrant to search for contraband founded on probable cause implicitly carries with it the limited authority to detain the occupants of the premises while a proper search is conducted" (p. 704). Although the police may detain people who are on the premises to be searched, they cannot search the people unless probable cause exists (*Ybarra v. Illinois*, 444 U.S. 85 [1979]). A frisk is permissible, though, as long as the police have a reasonable suspicion that there is a risk to officer safety. If a person does not live on the premises, does not house personal belongings there, and is not a threat, he or she will probably be allowed to leave.

As discussed in the section "Arrest with Warrants," federal law authorizes the police to break open doors and containers if they are refused admittance (18 U.S.C. Section 3109). Still, there are restrictions. Basically, the manner of the search must be limited to what is reasonably necessary to find the evidence in question. The Supreme Court has stated that "[e]xcessive or unnecessary destruction of property in the course of a search may violate the Fourth Amendment, even though the entry itself is lawful and the fruits of the search not subject to suppression" (*United States v. Ramirez*, 523 U.S. 65 [1998], p. 71). Additionally, the occupant of the place searched can be detained—even in handcuffs—for the duration of the search (*Muehler v. Mena*, 544 U.S. 93 [2005]).

PROCEDURE AFTER SERVICE OF A SEARCH WARRANT After a search warrant has been served, the police are required to inventory the items that were seized. Usually the inventory is taken by the searching officer in the presence of whose property was searched. This procedure not only protects against claims of police theft but also helps assure the person whose premises were searched that his or her property has been accounted for. A copy of the inventory is given to the person whose property was searched, and if no one was on the premises during the time of the search, the list must be left at the scene in a prominent place. Also, the police typically have to complete some type of a search record form to be kept on file with the department. Interestingly, the police are not required to notify the property owner of the steps

DECISION-MAKING EXERCISE 4.8
Defining Daytime

On August 26, at approximately 7:30 p.m., the Sunny County Sheriff's Department executed a search warrant on the premises of 5678 Cherry Lane. The defendants later argued that the search warrant and its execution were defective because the warrant directed that it be executed during the *daytime*. In fact, the warrant was executed at approximately 7:30 p.m., and sunset occurred at 6:43 p.m., according to the National Weather Service. Given this, was the warrant therefore defective?

DECISION-MAKING EXERCISE 4.9

Where Can Police Reasonably Look?

Sheriff's deputies had a search warrant to look for a rare, stolen koala in the house of the local taxidermist. When serving the warrant, they looked through the kitchen cupboards, wherein they found small baggies of a white, powdery substance as well as a scale. They seized the items and arrested the taxidermist for drug possession. The koala was never found. May the seized items be admitted into evidence? What if the officers had been looking for a stolen circus elephant?

necessary for the return of the property or to remedy any perceived constitutional violation (see *City of West Covina v. Perkins*, 525 U.S. 234 [1999]).

City of West Covina v. Perkins *(525 U.S. 234 [1999])*

MEDIA PRESENCE   In *Wilson v. Layne* (526 U.S. 603 [1999]), the Supreme Court decided whether the police can bring members of the media along during the service of a arrest warrant. The facts of the case are as follows: Early in the morning on April 16, 1992, deputy U.S. marshals and Montgomery County police officers entered the suspected home of Dominic Wilson. They were joined by a *Washington Post* reporter and a photographer as part of a marshals' service ride-along policy. Dominic's parents were asleep in bed when the officers arrived. They heard the officers enter the home and ran into the living room to investigate the disturbance. A verbal altercation ensued, and both the Wilsons were subdued. Dominic Wilson was never found. Even though the reporter observed what occurred and the photographer took pictures of what transpired, the story was never printed and the pictures were never published. The parents, Charles and Geraldine Wilson, nonetheless brought a *Bivens* action (the Section 1983 counterpart for lawsuits against *federal* officials) against the marshals, alleging the officers violated their Fourth Amendment rights by bringing the media into their home.

The case worked its way up through the courts and was ultimately heard by the Supreme Court, which decided that media presence during the service of arrest warrants violates the Fourth Amendment, as long as the presence serves no "legitimate law enforcement objectives." The Court declared that "it is a violation of the Fourth Amendment for police to bring members of the media or other third parties into a home during the execution of a warrant when the presence of the third parties in the home was not in aid of the execution of the warrant" (p. 614).

Chief Justice Rehnquist, writing for the majority, began by stating that the Fourth Amendment embodies the "centuries-old principle of respect for the privacy of the home" (p. 610). He went on to note that although the law enforcement officers were authorized to enter the Wilsons' home, "it does not necessarily follow that they were entitled to bring a

DECISION-MAKING EXERCISE 4.10

Detention of a Third Party during an Arrest

As officers arrived at a house to serve a search warrant, they encountered Larry McVee descending the front steps. The officers asked McVee to help them gain entry into the house. McVee replied that he did not have keys to the house but would ring someone over the intercom. When he did so, another occupant answered the door but refused to allow the officers into the house. The officers then forced the door open and detained McVee as well as eight other people who were in the house. All nine people were frisked because the officers feared for their safety. One of the people had a gun on his person. The officers arrested that man, and in his later trial for weapons offenses, he moved to suppress the gun on the grounds that the officers did not have justification to detain him (or the other people in the house) during the execution of a search warrant. Will his motion be granted?

newspaper reporter and photographer with them" (p. 611). The Court then considered whether the actions of both parties—the reporters and the police—were related to the objectives of the intrusion into the Wilsons' home. It ruled that they were not. Since the reporters were in the Wilsons' residence for their own purposes, they "were not present for any reason related to the justification for police entry into the home" (p. 611). However, if media presence *does* serve legitimate law enforcement objectives, then the Fourth Amendment will not be violated.

Wilson v. Layne
(526 U.S. 603 [1999])

To many observers, the Court's decision in *Wilson v. Layne* seemed to decide the fate of the so-called reality-based police television shows—and to an extent, it did. The police cannot take a camera crew with them when a arrest warrant is served. Media accompaniment is still permissible outside people's homes, however. Figure 4.9 provides a summary of the restrictions on the service of arrest warrants. The last sections of this chapter focus on special circumstances that arise in the arrest-warrant context.

SPECIAL CIRCUMSTANCES

Added restrictions govern bodily intrusions. The same is true of tracking devices, recording instruments, and electronic surveillance in general. The following subsections touch on the special circumstances in each of these areas.

Search Warrants and Bodily Intrusions

The Supreme Court has been especially restrictive with regard to intrusions into the human body. The most well-known case that serves as an example is *Rochin v. California* (342 U.S. 165 [1952]). In that case, the police had information that a man was selling narcotics. They entered his home and forced their way into his bedroom. When the police asked the man about two capsules that were lying on his bed, he put the capsules in his mouth. The officers could not successfully remove the drugs from the man's mouth, so they took him to the hospital, where his stomach was pumped. Drugs were found and the man was convicted in California state court for possession of morphine. *Rochin* was decided in 1952, prior to when the exclusionary rule was applied to the states. As a result, the Court ruled that the way the police handled the man shocked the conscience, thereby violating his Fourteenth Amendment right to due process.

In another case, *Winston v. Lee* (470 U.S. 753 [1985]), the Supreme Court decided whether the government could require a bullet to be surgically removed from a suspected robber. The Court required not only that a warrant be obtained before allowing such an intrusion but also that the suspect's safety and privacy interests should be weighed against society's interest in capturing lawbreakers. The Court noted,

FIGURE 4.9

Summary of Search Warrant Restrictions

1. Time Constraints
   a. Search must be executed promptly after issuance
   b. Search must be conducted during daylight hours if possible
   c. Search must not last indefinitely
2. Scope and Manner
   a. Search must be based on object sought
   b. Search must avoid causing excessive and unnecessary property damage
   c. Cannot search guests or third parties if probable cause to do so is lacking

A compelled surgical intrusion into an individual's body for evidence . . . implicates expectations of privacy and security of such magnitude that the intrusion may be "unreasonable" even if likely to produce evidence of a crime. . . . The reasonableness of surgical intrusions beneath the skin depends on a case-by-case approach, in which the individual's interests in privacy and security are weighed against society's interests in conducting the procedure. In a given case, the question whether the community's need for evidence outweighs the substantial privacy interest at stake is a delicate one admitting of few categorical answers. (pp. 759–760)

The Court did not expressly decide what the appropriate procedure would be before surgery would be permitted, but it did cite a lower court decision, *United States v. Crowder* (543 F.2d 312 [1977]), in which the D.C. Circuit Court of Appeals decided that before surgery would be permissible (even if a warrant were obtained), an adversarial hearing with appellate review must occur. Thus, under certain circumstances, it would appear that certain types of bodily intrusions require more than a warrant.

Given the importance of bodily intrusions vis-à-vis civil liberties, police departments should take special care for engaging in them. Accordingly, the San Bernardino, California, Police Department's policy for strip and body cavity searches is reprinted in Figure 4.10.

FIGURE 4.10

Strip and Body Cavity Search Policy (San Bernardino, CA, Police Department)

STANDARD OPERATING PROCEDURE   CHAPTER #29   PROCEDURE #1

STRIP and BODY CAVITY SEARCHES   (Revised)   4-8-91

PURPOSE

A. To establish a policy governing strip and body cavity searches, and to protect arrested persons from unwarranted intrusions.

B. To conform to the requirements of Penal Code Section 4030.

DEFINITIONS

A. <u>Strip Search</u> – Means a search that requires a person to remove or arrange some or all of his/her clothing so as to permit a visual inspection of the underclothing, breasts, buttocks, or genitalia of that person.

B. <u>Body Cavity</u> – Means the stomach or rectal cavity of any person and the vagina of a female person.

C. <u>Visual Body Cavity Search</u> – The visual inspection of a body cavity.

D. <u>Physical Body Cavity Search</u> – Mean physical intrusion into a body cavity for the purpose of discovering any object concealed in that cavity.

PROCEDURES

A. When an arrestee is taken into custody, that person may be subjected to a pat down search, metal detector search, and thorough clothing search in order to discover and retrieve concealed weapons and/or contraband prior to being transported to County Jail.

Figure 4.10 continued

B. Before requesting authority for a strip search or body cavity search, an officer must determine there is a reasonable suspicion based on specific and articulable facts to believe an arrestee is concealing a weapon or contraband, and that a strip search or body cavity search will result in the discovery of the weapon or contraband.

No strip search or visual body cavity search may be conducted on a misdemeanor or infraction arrestee, without the prior written authorization of the supervisor on duty. A copy of the written authorization shall remain with the case file and shall be made available upon request. The time, date, and place of the search, the name and sex of the person conducting the search, and a statement of the results of the search, including a list of any items removed from the person searched shall be recorded in the case file and made available upon request of the person search or his/her authorized representative. The authorization shall include specific and articulable facts and circumstances upon which the reasonable determination was made by the supervisor.

C. No arrestee shall be subjected to a physical body cavity search except under the authority of a search warrant issued by a magistrate specifically authorizing the physical body cavity search.

A physical body cavity search shall be conducted under sanitary conditions, and only by a physician, nurse practitioner, registered nurse, licensed vocational nurse, or emergency medical technician licensed to practice in the State of California. Any physician engaged in providing health care to detainees or inmates of a facility may conduct the physical body cavity search. A copy of the warrant shall remain in the case file and shall be made available upon request of the person searched or his/her authorized representative. The time, date, and place of search, the name and sex of the person conducting the search, and a statement of the results of the search including a list of items removed from the person searched shall be recorded in the case file.

D. A person conducting a strip search or a visual body cavity search shall not touch the breasts, buttocks, or genitalia of the person being searched.

E. All persons conducting or present during a strip search or visual or physical body cavity search shall be of the same sex as the person being searched, except for physicians or licensed medical personnel.

F. All strip, visual, and physical body cavity searches shall be conducted in an area of privacy so that the search cannot be observed by persons not participating in the search. A person is considered to be participating in the search if his/her official duties relative to search procedure require him/her to be present at the time the search is conducted.

G. No strip or body cavity search shall be conducted on persons not under arrest, without their consent, or a valid search warrant for that person and the rules herein apply to infraction or misdemeanor arrestees. Officers will also adhere to all procedures when dealing with felony arrestees, except that no prior written authorization of the supervisor is required.

H. Employees are reminded that willful violations of Penal Code Section 4030 relating to strip searches and body cavity searches by persons authorizing or conducting such searches are punishable as misdemeanors and civil actions as well punitive damages are available to a person improperly searched.

Source: Chapter 29, Procedure 1, "Use of Force," from *Standard Operating Procedure*, San Bernardino, California, Police Department (rev. December 22, 2004). Reprinted with permission.

The body cavity discussion, in particular, deserves careful attention, as this type of search enjoys a high level of Fourth Amendment protection.

Tracking Devices, Video Recordings, and Detection Devices

One of the more common types of tracking devices, known as a *beeper*, emits a signal that can be tracked by law enforcement officials. Beepers have been around for some time and are relatively crude in terms of their technology. Far more sophisticated types of devices are available nowadays, some that employ GPS technology. These newer devices have attracted little attention by the courts, but beepers have. For example, in *United States v. Knotts* (460 U.S. 276 [1983]), federal agents placed a beeper in a container of chloroform in a store without a warrant but with the consent of the store's owner. The container was later picked up, and the police tracked it to a cabin. The officers then obtained a warrant to search the cabin. The Supreme Court upheld their actions, even though they did not obtain a warrant in advance.

A key feature of *Knotts* was that the beeper led the police *to* the cabin, not inside it. When the police use beepers to track persons and items indoors, the story is different. In *United States v. Karo* (468 U.S. 705 [1984]), the police, using a beeper, tracked a suspect's movements *inside* a residence. The beeper was placed inside a can of ether. The Court ruled that this action was a violation of the Fourth Amendment.

Video recordings are another method of conducting electronic surveillance. Whether using such devices requires a warrant depends on whether the recording is of a private or a public place. With regard to private places, video recordings are usually governed, according to certain courts anyway, by Title III of the Omnibus Crime Control and Safe Streets Act of 1968, even though the act does not explicitly refer to video recorders. A key case in this area is *United States v. Torres* (751 F.2d 875 [7th Cir. 1984]). In it, the FBI obtained authorization from a judge to place cameras in so-called safehouses used by a Puerto Rican separatist group. The agents followed the guidelines set forth in Title III, and the Seventh Circuit Court of Appeals upheld their actions. Other courts, however, have held that Title III's restrictive guidelines need not apply to video recordings. Rather, they have argued that the traditional Fourth Amendment approach should be used (see, e.g., *United States v. Cuevas-Sanchez*, 821 F.2d 248 [5th Cir. 1987]).

The foregoing does not apply to video cameras in public places. Several cities throughout America use networks of strategically located video cameras to look for crime. While this may smack of Orwellian society, to date, the use of such cameras has been entirely constitutional. In a similar vein, several cities throughout the United States are using so-called red-light cameras to capture motorists who run red lights. Similar cameras are used to catch speeders, as well. While civil libertarians groan at the increased use of such cameras, they remain an effective law enforcement tool and are not considered unconstitutional.

Finally, detection devices are another method of engaging in what amounts to electronic surveillance. One of these devices, the thermal imager (infrared heat sensor), was discussed in Chapter 3. The Supreme Court decided in *Kyllo v. United States* (533 U.S. 27 [2001]) that a thermal imager cannot be used to scan a private residence without a warrant. Other types of detection devices, such as gun detectors—which can actually help police determine when persons are armed—are being developed, and some are even being used. It will be interesting to see if and when these come to the attention of the Supreme Court, as they almost certainly will.

Electronic Surveillance

The term *electronic surveillance* includes a variety of methods for spying on the activities of suspected criminals, including conversations as well as criminal actions.

The methods used to spy on criminal suspects are quite diverse and include wiretapping, "bugging," hacking into computer transmissions, tracking movements of persons and equipment, video surveillance, and seeing through opaque surfaces using devices such as thermal imagers and "gun detectors."

Electronic surveillance law is exceedingly complex and rapidly changing, so a thorough introduction is beyond the scope of this text. However, by focusing some attention on legislative developments over time, sufficient familiarity can be developed with the general contours of the law in this important area of criminal procedure. The following subsections begin by looking at early legislative requirements in the area of electronic surveillance, then move into Title III of the Omnibus Crime Control and Safe Streets Act of 1968 (and its 1986 amendments), and finally consider the PATRIOT Act, which was passed following the September 11 terrorist attacks.

Most of the law in this area, especially Title III and the PATRIOT Act, restricts government interception of private communications. Thus, the bulk of the discussion that follows concerns the use of wiretaps and similar strategies to intercept people's communications. Other types of electronic surveillance—namely, the use of tracking devices, video recorders, and detection devices—are discussed in a separate subsection, as these types of activities are governed mostly by Supreme Court decisions.

Prior to the Supreme Court's decision in *Katz v. United States* (389 U.S. 347 [1967]), the constitutionality of searches and seizures was governed by the so-called trespass doctrine (see Chapter 3). The leading case was *Olmstead v. United States* (277 U.S. 438 [1928]), in which the Court held that a warrantless wiretap was constitutional because it did not "trespass" on the defendant's property. Then, in *Goldman v. United States* (316 U.S. 129 [1942]), the Court upheld the use of a "detectaphone" placed against an office wall because it did not amount to a trespass. But in *Katz v. United States*, the Supreme Court abandoned the trespass doctrine, holding that the appropriate inquiry is whether the law enforcement action in question infringed on a person's reasonable expectation of privacy.

Following *Katz*, the Supreme Court decided *Berger v. New York* (388 U.S. 41 [1967]), in which it decided on the constitutionality of a statute that permitted eavesdropping orders to be issued by magistrates if the police showed reasonable grounds that evidence of a crime would be discovered. The Court declared the statute unconstitutional, holding that a warrant supported by probable cause is necessary to secure permission to intercept people's communications. Importantly, though, *Katz* and *Berger* do not apply to the interception of communications that can be considered consensual, such as when the government plants a listening device on an informant (see *On Lee v. United States*, 343 U.S. 747 [1952]; *Lopez v. United States*, 373 U.S. 427 [1963]).

In addition to being governed by the Supreme Court's decisions in *Olmstead*, *Katz*, and *Berger*, electronic surveillance was also subject to the restrictions in Section 605 of the **Federal Communications Act** of 1934. In it, Congress provided that "no person not being authorized by the sender shall intercept any communication and divulge or publish the existence, contents, purport, effect or meaning of such intercepted communications to any person." However, if the person whose conversation was intercepted consented to the conversation, any resulting evidence would be admissible (see *Rathbun v. United States*, 355 U.S. 107 [1957]). In summary, Supreme Court decisions and Section 605 restricted the surveillance of conversations in which the suspect did not consent to the conversation. Importantly, the suspect did not have to consent to the use of a recording device, only the conversation during which it was used.

Electronic surveillance law is rapidly changing. There are several "hoops" authorities have to jump through in order to conduct electronic surveillance of the sort depicted in this picture.

TITLE III AND THE ELECTRONIC COMMUNICATIONS PRIVACY ACT   In 1968, Congress passed **Title III of the Omnibus Crime Control and Safe Streets Act** (18 U.S.C. Sections 2510–20). Then, in 1986, Congress amended the act by passing the **Electronic Communications Privacy Act** (ECPA) (Pub. L. No. 99-508 [1986]). Both acts govern law enforcement electronic surveillance activities at both the federal and state levels. Both acts are of particular importance in the present context because they preempt state laws addressing electronic surveillance. That is, for electronic surveillance to conform to constitutional requirements, it must not only abide by state law but also by the 1968 and 1986 acts.

Title III restricts the *interception* of "wire, oral or electronic communications," unless such interception is authorized by statute (see the act for definitions of each). The 1986 amendments to the act added *electronic communications* to the list of protected activities. The amendments also covered the electronic storage and processing of information. In short, both acts protect virtually all wire, oral, and electronic communications among private parties. That is to say, for the government to intercept such information, it must obtain a valid search warrant.

In contrast to communications between private parties, communications among government employees and communications between private parties and the general public are not protected. For example, if an individual posts a message to the World Wide Web, it will not be protected in any way. Also, as discussed earlier, communications that are consensual in nature—such as between a suspect and a government informant—do not come under the protection of Title III or its amendments.

The requirements for obtaining a Title III warrant go beyond those for obtaining a typical warrant, as discussed earlier in this chapter. There are seven of them:

- The application for a Title III warrant must identify both the officer filing and the officer approving the application.
- The warrant application must contain "a full and complete statement of the facts and circumstances relied upon by the applicant to justify his belief that an order should be issued."

- The application should contain "a particular description of the nature and location of the facilities from which or the place where the communication is to be intercepted."
- The application must contain a "full and complete statement as to whether or not other investigative procedures have been tried and failed or why they reasonably appear to be unlikely to succeed if tried or to be too dangerous."
- The application must contain "a statement of the period of time for which the interception is required to be maintained," including, if deemed necessary, "a particular description of facts establishing probable cause to believe that additional communications of the same type will occur" after "the described type of communication has been first obtained."
- The warrant application must contain "a full and complete statement of the facts concerning all previous applications . . . involving any of the same persons, facilities, or places specified in the application, and the action taken by the judge on each such application."
- The warrant application must contain "a statement setting forth the results thus far obtained from the interception, or a reasonable explanation of the failure to obtain such results."

When preparing to serve a Title III warrant, authorities can covertly enter the place where the interception is to take place (see *Dalia v. United States*, 441 U.S. 238 [1979]). The entry must be reasonable and not result in excessive property damage. Indeed, too much, if any, property damage would alert that suspect that an investigation is taking place. Also, if the circumstances of the interception change during the course of the investigation, the Title III warrant will need to be amended. For example, if when listening to conversations, the police are alerted to additional criminal conduct that they would like to hear about, they must seek an amendment to the original warrant.

If all Title III requirements are not met, the remedy is suppression. That is, the exclusionary rule will apply. In fact, Title III has its own set of exclusionary rules, but they are more or less the same as the rule described in Chapter 2. For example, if a Title III warrant fails to describe with particularity the communications to be intercepted, and assuming this is called to the attention of the court, any evidence resulting from the interception will be inadmissible in court. However, if authorities make a reasonable mistake, then the "good faith" exception announced in *Leon* (468 U.S. 897 [1984]) will apply. Also, only those persons who have *standing* (i.e., who can show that the interception infringed on a reasonable expectation of privacy) can succeed in having intercepted communications excluded from trial (see *Alderman v. United States*, 394 U.S. 165 [1969]). Finally, in *United States v. Giordano* (416 U.S. 505 [1974]), the Court held that suppression of evidence is only required when the part of the act that has been violated "was intended to play a central role in the statutory scheme." In other words, trivial violations of the act will not likely result in suppression. For example, if fewer than all of the law enforcement officers involved in the investigation are identified in the warrant, then evidence will not be suppressed (see *United States v. Donovan*, 429 U.S. 413 [1977]).

THE FOREIGN INTELLIGENCE SURVEILLANCE ACT   The **Foreign Intelligence Surveillance Act** (FISA), passed in 1978, regulates electronic surveillance as it pertains to foreign intelligence gathering. In contrast, Title III and ECPA are mostly for domestic law enforcement purposes. FISA regulates a number of specific activities, including physical searches for intelligence-gathering purposes, the use of pen registers and so-called "trap-and-trace" devices, access to business records, and, of course, electronic surveillance. FISA also created the secretive **Foreign Intelligence Surveillance Court** (50 U.S.C. Section 1802[a][1][A]). The court hears requests for surveillance warrants. Before a warrant is issued, the court must find probable cause that:

- the target of the surveillance is a "foreign power" or "agent of a foreign power,"
- the places at which surveillance is sought are being used or will be used by the foreign power or agent,
- U.S. persons are properly protected (50 U.S.C Section 1805; 50 U.S.C. Section 1801[5]).

Electronic surveillance law continues to change at a feverish pace. What's more, when changes are made, they often incorporate "sunset" clauses that essentially terminate the legislation at a specified date. One example of this is the **Protect America Act**, signed into law on August 5, 2007. Among other things, the act removed the warrant requirement for government surveillance of foreign intelligence targets. A sunset clause was included partly because of the controversy surrounding the legislation, but certain provisions have since been reauthorized by the **FISA Amendments Act of 2008**. The latter is set to expire at the end of 2012.

Summary

1. OUTLINE THE COMPONENTS OF SEARCH AND ARREST WARRANTS.

A warrant has three required components: (1) a neutral and detached magistrate; (2) a showing of probable cause; and (3) particularity. A prosecutor or law enforcement official cannot be considered neutral and detached. Neither can a judge who is paid for issuing warrants. *Probable cause* was defined in Chapter 3, but in this chapter, it was pointed out that the showing of probable cause differs, depending on the type of warrant. An *arrest warrant* requires showing probable cause that the person to be arrested committed the crime. A *search warrant* requires showing probable cause that the evidence to be seized was connected with a crime *and* that it will be found in the place to be searched. Particularity in an arrest warrant is satisfied when the suspect's name or a detailed description of the person is given. Particularity in a search warrant is satisfied when the place to be searched and the item or items to be seized are described in detail.

2. DESCRIBE HOW SEARCH AND ARREST WARRANTS ARE EXECUTED.

Arrest warrants are required in two situations: (1) arrests in the home and (2) arrests in third-party homes. Arrests in public do not require warrants. Similarly, arrests in the presence of exigent circumstances do not require warrants, regardless of location. The police are required to announce their presence during the execution of a search warrant unless exigent circumstances are present.

The police will generally not be liable for property damage during the service of a warrant; however, due process can be violated if the property damage is excessive. Deadly force can be used to effect an arrest, but only when the suspect seeks to escape and poses a significant threat to other officers or citizens. Finally, the courts will admit evidence resulting from a wrongful arrest, as long as the mistake was a reasonable one.

Searches with warrants are subject to many of the same restrictions as *arrests* with warrants. However, search warrants are also constrained in terms of time, insofar as the police cannot wait too long to serve the warrant or take too long to look for evidence. Also, the courts frequently require that search warrants be served during daylight hours. The scope of the search must be limited to the object of the search, the seized evidence must be inventoried and a list given to the homeowner, and the police cannot bring members of the media along when serving a search warrant if the media presence serves no legitimate law enforcement objectives.

3. EXPLAIN HOW BODILY INTRUSIONS, THE USE OF TRACKING DEVICES, AND ELECTRONIC SURVEILLANCE CREATE "SPECIAL CIRCUMSTANCES" FOR FOURTH AMENDMENT PURPOSES.

The traditional Fourth Amendment approach to determining constitutionality does not always work in the case of bodily intrusions or when tracking devices, video recordings, or detection devices are used. Additionally, the interception of communications, in particular, is governed by a restrictive body of law (e.g., Title III of the Omnibus Crime Control and Safe Streets Act of 1968).

Key Terms

Key Cases

Warrant Components

- *Coolidge v. New Hampshire*, 403 U.S. 443 (1971)
- *Lo-Ji Sales, Inc. v. New York*, 442 U.S. 319 (1979)
- *Maryland v. Garrison*, 480 U.S. 79 (1987)
- *Andresen v. Maryland*, 427 U.S. 463 (1976)

Arrests with Warrants

- *Davis v. Mississippi*, 394 U.S. 721 (1969)
- *Payton v. New York*, 445 U.S. 573 (1980)
- *Steagald v. United States*, 451 U.S. 204 (1981)

- *Hudson v. Michigan*, 547 U.S. 586 (2006)
- *Sabbath v. United States*, 391 U.S. 585 (1968)
- *Tennessee v. Garner*, 471 U.S. 1 (1985)
- *Graham v. Connor*, 490 U.S. 386 (1989)

Searches with Warrants

- *Gooding v. United States*, 416 U.S. 430 (1974)
- *Harris v. United States*, 331 U.S. 145 (1947)
- *Michigan v. Summers*, 452 U.S. 692 (1981)
- *City of West Covina v. Perkins*, 525 U.S. 234 (1999)
- *Wilson v. Layne*, 526 U.S. 603 (1999)

Review Questions

1. Explain the three components of a valid warrant.
2. How does the showing of probable cause differ for an arrest warrant versus a search warrant?
3. How does particularity differ for an arrest warrant versus a search warrant?
4. Distinguish between a stop and an arrest.
5. Distinguish between a stop and a nonstop.
6. When is an arrest warrant required?
7. What reasons have been offered for the so-called announcement requirement with regard to arrest and search warrants?
8. When can the announcement requirement be dispensed with?
9. Briefly summarize the Supreme Court's view on property damage during the service of a warrant.
10. Summarize the Supreme Court's decisions in *Tennessee v. Garner* and *Graham v. Connor*. Why are these decisions important to criminal procedure?
11. What restrictions exist concerning the scope and manner of a search with a warrant?
12. What is the Supreme Court's view on the media's presence during the service of a search warrant? What is the leading case in this area?
13. Explain the two leading cases that address bodily intrusion during the course of a search.
14. What are the main statutes regulating electronic surveillance?

Web Links and Exercises

1. Developing a policy manual: Read Chief W. Dwayne Orrick's article "Developing a Police Department Policy-Procedure Manual," published in the International Association of Chiefs of Police *Big Ideas for Smaller Police Departments* newsletter. What, according to him, is the best way to develop a policy-procedure manual? What role do court recommendations play in his recommendations? You can find the article on page 4 here: http://www.theiacp.org/LinkClick.aspx?fileticket=On6JRot3kSc%3d&tabid=392 (accessed February 16, 2011).

2. Foreign Intelligence Surveillance Act: Read about recent developments in FISA. What activities has the FISA Court reported to Congress?

Suggested URL: http://www.fas.org/irp/agency/doj/fisa (accessed February 16, 2011).

3. Knock and announce: Read more about the knock-and-announce rule at the Federal Law Enforcement Training Center's website. Summarize the federal knock-and-announce rule. Is federal procedure different from state and local procedure?

Suggested URL: http://www.fletc.gov/training/programs/legal-division/the-informer/research-by-subject/4th-amendment/knockandannounce.pdf/view (accessed April 6, 2011).

LEARNING OBJECTIVES

When you complete this chapter, you should be able to:

▶ Summarize the issues involved in warrantless searches and seizures.

▶ Explain the search incident to arrest doctrine.

▶ Explain the concept of hot pursuit.

▶ Summarize the special issues involved in automobile searches.

▶ Summarize the plain view doctrine.

▶ Describe the situations in which warrantless arrests may be made.

Searches and Arrests without Warrants

INTRODUCTION

Moving beyond the Warrant Requirement

If it was not for exceptions to the warrant requirement, the Fourth Amendment would take substantially less effort to understand. At the same time, however, the many exceptions to the Fourth Amendment's warrant requirement are what make the Fourth Amendment interesting. The so-called warrantless searches and seizures discussed in this chapter are based on Supreme Court decisions, in which it was believed that to require a warrant would constitute an undue burden on law enforcement officials. Still, though, a warrant is *always* preferable; whenever circumstances permit, one should be obtained.

The exceptions to the Fourth Amendment's warrant requirement considered in this chapter are those requiring probable cause. This chapter's first main section covers warrantless searches, but warrantless arrests are also considered. There are other exceptions to the warrant requirement that do not require probable cause; they are discussed in the next two chapters. Chapter 6 examines the law of stop-and-frisk, and Chapter 7 looks at searches and seizures based on administrative justification as well as consent.

WARRANTLESS SEARCHES

Broadly, there are four types of warrantless searches that require probable cause. They are called **exceptions to the warrant requirement** because the actions at issue do not need to be supported by a search warrant. The four types of warrantless searches are (1) searches incident to (i.e., following) arrest; (2) searches in the presence of exigent circumstances; (3) searches involving automobiles; and (4) searches based on the "plain view" doctrine. Other warrantless searches exist, such as consent searches, but they do not require probable cause. One may be inclined to put "frisks" in the warrantless search category, but they are not technically "searches." Consent, frisks, and other warrantless actions that require *less* than probable cause are taken up in the next two chapters.

Searches Incident to Arrest

Imagine a situation in which a police officer has lawfully (i.e., with probable cause) arrested a suspect, is leading him away, and observes the suspect reach into his pocket. What would be going through the police officer's mind as he or she observed this behavior? Scenarios like this illustrate the reasoning behind the **search incident to arrest** exception. Namely, police officers must be permitted to engage in a search of a suspect incident to arrest (i.e., following an arrest). It would be impractical, even dangerous, to wait for a warrant before conducting such a search.

Chimel v. California
(395 U.S. 752 [1969])

The leading case in the area of incident searches is *Chimel v. California* (395 U.S. 752 [1969]). As the Supreme Court stated, a search incident to arrest is permitted "to remove any weapons that the [arrestee] might seek to use in order to resist arrest or effect his escape" and to "seize any evidence on the arrestee's person in order to prevent its concealment or destruction" (p. 763).

RESTRICTIONS   The most basic requirement concerning searches incident to arrest—and one that often goes overlooked—is that the arrest must be lawful. When the arrest itself is not lawful (i.e., when it is not based on probable cause), any search that follows is unlawful (see *Draper v. United States*, 358 U.S. 307 [1959]).

Another important threshold issue with regard to searches incident to arrest concerns the nature of the offense. Courts have grappled with the question as to whether a search should be permitted when the offense on which the arrest is based is not serious. Because the rationale of the exception is to provide officer safety, then is officer safety likely to be compromised when a minor offense, as opposed to a serious offense, justifies the arrest?

Two important Supreme Court cases have sought to answer these questions. First, in *United States v. Robinson* (414 U.S. 218 [1973]), the Court reversed a lower court's decision that only a patdown of the suspect's outer clothing was permissible following an arrest for driving with a revoked license. And in a companion case to *Robinson*, *Gustafson v. Florida* (414 U.S. 260 [1973]), the Court upheld the search of a suspect after his arrest for failure to have his driver's license.

The Supreme Court offered two reasons for its opinions in *Robinson* and *Gustafson*. First, according to Chief Justice Rehnquist, "It is scarcely open to doubt that the danger to an officer is far greater in the case of the extended exposure which follows the taking of a suspect into custody and transporting him to the police station than in the case of the relatively fleeting contact resulting from the typical

Terry-stop" (*United States v. Robinson*, p. 234). Second, the Court believed a bright-line rule was in order given the stakes involved (i.e., officer safety): "A police officer's determination as to how and where to search the person of a suspect whom he has arrested is necessarily a quick *ad hoc* judgment which the Fourth Amendment does not require to be broken down in each instance into an analysis of each step in the search" (p. 235).

Thus, *any* arrest justifies a warrantless search incident to that arrest. A key restriction, however, is that the arrest must result in a person being *taken into custody*. This was the ruling from *Knowles v. Iowa* (525 U.S. 113 [1998]). In that case, a police officer stopped a person for speeding, and rather than arresting him (which the officer had justification to do), the officer issued him a citation. Then, the officer conducted a search of the car and found a marijuana pipe. The Court noted that traffic stops rarely pose the same threat to officer safety as arrests. This is not to suggest, however, that police officers cannot search people incident to lawful arrest for minor vehicle-related infractions. If the authority to arrest is present, an incident search is permissible. The key restriction is that the person must actually be arrested and taken into custody. Otherwise, the search will not conform with Fourth Amendment requirements.

Knowles v. Iowa
(525 U.S. 113 [1998])

TIMING OF THE SEARCH   Another key restriction pertaining to searches incident to arrest has to do with the timing of the search. In particular, probable cause to arrest must *precede* the warrantless search (*Sibron v. New York*, 392 U.S. 40 [1968]). The reason for this is to restrict officers from engaging in "fishing expeditions," or searches based on less than probable cause that would presumably result in probable cause to make an arrest. Note, however, that if probable cause to arrest is in place, the officer is not required to formally arrest the suspect before engaging in the search (see *Rawlings v. Kentucky*, 448 U.S. 98 [1980]).

Preston v. United States
(376 U.S. 364 [1964])

If the search follows an arrest, then it must take place *soon* after the arrest. In legal parlance, the search must be *contemporaneous* to the arrest. In *Preston v. United States* (376 U.S. 364 [1964]), the case that established this rule, Justice Black observed that the "justifications [for the search incident to arrest] are absent where a search is remote in time or place from the arrest" (p. 367). In *Preston*, police officers arrested the occupants of a car and took them to jail. After this, the officers searched the car, which had been towed to an impound lot. The Supreme Court noted that the possibilities of destruction of evidence and danger to the officers were no longer in place, as the suspects were no longer even present (see also *Chambers v. Maroney*, 399 U.S. 42 [1970]).

Note that while a noncontemporaneous search is not justified under the search incident to arrest exception, it is authorized under the automobile exception discussed later. Also, the Supreme Court authorizes inventory searches of automobiles that have been lawfully impounded. Inventory searches are discussed later, as well.

There is one significant exception to the contemporaneousness requirement. In *United States v. Edwards* (415 U.S. 800 [1974]), the Supreme Court, in a 5 to 4 decision, upheld the warrantless search and seizure of an arrestee's clothing 10 hours after his arrest, during which time he was in jail. The Court noted that "searches and seizures that could be made on the spot at the time of arrest may legally be conducted later when the accused arrives at the place of detention" (p. 803). The Court did point out, however, that the taking of the individual's clothing at the time of the arrest would have been impractical because it "was late at night[,] no substitute clothing was then available for Edwards to wear, and it would certainly have been unreasonable for the police to have stripped respondent of his clothing and left him exposed in his cell throughout the night" (p. 805). Thus, the *Edwards* decision established the rule that a noncontemporaneous search incident to arrest is permissible when (1) an immediate search is nearly impossible and (2) the exigency still exists at the time of the later search.

SCOPE OF THE SEARCH   The case of *United States v. Rabinowitz* (339 U.S. 56 [1950]) was the first to set limits on the scope of a search incident to arrest. In that case, the officers, armed with a valid arrest warrant, arrested a man and then conducted a warrantless search of his one-room business, including the desk, safe, and file cabinets. The Supreme Court upheld the search because the room "was small and under the immediate and complete control of the respondent" (p. 64).

Nearly 20 years after *Rabinowitz*, however, the Supreme Court voted to overturn its earlier decision. In the case of *Chimel v. California*, the Court argued that the *Rabinowitz* decision had been construed to mean that "a warrantless search 'incident to a lawful arrest' may generally extend to the area that is considered to be in the 'possession' or under the 'control' of the person arrested" (p. 759). Further, the Court noted that the *Rabinowitz* standard gave police "the opportunity to engage in searches not justified by probable cause, [but] by the simple expedient of arranging to arrest suspects at home rather than elsewhere" (p. 767). To get around this problem, Justice Stewart argued in favor of a new **armspan rule**. In the Court's words, a search incident to arrest would now be limited to the area "within [the] immediate control" of the person arrested—that is, "the area from within which he might have obtained either a weapon or something that could have been used as evidence against him" (p. 768).

An interesting twist on the aforementioned cases can be found in *Washington v. Chrisman* (455 U.S. 1 [1982]). In that case, an officer stopped a student on suspicion of drinking under age, an action that the Court considered an arrest. The officer asked the student for his identification and followed him to his dorm room, where the student's identification was presumably located. While at the student's room, the officer observed in plain view marijuana and drug paraphernalia. The officer seized the evidence. The Supreme Court upheld the seizure of the evidence, stating that "[e]very arrest must be presumed to present a risk of danger to the arresting officer. . . . Moreover, the possibility that an arrested person will attempt to escape if not properly supervised is obvious" (p. 7). Thus, "it is not unreasonable, under the Fourth Amendment for an officer, as a matter of routine, to monitor the movements of an arrested person, as his judgment dictates, following the arrest" (p. 7).

The cases discussed thus far have focused narrowly on the scope of the incident search exception with reference to the arrestee. What if another person *besides* the arrestee poses a threat to the police? This concern has led to several exceptions to the armspan rule.

First, in *Maryland v. Buie* (494 U.S. 325 [1990]), the Supreme Court expanded the scope of the incident search in two ways. It held that the police may, as part of a search incident to arrest, look in areas immediately adjoining the place of arrest for other persons who might attack the officers; no justification is required. The key, however, is that

DECISION-MAKING EXERCISE 5.1
Timing of a Search Incident to Arrest

A locked suitcase was transported by police officers to the police station, after having been lawfully seized from the open trunk of a parked automobile during the arrests of those who were in its possession. After being back at the police station for over an hour, the officers opened the suitcase. They acted without a search warrant and without the consent of the arrested persons, but they did have probable cause to believe that the container held contraband. In fact, the suitcase contained large amounts of marijuana. Can this be considered a valid search incident to arrest?

such a search must occur incident to arrest. Next, the Court held that at any point up to the time the arrest is completed, the police may engage in a **protective sweep** (i.e., "a cursory visual inspection of those places in which a person might be hiding"), but reasonable suspicion must exist for such a sweep to be justified. Thus, no justification is required *after* arrest, but reasonable suspicion is required to engage in a sweep up to the point of the arrest.

Aside from the possible danger to police officers from "confederates," there is the potential for such third parties to engage in the destruction of evidence. Only one Supreme Court case appears to address this issue: *Vale v. Louisiana* (399 U.S. 30 [1970]). In that case, police officers had warrants authorizing the arrest of the defendant. While engaged in surveillance of the house, the officers observed the defendant come out of the house and engage in what appeared to be a drug sale. They arrested the defendant outside the home but then went back inside and searched it, according to the officers, because two of the defendant's relatives had arrived at the house in the meantime and could have destroyed evidence. *Vale* was actually a case concerning exigent circumstances (see later in this chapter), and the Court reversed the Louisiana Supreme Court's decision that upheld the search. But, in fact, the Court's opinion was not particularly instructive. It stated, in relevant part, that "no reason, so far as anything before us appears, to suppose that it was impracticable for [the officers] to obtain a search warrant as well" (p. 35), but it did not expressly state that related searches would always be unconstitutional. Indeed, several lower courts have upheld warrantless searches of homes for evidence after arrest on less than probable cause (e.g., *United States v. Hoyos*, 892 F.2d 1387 [9th Cir.1989]; *United States v. Rubin*, 474 F.2d 262 [3rd Cir. 1973]).

Another type of warrantless search of a house following a lawful arrest has been authorized based on the need to secure the premises, usually pending the procural of a search warrant. Thus, if the police believe another person or persons are in the house and could potentially destroy evidence, the house may be secured but not searched until a warrant has been obtained. This was the decision reached in *Segura v. United States* (468 U.S. 796 [1984]). In that case, the Supreme Court, in another 5 to 4 decision, declared "that where officers, having probable cause, enter premises . . . , arrest the occupants . . . and take them into custody and, for no more than the period here involved [19 hours in this case], secure the premises from within to preserve the status quo while others, in good faith, are in the process of obtaining a warrant, they do not violate the Fourth Amendment's proscription against unreasonable seizures" (p. 798).

It is appropriate at this juncture to note that the Court has authorized the police to rely on the incident search exception to engage in searches well beyond the arrestee's armspan—and when no threat exists from people sympathetic to the arrestee. In particular, the Supreme Court has held that officers may engage in a warrantless, suspicionless search of a car and containers within it following the lawful arrest of the car's driver (*New York v. Belton*, 453 U.S. 454 [1981]) but "only if it is reasonable to believe that the arrestee might access the vehicle at the time of the search or that the vehicle contains evidence of the offense" in question (*Arizona v. Gant*, No. 07-542 [2009]). This issue is discussed at greater length later in this chapter in the section "Automobile Searches."

Summary.   A search incident to arrest may be conducted without a warrant, but it is subject to four restrictions. First, the arrest must be based on probable cause and result in custodial detention. Second, the search must follow the arrest closely in time (i.e., be contemporaneous). Third, the police must limit their search to (1) the person arrested and any containers discovered from that search; (2) the arrestee's immediate grabbing area; (3) a protective sweep of the premises without justification following an arrest but with reasonable suspicion leading up to the arrest; and/or (4) securing

FIGURE 5.1

Permissible Scope of a Search Incident to Arrest (assuming a valid arrest)

Level of Intrusion	Justification Required
Search of arrestee	None
Search of arrestee's grabbing area	None
Protective sweep	Reasonable suspicion that confederates are present
Secure residence	Reasonable suspicion to fear destruction of evidence

the premises, if they have a reasonable belief that evidence may be destroyed by someone sympathetic to the arrestee (see Figure 5.1). Finally, the premises to be searched can be secured prior to procural of a warrant, but reasonable suspicion is required. Figure 5.2 presents the Gallatin, Tennessee, Police Department's policy for a search incident to arrest.

FIGURE 5.2

Search Incident to Arrest Policy (Gallatin, TN, Police Department)

9.7.2 Incident to Arrest

When an officer places a person under arrest, the officer will conduct a thorough search of the person and the area in his/her immediate reach. All items on the person of the subject will be removed and secured by the officer. The search of the immediate reach of the subject is intended to disclose weapons and any possible evidence. If these kinds of items are found, they may also be secured by the officer and placed into evidence.

A search incident to arrest will be conducted only after the subject has been placed in restraints (i.e., handcuffs). Whenever possible, the search will be conducted by two officers, one conducting the search, the other providing cover. The search should begin in the immediate area around the subject's hands, including an inspection of the subject's waistband. The officer should then search the subject methodically by searching one-half of the subject's body from head to foot and then returning to the top of the head and search the other side of the subject's body in the same manner. Only by searching a subject in such a methodical manner will an officer ensure his/her safety in knowing that the subject is not in possession of any weapons.

This method for searching an individual incident to an arrest is only offered as one way to search a subject. Under no circumstances is this method considered as the only option an officer has in searching a subject; however, it is a method that has been demonstrated to be effective when used consistently. Any method is acceptable as long as the search is thorough, complete, and effective in discovering weapons and evidence that are occasionally concealed on a subject's person.

Source: From *General Directives Manual*, Gallatin, Tennessee, Police Department (December 28, 1999). Used courtesy of the Gallatin Police Department.

DECISION-MAKING EXERCISE 5.2

Proper Scope for a Search Incident to Arrest

Two police officers arrived at Bobby Sheen's house with a valid warrant for his arrest. The officers were informed by a nosy neighbor that two of Sheen's accomplices were in the house with him. The officers knocked, announced their presence, and entered the house. They encountered Sheen as he was descending the stairs. He was placed under arrest. Immediately after the arrest, one of the officers went upstairs and found drug paraphernalia on a nightstand. May this evidence be lawfully seized? What if the drug paraphernalia had been found in a drawer instead?

Searches Based on Exigent Circumstances

As indicated earlier, the exceptions to the search warrant requirement are premised on the impracticality of obtaining a warrant. Perhaps no exception illustrates this better than the **exigent circumstances** exception. Simply put, when the exigencies, or emergencies, of the situation require the police to act immediately at the risk of danger to themselves, danger to others, the destruction of evidence, or the escape of the suspect, it would be unreasonable to require the police to take time to obtain a warrant.

Generally, three types of exigencies are recognized by the courts as authorizing the police to act without a warrant: (1) hot pursuit; (2) likelihood of escape or danger to others absent hot pursuit; and (3) evanescent evidence. Despite the fact that these exceptions allow the police to act without a warrant, probable cause is still required. For example, probable cause that the person being pursued is the suspect is required before the police can enter a home or building without a warrant to arrest him or her.

HOT PURSUIT   The Supreme Court first recognized the **hot pursuit** exception in the case of *Warden v. Hayden* (387 U.S. 294 [1967]), in which the police were called by taxicab drivers who reported that their taxi company had been robbed. The police followed the suspect to a house, where they were granted entry by the suspect's wife. The suspect was upstairs in the house, pretending to be asleep. While searching the house for the suspect, the police found and seized clothing, a shotgun, and a pistol, all of which were used against the suspect at trial. The Court found the warrantless entry reasonable because the "exigencies of the situation made that course imperative" (p. 298). Several reasons were offered for the decision. First, Justice Brennan stated that "[t]he Fourth Amendment does not require police officers to delay in the course of an investigation if to do so would gravely danger their lives or the lives of others" (pp. 298–299). Also, "[s]peed . . . was essential, and only a thorough search of the house for persons and weapons could have insured that Hayden was the only man present and that the police had control of all weapons which could be used against them or to effect an escape" (p. 299). Despite the sweeping language from the *Hayden* decision, the Supreme Court has imposed five restrictions on searches and seizures premised on hot pursuit.

Warden v. Hayden
(387 U.S. 294 [1967])

- Hot pursuit permits warrantless entry only when, first, the police have probable cause to believe that the person they are chasing has committed a crime and is on the premises entered.
- The police are also required to have reason to believe the suspect will escape or that further harm, either to evidence or to other people, will occur if the suspect is not immediately apprehended. With regard to this second restriction, one court has observed that "[a] hot pursuit, by itself, creates no necessity for dispensing with a warrant" (*State v. Wren*, 115 Idaho 618 [1989], p. 625). Similarly, the Ninth Circuit has stated that police officers must reasonably believe (1) "that the suspect either know[s] or will learn at any moment that they are in immediate

danger of apprehension"; (2) that "evidence is being currently removed or destroyed and it is impractical to advert the situation without immediately arresting the suspects or seizing the evidence"; or (3) that "a suspect is currently endangering the lives of themselves or others" (*United States v. George*, 883 F.2d 1407 [9th Cir. 1989]).

- Although it often goes without saying, the police must begin hot pursuit from a lawful starting point. If, for example, officers are unlawfully on someone's private property, they will not succeed in claiming hot pursuit to justify any further warrantless action. However, in *United States v. Santana* (427 U.S. 38 [1976]), the Supreme Court upheld the warrantless arrest of a woman in her house when the police *observed* a crime on private property from a public vantage point. In that case, police officers observed Santana standing in the open doorway of her house with a brown paper bag, which they had probable cause to believe contained narcotics. They pursued her into the house and arrested her. This decision suggests that the police can pursue from a public vantage point a suspect whom they observe on private property.

Welsh v. Wisconsin
(466 U.S. 740 [1984])

- The hot pursuit doctrine applies only to serious offenses, including felonies and some misdemeanors (see, e.g., *Welsh v. Wisconsin*, 466 U.S. 740 [1984]). This restriction on the hot pursuit doctrine—and, indeed, on exigent circumstance searches in general—is perhaps the most important one. As such, it is treated in a section by itself later.

- Generally, the scope of a search based on hot pursuit is broad. In *Hayden*, for example, the Supreme Court stated, "The permissible scope of search must, at the least, be as broad as may reasonably be necessary to prevent the dangers that the suspect at large in the house may resist or escape" (*Warden v. Hayden*, p. 299). However, the search must be "prior to or immediately contemporaneous with" the arrest of the suspect. Also, officers may only search where the suspect or weapons might reasonably be found. A simple rule of thumb, then, is that the nature of the exigency defines the scope of the search. Another rule of thumb with regard to hot pursuit is that if the police have a reasonable amount of time to obtain a warrant, they should always do so. In *Welsh*, for example, Justice Brennan argued that the government's "claim of hot pursuit . . . [was] . . . unconvincing because there was no immediate or continuous pursuit of the petitioner from the scene of [the] crime" (*Welsh v. Wisconsin*, p. 753).

ESCAPE AND ENDANGERMENT TO OTHERS ABSENT HOT PURSUIT Hot pursuit is justified, as just discussed, when, among other things, the suspect may escape or inflict harm on police officers or others. In some situations, however, a suspect can potentially escape or inflict harm absent hot pursuit. In *Minnesota v. Olson* (495 U.S. 91 [1990]), for example, the prosecution sought to justify a warrantless entry and arrest of a suspect in a duplex that the police had surrounded. There was probable cause to believe that Olson, the man in the duplex, had been the driver of a getaway car involved in a robbery/murder the day before. The Supreme Court ruled that the officers acted unconstitutionally under the circumstances because Olson was only the driver, not the murder suspect, and the weapon had been recovered, which diminished the urgency of the situation. In addition, it was unlikely Olson would escape because the building was surrounded. On its face, then, this case is not useful on this point. However, the Court seemed to suggest that had Olson *not* been the driver (i.e., had been the murderer), had the weapon *not* been recovered, and had the building *not* been fully surrounded, the warrantless action would have been lawful.

Minnesota v. Olson
(495 U.S. 91 [1990])

A more recent case, *Brigham City v. Stuart* (547 U.S. 398 [2006]) brought clarification. In that case, police were called to a house that received complaints about a loud party. On arriving at the scene, officers witnessed a fight involving four adults and one

DECISION-MAKING EXERCISE 5.3

Are Exigent Circumstances Present?

An officer attempted to stop a man for speeding 73 miles per hour in a 55-mile-per-hour zone. Instead of stopping, the man sped away and led the officer (and others who quickly joined) on a high-speed pursuit down two-lane roads at speeds of nearly 90 miles per hour. After several unsuccessful attempts to stop the fleeing car, one of the pursuing officers deliberately rammed the fleeing suspect's car, causing it to crash. The suspect was severely injured and rendered quadriplegic. Now he is suing under Section 1983 (see Chapter 2), alleging that the officer who rammed his car used excessive force to effect an unreasonable seizure under the Fourth Amendment. Should his lawsuit go forward?

juvenile. One of the adults hit the juvenile. The officers announced their presence, but they couldn't be heard above the commotion inside, so they entered without a warrant. In a unanimous decision, the Supreme Court held that such warrantless entries are constitutionally permissible so long as the police have an objectively reasonable basis to believe the occupant is "seriously injured or threatened with such injury."

EVANESCENT EVIDENCE In situations in which the search incident to arrest or hot pursuit exceptions do not apply, the Court has recognized an additional exception to the warrant required, one that permits warrantless searches for **evanescent evidence** (i.e., disappearing evidence). This can include evidence inside a person, as well as a house, a paper, or an effect.

The best example of vanishing or disappearing evidence inside a person is alcohol in the blood. In *Breithaupt v. Abram* (352 U.S. 432 [1957]), the Court upheld the warrantless intrusion (via a needle) into a man's body for the purpose of drawing blood to see if he had been drinking. The key in this case, however, was that medical personnel had conducted a *routine* blood test. The majority noted "that the indiscriminate taking of blood under different conditions or by those not competent to do so" (p. 438) would not be allowed. (Indeed, this is why *Breithaupt v. Abram* is an isolated case; police officers rarely, if ever, draw blood from suspects. Breathalyzers usually provide sufficient evidence of intoxication.)

Breithaupt v. Abram (352 U.S. 432 [1957])

The *Breithaupt* decision also established that warrantless searches for evanescent evidence are permissible only when (1) there is no time to obtain a warrant; (2) there is a "clear indication" that the search will result in obtaining the evidence sought; and (3) the search is conducted in a "reasonable manner." In support of the reasonable manner requirement, the Court offered the following from a later decision, *Schmerber v. California* (384 U.S. 757 [1966]):

> The interests in human dignity and privacy which the Fourth Amendment protects forbid any such intrusions on the mere chance that desired evidence might be obtained. In the absence of a clear indication that in fact such evidence will be found, these fundamental human interest require law officers to suffer the risk that such evidence may disappear unless there is an immediate search. (pp. 769–770)

In *Rochin v. California* (342 U.S. 165 [1952]), a case in which the *police* used a stomach pump to obtain evidence from a man's stomach, the Court declared that a due process violation occurred and that the officers' conduct shocked the conscience. The reason was that the police, not medical personnel, extracted the evidence. Another view is that the use of a stomach pump falls somewhat short of a routine medical procedure.

As for the clear indication requirement, the Court has been somewhat flexible. For example, in *United States v. Montoya de Hernandez* (469 U.S. 1204 [1985]), the Court treated the clear indication requirement from *Breithaupt* as being identical to the reasonable suspicion standard set forth in *Terry v. Ohio.* This case involved the detention for several hours of a woman who was suspected of smuggling narcotics in her alimentary canal.

Finally, it is important to remember that, like the hot pursuit exception, the exigency used to justify a warrantless search for evanescent evidence must be immediate. In other words, there must be good reason to believe that an immediate search will result in the seizure of the evidence in question. An example is *Cupp v. Murphy* (412 U.S. 291 [1973]). In that case, a man who had been informed of his wife's strangulation volunteered to come to the police station for questioning. While he was at the station, officers observed what appeared to be dried blood on the man's fingernails. The officers asked if they could take a scraping from his fingernails, and the man refused. He then started rubbing his hands behind his back and placing them in his pockets. At that point, the officers forcibly removed some of the material from under the man's fingernails. The Court upheld this action on the grounds that the police had probable cause to believe that "highly evanescent evidence" was in the process of being destroyed.

Cupp v. Murphy
(412 U.S. 291 [1973])

Recently, in *Kentucky v. King* (No. 09-1272 [2011]), the Supreme Court held that police can make a forcible warrantless entry into a private residence if they have reason to believe evidence is being destroyed. In that case, officers smelled marijuana outside an apartment, knocked loudly, and announced their presence. They then heard what they believed was the sound of evidence being destroyed. They announced their intent to enter, kicked in the door, and found drugs in plain view—and other evidence during the course of a protective sweep. The Supreme Court ruled that the evidence was admissible.

In certain rare situations, the police may have reason to suspect that evidence may be lost or destroyed not because of the actions of a person (the suspect or the suspect's confederates) but because of other causes. In *United States v. Chadwick* (433 U.S. 1 [1977]), for example, the Supreme Court noted that a warrant would not be required to search a footlocker if the officers believed that it contained evidence that would lose its value unless the footlocker were opened at once or if the officers had reason to believe that the footlocker contained explosives or other inherently dangerous items.

The American Law Institute's Code of Pre-Arraignment Procedure summarizes the law concerning exigencies. Section 206.5 of the code provides that warrantless entries based on reasonable cause are permissible when (1) individuals are in imminent danger of death or serious bodily harm; (2) items are present that are imminently likely

DECISION-MAKING EXERCISE 5.4

Immediacy and Evanescent Evidence

A motor home that federal drug agents believed to contain a methamphetamine laboratory was parked in a secluded area near a river. The agents maintained visual surveillance throughout the afternoon. Around 4 p.m., one of the agents smelled chemicals "cooking." Shortly after that, the agents observed a man dash out of the motor home, gasping for air. In light of this incident, the agents decided to search the motor home. They ordered all of the occupants out of the motor home and placed them under arrest. The agents then entered the motor home to see if any other people were inside, to turn off any cooking apparatus, and to inventory the contents. They found a methamphetamine laboratory behind a drawn curtain at the back of the motor home. Was this action justified?

to burn, explode, or otherwise cause death, serious bodily harm, or destruction of property; and/or (3) items subject to seizure are present that will cause or be used to cause death or serious bodily injury if not immediately seized.

OFFENSE SERIOUSNESS AND EXIGENT CIRCUMSTANCES   The Supreme Court has also noted that the *seriousness* of the offense for which the warrantless arrest is to be made may be relevant in determining whether exigent circumstances are present. For example, in *Welsh v. Wisconsin*, a witness one night reported that an automobile was being driven erratically. Eventually, the car swerved off the road and stopped in a field. The driver walked away before police could arrive at the scene. When they did arrive, the police checked the registration of the car and found out it belonged to Welsh. They went to Welsh's house, gained entry, and arrested Welsh without a warrant. The Supreme Court held that the warrantless nighttime entry of a suspect's home to make an arrest for a *nonjailable* offense is a violation of the Fourth Amendment:

> Before government agents may invade the sanctity of the home, it must demonstrate exigent circumstances that overcome the presumption of unreasonableness that attaches to all warrantless home entries. An important factor to be considered when determining whether any exigency exists is the gravity of the underlying offense for which the arrest is being made . . . [A]pplication of the exigent circumstances exception in the context of home entry should rarely be sanctioned when there is probable cause that only a minor offense has been committed. (p.750)

The majority also cited another case, *McDonald v. United States* (335 U.S. 451 [1948]), in its decision: "When an officer undertakes to act as his own magistrate, he ought to be in a position to justify it by pointing to some real immediate and serious consequences if he postponed action to get a warrant" (p. 460).

Welsh is controversial for at least two reasons. First, it is not always clear what constitutes a minor offense. The Court declared that warrantless entry to make an arrest for drunk driving is in violation of the Fourth Amendment, even though drunk driving is considered a serious offense in every state of the union. Second, although the Court did not say so, it implied that warrants are *not* required for warrantless home arrests in serious cases. The D.C. Circuit's opinion in *Dorman v. United States* (435 F.2d 385 [D.C. Cir. 1970]) highlighted seven factors that may permit warrantless entry, only one of which is an exigency discussed thus far:

- The offense is serious.
- The suspect is believed to be armed.
- The police have a high degree of probable cause for arrest.
- There is an especially strong reason to believe the suspect is on the premises.
- Escape is likely.
- The entry can be made peaceably.
- The entry can be made during the day.

Various lower courts have applied these criteria in their decisions (e.g., *United States v. Reed*, 572 F.2d 412 [2nd Cir. 1978]; *State v. Gregory*, 331 N.W.2d 140 [Iowa 1983]), but it is doubtful that the Supreme Court would uphold any one of the criteria besides the fifth and possibly the second.

Summary.   The common types of exigent circumstances recognized by the courts include hot pursuit, threats to persons, and threats to evidence. Warrantless action

DECISION-MAKING EXERCISE 5.5

Exigent Circumstances and the Severity of the Offense

Brian Corman was suspected of burglarizing an apartment while no one was home and stealing a checkbook and a television. But apparently, someone in the apartment complex witnessed Corman leaving the victim's unit and called the police. Officers responded and confronted Corman at the door to his apartment, which was in the same building. Without a warrant, the officers then entered Corman's apartment, searched it, found the items stolen in the burglary, and arrested him. Are these actions constitutionally valid?

based on a hot pursuit exigency is constitutional only if the police have probable cause to believe any of the following:

- The person they are pursuing has committed a serious offense.
- The person will be found on the premises the police seek to enter.
- The suspect will escape or harm someone or evidence will be lost or destroyed.
- The pursuit originates from a lawful vantage point.
- The scope and timing of the search are reasonable.

In situations in which the hot pursuit exception does not apply (and, presumably, the automobile and search incident to arrest exceptions do not apply), a warrantless search for evanescent evidence is permissible when (1) there is probable cause to believe that evidence will be destroyed, lost, or devalued; (2) the procedures employed are reasonable; and (3) the exigency was not police created. A broad interpretation of the latter condition suggests that the same applies in the case of hot pursuit, but the Supreme Court has not ruled on the problem of police-created exigencies. Also, a warrantless search is permissible absent hot pursuit or the potential for damage or destruction to evidence if probable cause exists to believe a person on the premises is in imminent danger of death or serious bodily harm.

Automobile Searches

Carroll v. United States
(267 U.S. 132 [1925])

In the landmark case of *Carroll v. United States* (267 U.S. 132 [1925]), the Supreme Court carved out an **automobile exception** to the Fourth Amendment's warrant requirement. The Court declared that the warrantless search of an automobile is permissible when (1) there is probable cause to believe the vehicle contains evidence of a crime and (2) securing a warrant is impractical. *Carroll*, which was decided in 1925, resulted from the vehicle stop of a suspect who was known to have previously engaged in the sale of bootleg whiskey (i.e., during Prohibition). A warrantless search of the car revealed 68 bottles of illegal liquor. The Supreme Court upheld the warrantless search on the grounds that the evidence would be lost if the police had been required to take the time to secure a warrant.

DECISION-MAKING EXERCISE 5.6

Police-Created Exigencies

The police knocked on the door of Patrick Warner, whom they suspected was an armed and dangerous narcotics dealer. When Warner came to the door, the police ordered him to place his hands on the glass door and then to slowly reach down and unlock it. Warner said he did not have a key and would need to go to another room to obtain one. Believing he would retrieve a gun from the other room, the officers kicked down the door and entered as the suspect retreated to another room. Once inside, the officers conducted a protective sweep of the apartment. During the course of the sweep, they found bales of marijuana. Were the entrance and the sweep justified?

Because vehicles are operated in public spaces, a lesser expectation of privacy is enjoyed, which means warrantless searches may be allowed.

Note that *Carroll* deals with vehicle *searches*, not stops. A different standard is applied to vehicle stops, which are discussed in a dedicated section in Chapter 6.

RATIONALE Three arguments can be offered in support of the automobile exception. First, because of the inherent mobility of vehicles, it is impractical to obtain warrants. According to the Court in *Carroll*:

> The guaranty (sic) of freedom from unreasonable searches and seizures by the Fourth Amendment has been construed, practically since the beginning of the Government, as recognizing a necessary difference between a search of a store, dwelling house or other structure in respect of which a proper official warrant readily may be obtained, and a search of a ship, motor boat, wagon or automobile, for contraband goods, where it is not practicable to secure a warrant because the vehicle can be quickly moved out of the locality in which the warrant must be sought. (p. 153)

The second reason for the automobile exception focuses on people's reasonable expectation of privacy. In particular, because vehicles are typically operated in public spaces, a lesser expectation of privacy is enjoyed. As the Court observed in *Cardwell v. Lewis* (417 U.S. 583 [1974]), people have a lesser expectation of privacy in an automobile because it serves a transportation function, not a privacy function; a car "seldom serves as one's residence or the repository of personal effects" (p. 590). Also, people have a lesser expectation of privacy in their automobiles because by their very nature, automobiles travel "public thoroughfares where [their] occupants and [their] contents are in plain view" (p. 590).

The third reason for the automobile exception hinges on the government regulations to which vehicles are subjected. The old adage that "driving is a privilege, not a right" applies in this context. The Court's opinion in *United States v. Chadwick* is illustrative. There, in deciding that the warrantless search of a man's footlocker, based on the automobile exception (because the footlocker was mobile), was unconstitutional, the Court pointed to five issues concerning the regulated nature of automobiles: Automobiles (1) travel on public roads; (2) are subject to state regulations and licensing requirements; (3) are subject to other strict regulations; (4) are subject to periodic inspections; and (5) may be impounded for public safety reasons. Thus, the Court declared that the automobile exception should not apply to the warrantless search of personal items, despite their mobility.

REQUIREMENTS Three general requirements must be met for a valid warrantless vehicle search: (1) the exception must only apply to automobiles; (2) with one exception, such a search must be premised on probable cause; and (3) it must be impractical to obtain a warrant (i.e., the vehicle stop must be such that it is impractical, burdensome, or risky to take time to obtain a warrant). The third requirement is unresolved, as the courts have relied on lesser expectation of privacy analysis rather than an exigency argument to support warrantless searches of automobiles. Figure 5.3 presents the vehicle search requirements of the Pine Bluff, Arkansas, Police Department.

So far, the term *automobile* has been tossed around with wild abandon. Note, though, that *automobile* has a very specific meaning. In other words, precise types of vehicles are covered by the automobile exception. Cars, boats (e.g., *United States v. Lee*, 274 U.S. 559 [1927]), and planes are all considered automobiles. However, what about the hybrid situation involving a vehicle serving the dual purpose of transportation and residence, such as a motor home or a tractor trailer with a sleeper cab?

California v. Carney
(471 U.S. 386 [1985])

The Court was confronted with this question in the case of *California v. Carney* (471 U.S. 386 [1985]). Unfortunately, the Court adopted another objective reasonableness standard and refused to define explicitly the types of automobiles covered by the automobile exception. The Court held that the test of whether a vehicle serves a transportation or residence function requires looking at the *setting* in which the vehicle is located. If the setting "objectively indicates that the vehicle is being used for transportation" (p. 386), then the automobile exception applies.

Four factors are used in determining whether a vehicle serves a transportation function: (1) whether it is mobile or stationary; (2) whether it is licensed; (3) whether it is connected to utilities; and (4) whether it has convenient access to the road. If, for example, a trailer is on blocks, unlicensed, connected to utilities, and in a trailer park, then it will almost certainly be treated in the same way that a residence is for purposes of the Fourth Amendment.

In *Carroll*, the Court noted that "where seizure is impossible except without warrant, the seizing officer acts unlawfully and at his peril unless he can show the court probable cause" (p. 156). Simply put, despite the fact that a vehicle search is permissible without a warrant, the search must still be based on probable cause. Note, however, that probable cause to *search* and probable cause to *arrest* are not one and the same. While probable cause to search may exist, this does not automatically create probable cause to arrest. In *Carroll*, for example, the police had probable cause to search the vehicle but not probable cause to arrest the occupants.

Similarly, probable cause to arrest does not authorize a full search of a vehicle, including the trunk, but it does authorize a search of the passenger compartment (*New York v. Belton*, 453 U.S. 454 [1981]). *Belton* was extended in *Thoraton v. United States* (541 U.S. 615 [2004]) to include searches where the initial contact between the officer and the suspect took place outside the vehicle, in a parking lot, but it was significantly restricted in an even more recent decision, *Arizona v. Gant* (No. 07-542 [2009]). In that case, a man was arrested for driving on a suspended license. He was handcuffed and placed in a patrol car, then officers searched his car and found cocaine in the pocket of a

Arizona v. Gant
(No. 07-542 [2009])

FIGURE 5.3

Vehicle Search Policy (Pine Bluff, AR, Police Department)

	SUBJECT:	POLICY NUMBER 352
PINE BLUFF POLICE DEPARTMENT ARK	SEARCH: MOTOR VEHICLE	ISSUE DATE 02/19/2008
	CHAPTER: INVESTIGATIONS	EFFECTIVE DATE 02/19/2008
	ISSUED By: Chief of Police John E. Howell	TOTAL PAGES 5

I. Policy

It is the policy of this department to conduct motor vehicle searches that are both legal and thorough. Such searches are to be conducted in strict observance of the constitutional rights of the owner and occupants of the motor vehicle being searched, and with due regard for the safety of all officers, other persons and property involved.

II. Definitions

MOTOR VEHICLE: Any vehicle operating or capable of being operated on public streets or highways, to include automobiles, trucks, trailers, recreational vehicles, mobile homes, motor homes, and any other type of vehicle, whether self-propelled or towed. This policy does not apply to vehicles of any type that have been immobilized is one location for use as a temporary or permanent residence or storage facility, or which are otherwise classified by the law as residencies or buildings.

SEARCH: An examination of all or a portion of the vehicle with an investigatory motive (i.e., for the purpose of discovering fruits, instrumentalities, or evidence of a crime or contraband). A vehicle search may also be conducted to determine the vehicle identification number or the ownership of the vehicle. Inventories of personal property conducted pursuant to impoundment of a vehicle are not covered by this policy.

III. Procedure

A. Whenever feasible, a warrant will be obtained for the search of a motor vehicle. Warranties searches are to be conducted only when lack of time or other exigencies make it impractical for officers to obtain a warrant.

B. When a vehicle has broken down, or there is otherwise no significant chance the vehicle will be driven away or that evidence contained within it will be removed or destroyed, the vehicle should be searched only after a warrant has be obtained, or the officer determines that some other exception to the warrant requirement is applicable. In other cases, vehicles may be searched:

1. When probable cause to search the vehicle exists;
2. With consent of the operator;
3. Incidental to an arrest of the occupants of the vehicle;
4. search for weapons
5. When necessary to examine the vehicle identification number or to determine the ownership of the vehicle; or
6. Under emergency circumstances not stated above

Figure 5.3 continued

C. SCOPE OF VEHICLE SEARCHES

1. *SEARCHES WITH A WARRANT.* When searching under a warrant, officers may search all areas of the vehicle unless the warrant states otherwise.

2. *PROBABLE CAUSE SEARCHES.* Officers may search a vehicle without warrants where there is probable cause to believe that the vehicle contains fruits, instrumentalities, or evidence of a crime or contraband. This type of warranties search shall be conducted only when the vehicle remains mobile. Probable cause searches may extend to all areas of the motor vehicle, unless the probable cause is limited to a specific area of the vehicle. Officers may not search areas of the vehicle that could not contain the fruits, instrumentalities or evidence of a crime or contraband being sought.

3. *CONSENT SEARCHES.* The extent of the consent search depends upon the terms of consent itself. If the consent is limited to specific areas of the vehicle, officers may search only portions of the vehicle covered by the consent. Officers may search a vehicle with the oral or written consent of the person in apparent control of the vehicle or the owner of the vehicle. Written consent should be obtained whenever possible before conducting these searches. Officers shall not obtain consent by any form of coercion or duress.

4. *SEARCH FOR WEAPONS.* Where there is an objectively reasonable belief that a driver or occupant of a vehicle is potentially dangerous, officers may conduct a search of the vehicle for weapons. Searches for weapons normally must be confined to the passenger area of the vehicle and those areas of the passenger compartment in which a weapon could be hidden. Areas may not be searched that are not immediately accessible to the vehicle's occupants, such as locked glove compartments.

5. *SEARCHES INCIDENT TO ARREST.* Searches of vehicles incident to arrest of the operator or an occupant shall be limited to areas within reach of the arrestee (normally the passenger area of the vehicle). The trunk, the engine compartment and locked compartments within the passenger area may not be searched. (See policy 260 for impounded vehicle inventory).

6. *ENTRIES TO EXAMINE VEHICLE IDENTIFICATION NUMBER OR DETERMINE OWNERSHIP OF THE VEHICLE.* Where circumstances require that officers determine the vehicle identification number of ownership of a vehicle, and such information cannot be acquired from the exterior of the vehicle, officers may enter the vehicle identification number or to determine the ownership of the vehicle must be limited to actions reasonably necessary to accomplish these goals.

7. *EMERGENCIES.* Officers may enter a vehicle without a warrant where emergency circumstances make it necessary for them to do so in order to protect life or property, or when the exigencies of the situation otherwise require such action. Search of a motor vehicle under emergency circumstances not otherwise listed above must be co-extensive with the nature of the emergency. The proper extent of the search must therefore be determined by search personnel in each specific situation, but in no event will the extent of the search exceed that necessary to respond properly to the emergency. Note: Where the initial search discloses probable cause to believe that order portions of the vehicle may contain fruits, instrumentalities or evidence of a crime or contraband, any additional portions of the vehicle may be searched that could reasonably contain the items being sought.

8. *SEARCH OF CONTAINERS FOUND IN A VEHICLE.* If any otherwise-lawful search of a vehicle is being conducted, containers found in the vehicle may be opened and searched. In no instance shall a container in a motor vehicle be searched unless it could contain the item(s) being sought. In addition:

   a. *UNLOCKED CONTAINER*
   Unlocked containers found in motor vehicles are governed by the nature of the search, as follows:

   b. *PROBABLE CAUSE SEARCH*
   In a probable cause search, containers such as paper bags, cardboard boxes, wrapped packages, etc., wherever found in the vehicle, may be opened provided they could contains items being searched or incident to arrest.

   c. *INCIDENT TO ARREST*
   When the passenger compartment of a vehicle is being searched incident to an arrest, such containers found within the passenger compartment may be opened.

d. *Consent*

Containers discovered during a consent search of the vehicle may be opened provided that the terms of the consent expressly permit or reasonably imply that the particular container may be opened.

e. *Other Circumstances*

Unlocked containers found in a vehicle under circumstances that do not justify an investigatory search of the container under any of the foregoing exceptions to the search warrant requirement should be secured but not searched until a warrant is obtained to search them.

9. Locked Containers

Locked containers such as attaché cases, suitcases and footlockers found during a vehicle search should be opened only if:

a. The search is being conducted under a warrant; or

b. There is probable cause to believe that a container located in the motor vehicle contains contraband or evidence.

c. A valid consent to open the locked container is first obtained. Where these conditions are not met, locked containers should be secured by search personnel and opened only after a warrant has been obtained.

10. Items Belonging to Passengers

Items belonging to passengers (e.g., wallets, handbags, purses) may be examined only in the following cases:

a. Officers have probable cause to search the vehicle, and the belonging in question is capable of concealing the item or items being searched for.

b. Officers have received valid consent to search the item.

c. A passenger has been placed under arrest, and the arrested passenger's belongings are being lawfully searched incident to that arrest.

D. Location and Time of Search

Whenever possible, search of a motor vehicle, and of containers found therein should be conducted at the location where the vehicle was discovered or detained. Under exigent circumstances, search of the vehicle or container may be delayed and/or conducted after the vehicle or container has been moved to another location. However, in all instances searches shall be conducted as soon as reasonably possible; that is, as soon as adequate personnel are available to conduct a thorough search with due regard for the safety of all officers, citizens and property concerned.

E. Conduct of the Search

Motor vehicle searches shall be conducted in a manner that minimizes the intrusiveness of the search and the inconvenience caused to vehicle owners, occupants and other persons involved. Where possible, damage to the vehicle or to other property in the course of the search should be avoided. When unavoidable, such damage should be confined to that reasonably necessary to carry out a safe and through search.

F. Abandoned Vehicles

If it is determined by an officer that a vehicle has been abandoned, the vehicle may be searched without a warrant.

G. Handling of Evidence Found During Vehicle Searches

Any evidentiary items discovered in the course of a motor vehicle search shall be collected, handled, packaged, marked, transported, and stored in accordance with applicable policies and procedures of this department. Where appropriate and feasible, itemized receipts for seized property shall be given to owner and/or occupants of the vehicle.

H. Security of Vehicles and Property Contained Therein

If a search of a vehicle leaves the vehicle or any property contained therein vulnerable to unauthorized entry, theft, or damage, search personnel shall take such steps as are reasonably necessary to secure and/or preserve the vehicle or property from such hazards.

Figure 5.3 continued

I.   RESPONSIBILITY OF SUPERVISING OFFICER

An officer supervising a vehicle search shall be responsible for ensuring that it is conducted in accordance with this policy. In the event that the vehicle search is conducted under a warrant, the officer shall ensure that the execution of the warrant is properly reported to the issuing court or other authority. The officer shall also be responsible for making any other reports regarding the search that may be required by law, policy, or procedure.

Source: Reprinted courtesy of Pine Bluff, AR, Police Department.

---

jacket. He was convicted of drug offenses. The Supreme Court held that a *Belton*-type search is permissible "only if it is reasonable to believe that the arrestee might access the vehicle at the time of the search or that the vehicle contains evidence of the offense of arrest." Whereas *Belton* was a bright-line decision, *Gant* now makes it somewhat difficult to determine whether a search is sanctioned. It forces officers to decide whether the vehicle contains evidence of the offense in question.

New York v. Belton
(453 U.S. 454 [1981])

There is one important exception to the rule that probable cause must be in place before a vehicle search can be conducted. In *New York v. Class* (475 U.S. 106 [1986]), the Court held in a 5 to 4 decision that the warrantless, suspicionless search of a car for the purpose of ascertaining the vehicle identification number (VIN) is permissible. All that is required is a valid traffic stop. This exception does not, however, authorize the police to enter cars at will, without any basis for a search. In support of its opinion, the Court pointed to the lesser expectation of privacy argument. Also, it noted that the search was minimally intrusive. The lower court in *Class* was not in agreement with the Supreme Court's decision: "The fact that certain information must be kept, or that it may be of a public nature, does not automatically sanction police intrusion into private space in order to obtain it" (p. 124).

A general rule concerning warrants is that they should be obtained whenever practical. However, given the circumstances surrounding most vehicle stops, it would seem foolish to require that the police obtain a warrant before engaging in the search of an automobile. As the Court observed in *Carroll*, in cases in which the securing of a warrant is reasonably practicable, a warrant must be used. In most situations involving the stop of an automobile, securing a warrant is not practical. In *Husty v. United States* (282 U.S. 694 [1931]), for example, a police officer followed up on a tip from an informant and found contraband in Husty's unattended car. Given that the car was unattended, one could argue that a warrant should have been secured, but the Court argued that the officer "could not know when Husty would come to the car or how soon it would be removed" (p. 701). Contrast *Husty* with *Coolidge v. New Hampshire* (403 U.S. 443 [1971]). In that case, the Court ruled that the automobile exception did not apply to a warrantless search and seizure of two cars located on the defendant's property because the police had probable cause to act more than two weeks before the search.

Husty and *Coolidge* suggest that the warrantless search of an automobile will only be upheld if it was impractical to obtain a warrant. This third requirement is unresolved, however. For example, in *Chambers v. Maroney*, the Court held that as long as the vehicle is readily mobile, a warrantless search is permissible, even if it is conducted away from the scene at the stationhouse. The actual search of the automobile in *Chambers* was made at the police station many hours after the car had been stopped on the highway, when the car was no longer movable. Furthermore, at that point, exigent circumstances no longer existed and a magistrate could have required a warrant. Yet the Court sanctioned the search (see also *Texas v. White*, 423 U.S. 67 [1975]).

One relatively recent case, *United States v. Johns* (469 U.S. 478 [1985]), seems to suggest that the rationale for the automobile exception is, at least in part, an exigency.

In that case, the Court held that the warrantless search of an automobile is impermissible if it "adversely affect[s] a privacy [or] possessory interest" (p. 487). This argument seems to suggest that a search under the automobile exception needs to be premised on the urgency of the situation; otherwise, a warrant should be secured. Nevertheless, the Court in *Johns* did state that a three-day delay between the initial stop and the arrest was permissible, partly because the car's owner did not claim that the delay caused hardship.

So, what is the role of exigency in the automobile exception? A safe rule of thumb is that the presence or absence of exigent circumstances is irrelevant. Instead, a showing that the automobile was readily mobile is enough to justify a warrantless search under the automobile exception (as long as probable cause is in place and the target of the search is, in fact, an automobile, as defined earlier).

SCOPE OF THE SEARCH   A number of court decisions have considered the scope of the search authorized under the automobile exception. Most of the decisions have focused on whether a container in an automobile can also be searched if probable cause to search the vehicle exists. In *Arkansas v. Sanders* (442 U.S. 753 [1979]), the Court ruled that the warrantless search of a suitcase was not permissible when the police waited for the suitcase to be placed in the vehicle. Similarly, in *Robbins v. California* (453 U.S. 420 [1981]), the Court held that a container discovered during a warrantless vehicle search can be seized but not searched until a warrant can be obtained.

Just one year after *Robbins*, the Court handed down its decision in *United States v. Ross* (456 U.S. 798 [1982]), which overturned *Robbins*. The Court declared that as long as the police have justification to conduct a warrantless vehicle search, they may conduct a search "that is as thorough as a magistrate could authorize in a warrant" (p. 800). The only limitation is "defined by the object of the search and the places in which there is probable cause to believe that it may be found" (p. 824). Accordingly, if the contraband sought is small (e.g., a syringe), the scope of the vehicle search exception is almost limitless. Recently, the Supreme Court held that even passengers' personal belongings can be searched (*Wyoming v. Houghton*, 526 U.S. 295 [1999]).

Fewer cases have focused on precisely how far the police can go during a vehicle search in terms of inflicting damage to the vehicle. On the one hand, based on a reading of the previous chapter, a due process violation may occur if the damage inflicted is excessive. On the other hand, it would appear that a certain degree of physical damage to an automobile is permissible. The *Carroll* decision, for example, was based on a warrantless search in which the police sliced open the vehicle's upholstery to look for contraband.

In another case, the Supreme Court considered whether allowing a drug dog to sniff a vehicle during a traffic stop violated the Fourth Amendment. In *Illinois v. Caballes* (543 U.S. 405 [2005]), an Illinois state trooper stopped a vehicle for speeding. During the 10-minute stop, while the trooper was going through all the usual motions associated

DECISION-MAKING EXERCISE 5.7

A Twist on *Carroll*

Two police detectives have probable cause to believe that several illegal automatic weapons are in the trunk of Carmine Lord's car. However, Lord's car is broken down and has been left with the local auto mechanic. Furthermore, Lord has proven to be a difficult customer and has refused to pay for the full amount of the repair. As such, the mechanic has locked Lord's car in a bay at his service station and refused to release it until he receives payment. Assuming they have the mechanic's blessing, may the detectives search Lord's car for the weapons while it is at the station?

with a traffic stop, another trooper arrived and allowed a drug dog to sniff the vehicle. The dog was alerted to the trunk. Marijuana was found, and the driver was arrested. The Supreme Court upheld the dog sniff, citing three factors: (1) the legality of the stop; (2) the short duration of the stop; and (3) no one can claim legal ownership to—and thereby assert a privacy interest in—contraband. This was a controversial decision, but one that clearly errs on the side of law enforcement.

Whren v. United States
(517 U.S. 806 [1996])

OTHER ACTIONS SANCTIONED IN A TRAFFIC STOP   The Supreme Court has permitted the police to stop a car based on the belief that a crime has been committed, which includes any traffic violation (*Whren v. United States*, 517 U.S. 806 [1996]). In addition, once a person has been stopped, the officer can order him or her to stand outside the vehicle without any justification (*Maryland v. Wilson*, 519 U.S. 408 [1997]; *Pennsylvania v. Mimms*, 434 U.S. 106 [1997]). The police can also engage in searches with consent (*Ohio v. Robinette*, 519 U.S. 33 [1996]), seize items that are in plain view (*Horton v. California*, 496 U.S. 128 [1990]), frisk the driver and/or search the passenger compartment of the vehicle out of concerns for safety (*Michigan v. Long*, 463 U.S. 1032 [1983]), and search the entire car if probable cause to arrest and/or search is developed (*New York v. Belton*). Finally, police are not required to provide the *Miranda* warnings when asking questions pursuant to a routine vehicle stop (*Miranda v. Arizona*, 384 U.S. 436 [1966]).

Some questions have been raised concerning the constitutional protections afforded to passengers who happen to be riding in a vehicle that is stopped. For example, in *Brendlin v. California* (551 U.S. 249 [2007]), the Supreme Court was presented with the question of whether a passenger is considered seized within the meaning of the Fourth Amendment when the vehicle is stopped. It held that passengers, like drivers, are seized in such situations. Why does this matter? Since the passenger was considered seized, he was able to challenge the constitutionality of the stop. He did so because police found contraband on his person.

WHEN OTHER DOCTRINES GOVERN SEARCHES OF AUTOMOBILES   Note that the automobile exception cases are *not* the only cases governing warrantless searches of vehicles. Many warrantless searches of vehicles are better analyzed under other exceptions to the Fourth Amendment's warrant requirement. For example, the Supreme Court has rejected the use of the automobile exception in analyzing searches of automobiles crossing international borders. Such cases are better analyzed under the border checkpoints exception discussed in Chapter 7.

Still other warrantless searches of automobiles are permissible based on other decisions unrelated to the automobile exception initially set forth in *Carroll*. These include searches (1) incident to arrest (see earlier discussion); (2) during the course of a stop-and-frisk (e.g., *Adams v. Williams*, 407 U.S. 143 [1972]; see Chapter 6); (3) under the

DECISION-MAKING EXERCISE 5.8
Proper Scope for an Automobile Search

Joan Lee was pulled over on Interstate 10 after a highway patrol officer observed her aggressively weaving from one lane to another. The officer had probable cause to search the vehicle for drugs. Accordingly, Lee opened the trunk, at which point the officer's attention was drawn to the spare tire. To the officer, it looked as though the spare was the wrong one for the vehicle. In addition, there appeared to be a white, powdery substance on the rubber. Based on his knowledge that narcotics are smuggled in such a fashion, the officer pulled the spare out of the vehicle, slashed it open with a knife, and found drugs inside. The drugs were seized and Lee was arrested. In terms of scope, was this search justified?

FIGURE 5.4

Levels of Justification for Automobile Searches

Level of Intrusion	Justification Required
Search of entire car, including containers	Probable cause to search
Search of passenger compartment and containers	Probable cause to arrest occupant
Weapons search of passenger compartment	Reasonable suspicion/fear for safety
Order occupants out of car	Reasonable suspicion to stop
Inventory search	Administrative

plain view doctrine (see later discussion); (4) based on the inventory search exception (see Chapter 7); and (5) with consent by the automobile's occupant (see Chapter 7). Therefore, searches of automobiles—like searches of other places as well as people—can simultaneously be governed by several different doctrines. Figure 5.4 summarizes the levels of justification required to conduct various types of vehicle searches.

RACIAL PROFILING   Clearly, the police have numerous opportunities to detect contraband during the course of a vehicle stop. And since almost every driver commits a violation of traffic law at some point or other, there is plenty of justification for stopping motorists to begin with. But whether every motorist is stopped for *legitimate* reasons is questionable. Further, even if the police have legal grounds to stop someone in his or her car, the question of pretext presents itself: Should the police be able to use traffic laws to stop people when they really have other motivations in mind (i.e., to gain consent to search)? The Supreme Court has yet to answer this question, which has led to the concern that the police have *too* much discretion in terms of their authority to stop motorists. Closely tied to this concern are allegations of **racial profiling**, which have emerged in recent years. Racial profiling occurs when the police use race or ethnicity as a factor in determining whether to stop someone.

A driver's race or ethnicity obviously does not provide the justification to stop him or her. But many argue that the police use existing traffic laws, which are numerous and easy to violate, to single out certain drivers based on their race or ethnicity. The Supreme Court has yet to decide on the constitutionality of this type of conduct directly, but at least one of its decisions has come close. For example, in *Whren v. United States* (517 U.S. 806 [1996]), Washington, D.C., police made a traffic stop and observed two bags of crack cocaine in the hands of a passenger who was seated in the front of the car. The police testified that they stopped the driver because he had violated traffic laws. In contrast, the defendants claimed that the stop was made based on their race and that the police used alleged traffic violations as a reason to stop them.

The Supreme Court concluded that the "constitutional reasonableness of traffic stops" does not depend "on the actual motivations of the individual officers" (p. 813). The Court also concluded that the only relevant inquiry is whether the officer had cause to stop the car (pp. 813–814). It rejected the argument that the Fourth Amendment requires a court to consider whether "the officer's conduct deviated materially from usual police practices, so that a reasonable officer in the same circumstances would not have made the stop for the reasons given" (p. 814). Simply put, the Supreme Court has stated that individual officers' motivations—whether racial or of any other substance—are irrelevant. The only question worth asking and answering, according to the Court, is whether the officer had cause to stop. Needless to say, this decision did not satisfy critics of racial profiling.

Justice Kennedy's dissent in *Maryland v. Wilson* summarizes the voices of racial profiling critics everywhere:

> The practical effect of our holding in *Whren*, of course, is to allow the police to stop vehicles in almost countless circumstances. When *Whren* is coupled with today's holding, the Court puts tens of millions of passengers at risk of arbitrary control by the police. If the command to exit were to become commonplace, the Constitution would be diminished in a most public way. As the standards suggested in dissent are adequate to protect the safety of the police, we ought not to suffer so great a loss. (p. 422)

The Court's opinion in *Whren* effectively closed the door on Fourth Amendment claims of racial discrimination. So what remedies are available? One answer is that motorists can sue, based on 42 U.S.C. 1983, for racial discrimination under the equal protection clause of the Fourteenth Amendment. At least two types of Fourteenth Amendment claims can be identified. The first is a challenge to a law or policy that intentionally classifies people based on race or some other classification. Second, plaintiffs can argue that a racially neutral policy or statute is being enforced in a discriminatory fashion. Another answer to the question of what remedies are available is that people targeted for profiling can seek relief under the Civil Rights Act of 1964.

Equal Protection Claims.   For the first type of equal protection claim to succeed, it must be shown that (1) a practice or policy intentionally classifies persons based on race and (2) the practice or policy withstands "strict judicial scrutiny" (*Adarand Constructors, Inc. v. Pena*, 515 U.S. 200 [1995], p. 227). These are known as *Pena's* first and second prongs.

Concerning *Pena's* first prong, one court has said that racial discrimination can be shown by a law that "expressly classifies persons on the basis of race" (*Hayden v. County of Nassau*, 180 F.3d 42 [2nd Cir. 1999]) or by a practice or policy that treats one differently from members of other racial groups. For example, if a police department's policy authorizes stops based on racial or ethnic characteristics, it would be discriminatory. According to another court, racial discrimination exists when law enforcement personnel "adopt a policy, employ a practice, or in a given situation take steps to initiate an investigation . . . based solely upon the citizen's race" (*United States v. Avery*, 128 F.3d 974 [6th Cir. 1997], p. 985).

In most situations, however, there are no formal policies or practices that authorize traffic stops based on race. What is necessary in such situations is to use statistical evidence to show that the police acted with intent to discriminate. However, because the saying "you can prove anything with statistics" is at least partly true, the courts have been mixed in terms of their willingness to rely on statistical evidence of racial discrimination. In *Hunter v. Underwood* (471 U.S. 222 [1985]), for instance, the Supreme Court sustained an equal protection claim by African Americans who claimed they were deprived of important rights for convictions under an Alabama law. The Court accepted statistical evidence to the effect that blacks were disenfranchised under the law at a rate 1.7 times more than whites.

However, in *McCleskey v. Kemp* (481 U.S. 279 [1987]), the Court rejected a statistical analysis related to the application of the death penalty in Georgia. The study presented in that case claimed that the race of the victim was the factor most likely to influence jury members in their death penalty decisions. The Court claimed that the study showed only a correlation between the race of the victim and the death penalty decision. The Court took a similar approach in *United States v. Armstrong* (517 U.S. 456 [1996]), in which it rejected the defendants' argument that the federal government engaged in the racially selective prosecution of "crack" cocaine offenders. It held that the defendants "failed to satisfy the threshold showing . . . that the Government declined to prosecute similarly situated suspects of other races" (p. 458). Both decisions suggest that it would be exceedingly difficult to show Fourteenth Amendment discrimination in the context of racial profiling.

As for *Pena's* second prong—that a policy or practice must withstand "strict judicial scrutiny"—the government must show the necessity of the classification scheme. Specifically, a Fourteenth Amendment equal protection claim will not succeed if the government can show that it has a compelling interest justifying the practice or policy. Or stated differently, if the government can show that unequal treatment is necessary to further some clear government purpose, an equal protection claim will not succeed (see, e.g., *Heller v. Doe*, 509 U.S. 312 [1993]; *Romer v. Evans*, 517 U.S. 620 [1996]). However, if the government cannot meet this strict scrutiny test, an equal protection claim will probably succeed, provided that *Pena's* first prong is also satisfied.

As for the second type of Fourteenth Amendment claim, courts sometimes hear lawsuits in which plaintiffs allege that a racially neutral policy or statute has been enforced in a racially discriminatory fashion. Indeed, as early as 1886, the Supreme Court recognized that laws and policies can be enforced in a discriminatory fashion. In *Yick Wo v. Hopkins* (118 U.S. 356 [1886]), the Supreme Court held that a racially neutral statute had been enforced "with a mind so unequal and oppressive as to amount to a practical denial by the state of that equal protection of the laws . . . which is secured . . . by the broad and benign provisions of the Fourteenth Amendment to the Constitution of the United States" (p. 373, n. 46).

Relatedly, some plaintiffs have argued that legal searches and seizures conducted with appropriate justification violate the Fourteenth Amendment if they are used to selectively target certain individuals over others. For example, a plaintiff may argue that even though he or she was detained lawfully, the police violated the Fourteenth Amendment's equal protection clause because they selectively targeted individuals for such actions based solely on race. These types of claims are fairly rare and not often successful, but one New Jersey court has stated that if a police department embarks "upon an officially sanctioned de facto policy of targeting minorities for investigation and arrest," then it may be held liable (*State v. Kennedy*, 588 A.2d 834 [N.J. Super. 1991]).

The recent case of *United States v. Travis* (62 F.3d 170 [6th Cir. 1995]) illustrates this type of Fourteenth Amendment–based allegation. In it, a woman argued that she was selected for questioning based on her race. A detective, who was assigned to the Cincinnati/Northern Kentucky airport, focused his attention on people arriving on a flight from Los Angeles because numerous passengers from the same flight had been arrested for drug offenses in the past. The woman was stopped by the detective and consented to a search. Drugs were found in her purse. The court held that because the detective did not need reasonable suspicion or probable cause (because of the woman's consent), no constitutional violation took place. However, the court did point out that consensual encounters based solely on race may violate the equal protection clause of the Fourteenth Amendment, even if the Fourth Amendment is not violated (see *Travis*, pp. 173–174).

Civil Rights Act of 1964.   Based on *Armstrong* and *McKleskey*, it is exceedingly difficult, if not currently impossible, to succeed with a Fourteenth Amendment equal protection–based claim. The remaining available remedy is Title VII of the Civil Rights Act of 1964, which requires a showing of **disparate impact**. Disparate impact is, in general, a method of acting that treats one group in a markedly different fashion than another. (In the present context, the focus is on police actions.)

Title VII states, in relevant part, that recipients of federal funds "may not . . . utilize criteria or methods of administration which have the effect of subjecting individuals to discrimination based on their race, color, national origin, or have the effect of defeating or substantially impairing accomplishment of the objectives of the program as respects individuals of a particular race, color, or national origin" (28 C.F.R. 42.104[b][2]).

This legislation looks attractive on its face, but it is primarily a method by which the federal government enforces certain rules against entities that receive federal funds—usually state and local units of government. The question of whether private parties (i.e., average citizens) can enforce Title VII is one that has been litigated extensively in the courts. Of particular interest has been the issue of *standing*. Specifically, a plaintiff must show that he or she was a direct participant in or intended beneficiary of a state or local program or activity that receives federal funds. Fortunately, the Civil Rights Act of 1987 defines *program or activity* as all operations of a governmental entity that receives federal funds. Thus, traffic stops would appear to fall within the meaning of the legislation. That is, in theory, people should be able to sue under Title VII for racially discriminatory traffic enforcement policies. The Supreme Court has not ruled on this issue, however.

Plain View Searches

Untrained observers frequently suggest that "plain view" applies in situations in which evidence can be seen without having to search for it. While this may be a *literal* interpretation of what it means for something to be in plain view, it is not the interpretation the courts use. Plain view has a very specific meaning in criminal procedure, and the doctrine applies only in certain situations.

Coolidge v. New Hampshire (403 U.S. 443 [1971])

The **"plain view" doctrine** first emerged in the Supreme Court's decision in *Coolidge v. New Hampshire* (403 U.S. 443 [1971]). The issue in *Coolidge* was whether evidence seized during a search of cars belonging to Coolidge was admissible. The police had a warrant to search the cars, but it was later deemed invalid, so the state argued that the evidence should still be admissible because the cars were in plain view from a public street and from the house in which Coolidge was arrested. The Court did not accept this argument, pointing out that just because the police could *see* the cars from where they were not enough to permit seizure of the evidence in question. However, the Court did point out that had the police been *in* an area, such as a car or a house, evidence that was "immediately apparent as such" and was discovered "inadvertently" would have been admissible. In other words, part of the reason the evidence was not admissible in *Coolidge* was that the police officers were not lawfully in the cars when the evidence was seized.

DECISION-MAKING EXERCISE 5.9

Racial Profiling

While on patrol, Officer James observed a white van with an African American driver inside, idling in a fire lane adjacent to a shopping mall. Rather than issuing the driver a citation, James parked his cruiser and entered the van's license plate number into his Law Enforcement Information Network ("LEIN") computer, which revealed that the van was registered to a Curtis Ellison, who had an outstanding felony warrant. Following department policy, James called for backup and continued to observe the van. Before backup arrived, another African American male got into the van and it drove away.

Officer James followed the van until his backup was close, at which point he activated his lights and stopped the van. James advised the driver that he was being stopped for parking in a fire lane and asked for his license, registration, and proof of insurance. When James learned that Ellison was the *passenger*, not the driver, he ordered Ellison out of the van, searched him, and found two firearms on his person. Ellison now alleges that he and his friend were victims of racial profiling and that the stop (and subsequent search) was invalid under the Fourth Amendment. Is this argument meritorious?

To summarize, the Court decided in *Coolidge* that a plain view seizure is authorized when (1) the police are lawfully in the area where the evidence is located; (2) the items are immediately apparent as subject to seizure; and (3) the discovery of the evidence is inadvertent. The first prong of the *Coolidge* ruling—the lawful access prong—has remained relatively stable over time. The second and third prongs, however, have undergone significant interpretation in recent years. The remainder of this section is therefore based on these three requirements.

THE LAWFUL ACCESS REQUIREMENT   For the plain view doctrine to apply, the police must have **lawful access** to the object to be seized. As the Supreme Court decided in *Coolidge*:

> [P]lain view *alone* is never enough to justify the warrantless seizure of evidence. This is simply a corollary of the familiar principle . . . that no amount of probable cause can justify a warrantless search or seizure absent "exigent circumstances." Incontrovertible testimony of the senses that an incriminating object is on premises belonging to a criminal suspect may establish the fullest possible measure of probable cause. But even where the object is contraband, this Court has repeatedly stated and enforced the basic rule that the police may not enter and make a warrantless seizure. (p. 468)

This excerpt from the Court's opinion in *Coolidge* reinforces the requirement that just because the police may *see* contraband does not necessarily mean they can *seize* it. If, for example, evidence is seen lying in a vacant lot or other public place, it may be seized. In such a situation, a search has not occurred. However, evidence that may be viewed from a public place but is, in fact, on private property cannot be seized unless a warrant is obtained or exigent circumstances are present. So, if a police officer on foot patrol observes a marijuana plant in the window of a private residence, he or she may not enter the premises and seize the plant, even though such observation establishes "the fullest possible measure of probable cause."

What is meant by *lawful vantage point?* There are four specific situations in which police officers can be found in a lawful vantage point for purposes of the plain view doctrine. The first is during a warranted search. For example, if an officer comes upon an article during the execution of a valid search warrant, the plain view doctrine may apply (subject to further restrictions described later). Second, officers are in a lawful vantage point during a valid arrest. This includes warrantless arrests in public, warrantless arrests based on exigent circumstances, and arrests with warrants. Third, when a warrantless search is conducted, the police officer is in a lawful vantage point—assuming, of course, that the warrantless search is based on probable cause. Finally, as illustrated in the previous paragraph, officers are always in a lawful vantage point during nonsearches.

THE "IMMEDIATELY APPARENT" REQUIREMENT   In addition to the requirement that the police have lawful access to an object for the plain view doctrine to apply, it must also be **immediately apparent** that the object is subject to seizure. *Immediately apparent* means that the officer has probable cause to seize the object.

This was the decision reached in *Arizona v. Hicks* (480 U.S. 321 [1987]). In that case, the police entered the defendant's apartment without a warrant because a bullet had been fired through his floor into the apartment below, injuring a person there. The warrantless entry was based on the exigency of looking for the shooter, for other potential victims, and for the weapon used in the incident. Once inside the apartment, the officer observed new stereo equipment that seemed out of place, given the surroundings.

Arizona v. Hicks
(480 U.S. 321 [1987])

The officer suspected the stereo equipment was stolen but did not have probable cause to believe as such, so he picked up a turntable in order to obtain its serial number. He then called in the information and confirmed that it was stolen. The Court held that this warrantless action did not satisfy the plain view doctrine. It was not immediately apparent to the officer that the stereo equipment was stolen.

Remember that *probable cause to seize* and *immediately apparent* are one and the same. An officer does not need to be absolutely certain that the object is subject to seizure for the plain view doctrine to apply. That was the decision reached in *Texas v. Brown* (460 U.S. 730 [1983]). In that case, Brown was stopped late at night at a routine driver's license checkpoint. When he opened the glove box in order to look for his license, an opaque balloon, knotted at the opening, fell out onto the floor of the passenger side of the vehicle. The officer making the stop observed what he perceived to be drug paraphernalia in the glove compartment and ultimately seized the balloon and its contents. The balloon was later proven to contain heroin. Brown was convicted of narcotics offenses. The Texas Court of Criminal Appeals reversed Brown's conviction, pointing out that the plain view doctrine did not apply because the officer did not *know* incriminatory evidence was before him when he seized the balloon. A unanimous Supreme Court reversed the decision, stating, "The fact that [the officer] could not see through the opaque fabric of the balloon is all but irrelevant; the distinctive character of the balloon itself spoke volumes as to its contents—particularly to the trained eye of the officer" (p. 743).

THE ROLE OF INADVERTENCY   The role of *inadvertency* in the plain view determination has received considerable attention. The original position of the Supreme Court in *Coolidge v. New Hampshire* was that an object seized under the plain view doctrine must not have been anticipated by the police. For example, assume that a police officer obtains a warrant to search a suspect's home for the proceeds from a robbery. Assume further that the officer *expects* to find guns in the house but does not state in the warrant that guns will be sought. If, during the search, the officer finds guns, under the Supreme Court's old ruling, the guns will not be admissible because the officers expected to find them. This restriction on the plain view doctrine came to be known as the *inadvertency requirement.* The rationale for this restriction was that an officer who anticipates discovering evidence of a crime should seek prior judicial authorization (i.e., a warrant). Further, the Fourth Amendment's particularity requirement would be compromised if general searches were permitted.

Horton v. California
(496 U.S. 128 [1990])

In *Horton v. California* (496 U.S. 128 [1990]), the Court declared that inadvertency, although a "characteristic of most legitimate 'plain view' seizures, . . . is not a necessary condition" of the doctrine (p. 130). The Court offered two reasons for abandoning the inadvertency requirement imposed in *Coolidge*. First, according to *Horton*, as long as a warrant particularly describes the places to be searched and the objects to be seized, the

DECISION-MAKING EXERCISE 5.10

Considering the "Immediately Apparent" Requirement for Plain View

Police officers have a warrant for the arrest of Randy Whitbeck, who is the suspect in a rape. They lawfully execute the warrant and arrest Whitbeck in his home. While there, one of the officers observes a rifle leaning up against the wall in an adjacent bedroom. With probable cause to suspect that it is an illegal assault weapon, she enters the room and seizes the gun. May the gun be introduced into evidence? Assume further that the gun is not connected in any way to the rape. Does it matter that the seizure of the gun is not connected with the rape? Finally, if the officers knew the rifle was contraband *prior* to serving the warrant and if the rifle was not named in the search warrant accompanying the arrest warrant, could they still seize it lawfully?

officer cannot expand the area of the search once the evidence has been found. In other words, it is unlikely that once officers have found the evidence listed in the warrant, they will go on a "fishing expedition," looking for evidence not listed in the warrant. According to the Court, the particularity requirement itself ensures that people's privacy is protected.

Second, the Court noted that "evenhanded law enforcement is best achieved by the application of objective standards of conduct, rather than standards that depend upon the subjective state of mind of the officer" (p. 138). An inadvertency requirement would force the courts to dwell on police officers' subjective motivations, which would be both time consuming and distracting. The Court went on to note that "[t]he fact that an officer is interested in an item of evidence and fully expects to find it in the course of a search should not invalidate its seizure if the search is confined in area and duration by the terms of the warrant or a valid exception to the warrant requirement" (p. 138).

PLAIN TOUCH, FEEL, AND SMELL   The term *plain view* suggests that the plain view doctrine is limited to items that the police can see with their eyes. Actually, in recent years, the Court has extended the plain view doctrine to incorporate items discovered using additional senses, especially smell (*United States v. Place*, 462 U.S. 696 [1983]) and feel (Cf., *Minnesota v. Dickerson*, 508 U.S. 366 [1993]). In *Dickerson*, for example, a police officer spotted Dickerson acting suspiciously near a notorious "crack house." The officer frisked Dickerson for a weapon, pursuant to *Terry v. Ohio*, but instead of finding a weapon, the officer found a small lump that he could not immediately identify. Instead of terminating the frisk, the officer carefully examined the object in Dickerson's pocket, which turned out to be cocaine. The Court ruled that this action was unlawful, arguing that the officer's actions fell outside the permissible scope of a seizure based on plain touch. Had it been immediately apparent to the officer that the object was contraband, the seizure would have been permissible. Additionally, the plain view doctrine can be extended to what police officers hear, as long as probable cause is in place and all the aforementioned requirements have been satisfied (see, e.g., *United States v. Jackson*, 588 F.2d 1046, 5th Cir., *cert. denied*, 442 U.S. 941 [1979]).

PLAIN VIEW AS A FALLBACK MEASURE   There are countless situations in which the plain view doctrine would seem to apply but in which the courts have based their decisions on other doctrines. An example of such a case can be found in *Colorado v. Bannister* (449 U.S. 1 [1980]). In that case, a police officer approached a stopped vehicle and observed on the passenger seat chrome lug nuts of the same type that had reportedly been stolen in the vicinity. The occupants of the car also matched the description of those described by the victim. The officer engaged in a warrantless search of the vehicle and seized the lug nuts. The Supreme Court did not apply the plain view doctrine in this case but instead relied on the automobile exception to the warrant requirement set forth in *Carroll v. United States* (see earlier discussion). The Court argued that the warrantless search and seizure of the evidence was permissible, given the inherent mobility of the car, so the plain view doctrine did not apply.

Thus, the plain view doctrine can be thought of as something of a fallback measure. If a warrantless search and/or seizure is not authorized by any other doctrine (e.g., search incident to arrest, search in the presence of exigent circumstances), plain view may apply. Consider, for example, the discussion concerning search warrant requirements in Chapter 4. Specifically, the particularity requirement states that the warrant must explicitly describe what is to be seized. However, if during the course of a warranted search, the police stumble across evidence that they believe can be seized but is not set forth in the search warrant, the plain view doctrine may apply. In such a situation, the original authorization to engage in the search (i.e., the search warrant) does not clearly permit seizure of the evidence, yet plain view provides another form of authorization to do so.

Similarly, evidence noticed during a hot pursuit (e.g., *Warden v. Hayden*), when accompanying an arrestee to his or her room (*Washington v. Chrisman*), when investigating a fire in a home (e.g., *Michigan v. Tyler*, 436 U.S. 499 [1978]), and many other such situations can be seized but not always on the warrantless action itself. For example, assume police officers during the course of a hot pursuit find a cache of illegal weapons in a house. The hot pursuit exception to the warrant requirement does not authorize seizure of the weapons, but the plain view doctrine does. Again, the plain view doctrine serves as a fallback measure. Another such fallback measure is the inventory search exception, discussed in Chapter 7.

In summary, the plain view doctrine will apply only in situations in which the police have lawful access to the object in question. Provided that the appropriate level of justification is in place to engage in the warrantless action in question (e.g., probable cause, reasonable suspicion, administrative justification, or when engaged in a nonsearch), the lawful access requirement will automatically be satisfied.

WARRANTLESS ARRESTS

Just as there are a number of searches that can be conducted without a warrant, the Supreme Court has also sanctioned certain arrests that can be made without a warrant. They include arrests in the presence of exigent circumstances and arrests in public places.

Arrests Based on Exigent Circumstances

Exigent (i.e., emergency) circumstances justify warrantless entry into a private home for the purpose of making an arrest. The five exigencies identified earlier in this chapter justify warrantless entry for this purpose. In other words, a warrantless arrest, with probable cause, is permissible if any of the following is present: (1) hot pursuit; (2) danger to officers; (3) danger to third parties; (4) escape; and (5) destruction of evidence. Figure 5.5 presents the San Bernardino, California, Police Department's policy for making warrantless arrests based on exigent circumstances.

Arrests in Public Places

United States v. Watson
(423 U.S. 411 [1976])

Unlike arrests made in the home (or in a third-party residence), arrests made in public do not require warrants. In *United States v. Watson* (423 U.S. 411 [1976]), the Supreme Court upheld the common-law rule that arrests made in public do not need to be predicated on a warrant. The Court expressed confidence in the ability of police officers to make probable cause determinations: "[W]e decline to transform [a] judicial preference [for arrest warrants] into a constitutional rule when the judgment of the Nation and Congress has for so long been to authorize warrantless public arrests on probable cause" (p. 423).

United States v. Santana
(427 U.S. 38 [1976])

The court extended this decision to the curtilage of a home in *United States v. Santana* (427 U.S. 38 [1976]). In that case, the police who had probable cause to arrest Santana arrived at her house to find her standing in the opening of her front door. When she saw the officers approaching, she retreated into the house. The officers followed her into the house and made the arrest. The Supreme Court declared that the officers' actions were constitutional because when Santana was standing in the doorway, "[s]he was not in an area where she had any expectation of privacy" (p. 42). The entry into Santana's house was justified on exigent circumstances—namely, hot pursuit.

FIGURE 5.5

Warrantless Arrest Policy (San Bernardino, CA, Police Department)

STANDARD OPERATING PROCEDURE   CHAPTER #2   PROCEDURE #9

ARREST IN RESIDENCE WITHOUT WARRANT   5-4-89

The "Ramey Decision" by the California Supreme Court commands that a police officer may not enter the residence of a suspect <u>for the purpose of effecting an arrest</u> without a warrant of arrest, unless "exigent (emergency) circumstances" justify such action, or lawful consent for entry is obtained.

The opinion defines exigent circumstances as "an emergency situation requiring swift action to prevent (1) <u>imminent</u> danger to life, (2) or <u>serious</u> damage to property, (3) or to forestall the <u>imminent</u> escape of a suspect, (4) or destruction of evidence."

The burden of proof of the existence of one or more of the exigent circumstances defined by the court will be upon the prosecution, and it appears that the courts will closely scrutinize any such claim of justification.

The prohibition includes arrests for felonies or misdemeanors whether by day or by night, and the prohibition encompasses arrest of adults and minors.

The Ramey rule will be applied to temporary residences such as hotels and motels. With the application of the "vicarious exclusionary rule", which acts to suppress evidence against any defendant when such evidence is obtained in the violation of any third party's rights, it appears that the prohibition will extend to residences of others where the suspect may be a guest regardless of the temporary nature of the suspect's tenancy.

The opinion of the court does not discuss the circumstances of "hot pursuit" or close pursuit from another place into a residence. It is believed that if probable cause for arrest exists during a pursuit but the arrest is not made due purely to the actions of the suspect in evading the officers and going into a residence, then the entry and arrest will be reasonable and justifiable in light of the imminent danger of escape.

Since the issue addressed by the court is the entry into a residence for the purpose of effecting the arrest and the necessity for judicial review of such process before the entry, it can be assumed that entry by means of a valid search warrant would satisfy the requirement for judicial review, and an arrest based on evidence uncovered during the search would be proper and not in violation of the rule in Ramey.

It appears also that if the officer enters the residence lawfully for any purpose other than the arrest of a suspect (in response to a call for service or in the legitimate course of an investigation) an ensuing arrest would be proper, although the courts would certainly scrutinize these circumstances.

In light of this opinion, the policy of the San Bernardino Police Department will be:

A warrant of arrest shall be obtained prior to any arrest of a suspect from a residence at any time for any offense except:

1. When one or more of the defined exigent circumstances are readily evident.
2. As a result of close pursuit wherein the arrest would have been lawful except for the suspect's evading the arrest and going into a residence.
3. When probable cause is developed during the execution of a valid search warrant for the residence and the suspect is present.
4. When entry has been lawfully made for another purpose (such as investigation of an offense or response to a call for service) and was not for the purpose of effecting an arrest.

Figure 5.5 continued

5. When lawful consent for entry for the purpose of effecting an arrest is obtained. In the case of minors, proper consent may be obtained from the parent/s or responsible adult in charge, or, in the absence of a responsible adult, from the minor himself.

During normal business hours, an arrest warrant may be obtained by contacting the District Attorney's Office. Outside of normal business hours, it will be necessary to contact the "on call" deputy district attorney for review and assistance and then a magistrate for the issuance of a warrant. There is no statutory provision for a telephonic arrest warrant, consequently it will be necessary to contact the magistrate in person.

A list of on-call deputies will be maintained in the watch commander's office along with a list of judges' telephone numbers and home addresses.

As has been the case prior to Ramey, it does not appear that the actual physical possession of a warrant of arrest is necessary as long as there is knowledge of the existence of a properly endorsed warrant.

Source: Chapter 2, Procedure 9, "Use of Force," from *Standard Operating Procedure*, San Bernardino, California, Police Department (rev. December 22, 2004). Reprinted with permission.

Watson and *Santana* therefore combine to permit another type of warrantless action authorized by the Fourth Amendment. As long as probable cause is in place, the police can make a warrantless arrest in a public place. A warrantless arrest in the curtilage of someone's home is also authorized. The key in *Santana*, though, was that the arrest was initiated by the police observing what they perceived to be criminal activity from a public place. This important qualification ensures that the police cannot just wander onto private property, looking for opportunities to make arrests. A crime must be observed from a lawful vantage point; otherwise, a warrant will be required.

What if the offense takes place out of view of the officer? The courts have stated that if probable cause exists, the police can arrest anyone for any offense, as long as the arrest is made in a public place. It is useful, though, to distinguish between (1) various types of offenses and (2) whether the offense in question was committed in the presence of the officer. Generally, any offense committed in an officer's presence permits an arrest. Also, there is no requirement that the offense for which a person is arrested be "closely related" to the conduct that led to the confrontation between officer and suspect (*Devenpeck v. Alford*, 543 U.S. 146 [2004]). Additionally, serious offenses (felonies) committed *out* of the officer's view permit a warrantless, public arrest—provided that probable cause exists. Less clear is the issue of a warrantless, public arrest for a misdemeanor committed out of the officer's presence.

ARRESTS FOR MINOR OFFENSES The Supreme Court has declared that "the Fourth Amendment does not forbid a warrantless arrest for a minor criminal offense, such as a misdemeanor seatbelt violation punishable only by a fine" (*Atwater v. City of Lago Vista*, 532 U.S. 318 [2001]). Texas law makes it a misdemeanor for a front-seat passenger in a car equipped with seatbelts not to wear the seatbelt. The law states that the police may arrest or issue only a citation to the passenger. Atwater was arrested and later filed suit under Section 1983, arguing that the officer violated her Fourth Amendment rights. In the Court's words, "Atwater has cited no particular evidence that those who framed and ratified the Fourth Amendment sought to limit peace officers' warrantless

Atwater v. City of Lago Vista (532 U.S. 318 [2001])

misdemeanor arrest authority to instances of actual breach of the peace, and the Court's review of framing-era documentary history has likewise failed to reveal any such design" (p. 336).

On its face, *Atwater* seems to be a controversial case. On closer examination, though, the decision is likely to have little impact on criminal procedure. The reason for this is, simply, that it is unpractical (and usually undesirable) to arrest people for violations as trivial as failing to wear a seatbelt. Just because the Court has now said that such warrantless arrests do not violate the Fourth Amendment does not mean that the police will alter their behavior consistent with the *Atwater* decision.

In another more recent case, *Virginia v. Moore* (553 U.S. 164 [2008]), police stopped a motorist for driving with a suspended license. Virginia state law required that the officers issue a citation and summons to appear in court. Instead, the officers arrested the driver. In a search incident to arrest, officers found cocaine. Moore's attorney sought suppression of the cocaine at trial. The trial court judge allowed the evidence, but the Virginia Supreme Court reversed. In a unanimous decision, the Supreme Court held that the officers did not violate Moore's constitutional rights. The *Moore* case is similar to *Atwater* in the sense that the offense that justified the arrest was relatively minor. And the Supreme Court sanctioned the officers' actions, even though they ran counter to Virginia law.

Virginia v. Moore
(553 U.S. 164 [2008])

Summary

1. SUMMARIZE THE ISSUES INVOLVED IN WARRANTLESS SEARCHES AND SEIZURES.

The situations in which law enforcement officials *can* search without a warrant almost outnumber the number of situations in which they *cannot* search without a warrant. The Supreme Court has carved out several exceptions to the Fourth Amendment's warrant requirement. While the exceptions vary considerably, a common thread runs through them: The Court has decided that it is not always practical to obtain a warrant. Warrantless searches include searches incident to arrest, hot pursuit, automobile searches, and plain view searches.

2. EXPLAIN THE SEARCH INCIDENT TO ARREST DOCTRINE.

Searches incident to arrest are constitutionally permissible, but the arrest must, of course, be legal (i.e., based on probable cause). Also, the arrest must result in someone being taken into custody. Next, the search must follow the arrest closely in time. Finally, the search incident to arrest is limited to (1) the person arrested and any containers discovered from that search and (2) the arrestee's immediate grabbing area. Prior to an arrest, the police may engage in a protective sweep of the premises, if they have a reasonable

belief that evidence may be destroyed by someone sympathetic to the arrestee. They may also engage in a protective sweep following arrest. No justification is required for such a postarrest sweep. Finally, the Supreme Court appears to agree that the premises can be searched for evidence that is likely to be destroyed, and probable cause is not required.

3. EXPLAIN THE CONCEPT OF HOT PURSUIT.

Hot pursuit, threats to persons, and threats to evidence are exigent circumstances that also permit dispensing with the Fourth Amendment's warrant requirement. Warrantless searches and arrests based on hot pursuit are constitutional only if the police have probable cause to believe (1) that the person they are pursuing has committed a serious offense; (2) that the person will be found on the premises the police seek to enter; and (3) that the suspect will escape or harm someone or that evidence will be lost or destroyed. Also, the pursuit must originate from a lawful vantage point and the scope and timing of the search must be reasonable. When hot pursuit does not apply, a warrantless search for evanescent evidence is permissible when (1) there is probable cause to believe that evidence will be destroyed, lost, or devalued; (2) the procedures employed are reasonable; and (3) the exigency was not police created. Finally, if neither hot pursuit nor the potential for damage or destruction to evidence exists, a warrantless search is permissible if the police have probable cause to believe a person on the premises is in imminent danger of death or serious bodily harm.

4. SUMMARIZE THE SPECIAL ISSUES INVOLVED IN AUTOMOBILE SEARCHES.

Warrantless automobile searches are constitutionally permissible because (1) automobiles are mobile, making it difficult to obtain warrants; (2) people enjoy a lesser expectation of privacy when in their cars; and (3) automobiles are subject to a host of government regulations. Even so, for an automobile search to be constitutional, it must be (1) directed at a vehicle ready to serve a transportation function; (2) premised on probable cause to believe the vehicle contains evidence of a crime; and (3) completed without unnecessary delay.

Racial profiling is of particular concern in the context of vehicle stops. It occurs when the police use race or ethnicity as a factor in determining whether they will stop someone. While a driver's race or ethnicity clearly does not provide justification to stop him or her, critics of profiling claim that the police can use existing traffic laws to single out certain individuals—say, for instance, pulling someone over for speeding regardless of whether that actually occurred. The Supreme Court has yet to decide directly on the constitutionality of this type of conduct, but at least one decision has come close to

the issue. In *Whren*, the Court stated that the "constitutional reasonableness of traffic stops" does not depend "on the actual motivations of the individual officers" (p. 813). Despite this controversial decision, Fourteenth Amendment due process claims and claims under Title VI of the Civil Rights Act of 1964 can still be raised.

5. SUMMARIZE THE PLAIN VIEW DOCTRINE.

Items in plain view can be seized if the police have lawful access to the items and if it is immediately apparent that the items are contraband. The discovery of such items does not have to be inadvertent. The "plain view" doctrine has been extended to include plain smell and plain feel. Finally, the plain view doctrine should be viewed as something of a fallback measure because the seizure of evidence can often be justified by other doctrines, such as hot pursuit, search incident to arrest, automobile searches, and so on.

6. DESCRIBE THE SITUATIONS IN WHICH WARRANTLESS ARRESTS MAY BE MADE.

Two types of warrantless arrests have been authorized by the Supreme Court. First, if exigent circumstances are present, the police may make a warrantless arrest. Probable cause is required, however. Second, an arrest in public can be made without a warrant. Even certain minor offenses can support arrest in public places.

Key Terms

armspan rule	152	exceptions to the warrant requirement	150	hot pursuit	155	protective sweep	153
automobile exception	160			immediately apparent	173	racial profiling	169
disparate impact	171	exigent circumstances	155	lawful access	173	search incident to arrest	150
evanescent evidence	157			"plain view" doctrine	172		

Key Cases

Searches Incident to Arrest

- *Chimel v. California*, 395 U.S. 752 (1969)
- *Knowles v. Iowa*, 525 U.S. 113 (1998)
- *Preston v. United States*, 376 U.S. 364 (1964)

Searches Based on Exigent Circumstances

- *Warden v. Hayden*, 387 U.S. 294 (1967)
- *Welsh v. Wisconsin*, 466 U.S. 740 (1984)

- *Minnesota v. Olson*, 495 U.S. 91 (1990)
- *Breithaupt v. Abram*, 352 U.S. 432 (1957)
- *Cupp v. Murphy*, 412 U.S. 291 (1973)

Automobile Searches

- *Carroll v. United States*, 267 U.S. 132 (1925)
- *California v. Carney*, 471 U.S. 386 (1985)
- *New York v. Belton*, 453 U.S. 454 (1981)

- *Arizona v. Gant*, No. 07-542 (2009)
- *Whren v. United States*, 517 U.S. 806 (1996)

Plain View Searches

- *Coolidge v. New Hampshire*, 403 U.S. 443 (1971)
- *Arizona v. Hicks*, 480 U.S. 321 (1987)
- *Horton v. California*, 496 U.S. 128 (1990)

Warrantless Arrests

- *United States v. Watson*, 423 U.S. 411 (1976)
- *United States v. Santana*, 427 U.S. 38 (1976)
- *Atwater v. City of Lago Vista*, 532 U.S. 318 (2001)
- *Virginia v. Moore*, 553 U.S. 164 (2008)

Review Questions

1. Explain the term *exceptions* as applied to the Fourth Amendment.
2. Summarize the requirements for a valid search incident to arrest.
3. What type of law enforcement activities fall under the banner of exigent circumstances?
4. Explain the Supreme Court's rationale for permitting warrantless searches of automobiles.
5. Summarize the requirements for a valid automobile search.
6. Explain the leading cases in the area of racial profiling.
7. What types of arrest are permissible without a warrant?
8. Why does the term *plain view* mean something different in criminal procedure than in everyday use?
9. Explain the lawful access prong of the plain view doctrine.
10. Explain the immediately apparent prong of the plain view doctrine.
11. To what extent is inadvertency relevant in the plain view context?
12. How has the plain view doctrine been extended by the Supreme Court?
13. What other Fourth Amendment doctrines may permit the seizure of evidence if the plain view doctrine does not apply?
14. Has the Supreme Court become too generous with exceptions to the Fourth Amendment's warrant requirement?

Web Links and Exercises

1. Technology and search incident to arrest: Read about some recent lower court cases dealing with the intersection of technology and the search incident to arrest exception to the warrant requirement. One particularly relevant case is *United States v. Finley* (477 F.3d 250 [5th Cir. 2007]).
   Suggested URL: http://cyb3rcrim3.blogspot.com/2007/05/search-incident-to-arrest.html (accessed February 16, 2011).
2. Police pursuits: Read about policies and training in the area of police vehicle pursuits. What is the key dilemma underlying the decision whether to pursue?
   Suggested URL: http://www.ncjrs.gov/pdffiles/164831.pdf (accessed February 16, 2011).
3. Profiling and the war on terror: Read about racial profiling before and after 9/11. How has the worst terrorist attack on our nation altered profiling?
   Suggested URL: http://www.scu.edu/ethics/publications/ethicalperspectives/profiling.html (accessed February 16, 2011).
4. Plain smell: Should the smell of burning marijuana justify a warrantless search? Read more in *United States v. Mowatt* (No. 06-4886 [4th Cir. 2008])
   Suggested URL: http://pacer.ca4.uscourts.gov/opinion.pdf/064886.P.pdf (accessed February 16, 2011).

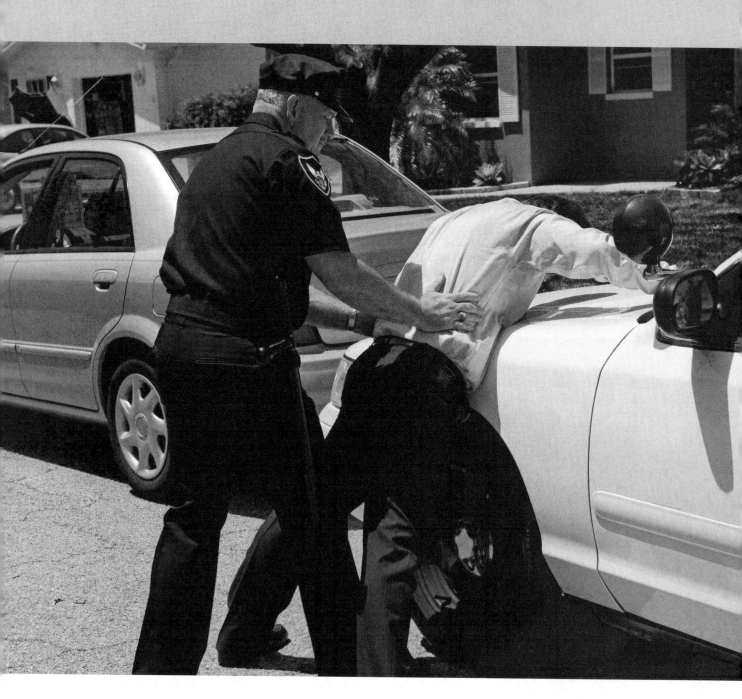

Actions Based on Reasonable Suspicion

INTRODUCTION

Loosening the Fourth Amendment's Restraints

Chapter 3 introduced reasonable suspicion as the appropriate standard of justification required for a police officer to conduct a stop-and-frisk. Reasonable suspicion was defined as a lesser degree of certainty than probable cause but a greater degree of certainty than a hunch or unsupported belief.

The term *reasonable suspicion* is found nowhere in the Constitution. Rather, reasonable suspicion is a standard created by the Supreme Court. The reason that the Court declared that certain confrontations between police and citizens can be based on reasonable suspicion is that crime control could not be accomplished without a lower standard than probable cause. If probable cause was always required, police officers would not even be able to question people about suspected involvement in criminal activity without a high degree of justification.

Reasonable suspicion can be understood in terms of the due process/crime control distinction raised in Chapter 1. The law governing stop-and-frisk attempts to achieve a balance between due process and crime control. On the one hand, most people find it desirable for the police to control crime. If crime ran rampant, people would curtail their activities by, for example, not going out at night. On the other hand, the Constitution is a highly prized guarantor of personal freedoms. Many people, despite their desire to see crime decline, would object to aggressive search-and-seizure tactics by the police. Reasonable suspicion is something of a compromise, then, between the conflicting goals of crime control and due process. It can be seen as achieving a balance between having unrestricted law enforcement and being able to apprehend lawbreakers.

Recall two critical points from Chapter 3. First, when police activity does not constitute a search, the Fourth Amendment does not apply. By extension, then, when the Fourth Amendment does not apply, probable cause is not required. Much the same logic applies to a stop and a frisk. If police conduct falls short of a stop or a frisk, the Fourth Amendment does not apply. Thus, when the Fourth Amendment does not apply, reasonable suspicion is not required. And if the police confront a person but such activity does not constitute a stop or a frisk, no justification is required. At the opposite extreme, though, if police conduct amounts to a more significant intrusion than a stop or a frisk, then a different standard of justification will be required—most likely, probable cause.

STOP AND FRISK: TWO SEPARATE ACTS

A *stop* is separate from a *frisk*. A stop always precedes a frisk, but a stop *does not* give a police officer permission to conduct a frisk. Rather, the officer must have separate justification for each act. Reasonable suspicion is required to stop a person, and it is also required to frisk a person.

Terry v. Ohio (392 U.S. 1 [1968])

In *Terry v. Ohio* (392 U.S. 1 [1968]), the Supreme Court ruled that in addition to the suspicion required to justify a stop, the officer must have reasonable suspicion that the person stopped is *armed* and *dangerous* in order to conduct a frisk. In support of this position, the Court used a balancing test: Each intrusion by the government must be justified by a legitimate objective. In other words, no legitimate law enforcement objective is served when a police officer frisks a person whom the officer does not perceive as threatening.

For example, assume a police officer observes two men in an area with much drug traffic activity, whispering to each other and passing items back and forth. Arguably, the officer would have reasonable suspicion that criminal activity is afoot, thus permitting him or her to question the men. However, if the officer does not perceive that either suspect is armed and dangerous, then a frisk would be inappropriate.

Between Reasonable Suspicion and Stop-and-Frisk

In *Terry*, the Supreme Court also held that before a frisk can take place, the officer must identify himself or herself as a police officer. However, if exigent circumstances exist, the identification may not be necessary. In *Adams v. Williams* (407 U.S. 143 [1972]), an officer, acting on a tip that a man in a nearby car had a gun at his waist, approached the car and asked the man to open the door. When the suspect rolled down his car window instead of opening the door, the officer reached into the car and removed a gun from the man's waistband. The officer did not identify himself, but the Supreme Court ruled that the seizure of the weapon was reasonable in light of the circumstances (see also Decision-Making Exercise 3.9).

In addition to requiring that an officer identify himself or herself, the Court in *Terry* also required an officer to make a "reasonable inquiry." Few cases have addressed the definition of *reasonable inquiry*, but as will be considered in the later discussion of confession and interrogation law, if the officer's questions become too accusatory, then they may fall outside the type permitted during the course of a *Terry* stop.

THE STOP

In many situations, it is clear when a police officer has stopped someone. For instance, when a patrol officer legally pulls a motorist over, it is safe to say that such activity constitutes a stop. Similarly, if a police officer handcuffs a suspect, that person has clearly been stopped (and arrested). But what about a simple confrontation between a foot patrol officer and a pedestrian? If the officer directs general questions—such as "What is your name?"—at the pedestrian, can this be considered a stop? Given that there are many situations such as this, the definition of a *stop* must be given special attention.

Definition of a Stop

Generally speaking, a **stop** is the detention of a person by a law enforcement officer for the purpose of investigation. Why does the definition of a stop matter? Remember, if the police officer's activities do not amount to a stop, then the Fourth Amendment does not apply. This is because a stop is the same thing as a seizure of a person. As the Court observed in *Terry v. Ohio*, "[W]henever a police officer accosts an individual and restrains his freedom to walk away, he has 'seized' that person" (p. 16).

In *Terry*, the Supreme Court stated that "obviously not all personal intercourse between policemen and citizens involves seizures of persons" (p. 20, n. 16). Instead, the Fourth Amendment applies only "when the officer, by means of physical force or show of authority, has in some way restrained the liberty of [a] citizen" (p. 20, n. 16). Thus, there is an important distinction to be drawn between (1) a forcible seizure or a stop and (2) a less intrusive type of confrontation in which, for example, the officer merely questions a person who is free to ignore the officer and leave. The seizure or stop requires reasonable suspicion (provided it is considered a *Terry* stop and not an arrest), but the simple questioning requires no justification.

United States v. Mendenhall (446 U.S. 544 [1980])

There is no easy way to distinguish a *stop* from a *nonstop*, but the Supreme Court has attempted to clarify the differences with an objective test. In *United States v. Mendenhall* (446 U.S. 544 [1980]), the Court observed:

> [A] person has been "seized" within the meaning of the Fourth Amendment only if, in view of all the circumstances surrounding the incident, a *reasonable person would have believed that he was not free to leave*. Examples of circumstances that might indicate a seizure, even where the person did not actually attempt to leave, would be the threatening presence of several officers, the display of a weapon by an officer, some physical touching of the person of the citizen, or the use of language or tone of voice indicating that compliance with the officer's request might be compelled. (p. 554, emphasis added)

The Court's decision in *Mendenhall* stemmed from a confrontation between plainclothes Drug Enforcement Agency (DEA) agents and a 22-year-old African American woman in the Detroit airport. The agents had asked the woman for her ticket and identification, and she complied. When they realized the name on the ticket did not match her name, the agents asked the woman to accompany them into a nearby private room. The Court did not actually decide whether the woman had been stopped, but it did create the objective test described in the previous quote. Figure 6.1 lists several criteria used to distinguish between a stop and a consensual encounter.

FIGURE 6.1

Factors Used to Distinguish between a Stop and a Consensual Encounter

1. Threatening behavior on the part of officers
2. The presence of several officers
3. Display of a weapon by an officer
4. Physical touching of the person by the officer
5. The issuing of orders as opposed to requests
6. The use of intimidating language or tone of voice
7. A lengthy time period
8. Intrusive actions, such as a full-body search
9. Use of lights or sirens
10. The officer blocking the person's path
11. Coercive police behavior
12. Taking place out of public view

Florida v. Royer (460 U.S. 491 [1983]) was the first case to apply the test set forth in *Mendenhall* in order to determine the conditions under which a seizure or stop may take place. The facts in *Royer* were virtually identical to the facts in *Mendenhall*, except that the officers did not return the detained individual's plane ticket or driver's license. The Supreme Court held, in a 5 to 4 decision, that given the circumstances, when the officers did not indicate that the individual was free to leave, a seizure had taken place. The Court wrote:

> The predicate permitting seizures on suspicion short of probable cause is that law enforcement interests warrant a limited intrusion on the personal security of the suspect. The scope of the intrusion permitted will vary to some extent with the particular facts and circumstances of each case. This much, however, is clear: *an investigative detention must be temporary and last no longer than is necessary to effectuate the purpose of the stop. Similarly, the investigative methods employed should be the least intrusive means reasonably available to verify or dispel the officer's suspicion in a short period of time.* (p. 500, emphasis added)

The detained individual was subjected to the functional equivalent of an arrest, and as a result, the agents needed probable cause to detain him for as long as they did (which, incidentally, was only about 15 minutes). Moving the subject from a public location to a private location was one of the key factors that helped turn the encounter from a stop into an arrest.

Contrast *Royer* with the Supreme Court's decision in *Florida v. Rodriguez* (469 U.S. 1 [1984]). In that case, the Court ruled that a seizure had *not* taken place when a plainclothes officer approached a man in an airport, displayed his badge, asked permission to talk with the man, and requested that he move approximately 15 feet to where the man's companions were standing with other police officers. The Court described this type of confrontation as "clearly the sort of consensual encounter that implicates no Fourth Amendment interest" (p. 5). It seems, therefore, at least in the airport context, that certain confrontations that take place in common areas do not amount to stops within the meaning of the Fourth Amendment.

In another case, *Michigan v. Chestnut* (486 U.S. 567 [1988]), police officers in their car followed a man who fled on foot when he spotted their patrol car. The officers did not activate their siren or lights, display weapons, ask the man to stop, or attempt to block the suspect's path. The Court acknowledged that this type of conduct can be "somewhat intimidating," but it ruled, nevertheless, that the act of police officers following the man did not amount to a stop. The situation would have been different, however, if the police officers had visibly chased the defendant. In the Court's words, "[W]hat constitutes a restraint on liberty prompting a person to conclude that he is not free to leave will vary, not only with the particular police conduct at issue, but also with the setting in which the conduct occurs" (p. 573).

Yet another case has applied the objective test set forth in *Mendenhall*. The case of *California v. Hodari D.* (449 U.S. 621 [1991]) involved the apprehension of an individual who was chased by the police on foot. The Court ruled that the individual had not been seized at the time he threw away a rock of cocaine because the police had not yet caught up with him. The individual argued that he was "stopped" when he was being pursued by the police officers because the chase was sufficient to cause a reasonable person to believe he was not free to leave. In other words, he argued that he was subjected to a "show of authority" stop. Accordingly, the individual argued in court that the cocaine should not be admissible as evidence. Rejecting his argument, the Court ruled that the seizure of a person during a pursuit occurs only when there is an application of force by the police or the suspect submits to police authority (i.e., gives up).

California v. Hodari D.
(449 U.S. 621 [1991])

Another case seeks to give meaning to the definition of a *stop*. In *Florida v. Bostick* (501 U.S. 429 [1991]), police officers approached a passenger on a bus and asked to inspect his ticket and identification and also his luggage. Both actions were conducted pursuant to a policy that permitted police officers to conduct suspicionless *Terry* stops for the purpose of detecting drug activity. The Supreme Court refused to adopt the Florida Supreme Court's analysis, which held that such drug sweeps were seizures, implicating the Fourth Amendment. Instead, the Court ruled that "in order to determine whether a particular encounter constitutes a seizure, a court must consider all the circumstances surrounding the encounter to determine whether the police conduct would have communicated to a reasonable person that the person was not free to decline the officer's requests or otherwise terminate the encounter" (p. 439). The Supreme Court remanded the case back to the Florida Supreme Court, instead of reversing it. Nevertheless, a portion of Justice O'Connor's opinion suggests that the majority was not satisfied with the Florida court's decision: The bus passenger's perception of not being free to leave was, according to O'Connor, "the natural result of his decision to take the bus."

Florida v. Bostick
(501 U.S. 429 [1991])

In *United States v. Drayton* (536 U.S. 194 [2002]), the U.S. Supreme Court held that *Bostick*-like bus detentions are permissible and that passengers need not be advised of their right to deny consent to search. And another recent decision requires suspects to provide identification if an officer so requests it (*Hiibel v. Sixth Judicial District of Nevada*, 5YZ U.S. 177 [2004]).

Alternative Definitions of a Stop

It is instructive to look toward the lower courts for further elaboration of the definition of a *stop*. Of course, the Supreme Court has the last word on that definition, but other courts have created interesting standards and/or looked to different factors than the reasonable person in their *Terry*-based analyses.

Instead of adopting the reasonable person test, some lower courts have, for example, focused on the degree of police coercion in determining what constitutes a stop. In *State v. Tsukiyama* (56 Haw. 8 [1974]), one of the leading state-level cases in this area, the Hawaii Supreme Court found that no search had occurred when police questioned a man after he had asked them for a flashlight so he could repair his car. The man was arrested and charged for weapons and drug offenses because when one of the officers on the scene asked him for his identification, he attempted to reach into the glove box of the car for a weapon. At issue in the case before the Hawaii Supreme Court, though, was whether the initial confrontation between the man and the police was a stop.

The Hawaii Supreme Court pointed to the lack of "command, authority, force, threat, coercion, physical stopping or restraint" (p. 17) at the point when the man asked for a flashlight. It further stated, "Since there was no 'stop' or 'seizure' of the defendant prior to his overtly unlawful act, we do not have to decide whether the circumstances could have given rise to a belief that 'criminal activity may have been afoot' and thus justify a 'stop' or 'seizure' " (pp. 17–18). Had the court declared the initial confrontation a stop, the "fruit of the poisonous tree" doctrine (see Chapter 2) could have potentially applied.

In another case, *Login v. State* (394 So.2d 183 [1981]), the Florida District Court of Appeals had occasion to define when a stop took place. In that case, a man walking in the Miami airport was confronted by a police officer, who displayed his badge and asked the man for identification. The officer asked the man if he could talk for a minute, at which point the officer observed cocaine residue around the man's nostrils. This raised a question similar to that in the *Tsukiyama* case: Did a stop occur when the officer asked the man if they could talk?

The court declared that a stop had not occurred and went on to note that it would be risky to rule that a stop automatically occurs the moment a person is confronted. In the court's words, a rule that a stop occurs the moment a person is confronted by a police officer

> would cover a multitude of police-citizen encounters which in no way approach a police seizure of the person, such as police questioning of a probable witness to a crime or police inquiries directed to a stranded motorist in need of assistance. To label all police encounters with the public as seizures when accompanied by questioning, no matter how cordial, would tremendously impede the police in the effective performance of both their criminal investigation and community assistance functions. (p. 14)

However, the court did note that a *seizure* does occur when the language used by the police "in tone and content bespeak[s] an order to stop, particularly when employed during a fast moving criminal investigation on the street" (p. 13). This observation is similar to the analysis offered by the Hawaii Supreme Court in *Tsukiyama*. Perhaps the most significant factor, then, in determining when a stop occurs is the tone and content of the police officer's questioning.

Other cases, though, would seem to suggest that even the act of asking a person to halt, such as the rider of a bicycle, does not constitute a stop within the meaning of the Fourth Amendment (see *People v. King*, 72 Cal. App.3d 346 [1977]; *State v. Davis*, 543 So.2d 375 [Fla. 3d D.C.A. 1989]).

DECISION-MAKING EXERCISE 6.1

Looking for Illegal Aliens

Immigration and Customs Enforcement (ICE—formerly the INS) routinely conducts so-called factory surveys to determine whether illegal aliens are employed at certain worksites. In these surveys, uniformed and armed agents disperse themselves through the building and approach each employee in order to inquire about his or her citizenship. While this is going on, employees are free to continue with their work and move about the building. Does such activity amount to a stop, thereby implicating the Fourth Amendment?

Duration of a Stop

What is the proper duration of a stop? Better yet, when does a stop evolve into an arrest because it takes too long? There are no easy answers. In *Florida v. Royer*, discussed above, the Supreme Court held that a 15-minute detention exceeded the bounds of a proper stop—and became a *de facto* arrest. Yet, in certain exceptional circumstances, the Supreme Court has permitted detentions lasting much longer. For example, in *United States v. Sharpe* (470 U.S. 675 [1985]), officers followed two vehicles suspected of involvement in drug trafficking. One vehicle was stopped and the driver was detained for 40 minutes while the officers sought and stopped the second car and its driver. The Court did not establish a bright-line rule for what time period is considered permissible, but it did state that "in evaluating whether an investigative detention is unreasonable, common sense and ordinary human experience must govern over rigid criteria" (p. 685). Thus, the 40-minute detention of the driver of the first car was permissible.

In another case, *United States v. Montoya De Hernandez* (473 U.S. 531 [1985]), a woman who was traveling from Colombia was detained for 16 hours in an airport because she was suspected of being a "balloon swallower" (i.e., a person who smuggles narcotics by hiding them in his or her alimentary canal). This was actually a very controversial case. The woman was given two options: (1) to return on the next available flight to Colombia or (2) to remain in detention until she was able to produce a monitored bowel movement. She chose the first option, but officials were unable to place her on the next flight, and she refused to use toilet facilities. Officials then obtained a court order to conduct a pregnancy test (she claimed to be pregnant), an X-ray exam, and a rectal exam. The exams revealed 88 cocaine-filled balloons in her alimentary canal. She was convicted of numerous federal drug offenses, but the court of appeals reversed that decision, holding that her detention violated the Fourth Amendment. The Supreme Court, in turn, reversed the court of appeals decision and ruled that the 16-hour detention was permissible. According to the Court, "The detention of a traveler at the border, beyond the scope of a routine customs search and inspection, is justified at its inception if customs agents, considering all the facts surrounding the traveler and her trip, reasonably suspect that the traveler is smuggling contraband in her alimentary canal" (p. 541).

United States v. Montoya De Hernandez (473 U.S. 531 [1985])

In another case, *Courson v. McMillian* (939 F.2d 1479 [11th Cir. 1991]), the Eleventh Circuit Court ruled that an officer's act of stopping a car and holding the occupants at gunpoint for 30 minutes was not illegal because most of the time was spent waiting for backup to arrive. Citing *Adams v. Williams*, the court observed:

> The Fourth Amendment does not require a policeman who lacks the precise level of information necessary for probable cause to arrest to simply shrug his shoulders and allow a crime to occur or criminal to escape. On the contrary, *Terry* recognizes that it may be the essence of good police work to adopt an intermediate response. A brief stop of a suspicious individual, in order to determine his identity or to maintain the status quo momentarily while obtaining more information, may be most reasonable in light of the facts known to the officer at the time. (pp. 145–146)

DECISION-MAKING EXERCISE 6.2

Creating a "Constitutionally Cognizable" Policy

The city mayor, frustrated with a wave of serious and violent crime in the area, instructs the police to stop and demand identification from each citizen they encounter. As the mayor's legal counsel, what would you advise regarding the constitutionality of these instructions to the police?

Contrast the decision reached in *Courson v. McMillian* with that reached in *United States v. Luckett* (484 F.2d 89 [9th Cir. 1973]). In *Luckett*, the Second Circuit Court declared a jaywalker's detention invalid because it was based on a hunch that there was a warrant for the jaywalker's arrest. The court ruled that the stop effectively turned into an arrest, not just because of the duration of the stop but because there was no basis for an arrest at the time of the stop.

Are there any clear answers, then, as to what the appropriate duration of a stop is? Unfortunately, no, but the Supreme Court has stated that the reasonableness of a stop turns on the facts and circumstances of each case. In particular, the Court has emphasized "(1) the public interest served by the seizure, (2) the nature and scope of the intrusion, and (3) the objective facts upon which the law enforcement officer relied in light of his knowledge and expertise" (*United States v. Mendenhall*, p. 561). Moreover, the Court has ruled that "the use of a particular method to restrain a person's freedom of movement does not necessarily make police action tantamount to an arrest" and that "police may take reasonable action, based upon the circumstances, to protect themselves . . . or to maintain the status quo" (*United States v. Kapperman*, 764 F.2d 786 [11th Cir. 1985], p. 790, n. 4).

The Meaning of "Free to Leave"

If a person is confronted but not stopped, is he or she *really* free to leave? This question invariably arises in criminal procedure class. Many people tend to feel intimidated by police officers, even when asked nonincriminating, innocuous questions. Would it not appear strange to an officer for someone to simply walk away during a conversation with him or her? Would the officer just let the person walk away and go about his or her business? There are no easy answers to questions such as these, but they highlight the differences between theory and reality, as considered in Chapter 1.

Even though the Supreme Court has stated that a stop does not take place when a reasonable person would believe he or she is free to leave, actually leaving during the course of a conversation with a police officer could prove to be something of a risky endeavor. Much the same controversy applies to situations in which a motorist is legally permitted to decline to give a police officer permission to search his or her surroundings, even though doing so may create suspicion.

In a similar vein, does a person who is stopped have the right to refuse to answer questions? The answer is yes, for an obvious reason: A person cannot be *forced* to talk. However, refusing to answer questions could create enough fear on the part of the officer to justify a stop and could also factor into a probable cause determination that could justify an arrest. Despite all Supreme Court rulings to the contrary, then, it is risky to simply walk away from an inquisitive police officer and/or to refuse to provide answers to his or her inquiries.

Can Effects Be Seized?

Terry v. Ohio and subsequent similar cases have mostly focused on stops of *persons*, but a handful of cases have addressed the stop (i.e., seizure) of property based on less than probable cause. As indicated in Chapter 3, probable cause is required for the seizure of a person if that seizure amounts to an arrest. The same applies to *effects*, which are usually a person's personal items. If the detention or seizure of a person's effects amounts to an arrest, then probable cause is required.

The question, then, is, when does the seizure of a person's effects rise to the level of an arrest? The Supreme Court attempted to answer this question in *United States v. Place* (462 U.S. 696 [1983]). In that case, the Court ruled that a 90-minute detention of a person's luggage in an airport to arrange for a drug dog "sniff" to detect drugs was

DECISION-MAKING EXERCISE 6.3

Stretching the Time Limits of a Stop

Law enforcement officers had a plane under surveillance because they had reasonable suspicion to believe that it was being used to transport narcotics. They approached the aircraft, which was ready for takeoff. Standing near the left wing of the plane, one of the officers raised his badge, identified himself, and, shouting over the noise of the speeding engine, ordered the pilot to shut off the engine and get down. The pilot looked from side to side and appeared hesitant about what to do. At that moment, the officer moved in front of the aircraft, drew his gun, pointed it at the pilot, and again yelled to him to shut off the engine and get out of the plane. The officer identified himself and said he wanted to speak to the pilot because he was suspected of narcotics smuggling. He then patted down the pilot in search of weapons; finding none, he placed his gun back in the holster. The officers then questioned the pilot about the plane's ownership. The pilot was evasive and ended up supplying inaccurate and contradictory information about who owned the plane. The officers then detained him for over an hour while *they* attempted to determine who owned the plane. Was this action justified?

unconstitutional because the detention was too long. Also, the Court stated that "the failure of the agents to accurately inform respondent of the place to which they were transporting his luggage, of the length of time he might be dispossessed, and of what arrangements would be made for return of the luggage if the investigation dispelled the suspicion" (p. 710) contributed to the unconstitutional nature of the detention. The Court went on to note that "some brief detentions of personal effects may be so minimally intrusive of Fourth Amendment interests that strong countervailing governmental interests will justify seizure based only on specific articulable facts that the property contains contraband or evidence of a crime" (p. 706).

In another case, *United States v. Leeuwen* (397 U.S. 249 [1970]), the Supreme Court confirmed that there are some situations in which restraints on people's effects do not amount to a Fourth Amendment seizure. In that case, the police, who were contacted by a suspicious postal clerk, asked post office officials to hold two packages for 29 hours while they investigated the situation and obtained a search warrant. A unanimous Court ruled that the circumstances "certainly justified detention, without a warrant, while an investigation was made" (p. 252). Also, the Court ruled that "[n]o interest protected by the Fourth Amendment was invaded by forwarding the packages the following day rather than the day when they were deposited" (p. 253). In short, because the detention of the package did not invade any privacy interest in the package, a Fourth Amendment seizure did not take place.

Summary.   A *Terry* stop/seizure is characterized by two specific events: (1) The police question a person or communicate with him or her and (2) a reasonable person would believe that he or she is not free to leave. Reasonable suspicion is required in order to make a *Terry* stop conform to Fourth Amendment requirements. Conversely, if an officer detains a person in such a manner that a reasonable person would believe he or she *is* free to leave, the protections of the Fourth Amendment do not apply and reasonable suspicion is not required. If the officer wishes to conduct a frisk—a separate act from a stop—he or she must have reasonable suspicion that the suspect is armed and dangerous, not just reasonable suspicion, as required for a *Terry* stop.

There are no clear answers as to what is the appropriate duration for a stop. However, as the Supreme Court suggested in *United States v. Mendenhall*, a lengthy stop is constitutionally permissible when (1) the public interest is served by the seizure; (2) the nature and scope of the intrusion are not excessive; and (3) the officer possesses enough in the way of objective facts to justify the stop (p. 561). Thus, if a person is stopped and detained for a long time based on an officer's hunch but poses no

DECISION-MAKING EXERCISE 6.4
What Constitutes a Proper Stop?

On a Wednesday afternoon at 3:00 p.m., Officer Weber was on patrol in a neighborhood that had experienced several daytime burglaries. Her attention was drawn to a car in the driveway of one residence, which had its trunk open. In the trunk were several plastic trash bags of the type reportedly used by the burglar to carry away the loot. Weber pulled her cruiser into the driveway behind the vehicle, blocking its path. At that point, the driver of the car was closing the trunk and preparing to leave. The driver approached Weber, appearing quite nervous, and asked her to move the cruiser. Instead of doing so, Weber asked the driver for identification, which he produced. The identification indicated an address on the other side of town. Weber then frisked the driver, found a gun in his left coat pocket, and arrested him. No evidence connected the driver to the burglaries, but he was prosecuted for unlawfully carrying a concealed weapon. He moved to exclude the gun on the grounds that the initial stop was illegal and that the gun was the fruit of that illegal stop. What should the court decide?

threat to public safety, then the stop will probably be declared illegal. In such a situation, the stop would need to be justified by probable cause because it would amount to a *de facto* arrest.

THE FRISK

As indicated, the additional step of frisking a suspect is a Fourth Amendment intrusion that requires justification apart from that required to stop the person. Specifically, in order to conduct a **frisk** (a superficial examination by the officer of the person's body surface or clothing to discover weapons or items that could be used to cause harm), the officer needs reasonable suspicion that the suspect is armed and dangerous. This is in addition to the reasonable suspicion required to stop the person for questioning.

Permissible Grounds for a Frisk

While *Terry* held that a frisk is permissible only when an officer reasonably fears for his or her safety, there is still considerable dispute over the situations in which a frisk is appropriate. What does it mean, in other words, to *fear for one's safety*? A number of court decisions have wrestled with this question.

Pennsylvania v. Mimms
(434 U.S. 106 [1977])

For example, in *Pennsylvania v. Mimms* (434 U.S. 106 [1977]), police officers observed a man driving a vehicle with expired plates. The officers stopped the vehicle in order to issue the man a traffic summons. When the officers asked the man to step out of the car, the officers observed a large bulge in the pocket of his jacket. Fearing that the bulge might be a weapon, one of the officers frisked the man. It turned out that the bulge was a .38 caliber revolver. The man claimed at his trial that the gun was seized illegally, but the Supreme Court upheld the frisk. Even though a bulge in one's pocket does not necessarily indicate he or she has a weapon, the Court granted some latitude in its decision to law enforcement personnel.

Ybarra v. Illinois
(444 U.S. 85 [1979])

However, in *Ybarra v. Illinois* (444 U.S. 85 [1979]), the Court ruled that officers did not have grounds to frisk 12 bar patrons during a search of the bar itself. Justice Stewart stated in *Ybarra* that "[t]he 'narrow scope' of the *Terry* exception does not permit a frisk for weapons on less than reasonable belief or suspicion directed at the person to be frisked, even though that person happens to be on premises where an authorized narcotics search is taking place" (p. 94). Thus, just because someone happens to be in an area in which criminal activity is supposedly taking place does not make him or her eligible for a frisk.

Despite the limitations on frisks imposed by the *Ybarra* decision, the Court has since gone back somewhat on its decision in that case. In *Minnesota v. Dickerson* (508 U.S. 366 [1993]), police officers observed a man leaving a "crack" house. As he approached and saw the officers, he turned and began walking in the opposite direction. The officers stopped and frisked him and found drugs on him. The frisk was conducted without reasonable suspicion or any other level of justification. The Court ruled that the police exceeded the bounds of a valid frisk when they found drugs on the man's person, but the Court did *not* rule that the frisk was unconstitutional. It would seem, then, that under certain circumstances, a frisk is permissible on less than reasonable suspicion. Apparently, the act of leaving a "crack" house and acting evasively was sufficient justification to conduct a frisk, even though the police went too far in doing so.

Minnesota v. Dickerson (508 U.S. 366 [1993])

In *Arizona v. Johnson* (No. 07-1122 [2009]), the Court further expanded the frisk doctrine. In that case, gang task force officers were patrolling and stopped a vehicle for a traffic violation. The officers had no reason to suspect the vehicle's occupants of criminal activity, but they nevertheless ordered them out of the car. One of them was frisked and a weapon was found. The Court sanctioned this activity, noting that "a passenger's motivation to use violence during the stop to prevent apprehension for a crime more grave than a traffic violation is just as great as that of the driver."

So, are there any clear rules that establish when an officer can reasonably fear for his or her safety? The answer is no. Ultimately, the determination of a potential threat is a subjective one. Almost without exception, the courts will defer to the judgment of the officer, assuming that he or she is able to articulate some specific facts that contributed to reasonable suspicion that the suspect was armed and dangerous. Figure 6.2 summarizes the circumstances as to when a frisk is permissible.

Scope of a Frisk

A number of cases have focused specifically on the permissible scope of a frisk. Two issues have been raised: (1) the definition of a *frisk*—that is, what the officer can physically do to a person that does not rise to the level of a search; and (2) the items that can be felt for during the course of a frisk.

With regard to the first issue, the Supreme Court in *Terry* described a *frisk* as "a carefully limited search of the outer clothing . . . in an attempt to discover weapons which might be used to assault [a police officer]" (p. 30). In *Sibron v. New York* (392 U.S. 40 [1968]), the Court offered additional clarification by declaring that the act of reaching into a suspect's pockets is impermissible when the officer makes "no attempt at an initial limited exploration for arms" (p. 65). Generally, then, a frisk is little more than an open-handed patdown of someone's outer clothing. Only if the officer feels something that resembles a weapon can he or she then reach into the suspect's pocket (or other area used to conceal it) to determine what the item is. And as the Supreme Court

Sibron v. New York (392 U.S. 40 [1968])

FIGURE 6.2

When a Frisk Is Permissible

1. When the person has a reputation for dangerousness
2. When the person is suspected of having committed a dangerous felony
3. When visual cues suggest the presence of a weapon or similar dangerous instrument
4. When the suspect makes suggestive or furtive gestures

observed in *United States v. Richardson* (949 F.2d 851 [6th Cir. 1991]), "When actions by the police exceed the bounds permitted by reasonable suspicion, the seizure becomes an arrest and must be supported by probable cause" (p. 856).

With regard to the second issue, or the items that can be felt for during the course of a frisk, the Supreme Court in *Ybarra v. Illinois* emphasized that frisks must be directed at discovering weapons, not criminal evidence. In *Ybarra*, one of the police officers had removed what he described as a "cigarette pack with objects in it" from the suspect. The Court basically decided that the officer's actions were too intrusive; the package could not have been considered a threat to the safety of the officers conducting the search. Significantly, the Court did not declare the seizure illegal because the officer was not looking for weapons but because the officer did not have reasonable suspicion to frisk every patron in the bar. Nevertheless, a frisk should not be used as a "fishing expedition" to see if some kind of usable evidence can be found on the person.

Two additional points concerning the scope of a frisk need to be underscored at this juncture. First, just because the Supreme Court has declared that a frisk should be conducted based on the motive to preserve officer safety, this does not mean the officer cannot seize contraband found during the course of a lawful frisk. This issue is discussed in the section on plain touch and feel later in this chapter. What is important now, though, is that a frisk is supposed to be *motivated* by the desire to remove weapons and other instruments of potential harm from a criminal suspect.

Second, remember that a valid frisk can always evolve into a Fourth Amendment search, provided that probable cause develops along the way. For example, assume that a Chicago police officer frisks a suspect because she fears he may be carrying a gun. If it turns out that the suspect is carrying a pistol, which is illegal in the city of Chicago, she could arrest the suspect and conduct a full search incident to arrest. In this example, though, the object seized during the frisk (i.e., the gun) must be immediately apparent to the officer for the seizure to be legal. As the Supreme Court stated in *Minnesota v. Dickerson*:

> Although the officer was lawfully in a position to feel the lump in respondent's pocket, because *Terry* entitled him to place his hands upon respondent's jacket, the court below determined that the incriminating character of the object was not immediately apparent to him. Rather, the officer determined that the item was contraband only after conducting a further search, one not authorized by *Terry* or by any other exception to the warrant requirement. (p. 379)

In the example, then, had the seizure followed careful manipulation of the object by the officer, then a seizure based on the frisk would not conform to Fourth Amendment requirements. Figure 6.3 provides additional examples of proper and improper frisks.

Summary. A frisk is permissible when an officer reasonably fears for his or her safety. However, there is no easy way to discern the facts that would *cause* an officer to reasonably fear for his or her safety. If an officer can offer no facts or testimony to support the frisk, it will probably be declared unconstitutional. On the other hand, if the officer possesses some objective information that served as the basis for a frisk (e.g., observing a bulge in a suspect's pocket), the frisk will probably be legal.

A number of cases have focused on the permissible scope of a frisk, and three important restrictions have been imposed. First, a frisk can be nothing more than a patdown of someone's outer clothing. Groping or squeezing is not permissible. Second, a frisk must be motivated by the desire to promote officer safety, not by the desire to seek out any form of contraband. That is, the sole purpose of a *Terry* patdown is to protect

FIGURE 6.3

Examples of Proper and Improper Frisks

Proper: An officer notices a vehicle being driven erratically and stops it. The driver gives false identification, admits having done time for robbery, and is wearing a bulky jacket that he is having a hard time keeping his hands out of. The officer orders him out of the car, pats him down, and finds syringes in the suspect's jacked pockets (*People v. Autry*, 232 Cal. App. 3d 365 [1991]).

Proper: At 1:15 a.m., officers stop a vehicle for driving with its lights off. The driver gets out of the vehicle and heads toward the officers, leaving two other individuals in vehicle. When the officers asked for the driver's license, he says it is in his socks. Fearing for his safety, the officer quickly frisks the driver and finds a knife in the driver's sock (*People v. Barnes*, 141 Cal. App. 3d 854 [1983]).

Proper: Two officers observe a young man looking into two parked cars in a back alley where there have been several complaints of criminal activity. The suspect tries to stay out of view of the officers when he noticed them by hiding behind a dumpster. When the officers approach the suspect and ask questions, he becomes combative. They frisk him for weapons (*People v. Michael S.*, 141 Cal. App. 3d 814 [1983]).

Proper: An officer responds to a report of several suspicious individuals in a restaurant parking lot. On arriving at the scene, one of the suspects turns and walks away, whereupon the officer notices a large bulge in his pocket. The officer stops the man, frisks him, and finds a weapon (*People v. Miles*, 196 Cal. App. 3d 612 [1987]).

Proper: In response to a "panhandler" complaint, an officer frisks a man after observing a large bulge in the front waistband of his pants (*People v. Snyder*, 11 Cal. App. 4th 389 [1992]).

Proper: An officer is serving a search warrant and pats down a man who is sitting on the couch in the living room. The man is passive and nonthreatening—and the warrant did not authorize any searches of persons (*People v. Thurman*, 209 Cal. App. 3d 817 [1989]).

Proper: An officer responds to a reported "prowler" call and frisks two individuals who could produce no identification and speak only Spanish (*People v. Castaneda*, 35 Cal. App. 4th 1222 [1995]).

Proper: An officer encounters a suspect walking along a street, carrying a television set in an area known for excessive burglaries. He pats the suspect down, checking for weapons (*People V. Myles*, 50 Cal. App. 3d 1107 [1975]).

Proper: An officer is having a consensual encounter with a man on the street. The man reaches into his pocket, at which point the officer notices a bulge therein. The officer grabs the man's wrist to prevent him from reaching into the pocket (*People v. Rosales*, 211 Cal. App. 3d 325 [1989]).

Improper: An officer frisks a man who was sitting in a parked car, with the engine running, in the middle of a rural dirt road. The man had no identification or license and refused to the let the officer search the vehicle. He was also nervous (*People v. Dickey*, 21 Cal. App. 4th 952 [1994]).

Source: From *California Peace Officers Legal Sourcebook*, electronic edition, revision 113 (Sacramento, CA: California Department of Justice, Office of the Attorney General), section 2.20.

the officer from weapons that might be used by the suspect during the encounter. Finally, for an officer to legally seize an item during the course of a frisk, that item must be immediately apparent to the officer as contraband.

For something of a summary of stop-and-frisk law, see Figure 6.4, which contains the San Bernardino, California, Police Department's stop-and-frisk policy. It succinctly summarizes the discussion thus far.

DECISION-MAKING EXERCISE 6.5
The Permissible Scope of a Frisk

Two police officers were approached by a person (previously unknown to them) who stated that Jack Smith was in the Valley Grill on First Street and that he had several bags of cocaine for sale. The person provided detailed information concerning Smith and described the clothing he was wearing. The officers went to the Valley Grill and found no one of that description. After the officers left the bar, however, they observed a person walking on the sidewalk who matched the description they had been given. The officers approached him, blocked his path, and asked for his identification. The man's identification revealed that his name was Jack Smith. At that point, the officers ordered Smith to remove his shoes. He did so as the officers continued to ask him questions. Was this action appropriate?

FIGURE 6.4
Stop-and-Frisk Policy (San Bernardino, CA, Police Department)

STANDARD OPERATING PROCEDURE   CHAPTER #29   PROCEDURE #3

CURSORY PATDOWN and CUSTODIAL SEARCHES   12-4-02

PURPOSE

To establish a policy governing cursory patdown and custody searches of detained and arrested subjects.

DEFINITIONS

    A. Search – A reasonable infringement of an individual's expectation of privacy. Every individual has the right to be protected from unreasonable searches as set forth by the Fourth Amendment of the United States Constitution and made applicable to the states by the Fourteenth Amendment.

    B. Cursory Patdown Search – A search conducted of detained subject for the purpose of detecting weapons.

    C. Custody Search – A search conducted of an arrested or detained subject where probable cause exists to arrest, to recover weapons, contraband, or other evidence. Normally custody searches are done during the booking procedure; however, this policy does not preclude in-field custody searches from occurring.

POLICY and PROCEDURES

Cursory Patdown Search

    A. Detaining/Arresting

        1. When an officer detains any subject suspected of committing a criminal offense and the officer has reasonable suspicion that subject may have a weapon, the officer shall conduct, or arrange for a cursory patdown search for weapons as soon as practical.

        2. When an officer arrests any subject, the officer shall conduct or arrange for a cursory patdown or custody search prior to placing the suspect in a vehicle for transportation.

        3. The cursory patdown search for weapons or contraband shall consist of patting the suspect's body and clothing. The squeezing of loosely fitting clothing, such as jacket seams and pockets or other unexplained masses is permitted. Detected potential weapons and contraband, or containers capable of concealing

weapons or contraband shall be removed for inspection. Officers shall be cautious of the potential presence of sharp or pointed objects.

B. In the absence of consent or plain sight, other detected objects may not be removed or inspected unless the subject is under arrest or probable cause exists to arrest the subject. Officers are cautioned that probable cause to arrest must exist before non-weapon objects can be removed for inspection.

C. Absent exigent circumstances, an officer of the same sex <u>shall</u> conduct the cursory search. Exigent circumstances are defined as:

- An immediate articulable threat to the officer, public safety, or the potential destruction/disposal of physical evidence.

- Response of a same sex officer will result in an unreasonable period of detention.

Whenever possible, cursory patdown searches by an officer of the opposite sex of the detainee should be in direct sight of a second witnessing officer. Every reasonable effort shall be made to protect the dignity of the arrestee or detainee during the cursory patdown search.

<u>Custody Search</u>

A. Custody searches shall be conducted of every individual who is arrested and maintained in police custody. A custody search should be conducted as soon as practical. Custody searches may be conducted in the field prior to transport, but must be conducted before an arrestee is allowed to enter the prisoner holding areas of a custodial facility. Most custodial facilities include secure areas away from confined prisoners for the purpose of searching and processing prisoners. Officers will make every reasonable effort to prevent weapons or contraband from entering any jail facility.

B. Custody searches are conducted for the purpose of detecting any and all objects in the possession of the arrestee. Custody searches include the removal of footwear, headwear, or outer clothing such as jackets, coats, sweaters, overpants, coveralls, etc. Non-surgically attached artificial apparatus such as a hairpiece or prosthesis capable of concealing weapons or contraband shall be removed.

C. Absent justification and authorization for a "strip search or body cavity search" (SOP Chapter #29, Procedure #1), arrestees shall not be required to remove shirts, blouses, trousers, pants, skirts, and shorts so long as such clothing items are not so thick to prevent the detection of weapons or contraband, or said items are determined to be of evidentiary value.

D. Absent exigent circumstances, officers of the same sex as the arrestee shall conduct custody searches. Exigent circumstances are defined as:

- <u>The immediate destruction of evidence</u>. Opposite sex officers who become aware of evidence or contraband during a cursory patdown search or other legal means and delaying the custody search would result in the immediate destruction of the evidence or contraband, may conduct a limited custody search for the purpose of recovering the evidence or contraband. If reasonable control techniques such as handcuffing the prisoner would prevent the destruction of the evidence or contraband, the custody search shall be delayed until a same sex officer is available.

- <u>The non-availability of a same sex officer or jail custodian</u>. When a same sex officer or jail custodian is not available, a supervisor or watch commander shall authorize an opposite sex custody search. A second opposite sex officer or jail custodian will witness all opposite sex custody searches. Every reasonable effort shall be made to protect the dignity of the arrestee during the custody search.

E. The department recognizes that there are a limited number of female officers and female jail custodians. It is not the intent of this policy to significantly delay or paralyze the processing of an arrestee due to the non-availability of same sex officers or jail custodians. Nor is it the intent of this policy to delay officers conducting cursory patdown searches from immediately seizing evidence from subjects under arrest or where probable cause exists to arrest. In such cases, officers shall take immediate action and notify a supervisor of that action as soon as practical. Officers will document the circumstances of the search and the results of the search in a report.

F. Officers and/or jail custodians shall document all property discovered during a custody search in a report. Normally this will be accomplished by means of an arrest follow up report or approved prisoner property inventory report.

Source: Chapter 29, Procedure 3, "Use of Force," from *Standard Operating Procedure*, San Bernardino, California, Police Department (rev. December 22, 2004). Reprinted with permission.

THE EVOLVING NATURE OF STOP-AND-FRISK LAW

In *Terry v. Ohio*, the Supreme Court created an exception to the Fourth Amendment's requirement that probable cause is required for searches by holding that police officers can stop and frisk people based on reasonable suspicion. In the wake of *Terry*, a number of significant and controversial Supreme Court decisions have modified the scope of the stop-and-frisk exception to the Fourth Amendment's probable cause requirement. Illustrative cases fall into four categories:

- vehicle stops and weapons searches of automobiles,
- protective sweeps of residences,
- plain touch and feel, and
- stops for loitering.

Vehicle Stops and Weapons Searches of Automobiles

Delaware v. Prouse (440 U.S. 648 [1979])

Automobile searches were covered in Chapter 5, but it is appropriate to mention here, during the discussion of stop-and-frisk, what police officers can do with automobiles in the presence of reasonable suspicion. *Delaware v. Prouse* (440 U.S. 648 [1979]) set forth the rule that police officers can stop and detain motorists in their vehicles so long as the officers have "at least articulable and reasonable suspicion" that the motorists are violating the law. For example, if a police officer observes a driver run a stop sign, the officer is justified in pulling the person over and detaining him or her because reasonable suspicion is present. The decision in *Pennsylvania v. Mimms* also authorizes a police officer to order a driver out of a car. The logic is that doing so is a minimal intrusion that can be justified by safety concerns. These decisions (as well as *Terry*) also permit a police officer to frisk a motorist who has been pulled over if the officer reasonably fears for his or her safety.

Interestingly, if a police officer orders a driver (or a passenger, or both) out of the car, is reasonably suspicious that the driver is armed and dangerous, and frisks the driver, the officer may also search the area of the interior of the car within the suspect's immediate control. Such a search is permissible even when the driver has already been ordered to step out of the vehicle. The case that established this ruling was *Michigan v. Long* (463 U.S. 1032 [1983]). In *Long*, police officers saw a car swerve into a ditch and after stopping to investigate, they observed that the driver was intoxicated and that there was a large hunting knife on the floor of the vehicle. The Supreme Court ruled that the officers were justified in searching the passenger compartment and frisking the driver.

Michigan v. Long is an important decision because a search almost always requires probable cause. Note, however, that the scope of the search in this case was limited to the vehicle occupant's grabbing area, which included the whole of the interior of the car. Neither containers inside the car nor any in the trunk of the car (if any) can be searched during the course of a vehicle weapons search based on reasonable suspicion.

Protective Sweeps of Residences

Another decision that essentially expands *Terry* is *Maryland v. Buie* (494 U.S. 325 [1990])—a case that was already discussed in the search incident to arrest section of the previous chapter. If police lawfully make an arrest in a person's residence, a protective sweep (defined in Chapter 5 and the glossary) of the home is permitted based on the *Terry* rationale. A *sweep* is when one or more officers disperse throughout the home with the intent of looking for other people that could pose a threat to the officers making the arrest. In the Court's words, a *protective sweep* is a "quick and limited search of the premises, incident to arrest, and conducted to protect the safety of police officers or others" (p. 325). This protective sweep, which requires reasonable suspicion, should be distinguished from the automatic but more limited sweep that is permitted incident to a lawful arrest (see Chapter 5).

Maryland v. Buie
(494 U.S. 325 [1990])

According to the Supreme Court, a sweep is permitted if the officer possesses "a reasonable belief based on specific and articulable facts that an area to be swept harbors an individual posing a danger to those at the arrest scene" (p. 337). In addition, a sweep "may extend only to a cursory inspection of those spaces where a person may be found" and may last only as long as is necessary to eliminate the suspicion of danger. The case of *Maryland v. Buie* thus expands *Terry* in the sense that police officers can do more than just frisk a person who is arrested in a private residence. Note, however, that this case does not permit officers to *search* but only to *sweep* the area. A search would have to be supported by probable cause. However, items in plain view can be seized (see Chapter 5).

The Court's decision in *Maryland v. Buie* is not without its critics, however—the dissenters in the case being perhaps the most vocal. Consider Justice Brennan's observations in the dissent he wrote:

> *Terry* and its early progeny permitted only brief investigative stops and extremely limited searches based on reasonable suspicion . . . but this Court more recently has applied the rationale underlying *Terry* to a wide variety of more intrusive searches and seizures prompting my continued criticism of the emerging tendency on the part of the Court to convert the *Terry* decision from a narrow exception into one that swallows the general rule that [searches] are reasonable only if based on probable cause. (p. 339)

DECISION-MAKING EXERCISE 6.6

A Vehicle Search

A police officer pulled a woman motorist over for exceeding the posted speed limit. The officer then ordered the woman out of the car. Without her consent and without probable cause, the officer searched the interior passenger compartment of the vehicle. He found marijuana and a "bong" under the seat and so arrested the woman. Was the search of the passenger compartment justified?

The exception Justice Brennan refers to is Terry's exception to the Fourth Amendment's requirement that reasonable searches be supported by probable cause. In a sense, *Terry* chipped away at the Fourth Amendment. Brennan's concern in this case, then, is that the Fourth Amendment continues to be weakened in cases that continue to uphold police actions that would otherwise be considered searches, but for the Court's decision in *Terry v. Ohio*.

This is an important area of law about which to remain informed. No doubt, the Supreme Court will continue to decide cases that involve the relationship among probable cause, reasonable suspicion, and the police activities that each permits.

Plain Touch and Feel

In *Minnesota v. Dickerson*, discussed earlier in this chapter, the ruling was that police officers exceeded the bounds of *Terry* when they frisked the suspect because the officer "squeezed, slid, and otherwise manipulated the packet's content" before learning that it was cocaine. Despite that decision, *Dickerson* is considered by many to be the case that officially recognized the doctrine known as *plain touch* (sometimes called *plain feel*). The Supreme Court has long recognized that the items in plain view fall outside Fourth Amendment protections because they are in plain view to the police. *Dickerson* is something of a cross between a *Terry*-based frisk and the "plain view" doctrine. According to one source, "[I]f the officer, while staying within the narrow limits of a frisk for weapons, feels what he has probable cause to believe is a weapon, contraband or evidence, the officer may expand the search or seize the object."[1]

The reason the Supreme Court frowned on the frisk conducted by the police in *Dickerson* was that it was not immediately apparent to the officers that the suspect had contraband in his pocket. Thus, for the plain feel doctrine to apply, two conditions must be met: (1) Police must have reasonable suspicion to frisk, *and* (2) contraband must be immediately apparent for it to be lawfully seized. Stated more formally, "[T]he police may seize contraband detected solely through the officer's sense of touch, if, as with the plain-view doctrine, the officer had a right to touch the object in question (lawful vantage point and lawful access) and, upon tactile observation, the object's identity as contraband was immediately apparent."[2] Figure 6.5 presents examples of proper seizures based on plain view, touch, and feel during stop-and-frisk situations.

Stops for Loitering

A somewhat lesser known but equally controversial expansion of *Terry* has been applied to stops for loitering. Generally, a person cannot be stopped with anything less than reasonable suspicion. However, certain statutes, known collectively as *loitering statutes*, authorize the police to stop or arrest suspicious-looking individuals based on a lesser degree of certainty than even reasonable suspicion. Because these statutes often permit the police to stop people based on less than reasonable suspicion, many of them have been declared unconstitutional on the grounds that they are too vague.

Papachristou v. City of Jacksonville (405 U.S. 156 [1972])

An illustrative case is *Papachristou v. City of Jacksonville* (405 U.S. 156 [1972]). In that case, the Supreme Court declared unconstitutional a municipal ordinance that targeted "vagrants" and "rogues and vagabonds, or dissolute persons who go about begging . . . common drunkards, lewd, wanton and lascivious persons, . . . persons wandering or strolling around from place to place without any lawful purpose or object, habitual loafers, [and] disorderly persons" (p. 157, n. 1). The Court concluded that the ordinance provided "no standards governing the exercise of . . . discretion" and thereby

---

[1] S. L. Emanuel and S. Knowles, *Emanuel Law Outlines: Criminal Procedure* (Larchmont, NY: Emanuel, 1998), p. 129.
[2] J. Dressler, *Law Outlines: Criminal Procedure* (Santa Monica, CA: Casenotes, 1977), pp. 12–15.

FIGURE 6.5

Examples of Proper Seizures Based on Plain View, Feel, and Touch during the course of Stop-and-Frisks

Example 1: During a patdown, an officer felt a lumpy object near the suspect's knee. The officer had already discovered a gram scale and the smell of methamphetamine and, so, was justified in making an arrest. The item near the suspect's knee turned out to be a baggie of methamphetamine. The officer was justified in seizing the contraband and it could be used at trial (*People v. Dibb*, 37 Cal. App. 4th 832 [1995]).

Example 2: While searching an individual for weapons, an officer felt a small clump of firm objects. He knew it is not a weapon, but based on his experience, he was sure he touched cocaine-filled balloons. He reached into the suspect's jacket and removed two clear bags, each containing 50 cocaine-filled balloons. The seizure was justified because the officer had probable cause to arrest (*People v. Lee*, 194 Cal. App. 3d 975 [1987]).

Example 3: While serving a search warrant, an officer frisked a man who appeared to have a large bulge in his pocket. Fearing it was a weapon, the officer reached into the man's pocket and found what turned out to be large rocks of cocaine. The seizure was justified (*People v. Thurman*, 209 Cal. App. 3d 817 [1989]).

Example 4: An officer responds to a complaint and noticed a large bulge in the suspect's pants. He reached in and found a bottle. The officer's actions were legal (*People v. Snyder*, 11 Cal. App. 4th 389 [1992]).

Source: From *California Peace Officers Legal Sourcebook*, electronic edition, revision 113 (Sacramento, CA: California Department of Justice, Office of the Attorney General), section 2.21.

"permit[ted] and encourage[d] an arbitrary and discriminatory enforcement of the law" and resulted "in a regime in which the poor and the unpopular are permitted to 'stand on the sidewalk . . . only at the whim of any police officer' " (p. 170).

In a more recent case, *Kolender v. Lawson* (461 U.S. 352 [1983]), the Supreme Court struck down another statute that made a misdemeanant of any person "[w]ho loiters or wanders upon the streets or from place to place without apparent reason or business and who refuses to identify himself and to account for his presence when requested by any peace officer to do so, if the surrounding circumstances are such as to indicate to a reasonable man that the public safety demands such identification" (p. 354, n. 1). The Court ruled that the statute was too vague because it "vests virtually complete discretion in the hands of the police to determine whether the suspect has satisfied the statute and must be permitted to go on his way in the absence of probable cause to arrest" (p. 358).

Kolender v. Lawson
(461 U.S. 352 [1983])

DECISION-MAKING EXERCISE 6.7

The Bounds of a Proper Frisk

An officer on foot patrol observed a known gang member leaving a notorious crack house. When the gang member spotted the officer, he turned and ran in the opposite direction. The officer gave chase, caught up with him, and ordered him to stop. The gang member did stop, at which point the officer administered a patdown frisk. No weapons were revealed, but the officer felt a lump in the gang member's pocket. Upon careful examination with her fingers, the lump was revealed to be a package of cellophane of the type commonly used to package "crack" cocaine. The officer seized the bag. May it be introduced as evidence at the gang member's trial for narcotics possession?

Even after *Kolender*, a number of jurisdictions have attempted to devise sufficiently specific loitering statutes. For example, the city of Chicago passed a statute providing that "whenever a police officer observes a person whom he reasonably believes to be a criminal street gang member loitering in any public place with one or more other persons, he shall order all such persons to disperse and remove themselves from the area." *Loitering* was defined as "to remain in any one place with no apparent purpose." Despite the more specific language of this statute, though, the Supreme Court also struck it down. Specifically, in *Chicago v. Morales* (527 U.S. 41 [1999]), the Supreme Court ruled that the statute was unconstitutionally vague. The majority believed that the statute still gave police too much discretion to decide which people could be classified as gang members. The Court suggested it may have upheld the statute if it had applied to gang members or to those with "an apparently harmful purpose or effect," but instead, that statute applied to "everyone in the city who may remain in one place with one suspected gang member as long as their purpose is not apparent to an officer observing them" (p. 41).

Stops, even arrests, for loitering, then, would seem to be constitutionally questionable. Several of the statutes that authorized stops for loitering have been struck down by the Supreme Court. Certainly, loitering statutes can still be found on the books elsewhere in the United States (some of which might not be too vague), but to be safe, the police should limit their stops of people to those that are based on reasonable suspicion that criminal activity is afoot. Any stop based on less than reasonable suspicion opens the police officer's actions to a great deal of constitutional scrutiny.

DRUG COURIER PROFILING

An especially controversial variety of *Terry*-like investigative stops includes those based on so-called drug courier profiles. This chapter gives detailed attention to **drug courier profiling** not just because it is a controversial criminal justice topic but also because it is an appropriate topic for a chapter on stop-and-frisk. Almost without exception, drug courier profiling occurs in the stop-and-frisk context—that is, when a person is stopped and questioned because he or she appears suspicious in some way. Drug courier profiling is most common in airports but also occurs on U.S. highways and elsewhere.

Indeed, profiling of offenders occurs for other offenses, as well. Law enforcement officials have developed profiles of a number of other varieties of offenders, including car thieves (*People v. Martinez*, 12 Cal. Rptr. 2d 838 [Cal. Ct. App. 1992]), child abusers (*Flanagan v. State*, 586 So.2d 1085 [Fla. Dist. Ct. App. 1991]), child batterers (*Commonwealth v. Day*, 569 N.E.2d 397 [Mass. 1991]), and sexual abusers (*State v. McMillan*, 590 N.E.2d 23 [Ohio Ct. App. 1990]), among others.

DECISION-MAKING EXERCISE 6.8

Putting It All Together

Deputy Smith was on patrol in his police cruiser when he heard a report over the radio that a bank had just been robbed and that four male perpetrators had fled in a blue 1976 Ford pickup without license plates. Several minutes later, Smith observed a vehicle matching the description given over the radio except that it *had* license plates. He followed the truck and, after turning on his flashers, ordered the driver of the truck to pull over to the side of the road, which he did. Smith approached the truck and observed three men and a woman inside, each of whom appeared nervous and upset by the fact that they had been pulled over. After Smith ordered the occupants out of the car, he observed a bulge in the driver's pocket. He frisked the driver and found a weapon. Was Smith justified in stopping the vehicle and frisking the driver?

The carrying of controlled substances by airline passengers is a common way that drugs enter the United States from foreign countries. Law enforcement agents *could* conceivably search every person who passes through an airport, but such an effort would be costly, time consuming, unacceptable to passengers, and almost certainly unconstitutional. Warrantless searches that are based on no articulable justification are always unreasonable under the Fourth Amendment, unless one of a few "specifically established and well-delineated exceptions" applies (*Katz v. United States*, 389 U.S. 347 [1967], p. 357). In other words, such searches violate the Fourth Amendment because they are not based on probable cause, as the amendment requires.

Given that suspicionless searches are illegal, then, the police are left with two options when it comes to confronting people suspected of being drug couriers. These two options are "consensual encounters in which contact is initiated by a police officer without any articulable reason whatsoever and the citizen is briefly asked some questions [and] a temporary involuntary detention ... which must be predicated on 'reasonable suspicion' " (*United States v. Bueno*, 21 F.3d [1978]). Both consensual encounters and investigative detentions are not considered searches, so they fall outside the Fourth Amendment's probable cause requirement.

Consent searches are covered in Chapter 7, but suffice it to say for now that when a person gives consent to the police to conduct a search or ask questions, the Fourth Amendment does not apply. Assuming the citizen remains free to decline the officer's request to conduct a search, the officer can legally ask a person to look in his or her car, bag, house, or other area. The logic behind consent searches was touched on in *Terry v. Ohio*, in which the Supreme Court stated that "there is nothing in the Constitution which prevents a policeman from addressing questions to anyone on the streets" (p. 27). There is one significant restriction, though, for a consent search (or stop) to be truly consensual, and it goes directly to the definition of *stop* covered earlier in this chapter: "[T]he Fourth Amendment permits police officers to approach individuals at random in airport lobbies and other public places to ask them questions and to request consent to search their luggage, so long as a reasonable person would understand that he or she could refuse to cooperate" (*Florida v. Bostick*, p. 431). In other words, the constitutionality of a consent search is premised on the requirement that the person is truly free to decline when asked by a police officer to allow a search.

Drug courier profiling often takes place at airports. Some profiling is very visible, but much of it is conducted by officials who work undercover. Most profiling also takes place away from checkpoints, such as the one depicted here. If authorities have reasonable suspicion to stop an individual anywhere in an airport, they will do so.

Perhaps more common in the practice of drug courier profiling is the use of investigative detentions, or *Terry* stops. *Terry*, as addressed throughout the bulk of this chapter, permits police officers to stop people based on reasonable suspicion that criminal activity is afoot. *Terry* stops occur in airports and elsewhere when a person is involuntarily detained. For this type of stop to occur, however, the officer needs to show that there is, in fact, reasonable suspicion that the person is a drug courier. The primary question that makes drug courier profiling a controversial topic is this: What characteristics must a person display for reasonable suspicion to be established?

Clearly, not every person walking through an airport can be stopped. Thus, law enforcement officials must look for specific characteristics of drug couriers. As the Supreme Court observed in *United States v. Mendenhall*, "Much . . . drug traffic is highly organized and conducted by sophisticated criminal syndicates . . . And many drugs . . . may be easily concealed. As a result, the obstacles to detection . . . may be unmatched in any other area of law enforcement" (pp. 545–546). Further, one of the most significant impediments in the war on drugs is the "extraordinary and well-documented difficulty of identifying drug couriers" (*Florida v. Royer*, p. 519).

The drug courier profile is generally attributed to Paul Markonni, a DEA agent who identified a number of suspicious characteristics of likely drug couriers when he was assigned to a drug interdiction unit at the Detroit airport. That profile has since been described as an "informally compiled abstract of characteristics thought typical of persons carrying illicit drugs" (*United States v. Mendenhall*, p. 547). There is no single, nationally recognized drug courier profile or set of characteristics indicative of drug courier profiling. Instead, specific cases must be considered to ascertain which types of characteristics fit the drug courier profile.

The first drug courier profile case of note, *United States v. Van Lewis* (409 F. Supp. 535 [E.D. Mich. 1976]), listed several characteristics to be used in identifying drug couriers: (1) the use of small denominations of currency for ticket purchase; (2) travel to and from major drug import centers; (3) the absence of luggage or use of empty suitcases on trips that normally require extra clothing; and (4) travel under an alias. In a similar case, the Fifth Circuit Court, in *Elmore v. United States* (595 F.2d 1036 [5th Cir. 1979]), described these common characteristics of drug couriers:

> (1) arrival from or departure to an identified source city; (2) carrying little or no luggage; (3) unusual itinerary, such as rapid turnaround time for a very lengthy airplane trip; (4) use of an alias; (5) carrying unusually large amounts of currency in the many thousands of dollars, usually on their person, or in briefcases or bags; (6) purchasing airline tickets with a large amount of small denomination currency; and (7) unusual nervousness beyond that ordinarily exhibited by passengers. (p. 1039, n. 3)

Some secondary characteristics of drug couriers were also identified in *Elmore v. United States*, including "(1) the almost exclusive use of public transportation, particularly taxicabs, in departing from the airport; (2) immediately making a phone call after deplaning; (3) leaving a false or fictitious call-back telephone number with the airline being utilized; and (4) excessively frequent travel to source or distribution cities" (p. 1039, n. 3).

Still other characteristics of drug couriers include unusual dress, age between 25 and 35, and extreme paleness consistent with being extremely nervous.[3] Another study points to characteristics such as "not checking bags at the airport, not using identification

---

[3] B. Wilson, "The War on Drugs: Evening the Odds through the Use of the Airport Drug Courier Profile," *Boston University Public Interest Journal* 6 (1994): 202–232.

FIGURE 6.6

Typical Characteristics of Drug Couriers

1. Use small denominations of currency for ticket purchases
2. Travel to and from major drug import centers
3. Have no luggage or use empty suitcases on trips that normally require extra clothing
4. Travel under an alias
5. Have an unusual itinerary, such as a rapid turnaround time for a very lengthy airplane trip
6. Carry unusually large amounts of currency (i.e., many thousands of dollars)
7. Display unusual nervousness beyond that ordinarily exhibited by passengers
8. Use public transportation almost exclusively upon departing the airport
9. Immediately make a phone call after deplaning
10. Leave a false or fictitious call-back telephone number with the airline
11. Dress in an unusual manner
12. Are between 25 and 35 years old
13. Are extremely pale (consistent with being extremely nervous)
14. Do not use identification tags on luggage
15. Purchase tickets on the day of the flight
16. Exit first or last from the plane
17. Walk quickly through the terminal while continuously checking over his or her shoulder
18. Quickly leave the airport on arrival

tags on luggage, purchasing tickets on the day of a flight, exiting first or last from the plane, visually scanning the terminal for law enforcement, making no eye contact with airport personnel, walking quickly through the terminal while continuously checking over one's shoulder, and quickly leaving the airport on arrival."[4] See Figure 6.6 for a fairly comprehensive list of the typical characteristics of drug couriers.

Landmark Cases

Reid v. Georgia (448 U.S. 438 [1980]) was one of the first Supreme Court cases to address drug courier profiling. The petitioner, Reid, arrived at the Atlanta airport on an early morning flight. A narcotics agent on duty at the time observed that Reid repeatedly looked over his shoulder at another man and that both were carrying shoulder bags. As the two men left the airport, the narcotics officer approached them and asked them for identification and to consent to a search. Reid tried to run away and, in doing so, left his bag behind, which turned out to contain cocaine. He was later apprehended and brought to trial on drug possession charges. He attempted to have the cocaine thrown out under the exclusionary rule, claiming that he had been unconstitutionally detained as he was leaving the airport with the other man.

Reid v. Georgia
(448 U.S. 438 [1980])

---

[4] C. R. Williams and B. A. Arrigo, "Discerning the Margins of Constitutional Encroachment: The Drug Courier Profile in the Airport Milieu," *American Journal of Criminal Justice* 24 (1999): 31–46.

The trial court granted Reid's motion to suppress the cocaine; however, the Georgia Court of Appeals reversed the lower court's decision and ruled that the narcotics agent had performed a permissible stop based on the so-called drug courier profile. In its decision, the Georgia Court of Appeals noted that Reid (1) had arrived from Fort Lauderdale, Florida, a place of origin for drugs; (2) was traveling at an unusual hour; (3) was attempting to conceal the fact that he was traveling with another person; and (4) was not traveling with any luggage, other than the shoulder bag (p. 441).

The U.S. Supreme Court granted *certiorari*, holding that "the judgment of the appellate court cannot be sustained insofar as it rests on the determination that the DEA agent lawfully seized the petitioner when he approached him" (p. 441). The Court went on to note that the agent "could not . . . have reasonably suspected the petitioner of criminal activity on the basis . . . that the petitioner preceded another person and occasionally looked backward at him" (p. 441). The other reasons for stopping Reid were also criticized by the Court because the unusual hour, lack of luggage, and place of origin "describe a very large category of presumably innocent travelers, who would be subject to virtually random seizures were the Court to conclude that as little foundation as there was in this case could justify the seizure" (p. 441). The Court declared that the DEA agent did not have reasonable suspicion to detain Reid.

By now, *United States v. Mendenhall* should be something of a familiar case; it was covered at length in defining the *stop* in stop-and-frisk. However, *Mendenhall* has also had important implications for drug courier profiling in the United States. In that case, DEA agents, who were "present for the [purpose] of detecting unlawful traffic in narcotics" (p. 545), observed Mendenhall in the Detroit airport. They approached her in the airport and identified themselves. They then asked Mendenhall for her identification and airline ticket. When she complied, they noticed that the plane ticket was in another name. At that point, the agents asked Mendenhall if she would accompany them to a private room and consent to a search of her bags. She was told that she had the right to decline, but she handed over her purse and agreed to the search. A female police officer then arrived to search Mendenhall's person. When she removed her clothing, a package that appeared to contain heroin was revealed. The Supreme Court sanctioned this action and declared that a certain degree of deference should be given to law enforcement agents to interpret the circumstances in each case, based on their experience and expertise. The Court reasoned that an experienced law enforcement officer may be "able to perceive and articulate meaning in given conduct which would be wholly innocent to the untrained observer" (*United States v. Mendenhall*, p. 557).

DECISION-MAKING EXERCISE 6.9

An Application of Drug Courier Profiling

DEA agents at the Dallas/Fort Worth airport observed a woman exiting a plane that had just arrived from Miami. She was carrying a small bag on her shoulder and looking around as if she was expecting to meet another person. Still alone, she walked quickly into a restroom. When she came out, she went directly to a pay phone, where she made a phone call lasting 30 minutes. Finding her conduct suspicious, the DEA agents approached the woman, identified themselves, and asked if they could speak with her. The woman appeared very nervous, and her voice cracked when she conversed with them. The agents asked for the woman's identification and plane ticket. She furnished her plane ticket but stated that she had lost her identification. The agents asked how long she was going to stay in the Dallas/Fort Worth area. She replied that she would remain for one week, but one of the agents noticed that her ticket indicated that she would be leaving later that same day. Do the agents have justification to further detain the woman?

Another significant drug courier profiling case decided by the Supreme Court is *Florida v. Royer* (460 U.S. 491 [1983]). In that case, two detectives at the Miami International Airport observed Royer, who had purchased a one-way ticket to New York under an assumed name. Believing that Royer displayed characteristics associated with the drug courier profile, the officers approached him. Royer produced his ticket and identification after being requested to do so. The officers did not return his ticket and identification and instead asked Royer to accompany them to a nearby room. One of the detectives retrieved the luggage that Royer had checked and brought it to the room. Royer produced a key for the suitcases, and upon opening one of them, marijuana was found. Royer was convicted for felony possession; however, the Florida Court of Appeals reversed the trial court's decision, holding that the officers detained Royer without probable cause, which was required because of the intrusive nature of the stop.

The detectives argued that Royer fit the drug courier profile for a number of reasons. First, he was carrying luggage that appeared to be heavy. Second, he was young, dressed casually, and appeared nervous. Finally, he paid for his plane ticket in cash and did not complete the airline identification tag, opting instead to write only his name and destination on the tag. The court argued on appeal, however, that "any of these factors relied upon by Miami police may have been as consistent with innocence as with guilt" (p. 492) and that the drug courier profile alone was insufficient to establish reasonable suspicion, much less probable cause, to detain Royer. The case worked its way up to the U.S. Supreme Court, and the Court upheld the appeals court decision. According to the Supreme Court, Royer was detained illegally, in part because the detectives did not indicate at any point that he was free to leave. Further, the Court argued that "the detention . . . was a more serious intrusion on his personal liberty than is allowable on mere suspicion of criminal activity. What had begun as a consensual encounter . . . escalated into an investigatory procedure in an interrogation room, and [Royer] . . . was under arrest" (p. 503).

In *United States v. Sokolow* (490 U.S. 1 [1989]), DEA agents stopped Sokolow upon his arrival at Honolulu International Airport and found a large quantity of cocaine in his carry-on luggage. In support of the stop, the agents noted that Sokolow (1) had paid $2,100 for his airline ticket with a roll of $20 bills; (2) traveled under an assumed name; (3) had flown in from a major "source city," Miami; (4) had stayed in Miami for only 48 hours; (5) appeared nervous; and (6) did not check any luggage. The district court denied Sokolow's motion to suppress the drugs, finding that the agents had reasonable suspicion to stop him in the airport. However, the court of appeals declared that the stop was illegal, a violation of the Fourth Amendment. The court relied on a two-pronged test to assess the legality of the stop. It required a showing that (1) there was "ongoing criminal activity" and that there were (2) "personal characteristics" of drug courier profiles. While the second prong would seem to have been met in this case, the appeals court decided that the first prong had not been met because the government did not offer "empirical documentation that the combination of facts at issue did not describe the behavior of significant numbers of innocent persons" (p. 2). In other words, the court of appeals found no evidence of ongoing criminal activity and thus ruled that the stop was in violation of the Fourth Amendment.

The U.S. Supreme Court reversed the appeals court decision. It held that the agents *did* have reasonable suspicion that Sokolow was engaged in the transportation of narcotics. In criticizing the two-pronged test used by the appeals court, the Supreme Court noted that the test "created unnecessary difficulty in dealing with one of the relatively simple concepts embodied in the Fourth Amendment" (p. 3). In reference to the suspicious conduct observed by the agents, the Court went on to note that "although each of these factors [e.g., paying $2,100 for a plane ticket with small denomination

United States v. Sokolow (490 U.S. 1 [1989])

bills] is not by itself proof of illegal conduct and is quite consistent with innocent travel, taken together they amount to reasonable suspicion that criminal activity was afoot" (p. 4).

Race and Drug Courier Profiling

Critics of drug courier profiling have argued that the practice is racially discriminatory. One commentator has argued, for example, that "[a]lthough the DEA has refused to commit the entire profile to writing, the profile clearly contains a racial component."[5] In fact, in *United States v. Taylor* (956 F.2d 572 [6th Cir. 1992]), a case that went before the Sixth Circuit Court, an officer admitted that 75 percent of the persons detained through use of drug courier profiling were African Americans (p. 581, n. 1). In a strong dissent to that case, Judge Damon Keith wrote, "The disproportionate number of African-Americans who are stopped indicates that a racial imbalance against African-Americans does exist and is implicitly sanctioned by the law enforcement agency. . . . We cannot allow law enforcement officers to cloak what may fairly be characterized as a racist practice in a generic drug profile that openly targets African-Americans" (pp. 581–582).

Those who argue that race is not a factor in profiling claim, perhaps accurately, that the profile targets minorities because they are, in fact, more likely to be drug couriers than nonminorities. Nevertheless, if a disproportionate number of minorities are

---

DECISION-MAKING EXERCISE 6.10

Terrorist Profiling

In 2004, two Arab gentlemen, Tarik Farag and Amro Elmasry, traveled from San Diego to New York's JFK airport on American Airlines Flight 236. As soon as they deplaned at JFK, they were met by no less than 10 armed agents in paramilitary gear with guns and police dogs. They were ordered to raise their hands and were frisked, handcuffed, and whisked off to an interrogation room. The investigation yielded no evidence of wrongdoing. The men sued, arguing that their arrests were unjustified, but the government cited the following as justification for the airport detention (note that these facts were reported to the captain by two counterterrorism agents who were on the flight):

- At the beginning of the flight, despite sitting on opposite sides of the aisle, plaintiffs spoke to each other over the heads of other passengers in a mixture of Arabic and English;
- Elmasry made an allegedly "unusual" initial seat change "from a window seat . . . to a middle seat . . . between two other male passengers";
- After Elmasry changed seats, he and Farag talked to each other "loudly" over the heads of other passengers in a mixture of Arabic and English;

- Elmasry looked at his watch when the plane took off, when the plane landed, and at other points during the flight;
- After the meal service, Elmasry "got out of his seat . . . , went into the aisle, leaned over to Farag, and spoke a 'very short sentence' to Farag in a mixture of Arabic and English";
- Immediately thereafter, plaintiffs moved together to the back of the plane, and did not take their carry-on luggage with them;
- Plaintiffs got up to return to the front of the cabin at the very end of the flight, after the "fasten seatbelt" indicator was lit;
- Upon returning to the front of the plane, Farag did not sit in his original seat (17E), but rather, in Elmasry's original seat (18A), which was located directly behind Smith; [and]
- After the plane landed, Elmasry took out his cellular phone and deleted five or six numbers (*Farag v. United States*, 2008 U.S. Dist. LEXIS 95331 [2008], pp. 23–24).

Is there merit to the government's argument?

---

[5] S. L. Johnson, "Race and the Decision to Detain a Suspect," *Yale Law Journal* 93 (1983): 214–258, 234.

stopped during profiling, a serious problem is posed—that of a self-fulfilling prophecy. One author's observations regarding this matter are quite telling:

> If the profile assumes that racial minorities are more likely than Whites to be couriers, then the percentage of minorities in the group of people stopped will be higher than the percentage of minorities in the overall population. Even if minorities are in reality no more predisposed than Whites to serve as drug couriers, they will nevertheless appear to be more predisposed, because they will make up a larger proportion of the pool of those persons stopped.[6]

The race issue in drug courier profiling has yet to be addressed by the Supreme Court, just as the use of profiling itself has yet to be decided. It is likely, however, that the Court, in the not too distant future, will have an opportunity to settle this controversial issue once and for all. For now, it cannot be said with complete certainty that race is a factor in drug courier profiling.

INVESTIGATIVE DETENTIONS

The Supreme Court has held that certain police station detentions are justifiable on less than probable cause. One type of **investigative detention** a stationhouse detention, is less intrusive than an arrest but more intrusive than a *Terry* stop. Stationhouse detentions are used in many locations for such purposes as obtaining fingerprints and photographs, ordering lineups, administering polygraph examinations, and securing other types of evidence.

In *Davis v. Mississippi* (394 U.S. 721 [1969]), the Court excluded fingerprint evidence obtained from 25 rape suspects, but it did note that detention for fingerprinting could have been permissible if "narrowly circumscribed procedures" were in place. In other words, the Court suggested that to justify the detention, there had to be some objective basis for detaining a person, a clear investigation underway, and a court order stating that adequate evidence exists. In another case, *Hayes v. Florida* (470 U.S. 811 [1985]), the Court stated:

> Our view continues to be that the line is crossed when the police, without probable cause or a warrant, forcibly remove a person from his home or other place in which he is entitled to be and transport him to the police station, where he is detained, although briefly, for investigative purposes. We adhere to the view that such seizures, at least where not under judicial supervision, are sufficiently like arrests to invoke the traditional rule that arrests may constitutionally be made only on probable cause. (p. 816)

The key in *Hayes*, however, is that the detention was not consensual. In cases in which consent is obtained, probable cause is not necessary. In short, a stationhouse detention for the purpose of fingerprinting is permissible when (1) there is reasonable suspicion to believe the suspect has committed a crime; (2) there is a reasonable belief that the fingerprints will inculpate or exculpate the suspect; and (3) the procedure is carried out promptly. (Note that the Supreme Court has not addressed stationhouse detentions *not* involving fingerprinting.)

---

[6] T. Yin, "The Probative Values and Pitfalls of Drug Courier Profiles as Probabilistic Evidence," *Texas Forum on Civil Liberties and Civil Rights* 5 (2000): 141–190, 151.

Summary

1. DISTINGUISH BETWEEN A STOP AND A NONSTOP.

A number of specific conclusions can be drawn from the stop-and-frisk discussion in this chapter and from the introduction to reasonable suspicion presented in Chapter 3. First, a police/citizen encounter is not governed by the Fourth Amendment unless it is considered a *stop*, which is one type of *seizure*. When the police activity in question rises to the level of a stop, then the Fourth Amendment applies, and the officer is required to have the appropriate level of justification for the stop to be legal.

Factors to consider in determining whether a stop has taken place include (1) whether the police action was threatening; (2) how long the detention lasted; (3) whether the person was physically detained or physically touched by the police; (4) whether the detention took place in public view or removed from public view, such as in a private room; and perhaps most importantly, (5) whether a reasonable person would, under the circumstances, have believed that he or she was free to leave. With regard to the last factor, it is not necessary that police communicate to the detainee that he or she is free to leave. A situation involving only brief questioning, then, is unlikely to be considered a stop, implicating the Fourth Amendment.

2. EXPLAIN WHEN A STOP-AND-FRISK IS PERMISSIBLE.

The Fourth Amendment generally requires that probable cause be in place before a Fourth Amendment seizure can occur. However, the Supreme Court in *Terry* ruled that a person can be seized on less than probable cause to arrest. The second conclusion, then, focuses on when this can occur. Generally, a seizure based on less than probable cause (i.e., reasonable suspicion) can occur under three circumstances: (1) when the officer observes a person engaging in unusual activity and can point to specific, articulable facts that contribute to reasonable suspicion that criminal activity is afoot; (2) when the officer receives information from an informant who is reliable; and (3) when the officer receives a communication from another police department that the person to be stopped is suspected of involvement in criminal activity.

3. SUMMARIZE STOP-AND-FRISK PROCEDURE.

When reasonable suspicion is in place and a police officer is entitled to make a stop, he or she must make reasonable inquiries. These inquiries should be limited to testing the officer's suspicion. If the questioning becomes unreasonable, excessive, or too intrusive, probable cause may be required. Then, if the officer reasonably believes, during the course of questioning, that the person is armed and dangerous, he or she can frisk the person. Factors used in determining whether a frisk is reasonable include (1) whether the person has a reputation for dangerousness; (2) the type of criminal activity in which the person is presumably involved; (3) visual cues that suggest the presence of a weapon; and/or (4) suggestive or furtive gestures on the part of the suspect.

Frisks are limited. If one is authorized because the officer reasonably fears for his or her safety, it is limited to a patdown of the person's outer clothing. Recent decisions, however, permit a limited search of the area immediately surrounding the person, such as in automobiles and other situations in which several people may be found. Weapon-like objects and contraband can be removed during the course of the frisk, but both must be immediately apparent to the frisking officer. If a weapon or other item is not immediately apparent, then the officer risks exceeding the limits of a frisk, especially if he or she feels, gropes, or otherwise manipulates the object in an attempt to determine what it is. Such activity may arise to the level of a search, requiring probable cause.

4. EXPLAIN THE RELEVANCE OF DRUG COURIER PROFILING IN THE STOP-AND-FRISK CONTEXT.

Drug courier profiling remains a controversial practice. While the courts do commonly recognize characteristics of drug courier profiles, a number of cases concerning drug courier profiling have reached the Supreme Court. Even so, the Court has yet to rule on the constitutionality of drug courier profiling. Racial discrimination is also at issue in drug courier profiling. There is no shortage of criticism concerning the role of race in profiling, but since the Supreme Court has not decided on the legality of profiling, it is unlikely that racially motivated investigative stops, to the extent they exist, will cease.

5. COMPARE AND CONTRAST INVESTIGATIVE DETENTIONS WITH STOP-AND-FRISK.

Investigative detentions, also called a stationhouse detention, are less intrusive detentions than arrests but more intrusive than a *Terry* stop. Stationhouse detentions are used in many locations for such purposes as obtaining fingerprints and photographs, ordering lineups, administering polygraph examinations, and securing other types of evidence.

Key Terms

drug courier profiling   202   frisk   192   investigative detention   208   stop   185

Key Cases

Stop

- *Terry v. Ohio*, 392 U.S. 1 (1968)
- *United States v. Mendenhall*, 446 U.S. 544 (1980)
- *California v. Hodari D.*, 449 U.S. 621 (1991)
- *Florida v. Bostick*, 501 U.S. 429 (1991)
- *United States v. Montoya De Hernandez*, 473 U.S. 531 (1985)

Frisk

- *Pennsylvania v. Mimms*, 434 U.S. 106 (1977)
- *Ybarra v. Illinois*, 444 U.S. 85 (1979)
- *Minnesota v. Dickerson*, 508 U.S. 366 (1993)
- *Sibron v. New York*, 392 U.S. 40 (1968)

Evolving Nature of Stop-and-Frisk

- *Delaware v. Prouse*, 440 U.S. 648 (1979)
- *Maryland v. Buie*, 494 U.S. 325 (1990)
- *Papachristou v. City of Jacksonville*, 405 U.S. 156 (1972)
- *Kolender v. Lawson*, 461 U.S. 352 (1983)

Drug Courier Profiling

- *Reid v. Georgia*, 448 U.S. 438 (1980)
- *United States v. Mendenhall*, 446 U.S. 544 (1980)
- *United States v. Sokolow*, 490 U.S. 1 (1989)

Review Questions

1. Why is it important to view a stop and a frisk as two separate acts?
2. Assuming a police officer has reasonable suspicion to stop a person, what must the officer do before stopping him or her?
3. Define a *stop*.
4. Why is the duration of a stop important?
5. Can *effects* be seized? Explain.
6. Summarize the permissible grounds for a frisk.
7. Summarize the Supreme Court's view on the proper scope of a frisk.
8. In what ways has stop-and-frisk law been expanded? Summarize pertinent cases.
9. Why is it important to distinguish between theory and reality when discussing stop-and-frisk?
10. What is drug courier profiling?
11. Identify several characteristics of drug couriers.
12. Summarize the Supreme Court's view on drug courier profiling, citing relevant cases.
13. In what ways is race relevant to the drug courier profile?
14. What are investigative detentions? How do they differ from stops?
15. Reasonable suspicion is not mentioned in the Fourth Amendment. Has the Supreme Court overstepped its authority by essentially creating this level of justification? Why or why not?

Web Links and Exercises

1. Stop-and-frisk: Read more about police actions that fall short of arrest.
URL (read the article called "Police Intervention Short of Arrest"): http://www.fbi.gov/stats-services/publications/law-enforcement-bulletin/2006-pdfs/nov06leb.pdf (accessed February 16, 2011).
2. Traffic stops: Read about traffic stops and the risks. What does it mean to "take AIM" in traffic stops?
Suggested URL: http://www.fbi.gov/stats-services/publications/law-enforcement-bulletin/2008-pdfs/may08leb.pdf (accessed February 16, 2011).

3. Drug courier profiling: Identify additional characteristics of drug couriers. Which of these may lead police to detain innocent persons?
Suggested URL: http://www.cass.net/~w-dogs/lcour.htm (accessed February 16, 2011).
4. Terrorist profiling: Read about terrorist profiling.
Suggested URL (there is a section in the report at this URL): http://www.loc.gov/rr/frd/pdf-files/Soc_Psych_of_Terrorism.pdf (accessed February 16, 2011).

LEARNING OBJECTIVES

When you complete this chapter, you should be able to:

▸ Explain the justification for regulatory and administrative searches.

▸ Describe regulatory and administrative searches.

▸ Describe consent searches and the issues associated with them.

Actions Based on Administrative Justification and Consent

INTRODUCTION

Casting Off the Fourth Amendment's Restraints

As mentioned in Chapter 3, actions based on administrative justifications are those in which the primary purpose is noncriminal. They resemble searches because they intrude on people's privacy—and can lead to the discovery of evidence. Technically, however, they are not searches. Instead of being based on probable cause or reasonable suspicion, administrative actions invoke a balancing test, weighing citizens' privacy interests against the interest to ensure public safety. When the latter outweighs the former, an administrative "search" is allowed, subject to certain limitations (e.g., department policy). This chapter briefly introduces several types of actions that the Supreme Court has authorized based on administrative justification.

This chapter also introduces the topic of consent searches. When a person gives valid consent to search, neither a warrant nor probable cause is required. Closely tied to consent searches is the controversial police practice known as "knock and talk." The consent search section also delves into third-party consent or the extent to which one person can grant consent to have another person's property searched. Consent fits nicely in this chapter because neither it nor actions based on administrative justification require probable cause—or any real measure of proof that a crime is being or has been committed.

ACTIONS BASED ON ADMINISTRATIVE JUSTIFICATION

The Supreme Court has authorized numerous varieties of actions under the administrative justification exception to the Fourth Amendment's probable cause and warrant requirements. Sometimes they are described as *special needs beyond law enforcement searches*; other times, they are called *regulatory searches*. To avoid confusion, this book lumps all of them under the category of *administrative justification*. The actions that are considered include (1) inventories; (2) inspections; (3) checkpoints; (4) school discipline; (5) "searches" of government employees' offices; (6) drug and alcohol testing; and (7) parole and probation supervision. Note that when the term "search" appears in quotes, it is because while a particular action may look like a search, it is not the same as a true Fourth Amendment search.

Inventories

Like seizures based on plain view, inventories can be viewed as another fallback measure. An inventory can be of a vehicle and/or of a person's personal items. Usually, a search occurs under the automobile exception (in the case of an automobile) or a search incident to arrest (when a person is involved), and an inventory is taken after the fact for the purpose of developing a record of what items have been taken into custody. Both types of inventories are fallbacks in the sense that they often occur *after* an earlier search.

South Dakota v. Opperman (428 U.S. 364 [1976])

VEHICLE INVENTORIES   A **vehicle inventory** occurs in a number of situations, usually after a car has been impounded for traffic or parking violations. In *South Dakota v. Opperman* (428 U.S. 364 [1976]), the Supreme Court held that a warrantless inventory is permissible on administrative/regulatory grounds. However, it must (1) follow a *lawful* impoundment; (2) be of a routine nature, following standard operating procedures; and (3) not be a "pretext concealing an investigatory police motive." Thus, even though an inventory can be perceived as a fallback measure, which permits a search when probable cause is lacking, it cannot be used in lieu of a regular search requiring probable cause.

Why did the Court opt for another standard besides probable cause for the inventory, despite the fact that it is still a "search" in the conventional sense of the term? The Court noted that the probable cause requirement of the Fourth Amendment is "unhelpful" in the context of administrative care-taking functions (e.g., inventories) because the concept of probable cause is linked to criminal investigations. Probable cause is irrelevant with this type of administrative action, "particularly when no claim is made that the protective procedures are a subterfuge for criminal investigations" (p. 371).

The Court offered three reasons in support of vehicle inventories. First, an inventory protects the owner's property while it is in police custody. Second, an inventory protects the police against claims of lost or stolen property. Finally, an inventory protects the police and public from dangerous items (e.g., weapons) that might be concealed in a car.

Note that inventories include containers. That is, the police may examine *any* container discovered during the course of a vehicle inventory, but this should be mandated by departmental procedures. This was the decision reached in *Colorado v. Bertine* (479 U.S. 367 [1987]). That decision also helped the police insofar as the Court refused to alter the vehicle inventory exception to the Fourth Amendment when secure impound facilities are accessible. As the Court stated, "[T]he security of the storage facility does not completely eliminate the need for inventorying; the police may still wish to protect themselves or the owners of the lot against false claims of theft or dangerous instrumentalities" (p. 373).

*Colorado v. Bertine
(479 U.S. 367 [1987])*

In *Bertine*, the Court also rejected an argument that car owners should be able to make their own arrangements if their vehicles are impounded (e.g., have it towed by a private company, have a friend drive it home). The Court stated, "The reasonableness of any particular governmental activity does not necessarily or invariably turn on the existence of alternative 'less intrusive' means" (p. 374).

Reading *Opperman* and *Bertine* would suggest that inventories are relatively standard and intended mainly to take note of a car's contents. However, in *Michigan v. Thomas* (458 U.S. 259 [1982]), the Supreme Court concluded that the police could go even further. In that case, officers found a loaded .38 revolver in one of the impounded vehicle's air vents. The Court upheld the officers' actions because marijuana had been found in the vehicle shortly before the gun was detected.

In conclusion, two important issues must be understood with regard to vehicle inventories. First, if during the course of a valid inventory, the police discover evidence that gives rise to probable cause to search, then a more extensive search is permissible. However, according to *Carroll v. United States* (267 U.S. 132 [1925]), discussed in Chapter 5, one of the requirements for such action to be constitutional is the impracticality of securing a warrant.

Second, despite the Supreme Court's apparent willingness to give police wide latitude with vehicle inventories, what makes them constitutional is clear guidelines as to how the inventory should be conducted. In other words, the Court has authorized inventories without probable cause or a warrant only if, in addition to the other requirements discussed earlier, it is conducted in accordance with clear departmental policies and procedures. Requiring the police to follow appropriate policies minimizes discretion and the concern that inventories may be used for criminal investigation purposes. The inventory search policy from the Pine Bluff, Arkansas, Police Department's *Policy and Procedure Manual* is reprinted in Figure 7.1.

PERSON INVENTORIES The inventory exception to the Fourth Amendment's warrant requirement applies in the case of a **person inventory**, as well. The action permitted is often called an *arrest inventory*. The general rule is that the police may search an arrestee and his or her personal items, including containers found in his or her possession, as part of a routine inventory incident to the booking and jailing procedure. As decided in *Illinois v. Lafayette* (462 U.S. 640 [1983]), neither a search warrant nor probable cause is required. According to the Court:

*Illinois v. Lafayette
(462 U.S. 640 [1983])*

> Consistent with the Fourth Amendment, it is reasonable for police to search the personal effects of a person under lawful arrest as part of the routine administrative procedure at a police station incident to booking and jailing the suspect. The justification for such searches does not rest on probable cause, and hence the absence of a warrant is immaterial to the reasonableness of the search. Here, every consideration of orderly police administration— protection of a suspect's property, deterrence of false claims of theft against the police, security, and identification of the suspect—benefiting both the police and the public points toward the appropriateness of the examination of respondent's shoulder bag. (pp. 643–648)

FIGURE 7.1

Vehicle Inventory Policy (Pine Bluff, AR, Police Department)

	SUBJECT:	POLICY NUMBER 260
(Pine Bluff Police Department ARK badge)	TOWING & STORAGE OF VEHICLES	ISSUE DATE 02/19/2008
	CHAPTER: PATROL	EFFECTIVE DATE 02/19/2008
	ISSUED By: Chief of Police John E. Howell	TOTAL PAGES 6

I. PROCEDURES

A. GENERAL

1. The Impoundment of motor vehicles shall be accomplished by the use of contract commercial towing services, towing vehicles, and impoundment lots as authorized by this law enforcement agency. All towing agencies must be a member of the Arkansas Towing and Recovery Board, certified for and display inspection documentation indicating they are authorized for non-consent towing.

2. Vehicles impounded by or otherwise taken into the custody by this agency shall be inventoried in a manner consistent with this agencies policy on motor vehicle inventories as stated in Section F of this policy.

    a. Inventories should be performed at the scene or at a safe place nearby whenever this can be done safely and effectively.

    b. A Pine Bluff Police Department wrecker log will be completed on any impounded motor vehicles.

    c. Motor vehicles shall not be impounded for purposes other than those defined by statute or ordinance, (e.g., not as a form of punishment, or as a means of conducting vehicle searches when probable cause does not exist or consent to search cannot be obtained).

3. When impoundments are necessary, the operator and any passengers should not be stranded. Officers shall take those measures necessary to ensure that the operator and any passengers of the vehicle are offered transportation. To include but not limited to:

    a. Call a taxi cab for them.

    b. Call a friend or relative to pick them up.

    c. With supervisor approval, transport them to the nearest reasonably safe location.

4. If the driver/owner or passenger(s) decline assistance with transportation and the vehicle is towed at the direction of an officer for any reason, the officer shall document their refusal on an original Information/Incident Report, as Supplemental to and existing Information/Incident Report, or on an Accident Report, whichever is appropriate to the circumstances.

5. Vehicle operators may be permitted to remove unsecured valuables of a non-evidentiary nature from the vehicle prior to its removal for impoundment. The nature of these valuables shall be noted on the appropriate reporting document.

6. Impounded vehicles shall be released to owners with proof of ownership and personal identification, and following proof of payment of any impoundment, storage, or related fees and taxes.

Source: Reprinted courtesy of Pine Bluff, AR, Police Department.

It is important to understand that an inventory of person must follow a lawful arrest, so the probable cause to search requirement is essentially satisfied at the arrest stage.

The Supreme Court's decision in *Opperman*, discussed in the vehicle inventory section, has essentially been extended to person inventories. That is, as part of inventorying a person's possessions pursuant to a valid arrest, the police may also examine containers. The Court felt that it would be unduly burdensome on the police to require them to distinguish between which containers may or may not contain evidence of criminal activity.

Inspections

A variety of **inspections** is permissible without a warrant or probable cause. For all practical purposes, they are "searches." Even so, the courts have continually stressed that the justification for such searches is the "invasion versus need" balancing act—that is, the benefits of some inspections outweigh the costs of inconveniencing certain segments of the population. Most of these exceptions to the warrant requirement are based on the Court's decision in *Camara v. Municipal Court* (387 U.S. 523 [1967]), where it was concluded that "there can be no ready test for determining reasonableness other than by balancing the need to search against the invasion which the search entails" (pp. 536–537).

Camara v. Municipal Court (387 U.S. 523 [1967])

HOME INSPECTIONS   Two types of home inspection have been authorized by the Court. The first concerns health and safety inspections of residential buildings, such as public housing units. In *Frank v. Maryland* (359 U.S. 360 [1959]), for example, the Court upheld the constitutionality of a statute designed to punish property holders for failing to cooperate with warrantless health and safety inspections. The Court noted that such inspections "touch at most upon the periphery of the important interests safeguarded by the Fourteenth Amendment's protection against official intrusion" (p. 367). In 1967, however, the Court overruled the *Frank* decision in *Camara v. Municipal Court* (387 U.S. 523 [1967]).

In *Camara*, the Court noted that nonconsensual administrative inspections of private residences amount to a significant intrusion upon the interests protected by the Fourth Amendment. Today, a warrant is required for authorities to engage in a home inspection. However, the meaning of *probable cause* in such a warrant differs from that discussed earlier. The Court has stated that if an area "as a whole" needs inspection, based on factors such as the time, age, and condition of the building, then the probable cause requirement will be satisfied. The key is that probable cause in the inspection context is not *individualized* as in the typical warrant. That is to say, inspections of this sort are geared toward buildings, not persons.

A second type of home inspection is a welfare inspection. In *Wyman v. James* (400 U.S. 309 [1971]), the Supreme Court upheld the constitutionality of a statute that allowed welfare caseworkers to make warrantless visits to the homes of welfare recipients.

Wyman v. James (400 U.S. 309 [1971])

DECISION-MAKING EXERCISE 7.1

Inventoried and Inventoried Again

At the time of the defendant's arrest, police officers inventoried his automobile and seized several items. Approximately eight hours after the car was impounded, an officer, without obtaining a warrant, searched the car a second time, seizing additional evidence. Note that both searches were inventory searches. Do these searches appear, as many courts have stated it, to "pass Fourth Amendment muster"? What if only the second search was deemed unconstitutional?

The purpose of such inspections is to ensure that welfare recipients are conforming with applicable guidelines and rules. The Court declared that welfare inspections are not searches within the meaning of the Fourth Amendment, which means they can be conducted without a warrant *or* probable cause. Of course, such inspections should be based on neutral criteria and should not mask intentions to look for evidence of criminal activity.

BUSINESS INSPECTIONS Far more case law exists in the arena of business inspections. *See v. City of Seattle* (387 U.S. 541 [1967]), which was a companion case to *Camara*, was one of the first to focus on the constitutionality of business inspections. *See* involved a citywide inspection of businesses for fire code violations. The Court noted that "[t]he businessman, like the occupant of a residence, has a constitutional right to go about his business free from unreasonable official entries upon his private commercial property" (p. 543) and therefore that warrants were required to engage in business inspections.

However, soon after *See*, the Court created what came to be known as the **closely regulated business** exception to the warrant requirement set forth in *Camara* and *See*. Specifically, in *Colonnade Catering Corp. v. United States* (397 U.S. 72 [1970]), the Court upheld a statute criminalizing refusal to allow warrantless entries of liquor stores by government inspectors. According to the Court:

Colonnade Catering Corp. v. United States (397 U.S. 72 [1970])

> We agree that Congress has broad power to design such powers of inspection under the liquor laws as it deems necessary to meet the evils at hand. The general rule laid down in *See v. City of Seattle* . . . —"that administrative entry, without consent, upon the portions of commercial premises which are not open to the public may only be compelled through prosecution or physical force within the framework of a warrant procedure"—is therefore not applicable here. In *See*, we reserved decision on the problems of "licensing programs" requiring inspections, saying they can be resolved "on a case-by-case basis under the general Fourth Amendment standard of reasonableness." . . . What we said in *See* reflects this Nation's traditions that are strongly opposed to

---

DECISION-MAKING EXERCISE 7.2
Welfare-Related Home Inspections

These are the paraphrased facts from a real case, *Calabretta v. Floyd* (189 F.3d 808 [9th Cir. 1999]): An anonymous party called the Department of Social Services and said that she was awakened by a child screaming "No, Daddy, no" at 1:30 a.m. at the Calabretta home. Four days after the call, a social worker went to the Calabretta home to investigate. Mrs. Calabretta, the mother, refused to let the social worker in. Then, 10 days after the first visit, the social worker returned to the Calabretta house with a police officer. The officer met the social worker at the Calabretta house, knowing nothing about the case except that he had been assigned to assist her. She told him that they had received a report of the children crying, and he understood her to mean that they might have been beaten. When the police officer knocked on the door of the home, Mrs. Calabretta responded but did not open the door. The police officer said they were checking on the children's welfare because someone had reported children crying. Mrs. Calabretta still did not open the door and said she was uncomfortable letting them in without her husband at home. The police officer had the opinion that any check on the welfare of children involved an exigent circumstance and thus that no search warrant was needed. Once the two gained entry, the social worker took the children into one room while the officer remained in another room with the mother. The social worker asked the 12-year-old to pull down the 3-year-old's pants to check for bruises on her buttocks. The 12-year-old refused and the 3-year-old began crying. At that point, the mother rushed in. The social worker then demanded that the mother pull down the 3-year-old's pants, which she did. There were no bruises. The Calabrettas sued the social worker, the police officer, and other defendants for, among other things, a violation of their Fourth Amendment rights. Was the entrance into the Calabretta home constitutional?

using force without definite authority to break down doors. We deal here with the liquor industry long subject to close supervision and inspection. As respects that industry, and its various branches including retailers, Congress has broad authority to fashion standards of reasonableness for searches and seizures. (pp. 76–77)

Similarly, in *United States v. Biswell* (406 U.S. 311 [1972]), the Court upheld the war-rantless inspection of a firearms dealership. In *Biswell*, the Court observed that "[w]hen a dealer chooses to engage in this pervasively regulated business and to accept a federal license, he does so with the knowledge that his business records, firearms and ammunition will be subject to effective inspection" (p. 311). A key restriction on this ruling, however, is that authorities cannot use unauthorized force for the purpose of gaining entrance.

United States v. Biswell
(406 U.S. 311 [1972])

In a later case, *Donovan v. Dewey* (452 U.S. 494 [1981]), the Court modified the closely regulated business exception. The Court decided that it is not enough that an industry is "pervasively regulated" for the business inspection exception to apply. Three additional criteria must be met: (1) the government must have a "substantial" interest in the activity at stake; (2) warrantless searches must be necessary to the effective enforcement of the law; and (3) the inspection protocol must provide "a constitutionally adequate substitute for a warrant."

The Court clarified the *Dewey* criteria in *New York v. Burger* (482 U.S. 691 [1987]). In that case, the Court upheld the warrantless inspection of a vehicle junkyard for the purpose of identifying "vehicle dismantlers." Justice Blackman noted that *Dewey's* first criterion was satisfied because vehicle theft was a serious problem in New York. The second criterion was satisfied because surprise inspections were necessary if stolen vehicles and parts were to be identified, and the third criterion—adequate substitute—was satisfied because junkyard operators were notified that inspections would be unan-nounced and conducted during normal business hours. In the Court's words:

> The New York regulatory scheme satisfies the three criteria necessary to make reasonable warrantless inspections pursuant to [the statute in question]. First, the State has a substantial interest in regulating the vehicle-dismantling and automobile-junkyard industry because motor vehicle theft has increased in the State and because the problem of theft is associated with this industry . . . Second, regulation of the vehicle-dismantling industry reasonably serves the State's substantial interest in eradicating automobile theft . . . [and third, the statute] provides a "constitutionally adequate substitute for a warrant." . . . . The statute informs the operator of a vehicle dismantling business that inspec-tions will be made on a regular basis . . . . Thus, the vehicle dismantler knows that the inspections to which he is subject do not constitute discretionary acts by a government official but are conducted pursuant to the statute. (pp. 708–709)

DECISION-MAKING EXERCISE 7.3

Business Inspections

Komfortable Kitty Drug Company manufactures and pack-ages veterinary drugs. Several times during a one-year pe-riod, Federal Drug Administration (FDA) agents inspected the company's premises to ensure compliance with the Food, Drug, and Cosmetic Act (actual legislation). The agents cited Komfortable Kitty for several violations. Drugs that were allegedly in violation of the act were seized pursuant to an *in rem* arrest warrant (i.e., a warrant authorizing the arrest of property). Altogether, over $100,000 worth of drugs and equipment were seized. Komfortable Kitty has contested the constitutionality of the seizure. Does the company have a valid case?

It is important to point out, though, that when business inspections become non regulatory (e.g., for the purpose of criminal investigation/prosecution), then a warrant is required (see *G.M. Leasing Corp. v. United States*, 429 U.S. 338 [1977]).

Michigan v. Tyler
(436 U.S. 499 [1978])

FIRE INSPECTIONS   In *Michigan v. Tyler* (436 U.S. 499 [1978]), the Supreme Court authorized the warrantless inspection of a burned building/residence (i.e., fire inspection) immediately after the fire has been put out. The key is that the inspection must be contemporaneous, not several days or weeks after the fire. The justification offered by the Court was that it is necessary to determine the cause of a fire as soon as possible after it has been extinguished. A warrant in such an instance, felt the Court, would be unduly burdensome.

In a related case, *Michigan v. Clifford* (464 U.S. 287 [1984]), the Court decided on the constitutionality of a warrantless arson-related inspection that was conducted five hours after the fire was extinguished. While the inspection began as just that, when evidence of arson was found, a more extensive search was conducted. The Court required a warrant because the officials engaging in the search admitted it was part of a criminal investigation. According to the Court:

> The warrantless intrusion into the upstairs regions of the Clifford house presents a telling illustration of the importance of prior judicial review of proposed administrative searches. If an administrative warrant had been obtained in this case, it presumably would have limited the scope of the proposed investigation and would have prevented the warrantless intrusion into the upper rooms of the Clifford home. An administrative search into the cause of a recent fire does not give fire officials license to roam freely through the fire victim's private residence. (p. 298)

Interestingly, in *Clifford*, the Court stated that "the home owner is entitled to reasonable advance notice that officers are going to enter his premises for the purposes of ascertaining the cause of the fire" (p. 303), which suggests that notice, but not a warrant, is required for the typical fire inspection. More extensive searches, however, still require warrants supported by probable cause.

United States v. Ramsey
(431 U.S. 606 [1977])

INTERNATIONAL MAIL INSPECTIONS   The Supreme Court has permitted government officials to open incoming international mail. For example, in *United States v. Ramsey* (431 U.S. 606 [1977]), customs agents opened mail that was coming into the United States from Thailand, a known source of drugs. Further, the agents felt that a specific envelope was heavier than what would have been considered usual. Considering these factors, the Supreme Court upheld the warrantless search:

> The border-search exception is grounded in the recognized right of the sovereign to control, subject to substantive limitations imposed by the Constitution, who and what may enter the country. It is clear that there is nothing in the rationale behind the bordersearch exception which suggests that the mode of entry will be critical. It was conceded at oral argument that customs officials could search, without probable cause and without a warrant, envelopes carried by an entering traveler, whether in his luggage or on his person. . . . Surely no different constitutional standard should apply simply because the envelopes were mailed, not carried. The critical fact is that the envelopes cross the border and enter this country, not that they are brought in by one mode of transportation rather than another. It is their entry into this country from without it that makes a resulting search "reasonable." (p. 620)

Checkpoints

Several types of **checkpoints** are constitutionally permissible without warrants. A checkpoint is a means of investigating a large number of people and should be distinguished from an inspection. Whereas an *inspection* targets particular homes and/or businesses, a *checkpoint* possesses an element of randomness—or total predictability. Either *everyone* is stopped or every *n*th person (e.g., every tenth person) is stopped. A checkpoint is similar to an investigation insofar as its purpose is not criminal in the sense that a typical search is. And to the extent that some checkpoints border on looking for evidence of crime (e.g., illegal immigrants), they are often justified because they are not based on individualized suspicion.

BORDER CHECKPOINTS   In *Carroll v. United States* (267 U.S. 132 [1925]), the Supreme Court stated that brief border detentions are constitutionally permissible. Further, it is in the interest of "national self protection" to permit government officials to require "one entering the country to identify himself as entitled to come in . . . " (p. 154). More recently, in *United States v. Montoya de Hernandez* (473 U.S. 531 [1985]), the Court reaffirmed the need for warrantless border inspections: "Routine searches of the persons and effects of entrants [at the border] are not subject to any requirement of reasonable suspicion, probable cause, or a warrant . . . [O]ne's expectation of privacy [is] less at the border" (p. 538). The Court wrote:

> [This case reflects] longstanding concern for the protection of the integrity of the border. This concern is, if anything, heightened by the veritable national crisis in law enforcement caused by smuggling of illicit narcotics . . . and in particular by the increasing utilization of alimentary canal smuggling. This desperate practice appears to be a relatively recent addition to the smugglers' repertoire of deceptive practices, and it also appears to be exceedingly difficult to detect. (pp. 538–539)

Border checkpoints have also been upheld on U.S. waterways (*United States v. Villamonte-Marquez*, 462 U.S. 579 [1983]), at highway checkpoints well inside the international borders (*Almeida-Sanchez v. United States*, 413 U.S. 266 [1973]), and at international airports (*Illinois v. Andreas*, 463 U.S. 765 [1983]). According to a recent Supreme Court decision (*United States v. Flores-Montano*, 541 U.S. 149 [2004]), it also appears that more than just a detention is permissible at the border. In that case, the Supreme Court sanctioned the removal, disassembly, and reassembly of a vehicle's fuel tank.

ILLEGAL IMMIGRANT CHECKPOINTS   In *United States v. Martinez-Fuerte* (428 U.S. 543 [1976]), the Court upheld the decision of the Immigration and Naturalization Service (INS) to establish roadblocks near the Mexican border for the purpose of discovering illegal aliens. The Court offered a number of reasons for its decision. First, "[t]he degree of intrusion upon privacy that may be occasioned by a search of a house hardly can be compared with the minor interference with privacy resulting from the mere stop for questioning as to residence" (p. 565). Second, motorists could avoid the checkpoint if they so desired. Third, the Court noted that the traffic flow near the border was heavy, so individualized suspicion was not possible. Fourth, the location of the roadblock was not decided by the officers in the field "but by officials responsible for making overall decisions" (p. 559). Finally, a requirement that such stops be based on probable cause "would largely eliminate any deterrent to the conduct of well-disguised smuggling operations, even though smugglers are known to use these highways regularly" (p. 557). Importantly, law enforcement officers must have justification to examine the bags and personal effects of individuals who are stopped at immigration checkpoints (or during any immigration check) (*Bond v. United States*, 529 U.S. 334 [2000]).

United States v. Martinez-Fuerte
(428 U.S. 543 [1976])

DECISION-MAKING EXERCISE 7.4

Detecting Illegal Aliens

The U.S. Border Patrol relies on checkpoints north of the Mexican border to look for illegal aliens. (In California, these can be found as far as 90 miles north of the border.) These checkpoints are often stationed in the middle of major freeways, where every car must slow down and, at a minimum, be waved through by one of several agents standing between the lanes. In addition, there is little, if any, opportunity to exit the freeway in order to avoid the checkpoints. Can these checkpoints be considered administrative? What if, instead of having the cars slow down, the border patrol required all vehicles to *stop*, at which point they would briefly search the trunk, cargo compartment (i.e., for a pickup truck, van, or tractor trailer), and so on in an effort to detect illegal aliens? Could they legally do this?

Michigan Dept. of State Police v. Sitz (496 U.S. 444 [1990])

SOBRIETY CHECKPOINTS In *Michigan Dept. of State Police v. Sitz* (496 U.S. 444 [1990]), the Court upheld a warrantless, suspicionless checkpoint designed to detect evidence of drunk-driving. In that case, police checkpoints were set up, at which all drivers were stopped and briefly (approximately 25 seconds) observed for signs of intoxication. If such signs were found, the driver was detained for sobriety testing, and if the indication was that the driver was intoxicated, an arrest was made. The Court weighed the magnitude of the governmental interest in eradicating the drunk-driving problem against the slight intrusion to motorists stopped briefly at such checkpoints. Key to the constitutionality of Michigan's checkpoint were two additional factors: (1) evenhandedness was ensured because the locations of the checkpoints were chosen pursuant to written guidelines and every driver was stopped; and (2) the officers themselves were not given discretion to decide whom to stop. Significantly, the checkpoint was deemed constitutional even though motorists were *not* notified of the upcoming checkpoint *or* given an opportunity to turn around and go the other way. According to the Court:

> No one can seriously dispute the magnitude of the drunken driving problem or the State's interest in eradicating it. Media reports of alcohol-related death and mutilation on the Nation's roads are legion. The anecdotal is confirmed by the statistical. . . . For decades, this Court has "repeatedly lamented the tragedy." . . . Conversely, the weight bearing on the other scale—the measure of the intrusion on motorists stopped briefly at sobriety checkpoints—is slight. . . . In sum, the balance of the State's interest in preventing drunken driving, the extent to which this system can reasonably be said to advance that interest, and the degree of intrusion upon individual motorists who are briefly stopped, weighs in favor of the state program. We therefore hold that it is consistent with the Fourth Amendment. (pp. 451–455)

LICENSE AND SAFETY CHECKPOINTS In *Delaware v. Prouse* (440 U.S. 648 [1979]), the Supreme Court held that law enforcement officials cannot randomly stop drivers for the purpose of checking their drivers' licenses. The Court's reasoning is interesting:

> An individual operating or traveling in an automobile does not lose all reasonable expectation of privacy simply because the automobile and its use are subject to government regulation. Automobile travel is a basic, pervasive, and often necessary mode of transportation to and from one's home, workplace, and leisure activities. Many people spend more hours each day traveling in cars than walking on the streets. Undoubtedly, many find a greater sense of security and privacy in traveling in an automobile than they do in exposing themselves by pedestrian or other modes of travel. Were the

individual subject to unfettered governmental intrusion every time he entered an automobile, the security guaranteed by the Fourth Amendment would be seriously circumscribed. . . . Accordingly, we hold that except in those situations in which there is at least articulable and reasonable suspicion that a motorist is unlicensed or that an automobile is not registered, or that either the vehicle or an occupant is otherwise subject to seizure for violation of the law, stopping an automobile and detaining the driver in order to check his driver's license and the registration of the automobile are unreasonable under the Fourth Amendment. (pp. 662–663)

The Court did note, however, that "this holding does not preclude the State of Delaware or other States from developing methods for spot checks that involve less intrusion or that do not involve the unconstrained exercise of discretion" (p. 663). In particular, "Questioning of all oncoming traffic at roadblock-type stops is one possible alternative" (p. 663). If officers stopped every fifth, tenth, or twentieth vehicle, then this action would probably conform to the Court's requirement that roadblocks and checkpoints restrict individual officers' discretion to the fullest extent possible. See Figure 7.2 for an example of a vehicle safety checkpoint policy.

FIGURE 7.2

Vehicle Safety Checkpoint Policy (Pine Bluff, AR, Police Department)

[Pine Bluff Police Department ARK badge]	**SUBJECT:** **VEHICLE SAFETY CHECKPOINT**	**POLICY NUMBER** 403
		ISSUE DATE 02/19/2008
	CHAPTER: TRAFFIC	**EFFECTIVE DATE** 02/19/2008
	ISSUED By: Chief of Police John E. Howell	**TOTAL PAGES** 4

I. <u>POLICY</u>

This agency has a primary mission of creating a safer environment for the citizens within this community. In furtherance of this mission, this agency shall periodically conduct a vehicle safety checkpoint as directed by the Chief or his or her designee. All vehicle safety checkpoint operations shall be closely supervised as assigned by the Chief or his or her designee. The directives, as stated within this policy, shall be applied as a standard operating procedure in providing guidance to agency personnel in conducting all vehicle safety checkpoints. This policy applies only to vehicle safety checkpoints. It does not apply to sobriety checkpoints, drug interdiction checkpoints, or roadblocks for other purposes.

II. <u>PURPOSE</u>

To increase the effectiveness of this agency in checking for unsafe vehicles traveling upon the roadways. Vehicle safety checkpoints will also allow this agency the opportunity to periodically concentrate its efforts in checking for violations of Arkansas traffic and regulatory laws that will ultimately increase the safety of the citizens within the community.

Figure 7.2 continued

III. PROCEDURES:

A. A decision to implement a vehicle safety checkpoint operation must be approved either by the Chief or his or her designee.

B. The maximum duration of any vehicle safety checkpoint operation shall be four hours unless otherwise directed by the Chief or his or her designee.

C. A safety checkpoint operation shall only be conducted by utilizing the proper equipment. The following shall be considered as being proper equipment:

    1. At least three marked patrol units equipped with emergency lights, siren and communications devices. One of these marked units shall be positioned at the checkpoint central location and shall have emergency lights operational during the checkpoint operation. The other two patrol units shall be positioned at each end of the checkpoint area. Other patrol units, for prisoner transport, shall be called to the checkpoint area if necessary.

    2. At least one portable sign (when traffic is only stopped one way) to be placed alongside the roadway approximately 300 feet from the checkpoint area. The letters on the sign shall be large enough so that passing motorists are able to read it easily. The sign shall display the following messages:

        a. NOTICE————You are now entering a vehicle safety checkpoint under the direction of the Pine Bluff Police Department.

        b. Be prepared to stop.

    3. When traffic is being stopped from both directions a second sign shall be utilized and displayed as stated above.

    4. A vehicle safety checkpoint operation shall only be conducted by assigning the appropriate number of personnel. The following shall be considered an appropriate number of personnel:

        a. At least two or three officers (depending on the time of day and the traffic flow) conducting the checkpoint in full departmental uniform or in clothing, as approved by an immediate supervisor, that identifies him or her as a law enforcement officer. Two officers shall be utilized to approach the vehicles stopped and one officer will be utilized to take any enforcement action as necessary.

        b. At least one officer or a properly trained K-9 and K-9 handler occupying the other marked units. These officers shall be in full departmental uniform or in clothing, as approved by an immediate supervisor that identifies him or her as a law enforcement officer.

    5. A supervisor as assigned by the Chief or his or her designee.

    6. Law Enforcement officers of this agency participating in a vehicle safety checkpoint operation shall:

        a. Establish a checkpoint only in an area where there is complete visibility for a minimum of 500 feet from both directions of oncoming traffic to the checkpoint area.

        b. Establish a checkpoint whereby all vehicles or a designated number, every third vehicle for instance, is stopped. The Chief of Police or other supervisor assigned to the operation shall make a decision as to how the checkpoint will be conducted at the scene.

        c. Cautiously approach all vehicles and be particularly alert to suspicious movements or actions of the vehicle occupants. Policy 403 Page 3

        d. Allow the driver and occupants to remain inside their vehicle unless their removal from the vehicle is necessary due to facts leading the officer to reasonably suspect that:

            i. A crime has been or is being committed;

            ii. The vehicle occupant(s) presents some danger to the officer or others; or

            iii. The person is armed and presently dangerous.

    e. Courteously advise the driver of the vehicle the following: This is a vehicle safety checkpoint being conducted by the Pine Bluff Police Department. We are checking vehicles for the safety of all motorists within the city of Pine Bluff.

    f. Advise the operator of the vehicle to provide a driver's license, vehicle registration, and proof of vehicle insurance. Also advise the vehicle operator that a brief vehicle safety inspection, checking the general condition of the motor vehicle, will be completed.

    g. Complete the vehicle/document inspection and take any enforcement action deemed necessary or appropriate. Drivers of vehicles for which enforcement action is necessary will be directed to a "pull off area" that has been established prior to the beginning of the checkpoint operation. A pull off area is defined as a location such as the following:

        i. The shoulder of the roadway that is wide enough that three or more vehicles can be parked in a safe manner.

        ii. A parking area that can be utilized either by permission of the owner or a business parking lot for which the business is closed.

        iii. The pull off area is necessary to avoid any lane blockage for prolonged periods and to provide for motorists and officer safety.

    h. After completing the document/vehicle inspection or taking enforcement action and no arrests are made, law enforcement officers shall:

        i. Thank the vehicle operator/occupants for the cooperation extended.

        ii. Promptly release the vehicle and occupants.

    i. The additional patrol unit(s), positioned at each end of the checkpoint area, shall provide back-up for the officers conducting the checkpoint and shall conduct traffic stops in a situation where a vehicle, after observing the portable signs, takes evasive action to avoid entering the checkpoint area.

7. Upon completion of a vehicle safety checkpoint operation, all signs will be removed from alongside the roadway and returned to agency storage. Policy 403 Page 4

8. Agency personnel assigned to a vehicle safety checkpoint operation must first attend a briefing for which a supervisor or designee will further familiarize personnel with agency operational procedures, discuss the location of the checkpoint and emphasize officer safety.

9. Information about any vehicle safety checkpoint operation, or subsequent arrests or seizures as a result of the operation, will be released to the news media in accordance with departmental policy concerning Freedom of Information.

10. At the conclusion of a vehicle safety checkpoint operation, the Chief or supervising officer in charge will assign one of the officers involved in the checkpoint to complete a full report outlining the details associated with the operation. The report shall include the date, time, and location of the checkpoint; personnel assigned including the use of a K-9 and in what capacity each individual was utilized; results of the operation such as, arrests made, searches conducted and items seized subsequent to the search; and any other information specific to the particular event.

11. A completed report shall be forwarded to the supervising officer making the assignment. The supervising officer shall forward a copy to the Criminal Investigation Division for investigative purposes if necessary. The original report shall be filed within the Police Department in accordance with departmental filing procedures.

12. Law enforcement officers of this agency may conduct a Vehicle Checkpoint operation in conjunction with other law enforcement agencies within the City only if the cooperating agency will agree to comply with the specific requirements set forth within this policy.

Source: Reprinted courtesy of Pine Bluff, AR, Police Department.

CRIME INVESTIGATION CHECKPOINTS   In *Illinois v. Lidster* (540 U.S. 419 [2004]), the Supreme Court decided that checkpoints are also authorized for officers to ask questions related to crimes that had occurred earlier at the same area. In *Lidster*, police briefly detained motorists to ask them if they had any information about a hit-and-run accident between a vehicle and a bicycle that had taken place a week before at the same location. A driver entered the checkpoint, swerved, and nearly hit an officer. He was stopped and subjected to a field sobriety test. He was convicted of drunk-driving and later challenged the constitutionality of the checkpoint. The Supreme Court disagreed, thus permitting yet another type of checkpoint.

OTHER TYPES OF CHECKPOINTS   Still other types of checkpoints have come to the Supreme Court's attention. In *United States v. Villamonte-Marquez*, for example, the Court distinguished stops of boats on water from stops of vehicles on land. In that case, customs officers stopped and boarded a person's boat to inspect documents in accordance with 19 U.S.C. Section 1581(a), which permits officers to board any vessel, at any time, without justification, to examine the vessel's manifest or other documents. While onboard the defendant's boat, one of the customs officers smelled what he thought was marijuana. Looking through an open hatch, the officer spotted bales that turned out to contain marijuana. The Court noted that fixed checkpoints are not possible, given the expansiveness of open water, so it relied on different reasoning. The Court noted that boardings such as that in *Villamonte-Marquez* are essential to ensure enforcement of the law in waters, "where the need to deter or apprehend drug smugglers is great" (p. 593). Key restrictions the Court *did* impose, though, were that such detentions be brief and limited to the inspection of documents. The reason the seizure of the marijuana was upheld in *Villamonte-Marquez* was that the contraband was in plain view.

Airport checkpoints are also authorized, and there is no need for probable cause or reasonable suspicion in such situations. According to the Ninth Circuit, "The need to prevent airline hijacking is unquestionably grave and urgent. . . . A pre-boarding screening of all passengers and carry-on articles sufficient in scope to detect the presence of weapons or explosives is reasonably necessary to meet the need" (*United States v. Davis*, 482 F.2d 893 [9th Cir. 1973]). Another court reached a similar conclusion (*United States v. Lopez*, 328 F. Supp. 1077 [E.D.N.Y. 1971]). And the Fifth Circuit's opinion in *United States v. Skipwith* (482 F.2d 1272 [5th Cir. 1971]) is particularly helpful:

> [T]he intrusion which the airport search imposes on the public is not insubstantial. It is inconvenient and annoying, in some cases it may be embarrassing, and at times it can be incriminating. There are several factors, however, which make this search less offensive to the searched person than similar searches in other contexts. One such factor is the almost complete absence of any stigma attached to being subjected to search at a known, designated airport search point. . . . In addition, the offensiveness of the screening process is somewhat mitigated by the fact that the person to be searched must voluntarily come to and enter the search area. He has every opportunity to avoid the procedure by not entering the boarding area. Finally, the circumstances under which the airport search is conducted make it much less likely that abuses will occur. Unlike searches conducted on dark and lonely streets at night where often the officer and the subject are the only witnesses, these searches are made under supervision and not far from the scrutiny of the traveling public. Moreover, the airlines, which have their representatives present, have a

definite and substantial interest in assuring that their passengers are not unnecessarily harassed. The officers conducting the search under these circumstances are much more likely to be solicitous of the Fourth Amendment rights of the traveling public than in more isolated, unsupervised surroundings. (pp. 1275–1276)

Note that airport screenings are now conducted by *public* as opposed to *private* actors. Prior to the September 11, 2001, terrorist attacks on the World Trade Center and the Pentagon, airport inspections were conducted by private security companies. Now, they are conducted by Transportation Safety Administration (TSA) officials, who are employed by the federal government. This change is of no consequence to the constitutionality of airport screenings, however, even though such inspections are today sometimes more intrusive than prior to September 11 (e.g., "shoe searches" and searches at the boarding gate in addition to at the main security checkpoint).

UNCONSTITUTIONAL CHECKPOINTS The administrative rationale is *not* acceptable, by comparison, to detect evidence of criminal activity. This was the decision reached in *City of Indianapolis v. Edmond* (531 U.S. 32 [2000]), a case in which the Supreme Court decided whether a city's suspicionless checkpoints for detecting illegal drugs were constitutional. Here is how the Supreme Court described the checkpoints:

City of Indianapolis v. Edmond (531 U.S. 32 [2000])

> The city of Indianapolis operated a checkpoint program under which the police, acting without individualized suspicion, stopped a predetermined number of vehicles at roadblocks in various locations on city roads for the primary purpose of the discovery and interdiction of illegal narcotics. Under the program, at least one officer would (1) approach each vehicle, (2) advise the driver that he or she was being stopped briefly at a drug checkpoint, (3) ask the driver to produce a driver's license and the vehicle's registration, (4) look for signs of impairment, and (5) conduct an open-view examination of the vehicle from the outside. In addition, a narcotics-detection dog would walk around the outside of each stopped vehicle. (p. 32)

The Court held that stops such as those conducted during Indianapolis's checkpoint operations require individualized suspicion. In addition, "because the checkpoint program's primary purpose [was] indistinguishable from the general interest in crime control" (p. 44), it was deemed violative of the Fourth Amendment.

School Discipline

Public school administrators and teachers may "search" a student without a warrant if they possess reasonable suspicion that the action will yield evidence that the student has violated the law or is violating the law or rules of the school. However, such **school discipline "searches"** must not be "excessively intrusive in light of the age and sex of the students and the nature of the infraction" (p. 381). This was the decision reached in *New Jersey v. T.L.O.* (469 U.S. 325 [1985]). In *T.L.O.*, a high school student was caught smoking in a school bathroom (in violation of school policy) and was sent to the vice principal. When the vice principal searched the student's purse for cigarettes, he also found evidence implicating the student in the sale of marijuana. The Court held that the evidence was admissible because the administrator had sufficient justification to search the purse for evidence concerning the school's antismoking policy.

New Jersey v. T.L.O. (469 U.S. 325 [1985])

DECISION-MAKING EXERCISE 7.5

A Constitutionally Valid Checkpoint?

The facts from an actual case follow. Was this action constitutional?

During the spring and summer of 1992, street crime, including four drive-by shootings, escalated in the Soundview neighborhood of the Bronx. In response, the 43rd precinct instituted the so-called Watson Avenue Special Operation. This involved a temporary vehicular checkpoint in an eight square-block narcotics-ridden area where most of the drive-by shootings had taken place. The checkpoint was to be active three days a week on a random basis and for approximately six hours a day, primarily in the evening hours. When the checkpoint was in operation, officers manning the barricade were to stop every vehicle seeking to enter the area in order to ascertain the driver's connection to the neighborhood. Drivers who approached the checkpoint were to be allowed to avoid questioning by driving around the area or by parking their cars and entering the area on foot. Area residents and commercial vehicles were to be allowed into the neighborhood. Officers manning the barricades were verbally instructed that they could also allow cars dropping off small children or visiting the local church to enter the area. Other than that, vehicles were not permitted beyond the barricades. The operation was in effect for six weeks, between August 26 and October 10, 1992 (*Maxwell v. City of New York*, 102 F.3d 664 [2d Cir. 1996], p. 665).

In support of its decision in *T.L.O.*, the Court noted that a warrant requirement "would unduly interfere with the maintenance of the swift and informal disciplinary procedures needed in the schools . . . [and] . . . the substantial need of teachers and administrators for freedom to maintain order in the schools" (p. 376). The majority further stated that the reasonableness test for **school disciplinary "searches"** involves a twofold inquiry: "First, one must consider 'whether the . . . action was justified at its inception . . . ' second, one must determine whether the search as actually conducted 'was reasonably related in scope to the circumstances which justified the interference in the first place' " (p. 341).

There are important limits on school discipline searches, especially in light of the Supreme Court's decision in *Safford Unified School District v. Redding* (No. 08-479 [2009]). In that case, Savana Redding, an eighth grader, was "strip searched" by school officials on a belief that she was in possession of certain nonprescription medications, in violation of school policy. Writing for the majority, Justice Souter found that the search violated the Fourth Amendment because there was no " . . . indication of danger to the students from the power of the drugs or their quantity and any reason to suppose that (Redding) was carrying pills in her underwear." More than just reasonable suspicion is necessary, then, to support particularly intrusive searches of this nature—for school discipline, but also in the workplace.

Note that *T.L.O.* concerns students in kindergarten through grade 12. A different story emerges in the context of public and private universities. The courts have generally held that the Fourth Amendment is applicable at the university level. That is, for university personnel to conduct searches of students' dorm rooms, lockers, and so on, some level of justification is required.

LOCKER CHECKS AND DRUG DOG "SNIFFS" A handful of lower court decisions concern inspections of public school students' lockers as well as drug dog "sniffs" for the purpose of detecting illicit drugs. First, random, suspicionless locker inspections are generally permissible, assuming the students have been given some notification in advance that their lockers are subject to inspection at any time (see *Commonwealth v. Cass*, 709 A.2d 350 [Pa. 1998]). However, "searches" of *specific* lockers would still be subject to the reasonableness test set forth in *T.L.O.*

With regard to the use of drug dogs, the Fifth Circuit held that so-called sniffs of lockers and cars in public schools are constitutional (*Horton v. Goose Creek Independent School District*, 690 F.2d 470 [5th Cir. 1982]). The court reasoned that lockers and cars were inanimate objects located in a public place.

Then there is the Seventh Circuit's controversial holding in *Doe v. Renfrow* (631 F.2d 91 [7th Cir. 1980]) that the exploratory sniffing of *students* (as opposed to their property) was not a search. The Seventh Circuit affirmed the lower federal court's observation that "the presence of the canine team for several minutes was a minimal intrusion at best and not so serious as to invoke the protections of the Fourth Amendment" (*Doe v. Renfrow*, 475 F. Supp. 1012 [1979], p. 1020). In another appellate court case, though, the Ninth Circuit held that dog sniffs of students' possession implicate the Fourth Amendment and require probable cause (*B.C. v. Plumas Unified School District*, 192 F.3d 1260 [9th Cir. 1999]). This is a disagreement between federal circuits that is ripe for some Supreme Court resolution.

"Searches" of Government Employees' Offices

In a case very similar to *T.L.O.*, although not involving a public school student, the Court held that neither a warrant nor probable cause was required to "search" a government employee's office, but the "search" must be "a noninvestigatory work-related intrusion or an investigatory search for evidence of suspected work-related employee misfeasance" (*O'Connor v. Ortega*, 480 U.S. 709 [1987]). Justice O'Connor summarized the Court's reasoning: "[T]he delay in correcting the employee misconduct caused by the need for probable cause rather than reasonable suspicion will be translated into tangible and often irreparable damage to the agency's work, and ultimately to the public interest" (p. 724). It is important to note, however, that the Court was limiting its decision strictly to work-related matters: "[W]e do not address the appropriate standard when an employee is being investigated for criminal misconduct or breaches of other nonwork-related statutory or regulatory standards" (p. 729). The Court further noted in *Ortega* that the appropriate standard by which to judge such "searches" is *reasonableness*:

O'Connor v. Ortega
(480 U.S. 709 [1987])

> We hold, therefore, that public employer intrusions on the constitutionally protected privacy interests of government employees for noninvestigatory, work-related purposes, as well as for investigations of work-related misconduct, should be judged by the standard of reasonableness under all the circumstances. Under this reasonableness standard, both the inception and the scope of the intrusion must be reasonable. (pp. 725–726)

Recently, the Supreme Court was confronted with the question of whether a police officer's employer could examine the content of messages sent via a pager. Ontario, California, police officers were given department-issued pagers. When one of them exceeded the number of allotted monthly messages, the department acquired transcripts of the officer's messages, learned that some of them were sexually explicit, and then disciplined the officer accordingly. He sued under Section 1983, alleging his Fourth Amendment rights were violated. However, the Supreme Court disagreed, holding that the department's "search" of the pager message contents was reasonable (*City of Ontario v. Quon*, No. 08-1332 [2010]).

At the risk of confusing matters, it should be pointed out that *reasonableness* in the context of public school student and government employee "searches" is not the same as *reasonable suspicion*. The latter refers to a certain level of suspicion, while the former focuses on the procedural aspects of the actions in question (e.g., Did authorities go too far in looking for evidence?). The distinction between *reasonableness* and *reasonable suspicion* is a subtle but important one—hence, the reason for discussing disciplinary and work-related "searches" in the section on administrative justification.

Perhaps more important, none of the foregoing applies to individuals employed in *private* companies. The reason for this should be fairly clear: Private employees work for private employers, the latter not being bound by the strictures of the Fourth Amendment. Stated simply, private employers can search private employees' lockers, desks, and the like without infringing on any constitutional rights.

Drug and Alcohol Testing

The Supreme Court has, especially recently, decided on the constitutionality of **drug and alcohol testing** programs. Three lines of cases can be discerned: (1) employee testing, (2) hospital patient testing, and (3) school student testing. Cases involving drug and alcohol testing of each of these three groups are reviewed in the following subsections.

Skinner v. Railway Labor Executives' Association (489 U.S. 602 [1989])

DRUG AND ALCOHOL TESTING OF EMPLOYEES   The Supreme Court has permitted warrantless, suspicionless drug and alcohol testing of employees. In *Skinner v. Railway Labor Executives' Association* (489 U.S. 602 [1989]) and *National Treasury Employees Union v. Von Raab* (489 U.S. 656 [1989]), the Court upheld the constitutionality of certain regulations that permit drug and alcohol testing, citing two reasons for its decision. The first was deterrence; without suspicionless drug testing, there would be no deterrent to employees to stay off drugs. The second reason was that drug testing promotes businesses' interest in obtaining accurate information about accidents and who is responsible. In *Skinner*, Justice Stevens made this observation:

> Most people—and I would think most railroad employees as well—do not go to work with the expectation that they may be involved in a major accident, particularly one causing such catastrophic results as loss of life or the release of hazardous material requiring an evacuation. Moreover, even if they are conscious of the possibilities that such an accident might be a contributing factor, if the risk of serious personal injury does not deter their use of these substances, it seems highly unlikely that the additional threat of loss of employment would have any effect on their behavior. (p. 634)

Two interesting limitations should be noted about both these cases. The first is that the Court did not decide whether warrantless, suspicionless drug testing could be used

---

DECISION-MAKING EXERCISE 7.6
Searches of Government Employees

Federal law enforcement agents suspected that several employees in a government agency were engaged in criminal wrongdoing. Several of the agency's records were subpoenaed. To ensure that the records were being prepared in accordance with the subpoena, the agents visited the government agency. During the course of their visit, the director of the agency was asked to open an employee's office. Upon looking in the employee's office, the agents found incriminating documents and seized them. They also searched the employee's file cabinet and found more incriminating documents, which were also seized. Is this a valid search of a government employee's office, as authorized by *O'Connor v. Ortega* (480 U.S. 709 [1987])?

for *law enforcement* purposes. Rather, such testing was held to be constitutional for *regulatory* reasons. Second, both cases focused on federal regulations: Federal Railroad Administration guidelines in *Skinner* and U.S. Customs Service Policy in *National Treasury Employees Union*. Left open was the question of private business policy. Nevertheless, the courts have since upheld drug and alcohol testing of teachers, police officers, and several other groups.[1]

This line of cases would seem to suggest that employee drug testing is becoming increasingly common across the United States. While it is certainly true that more employees are subject to drug testing now than in the past, the Supreme Court has clearly stated that certain drug testing policies are unconstitutional. For example, in *Chandler v. Miller* (520 U.S. 305 [1997]), the Court struck down a Georgia statute that required every person seeking nomination or election to undergo a test for illegal drugs.

DRUG AND ALCOHOL TESTING OF HOSPITAL PATIENTS   In a recent case, *Ferguson v. Charleston* (532 U.S. 67 [2001]), the Supreme Court addressed the constitutionality of drug testing of hospital patients. In the fall of 1988, staff at the Charleston, South Carolina, public hospital became concerned over the apparent increase in the use of cocaine by patients who were receiving prenatal treatment. Staff at the hospital approached the city and agreed to cooperate in prosecuting pregnant mothers who tested positive for drugs. A task force was set up, consisting of hospital personnel, police, and other local officials. The task force formulated a policy for how to conduct the tests, preserve the evidence, and use it to prosecute those who tested positive. Several women tested positive for cocaine. The question before the Supreme Court was, Is the Fourth Amendment violated when hospital personnel, working with the police, test pregnant mothers for drug use without their consent? Not surprisingly, the Court answered "yes":

> Because the hospital seeks to justify its authority to conduct drug tests and to turn the results over to police without the patients' knowledge or consent, this case differs from the four previous cases in which the Court considered whether comparable drug tests fit within the closely guarded category of constitutionally permissible suspicionless searches . . . . Those cases employed a balancing test weighing the intrusion on the individual's privacy interest against the "special needs" that supported the program. The invasion of privacy here is far more substantial than in those cases. In previous cases, there was no misunderstanding about the purpose of the test or the potential use of the test results, and there were protections against the dissemination of the results to third parties. Moreover, those cases involved disqualification from eligibility for particular benefits, not the unauthorized dissemination of test results. The critical difference, however, lies in the nature of the "special needs" asserted. In each of the prior cases, the "special need" was one divorced from the State's general law enforcement interest. Here, the policy's central and indispensable feature from its inception was the use of law enforcement to coerce patients into substance abuse treatment. (pp. 77–78)

Ferguson v. Charleston
(532 U.S. 67 [2001])

---

[1] P. T. Bookspan, "Jar Wars: Employee Drug Testing, the Constitution, and the American Drug Problem," *American Criminal Law Review* 26 (1988): 359–400.

Vernonia School District 47J v. Acton   (515 U.S. 646 [1995])

DRUG AND ALCOHOL TESTING OF SCHOOL STUDENTS   The Supreme Court has recently extended its drug testing decisions to include public school students. Specifically, in *Vernonia School District 47J v. Acton* (515 U.S. 646 [1995]), the Court upheld a random drug testing program for school athletes. The program had been instituted because the district had been experiencing significant student drug use. Under the program, all students who wished to play sports were required to be tested at the beginning of the season and then retested randomly later in the season. The Court noted that athletes enjoy a lesser expectation of privacy, given the semipublic nature of locker rooms, which is where the testing took place. Also, athletes are often subject to other intrusions, including physical exams, so drug testing involved a "negligible" privacy intrusion, according to the Court.

Board of Education v. Earls   (536 U.S. 822 [2002])

Even more recently, the Supreme Court affirmed *Vernonia School District*. The case of *Board of Education v. Earls* (536 U.S. 822 [2002]) dealt with another student drug testing policy. The Student Activities Drug Testing Policy, implemented by the Board of Education of Independent School District no. 92 of Pottawatomie County, required students who participate in extracurricular activities to submit to random, suspicionless drug tests. Urine tests were intended to detect the use of illegal drugs. Together with their parents, two students, Lindsay Earls and Daniel James, brought a Section 1983 lawsuit against the school district, alleging that the drug testing policy violated the Fourth Amendment, as incorporated to the states through the due process clause of the Fourteenth Amendment. The district court found in favor of the school district, but the Tenth Circuit Court reversed the decision, holding that the policy violated the Fourth Amendment. It concluded that random, suspicionless drug tests would only be permissible if there were some identifiable drug abuse problem. However, the Supreme Court held that random, suspicionless drug testing of students who participate in extracurricular activities "is a reasonable means of furthering the School District's important interest in preventing and deterring drug use among its schoolchildren and does not violate the Fourth Amendment" (p. 822).

Probation and Parole Supervision

Griffin v. Wisconsin (483 U.S. 868 [1987])

A person on probation enjoys a lesser expectation of privacy than the typical citizen. In *Griffin v. Wisconsin* (483 U.S. 868 [1987]), the Supreme Court held that a state law or agency rule permitting probation officers to search a probationer's home without a warrant and based on reasonable suspicion was constitutional. The majority (of only five justices) concluded that probation supervision "is a 'special need' of the State permitting a degree of impingement upon privacy that would not be constitutional if applied to the public at large" (p. 875). The same principle almost certainly applies to parolees, but the Supreme Court has not addressed this issue.

The Court has also ruled that evidence seized by parole officers during an illegal search and seizure need not be excluded at a parole revocation hearing (see *Pennsylvania*

DECISION-MAKING EXERCISE 7.7

Drug Testing of Students

The school board approved a policy prohibiting a high school student from participating in any extracurricular activities or driving to and from school unless the student and his or her parent or guardian consented to and passed tests for drugs, alcohol, and tobacco in random, unannounced urinalysis examinations. (Extracurricular activities include not only athletic teams but also organizations such as the student council, foreign language clubs, and so on.) When consent for testing had been given and the individuals had taken and passed the tests, then participation in the extracurricular organizations or driving to and from school would be permitted. The testing was to be conducted by Acme Toxicology Services, which would collect the samples, and the local hospital's laboratory services division, which would perform the tests. Can this type of random, suspicionless drug testing be considered an administrative search?

Board of Probation and Parole v. Scott, 524 U.S. 357 [1998]). This latter decision can be interpreted to mean that the exclusionary rule does not apply in parole revocation hearings. A warrant requirement, the Court noted, "would both hinder the function of state parole systems and alter the traditionally flexible, administrative nature of parole revocation proceedings" (p. 364).

More recently, in *United States v. Knights* (534 U.S. 112 [2001]), the Supreme Court held that warrantless searches of probationers are permissible not only for probation-related purposes (e.g., to ensure that probation conditions are being conformed with) but also for investigative purposes. In that case, a probationer was suspected of vandalizing utility company facilities. A police detective searched the probationer's residence and found incriminating evidence. The Supreme Court held that "[t]he warrantless search of Knights, supported by reasonable suspicion and authorized by a probation condition, satisfied the Fourth Amendment" (p. 112).

Needless to say, all three of the aforementioned decisions do not provide a great deal of guidance to probation officers on the streets. *Griffin*, for example, dealt with the constitutionality of one statute in one state. This means that probation officers are mostly forced to turn to state-level supreme court decisions for guidance. The California Supreme Court has offered some clarification with regard to searches-and-seizures by probation officers that the Supreme Court has not; but of course, its decisions are limited to California. Some interesting decisions from that state are worth considering, nonetheless.

MORE LATITUDE AT THE STATE LEVEL   Probation officers are often given even more latitude at the state level. For example, two weeks after the Supreme Court decided *Griffin*, the California Supreme Court decided *People v. Bravo* (738 P.2d 336 [Cal. 1987]), *cert. denied*, 485 U.S. 904 [1988]). The issue in that case was the constitutionality of a warrantless search conducted in accordance with a probation contract that required the probationer to "submit his person and property to search or seizure at any time of the day or night by any law enforcement officer with or without a warrant" (p. 337, n. 1). Relying on the U.S. Supreme Court's decision in *Schneckloth v. Bustamonte* (412 U.S. 218 [1973]), California's high court ruled that because the search was conducted pursuant to the probationer's voluntary consent (i.e., consent given when the probationer agreed to the terms specified in the probation contract), it would violate the Fourth Amendment only if it exceeded the scope of the probationer's consent. The same holds true even for searches of probationers by other peace officers. However, the court also stated that probation searches of the type arising in *Bravo* can only be conducted for "legitimate law enforcement purposes" and not "for harassment or . . . arbitrary and capricious reasons" (p. 342).

Notwithstanding the restrictions just mentioned, the California Supreme Court requires no justification for probation searches. In fact, the California courts have distinguished *Griffin* by arguing that it only applies to searches conducted pursuant to a regulatory scheme, in which the administrative justification balancing act comes into play. For example, in *In re Marcellus L.* (279 Cal. Rptr. 901 [Ct. App. 1991]), the court of appeal for California's first district found that *Griffin* does not apply when the probationer expressly agrees to consent to searches as a condition of probation: "[T]he authority to search [in *Griffin*] existed by way of [Wisconsin's] regulation, not because the defendant specifically agreed to submit to warrantless, unexpected searches" (p. 940).

POLICE/PROBATION PARTNERSHIPS   A controversial practice closely connected to searches of probationers comes in the form of **police/probation partnerships**, a cutting-edge law enforcement strategy now being experimented with across the country. An example of one such approach is Boston's Operation Night Light. The program began in 1992 as an informal collaboration between probation officers and Boston's Anti-Gang Violence Unit. Teams composed of one probation officer and two police officers serving as backup make surprise visits to the homes, schools, and worksites of high-risk youth probationers, mostly during the hours of 7 p.m. to midnight. The program grew to the extent that 50 police officers and 50 probation officers worked together like this seven nights a week.

Another example of a police/probation partnership in action is the IMPACT project in San Bernardino, California. The program was virtually identical to Boston's. One difference was that the teams consisted of one San Bernardino police officer and one San Bernardino County probation officer. (Probation is a county-level function in California.) Also, *all* new probationers were under scrutiny.

What makes these and other police/probation partnerships interesting from a Fourth Amendment standpoint are the search-and-seizure implications. On one hand, these partnerships may be highly effective crime-reduction mechanisms. On the other hand, critics of police/probation partnerships claim that they are little more than a method of circumventing the Fourth Amendment's probable cause and warrant requirements. In other words, critics claim that police officers use probation officers as "stalking horses" to skirt the Fourth Amendment. The California Supreme Court's *Bravo* decision (discussed earlier), for example, permits warrantless, suspicionless searches of probationers, even by police officers.

Here again, due process and crime control collide. Police/probation partnerships may effectively reduce crime, but they may also compromise due process. Someday, the constitutionality of these partnerships will be decided in court. Most likely, the U.S. Supreme Court will decide on the matter in the near future. The Fourth Amendment implications are simply too serious to ignore.

A person who is on probation enjoys a lesser expectation of privacy than the average citizen.

PAROLE SUPERVISION   In *Samson v. California* 547 U.S. 843 [2006]), the Supreme Court extended its earlier probation decision to parole supervision. It held that "[t]he Fourth Amendment does not prohibit a police officer from conducting a suspicionless search of a parolee" (p. 843). What was the Court's logic for this decision? It stated, "Parolees, who are on the 'continuum' of state-imposed punishments, have fewer expectations of privacy than probationers, because parole is more akin to imprisonment than probation is" (p. 843).

Samson v. California (547 U.S. 843 [2006])

CONSENT SEARCHES

Technically, most administrative exceptions to having a warrant require no justification. Rather, the courts focus on public safety versus individual privacy. That said, there is one clear-cut situation in which absolutely no justification or balancing act is required in order to decide on the constitutionality of a search. That situation is *consent*. When a person consents to a search, no justification is required. This is known as a **consent search**.

Cases involving consent searches can be placed into three categories. Consent searches must be *voluntary*, so several cases have focused on the meaning of that term. Other cases have defined the *scope* of consent searches, and still others have focused on whether a *third-party individual* can give consent in order to subject another person's private effects to a search.

Voluntariness

The general rule is that validly obtained consent justifies a warrantless search, with or without probable cause. However, for consent to be valid, it must be voluntary. Consent cannot be "the result of duress or coercion, express or implied" (*Schneckloth v. Bustamonte*, 412 U.S. 218 [1973]). When does duress or coercion take place? There is no clear answer to this question. Instead, the Court has opted for a *totality of circumstances* test. This test requires looking at the *surrounding circumstances* of the consent, including whether a show of force was made; whether the person's age, mental condition, or intellectual capacities inhibited understanding; whether the person is or was in custody; and/or whether consent was granted "only after the official conducting the search [had] asserted that he possesses a warrant" (*Bumper v. North Carolina*, 391 U.S. 543 [1968]).

Schneckloth v. Bustamonte (412 U.S. 218 [1973])

Importantly, consent to search may be valid even if the consenting party is unaware of the fact that he or she can refuse consent (*Schneckloth v. Bustamonte*). As the Court stated in *Ohio v. Robinette* (519 U.S. 33 [1996]), "[J]ust as it 'would be thoroughly impractical to impose on the normal consent search the detailed requirements of an effective warning,' so too would it be unrealistic to require police officers to always inform detainees that they are free to go before a consent to search may be deemed involuntary" (pp. 39–40). This view was recently reaffirmed in *United States v. Drayton* (536 U.S. 194 [2002]), a case involving consent searches of bus passengers. Nevertheless, the issue of one's awareness of the right to refuse consent is still factored into the totality of circumstances analysis (e.g., *United States v. Mendenhall*, 446 U.S. 544 [1980]), although ignorance of the right to refuse is not enough, in and of itself, to render consent involuntary.

To err on the side of constitutionality, many police departments have suspects complete "consent to search" forms. An example of one such form, from the San Bernardino, California, Police Department, is shown in Figure 7.3.

Scope Limitations

The *scope* of a consent search is limited to the terms of the consent. In other words, the person giving consent delineates the scope. This was the decision reached in the case of *Florida v. Jimeno* (500 U.S. 248 [1991]). For example, if a person tells the police "You may look around," it does not necessarily mean the police can look *anywhere* for evidence of criminal activity.

Florida v. Jimeno (500 U.S. 248 [1991])

FIGURE 7.3

Example of a Consent to Search Form

Crime Report No._____

CONSENT TO SEARCH

I, _____ give the San Bernardino Police Department my consent to search the below listed property.

Address: _____City _____

_____ Country _____

Address: _____City _____

_____ Country _____

Vehicle/s: Make _____Year _____Veh. Lic. # _____

              Make _____Year _____Veh. Lic. # _____

Other: _____

_____

_____

_____

_____

_____

                                          Signed: _____

Date: _____   Time: _____

Witness _____   Witness _____

Source: San Bernardino, California, Police Department. Reprinted with permission.

Another issue concerning the scope of a consent search is whether consent can be withdrawn once given. In *State v. Brochu* (237 A.2d 418 [Me. 1967]), the Maine Supreme Court held that a defendant's consent to search his house for evidence of his wife's murder did not extend to another search carried out the day after he was arrested as a suspect. Thus, although the man did not expressly request that the search be terminated, the Maine court still decided that consent had been terminated. The Supreme Court has not directly decided whether consent can be withdrawn, however.

Third-Party Consent

A handful of Supreme Court cases have focused on whether a third party (the third party being someone other than the authority asking for consent to search and the individual whose property he or she hopes to search) can give consent to have another person's property searched (e.g., a landlord consenting to have a tenant's apartment searched;

parents consenting to have their child's room searched). As far as the immediate family is concerned, there are several general rules: (1) Wives and husbands can give consent to have their partners' property searched and (2) parents can give consent to have their children's property searched, but (3) children cannot give consent to have their parents' property searched. The reason children cannot give consent is that they are considered incompetent to give voluntary consent, given their age.

More confusing is the situation of a roommate, former girlfriend, friend, or extended family member. Two important Supreme Court cases are relevant here. First, third-party consent can be given if (1) the third-party individual possesses "common authority" over the area to be searched and (2) the nonconsenting party (e.g., the roommate) is not present (*United States v. Matlock*, 415 U.S. 164 [1974]). According to the Court, **common authority** rests on "mutual use of the property by persons generally having joint access or control for most purposes" (p. 172, n. 7). Thus, a third party could give consent to have a shared bathroom searched but not to have his or her roommate's bedroom searched. What happens, however, if the nonconsenting party is present and affirmatively objects to the search? The courts are divided on this issue.

*United States v. Matlock
(415 U.S. 164 [1974])*

There are some clear-cut situations, in which two people possess common authority over a particular area, but what happens when it is not clear to officers at the scene whether common authority exists? In response to this question, the Supreme Court has held that the warrantless entry of private premises by police officers is valid if based on the **apparent authority** doctrine. In other words, a warrantless entry of a residence is valid if it is based on the consent of a person whom the police reasonably believe has authority to grant consent, even if their beliefs are ultimately erroneous (*Illinois v. Rodriguez*, 497 U.S. 177 [1990]). The test for reasonableness in this situation, according to

*Illinois v. Rodriguez
(497 U.S. 177 [1990])*

DECISION-MAKING EXERCISE 7.8

What Constitutes Voluntary Consent?

Here are some interesting facts from a real-world case: Several undercover police officers went to the apartment where it was believed a robbery suspect was hiding out. They did not have probable cause that the suspect was at that location, and indeed, they did not even know the suspect's name, so no warrant was obtained. Rather, the visit was to be merely investigative, and it was hoped that enough information would be gleaned from the visit so a valid warrant could be obtained. The officers knocked on the apartment door, and the man who answered the door fit the description of the suspect. The officers identified themselves, arrested the man, and conducted a protective sweep of the apartment, fearing that other dangerous individuals may be present. Once the premises had been secured, the officers asked the suspect, who was seated at a table in handcuffs, to sign a "consent to search" form. The suspect said, "You go ahead and search, but I ain't signing nothing." Setting aside the issue of the constitutionality of the arrest and protective sweep, was the suspect's consent voluntary?

DECISION-MAKING EXERCISE 7.9

Scope of Consent

Hector Lopez is stopped by the highway patrol for speeding. The officer who approaches his car asks if he will consent to a search of his vehicle. As reinforcements arrive, the officer states that they are concerned about drug smuggling on this stretch of freeway. Lopez gives consent and says, "Yes, you can search my car," and so the officers subject the car to an intensive search. They remove every bag and every moveable item from the vehicle and scrutinize each one carefully. They further check the spare tire compartment, engine compartment, and glove box and even the panels providing access to lighting, electrical, and so on. Have the officers exceeded the scope of Lopez's consent? What if, instead, Lopez stated, "Yes you can search my car, but I'm late for a doctor's appointment, so I have to leave in no more than five minutes"?

the Court, is as follows: "[W]ould the facts available to the officer at the moment [of the entry] . . . warrant a man of reasonable caution in the belief that the consenting party had authority over the premises?" (p. 179). *Rodriguez* involved consent given by a former girlfriend who possessed apparent authority to grant consent because she still had a key to her ex-boyfriend's apartment.

Still other cases have focused on whether third-party individuals can give consent. Most cannot. For example, a landlord cannot give consent to search property rented to another person (*Stoner v. California*, 376 U.S. 483 [1964]), one lessor cannot give consent to search the premises of another lessor (*United States v. Impink*, 728 F.2d 1228 [9th Cir. 1985]), hotel clerks cannot give consent to search guests' rooms (*Stoner v. California*), and college officials cannot give consent to search students' dormitories (*Piazzola v. Watkins*, 442 F.2d 284 [5th Cir. 1971]). Note, however, that consent given by the driver of a vehicle to search any part of the vehicle is valid even if the driver is not the owner of the vehicle (*United States v. Morales*, 861 F.2d 396 [3rd Cir. 1988]).

What if both parties who have common authority are present when the police request consent, but one of them refuses consent and the other gives it? This issue came up in the case of *Georgia v. Randolph* (547 U.S. 103 [2006]), a case in which police were called to the scene of a domestic dispute. When the officers asked for consent to search, the husband unequivocally refused, but the wife readily consented. The officers took the wife up on her consent, searched the premises, and found cocaine. The husband was sought to have the cocaine excluded from his subsequent trial, but a Georgia trial court denied his motion. The Georgia Supreme Court reversed and the U.S. Supreme Court affirmed, holding that "a physically present co-occupant's stated refusal to permit entry renders warrantless entry and search unreasonable and invalid" (p. 103).

"Knock and Talk"

So-called **"knock and talk"** consent searches are popular with law enforcement officers because of the difficulty of securing warrants in particular instances. The typical "knock and talk" scenario plays out when police officers approach someone's house, knock on the front door, and request consent to search the home. In *State v. Smith* (488 S.E.2d 210 [N.C. 1997]), the North Carolina Supreme Court described the procedure as follows:

> The "knock and talk" procedure is a tactic used by law enforcement . . . when they get information that a certain person has drugs in a residence but the officers don't have probable cause for a search warrant. The officers then proceed to the residence, knock on the door, and ask to be admitted inside. Thereafter gaining entry, the officers inform the person that they're investigating information that drugs are in the house. The officers then ask for permission to search and apparently are successful in many cases in getting the occupant's "apparent consent." (p. 212)

"Knock and talk" searches are controversial because they are not predicated on warrants, probable cause, or both. Such searches strike at the cardinal Fourth Amendment principle that "physical entrance into the home of another without a warrant is the chief evil the Fourth Amendment has sought to alleviate" (*Payton v. New York*, 445 U.S. 573 [1980], p. 585). What makes "knock and talk" *legal*, in the strictest sense, however, is that the subsequent search is based on consent. Of course, though, the extent to which ordinary people are aware of their right to *refuse* consent is not altogether clear. To date, the Supreme Court has not ruled on the constitutionality of "knock and talk" practices. More than likely, the tactic will continue as long as consent is validly obtained. See Figure 7.4 for a list of questions that are commonly raised during a "knock and talk" situation.

FIGURE 7.4

Questions Often Raised with Regard to "Knock and Talk" Searches

1. *How is it known what was said?* The wording used by the officer to gain consent is of paramount importance.
2. *To what extent was a show of authority relied on by the officer?* A show of authority may diminish voluntariness.
3. *What is the scope of the search?* The scope may be limited by the wording used by the officer or the consenting party.
4. *Can the party that gives consent also terminate consent?* Generally, yes, but who is to be trusted: the officer(s) or the consenting party?
5. *What if the officer threatens to obtain a warrant?* Doing so diminishes voluntariness, if not eliminates it.
6. *What if the officer makes false statements to gain entry?* There is no prohibition against using false statements, but doing so diminishes voluntariness.
7. *Should the consenting party be advised of his or her* Miranda *rights?* Giving the *Miranda* warnings is not necessary unless a custodial interrogation takes place.
8. *Can a third party give consent?* A third party can give consent only if he or she has authority (or apparent authority) to do so.
9. *What if the consenting party is intoxicated?* This factors into the voluntariness determination.
10. *What if, during the course of a "knock and talk" procedure, exigent circumstances develop?* A full search would be permissible under such circumstances.

DECISION-MAKING EXERCISE 7.10

The Bounds of "Knock and Talk"

In response to a neighbor's complaint, two police officers arrive at a home where there is clearly a loud party taking place. They knock on the door and a person who is visibly intoxicated asks in a slurred manner, "What can I do for you, officers?" The officers respond, "We have received a complaint about the noise coming from your house. Would you please tone it down?" The drunk person at the door responds, "Yup, no problem." At that point, the officers ask, "Do you mind if we come in and take a look around?" The drunk responds, "Will you get a search warrant if I refuse?" The officers, in turn, respond, "Yes, we will." The drunk then gives the officers permission to enter. Is doing so acceptable? In particular, assuming the officers do not have probable cause to get a warrant but rather lied in an effort to gain entry, will any contraband that might turn up during the course of the search be considered admissible in a criminal trial?

Summary

1. EXPLAIN THE JUSTIFICATION FOR REGULATORY AND ADMINISTRATIVE SEARCHES.

Actions based on administrative justification and consent require neither reasonable suspicion nor probable cause. The term *administrative justification* is something of a euphemism. It is not really *justification* at all. Actions based on administrative justification require

that the government's interest in protecting public safety outweighs individual privacy interests. Consent searches, in contrast, need to be predicated on little more than validly given consent.

Actions based on administrative justification are rich in variety. They have been labeled *special needs searches* and *regulatory searches,* but to promote clarity, this chapter has used the language *administrative justification* to refer to all such actions. The most common actions based on administrative justification are inventories, inspections, checkpoints, school discipline, "searches" of government employees' offices, drug and alcohol testing, and parole and probation supervision.

2. DESCRIBE REGULATORY AND ADMINISTRATIVE SEARCHES.

Inventories fall into two categories: (1) vehicle inventories and (2) person inventories. A vehicle inventory must follow a lawful impoundment, be of a routine nature, follow department policy, and not be used as a pretext concealing an investigative police motive. A person inventory is justified on similar grounds, except that it must be preceded by a lawful arrest.

Four types of inspections have been recognized by the U.S. Supreme Court. First, a general home inspection, such as a code inspection, requires a specific type of warrant, but a welfare inspection, conducted for the purpose of determining compliance with welfare conditions, requires no warrant. Second, an inspection of a closely regulated business is permissible without a warrant if (1) the government has a substantial interest in the activity at stake; (2) the search promotes effective enforcement of the law; and (3) the inspection protocol provides a constitutionally adequate substitute for a warrant. Third, a fire inspection, usually tied to an arson investigation, is permissible without a warrant but must be contemporaneous to the fire. Finally, authorities may open and inspect international mail without a warrant.

Several types of checkpoints have also been sanctioned by Supreme Court. In general, for a checkpoint to conform to constitutional requirements, it must be minimally intrusive, brief, and not directly tied to a criminal investigation. More specifically, checkpoints at the nation's borders, well inside the borders, at airports, and on the nation's waterways are permissible but mainly for the purpose of identifying incoming individuals. Illegal alien checkpoints are permissible without a warrant or probable cause for the purpose of detecting illegal aliens entering the country but must conform to established policies and procedures. Checkpoints for determining sobriety, as well as license and safety checkpoints, are constitutionally permissible but must also conform to department policies. Other types of checkpoints, such as airport security checkpoints, have been acknowledged by the Supreme Court and deemed constitutional. Checkpoints intended for the sole purpose of detecting criminal activity are unconstitutional, however.

School disciplinary "searches" are constitutionally permissible, but they must be reasonable. Random, suspicionless locker inspections are permissible but only with ample notice to students. The foregoing applies only to schools for kindergarten through grade 12. A traditional Fourth Amendment approach has been adopted for searches of college students. Drug dog "sniffs" of public school students have not been ruled on by the Supreme Court. For now, it appears that the police have fairly wide latitude in this area.

"Searches" of government employees' offices are permissible with neither a warrant nor probable cause but must amount to noninvestigatory work-related intrusions or investigatory searches for evidence of suspected work-related employee misconduct. When the object of interest in the "search" is evidence of non-work-related criminal misconduct, a warrant is required. None of the foregoing applies to *private* employees. That is, private employees do not enjoy Fourth Amendment protection because their employers are not government actors.

As for drug and alcohol testing, employees and public school students can be screened for substance use but only by properly trained individuals following appropriate policies (e.g., nurses). Hospital patients, however, cannot be subjected to drug and alcohol testing. Probation supervision permits warrantless searches premised on reasonable grounds. Some state Supreme Court decisions have suggested that no justification is necessary—that such searches are consented to as a result of the probation agreement.

3. DESCRIBE CONSENT SEARCHES AND THE ISSUES ASSOCIATED WITH THEM.

Consent searches are constitutional, but consent must be voluntary, as determined by the totality of circumstances. The scope of a consent search is defined by the person giving consent. Third parties can give consent if they have actual or apparent authority over the premises or property to be searched. A controversial law enforcement practice tied to consent searches is "knock and talk," a strategy in which police seek to gain consent to enter a residence for the purpose of detecting evidence of criminal activity. This concludes Part II, the section on search-and-seizure. Figure 7.5 briefly summarizes, in question-and-answer format, the issues discussed in this and the last four chapters. It serves as a helpful guide for determining the constitutionality of searches, seizures, and similar types of law enforcement action.

FIGURE 7.5

Guide to the Fourth Amendment

A. Does the Fourth Amendment apply?

Each of the questions 1–4 must be answered yes for the amendment to apply.

   1. Does the person have standing?
   2. Is the evidence in question a person, house, paper, or effect?
   3. Is the conduct governmental?
   4. Has a reasonable expectation of privacy been infringed upon, or has a seizure occurred?

   If all of the questions were answered yes, then proceed to B.

B. Was the conduct in question justified?

   1. Identify the type of intrusion (e.g., search, stop, arrest, nonsearch).
   2. For the type identified, identify the level of justification required (e.g., probable cause, reasonable suspicion, administrative justification).

   If there is a mismatch, between the type and level of justification, then the conduct in question was not justified. If there is *not* a mismatch, go to C.

C. Was a warrant required?

   If yes, answer questions 1–3. If no, move to D.

   1. Was it issued by a neutral and detached magistrate?
   2. Was it supported by probable cause?
   3. Was the particularity requirement satisfied?

   All three questions must be answered yes for the warrant to be valid.

D. If a warrant was not required, were the prerequisites met for a warrantless search or seizure?
   The answer to this question requires revisiting the material set forth in this and earlier chapters.

E. Any no answers and/or inappropriate justification will result in exclusion of evidence.

Key Terms

apparent authority	237	common authority	237	"knock and talk"	238
checkpoints	221	consent search	235	person inventory	215
closely regulated business	218	drug and alcohol testing	230	police/probation partnerships	233

school disciplinary "searches" 227
vehicle inventory 214

Key Cases

Inventories

- *South Dakota v. Opperman*, 428 U.S. 364 (1976)
- *Colorado v. Bertine*, 479 U.S. 367 (1987)
- *Illinois v. Lafayette*, 462 U.S. 640 (1983)

Inspections

- *Camara v. Municipal Court*, 387 U.S. 523 (1967)
- *Wyman v. James*, 400 U.S. 309 (1971)
- *Colonnade Catering Corp. v. United States*, 397 U.S. 72 (1970)

- *United States v. Biswell,* 406 U.S. 311 (1972)
- *Michigan v. Tyler,* 436 U.S. 499 (1978)
- *United States v. Ramsey,* 431 U.S. 606 (1977)

Checkpoints

- *United States v. Martinez-Fuerte,* 428 U.S. 543 (1976)
- *Michigan Dept. of State Police v. Sitz,* 496 U.S. 444 (1990)
- *Illinois v. Lidster,* 540 U.S. 419 (2004)
- *City of Indianapolis v. Edmond,* 531 U.S. 32 (2000)

Other Administrative Searches

- *New Jersey v. T.L.O.,* 469 U.S. 325 (1985)
- *O'Connor v. Ortega,* 480 U.S. 709 (1987)

- *Skinner v. Railway Labor Executives' Association,* 489 U.S. 602 (1989)
- *Ferguson v. Charleston,* 532 U.S. 67 (2001)
- *Vernonia School District 47J v. Acton,* 515 U.S. 646 (1995)
- *Board of Education v. Earls,* 536 U.S. 822 (2002)
- *Griffin v. Wisconsin,* 483 U.S. 868 (1987)
- *Samson v. California,* 547 U.S. 843 (2006)

Consent

- *Schneckloth v. Bustamonte,* 412 U.S. 218 (1973)
- *Florida v. Jimeno,* 500 U.S. 248 (1991)
- *United States v. Matlock,* 415 U.S. 164 (1974)
- *Illinois v. Rodriguez,* 497 U.S. 177 (1990)

Review Questions

1. In what ways do actions based on administrative justification get around the requirements of the Fourth Amendment?
2. What types of inventories have been permitted by the Supreme Court? Explain the restrictions on each.
3. What types of inspections have been permitted by the Supreme Court? Explain the restrictions on each.
4. Distinguish between border checkpoints and illegal immigrant checkpoints.
5. Are sobriety and license and safety checkpoints valid? If so, when?
6. At what point do checkpoints become unconstitutional?
7. What are school disciplinary searches? What, if any, justification is required to conduct such searches?

8. Under what circumstances are suspicionless searches of government employees' offices constitutional?
9. Summarize the Supreme Court case law involving drug testing.
10. Explain the Supreme Court's decision in *Griffin v. Wisconsin.* How influential is this case in terms of probation supervision?
11. Why are police/probation partnerships controversial?
12. Summarize the requirements for a valid consent search.
13. Under what circumstances can a third party give consent to have another person's property searched?
14. Explain the law enforcement practice known as "knock and talk."

Web Links and Exercises

1. Border checkpoints: Read the Government Accountability Office's report concerning the performance of border checkpoints, particularly those located in interior areas.
URL: http://www.gao.gov/new.items/d05435.pdf (accessed February 16, 2011).
2. Vehicle checkpoints: Read about the opposition to vehicle checkpoints. Are the critics' argument meritorious?
Suggested URL: http://www.roadblock.org (accessed February 16, 2011)
3. Virtual strip searches: Read about how advanced imaging technology works.
Suggested URL: http://www.tsa.gov/approach/tech/ait/index.shtm (accessed February 16, 2011)

4. Police/probation partnerships: Read about varieties of police/probation partnerships. Which is likely to be most effective?
URL: http://www.ncjrs.gov/pdffiles1/175047.pdf (accessed February 16, 2011).
5. Consent searches: Read Carl Benoit's article about consent searches. Focus closely on the section about a "physically present objector." What rules should officers follow?
URL: http://www.fbi.gov/stats-services/publications/law-enforcement-bulletin/2008-pdfs/july08leb.pdf/at_download/file (accessed February 16, 2011)

Part 3

INTERROGATIONS, CONFESSIONS, AND IDENTIFICATION PROCEDURES

LEARNING OBJECTIVES

When you complete this chapter, you should be able to:

▸ Summarize how suspects may use the Fifth Amendment to protect themselves against self-incrimination.

▸ Explain *Miranda* rights and how they impact interrogations and confessions.

▸ Summarize how the Sixth Amendment impacts interrogations and confessions.

▸ Summarize how due process and voluntariness impact interrogations and confessions.

▸ Know when unconstitutionally obtained confessions are admissible in court to prove guilt.

Interrogations and Confessions

INTRODUCTION

Getting Suspects to Talk

This chapter turns to the law of confessions and interrogations. The Fifth Amendment is what protects suspects from improper interrogation procedures and from being forced to supply illegally obtained confessions, but it is not the *only* protection offered to suspects in the confession context. Other amendments, such as the Sixth and the Fourteenth, also apply, but the Fifth is most applicable. Accordingly, this chapter begins with an in-depth look at the protections afforded to criminal suspects by the Fifth Amendment.

THE FIFTH AMENDMENT AND SELF-INCRIMINATION

The Fifth Amendment protects against much more than self-incrimination (e.g., it also contains the so-called *eminent domain clause*), but such protections are beyond the scope of a criminal procedures text. Instead, this chapter focuses squarely on what is known as the *self-incrimination clause* of the Fifth Amendment, which states, in relevant part, that no person "shall be compelled in any criminal case to be a witness against himself."

The self-incrimination clause seems straightforward on its face, but it has been litigated extensively in the courts over the years. For ease of exposition, the self-incrimination clause can be broken into four specific components, each of which has come before the U.S. Supreme Court more than once. The four components are what it means to be (1) compelled and (2) in a criminal proceeding as well as what it means (3) to be a witness and (4) a witness against oneself.

What It Means to Be Compelled

Former chief justice Burger once wrote that "absent some officially coerced self-accusation, the Fifth Amendment privilege is not violated by even the most damning admissions" (*United States v. Washington*, 431 U.S. 181 [1977]). What Justice Burger meant by this was that voluntary (i.e., noncompelled) admissions are not subject to Fifth Amendment protection. That is, if a person fails to assert Fifth Amendment protection and a waiver is "voluntary and intelligent," then whatever that person says will be admissible (see *Garner v. United States*, 424 U.S. 648 [1976]).

Miranda v. Arizona
(384 U.S. 436 [1966])

When, then, can a confession or admission be considered *compelled*? According to the Supreme Court, compulsion can occur in a number of formal as well as informal circumstances. As noted in the landmark case of *Miranda v. Arizona* (384 U.S. 436 [1966]), discussed at length later in this chapter, if the Fifth Amendment applied only in formal settings, such as during trial, then "all the careful safeguards erected around the giving of testimony, whether by an accused or a witness, would become empty formalities in a procedure where the most compelling possible evidence of guilt, a confession, would have already been obtained at the unsupervised pleasure of the police" (p. 466).

Compulsion can occur via several means, but since our interest in this chapter lies with confessions and interrogations, we will limit the discussion to how compulsion can occur during questioning.

COMPULSION DURING QUESTIONING   Whether a person can be compelled to testify against himself or herself, in violation of the Fifth Amendment, requires attention to several distinct varieties of questioning as well as to *whom* is being asked the question: the suspect/defendant or a witness. Specifically, compulsion can occur when certain types of questions are asked of people suspected of being involved in criminal activity. By contrast, compulsion rarely occurs when witnesses are asked questions.

Questioning of Suspects/Defendants.   First, if a person is arrested and interrogated after asserting Fifth Amendment protection (and is not provided with counsel), then the Fifth Amendment will be violated. This simple rule stems from the *Miranda* decision, which, as already indicated, is reviewed in depth later in this chapter.

Second, a defendant in a criminal *trial* cannot be compelled to testify under *any* circumstances. The defendant enjoys absolute Fifth Amendment protection from self-incrimination during a criminal proceeding. However, once a defendant takes the stand, he or she can be compelled to answer questions. Indeed, the defendant can be held in contempt for failing to answer questions once he or she has taken the stand. The same rule applies to witnesses. The so-called **fair examination rule** ensures that witnesses at either a trial or a grand jury hearing can be compelled to answer questions once they waive their Fifth Amendment privilege and begin to testify (see, e.g., *Brown v. United States*, 356 U.S. 148 [1958]; *Rogers v. United States*, 340 U.S. 367 [1951]).

*Brown v. United States
356 U.S. 148 [1958]*

Questioning of Witnesses. Questioning of witnesses at trial, questioning of witnesses appearing before grand juries, and noncustodial questioning cannot be considered compelled. First, in stark contrast to the *Miranda* decision, which requires officials to notify people of their right to counsel before custodial interrogation, the Supreme Court has held that trial witnesses are not entitled to notification of their right to remain silent. No assessment as to whether the person's testimony at trial is the product of a voluntary and intelligent waiver is required, either. According to Justice Frankfurter in *United States v. Monia* (317 U.S. 424 [1943]), "[I]f [a witness] desires the protection of the [Fifth Amendment's privilege against self-incrimination], he must claim it or he will not be considered to have been 'compelled' within the meaning of the Amendment" (p. 427).

Trial witnesses do not need to be advised of their privilege against self-incrimination for two reasons. First, it is likely that testimony given at a public trial will be less coercive than any statements made out of view of the court. Second, since a trial witness is not the defendant, the process of questioning will likely be less adversarial; rather, the prosecution will simply question the witness.

Next, witnesses who testify before grand juries are not required to be advised of their privilege against self-incrimination and, as such, cannot be *compelled* in Fifth Amendment terms. This was the decision reached in the case of *United States v. Mandujano* (425 U.S. 564 [1976]), in which the respondent was charged with perjury for making false statements while testifying before a grand jury. He moved to have his false statements suppressed in his criminal trial, but the Supreme Court held that the failure of the state to provide him with *Miranda*-like warnings did not violate the Fifth Amendment (see also *United States v. Wong*, 431 U.S. 174 [1977]; *United States v. Washington*). The reasoning for this rule is simple: Since such testimony takes place before members of the public (i.e., the grand jury itself) and is usually monitored by the court, the potential for coercion is considerably less likely than is possible in a private setting.

Finally, noncustodial questioning of witnesses outside the courtroom contains the potential for coercion, but the courts have held that out-of-court witnesses do not need to be advised of their privilege against self-incrimination. As Justice Scalia noted in *Brogan v. United States* (522 U.S. 398 [1998]), it is "implausible" that people are not aware of their right to remain silent "in the modern age of frequently dramatized '*Miranda*' warnings" (p. 405). In other words, witnesses who are questioned outside court, in noncustodial situations, cannot be considered compelled for Fifth Amendment purposes.

Distinguishing between Criminal and Noncriminal Proceedings

The previous section considered several means by which the government can compel people to incriminate themselves. It is now necessary to focus on the definition of "criminal proceeding," one of the other important elements of the Fifth Amendment's self-incrimination clause. Stated simply, if a statement is compelled but is not used in a criminal proceeding, it cannot have been obtained in violation of the Fifth Amendment's self-incrimination clause. This is because the Fifth Amendment does not apply in noncriminal proceedings.

As a general rule, any criminal defendant has the right to remain silent at grand jury as well as trial proceedings. However, such an individual can also refuse "to answer official questions put to him in any . . . proceeding, civil or criminal, formal or informal, where the answers might incriminate him in *future* criminal proceedings" (*Lefkowitz v. Turley*). Criminal proceedings can thus include more than criminal trials.

It is important to note that just because an answer is compelled before a criminal proceeding, it will not necessarily be held in violation of the Fifth Amendment. For example, in *Estelle v. Smith* (451 U.S. 454 [1981]), the Supreme Court held that the state may compel answers from a defendant during pretrial hearings to determine his or her competence to stand trial. Such questioning is not considered criminal, for purposes of the Fifth Amendment.

SOME COMPLICATIONS   Outside the criminal trial context (i.e., in civil cases), determining whether a proceeding is criminal for Fifth Amendment purposes is not as easy as one might expect. To deal with this complex determination, the courts usually focus on the issue of *punitive sanctions*. That way, there is no need to distinguish between civil and criminal proceedings. Both types of proceedings possess the potential to hand down punitive sanctions (e.g., forfeiture of one's property or punitive damages in a liability lawsuit).

That a civil proceeding can be considered criminal for self-incrimination purposes is evidenced in *In re Gault* (387 U.S. 1 [1967]). In that case, the Supreme Court had the opportunity to determine whether a state's *civil* designation of juvenile proceedings diminished the Fifth Amendment's applicability in such proceedings. The Court noted that "our Constitution guarantees that no person shall be 'compelled' to be a witness against himself when he is threatened with deprivation of his liberty" (p. 50). Because juveniles' liberty is often at stake in juvenile trials (adjudicatory hearings as they are sometimes called), even if such trials are designated *civil*, the Fifth Amendment applies.

However, in *Minnesota v. Murphy* (465 U.S. 420 [1984]), the Court noted that questions asked of a probationer that were relevant only to his or her probationary status and "posed no realistic threat of incrimination in a separate criminal proceeding" (p. 435, n. 7) did not violate the Fifth Amendment. That is, the questions did not take place in a criminal proceeding.

In one interesting case, *Allen v. Illinois* (478 U.S. 364 [1986]), the Supreme Court noted that the *Gault* decision's deprivation of liberty criterion was "plainly not good law" (p. 372). Instead, the Court focused on "the traditional aims of punishment—retribution or deterrence" (p. 370). Specifically, the Court considered in *Allen* whether an Illinois statute that provided for the civil commitment of people deemed to be "sexually dangerous" was constitutional. The Court's decision was that civil confinement under the Illinois Sexually Dangerous Persons Act did *not* meet the traditional aims of punishment but was instead rehabilitative. According to the Court, had the civil confinement imposed on the offenders "a regimen which is essentially identical to that imposed upon felons with no need for psychiatric care, this might well be a different case" (p. 373).

So, what exactly is a *criminal proceeding*, for purposes of the Fifth Amendment? It is safe to conclude that a criminal proceeding is one that may result in criminal punishment. This includes not only criminal trials but also such proceedings as juvenile delinquency hearings, grand jury investigations, capital sentencing hearings, and the like. Civil commitment proceedings and other proceedings intended to serve a rehabilitative or similar purpose (i.e., other than punishment) are not considered criminal for purposes of the Fifth Amendment.

What It Means to Be a Witness

Still another issue is relevant concerning the scope of the Fifth Amendment's protection against self-incrimination—namely, the definition of a *witness*. Everyone knows what a *witness* is in the conventional sense of the term, but in this context, the Supreme Court

In re Gault   (387 U.S. 1 [1967])

has declared that the term *witness* can be defined as "one who supplies **testimonial evidence**." The Fifth Amendment protection against compelled self-incrimination also extends to things that people say which are communicative in nature—but not necessarily testimonial. An example is an incriminating statement given in a police interrogation room. *Testimony* thus comes in two forms: (1) that which is given at trial under oath and (2) that which is *communicative information* given by a person who is not under oath.

The testimonial evidence requirement does not cover **physical evidence** (e.g., tangible property and the like). In other words, physical evidence is *not* protected by the Fifth Amendment. As Justice Holmes pointed out, "[T]he prohibition of compelling a man in a criminal court to be witness against himself is a prohibition of the use of physical or moral compulsion to extort communications from him, not an exclusion of his body as evidence when it may be material" (*Holt v. United States*, 218 U.S. 245 [1910], pp. 252–253).

More recently, in *Schmerber v. California* (384 U.S. 757 [1966]), the Court held that "the privilege protects an accused only from being compelled to testify against himself, or otherwise provide the State with evidence of a testimonial or communicative nature" (p. 761). As a general rule, then, the government can compel any criminal defendant to supply incriminating *physical* evidence without violating the Fifth Amendment. Indeed, the government can force the accused to wear a particular outfit (e.g., *Holt*), to submit to the extraction of a blood sample (e.g., *Schmerber*), to participate in a lineup (e.g., *United States v. Wade*, 388 U.S. 218 [1967]), or to produce a sample of handwriting (e.g., *Gilbert v. California*, 388 U.S. 263 [1967]; *United States v. Mara*, 410 U.S. 19 [1973]) or a voice exemplar (e.g., *United States v. Dionisio*, 410 U.S. 1 [1973]).

In addition, the Fifth Amendment "offers no protection against compulsion to submit to fingerprinting, photography, or measurements, . . . to appear in court, to stand, to assume a stance, to walk, or to make a particular gesture" (*United States v. Wade*, p. 223). As long as the government does not seek testimonial evidence, the Fifth Amendment cannot be violated, even at trial.

It should be pointed out that *some* verbal responses to questions can be considered noncommunicative and thus exempt from the Fifth Amendment. For example, in *Pennsylvania v. Muniz* (496 U.S. 582 [1990]), the Court held unanimously that the inability to articulate words in a clear manner was not testimonial evidence and could be used against the defendant. In that case, the state introduced the defendant's slurred responses to numerous routine booking questions in order to prove he was guilty of drunk-driving.

What It Means to Be a Witness against Oneself

The fourth and last element of the Fifth Amendment's self-incrimination clause is that it is limited, not surprisingly, to the person *making* the incriminating statement. That is, the only person who can assert Fifth Amendment protection is the person being compelled to answer a question. According to the Supreme Court, "The Constitution explicitly prohibits compelling an accused to bear witness 'against himself': it necessarily does not proscribe incriminating statements elicited from another. Compulsion upon the person asserting it is an important element of the privilege" (*Couch v. United States*, 409 U.S. 322 [1973], p. 328).

Couch v. United States (409 U.S. 322 [1973], p. 328)

Furthermore, the Court noted that "[w]e cannot cut the Fifth Amendment completely loose from the moorings of its language and make it serve as a general protector of privacy—a word not mentioned in its text and a concept directly addressed in the Fourth Amendment" (*Fisher v. United States*, 425 U.S. 391 [1976], p. 401). Thus, in *Couch*, the Fifth Amendment did not protect a business owner whose accountant turned over documents that incriminated the owner.

There are some exceptions to the rule that only the person being compelled can assert Fifth Amendment privilege. For example, when documents are transferred to an attorney for the purpose of obtaining legal advice, the attorney may assert Fifth Amendment protection in place of his or her client. This exception is not based on the Fifth Amendment, however. (Rather, it is a privileged communication.)

INTERROGATIONS AND CONFESSIONS

Most of the law concerning confessions and admissions has arisen in the context of police interrogation. The courts have imposed a litany of restrictions on what law enforcement officials can do in order to elicit incriminating statements from suspected criminals.

It is worthwhile, before continuing, to define the terms *confession* and *admission*. A **confession** occurs when a person implicates himself or herself in criminal activity following police questioning and/or interrogation. An **admission**, by contrast, need not be preceded by police questioning; a person can simply admit to involvement in a crime without any police encouragement. Despite these differences, a confession and an admission will be treated synonymously throughout the remainder of this chapter. Toward the end of the chapter, the discussion will turn to what steps law enforcement officials should take to secure a valid, documented confession.

Various Approaches to Confession Law

Confessions and admissions are protected by the Fifth Amendment. The *Miranda* rights, for example, stem from the Fifth Amendment. However, confessions and admissions are also protected by the Fourteenth Amendment's due process clause as well as the Sixth Amendment's right to counsel clause.

The primary focus in this chapter is on the Fifth Amendment, but for the sake of placing Fifth Amendment confession law into context, it is important to briefly consider the extent to which confessions are protected by other constitutional provisions. Indeed, the very fact that *three* amendments place restrictions on what the government can do in order to obtain confessions suggests that the U.S. Constitution places a high degree of value on people's rights to be free from certain forms of questioning.

The Due Process Voluntariness Approach

One approach to confessions and admissions can be termed the **due process voluntariness approach**. In general, when a suspect makes an involuntary statement, his or her statement will not be admissible in a criminal trial (or, as indicated earlier, in any other criminal proceeding) to prove his or her guilt.

Brown v. Mississippi *(297 U.S. 278 [1936])*

At one time, the Fifth and Sixth Amendments did not apply to the states. An illustrative case is *Brown v. Mississippi* (297 U.S. 278 [1936]). There, police officers resorted to whippings and other brutal methods in order to obtain confessions from three African American defendants who were later convicted based on their confessions alone. The Supreme Court analyzed this case under the Fourteenth Amendment's due process clause and found the convictions invalid because the interrogation techniques had been so offensive.

When, then, is a confession involuntary? As decided in *Fikes v. Alabama* (352 U.S. 191 [1957]), the answer is when, under the "totality of circumstances that preceded the confessions," the defendant is deprived of his or her "power of resistance" (p. 198). This answer, unfortunately, does not provide any uniform criteria for determining voluntariness. Instead, the courts take a case-by-case approach to determining voluntariness. Usually, this requires focusing on two issues: (1) the police conduct in question and (2) the characteristics of the accused.

POLICE CONDUCT   It has been made patently clear that physical brutality to coerce a confession violates the Fourteenth Amendment. As Justice Douglas stated in *Williams v. United States* (341 U.S. 97 [1951]), "Where police take matters into their own hands, seize victims, and beat them until they confess, they deprive the victims of rights under the Constitution" (p. 101).

Williams v. United States *(341 U.S. 97 [1951])*

In many other situations, however, the police conduct in question may not rise to the level of torture but may still be questionable. For example, in *Rogers v. Richmond* (365 U.S. 534 [1963]), a man confessed after the police told him they were going to take his wife into custody. And in *Lynumm v. Illinois* (372 U.S. 528 [1963]), a defendant confessed after being promised leniency. Both confessions were found to be coerced. This is not to suggest that deception on the part of the police necessarily gives rise to an involuntary confession but only that it is one of several considerations in determining voluntariness.

It is safe to conclude that psychological pressures, promises of leniency, and deception are rarely *by themselves* enough to render a statement involuntary, but two or more such acts (especially if coupled with physical force) will more than likely result in an involuntary confession. Some illustrative cases are worth considering.

For example, in *Spano v. New York* (360 U.S. 315 [1959]), detectives relied on a police officer who was a friend of the accused to question him. The officer falsely stated that his job would be in jeopardy if he did not get a statement from the accused. The Supreme Court concluded that the false statement, including the sympathy thereby obtained, was sufficient to render the accused's statement involuntary.

Next, in *Leyra v. Denno* (347 U.S. 556 [1954]), police relied on a psychiatrist who posed as a doctor in order to give the accused relief from a sinus problem. The psychiatrist used subtle forms of questions and ultimately obtained a statement from the accused. The Court felt that the suspect was unable to resist the psychiatrist's subtle questioning.

Contrast *Spano* and *Denno* with *Frazier v. Cupp* (394 U.S. 731 [1969]). There, the Supreme Court held that a police officer's false statement that a co-defendant implicated the accused was not sufficient to produce an involuntary statement. However, if the accused is questioned far from home and denied access to friends and family for several days, his or her resulting statements will probably be deemed involuntary (see *Fikes v. Alabama*). Similarly, an overly lengthy period of questioning and/or a denial of basic amenities, such as food, may result in a determination of involuntariness (see, e.g., *Crooker v. California*, 357 U.S. 433 [1958]; *Payne v. Arkansas*, 356 U.S. 560 [1958]; *Ashcraft v. Tennessee*, 322 U.S. 143 [1944]; *Chambers v. Florida*, 309 U.S. 227 [1940]).

CHARACTERISTICS OF THE ACCUSED   As far as characteristics of the accused are concerned, conditions such as disabilities and immaturity have resulted in excluded confessions. For example, in *Haley v. Ohio* (332 U.S. 596 [1948]), the Supreme Court reversed a 15-year-old boy's confession. In the Court's words, "Mature men possibly

DECISION-MAKING EXERCISE 8.1

Police Conduct and Voluntariness

A suspect was interrogated by five officers who, with their guns drawn, stood over him as he lay handcuffed on the ground, semiconscious from a gunshot he had received earlier (a wound that was not inflicted by the officers). The officers did not threaten to shoot the suspect if he failed to confess. Rather, they simply pointed their guns at him. Assuming the suspect confessed, would his confession be considered involuntary under the Fourteenth Amendment?

might stand the ordeal from midnight to 5 a.m. but we cannot believe that a lad of tender years is a match for the police in such a contest" (pp. 599–600).[1]

In some instances, fatigue and pain (e.g., as the result of an injury) can also render an accused's statement involuntary; however, such a result usually requires some questionable conduct on the part of the officials engaged in questioning of the accused (see *Ashcraft v. Tennessee*; *Mincey v. Arizona*, 437 U.S. 385 [1978]; and *Beecher v. Alabama*, 408 U.S. 234 [1972]).

As a general rule, voluntariness is overcome when (1) the police subject the suspect to coercive conduct and (2) the conduct is sufficient to overcome the will of the suspect. Another requirement is to look at the totality of circumstances to determine if the suspect's vulnerabilities and condition, coupled with the police conduct, led to giving an involuntary confession (see *Colorado v. Connelly*, 479 U.S. 157 [1986]). See Figure 8.1 for a list of factors used to determine whether a confession is voluntary.

Colorado v. Connelly
(479 U.S. 157 [1986])

The Sixth Amendment Approach

The Sixth Amendment also places restrictions on what the police can do to obtain confessions and admissions from criminal suspects. In particular, the Supreme Court's decision in *Massiah v. United States* (377 U.S. 201 [1964]) led to the rule that the Sixth Amendment's guarantee to counsel in all "formal criminal proceedings" is violated when the government "deliberately elicits" incriminating responses from a person. The two key elements to the Sixth Amendment approach are deliberate elicitation and formal criminal proceedings. The following subsections define each element.

Massiah v. United States
(377 U.S. 201 [1964])

DELIBERATE ELICITATION In the *Massiah* case, the defendant was released on bail pending a trial for violations of federal narcotics laws and subsequently made an incriminating statement in the car of a friend who had allowed the government to install a radio designed to eavesdrop on the conversation. Justice Stewart, writing for the majority, argued that if the Sixth Amendment's right to counsel is "to have any efficacy it must apply to indirect and surreptitious interrogations as well as those conducted in the jailhouse" (p. 206). Furthermore, "Massiah [the defendant] was more seriously imposed

FIGURE 8.1

Factors Considered in Determining Voluntariness

Police Behavior	Characteristics of the Suspect
• Psychological pressure by the police	• Disability
• Promises of leniency	• Immaturity
• Deception	• Intoxication
• Length of detention	• Fatigue
• Duration of questioning	• Pain
• Intensity of questioning	• Age
• Deprivation of access to family, friends, nourishment, and counsel	• Level of education
• Whether the suspect was advised of his or her right	• Familiarity with the criminal process

---

[1] Note that *Haley* dealt with due process, not *Miranda*. The Court held in *Fare v. Michael C.* (442 U.S. 707 [1979]) that juveniles are not to be treated differently than adults in the *Miranda* context.

upon . . . because he did not even know that he was under interrogation by a government agent" (p. 206). These are issues of **deliberate elicitation**, in which police officers create a situation likely to induce a suspect into making an incriminating statement.

In another Sixth Amendment case, *Brewer v. Williams* (430 U.S. 387 [1977]), a defendant was suspected of killing a 10-year-old girl. Before he was to be taken by police officers to another city, his attorneys advised him not to make any statements during the trip. The attorneys were also promised by the police officers that they would not question the defendant during the trip. Nevertheless, during the trip, one of the officers suggested that the girl deserved a "Christian burial." The officer further mentioned that an incoming snowstorm would make it difficult to find the girl's body. The officer then stated, "I do not want you to answer me. I don't want to discuss it further. Just think about it as we're riding down the road" (p. 432). Shortly thereafter, the defendant admitted to killing the girl and directed the police to her body. The Court reversed the defendant's conviction, arguing that the officer had "deliberately and designedly set out to elicit information from Williams [the defendant] just as surely as—and perhaps more effectively than—if he had formally interrogated him" (p. 399).

Brewer v. Williams (430 U.S. 387 [1977])

In a related case, *United States v. Henry* (447 U.S. 264 [1980]), the Supreme Court focused on whether the officers "intentionally creat[ed] a situation likely to induce Henry [the defendant] to make incriminating statements without the assistance of counsel" (p. 274). In that case, a man named Nichols, who was in jail with Henry, was enlisted by the police to be alert to any statements Henry made concerning a robbery. The police did not ask Nichols to start a *conversation* with Henry, only to be alert to what he said. The Supreme Court found that the officers created a situation likely to elicit an incriminating response but only because Nichols was a paid informant.

United States v. Henry (447 U.S. 264 [1980])

However, when law enforcement officers place an informant who is not paid but is working closely with the police in the same cell as the defendant, deliberate elicitation does not necessarily occur. This was the decision reached in *Kuhlmann v. Wilson* (477 U.S. 436 [1986]). Kuhlmann, the informant, did not ask the defendant any questions concerning the crime for which the defendant was charged but instead listened to (and later reported on) the defendant's "spontaneous" and "unsolicited" statements. Clearly, the line between these two cases is thin. The only distinction appears to be that Nichols, the informant in *Henry*, had worked with the police in the past and was being paid.

FORMAL CRIMINAL PROCEEDINGS   A case closely related to *Massiah* (and decided shortly after it) is *Escobedo v. Illinois* (378 U.S. 478 [1964]). Escobedo was arrested for murder, questioned, and released. Then, 10 days later, an accomplice implicated Escobedo and he was rearrested. He requested to consult with his attorney, but that

DECISION-MAKING EXERCISE 8.2

Suspect Characteristics and Voluntariness

Ed Hornby approached a police officer on the street and said that he had killed someone and wanted to talk about it. He later confessed to an unsolved murder that had occurred several years earlier. Prior to trial, Hornby sought to have his confession excluded, arguing that it was involuntary. At trial, a psychiatrist testified for the defense that Hornby suffered from *command auditory hallucinations*, a condition that rendered him unable to resist what the "voices in his head" told him to do. How should the court decide? What if, instead, Hornby had become hesitant to talk and his confession had been preceded by a lengthy middle-of-the-night interrogation, during which he had been denied food and a desperately needed trip to the restroom?

request was denied. Escobedo was convicted of murder, based partly on the statement provided by his accomplice. The Supreme Court reversed this decision, however:

> We hold . . . that where, as here, the investigation is no longer a general inquiry into an unsolved crime but has begun to focus on a particular suspect, the suspect has been taken into police custody, the police carry out a process of interrogations that lends itself to eliciting incriminating statements, the suspect has requested and been denied an opportunity to consult with his lawyer, and the police have not effectively warned him of his absolute constitutional right to remain silent, the accused has been denied "the Assistance of Counsel" in violation of the Sixth Amendment . . . and that no statement elicited by the police during the interrogation may be used against him at a criminal trial. (pp. 490–491)

Unfortunately, *Escobedo* was cause for some confusion. In *Massiah*, the Court held that the Sixth Amendment right to counsel applies once formal proceedings have begun (e.g., a preliminary hearing, trial, or anything in between). However, in *Escobedo*, the Court seemed to broaden the scope of the Sixth Amendment by holding that it also applies once the accused becomes the focus of an investigation by the police. This left a significant question unanswered: When does a person become an accused? That is, when do formal criminal proceedings commence?

Massiah was indicted, so many courts have concluded that **formal criminal proceedings** begin with indictment (e.g., *United States ex rel. Forella v. Follette*, 405 F.2d 680 [2nd Cir. 1969]). However, eight years after *Massiah* (and after *Miranda*), the Supreme Court decided *Kirby v. Illinois* (406 U.S. 682 [1972]). In that case, the Court held that the Sixth Amendment is implicated whenever the "adverse positions of the government and defendant have solidified" so that "a defendant finds himself faced with the prosecutorial forces of organized society, and immersed in the intricacies of substantive and procedural criminal law" (p. 689). Fortunately, the Court clarified this statement by noting that the Sixth Amendment applies "whether by way of *formal charge, preliminary hearing, indictment, information, or arraignment*" (p. 689, emphasis added). This was echoed in *Rothgery v. Gillespie County* (554 U.S. 1 [2008]), wherein the Court held that the Sixth Amendment right to counsel can attach at the initial appearance (see Chapter 10 for more on the initial appearance).

Massiah does not apply simply because a suspect or arrestee has retained the services of counsel. In *Moran v. Burbine* (475 U.S. 412 [1986]), the Supreme Court held that what is important in determining whether the Sixth Amendment right to counsel applies is whether "the government's role [has] shift[ed] from investigation to accusation" (p. 430). Similarly, in *Maine v. Moulton* (474 U.S. 159 [1985]), the Court held that "to exclude evidence pertaining to charges as to which the Sixth Amendment right to counsel had not attached at the time the evidence was obtained, simply because other charges were pending at that time, would unnecessarily frustrate the public's interest in the investigation of criminal activities" (p. 180).

It should be noted that the Sixth Amendment approach to interrogations and confessions is offense-specific. This was reiterated by the Supreme Court in *Texas v. Cobb* (531 U.S. 162 [2001]), where it held that a man's confession to a crime with which he had not been charged did not violate the Sixth Amendment. In that case, the defendant was indicted for burglary and given access to counsel, which obviously prohibits deliberate elicitation of incriminating information. However, he confessed to murdering the woman and child who lived in the home he allegedly burglarized. He later sought to have his confession excluded, but the Supreme Court disagreed, in essence, finding that the burglary charge did not trigger the Sixth Amendment protection for the murder charge.

WAIVER OF THE SIXTH AMENDMENT RIGHT TO COUNSEL (CONFESSIONS)   One's Sixth Amendment right to counsel can be waived in the confession context (just as in the case of trial context, as you will see in Chapter 11). In *Michigan v. Jackson* (475 U.S. 625 [1986]), the Supreme Court held that once an accused individual has asserted his or her Sixth Amendment right to counsel, any statements obtained from subsequent questioning would be inadmissable at trial unless the accused initiated the communication.

This decision was recently overturned, however, in *Montejo v. Louisiana* (No. 07-1529 [2009]). Unbeknownst to police, Montejo had been appointed an attorney, but he was encouraged by a detective to write a letter of apology to the wife of the man he had killed. Before doing so, he was advised of his *Miranda* rights, but again, he had been appointed counsel—it was just that police did not know this. The prosecution introduced the apology letter at trial. Montejo sought to have it excluded since, he felt, his attorney was not present when it was written. The Supreme Court disagreed. It felt that *Miranda* and other decisions offer sufficient protection. Also, had Montejo asserted his right to counsel, the outcome would have likely been different.

What is the practical meaning of the *Montejo* decision? Law enforcement is now allowed, after reading a suspect the *Miranda* rights and receiving a voluntary waiver of the right to counsel, to interrogate a suspect who has been appointed counsel, provided that the suspect (1) has not previously asserted *Miranda* protection or (2) has previously asserted *Miranda* protection and subsequently waived it. The decision is beneficial to law enforcement because it offers more opportunities for them to secure incriminating statements from criminal suspects.

The *Miranda* Approach

In a very important yet frequently overlooked case, *Malloy v. Hogan* (378 U.S. 1 [1964]), the Supreme Court held that the Fifth Amendment's self-incrimination clause applies to the *states*. In announcing that ruling some 40 years ago, the Court said that "today the admissibility of a confession in a state criminal prosecution is tested by the same standard applied in federal prosecution since 1897" (p. 7).

Not long after that decision, the Supreme Court moved beyond *Massiah*, *Escobedo*, and the due process voluntariness approaches to interrogation law, focusing instead on the Fifth Amendment. In *Miranda v. Arizona* (384 U.S. 436 [1966]) the Court announced the following important rule: "[T]he prosecution may not use statements, whether exculpatory or inculpatory, stemming from *custodial interrogation* of the defendant unless it demonstrates the use of procedural safeguards effective to secure the privilege against self-incrimination" (p. 444, emphasis added). This wording clearly established that the Fifth Amendment should serve as the basis for determining the constitutionality of a confession.

Importantly, the Sixth and Fourteenth Amendments still apply to interrogations and confessions in certain situations. For example, if the police conduct in question is not a custodial interrogation (as in *Miranda*) but formal charges have been filed, the Sixth Amendment will apply. Similarly, if custody and interrogation do not take place *and* formal charges are not filed, the due process voluntariness test can still be relevant for the purpose of determining the constitutionality of a confession or admission. In fact, think of the Fourteenth Amendment's due process clause, in particular, as being something of a fallback. If no other constitutional protections apply, the guarantee of due process almost always does.

The *Miranda* **warnings**, which are most often read by police to an arrestee, often comprise a series of statements like this: "You have the right to remain silent. Anything you say can and will be used against you in a court of law. You also have the right to an attorney. If you cannot afford an attorney, one will be provided to you at no cost. Do you understand these rights as they have been read to you?"

DECISION-MAKING EXERCISE 8.3

Formal Criminal Proceedings

An arrest warrant was issued for Mark Eddie for the crime of burglary, following an indictment for his latest heist. A detective arrested Eddie, brought him to the stationhouse, and then interrogated him at length concerning the burglary without counsel present. The detective also interrogated Eddie about additional burglaries of which he was suspected of being involved in. While Eddie refused to talk about the most recent burglary (in which he made off with a substantial amount of money), he did admit to two prior burglaries. Was the questioning constitutional?

The discussion will return to some Supreme Court cases addressing the substance and adequacy of these warnings, particularly when they are read differently. But for now, the concepts of custody and interrogation require attention. Since the Supreme Court limited its decision in *Miranda* to custodial interrogations, it is important to understand the definitions of these two important terms: *custody* and *interrogation*.

CUSTODY   Many people believe that *Miranda* rights apply whenever the police begin to question a person. This is not the case; if the person being questioned is not in *custody*, *Miranda* rights do not apply. Simple police questioning, or even a full-blown interrogation, is not enough to trigger the protections afforded by the Fifth Amendment. The person subjected to such questioning must be in police custody.

What is **custody**? The Court announced that *Miranda* applies when "a person has been taken into custody or otherwise deprived of his freedom of action in any significant way." An arrest is a clear-cut case of police custody, but what about a lesser intrusion? Unfortunately, there is no easy answer to this question. Instead, the courts have chosen to focus on the circumstances surrounding each individual case. The Court has stated, however, that "the only relevant inquiry [in analyzing the custody issue] is how a reasonable man in the suspect's position would have understood his situation" (*Berkemer v. McCarty*, 468 U.S. 420 [1984], p. 442).

Berkemer v. McCarty
468 U.S. 420 [1984], p. 442

In the absence of a full-blown arrest, the courts have focused on four types of police/citizen encounters in determining whether custody exists for purposes of *Miranda*: (1) traffic and field stops; (2) questioning in the home; (3) questioning at the police station or equivalent facility; and (4) questioning for minor crimes.

First, custody does not take place in the typical traffic stop. This was the decision reached in *Berkemer v. McCarty*. There, a motorist was stopped for weaving in and out of traffic. After he admitted to drinking and smoking marijuana, the officer arrested him. The motorist argued that he should have been advised of his right to remain silent, but the Supreme Court disagreed, noting that vehicle stops are "presumptively temporary and brief" and sufficiently public to avoid the appearance of being coercive. The Court added, "From all that appears in the stipulation of facts, a single police officer asked [the defendant] a modest number of questions and requested him to perform a simple balancing test at a location visible to passing motorists" (p. 442) and thus did not violate the Fifth Amendment.

The same applies to stops not involving vehicles. *Miranda* permits law enforcement officers to engage in "[g]eneral on-the-scene questioning as to facts surrounding a crime or other general questioning of citizens in the factfinding process" (p. 477). With regard to *Terry* stops in particular, "[t]he comparatively nonthreatening character of [investigative] detentions explains the absence of any suggestion in our opinions that *Terry* stops are subject to the dictates of *Miranda*" (p. 440). But what if an investigative stop becomes more intrusive than a *Terry* stop, say, by taking place over a long period of time and/or in a private setting? Then, the Fifth Amendment's self-incrimination clause, made known to suspects through the *Miranda* warnings, will usually apply.

Second, it is possible for questioning in one's home to rise to the level of custody. In *Orozco v. Texas* (394 U.S. 324 [1969]), the Supreme Court declared that custody existed when four police officers woke a man in his own home and began questioning him. However, in contrast to *Orozco* is *Beckwith v. United States* (425 U.S. 341 [1976]). There, Internal Revenue Service (IRS) agents interviewed a man in his home, an action that the Supreme Court declared noncustodial. The man argued that because he was the focus of a criminal investigation, he should have been advised of his right to remain silent. However, Chief Justice Burger noted that "*Miranda* specifically defined 'focus,' for its purposes, as 'questioning initiated by law enforcement officers *after* a person has been taken into custody or otherwise deprived of his freedom of action in any significant way' " (p. 347).

Third, questioning at the police station or an equivalent facility can also rise to the level of custody. However, not all stationhouse questioning can be considered custodial. Consider what the Supreme Court said in *Oregon v. Mathiason* (429 U.S. 492 [1977]), a case involving a man who voluntarily agreed to meet officers at the police station for questioning. He admitted to involvement in a crime but later argued that his visit to the stationhouse was custodial because of its inherently coercive nature. The Court said:

> Any interview of one suspected of a crime by a police officer will have coercive aspects to it, simply by virtue of the fact that the police officer is part of a law enforcement system which may ultimately cause the suspect to be charged with a crime. But police officers are not required to administer *Miranda* warnings to everyone whom they question. Nor is the requirement of warnings to be imposed simply because the questioning takes place in the stationhouse, or because the questioned person is one whom the police suspect. (p. 495)

In a later case, *California v. Beheler* (463 U.S. 1121 [1983]), the Court offered some clarification concerning its decision in *Mathiason*. It pointed out that *Miranda* is not implicated "if the suspect is not placed under arrest, voluntarily comes to the police station, and is allowed to leave unhindered by the police after a brief interview" (p. 1121).

California v. Beheler
(463 U.S. 1121 [1983])

Interestingly, the *Beheler* decision seems to hold even if a person is pressured to come to the police station for questioning (see, e.g., *Yarborough v. Alvarado*, 541 U.S. 652 [2004]). For example, in *Minnesota v. Murphy*, a probationer was ordered to meet with his probation officer for questioning. During the meeting, the probationer confessed to a rape and a murder. He later argued that he should have been advised of his *Miranda* rights, but the Court disagreed, holding that Murphy's "freedom of movement [was] not restricted to the degree associated with formal arrest" (p. 430). Furthermore, while "[c]ustodial arrest is said to convey to the suspect a message that he has no choice but to submit to the officers' will and to confess . . . [i]t is unlikely that a probation interview, arranged by appointment at a mutually convenient time, would give rise to a similar impression" (p. 433). The Court commented further in *Murphy*:

> Many of the psychological ploys discussed in *Miranda* capitalize on the suspect's unfamiliarity with the officers and the environment. Murphy's regular

FIGURE 8.2

Distinguishing between Custodial and Noncustodial Situations

Custodial Situation	Noncustodial Situation
Arrest	Typical traffic stop
Excessively lengthy confrontation	General on-the-scene questioning
Not free to leave	Free to leave
Involuntary encounter	Voluntary encounter
Private place, such as a police station	Public place, where movement is not restricted

meetings with his probation officer should have served to familiarize him with her and her office and to insulate him from psychological intimidation that might overbear his desire to claim the privilege. Finally, the coercion inherent in custodial interrogation derives in large measure from an interrogator's insinuation that the interrogation will continue until a confession is obtained. . . . Since Murphy was not physically restrained and could have left the office, any compulsion he might have felt from the possibility that terminating the meeting would have led to revocation of probation was not comparable to the pressure on a suspect who is painfully aware that he literally cannot escape a persistent custodial interrogator. (p. 433)

Fourth, the Supreme Court has had occasion to determine whether *Miranda* applies—specifically, whether people can be considered in custody for minor offenses. Again, *Berkemer* was a case involving a traffic stop. The second issue before the Court in that case was whether an exception to *Miranda* should exist for relatively minor crimes, such as misdemeanors. The Court declared that no distinction should be drawn between types of crimes as far as *Miranda* is concerned. Instead, the only relevant issue is whether a person is in custody (and, of course, interrogated). Even for a misdemeanor, the incentive for police to try to induce the defendant to incriminate himself or herself may well be significant.

It should be underscored before moving on that a key component of *Miranda* is that the questioning (and detention) must be conducted by government actors. If the people engaged in questioning cannot be considered government actors, then Fifth Amendment protections do not apply. However, when a private individual conducts a custodial interrogation as an agent of the police (i.e., working for the police), *Miranda* applies (see, e.g., *Wilson v. O'Leary*, 895 F.2d 378 [7th Cir. 1990]). Figure 8.2 provides a list of factors that are used to distinguish custodial from noncustodial encounters.

DECISION-MAKING EXERCISE 8.4

The Nature of Custody

Carole Reynolds was being held in jail while awaiting trial on narcotics offenses. The police had been unable to get her to make an incriminating statement, so they decided to place an undercover agent in her cell. The two women eventually struck up a conversation, and the agent asked Reynolds, "What do you do for a living?" She responded, "I'm a drug kingpin." Could Reynolds's statement be used against her at her trial for narcotics offenses?

DECISION-MAKING EXERCISE 8.5

Can Reading the *Miranda* Rights Create a Custodial Situation?

Assume that with reasonable suspicion, police officers approach a man whom they suspect of recently robbing the First National Bank. They confront the man, and before initiating any questioning, they immediately read him his *Miranda* rights. Shortly after being read his rights but before questioning, the suspect states, "I'm glad you guys found me. I can't go on like this. I robbed First National." Does the officers' reading of *Miranda* convert a noncustodial situation (the case here) into a custodial one?

INTERROGATION   The second major component of *Miranda* is interrogation. Custody by itself is not enough to require that the *Miranda* warnings be given. For a person to be afforded Fifth Amendment protection—and particularly, to be advised of his or her right to remain silent—he or she must be subjected to interrogation.

Miranda defined **interrogation** as "questioning initiated by law enforcement officers." Then, in *Rhode Island v. Innis* (446 U.S. 291 [1980]), the Court noted that interrogation "must reflect a measure of compulsion above and beyond that inherent in custody itself" (p. 300). Thus, any questions that tend to incriminate—that is, those that are directed toward an individual about his or her suspected involvement in a crime—are considered interrogation.

Rhode Island v. Innis
(446 U.S. 291 [1980])

Unfortunately, many *questions* are not readily identifiable as such. In *Innis*, the Supreme Court noted that in addition to "express questioning," the "functional equivalent" of a question is also possible. The **functional equivalent of a question** includes "any words or actions on the part of the police (other than those normally attendant to arrest and custody) that the police should know are reasonably likely to elicit an incriminating response from the suspect" (p. 302, n. 8).

In *Innis*, while police officers were driving the defendant to the police station after his arrest for armed robbery, they engaged in a conversation about the danger the missing robbery weapon posed to schoolchildren with disabilities. Apparently in response to the conversation, the defendant directed the officers to the location of the weapon. Interestingly, though, the Supreme Court held that the officers' conversation did not constitute interrogation: It was "nothing more than a dialogue between the two officers

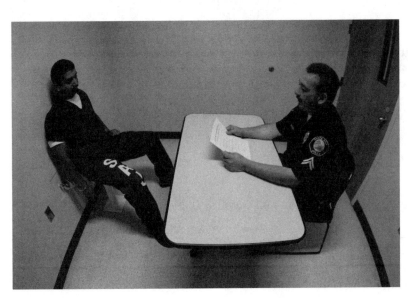

Suspects who are custodially interrogated must be advised of their *Miranda* rights. If the suspect is not in custody or is not interrogated, the *Miranda* rights do not need to be read.

to which no response from the respondent was invited" (p. 315). The majority assumed implicitly that suspects will not respond to "indirect appeals to . . . humanitarian impulses," but Justice Stevens dissented and argued that such an assumption "is directly contrary to the teachings of police interrogation manuals, which recommend appealing to a suspect's sense of morality as a standard and often successful interrogation technique" (p. 315).

Even though *Innis* did not ultimately involve the functional equivalent of a question, the Court essentially expanded the definition of *questioning*. Namely, a mere conversation between police officers designed to elicit an incriminating response—even if the conversation is not directed toward the suspect—can require giving the *Miranda* warnings. Of course, the person must also be in custody for the *Miranda* warnings to apply. Figure 8.3 lists some of the factors considered when distinguishing between interrogation and general questioning.

OTHER *MIRANDA* ISSUES   A number of important Supreme Court cases have hinged on (1) the substance and adequacy of the *Miranda* warnings and (2) waivers of *Miranda*. If, for example, the *Miranda* warnings are not given adequately, then the police risk having a confession being thrown out of court. Also, like many rights, those provided by *Miranda* can be waived. That is, suspects can elect *not* to remain silent. Finally, suspects are not required to be advised of their *Miranda* rights when doing so could compromise public safety. These and other *Miranda* issues are considered in the four subsections that follow.

Substance and Adequacy of the Warnings.   There is a long line of cases involving people who have sought to have their confessions excluded at trial because all or some of the *Miranda* warnings were not read adequately. For example, in *California v. Prysock* (453 U.S. 355 [1981]), the juvenile defendant was told, "You have the right to talk to a lawyer before you are questioned, have him present with you while you are being questioned, and all during the questioning" (p. 359). The defendant was then told that he had the right to a court-appointed lawyer but not that one would be provided for him if he was indigent.

California v. Prysock
(453 U.S. 355 [1981])

The defendant challenged his conviction, but the Court concluded that the warnings given to him were sufficient and that "*Miranda* itself indicates that no talismanic incantation was required to satisfy its strictures" (p. 359).

In another interesting case, *Duckworth v. Eagan* (492 U.S. 192 [1989]), the following warnings were given:

> Before we ask you any questions, you must understand your rights. You have the right to remain silent. Anything you say can be used against you in court. You have the right to talk to a lawyer for advice before we ask you any questions, and to have him with you during questioning. You have this right to the advice and presence of a lawyer even if you cannot afford to hire one. We have no way of giving you a lawyer, but one will be appointed for you, if

FIGURE 8.3

Distinguishing between Interrogation and General Questioning

Interrogation	General Questioning
Guilt-seeking questions	Information-gathering questions
Conversation intended to elicit a response	Conversation not intended to elicit a response

DECISION-MAKING EXERCISE 8.6

Incriminating Evidence and Interrogation

Police officers lawfully executed a search warrant on Don Cheney's house. Cheney was not at home, but the officers were let into the house by his wife. When Cheney arrived at home, he was immediately arrested. He was then seated on the living room couch, and one of the officers brought in a potted marijuana plant and placed it on the coffee table in front of him. When Cheney saw the plant, he began crying and said, "OK, you got me. The plant is mine. As you probably know, there are plenty more where that came from." At trial, Cheney sought to have his statement suppressed on the grounds that a custodial interrogation without the *Miranda* warnings took place in his living room on the night of the search. How should the court decide?

DECISION-MAKING EXERCISE 8.7

Another Interrogation?

The police permitted a man who was the suspect in a murder investigation to converse with his wife at the police station where he was being held. Their conversation occurred during the presence of a police officer and was recorded. The man made an incriminating response during the conversation, which was later introduced at his trial for the murder of his child. The man argued that he had been subjected to the functional equivalent of an interrogation when the police officer was present with a tape recorder. Is he correct?

you wish, if and when you go to court. If you wish to answer questions now without a lawyer present, you have the right to stop answering questions at any time. You also have the right to stop answering at any time until you've talked to a lawyer. (p. 198)

Even though the warnings in this version suggested that counsel would only be provided at court, the Supreme Court held, in a 5 to 4 decision, that these warnings "touched all the bases required by *Miranda*" (p. 203). Thus, as long as all the essential *Miranda* information is communicated, simple departures will not render a confession thereby obtained inadmissible in a criminal trial.

Another factor involving the substance and adequacy of the *Miranda* warnings concerns the role of additional, unnecessary information. If more information than the original *Miranda* warnings is provided to a suspect, will any subsequent confession be inadmissible? For example, must the defendant be advised of the consequences of deciding to answer questions? The case of *Colorado v. Spring* (479 U.S. 564 [1987]) is a useful point of departure. There, the defendant was arrested and questioned on suspicion of transporting stolen firearms. He was also questioned about a homicide. He admitted that he had been given his *Miranda* warnings and that he understood them; however, he argued that the statements he made about the homicide were not admissible because he had not been informed that he was going to be questioned about the homicide (i.e., he was arrested on suspicion of transporting stolen firearms). Unfortunately for the defendant, the majority held that "a suspect's awareness of all the possible subjects of questioning in advance of interrogation is not relevant to determining whether the suspect voluntarily, knowingly, and intelligently waived his Fifth Amendment privilege" (p. 577).

A similar issue came up in *Florida v. Powell* (No. 08-1175 [2010]), a case in which the following was added to the *Miranda* warning: "You have the right to use any of these rights at any time you want during this interview." The Supreme Court held that advising a suspect that he or she has the right to talk with an attorney before answering any questions *and* that the suspect can invoke that right at any time during questions conformed to *Miranda*.

To ensure that the *Miranda* warnings are read properly, most police departments have a policy describing what that should entail. Figure 8.4 provides an example of one such policy, from the San Bernardino, California, Police Department.

Waiver of Miranda.   In *Miranda*, the Supreme Court stated that if a person talks after he or she has been read the warnings, "a heavy burden rests on the government to demonstrate that the defendant knowingly and intelligently waived his privilege against self-incrimination and his right to retained or appointed counsel" (p. 475). Furthermore, "a valid waiver will not be presumed simply from the silence of the accused after warnings are given or simply from the fact that a confession was in fact eventually obtained" (p. 475). According to the Supreme Court:

> Whatever the testimony of the authorities as to waiver of rights by an accused, the fact of lengthy interrogation or incommunicado incarceration before a statement is made is strong evidence that the accused did not validly waive his rights. In these circumstances the fact that the individual eventually made a statement is consistent with the conclusion that the compelling influence of the interrogation finally forced him to do so. It is inconsistent with any notion of a voluntary relinquishment of the privilege. Moreover, any evidence that the accused was threatened, tricked, or cajoled into a waiver will, of course, show that the defendant did not voluntarily waive his privilege. (p. 476)

In recent years, the courts have interpreted this language loosely. That is, whereas *Miranda* declared that a waiver should be viewed with considerable caution, later decisions have suggested that the burden of demonstrating a valid waiver is not difficult to meet. For example, in *Colorado v. Connelly*, the Court held that the government need only show the validity of a waiver by a "preponderance of evidence." And in *Fare v. Michael C.*, the Court held that the "totality of the circumstances approach is adequate to determine whether there has been a waiver" (p. 725). This latter test is not unlike the due process voluntariness test, discussed earlier in this chapter. It is used to assess juvenile waivers, as well.

Must the waiver be express? That is, must a person affirmatively state something to the effect that "I am willing to answer questions" for a waiver of *Miranda* to take place? The answer to this question is, "no." In the past, the Court preferred an

DECISION-MAKING EXERCISE 8.8

Were the *Miranda* Rights Read Properly?

William Wentworth was interrogated while in police custody. He wore an expensive suit, sported lavish jewelry, and otherwise exhibited an aura of financial success. Before being interrogated, he was read the following rights: "You have the right to remain silent. Anything you say can and will be used against you in court. You have the right to talk with an attorney, either retained by you or appointed by the court, before giving a statement, and to have your attorney present when answering any questions." Wentworth made an incriminating statement during the interrogation and later moved to suppress it on the grounds that he was not informed that counsel would be provided if he was indigent. How should the court decide?

FIGURE 8.4

Miranda Advisement Policy (San Bernardino, CA, Police Department)

STANDARD OPERATING PROCEDURE   CHAPTER #15   PROCEDURE #1

PROCEDURE FOR MIRANDA ADVISEMENT   (Revised)   10-26-88

PURPOSE

To ensure uniformity when advising persons of their Miranda rights.

PROCEDURE

It is <u>not</u> necessary that the defendant sign a written waiver of his rights. The law only requires that the waiver be free, intelligent, and voluntary.

The Miranda warning should always be <u>read</u> to the suspect rather than relying on memory, using the following wording:

1. You have the right to remain silent.
2. Anything you say can and will be used against you in court.
3. You have the right to talk with an attorney and to have an attorney present before and during any questioning.
4. If you cannot afford an attorney, one will be appointed free of charge to represent you before and during any questioning.

After the warning and in order to secure a waiver, the following questions should be asked and an affirmative reply secured to each question. The officer should always make a record of the <u>exact words</u> used by the defendant when he answers each of the following questions.

1. Do you understand the rights I have just explained to you?
2. With these rights in mind, do you wish to talk to me/us now?

When the person being advised of his Miranda rights speaks only Spanish, the following waiver shall be read:

1. Usted tiene el derecho de no decir nada.
2. Cualquier cosa que usted diga puede usarse contra usted y se usara contra usted en una corte de leyes.
3. Usted tiene el derecho de hablar on un abogado, y de tener un abogado presente antes y durante cualquier interrogacion.
4. Si usted no puede pagarle a un abogado, uno le sera nombrado gratis para que le represente a usted antes ye durante la interrogacion.

Renucia

1. ¿Entiende usted cada uno de los derechos que acabo de explicarle a usted? ¿Si o no?
2. ¿Teniendo en cuenta estos derechos suyos, desea usted hablar on nosotros ahora? ¿Si o no?

Source: Chapter 15, Procedure 1, "Use of Force," from *Standard Operating Procedure*, San Bernardino, California, Police Department (rev. December 22, 2004). Reprinted with permission.

express waiver. But in *Miranda*, the Court noted that "a valid wavier will not be presumed." Similarly, in *Westover v. United States* (a case joined with *Miranda*), the Court stated that an *articulated waiver* is required before a confession will be considered admissible.

However, in *North Carolina v. Butler* (441 U.S. 369 [1979]), the Court decided otherwise. According to Justice Stewart, "The question [of a waiver] is not one of form, but rather whether the defendant in fact knowingly and voluntarily waived his rights delineated in the *Miranda* case" (p. 373). Further, a "course of conduct indicating waiver" (such as the suspect deciding to converse with the police) is sufficient for a valid waiver to take place. Based on this decision, the current rule is that the government must show a valid waiver based on "the particular facts and circumstances surrounding [the] case, including the background, experience, and conduct of the accused" (pp. 374–375). In other words, the courts now take a case-by-case approach in determining whether *Miranda* waivers are obtained legally.

As was made clear in *Butler*, a valid *Miranda* waiver requires a showing that the waiver was knowing and intelligent. What, then, is a *knowing and intelligent waiver*? There is no clear answer to this question, but the Court has noted that a full and complete understanding of the *Miranda* warnings is not necessary for a valid waiver to take place. This was the decision reached in *Connecticut v. Barrett* (479 U.S. 523 [1987]). In that case, the defendant refused to give the police any written statements before he talked to an attorney. He did state, however, that he had no problem *talking* to the police. As it turned out, the defendant thought that only written statements could be used against him in court. The Court called his actions "illogical" but nonetheless held that his oral statements were admissible. A similar conclusion was reached in *Berghuis v. Thompkins* (08-1470 [2010]). The Court held that "where the prosecution shows that a *Miranda* warning was given and that it was understood by the accused, an accused's uncoerced statement establishes an implied waiver of the right to remain silent."

Another case focusing on the knowing and intelligent requirement was *Wyrick v. Fields* (459 U.S. 42 [1982]). In that case, the defendant expressed some confusion about the duration of a *Miranda* waiver. He had agreed to take a polygraph examination without counsel present. After the examination, he also answered questions from the examiner about his feelings concerning the examination, which led to him supplying incriminating information. When the defendant's statements were used against him, he argued that neither he nor his attorney believed that the polygraph procedure also included post-examination questioning. However, the Supreme Court pointed out that "it would have been unreasonable for Fields [the defendant] and his attorney to assume that Fields would not be informed of the polygraph readings and asked to explain any unfavorable result" (p. 47). In addition, the Court concluded that "the questions put to Fields after the examination would not have caused him to forget the rights of which he had been advised and which he had understood moments before" (p. 49).

Two additional Supreme Court decisions focused on whether the police can use trickery to obtain a *Miranda* waiver and/or statement. In *Colorado v. Spring*, the Court held that trickery *had not* taken place when the police failed to advise the defendant that he would be questioned about a different crime than the one for which he was arrested. It did point out, however, that "any evidence that the accused was . . . tricked . . . into a waiver will, of course, show that the defendant did not voluntarily waive his privilege" (p. 575).

In another interesting case, *Moran v. Burbine*, the Supreme Court held that a confession was validly obtained even though the police questioned the defendant after assuring his attorney that he would not be questioned until the following day. In a 6 to 3 decision, the Court held that this action did not result in a coerced confession. As Justice O'Connor noted, "[T]he same defendant, armed with the same information and confronted with precisely the same police conduct, would have knowingly waived his *Miranda* rights had a lawyer not telephoned the police station to inquire about his status" (p. 422).

In light of these two cases, it seems somewhat difficult to determine what constitutes trickery. A general rule is this: If officials lead a defendant to believe that he or she has no right to remain silent, then trickery is taking place. However, if the police merely lead a defendant to believe there is no point in remaining silent (as in *Butler*, *Barrett*, *Fields*, *Spring*, and *Burbine*), then any subsequent incriminating statements that are made will probably be viewed as knowing and intelligent.

Before moving on, it is worth mentioning that in addition to the requirement that a valid *Miranda* waiver must be knowing and intelligent, it must also be voluntary. The test for voluntariness is similar to the due process voluntariness test discussed earlier in this chapter. Threats, physical force, and the like can lead to defendants issuing involuntary confessions. However, in *Fare v. Michael C.*, the Court held that the confession obtained from a 16-year-old was not involuntary. In a strongly worded dissent, Justice Powell argued that the juvenile in this case "was immature, emotional, and uneducated, and therefore was likely to be vulnerable to the skillful, two-on-one, repetitive style of interrogation to which he was subjected" (p. 733). A safe rule is that the police must engage in seriously questionable conduct for the voluntariness requirement of a *Miranda* waiver to be violated.

Again, to be safe, many police departments require that each suspect completes a *Miranda* waiver before interrogation commences. Doing so helps ensure that the waiver is documented. An example of a *Miranda* waiver form, from the San Bernardino, California, Police Department, is reprinted in Figure 8.5.

In a recent twist on the notion of *Miranda* waivers (*United States v. Patane*, 542 U.S. 630 [2004]), the Supreme Court considered whether police officers' failure to complete the *Miranda* warnings—after the suspect interrupted midway through by saying, "I understand my rights"—violated the Fifth Amendment. In that case, after the suspect had interrupted the reading of *Miranda* and said he understood his rights, he informed police of the location of a pistol. He was indicted for possession of a firearm by a convicted felon and sought suppression of the pistol, claiming his Fifth Amendment privilege was violated. The Supreme Court disagreed.

Questioning after Assertion of One's Right to Remain Silent.   As a general rule, questioning must cease once the accused asserts his or her right to remain silent. According to the Supreme Court in *Miranda*:

> If the individual indicates in any manner, at any time prior to or during questioning, that he wishes to remain silent, the interrogation must cease. . . . Without the right to cut off questioning, the setting of in-custody interroga-

---

DECISION-MAKING EXERCISE 8.9

The Circumstances for a Voluntary Waiver

Fred Nicholas was arrested for murder, taken to the police station, and advised of his *Miranda* rights. He stated that he wished his attorney could be present but that he was away on business. Given that, Nicholas said that he "might as well talk." Unknown to Nicholas, his attorney was in town after all, had heard about Nicholas's arrest, and had tried unsuccessfully to contact him. In fact, the police had explicitly refused to let Nicholas meet with his attorney. Nicholas made an incriminating statement. Should it be admissible at trial?

FIGURE 8.5

Miranda Waiver Form (San Bernardino, CA, Police Department)

WAIVER

I have been advised that:

1. I have the absolute right to remain silent.

2. Anything i say can and will be used as evidence against me in court.

3. I have the right to be represented by an attorney and to consult with him before making any statement or answering any questions and I have the right to have an attorney present during any questioning.

4. If I cannot afford an attorney, one will be appointed by the court, free of charge, to represent me before any questioning, if I desire.

I understand these rights. these rights have been explained to me. With these rights in mind, I am willing to talk to officers about the charges against me.

Date_____   Signed_____

Witness_____   Witness_____

Source: San Bernardino, California, Police Department. Reprinted with permission.

---

tion operates on the individual to overcome free choice in producing a statement after the privilege has been once invoked. If the individual states that he wants an attorney, the interrogation must cease until an attorney is present. . . . If the individual cannot obtain an attorney and he indicates that he wants one before speaking to police, they must respect his decision to remain silent. . . . If authorities conclude that they will not provide counsel during a reasonable period of time in which investigation in the field is carried out, they may refrain from doing so without violating the person's Fifth Amendment privilege so long as they do not question him during that time. (pp. 473–474)

Michigan v. Mosley
(423 U.S. 96 [1975])

However, there is at least one circumstance in which the police can question a suspect after he or she has asserted the *Miranda* rights. In *Michigan v. Mosley* (423 U.S. 96 [1975]), the Supreme Court permitted questioning after an assertion of *Miranda*. In that case, two hours after the defendant had stated that he did not want to talk, a different police officer confronted him in a different room about another crime and read him the *Miranda* rights for a second time. After this, the man made incriminating statements. In a 7 to 2 decision, the Court held that the suspect's *Miranda* rights had been "scrupulously honored." The Court said that the second officer's actions were acceptable because "the police here immediately ceased the interrogation, resumed questioning only after the passage of a significant period of time and the provision of a fresh set of warnings, and restricted the second interrogation to a crime that had not been a subject of the earlier interrogation" (p. 106).

The key to *Michigan v. Mosley* was that the second set of questions concerned a *separate crime*. What if police had continued to ask questions about the same crime? Had they done so immediately, the questioning would have been inappropriate. But the issue is less than black and white according to the Supreme Court's recent decision in *Maryland v. Shatzer* (08-680 [2010]). In that case, police (albeit a different officer) resumed questioning about the same crime more than *two weeks* after the suspect was released following initial questioning. The suspect was reread his *Miranda* rights, which he then waived. He confessed to various crimes of sex abuse. The Supreme Court decided that his confession was admissible, in part because "[h]is change of heart [was] . . . likely attributable to the fact that further deliberation in familiar surroundings [had] caused him to believe (rightly or wrongly) that cooperating with the investigation [was] in his interest."

Maryland v. Shatzer
(08-680 [2010])

The Public Safety Exception to *Miranda*. On some occasions, custodial interrogation is permissible without the *Miranda* warnings. Specifically, if public safety is in jeopardy, no warnings are required. This was the decision reached in *New York v. Quarles* (467 U.S. 649 [1984]). There, the Court held that the warnings need not be given if the suspect could have endangered public safety.

New York v. Quarles
(467 U.S. 649 [1984])

The facts from *Quarles* are as follows: After receiving information that a man with a gun had just entered a supermarket, Officer Kraft, along with three other officers, entered the store. Kraft spotted the defendant, drew his gun, and ordered the man to stop and put his hands over his head. When the officers frisked the man, they found an empty shoulder holster on him. When they asked where the man had put the gun, he replied, "The gun is over there." Officer Kraft retrieved the revolver and then placed the man under arrest and read him the *Miranda* warnings. The trial court and the lower appellate courts excluded the gun on the grounds that it was obtained in violation of *Miranda* (i.e., the man had not been advised of his right to remain silent at the time the gun was found).

The Supreme Court disagreed. Justice Rehnquist wrote the majority opinion, arguing that rigid application of *Miranda* is not always warranted, particularly when public safety is a concern:

> [T]he need for answers to questions in a situation posing a threat to public safety outweighs the need for the prophylactic rule protecting the Fifth Amendment's privilege against self-incrimination. We decline to place officers such as Officer Kraft in the untenable position of having to consider, often in a matter of seconds, whether it best serves society for them to ask the necessary questions without the *Miranda* warnings and render whatever probative evidence they uncover inadmissible, or for them to give the warnings in order to preserve the admissibility of evidence they might uncover but possibly damage or destroy their ability to obtain that evidence and neutralize the volatile situation confronting them. (pp. 657–658)

The Court also made it clear that the appropriate test for determining whether a threat to public safety exists is an objective one—that is, one based on what a reasonable person in the same circumstances would believe: "[W]here spontaneity rather than adherence to a police manual is necessarily the order of the day, the application of the [public safety] exception . . . should not be made to depend on *post hoc* findings at a suppression hearing concerning the subjective motivation of the arresting officer" (p. 656). The majority in *Quarles* apparently believed that an objective threat to public safety existed. Insofar as the officers did not know where the gun was located, not knowing "obviously posed more than one danger to the public safety: an accomplice might make use of it [or] a customer or employee might later come upon it" (p. 657).

The *Quarles* decision is a controversial one. As Justice O'Connor noted in disagreement with the newly issued public safety exception to *Miranda* (though not with the majority's ultimate decision):

> *Miranda* has never been read to prohibit the police from asking questions to secure the public safety. Rather, the critical question *Miranda* addresses is who shall bear the cost of securing the public safety when such questions are asked and answered: the defendant or the state. *Miranda*, for better or worse, found the resolution of that question implicit in the prohibition against compulsory self-incrimination and placed the burden on the State. (p. 664)

Quarles, by contrast, appears to place the burden on the defendant. It does so, in Justice O'Connor's view, not by ensuring that public safety is preserved but by creating a *Miranda* loophole that helps ensure that otherwise inadmissible evidence can be used against the defendant.

CHALLENGING *MIRANDA*   The *Miranda* decision was not without controversy. In 1968, shortly after the decision was announced, Congress passed a Crime Control Act that, among other things, attempted to overrule the *Miranda* decision. The statute, codified as **18 U.S.C. Section 3501**, states that in any federal prosecution, a confession "shall be admissible in evidence if it is voluntarily given." Under the law, suspects are not required to be advised of their right to counsel, their right not to incriminate themselves, and so on.

For several years, Section 3501 remained dormant. The U.S. attorneys general have known that to utilize the statute would be to challenge the authority of the U.S. Supreme Court. But critics of *Miranda* were looking for an opportunity to bring Section 3501 before the Court. That opportunity arose in 2000: Charles Dickerson was indicted for bank robbery and related crimes. He moved to suppress a statement he made to Federal Bureau of Investigation (FBI) agents on the ground that he had not received his *Miranda* warnings. The district court granted Dickerson's motion to suppress but also noted that the confession was voluntary, despite the apparent *Miranda* violation.

Dickerson v. United States (530 U.S. 428 [2000])

Then, the Court of Appeals for the Fourth Circuit held (in a 2 to 1 decision) that "Congress, pursuant to its power to establish the rules of evidence and procedure in the federal courts, acted well within its authority in enacting Section 3501, [and] Section 3501, rather than *Miranda*, governs the admissibility of confession in federal court" (*United States v. Dickerson*, 166 F.3d 667 [4th Cir. 1999], p. 671). The case, *Dickerson v. United States* (530 U.S. 428 [2000]), then went before the Supreme Court. In a 7 to 2 opinion, Chief Justice Rehnquist wrote for the Court:

> We hold that *Miranda*, being a constitutional decision of this Court, may not be in effect overruled by an Act of Congress, and we decline to overrule *Miranda* ourselves. We therefore hold that *Miranda* and its progeny in this Court govern the admissibility of statements made during custodial interrogation in both state and federal courts. (p. 431)

The Court further noted:

> Whether or not we would agree with *Miranda's* reasoning and its resulting rule, were we addressing the issue in the first instance, the principles of *stare decisis* weigh heavily against overruling it now. . . . While *stare decisis* is not an inexorable command, particularly when we are interpreting the Constitution, even in constitutional cases, the doctrine carries such persuasive force that we have always required a departure from precedent to be supported by some special justification.
>
> We do not think there is such justification for overruling *Miranda*. *Miranda* has become embedded in routine police practice to the point where the warnings have become part of our national culture. (p. 443)

OTHER RECENT *MIRANDA* DECISIONS In *Chavez v. Martinez* (538 U.S. 760 [2003]), the Supreme Court seems to have shifted its view on *Miranda*. In that case, a police officer interrogated a man while he was receiving treatment for a gunshot wound. The man was *not* advised of his *Miranda* rights. He was never charged with a crime, but later sued under 42 U.S.C. Section 1983 (see Chapter 2), arguing that his constitutional rights were violated. The Supreme Court disagreed because the man was not compelled to be a "witness" against himself in a "criminal case." This decision would seem to suggest *Miranda* warnings are never required, unless statements obtained without the warnings are actually used against the accused in a criminal case.

In *Missouri v. Seibert* (542 U.S. 600 [2004]), the Supreme Court made it clear that *Miranda* warnings must be given *before* interrogation commences. In that case, the accused was interrogated—without *Miranda* warnings having been read—and she confessed. She was then advised of her *Miranda* rights and "re-confessed." The Supreme Court declared that the interrogating officer's pre-*Miranda* questioning was improper. The confession was deemed inadmissible at trial.

The Exclusionary Rule and Confession Analysis

It is important to focus on the role of the *exclusionary rule* in the confession analysis. It is often said that the exclusionary rule applies only to the Fourth Amendment. Part of the reason for this is that the Fifth Amendment essentially contains its own exclusionary rule by prohibiting compulsion of testimony. Whatever view one takes, the debate is largely semantic. In the end, evidence obtained in violation of *any* constitutional amendment will not be admissible in a criminal trial.

Generally speaking, a confession obtained in violation of *Miranda* or some constitutional provision will be excluded. However, just because a confession is obtained illegally does not mean that any subsequently obtained evidence will automatically be excluded. In fact, illegally obtained statements are themselves considered admissible in certain instances. Accordingly, the following subsections focus on three lines of cases involving confessions and the exclusionary rule: (1) standing cases, (2) impeachment cases, and (3) "fruit of the poisonous tree" cases.

CONFESSIONS AND STANDING For a confession (or evidence thereby obtained) to be excluded, the person arguing for exclusion must have *standing*; that is, one person cannot seek to exclude the confession of another, even if that confession was obtained in violation of *Miranda*. As noted in *Couch v. United States* (409 U.S. 322 [1973]), being advised of *Miranda* is considered a personal right. Thus, a person arguing for exclusion of an (unconstitutionally obtained) incriminating statement must have standing;

Couch v. United States (409 U.S. 322 [1973])

otherwise, the statement and subsequent evidence will be deemed admissible. (Standing was covered in Chapter 3.)

CONFESSIONS AND IMPEACHMENT   Another situation in which improperly obtained incriminating statements may be admissible is when such statements are used for purposes of impeachment. A key restriction on this rule, however, is that the statement must be obtained voluntarily in the due process sense. Also, the rules vary depending on whether it is a *Miranda* case or Sixth Amendment right to counsel case.

Harris v. New York
(401 U.S. 222 [1971])

For an example of a *Miranda* case, consider *Harris v. New York* (401 U.S. 222 [1971]). The prosecution sought to introduce an out-of-court statement that was inconsistent with the defendant's in-court testimony, even though the out-of-court statement was obtained in violation of *Miranda*. The Supreme Court held that the out-of-court-statement was admissible—to only for impeachment purposes, not to be used as evidence against Harris. The Court noted further that such a statement must be obtained voluntarily, which it was in Harris's case (see also *Oregon v. Hass*, 420 U.S. 714 [1975]; *New Jersey v. Portash*, 437 U.S. 385 [1978]).

Note that for a statement obtained in violation of *Miranda* to be admissible for impeachment purposes, the statement must, in fact, be an oral communication. The prosecution cannot introduce evidence of an accused's out-of-court *silence* for impeachment purposes. This issue arose in the case of *Doyle v. Ohio* (426 U.S. 610 [1976]), in which after the defendant's in-court exculpatory story, the prosecution sought to introduce evidence that the defendant did not offer the same explanation to the police. The Supreme Court held that the defendant's silence was not admissible for purposes of impeachment (see also *Wainwright v. Greenfield*, 474 U.S. 284 [1986]).

As for the Sixth Amendment approach, in *Michigan v. Harvey* (494 U.S. 344 [1990]), the Supreme Court held that a statement obtained in violation of the right to counsel (police questioned with the defendant after he invoked his right to counsel and later waived it) could be admitted for impeachment purposes. Recently, in *Kansas v. Ventris* (No. 07-1356 [2009]), the Supreme Court reached a similar conclusion. In that case a police relied on an informant to obtain a statement from Ventris—after Ventris had been formally charged with a crime. It admitted the statement, but for impeachment purposes, not as part of the government's case in chief, even though the incriminating statement was obtained in violation of the Sixth Amendment. The difference is subtle, but important.

CONFESSIONS AND "FRUIT OF THE POISONOUS TREE"   As discussed in Chapter 2, unconstitutionally obtained derivative evidence is not admissible under the so-called "fruit of the poisonous tree" doctrine. However, the Supreme Court has not been so quick to apply the same rule in the case of illegally obtained confessions. It has held that physical evidence obtained in violation of *Miranda* is admissible, as long as the information supplied by the accused is voluntary in the due process sense.

United States v. Bayer
(331 U.S. 532 [1947])

The first case of note concerning the derivative evidence doctrine in the confession context was *United States v. Bayer* (331 U.S. 532 [1947]), a case decided well before the *Miranda* decision was handed down. There, the Court held that the Fourth Amendment "fruit of the poisonous tree" doctrine did not control the admissibility of improperly obtained confessions.

Then, in *Michigan v. Tucker* (417 U.S. 433 [1974]), a case decided after *Miranda*, but involving an interrogation that took place *before Miranda*, the Court suggested that it had not changed its position. In *Tucker*, a suspect was questioned about a rape without being advised of his right to counsel. Tucker claimed he was with a friend at the

DECISION-MAKING EXERCISE 8.10

Should the Exclusionary Rule Apply?

Assume the police have Jack Richter in custody and are inter-rogating him about his suspected involvement in a gruesome murder. They do not advise him of his *Miranda* rights. Further, one of the officers, who is notorious for his aggres-sive interrogation techniques, holds a .357 revolver (loaded with one round) to Richter's head and plays "Russian roulette" in order to obtain a confession. Richter succumbs to the pressure and admits to the murder. He also points the police to the location of the murder weapon. Obviously, his statement will not be admissible. What about the murder weapon?

time of the crime. The police then obtained incriminating evidence against Tucker from the friend. Although this information was clearly fruit of the initial interroga-tion, the Court stated that "[t]he police conduct at issue here did not abridge respon-dent's constitutional privilege against compulsory self-incrimination, but departed only from the prophylactic standards later laid down by this Court in *Miranda* to safe-guard this privilege" (p. 446). In other words, the Court saw no reason to exclude the friend's statement.

In *Oregon v. Elstad* (470 U.S. 298 [1985]), the Court reaffirmed its *Tucker* decision, making clear that it would continue to treat *Miranda* as a prophylactic rule, at least inso-far as it governs the admissibility of derivative evidence. What's more, derivative evidence obtained from a violation of *Miranda* is admissible but only if voluntarily obtained. In sum, these decisions govern derivative evidence, not the initial incriminat-ing statements (such as Tucker's claim that he was with a friend). The latter are inadmissible when obtained in violation of the Fifth Amendment.

THE IMPORTANCE OF DOCUMENTING A CONFESSION

So far, this chapter has been concerned with the methods by which the police can extract incriminating information from a criminal suspect. Assuming the police are suc-cessful in terms of eliciting an incriminating response, it is not enough for the suspect to say, "I did it" or to otherwise offer some form of verbal confession. In fact, if the police hand the suspect a pencil and paper and say, "Write down your confession," this will not be enough, either. Instead, the police need to follow specific procedures for docu-menting and reporting a confession.

According to one source,[2] the police should document every interrogation and even keep an *interview log*: a document containing information about the individuals in-volved in the interrogations and actions taken by both sides. A list of topics to be cited in an interview log is shown in Figure 8.6.

Also, a signed statement from the accused should be secured. First, the signed statement should identify the suspect, the investigators, and the crime involved. Second, the statement should describe, in language the suspect can understand, the details of the crime, what the suspect did, and how he or she did it. The statement should then be carefully reviewed with the suspect, even read aloud, so its content is clear. Finally, the statement should be signed by the suspect, the officer who conducted the interrogation, and at least one witness—preferably another officer. Figure 8.7 shows a model statement form for securing a written confession from a criminal suspect.

---

[2] T. T. Burke, "Documenting and Reporting a Confession with a Signed Statement: A Guide for Law Enforcement," *FBI Law Enforcement Bulletin* 70 (2001): 17–22.

FIGURE 8.6

Content of Typical Interview Log

Interview Log

1. Identity of person interviewed
2. Identity of officers conducting interview
3. Location of interview
4. Date of interview
5. Time of arrest, if applicable
6. Location of arrest
7. Identity of officers making arrest
8. Time interview began
9. Time officers informed subject or suspect of his or her rights, and if more than one officer, name of officer advising subject or suspect
10. Time subject or suspect waived his or her rights
11. Time interview concluded
12. Time preparation of statement commenced
13. Identity of person preparing statement
14. Time statement completed
15. Time subject or suspect reviewed statement
16. Time subject or suspect signed written statement
17. A record of request and complaints of subject and the action taken thereon, such as the time a subject requests permission to call an attorney, the time he or she made a call to his attorney, the time subject complained of illness, the time and action taken on this complaint, the time subject requested food, the time and action taking on this request, and the details as to how this request was handled.

Source: T. T. Bruke, "Documenting and Reporting a Confession with a Signed Statement: A Guide for Law Enforcement," *FBI Law Enforcement Bulletin* (February 2001): 21.

FIGURE 8.7

Sample Form for Securing a Written Confession: White-Collar Crime

Signed Statement Format
White Collar Crime Sample

I, (*subject's name and address*) hereby make the following free and voluntary statement to (*officer's official name and title*) who has identified himself/herself as a (*title of officer and name of department or agency*). I have been advised that I have been interviewed concerning my involvement in (*phrase describing scheme or nature of crime and victim, such as "the misappropriation and theft of $100,000 from the First National Bank while I was employed there during 1999"*).

I was born on (*subject's date of birth*) at (*subject's place of birth*). I attended (*last school attended*) and completed (*last grade or graduation date*). I read and write the English language.

> Officers should use the next few paragraphs to summarize what the subject did and how the subject did it, in his own words. Because this statement occurs after the subject's confession, officers can assist the subject in formulating the statement, using information previously provided. Officers should include any information the subject provides regarding what happened to the stolen money, how it was spent, items purchased, and other related details.

I knew that what I was doing was wrong, and I regret my actions. I wish to cooperate with the (*name of agency*) investigation and get this matter resolved. (*Optional paragraph, depending on circumstances and subject's remorse*)

I have read this (*number of pages*) page statement, have initialed all corrections, and I am signing it because it is true and correct. (*The subject writes this after reading the statement aloud and accepting its contents.*)

_____

(subject's signature and date)

First witness: _____

(officer taking statement, title, agency, location, and date)

Second witness:_____

(third-party individual, title, agency, location, and date)

(*NOTE: Officers should always have the subject read the statement aloud to them and initial any corrections. Also, they should avoid blank lines between sentences and paragraphs in the statement.*)

Source: T. T. Burke, "Documenting and Reporting a Confession with a Signed Statement: A Guide for Law Enforcement," *FBI Law Enforcement Bulletin* (February 2001): 19.

Summary

1. SUMMARIZE HOW SUSPECTS MAY USE THE FIFTH AMENDMENT TO PROTECT THEMSELVES AGAINST SELF-INCRIMINATION.

The Fifth Amendment's self-incrimination clause is frequently relied on in challenges to the constitutionality of confessions. However, for the Fifth Amendment to be successfully invoked, several requirements must be met. First, the police must compel a statement that is incriminating as well as testimonial. And, of course, the accused individual is the only one who can assert his or her Fifth Amendment protection against an unconstitutionally obtained confession.

2. EXPLAIN *MIRANDA* RIGHTS AND HOW THEY IMPACT INTERROGATIONS AND CONFESSIONS.

A confession will be thrown out, as was the decision in *Miranda v. Arizona*, if a suspect's incriminating statement is a result of custodial interrogation in which the suspect was not advised of his or her constitutional right to have counsel present. Before custodial interrogation can commence, suspects must be advised of their so-called *Miranda* rights.

3. SUMMARIZE HOW THE SIXTH AMENDMENT IMPACTS INTERROGATIONS AND CONFESSIONS.

Confessions are also governed by the Sixth Amendment's right to counsel clause but only when formal charges have been filed. If the police deliberately elicit information from a person who has already been charged with a crime, the charged individual has the right to have counsel present during questioning.

4. SUMMARIZE HOW DUE PROCESS AND VOLUNTARINESS IMPACT INTERROGATIONS AND CONFESSIONS.

An involuntarily obtained confession violates due process. Figure 8.8 illustrates the relationships among

FIGURE 8.8

Relationship among the Various Approaches to Confession Law

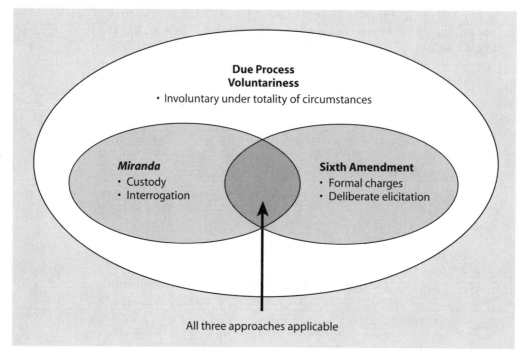

Source: Adapted from R. M. Bloom and M. S. Brodin, *Criminal Procedure: Examples and Explanations,* 2nd ed. (New York: Little, Brown, 1996)

the various constitutional provisions governing police interrogation procedures. The due process voluntariness approach acts as a fallback and is always applicable. The Sixth and Fifth Amendments, by contrast, apply in specific circumstances, as described. And it is possible (albeit rare) for all three provisions to come into play.

5. KNOW WHEN UNCONSTITUTIONALLY OBTAINED CONFESSIONS ARE ADMISSIBLE IN COURT TO PROVE GUILT.

For a confession (or evidence thereby obtained) to be excluded, the person arguing for exclusion must have

standing; that is, one person cannot seek to exclude the confession of another, even if that confession was obtained in violation of *Miranda.* Another situation in which improperly obtained incriminating statements may be admissible is when such statements are used for purposes of impeachment. A key restriction on this rule, however, is that the statement must be obtained voluntarily in the due process sense. Finally, the Supreme Court has held that physical evidence obtained in violation of *Miranda* is admissible, as long as the information supplied by the accused is voluntary in the due process sense.

Key Terms

18 U.S.C. Section 3501	268	deliberate elicitation	253	fair examination rule	246	interrogation	259
admission	250	due process		formal criminal proceeding	254	*Miranda* warnings	255
confession	250	voluntariness		functional equivalent		physical evidence	249
custody	256	approach	250	of a question	259	testimonial evidence	249

Key Cases

Fifth Amendment in General

- *Brown v. United States*, 356 U.S. 148 (1958)
- *In re Gault*, 387 U.S. 1 (1967)
- *Couch v. United States*, 409 U.S. 322 (1973)

Due Process Voluntariness Approach

- *Brown v. Mississippi*, 297 U.S. 278 (1936)
- *Williams v. United States*, 341 U.S. 97 (1951)
- *Colorado v. Connelly*, 479 U.S. 157 (1986)

Sixth Amendment Approach

- *Massiah v. United States*, 377 U.S. 201 (1964)
- *Brewer v. Williams*, 430 U.S. 387 (1977)
- *United States v. Henry*, 447 U.S. 264 (1980)

Miranda

- *Miranda v. Arizona*, 384 U.S. 436 (1966)
- *Berkemer v. McCarty*, 468 U.S. 420 (1984)
- *California v. Beheler*, 463 U.S. 1121 (1983)
- *Rhode Island v. Innis*, 446 U.S. 291 (1980)
- *California v. Prysock*, 453 U.S. 355 (1981)
- *Michigan v. Mosley*, 423 U.S. 96 (1975)
- *Maryland v. Shatzer*, 08-680 (2010)
- *New York v. Quarles*, 467 U.S. 649 (1984)
- *Dickerson v. United States*, 530 U.S. 428 (2000)

Exclusionary Rule and Confessions

- *Couch v. United States*, 409 U.S. 322 (1973)
- *Harris v. New York*, 401 U.S. 222 (1971)
- *United States v. Bayer*, 331 U.S. 532 (1947)

Review Questions

1. Explain the means by which compulsion can occur, in Fifth Amendment terms.
2. What is the difference between a criminal and a noncriminal proceeding?
3. What does it mean to be a witness, in Fifth Amendment terms?
4. What does it mean, in Fifth Amendment terms, to be a witness against oneself?
5. Summarize the due process voluntariness approach to interrogations and confessions.
6. What factors affect voluntariness?
7. Summarize the Sixth Amendment approach to interrogations and confessions.
8. Explain deliberate elicitation.
9. What are formal criminal proceedings, for purposes of the Sixth Amendment approach to interrogations and confessions?
10. What are the *Miranda* warnings?
11. When does *Miranda* apply?
12. Citing relevant cases, distinguish between custody and interrogation, for *Miranda* purposes.
13. Summarize the requirements for a valid *Miranda* waiver.
14. What is the public safety exception to *Miranda*?
15. How does the exclusionary rule operate in the context of confessions and interrogations?

Web Links and Exercises

1. Interviewing: Read Simon and Boetig's article about how to conduct a structured investigative interview.
URL (read the article, "The Structured Investigative Interview"): http://www.fbi.gov/stats-services/publications/law-enforcement-bulletin/2007-pdfs/june07leb.pdf (accessed February 16, 2011).
2. More on *Miranda*: Learn more about the Supreme Court's important decision in *Miranda v. Arizona*.
URL: http://www.mirandawarning.org (accessed February 16, 2011).
3. Vague invocations of the right to counsel: What if a suspect makes an ambiguous reference to his or her right to counsel in the interrogation context?
Suggested URL: http://www.aele.org/interrogations.html (accessed February 16, 2011).
4. How interrogation works: Read more about how interrogation actually plays out.
Suggested URL: http://people.howstuffworks.com/police-interrogation4.htm (accessed February 16, 2011).

LEARNING OBJECTIVES
When you complete this chapter, you should be able to:

▸ Outline pretrial suspect identification techniques.

▸ Explain the problem of witness misidentification.

▸ Summarize identification techniques during the trial and issues involving witness credibility.

▸ Explain how the exclusionary rule operates in the identification context.

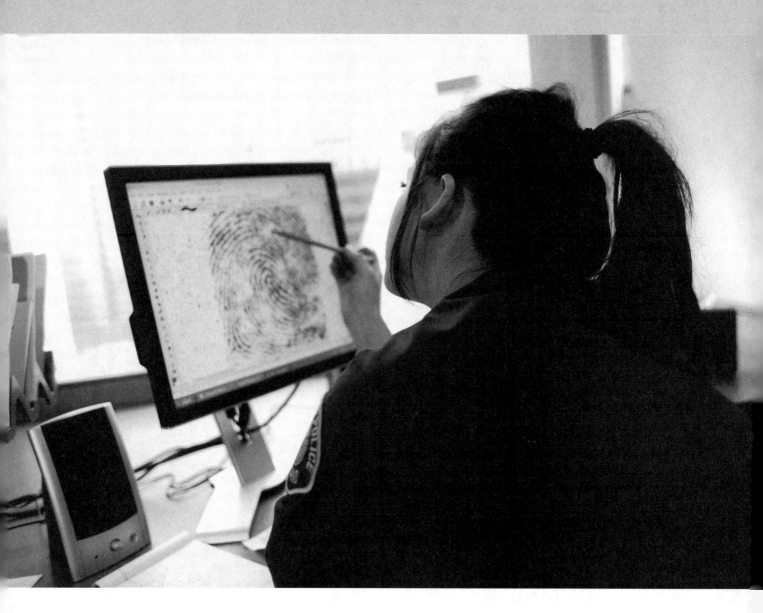

CHAPTER 9

Identification Procedures and the Role of Witnesses

INTRODUCTION

Dealing with Witnesses to Crimes

Identification procedures include those systems and activities that allow witnesses of crimes to identify suspected perpetrators. The three most common types of identification procedures are lineups, showups, and photographic arrays. In a **lineup**, the suspect is placed alongside several other people (sometimes called "fillers," "foils," or "distractors") who resemble him or her, and the witness (or victim) picks the suspect out of the lineup. The fillers may be jail inmates, actors, or volunteers. In a **showup**, the suspect is brought before the witness alone, so the witness can be asked whether that person is the perpetrator. Finally, in a **photographic array** (or photographic display), several photographs, including one of the suspect, are shown to a witness or victim, and he or she is asked to pick out the perpetrator.

Identification procedures fall into two broad categories: (1) out of court and (2) in court. The three identification procedures just described—lineups, showups, and photographic arrays—occur *out of court* and prior to trial. There are, however, many occasions in which the prosecution may wish to have a witness identify the suspect *in court* and during trial. Of course, not all witnesses recollect accurately and/or can be trusted with regard to a suspect's identification. It is therefore important to consider the *witness examination process* with an eye toward witness identification.

Naturally, it is in the prosecution's interest to introduce evidence that a witness or victim picked the perpetrator out of a lineup. However, it is not as simple as demonstrating that a witness identified the perpetrator. The identification procedure must be fair as well as conform to constitutional requirements. Those constitutional requirements place restrictions on what officials can do in terms of arranging lineups, showups, and photographic arrays. And these restrictions are critical because witnesses to crimes are frequently inaccurate in their descriptions.

Accordingly, this chapter begins with a discussion of the constitutional restrictions that govern the identification process. Next, out-of-court identification procedures are considered followed by in-court identification procedures and the witness examination process. The chapter concludes with a look at the role of the exclusionary rule as it applies to in-court and out-of-court identification procedures.

CONSTITUTIONAL RESTRICTIONS ON IDENTIFICATION PROCEDURES

Identification procedures have been challenged on several grounds, stemming from the Fourteenth Amendment's due process clause, the Fifth Amendment's self-incrimination clause, and the Sixth Amendment's right to counsel clause. People have also challenged the constitutionality of identification procedures on Fourth Amendment grounds.

Right to Counsel

United States v. Wade (388 U.S. 218 [1967])

In *United States v. Wade* (388 U.S. 218 [1967]), a defendant was placed in a police lineup, without his attorney present, *after* he had been indicted for a crime. The Supreme Court held that this violated the Sixth Amendment because a postindictment lineup is a "critical stage" in the criminal process. Further, "the presence of counsel [at postindictment lineups] is necessary to preserve the defendant's basic right to a fair trial" (p. 227). Indeed, the right to counsel extends well beyond the identification stage (see Chapter 11).

The key in *Wade* was that the lineup was postindictment—that is, conducted after charges had been filed. Had charges *not* been filed, a different decision would have probably resulted. Another important feature of the *Wade* decision was that it distinguished lineups from "various other preparatory steps, such as systematized or scientific analyzing of the accused's fingerprints, blood sample, clothing, hair and the like" (p. 227). Counsel is not required for these types of activities because

> [k]nowledge of the techniques of science and technology is sufficiently available, and the variables in techniques few enough, that the accused has the opportunity for a meaningful confrontation of the Government's case at trial through the ordinary processes of cross-examination of the Government's expert witnesses and the presentation of the evidence of his own experts. (pp. 227–228)

Recently, the Supreme Court has extended the Sixth Amendment right to counsel to include other hearings, such as preliminary hearings and arraignments (see, e.g., *Kirby v. Illinois*, 406 U.S. 682 [1972]).

DECISION-MAKING EXERCISE 9.1

Counsel during a Lineup

Sam Linde has been arrested and charged with burglarizing Paul's Appliance Store. Authorities also suspect that Linde has burglarized several other appliance stores in the area, including John's Appliance Store. Suppose the police want to place Linde in a lineup for a witness who saw him leave John's Appliance Store in the middle of the night. Must counsel be present? (You may recall a similar exercise from the previous chapter, which dealt with confessions, but here the issue is a lineup.)

Due Process

The Supreme Court has also clearly stated that the Fourteenth Amendment's due process clause bears on the constitutionality of identification procedures. For example, in *Stovall v. Denno* (388 U.S. 293 [1967]), the Court held that the accused is entitled to protection against procedures "so unnecessarily suggestive and conducive to irreparable mistaken identification" (p. 293) as to amount to a due process violation. In general, for an identification procedure to satisfy the due process clause, it must be (1) reliable and (2) minimally suggestive.

Stovall v. Denno
(388 U.S. 293 [1967])

Whether an identification procedure is *reliable* is determined in light of the facts and circumstances surrounding the case. The following factors are used in determining whether an identification procedure is reliable:

> The opportunity of the witness to view the criminal at the time of the crime, the witness's degree of attention, the accuracy of the witness's prior description of the criminal, the level of certainty demonstrated by the witness at the confrontation, and the length of time between the crime and the confrontation. (*Neil v. Biggers*, 409 U.S. 188 [1972], p. 199)

Indeed, the Court stated in *Biggers* that reliability is more important than *suggestiveness*. In the Court's words, it is "the likelihood of misidentification which violates a defendant's right to due process" (p. 199). This position was reaffirmed in the case of *Manson v. Braithwaite* (432 U.S. 98 [1977]), where the Court held that the totality of circumstances determines whether an identification procedure is unreliable.

Manson v. Braithwaite
(432 U.S. 98 [1977])

Suggestiveness has also been important in determining whether an identification procedure violates the due process clause. If the procedure is set up such that the witness or victim is almost guaranteed to pick the perpetrator, it is unnecessarily suggestive. If, for example, an offender is 6 feet tall and placed in a lineup with several others who are considerably shorter, then the procedure will be considered suggestive.

Self-Incrimination

The Fifth Amendment's self-incrimination clause has been invoked with regard to identification procedures. In particular, some defendants have argued that being forced to participate in a lineup or photographic array is itself incriminating and, as such, violates the Fifth Amendment. However, in *United States v. Wade*, the Court held that the privilege against self-incrimination does not limit the use of identification procedures.[1]

---

[1] Note that the Fifth Amendment would apply if a defendant in a lineup was forced to answer questions from the police or witnesses.

The reason the Court offered is that even though incriminating information can result from identification procedures, such evidence is physical or real as opposed to testimonial. In *Wade*, the Court decided on the constitutionality of an identification procedure, in which the accused was required to utter words that were presumably uttered by the perpetrator. The Court concluded that this type of identification procedure was valid because the defendant's voice was used as an identifying characteristic, not as a means to get him to express his guilt. Thus, the Fifth Amendment does not apply to identification procedures.

The Fourth Amendment

Lastly, identification procedures have been challenged on Fourth Amendment grounds. Like the Fifth Amendment, the Fourth Amendment has yet to be successfully invoked with regard to identification procedures. According to the Supreme Court, no one enjoys a reasonable expectation of privacy in characteristics that are exposed to the public. For example, if an offender is viewed by a witness, the witness's identification of the offender will be admissible in court, even though the identification is incriminating. The offender/defendant may argue that the act of being viewed by the witness is incriminating, but the courts consider this sort of knowing exposure as beyond constitutional protection.

Schmerber v. California
(384 U.S. 757 [1966])

One of the leading cases in this area is *Schmerber v. California* (384 U.S. 757 [1966]). There, a sample of the defendant's blood was taken by a doctor in a hospital following the defendant's arrest. The sample was used as evidence in the defendant's trial for drunk-driving. The defendant argued that the blood sample was incriminating and should be excluded from trial. The Supreme Court disagreed:

> Particularly in a case such as this, where time had to be taken to bring the accused to a hospital and to investigate the scene of the accident, there was no time to seek out a magistrate and secure a warrant. Given these special facts, we conclude that the attempt to secure evidence of blood-alcohol content in this case was an appropriate incident to petitioner's arrest. (pp. 770–771)

Obviously, if the police want to seize a person so as to obtain fingerprints, a voice exemplar, or some other form of evidence, they are bound by Fourth Amendment restrictions. As noted elsewhere in this book, probable cause is required before the police can seize a person. Assuming a seizure is justified, however, then any real or physical evidence obtained by the arrestee will be admissible.

Hayes v. Florida
(470 U.S. 811 [1985])

There is at least one exception to the Fourth Amendment's probable cause requirement as it pertains to identification procedures. In *Hayes v. Florida* (470 U.S. 811 [1985]), the Court stated:

> There is ... support in our cases for the view that the Fourth Amendment would permit seizures for the purpose of fingerprinting, if there is reasonable suspicion that the suspect has committed a criminal act, if there is a reasonable basis for believing that fingerprinting will establish or negate the suspect's connection with that crime, and if the procedure is carried out with dispatch. (p. 817)

However, if conducted in the home, such a seizure must be preceded by judicial authorization.

Summary.   Only two constitutional provisions actually place restrictions on identification procedures: the Fourteenth Amendment's due process clause and the

FIGURE 9.1

Summary of Constitutional Issues in Identification Procedures

- **Fourth Amendment:** The Fourth Amendment protects from an unlawful search or seizure conducted for the purpose of securing an identification. There is an exception, however: A witness can identify a suspect who is wrongfully seized if the identification is sufficiently independent of the illegal seizure.
- **Fifth Amendment:** Technically, the Fifth Amendment does not apply to identification procedures. This is true even if a suspect is asked to supply a voice exemplar, if this is done for the purpose of identification (and not a confession or admission).
- **Sixth Amendment:** The Sixth Amendment right to counsel exists in the context of making an identification but only in limited circumstances. First, the right to counsel only applies if formal adversarial charges have commenced. Second, a suspect in a photographic array does not enjoy Sixth Amendment protection, regardless of whether charges have been filed.
- **Fourteenth Amendment:** The Fourteenth Amendment's due process clause always applies to identification procedures. In particular, if an identification procedure is too suggestive, it will violate the Fourteenth Amendment.

Sixth Amendment's right to counsel clause. The Fifth Amendment, while important to confession law, does not come into play when identification procedures are at issue. Similarly, the Fourth Amendment does not apply to identification procedures directly, but it does apply indirectly insofar as probable cause is required if law enforcement officials plan to seize somebody for the purpose of identifying him or her. See Figure 9.1 for a summary of these issues.

PRETRIAL IDENTIFICATION TECHNIQUES

As described earlier, there are three types of pretrial identification techniques: lineups, showups, and photographic arrays. Each of these identification procedures is described in a following section, with particular focus on how the constitutional restrictions already discussed apply to it.

Lineups

Suspects can be forced to participate in lineups because lineups exhibit physical characteristics, not testimonial evidence. Indeed, suspects placed in lineups can also be required to supply voice exemplars but solely for identification purposes, not as a confession. If a suspect refuses to participate in a lineup, he or she can be cited with contempt (*Doss v. United States*, 431 F.2d 601 [9th Cir. 1970]), and the prosecutor can comment at trial about the suspect's refusal to cooperate (*United States v. Parhms*, 424 F.2d 152 [9th Cir. 1970]).

STEPS TO MINIMIZE SUGGESTIVENESS As noted earlier, the due process clause restricts identification procedures. In particular, an overly **suggestive lineup** violates due process. In *United States v. Wade*, the Supreme Court noted that a lineup becomes suggestive when, for instance,

> all in the lineup but the suspect were known to the identifying witness, . . . the other participants in a lineup were grossly dissimilar in appearance to the suspect, . . . only the suspect was required to wear distinctive clothing

which the culprit allegedly wore, . . . the suspect is pointed out before or during a lineup, and . . . the participants in the lineup are asked to try on an article of clothing which fits only the suspect. (p. 233)

The Project on Law Enforcement Policy and Rulemaking proposes several guidelines for minimizing suggestiveness in a police lineup:

- The lineup should consist of at least five people, including the suspect.
- The persons in the lineup should have similar physical characteristics.
- The suspect should be permitted to choose his or her place in line.
- Each person in the lineup should be required to take whatever specialized action is required (e.g., to utter certain words).
- The persons in the lineup should be warned to conduct themselves such that the suspect does not stand out.
- A lineup should be photographed or videotaped.[2]

The International Association of Chiefs of Police (IACP) Legal Center has recommended similar guidelines:

- A lineup should consist of five to six people.
- Each participant in the lineup must sign the appropriate waiver form, unless his or her counsel is present.
- Everyone in the lineup should be of the same sex and race, approximately the same age, and approximately the same height, weight, coloring, build, and so on.
- Everyone in the lineup should wear approximately the same clothing.
- The accused should be placed in the lineup at random, so as not to stand out.
- Persons known to the witness should not be placed in the lineup.
- Private citizens participating in the lineup (if insufficient numbers of prisoners are available) should sign a written consent form indicating they are aware that no charges have been filed against them, that they are free to leave at any time, and so on.
- Each witness should view the lineup separately so one witness does not unduly influence another in his or her identification of the perpetrator.
- Each participant in the lineup should be given the same instructions and should perform the same acts (e.g., supply a voice exemplar).
- Participants in the lineup should be instructed not to make any statements or comments unless ordered to do so.
- Frontal and side-profile photographs of the lineup should be taken.
- A single officer should oversee the lineup procedure.
- A written waiver of counsel should be obtained if the suspect waives his or her Sixth Amendment right to have counsel present at a *postindictment lineup*.[3]

An important restriction concerning lineups is that people cannot be indiscriminately picked off the street for participation. If a person is *not* already in custody, the police must have reasonable suspicion that he or she has committed the crime in question (see *Hayes v. Florida*). However, if the person *is* in custody prior to the lineup, then he or she can be forced to stand in a lineup without any judicial authorization (see *United States v. Anderson*, 490 F.2d 785 [D.C. Cir. 1974]).

---

[2] From Project on Law Enforcement Policy and Rulemaking, "Eyewitness Identification," *Model Rules for Law Enforcement* (Tempe, AZ: Arizona State University, 1974).
[3] International Association of Chiefs of Police, "Eyewitness Identification," in *Legal Points* (Gaithersburg, MD: IACP Legal Center, 1975).

Showups

A showup is a one-on-one victim/offender confrontation, usually conducted outside the courtroom setting. Specifically, a showup is usually held when the suspect has been apprehended shortly after having committed the crime and the witness is still at or near the scene of the crime. A lineup is always preferable to a showup (because a lineup consists of several potential suspects); however, a showup is necessary under certain circumstances.

For example, when a witness is immobile and cannot be present at a lineup, a showup is an effective alternative. In *Stovall v. Denno*, the Supreme Court noted, "Faced with the responsibility for identifying the attacker, with the need for immediate action and with the knowledge that [the victim] could not visit the jail, the police followed the only feasible procedure and took [the accused] to the hospital room" (p. 295). In a similar vein, a showup is preferable when the *suspect* is immobile (see *Jackson v. United States*, 412 F.2d 149 [D.C. Cir. 1969]).

A showup is sometimes desirable to facilitate prompt identification when time is of the essence. If the witness is required to wait for a lineup, for instance, misidentification is more likely to result. A showup conducted more than 60 minutes after the crime, however, will usually not be upheld (see *United States v. Perry*, 449 F.2d 1026 [D.C. Cir. 1971]). But in at least one case, the Supreme Court upheld a stationhouse showup in which no emergency existed. In *Neil v. Biggers* (409 U.S. 188 [1972]), the Court sanctioned an arranged one-on-one showup, even though it took place well after the point at which the crime in question was committed. The Court noted, given the facts, that there was "no substantial likelihood of misidentification" (p. 201). This was because the witness had an opportunity to view the suspect for almost 30 minutes, under good lighting, prior to the showup.

Neil v. Biggers
(409 U.S. 188 [1972])

The same constitutional provisions that govern lineups also govern showups. Specifically, the Sixth Amendment right to counsel applies but only after adversarial proceedings have commenced (see *Moore v. Illinois*, 434 U.S. 220 [1977]). Due process

Moore v. Illinois
(434 U.S. 220 [1977])

DECISION-MAKING EXERCISE 9.2
Altering the Suspect's Appearance

On December 24, the Toy Emporium was robbed. The suspect escaped before security guards and police could capture him, but store security cameras and several witnesses indicated that the crime was committed by a white male who was 6 feet, 3 inches tall, approximately 270 pounds, between 25 and 30 years of age, wearing a green trench coat, and having long hair. Two hours after the robbery, a man was arrested in a nearby town because he fit the general description of the robber. However, he was bald and wearing a brown trench coat. A lineup was conducted, in which the suspect was required to wear a wig resembling the long hair of the perpetrator. He was positively identified by several witnesses. Does the act of requiring the suspect to alter his appearance conform to constitutional requirements?

DECISION-MAKING EXERCISE 9.3
What Constitutes a Valid Showup?

The police believe that Anna Delgado was involved in a hit-and-run car accident in which a man was killed. They do not have the reasonable suspicion required to seize Delgado for appearance in a lineup, but they do have a witness to the accident. The police decide to take the witness to Delgado's place of work to make an identification. Delgado is identified at her place of employment. Is this type of showup valid?

protections also exist. If the showup is unnecessarily suggestive under a totality of circumstances analysis, then any identification that comes from it will not be admissible in court.

IN-COURT SHOWUPS What happens when a witness identifies the accused for the first time in *court*? This has happened on occasion and is best described as an **in-court showup**. The key feature of an in-court showup is that the witness has *not* identified the suspect, either in a lineup or related procedure, prior to trial. How do the courts deal with this? The answer is important because an in-court identification is highly suggestive. Namely, the suspect has already been identified by virtue of having been charged with the crime.

The leading case dealing with in-court showups is *Moore v. Illinois*, although the focus of the case was on the preliminary hearing, not the trial. The Court's decision would be expected to apply to criminal trials, as well as other adversarial proceedings, however. Here are the facts from that case, as described by the Supreme Court:

> After petitioner had been arrested for rape and related offenses, he was identified by the complaining witness as her assailant at the ensuing preliminary hearing, during which petitioner was not represented by counsel nor offered appointed counsel. The victim had been asked to make an identification after being told that she was going to view a suspect, after being told his name and having heard it called as he was led before the bench, and after having heard the prosecutor recite the evidence believed to implicate petitioner. Subsequently, petitioner was indicted, and counsel was appointed, who moved to suppress the victim's identification of petitioner. The Illinois trial court denied the motion on the ground that the prosecution had shown an independent basis for the victim's identification. At trial, the victim testified on direct examination by the prosecution that she had identified petitioner as her assailant at the preliminary hearing, and there was certain other evidence linking petitioner to the crimes. He was convicted and the Illinois Supreme Court affirmed. (p. 220)

Notwithstanding the clear violation of the Sixth Amendment in this case (which the Supreme Court also pointed out), the Court pointed to the suggestiveness that occurs when a witness identifies a suspect for the first time at a formal hearing:

> It is difficult to imagine a more suggestive manner in which to present a suspect to a witness for their critical first confrontation than was employed in this case. The victim who had seen her assailant for only 10 to 15 seconds, was asked to make her identification after she was told that she was going

DECISION-MAKING EXERCISE 9.4

Making a Valid Identification

Wilma Hobbes was unable to identify the man suspected of raping her, even after the police presented her with a photographic array *and* a lineup. Some weeks later, in a chance encounter while walking through the local courthouse, Wilma passed a person whom she believed was her rapist. He was subsequently arrested, and she identified him at the trial. Should this identification be considered valid?

to view a suspect, after she was told his name and heard it called as he was led before the bench, and after she heard the prosecutor recite the evidence believed to implicate petitioner. Had petitioner been represented by counsel, some or all of this suggestiveness could have been avoided. (pp. 229–230)

What message is to be gleaned from *Moore v. Illinois*? In general, law enforcement officials should have witnesses identify suspects via lineups, showups, or photographic arrays *prior* to the point at which adversarial proceedings commence. Any of these identification procedures would result in a less suggestive identification than would be likely at trial. Clearly, though, lineups, showups, and photographic arrays can also be suggestive.

Photographic Identifications

The last type of identification procedure to be considered in this text is the photographic identification array. It involves displaying a picture of the suspect along with pictures of several other people to a victim or witness for the purpose of identification.

Photographic identification procedures approximate real-life lineups by including several people, but they are not subjected to the same constitutional restrictions that lineups are. In particular, there is no Sixth Amendment right to counsel during a photographic identification. However, due process protections *do* apply.

To minimize due process problems, several photographs of like individuals should be shown to the witness or victim so as to minimize unnecessary suggestiveness. In *Simmons v. United States* (390 U.S. 377 [1968]), the Supreme Court shed some light on the importance of a carefully constructed photographic array:

Simmons v. United States
(390 U.S. 377 [1968])

> Despite the hazards of initial identification by photograph, this procedure has been used widely and effectively in criminal law enforcement, from the standpoint both of apprehending offenders and of sparing innocent suspects the ignominy of arrest by allowing eyewitnesses to exonerate them through scrutiny of photographs. The danger that use of the technique may result in convictions based on misidentification may be substantially lessened by a course of cross-examination at trial which exposes to the jury the method's potential for error. We are unwilling to prohibit its employment, either in the exercise of our supervisory power or, still less, as a matter of constitutional requirement. Instead, we hold that each case must be considered on its own facts, and that convictions based on eyewitness identification at trial following a pretrial identification by photograph will be set aside on that ground only if the photographic identification procedure was so impermissibly suggestive as to give rise to a very substantial likelihood of irreparable misidentification. (p. 384)

As indicated, to conform to due process requirements, multiple photographs of like individuals are ideal for a photographic array. However, in one case, the Supreme Court sanctioned a photographic array consisting of one picture. In *Manson v. Braithwaite* (432 U.S. 98 [1977]), the Court sanctioned an in-court identification based on an earlier identification from a single photograph because it was reliable based on the totality of circumstances. The reasons the Court cited are illustrative. In particular, the Court described how Glover, the witness, who was also a police

Manson v. Braithwaite
(432 U.S. 98 [1977])

officer, arrived at his conclusion that the suspect (referred to below as the *vendor* of illegal drugs) in the photograph was, in fact, the perpetrator. Here are the criteria on which the Court focused:

- *The opportunity to view.* Glover testified that for two to three minutes he stood at the apartment door, within two feet of the respondent. The door opened twice, and each time the man stood at the door. The moments passed, the conversation took place, and payment was made. Glover looked directly at his vendor. It was near sunset, to be sure, but the sun had not yet set, so it was not dark or even dusk or twilight. Natural light from outside entered the hallway through a window. There was natural light, as well, from inside the apartment.

- *The degree of attention.* Glover was not a casual or passing observer, as is so often the case with eyewitness identification. Trooper Glover was a trained police officer on duty—and specialized and dangerous duty—when he called at the third floor of 201 Westland in Hartford on May 5, 1970. . . . It is true that Glover's duty was that of ferreting out narcotics offenders and that he would be expected in his work to produce results. But it is also true that, as a specially trained, assigned, and experienced officer, he could be expected to pay scrupulous attention to detail, for he knew that subsequently he would have to find and arrest his vendor. In addition, he knew that his claimed observations would be subject later to close scrutiny and examination at any trial.

- *The accuracy of the description.* Glover's description was given to D'Onofrio [a backup officer] within minutes after the transaction. It included the vendor's race, his height, his build, the color and style of his hair, and the high cheekbone facial feature. It also included clothing the vendor wore. No claim has been made that respondent did not possess the physical characteristics so described. D'Onofrio reacted positively at once. Two days later, when Glover was alone, he viewed the photograph D'Onofrio produced and identified its subject as the narcotics seller.

- *The witness's level of certainty.* There is no dispute that the photograph in question was that of respondent.

- *The time between the crime and the identification.* Glover's description of his vendor was given to D'Onofrio within minutes of the crime. The photographic identification took place only two days later. We do not have here the passage of weeks or months between the crime and the viewing of the photograph. (pp. 114–116)

Taken together, these five considerations led the Court to this conclusion:

These indicators of Glover's ability to make an accurate identification are hardly outweighed by the corrupting effect of the challenged identification itself. Although identifications arising from single-photograph displays may be viewed in general with suspicion, see *Simmons v. United States*, 390 U.S., at 383, we find in the instant case little pressure on the witness to acquiesce in the suggestion that such a display entails. D'Onofrio had left the photograph at Glover's office and was not present when Glover first viewed it two days after the event. There thus was little urgency and Glover could view the photograph at his leisure. And since Glover examined the photograph alone, there was no coercive pressure to make an identification arising from the presence of another. The identification was made in circumstances allowing care and reflection. (p. 116)

The *Manson* decision suggests that single-photograph arrays are constitutionally permissible, but understand that the witness in this case was a police officer and that the facts were somewhat unusual. It is doubtful that the Supreme Court would

FIGURE 9.2

Lineup, Showup, and Photographic Array Policy (Gallatin, TN, Police Department)

9.29 Showup, Lineup, and Photographic Identification

9.29.1 Showup

A showup is the presentation of a suspect to an eyewitness a short time after the commission of a crime. Many courts have suppressed evidence from a showup due to the inherent suggestiveness of the event. Because of this, a lineup is preferred over a showup when possible. However, when exigent circumstances require the use of a showup, the following guidelines will be used:

1. A showup will not be conducted when the suspect is in a cell, restrained, or dressed in jail clothing;
2. A showup will not be conducted with more than one witness present at a time. Witnesses will not be allowed to communicate with each other regarding the identification of the suspect;
3. The same suspect will not be presented to the same witness more than once;
4. The suspect will not be required to put on clothing worn by the perpetrator, speak words uttered by the perpetrator, or perform other actions of the perpetrator; and
5. Officers will not say or do anything that might suggest to the witness that the suspect is or may be the perpetrator.

9.29.2 Photographic Identification

In conducting a photographic identification, an officer must use multiple photographs shown individually to a witness or simultaneoulsy in a book or array. Additionally, an officer will adhere to the following guidelines when conducting a photographic identification:

1. Use at least six photographs of individuals who are reasonably similar in age, height, weight, and general appearance and of the same sex and race;
2. Whenever possible, avoid mixing color and black and white photos, use photos of the same size and basic composition, and never mix mug shots with other snapshots or include more than one photo of the same suspect;
3. Cover any portions of mug shots or other photographs that provide identifying information on the subject, and similarly cover those used in the array;
4. Show the photo array to only one witness at a time;
5. Never make suggestive statements that may influence the judgement or perception of the witness; and
6. Preserve the photo array, together with full information about the identification process, for future reference.

9.29.3 Lineup

A lineup is the live presentation of at least five individuals to a victim. In conducting a lineup, an officer will schedule the lineup on a date and at a time that is convenient for all concerned parties. Additionally, the officer must fulfill necessary legal requirements for the transfer of a subject to the lineup location should he/she be incarcerated at a detention center; make timely notice to the detention center concerning the pickup; and make arrangements for picking up the prisoner. Finally, the officer must make arrangements to have at least four other persons act as "fill ins" at the lineup who are of the

Figure 9.2 continued

same race, sex, and approximate height, weight, age, and physical appearance and who are similarly clothed.

The officer in charge of conducting the lineup will ensure that the following requirements are adhered to:

1. Ensure that the prisoner has been informed of his/her right to counsel if formal charges have been made against him/her, and also ensure that he/she has the opportunity to retain counsel or request that one be provided;
2. Obtain a written waiver on the prescribed departmental form should the prisoner waive his/her right to counsel;
3. Allow counsel representing the accused an opportunity to observe the manner in which the lineup is conducted;
4. Advise the accused that he/she may take any position in the lineup which he/she prefers and may change positions prior to summoning a new witness;
5. Ensure that all persons in the lineup are numbered consecutively and are referred to only by number;
6. Ensure that a complete written, audio, and video record of the lineup proceedings are made and retained when possible;
7. Ensure that witnesses are not permitted to see nor are they to be shown any photographs of the accused immediately prior to the lineup;
8. Ensure that not more than one witness views the lineup at a time and that they are not permitted to speak with one another during lineup proceedings; and
9. Scrupulously avoid using statements, clues, casual comments, or providing unnecessary or irrelevant information that in any manner may influence the witnesses' decision-making process or perception.

Source: From *General Directives Manual*, Gallatin, Tennessee, Police Department (December 28, 1999). Used courtesy of the Gallatin Police Department.

uphold a similar identification today. It is always preferable to place multiple pictures of like individuals in a photographic array.

To summarize the points made thus far, see Figure 9.2. It contains the Gallatin, Tennessee, Police Department's policy for the use of showups, lineups, and photographic arrays.

IDENTIFICATION PROCEDURES: FLAWS AND FIXES

Nearly every suspect identification procedure can be flawed in some fashion, some more than others. Consider showups. No matter what steps police take to ensure fairness, showups are prone to mistaken identification. And the consequences of mistaken identification can be serious:

> Billy Wayne Miller was asleep in a back bedroom of his father's modest Oak Cliff home when three Dallas police officers burst through the front door around 3 a.m., guns in hand, yelling another man's name. Still groggy and clad only in his underwear, Mr. Miller was taken to the front porch. There he spotted a woman in a squad car glance at him and nod to an officer seated beside her before the car drove away. That split-second, one-man lineup cost Mr. Miller 22 years of his life on a rape conviction that DNA evidence later invalidated.[4]

---

[4] S. McGonigle and J. Emily, "DNA Exoneree Fell Victim to 'Drive-by' Identification," *Dallas Morning News*, October 13, 2008: http://www.dallasnews.com/sharedcontent/dws/dn/latestnews/stories/101308dnproDNA showups.264c41d.html (accessed November 4, 2008).

DECISION-MAKING EXERCISE 9.5

Creating a Valid Photographic Array

A rapist tells each of his victims that he has already been imprisoned for rape. His latest victim, Sandy, tells the police what he said. The police then show Sandy a single photograph of a rape suspect who was previously imprisoned. Sandy identifies the man in the photo as her rapist. Is this photographic array constitutional? Next, assume that the rapist does not tell his victims he has previously been imprisoned and that the police place his photo in a photographic array with the photos of two other individuals. Is this procedure appropriate? What if five photos are shown: three of the rapist (each from different points in time, with different clothes, etc.) and one each of the other two individuals?

DECISION-MAKING EXERCISE 9.6

The Photo Array Revisited

What if for purposes of having several of a suspected rapist's victims identify him in a photographic lineup, the police tell the second witness who the first witness identified, the third witness who the first and second witnesses identified, and so on? What if, instead, the police show five different photographic arrays to a single witness, but the suspected rapist appears once in each array?

Stories like Billy Wayne Miller's could be less common if authorities relied exclusively on lineups and photographic identification procedures. However, even lineups can be flawed. And so can photographic arrays. The Innocence Project, an organization that works to exonerate wrongfully convicted inmates, claims that "eyewitness misidentification is the single greatest cause of wrongful convictions nationwide."[5] The organization highlights some situations in which lineups and photographic procedures led to wrongful convictions:

- A witness in a rape case was shown a photo array where only one photo—of the person police suspected was the perpetrator—was marked with an "R."
- Witnesses substantially changed their description of a perpetrator (including key information such as height, weight, and presence of facial hair) after they learned more about a particular suspect.
- Witnesses only made an identification after multiple photo arrays or lineups—and then made hesitant identifications (saying they "thought" the person "might be" the perpetrator, for example), but at trial the jury was told the witnesses did not waver in identifying the suspect.[6]

Some might take issue with the Innocence Project's arguments, but many researchers have also found that identification procedures can be problematic, so much so that in May of 1998, then U.S. attorney general Janet Reno organized a working group of prosecutors, defense attorneys, police officers, and other experts who were tasked with creating a set of "best practices" for identification procedures. The working group's findings were echoed in an article published by a group of psychologists at around the same time. They identified "four simple rules of procedure that follow from the scientific literature that we argue could largely relieve the

---

[5] http://www.innocenceproject.org/understand/Eyewitness-Misidentification.php (accessed November 4, 2008).
[6] Ibid.

criminal justice system of its role in contributing to eyewitness identification problems."[7] The rules were:

- The person who conducts the lineup or photospread should not be aware of which member of the lineup or photospread is the suspect.
- Eyewitnesses should be told explicitly that the person in question might not be in the lineup or photospread and therefore should not feel that they must make an identification. They should also be told that the person administering the lineup does not know which person is the suspect in the case.
- The suspect should not stand out in the lineup or photospread as being different from the distractors based on the eyewitness's previous description of the culprit or based on other factors that would draw extra attention to the suspect.
- A clear statement should be taken from the eyewitness at the time of the identification and prior to any feedback as to his or her confidence that the identified person is the actual culprit.[8]

Double-Blind Lineups

When the investigator conducting a lineup knows who the suspect is, he or she can unintentionally (and even intentionally) influence the witness and thereby taint the identification procedure. For example, the investigator may say to the witness, "Why don't you take another look at number three." Assuming the suspect is in the number three position in a lineup, clearly this comment could sway the witness in the direction the investigatory prefers.

A **double-blind lineup** is one in which the investigator conducting the lineup (or assembling a photo array) does not know who the suspect is. This helps ensure that the investigator will not lead the witness in a particular direction. Studies indeed show that double-blind procedures reduce the risks of mistaken identifications.[9] Here is a summary of the findings from one of the most recent studies in this area:

DECISION-MAKING EXERCISE 9.7

Mistaken Identification?

Janice Bolan, a rape victim, was examined at a hospital and a rape kit was collected. No sperm cells were identified in the first examination of the swabs. Bolan then gave police a description of her attacker, saying he was an African American male between 25 and 30 years of age, approximately 6 feet tall, and had a beard. She then helped officers create a sketch of the perpetrator, which was circulated throughout the community. A week later, police received a call that a man fitting the description was working in a nearby grocery store. Police took Bolan by the store and asked if the man, Dean Cage, was her attacker. She answered yes. Police then conducted a lineup at the police station. Once again, Bolan identified Cage as her attacker. Cage was arrested and convicted in a bench trial, after she testified in court that she was "100 percent sure" Cage was the rapist—and pointed to him in court. Is there anything wrong with these events?

---

[7] G. L. Wells, M. Small, S. Penrod, R. S. Malpass, S. M. Fulero, and C. A. E. Brimacombe, "Eyewitness Identification Procedures: Recommendations for Lineups and Photospreads," *Law and Human Behavior* 22 (1998): 603–647.

[8] Ibid., pp. 627–635.

[9] See, e.g., S. M. Greathouse and M. B. Kovera, "Instruction Bias and Lineup Presentation Moderate the Effects of Administrator Knowledge on Eyewitness Identification," *Law and Human Behavior* 33 (2009): 70–82; R. M. Haw and R. P. Fisher, "Effects of Administrator-Witness Contact on Eyewitness Identification Accuracy," *Journal of Applied Psychology* 89 (2004): 1106–1112; M. B. Russano, J. J. Dickinson, S. M. Greathouse, and M. B. Kovera, "Why Don't You Take Another Look at Number Three: Investigator Knowledge and Its Effects on Eyewitness Confidence and Identification Decisions," *Cardozo Public Law, Policy, and Ethics Journal* 4 (2006): 355–379.

Administrator knowledge had the greatest effect on identifications of the suspect for simultaneous photospreads paired with biased instructions, with single-blind administrations increasing identifications of the suspect. When biased instructions were given, single-blind administrations produced fewer foil identifications than double-blind administrations. Administrators exhibited a greater proportion of biasing behaviors during single-blind administrations than during double-blind administrations.[10]

Virtual Officer Lineups

A problem with double-blind lineups is that they are resource intensive. They require at least two investigators instead of the usual one—one to know the identity of the suspect and another to administer the lineup without knowing the suspect's real identity. One solution to this problem is to use a "virtual officer" to conduct the procedure.[11] One team of researchers has gone so far as to develop software in which a virtual officer (called "Officer Garcia") conducts a photographic display. Because the virtual officer does not know the identity of the suspect or his or her placement in the array, the procedure is not susceptible to investigator influence. A "YouTube" demonstration is available online.[12]

IDENTIFICATION DURING TRIAL

Often, a witness will be called on to identify the perpetrator of a crime (usually, the defendant) *during* the trial. Sometimes, this process is straightforward and subject to little dispute by either party to the case. Other times, an in-court identification can be tainted by an out-of-court identification. (This problem is discussed in the exclusionary rule section toward the end of this chapter.) Accordingly, it is worth considering the witness questioning process.

A criminal trial is a carefully choreographed event, in which each party—the defense and the prosecution—has the right to ask questions as well as attack the credibility or believability of a witness's testimony. By custom, the plaintiff in a *civil case* has the burden of persuasion, so he or she goes first. That is, the plaintiff calls all his or her witnesses and presents the evidence required to build the case. When the plaintiff rests, then the defense has its turn.

Criminal cases are similarly choreographed. First, the prosecutor presents the state's case, and, then, the defendant presents his or her case. The process of examining witnesses, however, is much more complicated than this simple description. The following subsections are designed to shed light on this often confusing aspect of criminal procedure.

Forms of Questions

Witness questioning in a criminal trial proceeds through four stages. The first is **direct examination**, in which the witness is questioned by one party. Next, **cross-examination** takes place. This is where the other party to the case has an opportunity to question the witness. The next two stages are redirect and recross-examination, in which both parties ask further questions of witnesses pursuant to direct and cross-examination.

As a general rule, on direct examination, the questions must be specific but not leading. A **specific question** is one that does not call for a narrative. If the party calling the witness says, "Tell us what happened on the day of the incident," the opposing side

---

[10] Greathouse and Kovera, p. 70.
[11] O. H. MacLin, L. A. Zimmerman, and R. S. Malpass, "PC-Eyewitness and the Sequential Superiority Effect: Computer-Based Lineup Administration," *Law and Human Behavior* 29 (2005): 303–321.
[12] http://www.youtube.com/watch?v=SEhcLQmwtjQ (accessed November 4, 2008).

A witness is often called on to identify a suspect at trial.

will probably object. Instead, it is proper to ask something along the lines of, "Were you the victim of a burglary on August 6 of this year?"

At the other extreme, it is possible to be too specific, such that a question becomes leading. A **leading question** is, according to the *California Evidence Code*, one "that suggests to the witness the answer that the examining party desires."[13] An example of a leading question is, "Isn't that the perpetrator sitting right there at the defense table?" Leading questions are generally impermissible on direct examination (subject to some exceptions, described later) but permissible on cross-examination. Further, leading questions are permissible on redirect examination but not on recross-examination.

Figure 9.3 lists a number of other means for challenging the questions asked of witnesses, which are raised in the form of *objections*. If the judge sustains an objection raised by either party, the witness cannot answer the question. If the witness answers the question anyway, his or her response will be stricken from the record.

Refreshing a Witness's Memory

Witnesses frequently forget the facts to which they are supposed to testify, particularly if a great deal of time has expired between the event witnessed and the date of the in-court testimony. To remedy this problem, the *Federal Rules of Evidence* provide that a witness's prior experience may be *revived* by referral to the witness's prior statements.[14] Of course, if a witness has no memory whatsoever of the event to which he or she is to testify, then he or she is an incompetent witness. But if a refresher is all that is needed, then the examining party should be able to remind the witness of what he or she said in the past.

The process of refreshing a witness's memory involves two important concepts: (1) present memory revived and (2) past memory recorded. With regard to *present*

---

[13] *California Evidence Code*, Section 764. Available online: http://www.leginfo.ca.gov (accessed November 3, 2008).

[14] Ibid., Rule 612.

FIGURE 9.3

Common Objections to the Questions Asked of Witnesses

1. *"Asked and answered."* The question simply asked the witness to repeat testimony previously offered in response to a question.
2. *"Assumption of facts not in evidence."* The question asked the witness to comment on information that has not been introduced as evidence.
3. *"Argumentative."* The question was intended to argue with the witness, rather than elicit information from him or her. Such questions are designed to win over the jury.
4. *"Compound."* The question asked more than one question, thus requiring more than one clear-cut answer.
5. *"Misleading."* The question was based on inaccurate evidence or a misinterpretation of events.
6. *"Speculation and conjecture."* The question asked the witness to offer a guess or expectation. Witnesses, especially lay witnesses, are supposed to answer questions based on what they know.
7. *"Uncertain, ambiguous, or unintelligible."* The question has either many meanings or none at all.
8. *"Nonresponsive to the question."* When asked a yes or no question, the witness responded evasively or vaguely.
9. *"Substantive objection."* A rule of evidence has been violated.

memory revived, the in-court testimony of the witness is the evidence. By contrast, *past memory recorded* refers to a written account as being the evidence, not the witness's in-court testimony.

In the first concept, where a witness's present memory is revived when, for example, he or she is asked to refer to records or other written documents. After the witness views the documents and has his or her memory refreshed, his or her statement to this effect is admitted as evidence. The document(s) shown to the witness is not read or shown to the jury because the *document* is not evidence, only the witness's testimony. Assume, for example, that a witness to a car accident is asked whether she remembers the license plate number of the car that sped away from the scene. She replies that she is uncertain but may be able to recall the number if she can consult some notes she wrote on the day she witnessed the car leaving the scene. If the witness is permitted to rely on her notes and she then remembers the license plate number, then she will be permitted to testify to this effect under a theory of present memory revived.

The second theory of refreshing a witness's memory is, as indicated, *past recollection recorded*. Recall that in such an instance, it is the recording itself that is admitted

DECISION-MAKING EXERCISE 9.8

Identify the Leading Questions

What follows are several hypothetical questions that a prosecutor would ask a witness. Decide whether each is a leading question: (1) "Is the man who assaulted you in the courtroom today?" (2) "Could you point to the man who assaulted you?" (3) "Isn't the man who assaulted you sitting in this courtroom today?" (4) "Isn't that the man who assaulted you?" (5) "Isn't it true that the man who assaulted you is sitting right there?"

as evidence. That is, the jury considers the document as opposed to the witness's testimony. The written document essentially becomes a substitute for the witness's memory.

Certain requirements must be met before a past recollection recorded will be admitted into evidence. First, the witness must testify that he or she had personal knowledge of the facts at one time. Second, the witness must testify that the recording was accurate. Third, the witness must testify that he or she does not have adequate recollection of the facts such that he or she could testify to them in court. In addition, the trial judge must be satisfied with the document in order for it to be admissible into evidence. Finally, once a past recollection recorded has been admitted into evidence, the opposing side should have the opportunity to view the document (see *United States v. Kelly*, 349 F.2d 720 [2nd Cir. 1965]; *People v. Banks*, 50 Mich. App. 622 [1974]).

Witness Credibility

Credibility, first off, should be distinguished from *competence*. **Competence** pertains to a witness's ability to remember events, communicate effectively, and understand the importance of telling the truth, as well as the consequences of not doing so. **Credibility** pertains to whether the witness's testimony should be believed. In other words, can the witness's statements be judged as truthful? If the witness is able to remember events, communicate clearly to the jury, and come across as convincing, he or she will probably be regarded as credible.

When discussing competence, courts often refer to the processes of **accrediting** and **discrediting**. A witness can be *discredited* when the prosecution or defense challenges his or her credibility. The process of *accrediting* is the opposite, or when the prosecution or defense attempts to support, bolster, or improve a witness's credibility.

It is important to note that specific rules govern the processes of accrediting and discrediting. First, it is universally agreed on that in absence of an attack on a witness's credibility, no evidence may be introduced to support or bolster his or her credibility. According to the court in *United States v. Price* (722 F.2d 88 [5th Cir. 1983]), "[T]here is no reason why time should be spent in proving that which may be assumed to exist. Every witness must be assumed to be of normal moral character for veracity, just as he is assumed to be of normal sanity" (p. 90). Simply put, a witness generally cannot be accredited until someone, whether the prosecution or the defense, attempts to *discredit* him or her.

Consider the situation in which a witness is asked to introduce himself or herself and describe his or her background. The prosecution or defense may ask direct questions about the witness's familiarity with the case or, in the case of an expert witness, questions about the witness's occupation, background, and professional accomplishments. This type of questioning would appear to be accrediting, but a certain amount of background information can be supplied by introductory witness questioning without it being considered accreditation. However, there is a point where accrediting must stop, absent an attack on the witness's credibility. Unfortunately, there are few answers as to what amount of accrediting background information is permissible. According to the court in *Government of Virgin Islands v. Grant* (938 F.2d 401 [1985]):

> The jurisprudence of "background" evidence is essentially undeveloped. "Background" or "preliminary" evidence is not mentioned in the evidence codes, nor has it received attention in the treatises. One justification for its admission, at least in terms of the background of a witness qua witness, is that it may establish absence of bias or motive by showing the witness's relationship (or non-relationship) to the parties or to the case. (p. 513)

It is safe to conclude, though, that when the introduction process turns aggrandizing—that is, into more than an introduction—the accrediting of a witness must stop.

In one interesting case, *Pointer v. State* (74 So.2d 615 [Ala. Ct. App. 1954]), the prosecutor, during his closing statement, said that if the prosecution witness had been of bad character, the issue would have been raised by the defense. The court reversed the ensuing conviction, holding that because there was no attack on the witness's credibility during trial, the prosecutor was not permitted to bolster the witness's credibility (see also *Poole v. Commonwealth*, 176 S.E.2d 917 [Va.1970]).

A controversial issue with regard to accrediting concerns what can be done to bolster a witness's credibility when he or she cannot remember important events. If, for example, a witness testifies to a series of events but states that she is unable to remember everything, may another witness be called to offer reasons for the woman's memory lapse? A question similar to this was raised in *United States v. Awkward* (597 F.2d 667 [9th Cir.], *cert. denied*, 444 U.S. 885 [1979]). In that case, the Ninth Circuit Court of Appeals ruled that it was wrong for a prosecution witness to testify that he had been hypnotized and to permit a prosecution expert who had hypnotized that individual to testify about the effects of hypnosis on him or her. As the court observed:

> [U]nless an adverse party attacks the witness's ability to recall by bringing out or exploring the fact of hypnosis, the use of expert testimony to support the efficacy of hypnosis is improper. The party calling a witness should not be permitted to inquire in any way into the witness's ability to recall, or methods of pretrial memory refreshment, until such questions have been raised by the adversary. (p. 679)

In sum, witness accrediting is permissible, but usually "only after the character of the witness for truthfulness has been attacked by opinion or reputation evidence or otherwise" (*Blake v. Cich*, 79 F.R.D. 398 [D. Minn. 1978], p. 403). In legal parlance, accrediting of this sort is also known as *witness rehabilitation*, which is addressed following the discussion of impeachment. Note, however, that this restriction on accrediting is not recognized in most modern evidence statutes, except with regard to character evidence. That is, most modern statutes do not allow accrediting of a witness's character but remain silent as to other types of accrediting.[15]

IMPEACHMENT   The formal term for attacking a witness's credibility is **impeachment**. When faced with a witness who is not believed to be telling the truth, the prosecution or defense may decide to challenge the witness's believability before the jury. The jury will then draw its own conclusions as to the witness's truthfulness and believability.

How does impeachment occur? It is most often used by one party to a case against another. Generally, the process begins on cross-examination. The prosecution or the defense can attack a witness's credibility for a number of different, well-established reasons (see Figure 9.4). However, there is little value in attempting to impeach a witness if his or her testimony does not carry much weight or is unpersuasive to the jury. Alternatively, if there is no basis for an attack on a witness's credibility but the opposing side attempts to do so anyway, the impeachment effort could backfire.

---

[15] Ibid., Rule 608(a)(2).

FIGURE 9.4

Methods of Witness Impeachment

1. Establish bias or prejudice.
2. Point to prior convictions.
3. Allege uncharged crimes and immoral acts.
4. Identify contradictions and prior inconsistent statements.
5. Suggest inability to observe events.
6. Challenge reputation.

REHABILITATION When the credibility of a witness is attacked, the side that produced the witness can take steps to bolster his or her credibility, either by calling other witnesses or introducing other evidence. This process is known as **rehabilitation**. Rehabilitation occurs during redirect examination, which follows cross-examination. For example, assume the defense calls a witness. The defense attorney will question the witness in an effort to absolve the defendant of guilt. If the prosecution sees fit to impeach the defense witness and succeeds in doing so, the defense attorney will work to rehabilitate its witness during the redirect examination stage.

In discussing the importance of rehabilitation, one court observed that "it is well recognized that once a witness's credibility has been attacked, whether it be by the introduction of evidence of bad reputation, conviction of crime, inconsistent statements, evidence of misconduct, or by incisive cross-examination, the party calling the witness has a right to present evidence designed to rehabilitate the witness's credibility" (*State v. Bowden*, 439 A.2d 263 [R.I. 1982]).

Three common approaches are used to rehabilitate witnesses. The first is to argue that the witness was untruthful in the past but is telling the truth now. Perhaps the witness was once a deceptive miscreant but has been reformed to the extent that he or she can now be trusted. Alternatively, if a witness lies in order to avoid prosecution, it is possible that evidence could be admitted to show that he or she does not have a reputation for telling the truth (*United States v. Lechoco*, 542 F.2d 84 [D.C. Cir. 1976]).

Second, the party seeking to rehabilitate its own witness may argue that a contradictory or inconsistent statement alluded to by the other side was taken out of context. For example, suppose that part of a police report is used to impeach an officer who is giving testimony. The party seeking to rehabilitate the officer may then introduce other portions of the police report that shed light on the part used to impeach the officer (see *Short v. United States*, 271 F.2d 73 [9th Cir. 1959]).

A third way to rehabilitate a witness is to introduce other evidence to bolster his or her credibility. For example, suppose that a witness makes a statement *prior* to trial that contradicts his or her statement *at* trial. The other side may then elect to introduce additional pretrial statements supportive of his or her statements at trial. Refer to the infamous O. J. Simpson case and recall that Detective Mark Fuhrman was impeached by the defense because he had made racially discriminatory statements in the past. Had the prosecution called other police witnesses to testify as to Fuhrman's objectivity with regard to race, their testimony may have rehabilitated Fuhrman as a witness.

Given the importance of witness identification, it is useful to know how to be a good witness to criminal activity as well as a good in-court witness. This information is provided in Figures 9.5 and 9.6, respectively.

FIGURE 9.5

Tips for Being a Good Witness to Criminal Activity

1. Try to remember the basics:
   a. *Who* was the person?
   b. *What* did he or she do?
   c. *When* and *where* did he or she do this?
2. Was the offender an acquaintance or a stranger? Would you recognize the offender if you saw him or her again?
3. Pay attention to details: Was the offender male or female? What race or ethnicity was he or she? What was his or her approximate age? Height? Weight? Body build? Hair color and length? Any distinguishing features? What clothes was he or she wearing? Was he or she wearing a coat? Hat? Glasses? Did he or she have any weapons? What car was he or she driving, if any? What was the license plate number? What were the make, model, and color of the car? Features of the vehicle?
4. What did the offender say? What did he or she do? How did he or she act? Was anyone injured?
5. Where is the offender, or where did he or she go? How did he or she leave? How long ago did this happen?

FIGURE 9.6

Tips for Testifying in Federal Court

TIPS FOR TESTIFYING IN FEDERAL COURT

United States Department of Justice

1. A neat and clean appearance is very important for court. You should be comfortable, yet appropriately dressed for court (i.e., no hats, shorts, etc.). Avoid distracting mannerisms such as chewing gum.
2. Jurors who are, or will be, sitting on the case in which you are a witness may be present in the same public areas as you. For that reason, you should not discuss the case with anyone. Remember, too, that jurors may have the opportunity to observe how you act outside of the courtroom. If you see a juror, you are not allowed to speak to the juror, even to say hello.
3. When you are called to testify, you will first be sworn in. When you take the oath, pay attention to the clerk, and say "I do" clearly.
4. When a witness gives testimony, he/she is first asked some questions by the lawyer calling him or her to the stand; in your case, this is an Assistant United States Attorney. This is called the "direct examination." Then, the witness is questioned by the opposing lawyer (the defense counsel) in "cross examination." (Sometimes the process is repeated two or three times to help clear up any confusion.) The basic purpose of direct examination is for you to tell the judge and jury what you know about the case. The basic purpose of cross examination is to explore the accuracy of your testimony. Don't get mad if you feel you are being doubted in cross examination.

DO NOT LOSE YOUR TEMPER. An angry or impolite witness will probably not be believed. Always be polite and courteous.

Figure 9.6 continued

5. OBJECTION is a legal term that means one of the attorneys feels you are being asked an improper kind of question. When you hear a lawyer say "objection," simply stop speaking and wait for the judge to rule on the objection. If the judge decides the question is proper, he/she will OVERRULE the objection. If the judge decides the question is not proper, he/she will SUSTAIN the objection. You will be told either by the judge or the attorney whether to answer that question or another question.

   Whenever you are asked a question, listen to the whole question before you start to answer. Make sure you understand the question and then give your answer. If you do not understand the question or if you want it repeated, say so.

6. A SIDEBAR is when the judge and the attorneys meet at the judge's bench to discuss various matters, including technical disputes over the Federal Rules of Evidence. They meet at the judge's bench so the jury cannot hear their discussion.

7. Before you testify, try to picture the scene, the objects there, the distances, and exactly what happened so that you can recall the facts more accurately when you are asked. If the question is about distances or time, and if your answer is only an estimate, be sure you say it is only an estimate. Beware of suggestions by attorneys as to distances or times when you do not recall the actual time or distance. Do not agree with their estimate unless you independently arrive at the same estimate.

8. Speak in your own words. Don't try to memorize what you are going to say. Doing so will make your testimony sound rehearsed and unconvincing. Instead, be yourself, and prior to trial go over in your own mind those matters about which you will be questioned.

9. Most important of all, you are sworn to TELL THE TRUTH. Tell it. Every true fact should be readily admitted. Do not stop to figure out whether your answer will help or hurt either side. As a witness you are expected to be an impartial spokesperson for the facts as you know them.

10. Try to answer questions by stating what you saw or heard. You should not give an opinion unless you are asked to do so. You should not say what somebody else saw or heard unless you are asked.

11. Give positive, definite answers when at all possible. Avoid saying, "I think," "I believe," or "In my opinion," if you can be positive. If you do know, say so. Don't make up an answer. Be positive about things which you remember. If you are asked about details which you do not remember, simply say you don't remember.

12. You should answer only the questions asked and not volunteer information.

13. Unless you are sure, don't say "that's all of the conversation," or "nothing else happened". Instead, say "that's all I recall," or "that's all I remember happening". It is possible that after more thought or another question, you will remember something important.

14. The court reporter must be able to hear all your answers, so please don't nod your head for a "yes" or "no" answer. Speak loudly and clearly. Also, you will sound best if you don't use words like "yah", "nope", and "uh-huh".

15. When you answer a question, you may find it easiest to simply look at the person who asked the question. Use the same tone and effort when answering questions from both sides.

16. Do not exaggerate. Don't make overly broad statements that you may have to correct. Be particularly careful in responding to a question that begins, "Wouldn't you agree that . . . ?". The explanation should be in your own words. Do not allow an attorney to put words in your mouth.

17. Listen carefully to the questions you are asked. Understand the question, have it repeated if necessary, then give your answer.

18. If your answer was not correctly stated, correct it immediately. If your answer was not clear, clarify it immediately. It is better to correct a mistake yourself than to have the attorney discover an error in your testimony. If you realize you have answered incorrectly, say, "May I correct something I said earlier?"

19. Sometimes, witnesses give inconsistent testimony—something they said before doesn't agree with something they said later. If this happens to you, don't get flustered. Just explain honestly why you were mistaken. The jury, like the rest of us, understands that people make honest mistakes.

20. Sometimes an attorney may ask if you have talked to anybody about the case. It is perfectly proper for you to have talked to people before you testified, and you should, of course, respond truthfully to this question.

21. After you have completed testifying, you should not tell other witnesses what was said during your testimony until after the case is completed. Thus, do not ask other witnesses about their testimony and do not volunteer information about your own. Once you have been formally excused as a witness, you are free to go. Remember to fill out the witness voucher so you may be reimbursed.

Source: United States Attorney's Office, District of Colorado. Available online: http://www.justice.gov/usao/wie/vicwit/Tips.pdf (accessed February 16, 2011).

THE EXCLUSIONARY RULE AND IDENTIFICATIONS

When identification procedures violate constitutional protections, the results from such procedures cannot be considered admissible in a criminal trial. Generally, there are two means by which identifications will be excluded: (1) when an in-court identification is tainted by an out-of-court identification and (2) when a suspect is searched and/or seized improperly and then identified by a witness.

Tainted Identifications

In-court identifications are viewed cautiously. In most such situations, the defendant is sitting in the court room, not surrounded by anyone else matching his or her description (as in a lineup), and sometimes looking sinister or even guilty (e.g., wearing prison coveralls). Furthermore, given the fact that the defendant has been identified—at least, for trial purposes—as the one suspected of having committed a crime, witnesses often jump to the conclusion that the defendant is the one who should be held responsible.

Nevertheless, courts routinely permit in-court identifications. But if an in-court identification is tainted by an out-of-court identification, it may be excluded. This is known as a **tainted identification**.

Unfortunately, it is not always easy to decide whether an in-court identification is "fruit of the poisonous tree." In *United States v. Wade*, the Supreme Court held that an illegally conducted lineup does not invalidate later identifications resulting from an "independent source." The independent source in this context does not have to be another person. Instead, if the witness had plenty of time to view the perpetrator prior to the police lineup, showup, or photographic array, then his or her in-court identification may be admissible. Some factors that are considered include

the prior opportunity to observe the alleged criminal act, the existence of any discrepancy between any pre-lineup description and the defendant's actual description, any identification prior to lineup of another person, the identification by picture of the defendant prior to the lineup, failure to identify the defendant on a prior occasion, and the lapse of time between the alleged act and the lineup identification. (p. 241)

Also, if the witness did not experience intense anxiety or pressure during the criminal act (and thus had plenty of opportunity to absorb what was occurring), it is likely that his or her in-court identification will not be tainted by questionable police conduct during a lineup (see *United States v. Johnson*, 412 F.2d 753 [1st Cir. 1969], *cert. denied*, 397 U.S. 944 [1970]).

Identifications Resulting from Illegal Searches and Seizures

What happens if a person is wrongfully arrested—say, based on less than probable cause—and then placed in a lineup and identified by a witness? Can the witness's identification be considered admissible in a criminal trial? What if, further, the lineup is nonsuggestive and otherwise abides by constitutional requirements? Unfortunately, the Supreme Court has offered few answers to these questions.

United States v. Crews (445 U.S. 463 [1980])

Davis v. Mississippi (394 U.S. 721 [1969]) is a worthwhile point of departure. In *Davis*, the fingerprint identification of a rape suspect was deemed inadmissible because it was the product of an illegal arrest. However, in *United States v. Crews* (445 U.S. 463 [1980]), the Supreme Court decided otherwise. In that case, Crews was illegally arrested and photographed and then his photograph was shown to a witness, who identified him as the perpetrator. He was tried and convicted based, in part, on the witness's identification. The Supreme Court agreed with the trial court that the arrest was illegal but still upheld Crews's conviction. Three members of the majority justified this decision by arguing that the "fruit" was gathered at the point of the illegal arrest, as opposed to later, so the derivative evidence doctrine should not apply. The Court further noted that the identification had not " 'been come at by exploitation' of the violation of the defendant's Fourth Amendment rights" (p. 471).

Inasmuch as *Crews* was decided well after *Davis v. Mississippi*, it would seem that an identification resulting from an illegal search and/or seizure would be admissible. Think back, as well, to how the exclusionary rule applies in the *Miranda* context. The Supreme Court held in *United States v. Bayer* (331 U.S. 532 [1947]) that the "fruit of the poisonous tree" doctrine does not control the admissibility of physical evidence obtained from illegal confessions. These decisions, taken together, chip away at the

---

DECISION-MAKING EXERCISE 9.9

When Is an In-Court Identification Tainted?

Joan Vines heard noises emanating from Sarah Locklear's apartment and minutes later saw two men, one with black gloves and a brown paper bag, exit from the basement of the building and leave in a green 1956 Plymouth. Vines left her apartment immediately to check on things. She found the door to the Locklear apartment open, and she located a piece of stereo equipment just outside the building. Suddenly, the Plymouth returned, so Vines retreated to her apartment. Through her window, she watched the same two men put the piece of stereo equipment into the car. The men left again in the car, but not before Vines jotted down the license plate number. She later gave it to the police, together with physical descriptions of the two men. Vines was then brought to the station for the purpose of identifying one of the suspects. She was taken to a room in which the suspect was seated. The suspect was requested to stand and turn around, which he did. Vines identified him as one of the two participants in the burglary of Locklear's apartment. Vines later identified the man at his trial for burglary. Will the in-court identification be tainted by the stationhouse identification?

DECISION-MAKING EXERCISE 9.10

When Is an In-Court Identification Valid?

Valerie DeLuca's house has been burglarized so many times that she has given up all hope that the police will be able to find the perpetrator. She has told them the burglar's *modus operandi* several times and even that he has worn dark clothes and a black ski cap, but the police have still been unable to catch the burglar. Then, one night, the police apprehend a suspicious man, wearing dark clothing and a black ski cap, walking the streets of DeLuca's neighborhood. They don't have probable cause but arrest him anyway. They call DeLuca in to the stationhouse, hoping she can identify

the burglar in a lineup. In fact, she is not sure precisely who the burglar is, but she doesn't tell the police she is uncertain. Instead, she is so desperate to put an end to the burglaries that she plays the odds and identifies one of the men in the lineup. That man is then charged with burglary. Later, at trial, DeLuca identifies the man as the one who burglarized her house on several occasions. Will her in-court identification be valid? In other words, even though her testimony would not be truthful, would her in-court identification of the suspect conform to constitutional requirements?

exclusionary rule and reinforce the notion that the "fruit of the poisonous tree" doctrine applies in limited circumstances—primarily, when an illegal search and/or seizure (as opposed to an improper confession or identification) results in the subsequent seizure of tangible evidence.

Summary

1. OUTLINE PRETRIAL SUSPECT IDENTIFICATION TECHNIQUES.

Identification procedures are of three types: (1) lineups, (2) showups, and (3) photographic identifications or arrays. All are bound by the Fourteenth Amendment's due process clause. That is, if they are too suggestive, they will be declared unconstitutional. Lineups and showups are also restricted by the Sixth Amendment's right to counsel clause, but this clause does not apply to photographic identifications. Identification procedures are not protected by the Fifth and Fourth Amendments because an identification is not considered testimony or a seizure.

2. EXPLAIN THE PROBLEM OF WITNESS MISIDENTIFICATION.

Witnesses are prone to mistaken identification, especially in showup situations. Even lineups and photo arrays can result in mistaken identification. As such, various procedures have been developed to improve identification procedures. Two recent examples include double-blind lineups and virtual officer lineups.

3.SUMMARIZE IDENTIFICATION TECHNIQUES DURING THE TRIAL AND ISSUES INVOLVING WITNESS CREDIBILITY.

In addition to pretrial identification, identification during trial is important. As such, it is subject to a

number of important restrictions. A criminal trial is a carefully choreographed event, so the order of the questioning proceeds in specific stages. The form of questions, even if simply geared toward having a witness identify the defendant, is also significantly restricted. As a general rule, leading questions are not permissible except on cross-examination. Finally, since some witnesses tend to be untrustworthy, steps can be taken to cast doubt on their credibility. This process is known as impeachment.

4. EXPLAIN HOW THE EXCLUSIONARY RULE OPERATES IN THE IDENTIFICATION CONTEXT.

An identification, whether occurring during trial or prior to trial, can be excluded as evidence. First, if an in-court identification is tainted by an improper out-of-court identification, it will be inadmissible. Similarly, if an identification takes place following the illegal arrest and/or search of a suspect, it can be excluded, as well. There are exceptions to these rules, however. Usually, if the identification is sufficiently divorced from any prior illegality, it will be admissible at trial.

Key Terms

accrediting	294	discrediting	294	leading question	291	showup	277
Competence	294	double-blind		lineup	277	specific question	291
Credibility	294	lineup	290	photographic		suggestive lineup	281
cross-examination	291	impeachment	295	array	294	tainted	
direct examination	291	in-court showup	284	rehabilitation	296	identification	299

Key Cases

Constitutional Restrictions on Identifications

- *United States v. Wade*, 388 U.S. 218 (1967)
- *Stovall v. Denno*, 388 U.S. 293 (1967)
- *Manson v. Braithwaite*, 432 U.S. 98 (1977)
- *Schmerber v. California*, 384 U.S. 757 (1966)
- *Hayes v. Florida*, 470 U.S. 811 (1985)

- *Simmons v. United States*, 390 U.S. 377 (1968)
- *Manson v. Braithwaite*, 432 U.S. 98 (1977)

Exclusionary Rule and Identifications

- *United States v. Crews*, 445 U.S. 463 (1980)

Pretrial Identification

- *Neil v. Biggers*, 409 U.S. 188 (1972)
- *Moore v. Illinois*, 434 U.S. 220 (1977)

Review Questions

1. Explain how the Sixth Amendment right to counsel applies in the identification context.
2. Explain how due process applies in the identification context.
3. Why are the Fourth and Fifth Amendments not applicable in the identification context?
4. Explain the three types of pretrial identification procedures. How do they differ from one another?
5. What are some methods of reducing the suggestiveness of a lineup?
6. What is an in-court showup?
7. What does a constitutionally valid photographic array look like?
8. Explain how a witness is questioned during trial.
9. What is a leading question? Is it possible for the prosecutor to ask a leading question of a witness who is to identify the suspect in court? If so, how would such a question be phrased?
10. Distinguish between credibility and competence.
11. Distinguish between impeachment and rehabilitation.
12. What is a tainted identification? Why is it important in criminal procedure?
13. Explain the Supreme Court's view on identifications that result from illegal searches and/or seizures.
14. Summarize the tips for being a good witness to criminal activity.
15. Summarize the tips for being a good witness during court.

Web Links and Exercises

1. Improving identification procedure: What steps can be taken to improve identification procedures?
Suggested URL: http://www.ncjrs.gov/pdffiles1/nij/178240.pdf (accessed February 16, 2011).
2. Wrongful convictions: Read about the causes of wrongful convictions, according to the Innocence Project.
URL: http://innocenceproject.org (accessed February 16, 2011).

3. Double-blind lineups: Read more about making eyewitness identification more reliable. Do they improve on traditional lineup procedures?
Suggested URL: http://www.ojp.usdoj.gov/nij/journals/258/police-lineups.html (accessed February 16, 2011).
4. Virtual identification procedures: See a video demonstration with "Officer Garcia," the virtual officer.
URL: http://www.youtube.com/watch?v=SEhcLQmwtjQ (accessed February 16, 2011).

Part 4

THE BEGINNINGS OF
FORMAL PROCEEDINGS

LEARNING OBJECTIVES

When you complete this chapter, you should be able to:

▸ Explain the purpose and process of the initial appearance.

▸ Explain the purpose and the process of the probable cause hearing.

▸ Summarize bail and other types of pretrial release.

▸ Explain the purpose and process of the preliminary hearing.

▸ Summarize the arraignment process.

▸ Summarize the discovery process.

The Pretrial Process

INTRODUCTION

The Road to Trial

As indicated in Chapter 1, the criminal process begins with one of two events: a warrantless arrest or a criminal complaint. If a person is arrested without a warrant—say, for committing a crime in the presence of a police officer—then the arresting officer will file a criminal complaint against the individual and the formal criminal process will commence. On the other hand, if a warrant is obtained before making an arrest, the warrant must be preceded by a criminal complaint. Basically, the would-be arresting officer needs to convince a judge that a crime has been committed before an arrest warrant will be issued. The complaint serves as a basis for issuing an arrest warrant. The same logic applies if a private party complains as to someone's presumed involvement in criminal activity. In such a situation, an officer will probably investigate the private party's complaint and, if it is meritorious, the officer will apply for a warrant.

Once a person has been arrested, be it with or without a warrant, he or she will be booked at the arresting officer's police station or the sheriff's station (i.e., sheriffs usually run jails). **Booking** consists of filling out paperwork as to who was arrested, the time of the arrest, and the offense involved. Next, the arrestee's personal items will be inventoried. The arrestee may also be photographed and fingerprinted, depending on the offense and the jurisdiction involved. Finally, the arrestee will be placed in a holding cell, jail cell, or similar confinement facility and allowed to contact counsel, family, friends, and other individuals, as needed. (Contrary to popular depictions, more than one phone call is typically allowed.)

THE INITIAL APPEARANCE

Once arrested and booked, the suspect is then brought before a magistrate or judge in what is known as the **initial appearance**. Not all jurisdictions require an initial appearance (also referred to as *presentment*), but for those that do, the suspect must be brought before a judge in a relatively short period of time. Delays of more than six hours are usually unacceptable; they may be necessary on occasion, however, if the time of arrest precludes appearance before a judge (e.g., 1 a.m. on Monday).

The initial appearance is designed to serve a number of purposes. In a misdemeanor case, such as minor in possession, the trial may take place at this stage. In a more serious case, however, the accused will be advised of:

- the reason he or she is being detained (notification of formal charges often comes later at arraignment),
- his or her protection against self-incrimination, and
- his or her right to appointed counsel, if need be. The judge may also set bail at the initial appearance, but the bail determination often requires a separate hearing. (For ease of exposition, this chapter treats the bail determination as its own hearing, independent of the initial appearance.)

The initial appearance is usually swift and subject to few procedural constraints. In fact, only one Supreme Court decision has dealt explicitly with the initial appearance. In *Rothgery v. Gillespie County* (554 U.S. 191 [2008]), the Court held that the Sixth Amendment right to counsel applies at the initial appearance (we look closer at this decision in Chapter 13). In contrast, the probable cause, bail, and preliminary hearings have received much more of the Court's attention.

THE PROBABLE CAUSE HEARING

Gerstein v. Pugh
(420 U.S. 103 [1975])

In *Gerstein v. Pugh* (420 U.S. 103 [1975]), the Supreme Court held that the Fourth Amendment requires a so-called **probable cause hearing** either before or promptly after arrest.[1] A probable cause hearing *before* an arrest usually results in an arrest warrant being issued. Recall that an arrest warrant is issued based on a judge's determination as to whether probable cause is in place. No hearing to determine probable cause after such an arrest is necessary because it would be redundant. However, when an arrest is made *without* a warrant, then a probable cause determination must often be made. The purpose of the probable cause hearing is, in essence, to determine whether there is probable cause to keep a person detained.

---

[1] Probable cause hearings are not required in certain jurisdictions.

The *Gerstein* decision challenged the preliminary hearing system in Florida. Probable cause was determined at preliminary hearings in that state, but those hearings were not required until 30 days after arrest. Basically, a person could be held following a warrantless arrest for 30 days, sometimes longer. The Court held that such a lengthy detention required a judicial determination of probable cause *early on*:

> [W]hile the State's reasons for taking summary action subside, the suspect's need for a neutral determination of probable cause increases significantly. The consequences of prolonged detention may be more serious than the interference occasioned by arrest. Pretrial confinement may imperil the suspect's job, interrupt his source of income, and impair his family's relationship. . . . When the stakes are this high, the detached judgment of a neutral magistrate is essential if the Fourth Amendment is to furnish meaningful protection from unfounded interference with liberty. (p. 114)

The Court decided, in essence, that the prosecutor's decision to charge is not in itself enough to satisfy the probable cause requirement. However, the Court also noted that a probable cause hearing is *not* required after every arrest. An arrest with a warrant, as noted, need not be followed by a probable cause hearing. Likewise, when an arrest is based on a grand jury indictment, a probable cause hearing is not required, either. The logic for this is that the grand jury performs an investigative function, makes its probable cause determination, and then issues its indictment. Finally, if the detention in question is relatively short, such as when a preliminary hearing follows shortly after arrest, a probable cause hearing will not be required.

Procedural Issues Surrounding the Hearing

The lower court's decisions leading up to the Supreme Court's decision in *Gerstein* required that a probable cause hearing resemble an adversarial trial, complete with counsel, compulsory process, and the like. The Supreme Court reversed the lower courts' decisions as to these issues, declaring that the probable cause hearing is a not a "critical stage" of the criminal process. In support of its decision, the Court observed:

> Criminal justice is already overburdened by the volume of cases and the complexities of our system. The processing of misdemeanors, in particular, and the early stages of prosecution generally are marked by delays that can seriously affect the quality of justice. A constitutional doctrine requiring adversary hearings for all persons detained pending trial could exacerbate the problem of pretrial delay. (p. 122, n. 23)

Timing of the Hearing

The Court, in *Gerstein*, required that if it is to be held, the probable cause hearing must take place "promptly after arrest." It did not define what was meant by *promptly*, but in *Riverside County v. McLaughlin* (500 U.S. 44 [1991]), the Court offered some clarification. In a 5 to 4 decision, the Court held that a hearing that takes place within 48 hours of arrest conforms to Fourth Amendment requirements:

Riverside County v. McLaughlin (500 U.S. 44 [1991])

> In order to satisfy *Gerstein*'s promptness requirement, a jurisdiction that chooses to combine probable cause determinations with other pretrial proceedings must do so as soon as is reasonably feasible, but in no event later than 48 hours after arrest. Providing a probable cause determination

within that time frame will, as a general matter, immunize such a jurisdiction from systemic challenges. Although a hearing within 48 hours may nonetheless violate *Gerstein* if the arrested individual can prove that his or her probable cause determination was delayed unreasonably, courts evaluating the reasonableness of a delay must allow a substantial degree of flexibility, taking into account the practical realities of pretrial procedures. Where an arrested individual does not receive a probable cause determination within 48 hours, the burden of proof shifts to the government to demonstrate the existence of a bona fide emergency or other extraordinary circumstance, which cannot include intervening weekends or the fact that in a particular case it may take longer to consolidate pretrial proceedings. (p. 44)

Acceptable excuses for delay include "unavoidable delays in transporting arrested persons from one facility to another, handling late-night bookings where no magistrate is readily available, [and] obtaining the presence of an arresting officer who may be busy processing other suspects or securing the premises of an arrest" (p. 57). Unacceptable reasons for delay, by contrast, include the need to gather additional evidence to support the arrest in hindsight and issues of bad faith, such as to inconvenience an individual and make him or her wait for no legitimate reason.

DECISION-MAKING EXERCISE 10.1

The Probable Cause Hearing

Conner Case was arrested for robbery. He was taken to the police station, booked, and placed in detention. The police department maintains a policy that arrestees may be detained in the city detention facility at the request of an investigatory officer without having formal charges filed against them. Persons who are so detained are said to be "on hold." The main reason for doing so is to stage a lineup, in which a witness or a complainant can view and identify the suspect. If the arrestee is suspected of committing multiple offenses, the police department will hold several lineups, extending the period of detention longer than usual. The average time for investigative hold is 26 hours if no charges are filed and 35 hours if charges are filed. Case was held for 35 hours. He is now suing pursuant to 42 U.S.C. Section 1983, claiming that the police violated his Fourth Amendment rights and denied him a prompt probable cause hearing. In particular, he claims that the only valid reasons for delaying a probable cause hearing are those associated with transporting arrestees to the police station, booking them into the jail, and filing charges. How should the court rule?

DECISION-MAKING EXERCISE 10.2

Timing of the Probable Cause Hearing

With probable cause, Officer Jones arrested three men for impersonating police officers. The men were brought to the police station at 4:30 a.m. and subsequently fingerprinted, photographed, and given breathalyzer tests. The test results showed that all three men were legally intoxicated, with blood-alcohol levels well above the legal limit. The police department maintains a policy that arrestees with blood-alcohol levels of over 0.05 cannot be interviewed until they are sober, so the three men were placed into custody. Eighteen hours later, after sobering up, they were interviewed. All charges against them were dropped following the interviews. The three men sued Officer Jones under Section 1983, arguing that they were denied a prompt probable cause hearing. How should the court rule?

PRETRIAL RELEASE

Once a person has been arrested, the question as to whether he or she should be temporarily released (either via bail or on his or her own recognizance) invariably comes up. On the one hand, if the arrestee does not pose a significant risk of flight and has been arrested for a relatively minor offense, **pretrial release** seems a sensible approach. On the other hand, if the arrestee is likely to fail to appear in later proceedings, he or she should probably be jailed, pending additional court proceedings.

The Eighth Amendment states, "Excessive bail shall not be required." This simply means that bail cannot be set ridiculously high. Not everyone enjoys a constitutional right to bail, however. In capital cases, for example, bail has always been denied. Consider what the Supreme Court stated in *Carlson v. Landon* (342 U.S. 524 [1952]): "In England, [the Bail] clause has never been thought to accord a right to bail in all cases, but merely to provide that bail shall not be excessive in those cases where it is proper to grant bail. When this clause was carried over into our Bill of Rights, nothing was said that indicated any different concept" (p. 545).

Critics of some courts' decisions to deny bail have argued that because the U.S. criminal justice system presumes innocence, everyone should be released. After all, a defendant cannot be considered guilty until the state proves his or her guilt beyond a reasonable doubt. However, in *Bell v. Wolfish* (441 U.S. 520 [1979]), the Supreme Court stated that the presumption of innocence is merely "a doctrine that allocates the burden of proof in criminal trials" (p. 533).[2]

It is also important to point out that the Eighth Amendment prohibition against excessive bail *has not* been incorporated to the states. For example, in *Murphy v. Hunt* (455 U.S. 478 [1982]), a detainee sued under Section 1983 (see Chapter 2), claiming that his Eighth Amendment right was violated. The Supreme Court held that his suit was moot because he was convicted in Nebraska state court. This important decision, coupled with the realization that the Eighth Amendment's excessive bail provision has not been incorporated, explains some of the discrepancies in bail decisions.

The Pretrial Release Hearing

The Constitution does not specify whether bail should be set in a separate hearing, but numerous Court decisions seem to suggest a separate hearing is warranted. For example, in *Stack v. Boyle* (342 U.S. 1 [1951]), the Court stated that as part of the bail determination, the judge should consider "the nature and circumstances of the offense charged, the weight of the evidence against [the accused], [and] the financial ability of the defendant to give bail and the character of the defendant" (p. 6, n. 3). The Court also stated:

Stack v. Boyle
(342 U.S. 1 [1951])

> Since the function of bail is limited, the fixing of bail for any individual defendant must be based upon standards relevant to the purpose of assuring the presence of that defendant. The traditional standards as expressed in the Federal Rules of Criminal Procedure ... are to be applied in each case to each defendant.... It is not denied that bail for each petitioner has been fixed in a sum much higher than that usually imposed for offenses with like penalties and yet there has been no factual showing to justify such action in this case. The Government asks the courts to depart from the norm by assuming, without the introduction of evidence, that each petitioner is a pawn in a conspiracy and will, in obedience to a superior, flee the jurisdiction. To infer

---

[2] Note that some states have preset bail schedules for low-level offenses. For these states, some of the following discussion is not applicable.

from the fact of indictment alone a need for bail in an unusually high amount is an arbitrary act. Such conduct would inject into our own system of government the very principles of totalitarianism which Congress was seeking to guard against in passing the statute under which petitioners have been indicted. (pp. 5–6)

Assuming a bail hearing is required, it is also not clear whether a simple probable cause–type hearing is all that is needed or if a more adversarial proceeding is necessary. Since bail is set once charges have already been filed, it would seem that, at a minimum, counsel should be provided. In fact, in *United States v. Salerno* (481 U.S. 739 [1987]), the Court concluded that a federal preventive detention statute that provided for counsel, evidence presentation, and cross-examination was acceptable, but it did not state whether such rights should be afforded to the accused in every bail hearing. Thus, the question of what type of bail hearing is required, if any, remains unanswered. In some situations (and in certain jurisdictions), the bail decision is made during another hearing, such as the initial appearance.

The Pretrial Release Decision

The pretrial release decision has traditionally taken one of three forms. The first, and most common, results in release on bail. This is when the court collects a deposit from the individual being released in order to ensure that he or she will appear for later hearings. Second, some arrestees are released on their own recognizance, which means they simply promise to show up when required. Finally, in recent years, the courts have adopted a policy of preventive detention for certain individuals, which involves a calculation as to the arrestee's level of dangerousness and flight risk. Release is denied to those individuals likely to pose a threat to others or not likely to appear at their scheduled hearings.

RELEASE ON BAIL Pretrial release with **bail** is a common practice. Indeed, 18 U.S.C. Section 3142 provides that "upon all arrests in criminal cases, bail shall be admitted, except where the punishment may be death." Most states have adopted similar language in their constitutions. California's constitution, for example, provides that "all persons shall be bailable by sufficient sureties, unless for capital offenses when the proof is evidence or the presumption great" (Cal. Const. Art. I, Section 6). There is variability from state to state, however, because, once again, the Eighth Amendment's excessive bail provision has not been incorporated to the states through the due process clause of the Fourteenth Amendment.

The bail decision is sometimes problematic. More often than not, a judge sets bail according to the nature of the offense in question, not according to the accused's ability to pay.[3] The frequent result of this is that indigent defendants—no matter what they are accused of—languish in jail cells until their court dates because they cannot afford to post bail.

In response to many defendants' inability to post bail, the professional **bail bond agent** has stepped in.[4] These individuals collect a fee from the accused, usually a percentage of bail, and then post a bond so the accused can be released. If the accused shows up at trial, the agent collects his or her fee and gets his or her money

---

[3] See, for example, M. Paulsen, "Pre-Trial Release in the United States," *Columbia Law Review* 66 (1966): 109–125, 113.

[4] Not all states have bail bonds agents.

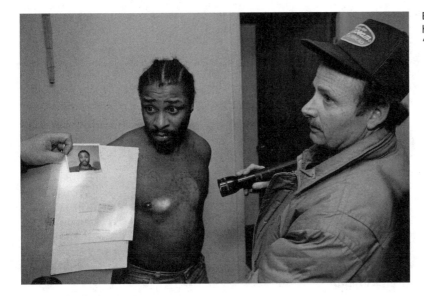

Bail bonds agents sometimes employ bounty hunters to apprehend individuals who have "skipped" bail.

back from the court. If the accused fails to show up, then the agent loses the amount posted. In order to avoid such an eventuality, bail bonds agents employ *bounty hunters*, whose job it is to catch the accused and bring him or her before the court. There is a misperception, however, that bail bonds agents can with impunity do whatever it takes to apprehend those who "skip" bail. Indeed, in response to concerns that such agents have been given too much authority, some states have adopted legislation to restrict their activities. Texas is perhaps most restrictive. Figure 10.1 reprints a Texas statute that sets forth the procedures bail bonds agents must follow to rearrest those who skip bail.

It is important to note an important flaw inherent in the bail bonds agent system. The problem is that the agents, not the courts, gain a certain degree of power. Regardless of what amount the court sets as bail, bonds agents can then decide who gets released or who stays in jail based on the accused's ability to pay. Those who can pay the fee effectively buy their freedom, if only temporarily. Those who cannot pay stay in jail. The courts sit on the sidelines, essentially, while the whole bail bonds process plays out. As described in the decision for *Pannell v. United States* (320 F.2d 698 [D.C.Cir. 1963]):

> Certainly the professional bondsman system as used in this District is odious at best. The effect of such a system is that the professional bondsmen hold the keys to the jail in their pockets. They determine for whom they will act as surety—who in their judgment is a good risk. The bad risks, in the bondsmen's judgment, and the ones who are unable to pay the bondsmen's fees, remain in jail. The court and the commissioner are relegated to the relatively unimportant chore of fixing the amount of bail. The result of this system in the District of Columbia is that most defendants, for months on end, languish in jail unable to make bond awaiting disposition of their cases. Instead of being allowed the opportunity of obtaining worthwhile employment to support their families, and perhaps to pay at least in part for their defense, almost 90 percent of the defendants proceed in forma pauperis, thus casting an unfair burden on the members of the bar of this community who are required to represent these defendants without pay. (p. 699)

FIGURE 10.1

Example of Bail Bonds Agent Rearrest Procedures

(a) Any [bail bond agent], desiring to [apprehend] his [bond recipient] and after notifying the [bond recipient's] attorney, if the [bond recipient] is represented by an attorney, in a manner provided by Rule 21a, Texas Rules of Civil Procedure, of the [bail bond agent's] intention to surrender the [bond recipient], may file an affidavit of such intention before the court or magistrate before which the prosecution is pending. The affidavit must state:

  (1) the court and cause number of the case;
  (2) the name of the defendant;
  (3) the offense with which the defendant is charged;
  (4) the date of the bond;
  (5) the cause for the [apprehension]; and
  (6) that notice of the [bail bond agent's] intention to surrender the [bond recipient] has been given as required by this subsection.

(b) If the court or magistrate finds that there is cause for the [bail bond agent] to [apprehend] his [bond recipient], the court shall issue a warrant of arrest for the [bond recipient]. It is an affirmative defense to any liability on the bond that:

  (1) the court or magistrate refused to issue a warrant of arrest for the principal; and
  (2) after the refusal to issue the warrant the [bond recipient] failed to appear.

(c) If the court or magistrate before whom the prosecution is pending is not available, the [bail bond agent] may deliver the affidavit to any other magistrate in the county and that magistrate, on a finding of cause for the [bail bond agent] to [apprehend] his [bond recipient], shall issue a warrant of arrest for the [bond recipient].

(d) An arrest warrant issued under this article shall be issued to the sheriff of the county in which the case is pending, and a copy of the warrant shall be issued to the [bail bond agent] or his agent.

(e) An arrest warrant issued under this article may be executed by a peace officer, a security officer, or a private investigator licensed in this state.

Source: Adapted from Texas Code of Criminal Procedures, Chapter 17, Article 17.19 (2002).

RELEASE ON ONE'S OWN RECOGNIZANCE Even though release on bail is the most common form of pretrial release, the courts have experimented with releasing people on their own recognizance. **Release on recognizance (ROR)** means that the accused is released with the assumption that he or she will show up for scheduled court hearings. Naturally, then, this method of pretrial release is reserved for those individuals who pose a minimal risk of flight.

New York City's Manhattan Bail Project was the first significant effort to explore the possibilities of ROR. This program, administered by the Vera Institute, focused on indigent defendants who, according to carefully set criteria, posed a minimal flight risk. Among the criteria considered were previous convictions, the nature of the offense, whether the accused was employed, and whether the accused had roots in the community (e.g., a family to go back to). The program was a resounding success: Only 1.6 percent of those individuals recommended for ROR intentionally failed to appear at court.

DECISION-MAKING EXERCISE 10.3

Amount of Bail

Mike Rhodes has been arrested for the crime of robbery, which carries a possible life sentence. The judge sets bail in the amount of $100,000. Rhodes has $12 to his name and no assets. (He rides the bus and lives with his parents.) As such, he cannot even afford the 10 percent deposit typically required to secure a bail bond. His only recourse is to sue under 42 U.S.C. Section 1983, claiming that his Fourteenth Amendment right to equal protection was violated when the judge set bail well beyond his means. Should his lawsuit succeed?

The results of the Manhattan Bail Project prompted other cities around the United States to adopt similar programs. And in 1984, Congress passed the federal Bail Reform Act, which provided that any person charged with a noncapital offense "be ordered released pending trial on his personal recognizance or upon the execution of an unsecured appearance bond in an amount specified by the judicial officer, unless the officer determines . . . that such a release will not reasonably assure the appearance of the person as required" (18 U.S.C. Sections 3146–3152).

An important feature of this new legislation was that bail was to be considered only as one of many options to ensure the accused's appearance at trial. Among the other options were restrictions on travel and association, along with other conditions that would ensure the appearance of the accused (see 18 U.S.C. Section 3146[a]). The Bail Reform Act also provided that when bail was to be used, the money should be deposited with the court, not with a bail bonds agent.

The Bail Reform Act further provided that

> the judge shall . . . take into account the available information concerning: the nature and the circumstances of the offense charged, the weight of evidence against the accused, the accused's family ties, employment, financial resources, character and mental condition, the length of his residence in the community, his record of convictions, and his record of appearances at court proceedings or of flight to avoid prosecution or failure to appear at court proceedings. (Section 3146[b])

This is in stark contrast to the notion that judges simply consider the nature of the offense in setting bail.

While the federal government and many states still release people on their own recognizance, this practice is not regularly relied on for serious offenses. In fact, when the offense in question is serious and the accused presents a significant risk of flight, bail may be altogether denied, as the following subsection attests.

PREVENTIVE DETENTION: DENYING PRETRIAL RELEASE Growing concern over crimes committed by defendants out on pretrial release prompted some reforms. In 1970, for example, the District of Columbia passed the first **preventive detention** statute, which authorized denial of bail to dangerous persons charged with certain offenses for up to 60 days (D.C. Code 1970 Section 23-1322). Then, Congress passed the federal Bail Reform Act of 1984 (18 U.S.C. Sections 3141–3150), which authorized judges to revoke pretrial release for firearms possession, failure to comply with curfew, and failure to comply with other conditions of release. The act also permitted detention for up to 10 days of an individual who "may flee or pose a danger to any other person or the community" (Section 3142[d]).

Somewhat controversially, the Bail Reform Act of 1984 permitted pretrial detention for *more than* 10 days of certain individuals. Thus, according to the act, if it is deemed that no pretrial release condition "will reasonably assure the appearance of the person as required and the safety of any other person and the community," then indefinite detention is acceptable. For a detention of this nature to conform to Fourth and Eighth Amendment restrictions, a hearing must be held to determine whether the case "involves a serious risk that the person will flee; [or] a serious risk that the person will obstruct or attempt to obstruct justice, or threaten, injure, or intimidate, a prospective witness or jury" (Section 3142[f]).

Criteria for Release

As indicated already, the Constitution does not guarantee the right to bail. Some people are denied bail, and others are granted bail. What criteria influence a judge's decision? Three factors are typically considered: (1) the accused's flight risk, (2) the level of dangerousness of the accused, and (3) the accused's financial status.

FLIGHT RISK   In *Stack v. Boyle*, the Supreme Court declared that the purpose of bail is to ensure the accused's appearance at trial:

> Like the ancient practice of securing the oaths of responsible persons to stand as sureties for the accused, the modern practice of requiring a bail bond or the deposit of a sum of money subject to forfeiture serves as additional assurance of the presence of an accused. . . . Since the function of bail is limited, the fixing of bail for any individual defendant must be based upon standards relevant to the purpose of assuring the presence of that defendant. (p. 5)

This does not mean, though, that a judge can set an unrealistic bail amount, in light of the Eighth Amendment's admonition:

> Admission to bail always involves a risk that the accused will take flight. That is a calculated risk which the law takes as the price of our system of justice . . . . In allowance of bail, the duty of the judge is to reduce the risk by fixing an amount reasonably calculated to hold the accused available for trial and its consequence. But the judge is not free to make the sky the limit, because the Eighth Amendment to the Constitution says: "Excessive bail shall not be required." (p. 8)

In short, a delicate balance needs to be struck to ensure the accused's appearance at trial. Bail should be set at an amount designed to minimize the risk of flight, yet the amount set should not be so much that the accused cannot reasonably afford to pay it, either by cash or by bond.

DECISION-MAKING EXERCISE 10.4
Preventive Detention

The Bail Reform Act of 1984 provided that judges can deny bail to certain individuals charged with specific crimes and after finding that "no condition or combination of conditions [attaching to release] will reasonably assure the appearance of the person as required and the safety of any other person and the community" (18 U.S.C. Section 3142[e]). Marty Corelli is a drug kingpin charged with serious narcotics offenses and is presumed to be a significant flight risk. Accordingly, the judge denies bail to Corelli, thereby requiring him to remain in jail until his trial. Is this action constitutional?

DANGEROUSNESS   Aside from the obvious risk of flight, some defendants are particularly dangerous individuals. Thus, the courts sometimes see fit either to deny bail or to set the amount relatively high because of perceived dangerousness. In *United States v. Salerno*, the Supreme Court dealt with a challenge to the Bail Reform Act of 1984 that, among other things, dangerousness cannot be considered. In the Court's words:

> Nothing in the text of the Bail Clause [of the Eighth Amendment] limits permissible government considerations solely to questions of flight. The only arguable substantive limitation of the Bail Clause is that the Government's proposed conditions of release or detention not be "excessive" in light of the perceived evil . . . . [W]hen the government has admitted that its only interest is in preventing flight, bail must be set by a court at a sum designed to ensure that goal, and no more . . . . We believe that when Congress has mandated detention on the basis of a compelling interest other than prevention of flight, as it has here, the Eighth Amendment does not require release on bail. (p. 754)

The issue of dangerousness, as it pertains to the bail decision, also came up in the case of *Schall v. Martin* (467 U.S. 253 [1984]). There, the Supreme Court upheld a statute that provided for detention of a juvenile who posed a serious risk of committing a crime while on release. The statute was criticized as essentially amounting to punishment without trial, but the Court decided that *punishment* only exists when the government's *intent* is to punish. And since the purpose of the state's detention policy was not to punish but rather to protect the community from a dangerous individual, it was deemed constitutional. Of course, given the problems inherent in predicting criminal behavior, the Court's argument is somewhat specious.

Schall v. Martin
(467 U.S. 253 [1984])

FINANCIAL STATUS   The courts usually take into account the accused's financial status in making a bail decision. Failure to do so can lead to irrational bail determinations. For example, if bail is set at a fixed amount, a poor individual will have a considerably more difficult time coming up with the required funds than a wealthy individual. Perhaps more important, if the wealthy individual views the amount as a "drop in the bucket," then he or she may not be motivated to show up for trial.

Surprisingly, bail can be denied simply because the accused is unable to pay it. In *Schilb v. Kuebel* (404 U.S. 357 [1971]), the Supreme Court took it upon itself to decide on the constitutionality of a state statute that provided that a criminal defendant who was not released on his or her own recognizance could (1) deposit 10 percent of the amount of set bail with the court, 10 percent of which would be forfeited to the court as *bail bonds costs*, or (2) pay the full amount of bail, all of which would be refunded if the accused showed up at court. The defendant argued that the statute unfairly targeted indigent individuals because they were forced to choose the first option. However, the Supreme Court upheld the statute because "[i]t should be obvious that the poor man's real hope and avenue for relief is the personal recognizance provision" (p. 369). Furthermore, in the words of the Court, "[I]t is by no means clear that [the second option, paying the full amount,] is more attractive to the affluent defendant" (p. 370).

Schilb v. Kuebel
(404 U.S. 357 [1971])

Treatment of Pretrial Detainees

The Supreme Court has dealt with several cases alleging unconstitutional conditions at pretrial detention facilities. For example, in *Bell v. Wolfish* (441 U.S. 520 [1979]), the Court upheld several of the rules promulgated by New York City's Metropolitan Correctional Center (MCC), including rules prohibiting inmates from receiving books from entities other than publishers, bookstores, and book clubs, as well as outside

Bell v. Wolfish
(441 U.S. 520 [1979])

packages. The Court also upheld unannounced searches of living quarters but was careful to state that when such prohibitions are intended to punish (i.e., instead of to serve some legitimate governmental purpose, such as to ensure the safety and security of inmates), they can violate due process. Quoting the Court:

> [If] a particular condition or restriction of pretrial detention is reasonably related to a legitimate governmental objective, it does not, without more, amount to "punishment." Conversely, if a restriction or condition is not reasonably related to a legitimate goal—if it is arbitrary or purposeless—a court permissibly may infer that the purpose of the governmental action is punishment that may not constitutionally be inflicted upon detainees *qua* detainees. (p. 539)

In one case, a pretrial detainee argued that unannounced searches of his cell violated the Fourth Amendment. The Court concluded, however, in *Hudson v. Palmer* (468 U.S. 517 [1984]), that prisoners do not enjoy a reasonable expectation of privacy in their cells:

> A prisoner has no reasonable expectation of privacy in his prison cell entitling him to the protection of the Fourth Amendment against unreasonable searches. While prisoners enjoy many protections of the Constitution that are not fundamentally inconsistent with imprisonment itself or incompatible with the objectives of incarceration, imprisonment carries with it the circumscription or loss of many rights as being necessary to accommodate the institutional needs and objectives of prison facilities, particularly internal security and safety. It would be impossible to accomplish the prison objectives of preventing the introduction of weapons, drugs, and other contraband into the premises if inmates retained a right of privacy in their cells. The unpredictability that attends random searches of cells renders such searches perhaps the most effective weapon of the prison administrator in the fight against the proliferation of weapons, drugs, and other contraband.

DECISION-MAKING EXERCISE 10.5

Financial Status and Bail Determination

A prosecution for mail fraud against a postal worker resulted in her conviction. During the trial, the defendant was 30 minutes late in returning after a recess, which the judge had granted so the defendant could go to her office to gather evidence for the defense. Because she was late, the judge ordered her to be held in jail for the balance of the trial. She had not been held in jail prior to the judge's decision. Is this action constitutional?

DECISION-MAKING EXERCISE 10.6

Treatment of Pretrial Detainees

Several pretrial detainees at the county jail brought a class action in federal district court against the county sheriff and other officials, claiming that the jail's policy of denying pretrial detainees contact visits with their spouses, relatives, children, and friends violates due process. Should pretrial detainees be constitutionally entitled to contact visits of this nature? If so, why?

A requirement that random searches be conducted pursuant to an established plan would seriously undermine the effectiveness of this weapon. (p. 517)

Furthermore, "society would insist that the prisoner's expectation of privacy always yield to what must be considered the paramount interest in institutional security" (p. 528). Prison guards, then, can seize "any articles which, in their view, disserve legitimate institutional interests" (p. 528, n. 8).

THE PRELIMINARY HEARING

The **preliminary hearing** is to be distinguished from the initial appearance, the probable cause hearing, and the pretrial release hearing. It almost always takes place after one of these hearings as well as after the charging decision. According to the decision in *Thies v. State* (178 Wis. 98 [1922]), the preliminary hearing is intended to prevent "hasty, malicious, improvident, and oppressive prosecutions" and to ensure that "there are substantial grounds upon which a prosecution may be based" (p. 103). Finally, the preliminary hearing resembles a criminal trial in that it is usually adversarial.

Just as the Constitution does not require a bail hearing, neither is a preliminary hearing required. This was the decision reached in *Lem Woon v. Oregon* (229 U.S. 586 [1913]) and reaffirmed in *Gerstein v. Pugh*. Thus, it is up to each state to determine if such a hearing is warranted.

Lem Woon v. Oregon (229 U.S. 586 [1913])

Fortunately, most states, as well as the federal government, require preliminary hearings, at least to a certain extent. Whether a preliminary hearing is required typically depends on a jurisdiction's method of filing criminal charges. In grand jury indictment jurisdictions (i.e., those that *require* that charges be filed in the form of a grand jury indictment), if the prosecutor secures an indictment within a specified time period, no preliminary hearing is required. However, if a prosecutor proceeds by information, then the defendant will usually be entitled to a preliminary hearing before the charges are filed.

Whether a jurisdiction proceeds by indictment or information has important implications concerning the defendant's rights. As discussed further in Chapter 11, the defendant does *not* enjoy the right to counsel during a grand jury proceeding. The defendant does not even enjoy the right to challenge the state's case. In a preliminary hearing, however, both rights exist. Thus, a zealous prosecutor in a jurisdiction that provides for either an indictment or an information-charging decision may opt for indictment because the accused will enjoy fewer rights. Of course, this issue may be moot because accused individuals can and often do waive their right to a preliminary hearing.

The Probable Cause Requirement

Assuming a preliminary hearing is required, the prosecutor has the burden of proving that the case should be *bound over* (i.e., handed over) to a grand jury or go to trial. The standard of proof is *probable cause*. Invariably, this step is confused with the probable cause hearing. The two hearings can be distinguished as follows: A probable cause hearing dwells on the justification to arrest, whereas a preliminary hearing dwells on whether probable cause exists to proceed with a trial. This is a critical distinction and is often responsible for holding separate probable cause and preliminary hearings in certain states.

The reason for setting probable cause as the appropriate standard for a preliminary hearing is that setting a *higher* standard would essentially make trial pointless.

To require proof beyond a reasonable doubt, for example, would make holding a later criminal trial redundant. On the other hand, some people favor having more proof than probable cause because once a probable cause hearing has taken place, the preliminary hearing seems somewhat redundant. To minimize some of the confusion, one court observed that "probable cause to arrest does not automatically mean that the Commonwealth has sufficient competent legal evidence to justify the costs both to the defendant and to the Commonwealth of a full trial" (*Myers v. Commonwealth*, 363 Mass. 843 [1973], p. 849).

Basically, the prosecutor needs to convince the judge that there is enough evidence to proceed with a trial. More specifically, there must be enough evidence to make a judge or jury contemplate which case is more convincing: that of the prosecution or the defense. If it is clear that the state has no case but perhaps had probable cause for arrest, the court will order that the would-be defendant be released.

Procedural Issues

Coleman v. Alabama
(399 U.S. 1 [1970])

Since a preliminary hearing is adversarial in nature, it seems sensible that the right to counsel should apply. According to the Supreme Court, in *Coleman v. Alabama* (399 U.S. 1 [1970]), it does, and the state must provide counsel if the accused is indigent. The Court declared that the preliminary hearing is a critical stage of the criminal process: "Plainly the guiding hand of counsel at the preliminary hearing is essential to protect the indigent accused against an erroneous and improper prosecution" (p. 9).

Evidence procedures in a preliminary hearing are markedly different than those in a criminal trial. First, the *Federal Rules of Criminal Procedure* allow hearsay evidence in preliminary hearings, though not explicitly.[5] By contrast, *hearsay evidence* (i.e., what one person previously heard and then repeats while testifying in court) is restricted in a criminal trial. Also, the exclusionary rule does not technically apply in preliminary hearings. Actually, it is not so much that the rule does not apply but rather that the preliminary hearing is an inappropriate stage of the criminal process in which to object to evidence. As the *Federal Rules of Criminal Procedure* also state, the defendant "may not object to evidence on the ground that it was unlawfully acquired."[6] (Note that the *Federal Rules of Criminal Procedure* apply to federal courts, not state courts. So some states may maintain different procedures.)

Another procedural matter in the preliminary hearing concerns the right to cross-examine witnesses as well as to use compulsory process to require their appearance. While these rights exist at criminal trials, preliminary hearings restrict them somewhat. In fact, the Supreme Court stated that there is no constitutional right to cross-examine at the preliminary hearing (*Goldsby v. United States*, 160 U.S. 70 [1895]). The court has discretion over the extent of cross-examination, but the bulk of it is reserved for trial.

Some have expressed concern that too much cross-examination at a preliminary hearing may turn it into a full-blown criminal trial. But one court has stated that "past experience indicates that trial strategy usually prevents such a result as both the prosecution and the defense wish to withhold as much of their case as possible" (*Myers v. Commonwealth*). Furthermore, "defense tactics usually mitigate against putting the defendant on the stand or presenting exculpatory testimony at the preliminary hearing unless defense counsel believes this evidence is compelling enough to overcome the prosecution's case" (pp. 856–857).

---

[5] The hearsay language was removed from the *Federal Rules* in 2002, but the Advisory Committee notes make it clear that hearsay can still be admitted. See http://www.law.cornell.edu/rules/frcrmp/NRule5_1.htm (accessed November 5, 2008).
[6] *Federal Rules of Criminal Procedure*, Rule 5.1(e). Available online at http://www.law.cornell.edu/rules/frcrmp/

DECISION-MAKING EXERCISE 10.7

Preliminary Hearings

Assume that a jurisdiction maintains a policy that people charged with misdemeanors will not be given preliminary hearings. Is such a restriction constitutional?

THE ARRAIGNMENT

Once a person has been formally charged, he or she will be arraigned. The purpose of the **arraignment** is to formally notify the defendant of the charge lodged against him or her. Also at the arraignment, the defendant enters one of three pleas: (1) **guilty**; (2) **not guilty**; or (3) **nolo contendere**. A plea of guilty is an admission by the defendant of every allegation in the indictment or information. Such a plea may be entered for a number of reasons. For example, the defendant may simply elect to be honest and admit responsibility. The defendant may also plead guilty after having made a plea agreement with the prosecution. (Plea bargaining is covered in Chapter 12.)

A plea of not guilty is fairly self-explanatory. The defendant formally contends that he or she did not commit the crime in question. A plea of not guilty will result in a full-blown criminal trial, especially for a serious crime. Finally, a plea of *nolo contendere* means, "I do not desire to contest the action." It resembles a guilty plea but is different in the sense that it may not be used against the defendant in any later civil litigation that arises from the acts that led to the criminal charge. Also, in some jurisdictions, if the defendant enters a plea of *nolo contendere*, the court may not ask the defendant whether he or she committed the crime in question. But with a guilty plea, the defendant is required to allocute. **Allocution** is when the defendant explains to the judge exactly what he or she did and why. The allocution is documented in court records and can be used against the defendant in related civil proceedings.

SUMMARY OF PRETRIAL PROCEEDINGS

So far, the discussion has distinguished among five potential pretrial proceedings: (1) the initial appearance; (2) the probable cause hearing; (3) the pretrial release hearing; (4) the preliminary hearing; and (5) the arraignment. The initial appearance usually always takes place, regardless of the method of arrest or even of the charges in question, but it is not constitutionally required. Indeed, for a misdemeanor, the trial may take place at this stage.

The probable cause hearing is also not *required* by the Constitution. Nevertheless, a probable cause determination needs to be made at some stage of the criminal process. If the arrest is by warrant, the hearing is not necessary. If the arrest is warrantless, then a probable cause hearing is necessary but only if a preliminary hearing is not set to take place immediately. Also, if the arrest is premised on a grand jury indictment, a probable cause hearing will not be necessary. In short, the purpose of the probable cause hearing is to avoid unnecessarily lengthy detention unsupported by probable cause.

A few court decisions seem to suggest that a separate pretrial release hearing is required, but the Supreme Court has offered no clarification on this matter. And as a practical matter, it is sometimes worthwhile to make the bail decision in another hearing, such as the initial appearance. Today, whether a bail hearing is required hinges on the jurisdiction in question and the nature of the offense.

Finally, the preliminary hearing is required but only in limited circumstances and for certain offenses—usually felonies. If a prosecutor obtains a grand jury indictment within a short period of time, a preliminary hearing may not be necessary. On the other hand, if the prosecutor proceeds with information, then a preliminary hearing may be required. Once a person has been charged with a crime, he or she will be arraigned. At the arraignment, the defendant will be notified of the charges against him or her and be allowed to enter a formal plea of guilty, not guilty, or *nolo contendere*.

DISCOVERY

If one learned of the criminal process only by watching courtroom dramas on prime-time television, his or her understanding of the process would be sorely limited. It is rarely the case that prosecutors and defense attorneys are mortal enemies or that one side springs surprise evidence on the other side. Instead, criminal (as well as civil) trials in the United States are carefully choreographed events with few unpredictable twists and turns. In fact, as many a litigator will attest, criminal trials are relatively boring and predictable. Even the most celebrated criminal trial of the 1990s, the O. J. Simpson trial, put the most attentive of observers to sleep at times.

Trials in this country are rarely exciting for several reasons. First, most prosecutors and defense attorneys are not great orators. And second, given the process of *discovery*, each side *knows* what evidence the other side will present, with few exceptions.

Discovery is the process by which each party to a case learns of the evidence that the opposition will present. The *Federal Rules of Criminal Procedure* provide that the defendant may, upon request, *discover* from the prosecution (1) any written statements or transcriptions of oral statements made by the defendant that are in the prosecution's possession; (2) the defendant's prior criminal record; and (3) documents, photographs, tangible items, results from physical and mental evaluations, and other forms of real evidence considered *material* to the prosecution's case.[7] Evidence is considered *material* if it is consequential to the case or, more simply, capable of influencing the outcome of the case. If the defense requests items in the second or third categories, then the prosecution will be granted *reciprocal discovery*, where it learns of the defense's evidence. Relevant portions of Rule 16 are reprinted in Figure 10.2.

Rule 16 of the *Federal Rules of Criminal Procedure* seems to permit a great deal of discovery, but it is actually restrictive. Several states permit even more discovery, such as the names and addresses of all persons known to have any information concerning the case. This means that the prosecution must provide the defense with a list of *all* individuals likely to give testimony at trial—and vice versa.

Discovery ends where strategy begins. That is, while both sides are given great latitude in terms of learning what evidence the opposition intends to use, strategy does not need to be shared. For example, the method of argument that the prosecution wishes to use in order to convince the jury of a particular fact is not subject to discovery. Similarly, the order in which the defense seeks to call witnesses need not be communicated to the prosecution. Strategy is also referred to as *work product*. Work product is not part of the discovery process.

The sections that follow focus on discovery by the prosecution, discovery by the defense, and constitutional issues raised in the discovery process. Be reminded that, consistent with the title of this chapter, discovery is part of the *pretrial process*. It takes place in the hours and days leading up to the criminal trial. But if, for example, a new

---

[7] *Federal Rules of Criminal Procedure*, Rule 16. Available online at http://www.law.cornell.edu/rules/frcrmp/

FIGURE 10.2

Types of Discovery under Rule 16

(a) **Government's Disclosure.**

(1) *Information Subject to Disclosure.*

(A) *Defendant's Oral Statement.*

Upon a defendant's request, the government must disclose to the defendant the substance of any relevant oral statement made by the defendant, before or after arrest, in response to interrogation by a person the defendant knew was a government agent if the government intends to use the statement at trial.

(B) *Defendant's Written or Recorded Statement.*

Upon a defendant's request, the government must disclose to the defendant, and make available for inspection, copying, or photographing, all of the following:

(i) any relevant written or recorded statement by the defendant if:
   • the statement is within the government's possession, custody, or control; and
   • the attorney for the government knows — or through due diligence could know — that the statement exists;

(ii) the portion of any written record containing the substance of any relevant oral statement made before or after arrest if the defendant made the statement in response to interrogation by a person the defendant knew was a government agent; and

(iii) the defendant's recorded testimony before a grand jury relating to the charged offense.

(C) *Organizational Defendant.*

Upon a defendant's request, if the defendant is an organization, the government must disclose to the defendant any statement described in Rule 16(a)(1)(A) and (B) if the government contends that the person making the statement:

(i) was legally able to bind the defendant regarding the subject of the statement because of that person's position as the defendant's director, officer, employee, or agent; or

(ii) was personally involved in the alleged conduct constituting the offense and was legally able to bind the defendant regarding that conduct because of that person's position as the defendant's director, officer, employee, or agent.

(D) *Defendant's Prior Record.*

Upon a defendant's request, the government must furnish the defendant with a copy of the defendant's prior criminal record that is within the government's possession, custody, or control if the attorney for the government knows—or through due diligence could know—that the record exists.

(E) *Documents and Objects.*

Upon a defendant's request, the government must permit the defendant to inspect and to copy or photograph books, papers, documents, data, photographs, tangible objects, buildings or places, or copies or portions of any of these items, if the item is within the government's possession, custody, or control and:

(i) the item is material to preparing the defense;

(ii) the government intends to use the item in its case-in-chief at trial; or

(iii) the item was obtained from or belongs to the defendant.

(F) *Reports of Examinations and Tests.*

Upon a defendant's request, the government must permit a defendant to inspect and to copy or photograph the results or reports of any physical or mental examination and of any scientific test or experiment if:

Figure 10.2 continued

> **(i)** the item is within the government's possession, custody, or control;
>
> **(ii)** the attorney for the government knows—or through due diligence could know—that the item exists; and
>
> **(iii)** the item is material to preparing the defense or the government intends to use the item in its case-in-chief at trial.

(G) *Expert Witnesses.*

At the defendant's request, the government must give to the defendant a written summary of any testimony that the government intends to use under Rules 702, 703, or 705 of the Federal Rules of Evidence during its case-in-chief at trial. If the government requests discovery under subdivision (b)(1)(C)(ii) and the defendant complies, the government must, at the defendant's request, give to the defendant a written summary of testimony that the government intends to use under Rules 702, 703, or 705 of the Federal Rules of Evidence as evidence at trial on the issue of the defendant's mental condition. The summary provided under this subparagraph must describe the witness's opinions, the bases and reasons for those opinions, and the witness's qualifications.

(2) *Information Not Subject to Disclosure.*

Except as Rule 16(a)(1) provides otherwise, this rule does not authorize the discovery or inspection of reports, memoranda, or other internal government documents made by an attorney for the government or other government agent in connection with investigating or prosecuting the case. Nor does this rule authorize the discovery or inspection of statements made by prospective government witnesses except as provided in 18 U.S.C. § 3500.

(3) *Grand Jury Transcripts.*

This rule does not apply to the discovery or inspection of a grand jury's recorded proceedings, except as provided in Rules 6, 12(h), 16(a)(1), and 26.2.

(b) Defendant's Disclosure.

(1) *Information Subject to Disclosure.*

(A) *Documents and Objects.*

If a defendant requests disclosure under Rule 16(a)(1)(E) and the government complies, then the defendant must permit the government, upon request, to inspect and to copy or photograph books, papers, documents, data, photographs, tangible objects, buildings or places, or copies or portions of any of these items if:

> **(i)** the item is within the defendant's possession, custody, or control; and
>
> **(ii)** the defendant intends to use the item in the defendant's case-in-chief at trial.

(B) *Reports of Examinations and Tests.*

If a defendant requests disclosure under Rule 16(a)(1)(F) and the government complies, the defendant must permit the government, upon request, to inspect and to copy or photograph the results or reports of any physical or mental examination and of any scientific test or experiment if:

> **(i)** the item is within the defendant's possession, custody, or control; and
>
> **(ii)** the defendant intends to use the item in the defendant's case-in-chief at trial, or intends to call the witness who prepared the report and the report relates to the witness's testimony.

(C) *Expert Witnesses.*

The defendant must, at the government's request, give to the government a written summary of any testimony that the defendant intends to use under Rules 702, 703, or 705 of the Federal Rules of Evidence as evidence at trial, if:

> **(i)** the defendant requests disclosure under subdivision (a)(1)(G) and the government complies; or
>
> **(ii)** the defendant has given notice under Rule 12.2(b) of an intent to present expert testimony on the defendant's mental condition.

This summary must describe the witness's opinions, the bases and reasons for those opinions, and the witness's qualifications[.]

(2) *Information Not Subject to Disclosure.*

Except for scientific or medical reports, <u>Rule 16(b)(1)</u> does not authorize discovery or inspection of:

(A) reports, memoranda, or other documents made by the defendant, or the defendant's attorney or agent, during the case's investigation or defense; or

(B) a statement made to the defendant, or the defendant's attorney or agent, by:

(i) the defendant;

(ii) a government or defense witness; or

(iii) a prospective government or defense witness.

(c) Continuing Duty to Disclose.

A party who discovers additional evidence or material before or during trial must promptly disclose its existence to the other party or the court if:

(1) the evidence or material is subject to discovery or inspection under this rule; and

(2) the other party previously requested, or the court ordered, its production.

(d) Regulating Discovery.

(1) *Protective and Modifying Orders.*

At any time the court may, for good cause, deny, restrict, or defer discovery or inspection, or grant other appropriate relief. The court may permit a party to show good cause by a written statement that the court will inspect ex parte. If relief is granted, the court must preserve the entire text of the party's statement under seal.

(2) *Failure to Comply.*

If a party fails to comply with this rule, the court may:

(A) order that party to permit the discovery or inspection; specify its time, place, and manner; and prescribe other just terms and conditions;

(B) grant a continuance;

(C) prohibit that party from introducing the undisclosed evidence; or

(D) enter any other order that is just under the circumstances.

Source: Federal Rules of Criminal Procedure, Rule 16. Available online: http://www.law.cornell.edu/rules/frcrmp/Rule16.htm (accessed February 16, 2011).

witness becomes available during the course of a trial, then discovery can take place later in the criminal process, as well.

Discovery by the Prosecution

Discovery by the prosecution is relatively limited because of the constitutional rights enjoyed by criminal defendants. For example, the defense cannot be compelled to provide the prosecution with incriminating information, particularly in the form of statements and admissions. The scope of prosecutorial discovery has been addressed repeatedly in the courts via the Fifth and Sixth Amendments.

FIFTH AMENDMENT RESTRICTIONS   What if the defense wishes to present an alibi at trial or to assert a defense to criminal liability? Should the prosecutor be permitted to discover this information? The Supreme Court faced the alibi issue in *Williams v. Florida*   *Williams v. Florida*
(399 U.S. 78 [1970])

(399 U.S. 78 [1970]). Florida had a *notice of alibi statute*, which provided that the defendant had to permit discovery of alibi defenses coupled with a list of witnesses who would support them. The Court found that this type of discovery does not violate the Fifth Amendment because it is not self-incriminating. In fact, the purpose of an alibi defense is to exculpate (i.e., clear) the defendant. According to the Court, "Nothing in the Fifth Amendment privilege entitles a defendant as a matter of constitutional right to await the end of the State's case before announcing the nature of his defense, any more than it entitles him to await the jury's verdict on the State's case-in-chief before deciding whether or not to take the stand himself" (p. 85).

The *Williams* decision extends to other defenses, as well. For example, if the defense intends to argue that the defendant is not guilty by reason of insanity, then the prosecutor needs to be notified in advance of this intention. Alternatively, if the defense intends to argue that the defendant acted in self-defense, then the prosecution should be notified. The reason for requiring this notification is that it provides the prosecutor with an opportunity to plan its argument to the contrary.

The defense often has to supply the prosecution with a witness list, also, and it must contain, at a minimum, the names of all the witnesses. Often, the defense also must provide the prosecution with information about how the witnesses will be testifying. Some people believe that compelling the defense to supply a witness list to the prosecution is incriminatory, but in fact, the prosecution would eventually discover the names and identities of the witnesses, as well as their testimony, at trial anyway.

One item concerning witnesses that the defense is *not* required to share with the prosecutor is whether the defendant will testify. In *Brooks v. Tennessee* (406 U.S. 605 [1972]), the Supreme Court declared unconstitutional a state statute that required the defendant, if he or she was to testify, to do so immediately after the prosecution rested its case. The Court held that the statute violated the Fifth Amendment's privilege against self-incrimination and diminished the defense counsel's ability to make such determinations as to when certain witnesses will testify. In reaching its decision, the Court cited *United States v. Shipp* (359 F.2d 185 [1966]):

> If the man charged with a crime takes the witness stand in his own behalf, any and every arrest and conviction, even for lesser felonies, can be brought before the jury by the prosecutor, and such evidence may have devastating and deadly effect, although unrelated to the offense charged. The decision as to whether the defendant in a criminal case shall take the stand is, therefore, often of utmost importance, and counsel must, in many cases, meticulously balance the advantages and disadvantages of the prisoner's becoming a witness in his own behalf. Why, then, should a court insist that the accused must testify before any other evidence is introduced in his behalf, or be completely foreclosed from testifying thereafter? . . . This savors of judicial whim, even though sanctioned by some authorities; and the cause of justice and a fair trial cannot be subjected to such a whimsicality of criminal procedure. (pp. 190–191)

It may prove useful, for example, to let the defendant take the stand at the *end* of the defense case if it is believed (1) that the defense's case was not particularly persuasive and (2) the defendant can offer testimony likely to sway the jury to support his or her version of events.

So far, the discussion has focused on Fifth Amendment restrictions to discovery in terms of defenses and witnesses. Of course, discovery extends beyond these areas to real evidence (e.g., a murder weapon) as well as documentary evidence (e.g., a falsified tax return). In general, the Fifth Amendment is not violated when the defense is compelled to disclose real and documentary evidence that will be introduced at trial. The reason for this should, by now, be clear: The Fifth Amendment's protection against self-incrimination is a personal right—that is, it applies to *people*, not to real or documentary evidence. However, the defense *cannot* be compelled to disclose evidence that will *not* be used at trial because of attorney/client privilege.

In summary, the Fifth Amendment is *not* violated when the defense is forced to provide the prosecution, in advance of trial, any of the following: (1) an alibi or other affirmative defense that will be raised at trial; (2) notice of witnesses who are to testify, including their statements; or (3) real or documentary evidence concerning the crime in question. By contrast, the Fifth Amendment *is* violated when the defense is compelled to (1) notify the prosecution as to whether the defendant intends to testify; (2) identify witnesses who will not testify at trial; or (3) disclose evidence that will not be introduced at trial.

SIXTH AMENDMENT RESTRICTIONS   The Sixth Amendment provides, in relevant part, that the accused enjoys the right "to have compulsory process for obtaining witnesses in his favor." As such, some constitutional challenges to the discovery process have been raised on these grounds.

As a first example, in *United States v. Nobles* (422 U.S. 225 [1975]), the defense attempted to call a private investigator to the stand whose testimony would have cast doubt on the prosecution's case. The trial judge ruled that the investigator could not testify until the prosecution received portions of the investigator's pretrial investigative report. The Supreme Court upheld this decision. The defense argued that this decision infringed on the accused's right to compulsory process—namely, to call the investigator to the stand. But according to the Court, "The Sixth Amendment does not confer the right to present testimony free from the legitimate demands of the adversarial system; one cannot invoke the Sixth Amendment as a justification for presenting what might have been a half-truth" (p. 241). The defense further argued that being forced to supply information from the investigator's report violated attorney/client privilege, but the Court countered by concluding that attorney/client privilege was basically waived when the defense decided to have the investigator testify about the contents of his report.

United States v. Nobles
(422 U.S. 225 [1975])

A second Sixth Amendment issue that has been raised with regard to discovery is whether the testimony can be excluded of a witness whom the defense does not inform the prosecution will testify. In *Taylor v. Illinois* (484 U.S. 400 [1988]), the defense called a witness who had not been on a witness list supplied to the prosecution before trial. The trial court excluded the witness's testimony, citing a violation of discovery procedure. The defendant appealed, arguing that exclusion of the witness's testimony violated the compulsory process clause of the Sixth Amendment. However, the Supreme Court ruled that exclusion of the testimony was appropriate and did not violate the Sixth Amendment. The purpose of discovery, the Court noted, is to "minimize the risk that fabricated testimony will be believed" (p. 413). (Also see *Michigan v. Lucas*, 500 U.S. 145 [1991], for further attention to the relationship between certain Sixth Amendment rights and the discovery process.)

In summary, *Nobles* and *Taylor* suggest that it is relatively difficult to infringe on a defendant's Sixth Amendment rights, as far as discovery is concerned. If the defense takes steps to secure a tactical advantage over the prosecution, either by failing to supply a complete list of witnesses or the documents about which witnesses will testify, then the Sixth Amendment right to compulsory process will not be violated. Thus, this particular Sixth Amendment right is a qualified one. Compulsory process must be preceded by granting the prosecution appropriate discovery.

DECISION-MAKING EXERCISE 10.8

Prosecutorial Discovery

Anne Tator, the local prosecutor, learns from defendant Fred Lyons that he has a list of potential witnesses who will testify on his behalf. Tator learns further that Lyons will not call at least half of the potential witnesses. Nevertheless, Tator demands that Lyons supply her with the full names of everyone on the list, even the names of those who will not testify. Is Tator constitutionally entitled to discover the identities of witnesses whom the defense will not call to testify?

Discovery by the Defense

Naturally, discovery should benefit the *defense* more than the *prosecution*. After all, the prosecution presents the state's case against the defendant; it is only sensible that the defense should learn the nature of the prosecution's case. Generally, though, the prosecution has the most information of both parties because it has to prove *beyond* a reasonable doubt that the defendant committed the crime. The defense, by contrast, only needs to raise reasonable doubt in the minds of the jurors that the defendant did *not* commit the crime.

CASES DEALING WITH DISCOVERY BY THE DEFENSE   It was already pointed out that in *Williams v. Florida*, the Supreme Court required the defense to notify the prosecution as to any defenses, alibi or otherwise, it would assert as well as a list of witnesses who would testify in support of those defenses. In *Wardius v. Oregon* (412 U.S. 470 [1973]), the Court declared that this type of discovery must be *reciprocal*. That is, the Court held that the prosecution must provide the defense with a list of witnesses who will testify in rebuttal to the defendant's alibi or defense:

Wardius v. Oregon
(412 U.S. 470 [1973])

> [I]n the absence of a strong showing of state interests to the contrary, discovery must be a two-way street. The State may not insist that trial be run as a "search for truth" so far as defense witnesses are concerned, while maintaining "poker game" secrecy for its own witnesses. It is fundamentally unfair to require a defendant to divulge the details of his own case while at the same time subjecting him to the hazard of surprise concerning refutation of the very pieces of evidence which he disclosed to the State. (pp. 475–476)

A key feature of the *Wardius* decision is that it applies only to evidence that is truly reciprocal. More specifically, if the defense supplies the prosecution with a list of witnesses who will testify, the prosecution is not necessarily required to supply the defense with something wholly disconnected from a witness list. This was the decision reached in *United States v. Armstrong* (517 U.S. 456 [1996]), in which the Supreme Court held that the prosecution need only supply the defense with evidence that is "material to the preparation of the defendant's case" (p. 462).

Basically, if the evidence the defense wants to discover is a "shield," or used to refute the state's case, access will be granted. If, by contrast, the evidence is a "sword," or intended to challenge prosecutorial conduct, access will not be granted.

In *State v. Eads* (166 N.W.2d 766 [Iowa 1969]), one court summarized the restrictions on defense discovery even for "shield" purposes. If a *state interest* is likely to be compromised, then the prosecution is not required to disclose evidence to the

DECISION-MAKING EXERCISE 10.9

Defense Discovery

The so-called Jencks Act (18 U.S.C. § 3500 [1976]) provides, in part, that "[i]n any criminal prosecution brought by the United States, no statement or report in the possession of the United States which was made by a Government witness or prospective Government witness (other than the defendant) shall be the subject of subpoena, discovery, or inspection until said witness has testified on direct examination in the trial of the case."

Assume that a defendant wishes to obtain a written statement made by one of the prosecution's witnesses *prior* to the witness's testimony. Clearly, the Jencks Act prohibits this. Thus, the defendant claims that the act seriously restricts his ability to conduct an effective defense. If you represented the appellate court charged with deciding on the constitutionality of this section of the Jencks Act, how would you decide?

defense, even if such evidence is intended to be used by the defense to challenge or refute the state's case. State interest precludes discovery by the defense under these circumstances:

> (1) It would afford the defendant increased opportunity to produce perjured testimony and to fabricate evidence to meet the State's case; (2) witnesses would be subject to bribe, threat and intimidation; (3) since the State cannot compel the defendant to disclose . . . evidence [protected by the Fifth Amendment], disclosure by the State would afford the defendant an unreasonable advantage at trial; and (4) disclosure is unnecessary in any event because of the other sources of information which defendant has under existing law. (p. 769)

In the wake of *Eads*, several states have imposed restrictions on defense discovery when certain state interests have been called into question. For example, many states prohibit discovery of the identities of prosecution witnesses until after they have testified so as to prevent defense tampering with (or threatening of) prosecution witnesses.

Nonreciprocal Discovery

With few exceptions, discovery is a two-way street: The defense must supply the prosecution with certain information and vice versa. For example, as already indicated, when the defense wants to assert an alibi, it must supply the prosecution with that alibi; the prosecution must, in turn, supply the defense with a list of witnesses who will testify in rebuttal to the alibi.

First, the restrictions on discovery discussed in the previous section, although controversial, do not leave the defense at a disadvantage. In fact, in some circumstances, the prosecution is required to supply information to the defense but *not* vice versa. Specifically, the prosecution has a constitutional duty to disclose exculpatory evidence to the defense. This is significant because, typically, the prosecution is interested in gaining a conviction. A requirement to disclose exculpatory evidence—evidence that would otherwise not be admitted at trial—would seem to damage the state's case, especially since the defense is not required to disclose evidence that *it* will not use at trial. But the Supreme Court disagrees with this position.

Second, the prosecution has a constitutional duty to preserve evidence, but the defense does not. These two methods of so-called **nonreciprocal discovery** are discussed in the two subsections that follow.

THE PROSECUTION'S DUTY TO DISCLOSE EXCULPATORY EVIDENCE As a matter of due process, the prosecution has a constitutional duty to reveal exculpatory evidence to the defense. Simply put, if the prosecution obtains evidence suggesting that the defendant is not guilty, it needs to inform the defense of this fact either before or well into the trial. Numerous Supreme Court cases have supported this important requirement. However, if the evidence clearly establishes factual innocence, it should be disclosed before the trial (*Unites States v. Ruiz*, 536 U.S. 622 [2002]).

First, in *Mooney v. Holohan* (294 U.S. 103 [1935]), the prosecution allegedly used perjured testimony to convict the defendant. The Court held that due process is violated when the prosecution "has contrived a conviction through the pretense of a trial which in truth is but used as a means of depriving a defendant of liberty through a deliberate deception of court and jury by the presentation of testimony known to be perjured" (p. 112). The key in *Mooney* was that the prosecution *arranged* to have a witness give false testimony. If perjured testimony is *not* arranged by the prosecution but, rather, given by a witness on his or her own volition, and if the prosecution learns of this, it will still be bound to notify the defense (*Alcorta v. Texas*, 355 U.S. 28 [1957]).

Next, in *Napue v. Illinois* (360 U.S. 264 [1959]), the Supreme Court held that falsification concerning the credibility of a witness constitutes a due process violation. In that case, a witness testified falsely that the prosecution had not promised him leniency for his willingness to cooperate. Since the prosecutor knew the witness's testimony was false and did nothing to correct it, the defendant's conviction was reversed, since "[t]he jury's estimate of the truthfulness and reliability of a given witness may well be determinative of guilt or innocence, and it is upon such subtle factors as the possible interest of the witness in testifying falsely that a defendant's life or liberty may depend" (p. 269). In a related case, *Giglio v. United States* (405 U.S. 150 [1972]), the promise of leniency was offered by a different prosecutor but the Court still required reversal, citing a due process violation.

Brady v. Maryland
(373 U.S. 83 [1963])

In *Brady v. Maryland* (373 U.S. 83 [1963]), perhaps the most important case in this area of law, the Supreme Court drastically altered its previous decisions concerning the prosecution's duty to disclose exculpatory evidence. The Court held that "the suppression by the prosecution of evidence favorable to an accused upon request violates due process where the evidence is *material either to guilt or to punishment*, irrespective of the good faith or bad faith of the prosecution" (p. 87; emphasis added). The Court also eloquently stated:

> Society wins not only when the guilty are convicted but when criminal trials are fair; our system of the administration of justice suffers when any accused is treated unfairly. An inscription on the walls of the Department of Justice states the proposition candidly for the federal domain: "The United States wins its point whenever justice is done its citizens in the courts." . . . A prosecution that withholds evidence on demand of an accused which, if made available, would tend to exculpate him or reduce the penalty helps shape a trial that bears heavily on the defendant. That casts the prosecutor in the role of an architect of a proceeding that does not comport with standards of justice, even though, as in the present case, his action is not "the result of guile." (pp. 87–88)

Whether evidence is *material* is not entirely clear, but in *United States v. Agurs* (427 U.S. 97 [1976]), the Supreme Court offered some clarification. In that case, the defendant stabbed and killed another man with the man's knife. She claimed self-defense but was nevertheless found guilty. The defense argued that because the prosecution had not disclosed that the victim had a prior criminal record, the conviction should be reversed. The Court disagreed, stating that the victim's prior criminal record was not material enough to the question of guilt or innocence. Important to this decision is the fact that the defense did not request information about the victim's prior criminal record at trial, only on appeal. Had the defense explicitly requested such information at trial, a different decision probably would have resulted.

An obvious problem is posed by the *Agurs* decision: If the defense does not know what exculpatory evidence the prosecution has, it cannot request that evidence. Does this mean that the defense should be denied access to exculpatory evidence if it does not request it? In *United States v. Bagley* (473 U.S. 667 [1985]), the Court sought to answer this question but, unfortunately, offered little clarification. In that case, the defense posed a broad request to the prosecution for discovery of "any deals, promises or inducements made to [prosecution] witnesses in exchange for their testimony" (pp. 669–670). The prosecution failed to disclose some of the requested information, but on appeal, the Supreme Court held that this action did not constitute a due process violation. According to the Court, there was no "reasonable probability" that the exculpatory evidence would have influenced the outcome of the case.

What amounts to a *reasonable probability* that the outcome of the case may be altered by failure to disclose exculpatory evidence? In *Kyles v. Whitley* (514 U.S. 419 [1995]), the Court sought to answer this question. Justice Souter's opinion in that case cited four elements of the reasonable probability standard that should be considered. First, reasonable probability does not mean a preponderance of evidence but something less. Second, when exculpatory evidence is included, the reasonable probability standard does not require the defense to show that the other evidence presented by the prosecution is insufficient to prove guilt. Third, once the defense demonstrates a reasonable probability of a different outcome, its job is done. Moreover, the appellate court cannot decide that the prosecution's failure to disclose evidence amounted to a harmless error. Finally, while the prosecution is not required to present every shred of evidence that may prove helpful to the defense, it "must be assigned the consequent responsibility to gauge the likely net effect of all such evidence and make disclosure when the point of 'reasonable probability' is reached" (p. 437).

Kyles v. Whitley
(514 U.S. 419 [1995])

In summary, the prosecution's constitutional duty to disclose exculpatory evidence hinges on whether such evidence would have a reasonable probability of changing the outcome of the case. The *Brady* decision, which created the reasonable probability standard, suggests that some of the Court's previous decisions in this area may have been altered. For example, it is possible that failure on the part of the prosecution to disclose that a witness presented perjured testimony (i.e., as in *Mooney*) may not amount to a due process violation if the exculpatory evidence does not have a reasonable probability of influencing the jury's decision. Thus, the purpose of *Brady*, *Kyles*, and the cases that followed is not to correct or deter prosecutorial misconduct but only to ensure that due process protections are not violated (see, e.g., *Smith v. Phillips*, 455 U.S. 209 [1982]).

Who makes the decision as to what constitutes a reasonable probability that the outcome of a case will be changed if exculpatory evidence is not disclosed? Depending on the case, it is usually the judge (i.e., court) or prosecutor who makes the decision. If the defense can show that the prosecution possesses exculpatory evidence, then a hearing to determine the reasonable probability issue may be required (see *DeMarco v. United States*, 415 U.S. 449 [1974]). However, if the defense has no knowledge of specific evidence possessed by the prosecution that may prove exculpatory, the prosecution can make the decision. In *Pennsylvania v. Ritchie* (480 U.S. 39 [1987]), for example, the Supreme Court held that the "defendant's right to discover exculpatory evidence does not include the unsupervised authority to search through the Commonwealth's files" (p. 59).

Arizona v. Youngblood *(488 U.S. 51 [1988])*

In *District Attorney v. Osborne* (No. 08-6 [2009]), the Court was confronted with the question of whether the due process clause requires the state to turn over DNA evidence to those found guilty of criminal activity. It decided that there is no such duty and that legislatures are the proper forum to set appropriate rules governing the release of DNA evidence. This decision makes clear, then, that there is no constitutional duty to disclose possibly exculpatory evidence *after* trial. However, "after trial" means post sentencing. If a prosecutor withholds evidence that could affect the defendant's sentence, then a due process violation occurs (see, e.g., *Cone v. Bell*, No. 07-1114 [2009]).

THE PROSECUTION'S DUTY TO PRESERVE EVIDENCE The prosecution is also constitutionally bound to *preserve* evidence. Simply put, the prosecution cannot destroy exculpatory evidence in an effort to gain a conviction. To do so would be a violation of due process. For the defense to convince the court that the prosecution has destroyed exculpatory evidence, it must demonstrate three facts: (1) that the evidence was expected to "play a significant role in the suspect's defense"; (2) that the evidence was of "such a nature that the defendant would be unable to obtain comparable evidence by other reasonably available means"; and (3) that the destruction of the evidence was a result of "official animus toward [the defendant] or . . . a conscious effort to suppress exculpatory evidence" (*California v. Trombetta*, 467 U.S. 479 [1984]). Note that the third requirement departs from the *Brady* decision discussed in the previous section. *Brady* did not consider the prosecution's state of mind relevant.

A case that offers some clarification concerning these three requirements is *Arizona v. Youngblood* (488 U.S. 51 [1988]). There, the Supreme Court stated that "unless a criminal defendant can show bad faith on the part of the police [or prosecution], failure to preserve potentially useful evidence does not constitute due process of law" (p. 58).

Not only must prosecutors preserve evidence but so, too, must police. Without a proper **chain of custody** (and sometimes even with one), the defense will allege that the evidence was tampered with or tainted in such a way that it cannot prove the defendant's involvement in a crime. As such, prosecutors' offices and police departments are very concerned with maintaining a proper chain of custody. Figure 10.3 presents portions of the Gallatin, Tennessee, Police Department's policy for processing and preserving evidence.

DECISION-MAKING EXERCISE 10.10
Disclosure of Exculpatory Evidence

Leonard Baum was convicted of first-degree murder and sentenced to death. In preparing an appeal, Baum's attorney learned that the state never disclosed certain evidence favorable to Baum. That evidence included eyewitness statements taken by the police following the murder; statements made to the police by an informant, who was never called to testify; and a list of the license numbers of cars parked at the crime scene on the night of the murder, which did not include Baum's car. Baum argues that had this evidence been disclosed at his trial, there would have been a reasonable probability that he would not have been found guilty. Should Baum be granted a new trial?

FIGURE 10.3

Example of a Chain of Custody Policy

9.30.2 Statutory Authority and Departmental Authorization

Any property used in commission or furtherance of certain crimes or used for the transportation of stolen property may be confiscated and forfeited as per TCA 40-33-101 through TCA 40-33-204.

Any time an officer wishes to seize or confiscate property under these circumstances (i.e. seizure of vehicle driven by an individual whose license is revoked), the officer will contact his/her shift supervisor for authorization. The shift supervisor will in turn notify the Field Operations Commander and/or the Chief of Police, or his/her designee, for authorization prior to the vehicle being seized by the requesting officer.

9.30.3 Processing Evidence

An officer that has evidence to be placed in the evidence room will make an inventory of the evidence at the location it was found or recovered. The seizing officer will properly handle, mark, and package all evidence, and place the evidence in the collection box in the processing room, if practical, or directly to the evidence room as soon as practical. The seizing officer must turn in evidence no later than the end of his/her tour of duty.

Evidence that cannot be marked directly for identification will be placed in a sealed container or package and the package will be marked for identification. Items will be placed in separate packages when the possibility of contamination exists. Items requiring lab analysis or processing must be placed in separate packages. Money and controlled substances will be counted or weighed by two officers, placed in envelopes separate from other evidence, and then sealed. Both officers will sign the envelopes.

Evidence of a hazardous nature will be appropriately packaged and stored in accordance with necessary safety precautions. Such substances include, but are not limited to, items that may have been exposed to or contaminated by communicable diseases, hazardous chemicals or waste products, or explosive or highly combustible products. When appropriate, the Property Officer will make arrangements and assume responsibility for storage and control of such items outside the evidence room.

An evidence envelope will be filled out and sealed for all evidence. If the items or evidence is too large to be placed into an envelope, only the evidence control form will be placed with the item. The chain of custody form will be forwarded with all required reports.

The reporting officer will document all evidence on the evidence control form. The reporting officer will fill out a chain of custody form. The departmental case number will be placed on all evidence forms.

If an officer needs a particular piece of property processed, the officer may request Investigations to make arrangements or assist in making arrangements, or may process the property himself/herself. Vehicles are to be processed at the scene, the impound lot, or other appropriate location.

9.30.4 Impounding Evidence

The Property Officer will be responsible for receiving, storing, maintaining, releasing, and accounting for all evidence in compliance with this policy. When evidence is deposited with the Property Officer or in an approved holding facility, an evidence

Figure 10.3 continued

receipt will be completed by the seizing officer. The evidence receipt will include all information necessary to both document and ensure the integrity or the chain of custody. All drugs will be weighed and monies counted by the Property Officer and recorded on the evidence receipt. The Property Officer will be responsible for developing and maintaining a master file of all evidence invoices and evidence tags completed. This file will be cross-indexed with the chain of custody file.

9.30.5 Storage of Evidence

The Property Officer will assign a storage location for each item of evidence and record this information on the evidence receipt and evidence tag. Evidence requiring added security, including money, precious metals, jewelry, gemstones, weapons, narcotics, and dangerous drugs, will be stored in a separate secured area. Perishable items will be stored in a refrigerator or other suitable container.

9.30.6 Access to the Evidence Room

Only employees authorized by the Chief may enter the evidence room. A log will be kept by the Property Officer to identify each authorized employee entering the evidence room.

9.30.7 Inspections of the Evidence Room

On a monthly basis, the Staff Services Commander will make an inspection of the evidence room to ensure adherence to appropriate policies and procedures. Unannounced inspections of the evidence room will be conducted semiannually as directed by the Chief. An annual inventory of evidence held by the Department will be conducted by a commanding officer, appointed by the Chief, not routinely or directly connected with evidence control.

9.30.8 Recording Transfers of Custody

The Property Officer will be responsible for developing and maintaining a file that documents all changes in custody of physical evidence. The file will be capable of readily identifying the individual or organization currently maintaining custody of all evidence. A written record of all transfers of physical evidence will be made. Officers who assume custody of evidence from the evidence room bear full responsibility for ensuring its security, proper storage, and maintenance, and for the ready retrieval of such evidence upon demand.

9.30.16 Removing Evidence from Storage

When evidence is needed for court, it may be obtained from the Property Room. This will be done during the Property Room hours. The officer will sign the Chain of Custody Form and assume full responsibility for the evidence. The Property Room Officer will note the officer's name and reason for removing the evidence on the appropriate log. All evidence will be returned at the end of the day's proceedings. If the Property Room Officer is not on-duty at the time the evidence is returned, the officer will have his/her supervisor place the evidence in the Evidence Locker. This will be noted on the Chain of Custody Form. If the evidence is in a sealed container or envelope, it will not be opened unless directed by the court or is needed for processing.

Source: From *General Directives Manual*, Gallatin, Tennessee, Police Department (December 28, 1999). Used courtesy of the Gallatin Police Department.

Summary

1. EXPLAIN THE PURPOSE AND PROCESS OF THE INITIAL APPEARANCE.

Before recapping what occurs at each stage of the pretrial process, it is important to underscore the fact that this process differs substantially across the United States. Some jurisdictions follow the procedures outlined in this chapter, in the order presented (see Figure 10.4). Others follow the same basic procedures but in a different order. Still others combine various hearings into a single hearing or do not require them at all. Readers are advised to familiarize themselves with the procedures followed where they reside.

That said, the pretrial process always begins with an initial appearance. This is where, at a minimum, the accused is advised of the charges against him or her. In a misdemeanor case, the trial may take place at this stage. Also, the accused may be advised of his or her privilege against self-incrimination as well as the right to appointed counsel, if he or she is indigent.

2. EXPLAIN THE PURPOSE AND THE PROCESS OF THE PROBABLE CAUSE HEARING.

Next, a probable cause hearing may be required. In particular, if the defendant is arrested without a warrant, a separate court hearing may be held to determine whether probable cause to arrest existed. This determination can be made independent of any other hearing. The probable cause hearing, if required, needs to be held promptly after arrest, usually within 48 hours.

3. SUMMARIZE BAIL AND OTHER TYPES OF PRETRIAL RELEASE.

After the probable cause hearing is the pretrial release determination. The accused may be released on bail, in which case he or she deposits a certain amount of money with the court (possibly through a bail bonds agent) as an incentive to show up for later hearings. Failure to show up will result in, among other things, forfeiture of the bail money. A defendant can also be released on his or her own recognizance (ROR). At the other extreme, a defendant who is presumed to pose a significant risk of flight may be held without bail. This tactic is known as preventive detention. Three different criteria are considered in making the pretrial release determination: the accused's (1) flight risk, (2) level of dangerousness, and (3) financial status.

4. EXPLAIN THE PURPOSE AND PROCESS OF THE PRELIMINARY HEARING.

The preliminary hearing is the next stage in the pretrial process. The preliminary hearing differs from the other hearings already discussed in that it is intended to be a check on the prosecution's charging decision. A preliminary hearing is generally not required, however, if (1) the defendant waives it or (2) the prosecutor proceeds by indictment. In the latter instance, the grand jury essentially serves as an appropriate check on the charging decision.

5. SUMMARIZE THE ARRAIGNMENT PROCESS.

After the preliminary hearing (or grand jury indictment), the arraignment is held. At this stage, the defendant is formally notified of the charges against him or her. In addition, he or she enters a plea of guilty, not guilty, or *nolo contendere*.

6. SUMMARIZE THE DISCOVERY PROCESS.

The last stage of the pretrial process discussed in this chapter is discovery. In actuality, however, discovery can take place early on, perhaps prior to a preliminary hearing, or well into a trial. Discovery is the process whereby the prosecution advises the defense of the evidence it will use to secure a conviction. The defense must also disclose the evidence it intends to use to exonerate the defendant. The prosecution has a duty to disclose the defendant's statements in its possession, tangible evidence that will be introduced at trial, test results that are material to the case, and a list of witnesses who will testify for the prosecution as well as the substance of their testimony. The defense, by contrast, must supply the defense with its intended alibi or other defense as well as a list of witnesses (and their statements) who will testify in support of the defense. Finally, the due process clause of the Fourteenth Amendment requires the prosecution to disclose exculpatory evidence to the defense *and* to preserve said evidence while in its custody.

FIGURE 10.4

Summary of the Pretrial Process.

Initial Appearance

a. Not required in all jurisdictions
b. Trial may take place at this stage for a misdemeanor
c. Accused informed of complaint against him or her, of protection against self-incrimination, of right to appointed counsel if need be

Probable Cause Hearing

a. Only required if arrest is warrantless
b. Must be held within 48 hours, but clear time limit has not been set

Pretrial Release/Bail Determination

a. Methods of ensuring defendant's return are bail, release on recognizance, preventive detention
b. Bail cannot be excessive

Preliminary Hearing

a. Serves as check on charging decision and is not same as probable cause hearing
b. May not be held if defendant waives it or prosecution proceeds by indictment

Arraignment

a. Suspect advised of formal charges filed against him or her
b. Suspect enters plea of guilty, not guilty, or *nolo contendere*

Discovery

a. Prosecution advises defense of evidence to be used in securing conviction
b. Defense advises prosecution of evidence to be used in securing acquittal
c. Prosecution must disclose exculpatory evidence and preserve it

Note: There are several variations to this order of events throughout the United States.

Key Terms

allocution	319	chain of custody	330	nonreciprocal
arraignment	319	discovery	320	discovery
bail	310	guilty	319	not guilty
bail bond agent	310	initial appearance	306	preliminary hearing
booking	306	*nolo contendere*	319	pretrial release

allocution   319
arraignment   319
bail   310
bail bond agent   310
booking   306

chain of custody   330
discovery   320
guilty   319
initial appearance   306
nolo contendere   319

nonreciprocal
   discovery   327
not guilty   319
preliminary hearing   317
pretrial release   309

preventive detention   314
probable cause
   hearing   306
release on recognizance
   (ROR)   312

Key Cases

Probable Cause Hearing

- *Gerstein v. Pugh*, 420 U.S. 103 (1975)
- *Riverside County v. McLaughlin*, 500 U.S. 44 (1991)

Pretrial Release

- *Stack v. Boyle*, 342 U.S. 1 (1951)
- *Schall v. Martin*, 467 U.S. 253 (1984)
- *Schilb v. Kuebel*, 404 U.S. 357 (1971)
- *Bell v. Wolfish*, 441 U.S. 520 (1979)

Preliminary Hearing

- *Lem Woon v. Oregon*, 229 U.S. 586 (1913)
- *Coleman v. Alabama*, 399 U.S. 1 (1970)

Discovery

- *Williams v. Florida*, 399 U.S. 78 (1970)
- *United States v. Nobles*, 422 U.S. 225 (1975)
- *Wardius v. Oregon*, 412 U.S. 470 (1973)
- *Brady v. Maryland*, 373 U.S. 83 (1963)
- *Kyles v. Whitley*, 514 U.S. 419 (1995)
- *Arizona v. Youngblood*, 488 U.S. 51 (1988)

Review Questions

1. What is booking?
2. What is the initial appearance? What is its purpose?
3. What is the probable cause hearing? What is its purpose? When is it required?
4. How soon after arrest must the probable cause hearing be held?
5. What methods of pretrial release are available? Define each.
6. What are the criteria for pretrial release? How have they been used in court decisions?
7. Summarize the key cases dealing with the treatment of pretrial detainees.
8. What is the preliminary hearing? What is its purpose? When is it required?
9. What rights does the defendant enjoy during the preliminary hearing?
10. What is discovery?
11. Citing cases, what are the restrictions on discovery by the prosecution?
12. Citing cases, what are the restrictions on discovery by the defense?
13. What is nonreciprocal discovery?
14. Explain what it means to require the prosecution to disclose exculpatory evidence. What are the consequences if the prosecution fails to do so?
15. Is the prosecution bound to preserve evidence? The police? If so, how?

Web Links and Exercises

1. The pretrial process: Read more about the pretrial process and browse back issues of *The Pretrial Reporter*.
URL (click on the "Resources" tab): http://www.pretrial.org (accessed February 16, 2011).
2. Bail: Read more about how bail works:
Suggested URL: http://www.aboutbail.com/news/articles/how_bail_works.php (accessed February 16, 2011).
3. Bail bonds agents: Read more about bail bonds agents at the Web site for the Professional Bail Agents of the United States. Click on the "Bail Information" tab and then on the "History of Bail" tab to read about the history of bail in the United States.
URL: http://pbus.com (accessed February 16, 2011).
4. *Federal Rules of Criminal Procedure*: Read about the rules of criminal procedure (including discovery rules) in federal court.
Suggested URL: http://www.law.cornell.edu/rules/frcrmp (accessed February 16, 2011).

LEARNING OBJECTIVES

When you complete this chapter, you should be able to:

▸ Describe the prosecutor's role, prosecutor's discretion, and the issues surrounding prosecutorial misconduct.

▸ Explain the concept of joinder and reasons for it.

▸ Explain the purpose, functions, and powers of a grand jury.

▸ Outline the development of the right to counsel.

▸ Be familiar with the courtroom workgroup and its functions.

CHAPTER 11

Prosecutors, Grand Juries, and Defense Attorneys

INTRODUCTION

Bringing Charges and Mounting a Defense

This chapter turns attention to the roles of the prosecutor, grand jury, and defense attorney. In a way, this chapter does not flow directly from the preceding chapter; for example, the right to counsel attaches to varying degrees well before the pretrial process is set into motion. Similarly, when the services of the grand jury are required, it can perform an investigative function well before the arrest stage of the criminal process. Prosecutors, too, perform a great deal of work before the pretrial process. Nevertheless, the functions of all three parties will be considered here for the sake of an orderly presentation. Just understand that the prosecutor, grand jury, and defense attorney do not necessarily enter the picture *after* the pretrial process has commenced.

This chapter begins by focusing on the prosecutor and, in particular, the decision whether or not to charge. In this vein, this chapter also introduces restrictions on the prosecutor's charging decision as well as the notion of *joinder*. Most of the discussion will be limited to the prosecutor's role leading up to a criminal trial. To delve into the prosecutor's role at trial (e.g., the order and method by which the state's case is presented) would take the discussion into another area. The prosecutor's role at trial is best understood in terms of the law of evidence, a topic not typically taken up in criminal procedure class.

Next, this chapter turns attention to the grand jury. The function of the grand jury is a source of some confusion to criminal procedure students. As such, the role of the grand jury is considered in detail, particularly when a grand jury is required and what roles it performs. This chapter also discusses the secrecy of grand juries, the rights of witnesses testifying before grand juries, and the various methods for challenging indictments. As with the section on the prosecutor, the grand jury section of this chapter is pretrial in nature. Indeed, the grand jury's function ceases once the charging decision has been made.

Finally, this chapter turns to the role of the defense attorney in criminal procedure. The Fourth Amendment and interrogation sections of this text have already discussed the function of defense counsel at various stages of the criminal process. Those functions are revisited briefly in this chapter, but the focus is primarily on the defense attorney's role at trial. The bulk of the defense attorney section of this chapter concerns the accused's right to effective assistance of counsel. This chapter also discusses the waiver of counsel and the distinctions between privately retained counsel and public defenders. It concludes with some attention to the so-called courtroom work group.

THE PROSECUTOR

The prosecutor performs a valuable function in reinforcing the notion that a crime is an offense against the state. In fact, Article II, Section 3, of the U.S. Constitution states that the executive branch of the federal government "shall take Care that the Laws be faithfully executed." This constitutionally mandated duty to execute the law usually falls on prosecutors. Of course, police officers, as part of the executive branch, do their part to execute the laws, but a strong argument can be made that prosecutors possess even more authority because of their ability to decide whether to bring formal charges against suspected criminals.

Just as police officers have the discretion to decide whether to make an arrest, so, too, do prosecutors have enormous discretion. As the Supreme Court noted in *Bordenkircher v.*

Hayes (434 U.S. 357 [1978]), "[S]o long as the prosecutor has probable cause to believe that the accused committed an offense defined by statute, the decision whether or not to prosecute, and what charge to file or bring before a grand jury, generally rests entirely on his discretion" (p. 364). Figure 11.1 presents portions of a federal prosecutor's charging document (a.k.a., "information").

Prosecutors do not have *unlimited* discretion, however. There are important restrictions on their decision to charge. Some stem from the Constitution, while others stem from statutes and other related sources.

FIGURE 11.1

Portions of a Federal Prosecutor's Charging Document (Information)

United States District Court
Northern District Of Illinois
Eastern Division

UNITED STATES OF AMERICA	)	
	)	
v.	)	No.____
	)	
ANTHONY MATTHEWS	)	Violations: Title 18, United States Code,
	)	Section 1343

COUNT ONE

The UNITED STATES ATTORNEY charges:

1. At times material to this information:
   a. Defendant ANTHONY MATTHEWS owned and controlled Express Mortgage, a licensed Illinois mortgage brokerage located on Wabash Street and on Western Boulevard in Chicago, Illinois.
   b. Bank One was a financial institution, the deposits of which were insured by the Federal Deposit Insurance Corporation ("FDIC"). Wells Fargo Home Mortgage was a subsidiary of Wells Fargo Bank.
   c. MIT Lending and St. Francis Mortgage were mortgage companies engaged in the business of issuing mortgage loans for the purchase of residential property.
2. Beginning no later than 2003 and continuing through at least 2006, at Chicago, in the Northern District of Illinois, Eastern Division, and elsewhere,

ANTHONY MATTHEWS,

defendant herein, together with other co-schemers known to the United States Attorney, devised, intended to devise, and participated in a scheme to defraud and to obtain money by means of materially false and fraudulent pretenses, representations, and promises, which scheme affected financial institutions. More specifically, defendant schemed to fraudulently obtain over $1 million in mortgage loan proceeds from various banks and mortgage lending institutions, including Bank One, Wells Fargo Bank. MIT Lending. St. Francis Mortgage and Wells Fargo Home Mortgage, among others (hereinafter referred to collectively as "lenders"), as described below.

Source: http://www.usdoj.gov/usao/iln/pr/chicago/2008/pr0619_01i.pdf (accessed November 7, 2008).

The Charging Decision

The prosecutor generally has the authority to decide whether to proceed with charges. This is known as **prosecutorial discretion**. He or she can elect not to charge for a number of reasons, even over strenuous objection on the part of the complainant or victim. The prosecutor's discretion can be further manifested by the act of *plea bargaining* (see Chapter 12); that is, he or she can accept a guilty plea for a lesser offense than the one charged. Finally, prosecutors sometimes have to answer to authorities that mandate, or at least strongly encourage, prosecution.

DECIDING NOT TO PROSECUTE   The most obvious reason for nonprosecution is lack of evidence. The prosecutor may determine that, based on the evidence presented to him or her by the police, the suspect is innocent. In such an event, there would be no point in proceeding to trial on the slight chance that a conviction would be obtained. Even if the prosecutor *believes* the suspect is guilty, if there is not enough *evidence* to obtain a conviction, then he or she will likely elect not to prosecute.

There are other reasons not to prosecute, as well. For example, even if the state's case is strong, there may be an incentive not to prosecute. In particular, if it appears the defense's case is *stronger*, then it may behoove the prosecutor to proceed with charges against a different individual.

Nonetheless, prosecutors are human and, as such, can be influenced by the facts of a particular case. Say, for instance, that a law mandates life in prison for growing in excess of 1,000 marijuana plants. Assume further that a suspect apprehended for violating such a law has a spotless record, is married, and has four children. Would life in prison be the best punishment for such an individual, or would a fine community service or other sanction be more appropriate? This decision is up to the prosecutor, and depending on the nature of the case, he or she may elect not to proceed with charges.

As another example, California's "three strikes" law requires life in prison for third-time felons. The first two felonies that qualify as "strikeable" under California's law can only be of certain varieties; typically, they are serious offenses. However, the third felony can be of *any* type. Critics of California's "three strikes" law often point to the man who was sentenced to prison for life for stealing a slice of pizza. Had the prosecutor who charged this individual been more sensible in exercising his or her discretion, then public outcry may not have been so significant.

Another reason for not charging traces to economic concerns. Simply put, it is not possible, given the resource restrictions that exist in most public agencies (prosecutors' offices included), to proceed with charges against every suspect. Not

---

DECISION-MAKING EXERCISE 11.1

Reasons for Nonprosecution

Another controversial reason for nonprosecution is a by-product of the United States' so-called war on drugs. Civil asset forfeiture statutes permit the forfeiture of money and property tied to criminal activity—most frequently, the illicit drug trade. Many asset forfeiture statutes permit forfeited proceeds to go to the executive branch, which usually means the police but sometimes prosecutors. Some have argued that when there is not enough evidence to proceed with a criminal case, prosecutors can opt to pursue civil forfeiture, for which the burden of proof is generally lower. And as an added bonus, if a forfeiture action succeeds and a person's property is forfeited to the state, then the prosecutor may reap a financial reward for selecting a civil proceeding instead of a criminal one. Is the possibility of civil asset forfeiture a legitimate reason not to prosecute? That is, if a prosecutor chooses not to press criminal charges against someone, instead opting for forfeiture, should the decision be considered constitutional?

having the time to build a case because of a high caseload may effectively force a prosecutor to be lenient with certain individuals.

CHALLENGING THE DECISION NOT TO PROSECUTE   A prosecutor's decision not to press charges is rarely challenged, but on occasion, higher authorities may get involved when they disagree with a prosecutor's decision. Failure to press charges can sometimes be questioned by a court, which can provide relief to individuals who disagree with the prosecutor's decision (e.g., *NAACP v. Levi*, 418 F. Supp. 1109 [D.D.C. 1976]). Other times, a prosecutor's supervisor or other high-ranking official may step in. According to one source, "Many states by statute confer upon the attorney general the power to initiate prosecution in cases where the local prosecutor has failed to act. In practice, however, attorneys general have seldom exercised much control over local prosecuting attorneys."[1]

Another way of preventing prosecutors from abusing their discretion (i.e., by failing to act) is to require them to abide by standards of conduct. These standards help prosecutors decide which cases are worthy of prosecution as well as what charges to pursue, all the while ensuring that they act in accordance with the law. Figure 11.2 presents portions of the *Code of Conduct for Judicial Employees*, published by the Administrative Office of the U.S. Courts.

Some U.S. jurisdictions require court approval of a prosecutor's decision not to pursue charges. The prosecutor is typically required to explain to the court in writing his or her reasons for failing to prosecute. While this approach may seem sensible on its

---

FIGURE 11.2

Code of Conduct for Judicial Employees

A. Code of Conduct for Judicial Employees.

CANON 1: A JUDICIAL EMPLOYEE SHOULD UPHOLD THE INTEGRITY AND INDEPENDENCE OF THE JUDICIARY AND OF THE JUDICIAL EMPLOYEE'S OFFICE

An independent and honorable Judiciary is indispensable to justice in our society. A judicial employee should personally observe high standards of conduct so that the integrity and independence of the Judiciary are preserved and the judicial employee's office reflects a devotion to serving the public. Judicial employees should require adherence to such standards by personnel subject to their direction and control. The provisions of this code should be construed and applied to further these objectives. The standards of this code shall not affect or preclude other more stringent standards required by law, by court order, or by the appointing authority.

CANON 2: A JUDICIAL EMPLOYEE SHOULD AVOID IMPROPRIETY AND THE APPEARANCE OF IMPROPRIETY IN ALL ACTIVITIES

A judicial employee should not engage in any activities that would put into question the propriety of the judicial employee's conduct in carrying out the duties of the office. A judicial employee should not allow family, social, or other relationships to influence official conduct or judgment. A judicial employee should not lend the prestige of the office to advance or to appear to advance the private interests of others. A judicial employee should not use public office for private gain.

Figure 11.2 continued

---

[1] Y. Kamisar, W. LaFave, and J. Israel, *Modern Criminal Procedure*, 9th ed. (St. Paul, MN: West, 1999), p. 894.

CANON 3: A JUDICIAL EMPLOYEE SHOULD ADHERE TO APPROPRIATE STANDARDS IN PERFORMING THE DUTIES OF THE OFFICE

In performing the duties prescribed by law, by resolution of the Judicial Conference of the United States, by court order, or by the judicial employee's appointing authority, the following standards apply:

A. A judicial employee should respect and comply with the law and these canons. A judicial employee should report to the appropriate supervising authority any attempt to induce the judicial employee to violate these canons.

Note: A number of criminal statutes of general applicability govern federal employees' performance of official duties. These include:

18 U.S.C. § 201 (bribery of public officials and witnesses);

18 U.S.C. § 211 (acceptance or solicitation to obtain appointive public office);

18 U.S.C. § 285 (taking or using papers relating to government claims);

18 U.S.C. § 287 (false, fictitious, or fraudulent claims against the government);

18 U.S.C. § 508 (counterfeiting or forging transportation requests);

18 U.S.C. § 641 (embezzlement or conversion of government money, property, or records);

18 U.S.C. § 643 (failing to account for public money);

18 U.S.C. § 798 and 50 U.S.C. § 783 (disclosure of classified information);

18 U.S.C. § 1001 (fraud or false statements in a government matter);

18 U.S.C. § 1719 (misuse of franking privilege);

18 U.S.C. § 2071 (concealing, removing, or mutilating a public record);

31 U.S.C. § 1344 (misuse of government vehicle);

31 U.S.C. § 3729 (false claims against the government).

In addition, provisions of specific applicability to court officers include:

18 U.S.C. § § 153,154 (court officers embezzling or purchasing property from bankruptcy estate);

18 U.S.C. § 645 (embezzlement and theft by court officers);

18 U.S.C. § 646 (court officers failing to deposit registry moneys);

18 U.S.C. § 647 (receiving loans from registry moneys from court officer).

This is not a comprehensive listing but sets forth some of the more significant provisions with which judicial employees should be familiar.

B. A judicial employee should be faithful to professional standards and maintain competence in the judicial employee's profession.

C. A judicial employee should be patient, dignified, respectful, and courteous to all persons with whom the judicial employee deals in an official capacity, including the general public, and should require similar conduct of personnel subject to the judicial employee's direction and control. A judicial employee should diligently discharge the responsibilities of the office in a prompt, efficient, nondiscriminatory, fair, and professional manner. A judicial employee should never influence or attempt to influence the assignment of cases, or perform any discretionary or ministerial function of the court in a manner that improperly favors any litigant or attorney, nor should a judicial employee imply that he or she is in a position to do so.

D. A judicial employee should avoid making public comment on the merits of a pending or impending action and should require similar restraint by personnel subject to the judicial employee's direction and control. This proscription does not extend to public statements made in the course of official duties or to the explanation of court procedures. A judicial employee should never disclose any confidential information received in the course of official duties except as required in the performance of such duties, nor should a judicial employee employ such information for personal gain. A former judicial employee should observe the same restrictions on disclosure of confidential information that apply to a current judicial employee, except as modified by the appointing authority.

E. A judicial employee should not engage in nepotism prohibited by law.

Note: See also 5 U.S.C. § 3110 (employment of relatives); 28 U.S.C. § 458 (employment of judges' relatives).

F. Conflicts of Interest.

(1) A judicial employee should avoid conflicts of interest in the performance of official duties. A conflict of interest arises when a judicial employee knows that he or she (or the spouse, minor child residing in the judicial employee's household, or other close relative of the judicial employee) might be so personally or financially affected by a matter that a reasonable person with knowledge of the relevant facts would question the judicial employee's ability properly to perform official duties in an impartial manner. . . .

CANON 4: IN ENGAGING IN OUTSIDE ACTIVITIES, A JUDICIAL EMPLOYEE SHOULD AVOID THE RISK OF CONFLICT WITH OFFICIAL DUTIES, SHOULD AVOID THE APPEARANCE OF IMPROPRIETY, AND SHOULD COMPLY WITH DISCLOSURE REQUIREMENTS

A. *Outside Activities.* A judicial employee's activities outside of official duties should not detract from the dignity of the court, interfere with the performance of official duties, or adversely reflect on the operation and dignity of the court or office the judicial employee serves. Subject to the foregoing standards and the other provisions of this code, a judicial employee may engage in such activities as civic, charitable, religious, professional, educational, cultural, avocational, social, fraternal, and recreational activities, and may speak, write, lecture, and teach. If such outside activities concern the law, the legal system, or the administration of justice, the judicial employee should first consult with the appointing authority to determine whether the proposed activities are consistent with the foregoing standards and the other provisions of this code. . . .

CANON 5: A JUDICIAL EMPLOYEE SHOULD REFRAIN FROM INAPPROPRIATE POLITICAL ACTIVITY

A. *Partisan Political Activity.* A judicial employee should refrain from partisan political activity; should not act as a leader or hold any office in a partisan political organization; should not make speeches for or publicly endorse or oppose a partisan political organization or candidate; should not solicit funds for or contribute to a partisan political organization, candidate, or event; should not become a candidate for partisan political office; and should not otherwise actively engage in partisan political activities.

B. *Nonpartisan Political Activity.* A member of a judge's personal staff, clerk of court, chief probation officer, chief pretrial services officer, circuit executive, and district court

Figure 11.2 continued

executive should refrain from nonpartisan political activity such as campaigning for or publicly endorsing or opposing a nonpartisan political candidate; soliciting funds for or contributing to a nonpartisan political candidate or event; and becoming a candidate for nonpartisan political office. Other judicial employees may engage in nonpartisan political activity only if such activity does not tend to reflect adversely on the dignity or impartiality of the court or office and does not interfere with the proper performance of official duties. A judicial employee may not engage in such activity while on duty or in the judicial employee's workplace and may not utilize any federal resources in connection with any such activity.

Note: See also 18 U.S.C. chapter 29 (elections and political activities).

Source: From *Code of Conduct for Judicial Employees.* Available Online: http://www.uscourts.gov/RulesAndPolicies/CodesOfConduct.aspx (accessed February 16, 2011).

face, the Supreme Court has been somewhat critical of judicial review of prosecutorial decisions. In *Wayte v. United States* (470 U.S. 598 [1985]), the Court gave this reason for avoiding judicial oversight: "Such factors as the strength of the case, the prosecution's general deterrence value, the Government's overall enforcement plan are not readily susceptible to the kind of analysis the courts are competent to make" (p. 606).

In general, if the prosecutor's decision not to press charges stems from legitimate factors, such as lack of evidence or case backlog, then the decision should be honored. The prosecutor's decision should be honored even if he or she agrees to dismiss criminal charges if the defendant agrees not to file a civil suit.

Restrictions on Bringing Charges

This section turns to situations in which charges are filed but for inappropriate reasons. In other words, whereas the previous sections considered situations in which the prosecutor *fails* to bring charges, this section considers situations in which the prosecutor *cannot* bring charges.

There are two primary reasons a prosecutor cannot bring charges against an accused individual: (1) if the prosecution is unfair and selective (i.e., targets a certain individual unfairly) and (2) if the prosecution is pursued for vindictive reasons. The following subsections focus in detail on these situations.

Before going ahead, it is important to point out that prosecutors may occasionally bring charges, say, for vindictive reasons. Assuming such conduct comes to the attention of someone in a higher position of authority, the prosecuting decision will essentially be overruled. That is, the charges against the accused will be dropped, or in the event that the person is charged and convicted, his or her conviction will be overturned. However, if a prosecutor brings charges for inappropriate reasons and this decision goes uncontested, then the charges will most likely stand.

UNFAIR AND SELECTIVE PROSECUTION   If the prosecutor's decision to press charges is *discriminatory* in nature, the Fourteenth Amendment's equal protection clause can be violated. For example, in *Yick Wo v. Hopkins* (118 U.S. 356 [1886]), the Supreme Court stated:

> Though the law itself be fair on its face and impartial in appearance, yet, if it is applied and administered by public authority with an evil eye and an unequal hand, so as practically to make unjust and illegal discriminations between persons in similar circumstances, material to their rights, the denial of equal justice is still within the prohibition of the Constitution. (pp. 373–374)

DECISION-MAKING EXERCISE 11.2

The Decision Not to Charge

Following are the facts reported by the U.S. District Court for the District of Columbia in *NAACP v. Levi*, discussed previously on Page xx:

> On May 31, 1971, Carnell Russ, a 24-year-old black, while operating his motor vehicle on an Arkansas highway, was arrested for an alleged speeding violation by Jerry Mac Green, a white state trooper. Russ was accompanied by his wife, their minor children, and an adult cousin. The trooper directed him to the county courthouse. Russ complied and upon arrival, parked his vehicle and was escorted into the courthouse by the arresting trooper and two other white law enforcement officers, Charles Ratliff and Norman Draper. Minutes later, Russ returned to the vehicle where his family awaited. He requested and received from his wife sufficient money to post the necessary collateral. He then joined the three officers who were close

> by observing his actions. The four retraced their steps with Russ again in custody. A short time thereafter, Mrs. Russ first observed two of the officers leave and minutes later an ambulance depart from the rear of the courthouse area where her husband had just entered in the officers' custody. She later learned that Mr. Russ, while under detention, had been shot in the center of his forehead by Ratliff and then transported to a hospital. Green and Draper were the sole witnesses to the shooting. Her husband died from the gunshot wound within hours. (p. 1112)

Ratliff was indicted and found not guilty of voluntary manslaughter pursuant to an investigation by the state police. Criminal charges were not brought against the other two officers, and the case was closed. Does the prosecutor's decision not to pursue charges against the other officers seem reasonable?

DECISION-MAKING EXERCISE 11.3

Another Decision Not to Charge

Chief Lord, of the Springfield Police Department, arrested Nancy Simpson for tampering with a witness, Terri Flanders, the alleged victim of an assault by a friend of Simpson's. Simpson hired an attorney, and discussions with the local prosecutor ensued. Simpson agreed to sign a written release—in which she promised not to sue the city, its officials, or the alleged victim of the assault—if the prosecutor dismissed the criminal charges. The criminal charges were dropped. Is fear of being sued a valid reason not to prosecute?

Simply put, if an individual is targeted for prosecution merely because he or she falls into a certain group (e.g., a minority group), then his or her constitutional rights will be violated. This is known as **selective prosecution**.

Since *Yick Wo*, the Court has become more specific as to what constitutes selective prosecution. In *Oyler v. Boles (368 U.S. 448 [1968])*, the Court held that prosecution becomes selective and in violation of the equal protection clause only when it is intentional and is intended to target "a certain class of cases . . . or specific persons." In that case, the defendant presented evidence that he was the only individual of six sentenced under a particular statute. The Court held that this was not discriminatory because the defendant was unable to demonstrate intent by the prosecutor or provide evidence that he fit the group targeted for prosecution. In fact, the Court noted:

Oyler v. Boles *(368 U.S. 448 [1968])*

> The conscious exercise of some selectivity in enforcement is not in itself a federal constitutional violation. Even though the statistics in this case might imply a policy of selective enforcement, it was not stated that the selection was deliberately based upon an unjustifiable standard such as race, religion, or other arbitrary classification. (p. 456)

Since the *Oyler* decision, the courts have imposed a three-pronged test for determining whether prosecution violates equal protection. It must be shown that (1) similarly situated individuals were not prosecuted, (2) the prosecutor intended for this to happen, and (3) the decision resulted from an arbitrary, rather than rational, classification scheme. An *arbitrary* classification scheme would be based on, for example, race or sex. A *rational* classification scheme would be one that considers the evidence against each individual without regard to the color of his or her skin, country of origin, religious preference, sex, or other such criteria.

Filing charges for discriminatory reasons is not the only type of unfair prosecution. Sometimes, prosecutors aggressively pursue *conspicuous individuals* and open themselves to criticism. This is not to say that highly public lawbreakers cannot be charged, however. Indeed, the courts have justified prosecution on the highest charge of certain individuals for the sole purpose of discouraging other people from committing the same offense. As one court noted, "Selective enforcement may . . . be justified when a striking example or a few examples are sought in order to deter other violators" (*People v. Utica Daw's Drug Co.*, 16 A.D.2d 12 [1962], p. 21).

In addition to being criticized for prosecuting high-profile offenders, prosecutors can also get into trouble for targeting the most *significant offender* in a group of offenders. To clarify, think of the conspicuous person cases discussed in the previous paragraphs, in which prosecutors opted to charge one offender instead of another, even though both were suspected of having committed the same offense. When a group of individuals is suspected of having committed various degrees of the same offense, why does the prosecutor only pursue the individual suspected of having committed the most serious offense?

An example of a case illustrating this practice is *State v. McCollum* (159 Wis.2d 184 [App. 1990]). In that case, the court dismissed prostitution charges against nude female dancers. In its decision, the court pointed out that the male patrons of these dancers were not charged, even though Wisconsin law criminalized their behavior, as well.

A fourth method by which prosecutors can open themselves to allegations of unfair and selective prosecution is through what is known as **pretextual prosecution**. This occurs when the prosecutor lacks the evidence to charge someone with a particular crime and so charges him or her with a lesser crime. However, prosecutors are rarely chastised for this type of conduct. For example, in *United States v. Sacco* (428 F.2d 164 [9th Cir. 1970]), a court noted that allowing a prosecutor to pursue lesser charges when the evidence to mount a more serious charge does not exist is perfectly acceptable.

The Supreme Court recently decided a case dealing with alleged discriminatory prosecution. Specifically, in *United States v. Bass* (536 U.S. 862 [2002]), the Court considered a defendant's request for discovery of the Department of Justice's charging practices in capital cases. He alleged that blacks were disproportionately charged in such cases and that he was charged because of his race. His argument did not succeed, however.

VINDICTIVE PROSECUTION   If a prosecutor's charging decision is motivated by revenge, then the resulting charge violates the due process clause of the Fourteenth Amendment. Specifically, if a prosecutor charges an individual simply because he or she is exercising his or her constitutional rights, such charges will not be allowed. This is known as **vindictive prosecution**.

Blackledge v. Perry
(417 U.S. 21 [1974])

This was the decision reached in *Blackledge v. Perry* (417 U.S. 21 [1974]). In that case, the defendant was convicted in a lower court for misdemeanor assault with a deadly weapon. After the defendant filed an appeal with the county superior court, the prosecutor obtained an indictment charging the offender with *felony* assault for the same conduct. The defendant pled guilty to this offense and was sentenced to five to seven years. Notwithstanding the obvious double-jeopardy concerns (covered further

DECISION-MAKING EXERCISE 11.4

What Is Selective Prosecution?

In July 1980, a Presidential Proclamation was issued requiring certain young males to register with the Selective Service System (the information is used for drafting potential soldiers if the need arises). David Elders refused to register and even went so far as the writing letters to government officials, including the President, in which he declared no intention to register. Elders' case, along with cases involving other men who refused to register, was placed in a "Selective Service" file. Only cases in the Selective Service file were selected for prosecution. Elders was prosecuted for failure to register. He claims the prosecution was selective. Is he right?

DECISION-MAKING EXERCISE 11.5

What Is Pretextual Prosecution?

The district attorney (D.A.) suspects that Corinne Dwyer is running a call-girl service out of her suburban home. The D.A. does not have enough evidence to prosecute Dwyer for her prostitution activities, but he does have sufficient evidence to prosecute Dwyer for abandoning an appliance. Dwyer had put a refrigerator at the end of her driveway with a "Free" sign on it, in violation of a statute that provides that "any person who discards or abandons or leaves in any place accessible to children, any refrigerator, icebox, deep freeze locker, . . . which is no longer in use, and which has not had the door removed or the hinges and such portion of the latch mechanism removed to prevent latching or locking of the door, is guilty of a misdemeanor." (This is an actual offense under the California Penal Code, Section 402b.) Dwyer is thus charged and argues that she has been unfairly targeted for pretextual prosecution, in violation of her Fourteenth Amendment right to equal protection. What should the court decide?

in Chapter 14) raised by the prosecutor's conduct in this case, the Supreme Court concluded that "vindictiveness against a defendant for having successfully attacked his first conviction must play no part in the sentence he receives after a new trial" (p. 33). The Court concluded further that such punishment after the fact must be overturned, unless the prosecutor can explain the increase in charges.

The Supreme Court's decision in *Blackledge* applies only in limited contexts, a point that cannot be overemphasized. Namely, it applies only after (1) the charged individual exercises his or her legal rights and (2) the prosecutor increases the charges after the first trial. With regard to the latter restriction, this means that if the prosecutor threatens the defendant with more serious charges during the pretrial phase, the Fourteenth Amendment will not be violated. New evidence could come along during this phase, which may legitimately warrant a more serious charge.

However, in *United States v. Goodwin* (457 U.S. 368 [1982]), the Supreme Court noted that it is possible for a prosecutor to act vengefully during the pretrial phase. It is possible, the Court noted, that "a defendant in an appropriate case might prove objectively that the prosecutor's [pretrial] charging decision was motivated by a desire to punish him for doing something that the law plainly allowed him to do" (p. 384). Furthermore, while "the defendant is free to tender evidence to the court to support a claim that enhanced charges are a direct and unjustifiable penalty for the exercise of a procedural right . . . only in rare cases [will] a defendant be able to overcome the presumptive validity of the prosecutor's actions through such a demonstration" (p. 384). In other words, if the more serious charging decision is made prior to trial, it is presumed that the prosecutor is not acting in a vindictive fashion, and the defendant must prove otherwise.

DECISION-MAKING EXERCISE 11.6

What Is Vindictive Prosecution?

Cesar Fresco was arrested for uttering (i.e., giving, offering, cashing, or passing or attempting to pass) a forged document, which is a felony punishable by a prison term of 2–10 years. He has an extensive criminal history and has committed forgery in the past. The prosecutor offers a plea bargain to Fresco, giving him two choices: (1) He can plead guilty to the crime and the prosecutor will recommend a five-year sentence; or (2) he can reject the plea, be prosecuted under the habitual offender statute, and face a potential life term. The prosecutor tells Fresco, "If you do not accept this agreement, I will prosecute you as a habitual offender and you will go to prison for the rest of your life." Fresco rejects the plea and is convicted. Later, he sues, claiming that the prosecution was vindictive. Will he succeed?

Dealing with Overzealous Prosecutors

By charging offenders, prosecutors serve as advocates for the government. In this capacity, they are immune from suit for charging suspects with crimes.[2] This is reasonable because imagine what would happen to the criminal process if prosecutors could be sued at every turn for charging offenders!

Prosecutors also act as advocates when they argue the government's case. And they can do almost anything in this capacity to secure a conviction without fear of being held liable. Prosecutors have been shielded from such actions as using false statements at pretrial hearings (*Burns v. Reed*, 500 U.S. 478 [1991]), using false testimony at trial (*Imbler v. Pachtman*, 424 U.S. 409 [1976]), failing to disclose exculpatory evidence (*Kalina v. Fletcher*, 522 U.S. 118 [1997]), fabricating evidence, influencing witnesses, and even breaching plea agreements. In a recent case, *Connick v. Thompson*, (No. 09-571 [2011]), the Supreme Court also held that a district attorney's office may not be held liable for failing to train its prosecutors in the event of a single *Brady* violation (i.e., failure to disclose exculpatory evidence).

Not everyone agrees prosecutors should enjoy absolute immunity, especially in light of recent DNA exonerations and high-profile scandals. According to one critic, prosecutors should only enjoy qualified immunity.

> Absolute immunity frustrates the purpose of civil rights legislation by failing to deter frequent and egregious misconduct. It also hinders the development of constitutional standards and the implementation of structural solutions for systemic problems. Prosecutorial liability—with the safeguard of qualified immunity to prevent vexatious litigation—is necessary to ensure the integrity of the criminal justice system.[3]

Qualified immunity was introduced in Chapter 2 in the Section 1983 context. In the prosecution context, it works somewhat differently. *Prosecutorial* qualified immunity attaches (1) when prosecutors act as administrators or investigators and (2) when they make reasonable mistakes. Alternatively, if the plaintiff in a lawsuit can show a prosecutor acted as an administrator or investigator and violated clearly established constitutional law, the prosecutor can be held liable.

---

[2] M. Z. Johns, "Reconsidering Absolute Prosecutorial Immunity," *Brigham Young University Law Review* 2005 (2005): 53–154.
[3] Ibid., p. 56.

RECOURSE   Despite the immunity they enjoy, there is recourse for dealing with overzealous prosecutors. Such recourse generally comes in one of four varieties:

- Private admonition or reprimand
- Public reprimand
- Suspension from law practice
- Permanent disbarment

Prosecutors' supervisors and state bar associations can take the first three actions. The fourth action, disbarment, is usually taken by bar associations alone. How often are prosecutors punished for their wrongdoing? Not very often. According to the Center for Public Integrity, out of more than 11,000 cases of prosecutorial misconduct, only two prosecutors were disbarred.[4] Reprimand was the most common sanction.

The story of Mike Nifong, the prosecutor in the infamous Duke lacrosse case (where three white Duke University lacrosse players were accused of rape by a black stripper), sheds some light on the problem of prosecutorial misconduct. He was the prototypical overzealous prosecutor. For example, he repeatedly made statements to the press that were unsupported and controversial. He also continued to pursue criminal charges, even as new evidence that would have made securing a conviction difficult came to light.

The state bar association filed complaints against Nifong. He was ultimately disbarred and held in contempt of court. Also, since some of Nifong's actions may not have been consistent with the role of an "advocate," his immunity may have been "qualified" rather than absolute. He was sued by the wrongfully accused lacrosse players and their families and claimed bankruptcy.

Joinder

Joinder refers to a situation in which the prosecutor either (1) brings multiple charges against the same individual in the same trial or (2) brings charges against multiple individuals in the same trial. In determining whether either is appropriate, two questions must be asked: First, based on the jurisdiction in question, is joinder appropriate? Second, if joinder is appropriate, will it be unfairly prejudicial? An answer of no to the first question and yes to the second requires what is known as a **severance**.

The question of whether joinder is appropriate is best resolved prior to trial, but sometimes joinder is not addressed until *after* trial. Assume, for example, that a single defendant is charged in the same trial for assault and robbery. Assume further that he is convicted on both counts. If he later claims that joinder was inappropriate (which, incidentally, means the burden of proof falls on him) and succeeds with this argument, what will the result be? According to the Supreme Court in *United States v. Lane* (474 U.S. 438 [1986]), if this joinder has "a substantial and injurious effect or influence in determining the jury's verdict" (p. 449), then new and separate trials must be held.

United States v. Lane
(474 U.S. 438 [1986])

MULTIPLE CHARGES AGAINST THE SAME INDIVIDUAL   According to the *Federal Rules of Criminal Procedure*, multiple charges can be brought against the same individual under the following circumstances: when the charges arise out of (1) the same criminal event (e.g., robbery of a convenience store and assault when fleeing the scene); (2) two separate criminal acts that are tied together in some fashion (e.g., a convenience store robbery to obtain cash to buy and sell illegal drugs); or (3) two criminal acts that are the

---

[4] Center for Public Integrity, *Harmful Error: Investigating America's Local Prosecutors*, http://projects.publicintegrity.org/pm (accessed November 7, 2008).

same or similar in character.[5] This latter circumstance is somewhat vague, but an example should clarify: If a serial killer uses the same *modus operandi* against his victims, he may be tried for several homicides in the same criminal trial.

When the defense argues against joinder, there are a number of motivating concerns. First, there is the concern that the jury (or the judge, if a bench trial is held) will not consider the criminal acts for which the accused is charged separately. Another concern is that the jury will view all the evidence against the accused in a cumulative, rather than separate, fashion. Say, for example, that the prosecution presents eyewitness testimony against a defendant accused of robbery. Also assume that the prosecution presents a murder weapon allegedly used by the defendant on the victim of the robbery. The jury may consider together the eyewitness testimony and the murder weapon and arrive at the conclusion that the accused is guilty. But if the robbery and homicide were tried separately, the jury may not arrive at this conclusion so easily. Finally, another defense argument against joinder is that by trying an individual on several charges in the same trial, he or she will have difficulty asserting separate defenses to the criminal acts at issue.

An obvious problem with joinder is the possibility of double jeopardy. When a prosecutor tries a person on several related crimes in the same trial, he or she must do so carefully. In short, the criminal acts alleged must be similar but not identical. Double jeopardy is considered in Chapter 14, but for now, an example may prove helpful: If the prosecutor charges an individual for first-degree as well as second-degree murder of the same victim in the same trial and the individual is convicted of both offenses, then it will be deemed unconstitutional.

CHARGES AGAINST MULTIPLE DEFENDANTS   The second form of joinder is when multiple defendants are charged in the same criminal trial. The *Federal Rules of Criminal Procedure* state, "Two or more defendants may be charged in the same indictment or information if they are alleged to have participated in the same act or transaction or in the same series of acts or transactions constituting an offense or offenses."[6] In other words, joinder of defendants is reserved in most instances for crimes of conspiracy (i.e., crimes where two or more individuals plot during a criminal act).

As with joinder of *charges*, joinder of *defendants* raises a number of concerns. For instance, the jury may get confused as to who, if anyone, is guilty and simply convict all of the defendants. Or the jury may convict one defendant who is perhaps less guilty than another defendant who is clearly guilty simply because they associated together. Also, it is conceivable that one defendant may testify against another but then refuse to answer questions on cross-examination, citing self-incrimination concerns.

There are clearly arguments against joinder, concerning both charges and defendants. However, there is one clear argument in favor of joinder—namely, efficiency. Allowing prosecutors to join charges and defendants reduces court backlog and speeds up the administration of justice.

THE GRAND JURY

According to the Fifth Amendment, "No person shall be held to answer for a capital, or otherwise infamous crime, unless on a presentment or indictment of a grand jury." This part of the Fifth Amendment cannot be fully appreciated without considering the time in which it was written. The framers favored **grand jury** indictments in certain

---

[5] *Federal Rules of Criminal Procedure*, Rule 8. Available online at http://www.law.cornell.edu/rules/frcrmp/
[6] Ibid.

The pool from which a grand jury is selected must be a fair cross-section of the community.

situations for fear that the prosecutor, a representative of government, could become too powerful in terms of making charging decisions. Indeed, the framers shared a clear sentiment that government should be kept in check, and the grand jury was one method of ensuring this.

Despite that intent, the grand jury is no longer so independent. Instead, the grand jury is now highly dependent on the actions of the prosecutor. Grand juries still perform important investigative functions, and they are quite powerful in terms of, for instance, being able to subpoena witnesses and records. But their role today is tied closely to the prosecutor. In fact, almost every state makes the prosecutor the main legal adviser of the grand jury and requires him or her to be present during all grand jury sessions. However, in some states, the grand jury functions independently of the prosecutor.

Even though the Fifth Amendment suggests that indictment by grand jury is guaranteed for certain offenses, this right has not been incorporated. In the 1884 decision of *Hurtado v. California* (110 U.S. 516 [1884]), the Supreme Court stated that indictment by a grand jury is not a right guaranteed by the due process clause of the Fourteenth Amendment. The Court stated:

Hurtado v. California
(110 U.S. 516 [1884])

> [W]e are unable to say that the substitution for a presentment or indictment by a grand jury of [a] proceeding by information after examination and commitment by a magistrate, certifying to the probable guilt of the defendant, with the right on his part to the aid of counsel, and to the cross-examination of the witnesses produced for the prosecution, is not due process of law. (p. 538)

It should be emphasized that just because the right to grand jury indictment has not been incorporated to the states, this does not mean that states do not require this method of prosecution. Several states do require that, for the most part, felonies are to be prosecuted only by grand jury indictment. The same is true for the federal system. Most states, however, permit prosecution by indictment or information. See Figure 11.3 for an overview of the mechanisms for filing serious charges in each state.

So, since most states permit indictment or information, under what circumstances is one or the other method used? Typically, grand jury indictment will be the charging mechanism of choice when (1) the case is of great public and/or political significance; (2) the investigative power of the grand jury is useful; (3) the grand jury may be able to

FIGURE 11.3

Charging Methods for Serious Crimes by State

Key
- Grand jury indictment required
- Grand jury indictment required only in capital and life imprisonment cases
- Grand jury indictment not required

Source: D. B. Rottman and S. M. Strickland, *State Court Organization, 2004* (Washington, DC: National Center for State Courts, 2004). Note that some states requiring grand jury indictment do so only for certain offenses. For example, Texas requires grand jury indictments for felonies, not misdemeanors.

issue an indictment more quickly compared to holding a preliminary hearing and then issuing an information indictment; or (4) one or more witnesses is hesitant to speak in open court, preferring the secrecy surrounding grand jury proceedings.

How a Grand Jury Is Constructed

A grand jury can be *impaneled* either by the court or by the prosecutor. Usually, the court has this responsibility, but prosecutors are becoming increasingly able to decide whether a grand jury is necessary.

The term *grand jury* should not be construed as singular; in larger jurisdictions, several grand juries may be acting at the same time. One or more could be performing investigative functions, and one or more others could be working on specific cases.

DURATION   Once a grand jury has been convened, its members serve for a specified period of time. A term can last from one to three months but sometimes less, if the court or prosecutor believes that further deliberation is unnecessary. Under the *Federal Rules of Criminal Procedure*, a regular grand jury cannot serve for a period longer than 18 months, unless the court extends the service "upon a determination that such extension is in the public interest."[7] Fortunately, people selected for grand juries do not have to meet every day; usually, a grand jury meets several days a month.

SIZE   Grand juries are larger than ordinary trial juries. In the past, grand juries consisting of 24 or so people were not uncommon. Today, grand juries are usually smaller, or in the neighborhood of 16–20 people. One state, Tennessee, permits a grand jury of 13 individuals, but the voting requirements in that state are fairly restrictive. See Figure 11.4 for an illustration of grand jury size requirements by state.

FIGURE 11.4

Grand Jury Size Requirements by State

Source: www.uday ton.edu/~grandjur/stategj/sizegj.htm (accessed March 10, 2011).

[7] Ibid., Rule 6.

VOTING REQUIREMENTS Grand jury voting requirements also vary by state. The most common voting requirement is that 12 grand jury members must agree on an indictment. However, one state, Virginia, requires only four votes for issuance of a **true bill**, which is the endorsement made by a grand jury when it finds sufficient evidence to warrant a criminal charge. Texas requires a vote of 9 out of 12.

As with a *petit jury* (i.e., that used in criminal trials), a grand jury is headed by a foreperson, who is charged with, among other duties, signing the indictment and keeping track of the votes of each member. Figure 11.5 presents portions of the indictment against Zacarias Moussaoui, one of the terrorists involved in the 9/11 attacks.

SELECTION OF MEMBERS People are selected for a grand jury in the same way they are selected for an ordinary trial (i.e., petit) jury: They are subpoenaed. In some states, grand jury members are selected from a list of eligible voters. In others, they are selected from a list of licensed drivers. Still other states select grand jury members from a list of tax returns, telephone directories, and so on. Most people do not get the opportunity to serve on a grand jury because grand juries are not convened that frequently.

The grand jury selection process usually involves two stages. First, a list of potential grand jury members is compiled by any of the methods (or others) just described. This list

FIGURE 11.5

Portions of Zacarias Moussaoui Indictment

IN THE UNITED STATES DISTRICT COURT
FOR THE EASTERN DISTRICT OF VIRGINIA
ALEXANDRIA DIVISION

UNITED STATES OF AMERICA	)	CRIMINAL NO:
	)	
-v-	)	Conspiracy to Commit Acts of Terrorism
	)	Transcending National Boundaries
ZACARIAS MOUSSAOUI,	)	(18 U.S.C. §§ 2332b(a)(2) & (c))
a/k/a "Shaqil,"	)	(Count One)
a/k/a "Abu Khalid al Sahrawi,"	)	
	)	Conspiracy to Commit Aircraft Piracy
	)	(49 U.S.C. §§ 46502(a)(1)(A) and (a)(2)(B))
Defendant.	)	(Count Two)
	)	
	)	Conspiracy to Destroy Aircraft
	)	(18 U.S.C. §§ 32(a)(7) & 34)
	)	(Count Three)
	)	
	)	Conspiracy to Use Weapons of Mass Destruction
	)	(18 U.S.C. § 2332a(a))
	)	(Count Four)
	)	
	)	Conspiracy to Murder United States Employees
	)	(18 U.S.C. §§ 1114 & 1117)
	)	(Count Five)
	)	
	)	Conspiracy to Destroy Property
	)	(18 U.S.C. §§ 844(f), (i), (n))
	)	(Count Six)

INDICTMENT

THE GRAND JURY CHARGES THAT:

COUNT TWO
(Conspiracy to Commit Aircraft Piracy)

1. The allegations contained in Count One are repeated.
2. From in or about 1989 until the date of the filing of this Indictment, in the Eastern District of Virginia, the Southern District of New York, and elsewhere, the defendant, ZACARIAS MOUSSAOUI, a/k/a "Shaqil," a/k/a "Abu Khalid al Sahrawi," and other members and associates of al Qaeda and others known and unknown to the Grand Jury, unlawfully, willfully and knowingly combined, conspired, confederated and agreed to commit aircraft piracy, by seizing and exercising control of aircraft in the special aircraft jurisdiction of the United States by force, violence, threat of force and violence, and intimidation, and with wrongful intent, with the result that thousands of people died on September 11, 2001.

Overt Acts

3. In furtherance of the conspiracy, and to effect its illegal objects, the defendant, and others known and unknown to the Grand Jury, committed the overt acts set forth in Count One of this Indictment, which are fully incorporated by reference.

(In violation of Title 49, United States Code, Sections 46502(a)(1)(A) and (a)(2)(B).)

COUNT THREE
(Conspiracy to Destroy Aircraft)

1. The allegations contained in Count One are repeated.
2. From in or about 1989 until the date of the filing of this Indictment, in the Eastern District of Virginia, the Southern District of New York, and elsewhere, the defendant, ZACARIAS MOUSSAOUI, a/k/a "Shaqil," a/k/a "Abu Khalid al Sahrawi," and other members and associates of al Qaeda and others known and unknown to the Grand Jury, unlawfully, willfully and knowingly combined, conspired, confederated and agreed to willfully destroy and wreck aircraft in the special aircraft jurisdiction of the United States, and to willfully perform acts of violence against and incapacitate individuals on such aircraft, so as likely to endanger the safety of such aircraft, resulting in the deaths of thousands of persons on September 11, 2001.

Overt Acts

3. In furtherance of the conspiracy, and to effect its illegal objects, the defendant, and others known and unknown to the Grand Jury, committed the overt acts set forth in Count One of this Indictment, which are fully incorporated by reference.

(In violation of Title 18, United States Code, Sections 32(a)(7) and 34.)

COUNT FOUR
(Conspiracy to Use Weapons of Mass Destruction)

1. The allegations contained in Count One are repeated.
2. From in or about 1989 until the date of the filing of this Indictment, in the Eastern District of Virginia, the Southern District of New York, and elsewhere, the defendant, ZACARIAS MOUSSAOUI, a/k/a "Shaqil," a/k/a "Abu Khalid al Sahrawi,"

Figure 11.5 continued

and other members and associates of al Qaeda and others known and unknown to the Grand Jury, unlawfully, willfully and knowingly combined, conspired, confederated and agreed to use weapons of mass destruction, namely, airplanes intended for use as missiles, bombs, and similar devices, without lawful authority against persons within the United States, with the results of such use affecting interstate and foreign commerce, and against property that was owned, leased and used by the United States and by departments and agencies of the United States, with the result that thousands of people died on September 11, 2001.

Overt Acts

3. In furtherance of the conspiracy, and to effect its illegal objects, the defendant, and others known and unknown to the Grand Jury, committed the overt acts set forth in Count One of this Indictment, which are fully incorporated by reference.

(In violation of Title 18, United States Code, Section 2332a(a).)

Source: http://www.usdoj.gov/ag/moussaouiindictment.htm (accessed February 16, 2011).

---

of grand jury members is known as the *venire*. Next, people are selected from the list to serve on the grand jury. At both stages, constitutional complications can arise.

First, special steps need to be taken to ensure that the list of potential grand jurors, like that for a typical petit jury, is fair and impartial. In particular, the defendant can raise constitutional challenges to the grand jury selection process if it is *not* fair and impartial. One such challenge is based on the *equal protection clause*. This requires showing that there is a significant disparity between a group's representation in the community and its representation on the grand jury (see *Casteneda v. Partida*, 430 U.S. 482 [1977]).

Another constitutional challenge against the composition of the grand jury pool stems from the *fair cross-section requirement* announced in *Taylor v. Louisiana* (419 U.S. 522 [1975]). There, the Court held that "systematic exclusion" of a "large distinct group" from the pool from which the (petit) jury is chosen violates the Sixth Amendment. The same logic carries over to the grand jury. If, for example, a grand jury consists of all white members and 40 percent of the community is black, the fair cross-section requirement will have been violated. By contrast, if the grand jury does not contain a snake handler, a militant feminist, a rabbi, or some such specific type of individual, the fair cross-section requirement will not have been violated because these and other individuals do not constitute large, distinct groups.

As for the selection of grand jury members from the pool, similar constitutional concerns can be raised. If, for instance, the grand jury pool is representative of a fair cross-section of the community, it is still possible that people could be excluded from the jury on a systematic basis. In *Rose v. Mitchell* (443 U.S. 545 [1979]), the Court held that the "right to equal protection of the laws [is] denied when [the defendant] is indicted from a grand jury from which members of a racial group purposefully have been excluded" (p. 556). The final composition of the grand jury can also be challenged on due process grounds (see *Beck v. Washington*, 369 U.S. 541 [1962]).

Taylor v. Louisiana
(419 U.S. 522 [1975])

Rose v. Mitchell
(443 U.S. 545 [1979])

Secrecy of Grand Jury Proceedings

Grand jury proceedings are intensely secret. In *United States v. Rose* (215 F.2d 617 [1954]), the Third Circuit Court of Appeals announced several reasons for this:

(1) to prevent the escape of those whose indictment may be contemplated;
(2) to insure the utmost freedom to the grand jury in its deliberations, and to

prevent persons subject to indictment or their friends from importuning the grand jurors; (3) to prevent subornation of perjury or tampering with the witnesses who may testify before the grand jury and later appear at the trial of those indicted by it; (4) to encourage free and untrammeled disclosures by persons who have information with respect to the commission of crimes; [and] (5) to protect the innocent accused who is exonerated from disclosure of the fact that he has been under investigation, and from the expense of standing trial where there was no probability of guilt. (pp. 628–629)

Notwithstanding these concerns, there are two categories of case law concerning grand jury secrecy: (1) cases addressing whether grand jury witness testimony should be supplied to the defense and (2) cases addressing the extent to which grand jury witnesses can share their testimony with other parties, such as other government officials.

DISCLOSURE OF WITNESS TESTIMONY TO THE DEFENSE According to the *Federal Rules of Criminal Procedure*, grand jury proceedings can be shared with the defense when the defendant makes "a showing that grounds may exist for a motion to dismiss the indictment because of matters occurring before the grand jury."[8] This type of disclosure is exceedingly rare and generally limited to situations in which there is evidence that prosecutorial misconduct occurred before the grand jury proceedings commenced.

DISCLOSURE OF WITNESS TESTIMONY TO OTHER PARTIES In *Butterworth v. Smith* (494 U.S. 624 [1990]), the Supreme Court declared that the First Amendment may provide an exception to the grand jury secrecy requirement. In that case, the Court held that a Florida statute that prohibited grand jury witnesses from recounting their own testimony violated freedom of speech.

*Butterworth v. Smith
(494 U.S. 624 [1990])*

Butterworth dealt with a defendant who wanted to share his testimony with third parties. However, many more cases deal with the issue of whether other third parties (i.e., besides the defense) should be able to access the records of grand jury proceedings. One such case is *Douglas Oil Co. of California v. Petrol Stops Northwest* (441 U.S. 211 [1979]). In that case, the Supreme Court held that parties seeking access to grand jury records "must show that the material they seek is needed to avoid a possible injustice to another judicial proceeding, that the need for disclosure is greater than the need for continued secrecy, and that their request is structured to cover only material so needed" (p. 222).

A third party that has traditionally been given greater latitude in terms of access to grand jury proceedings is the government. In fact, the *Federal Rules of Criminal Procedure* provide that no showing of "particularized need" is necessary in order to disclose information to other government attorneys who are assisting in prosecution.[9] However, when disclosure is sought by government officials who are *not* assisting in the prosecution, the Supreme Court has held that a showing of need *does* have to be made (see *United States v. Sells Engineering, Inc.*, 463 U.S. 418 [1983]).

Rights of Witnesses Testifying before Grand Juries

Grand juries rely heavily on witness testimony. However, the rights afforded to grand jury witnesses differ significantly from those afforded to witnesses in other settings (e.g., at trial). Also, the rights afforded to the individuals targeted by grand jury investigations differ from those afforded to criminal defendants.

---

[8] Ibid.

[9] Ibid.

The cases in this area revolve around three issues: (1) the right of the individual targeted by a grand jury investigation to testify, (2) whether grand jury witnesses are required to be advised of their right not to testify, and (3) the right to counsel as applied in grand jury proceedings.

RIGHT TO TESTIFY   It is well known that the defendant in a criminal trial has a constitutional right to testify or not testify in his or her own defense. In contrast, someone who is the target of a grand jury investigation usually *does not* enjoy the right to testify. Indeed, several states do not even grant the target of a grand jury investigation the right to be present. This restriction is justified on the same secrecy grounds discussed earlier. Also, since many grand jury proceedings are investigative, there may not be a specific target until the proceedings have reached a close. In such a situation, it would be cumbersome to allow all potential targets to be present in order to give testimony in their defense.

BEING ADVISED OF THE RIGHT NOT TO TESTIFY   When witnesses appear before grand juries, they enjoy the Fifth Amendment's privilege against self-incrimination. This is no different than in a criminal trial. However, a question has arisen in the courts over whether grand jury witnesses must be *told* that they can remain silent. In other words, the courts have grappled with whether the *Miranda* warnings should apply in the grand jury context.

As noted earlier in this book, the *Miranda* warnings are only required during custodial interrogation. Therefore, the following question must be asked: Are grand jury proceedings akin to custodial interrogations? At least one decision suggests that *Miranda* does not apply in the grand jury context because the proceedings are not as "inherently coercive" as traditional custodial interrogations (e.g., *Gollaher v. United States*, 419 F.2d 520 [9th Cir. 1969]). However, some states require by law that the targets of grand jury investigations, as well as grand jury witnesses, be advised of their right not to testify. The Supreme Court has yet to rule on this issue.

RIGHT TO COUNSEL   Should grand jury witnesses and the targets of grand jury investigations be provided with counsel? The Supreme Court has answered no to this question in at least two cases: *In re Groban's Petition* (352 U.S. 330 [1957]) and *United States v. Mandujano* (425 U.S. 564 [1976]). A person who has already been charged may have a right to counsel before a grand jury proceeding, but such an individual is rarely the target of such a proceeding (see, e.g., *Kirby v. Illinois*, 406 U.S. 682 [1972]). The typical grand jury witness is someone called upon to shed light on a particular case. Such witnesses do not enjoy the right to counsel in grand jury proceedings, but they can of course assert Fifth Amendment protection and refuse to incriminate themselves. As we will see shortly, though, the grand jury may offer a grant of immunity in exchange for a witness's testimony.

The Supreme Court has stated that grand jury proceedings take place before the initiation of adversarial criminal proceedings and, as such, are outside the scope of the Sixth Amendment's right to counsel. There are also several additional reasons for not allowing counsel to be present during grand jury proceedings: (1) the investigation could be delayed if the witness repeatedly confers with his or her attorney; (2) the investigation could be disrupted if the witness raises objections and arguments; and, of course, (3) secrecy could be compromised.

*United States v.
Mandujano   (425 U.S.
564 [1976])*

Investigative Powers of the Grand Jury

One of the main duties of a grand jury is to investigate alleged wrongdoing in order to determine whether an indictment should be issued. Because of this function, a grand

jury has a great deal of investigative power. For example, as decided in *United States v.* *United States v. Calandra*
Calandra (414 U.S. 338 [1974]), a grand jury "may compel the production of evidence or *(414 U.S. 338 [1974])*
the testimony of witnesses as it considers appropriate, and its operation generally is
unrestrained by the technical procedural and evidentiary rules governing the conduct
of criminal trials" (p. 343). In this vein, a grand jury can subpoena witnesses and
evidence. However, it can also extend grants of immunity to certain individuals in
exchange for their testimony, and it can find people in contempt for failing to cooperate
with an investigation.

SUBPOENAS   Two types of subpoenas are available to grand juries: (1) a **subpoena** *ad*
testificandum and (2) a **subpoena** *duces tecum*. The former compels a witness to
appear before the grand jury, and the latter compels the production of tangible
evidence (e.g., a suspected murder weapon). The power of the grand jury to utilize
both of these mechanisms is virtually unrestricted; however, there have been a few
constitutional objections to their use.

First, some have argued that a subpoena to appear before the grand jury amounts
to a seizure within the meaning of the Fourth Amendment. The Supreme Court
acknowledged in *United States v. Dioniso* (410 U.S. 1 [1973]) that being forced to appear
before a grand jury may be inconvenient but not in comparison to the "historically
grounded obligation of every person to appear and give his evidence before the grand
jury" (pp. 9–10). Furthermore, Fourth Amendment restrictions on the grand jury's
subpoena power "would assuredly impede its investigation and frustrate the public's
interest in the fair and expeditious administration of the laws" (p. 17).

As for tangible evidence, the Supreme Court has likewise held that a subpoena
duces tecum does not amount to a Fourth Amendment seizure. However, according to
the Court in *Hale v. Henkel* (201 U.S. 43 [1906]), such a subpoena must comport with the *Hale v. Henkel*
Fourth Amendment's particularity requirement. In *United States v. Gurule* (437 F.2d 239 *(201 U.S. 43 [1906])*
[10th Cir. 1970]), the Tenth Circuit announced a three-prong test for ensuring that a
grand jury subpoena satisfies the Fourth Amendment's reasonableness requirement:
"(1) the subpoena may command only the production of things relevant to the
investigation being pursued; (2) specification of things to be produced must be made
with reasonable particularity; and (3) production of records covering only a reasonable
period of time may be required" (p. 241).

It has already been noted that grand jury witnesses enjoy the Fifth Amendment
privilege, but could being forced to appear before a grand jury itself be incriminating?
Not surprisingly, people have objected to grand jury subpoenas for this reason. Few, if
any, have succeeded, however. Why? Someone who is appearing before a grand jury
does not know in advance what questions will be asked and, as such, cannot assert the
Fifth Amendment privilege prior to his or her appearance.

GRANTS OF IMMUNITY   Even though witnesses appearing before the grand jury enjoy
the Fifth Amendment privilege against self-incrimination, the grand jury can get around
this. In particular, the grand jury can extend *grants of immunity* to witnesses in exchange
for their testimony. A grant of transactional immunity prohibits future prosecution on the
acts for which the witness testifies. In contrast, so-called use and derivative use immunity
only bars the use of the witness's testimony against him or her in the future. If evidence is
obtained after the fact, independent of the witness's testimony before the grand jury, then
he or she can be charged (see *Kastigar v. United States*, 406 U.S. 441 [1972]).

FINDINGS OF CONTEMPT   When someone is subpoenaed to appear before the grand
jury but does not show up, the jury's **contempt power** can be utilized. That is, the
grand jury can impose civil and criminal sanctions on the individual. For example, an

DECISION-MAKING EXERCISE 11.7

Grand Jury Investigations

Assume that the grand jury is investigating a major case of corporate fraud. Assume further that the grand jury issues a subpoena *duces tecum*, calling for "all understandings, contracts or correspondence between the Fabulous Widgets Company and all of its business partners, as well as all reports made and accounts rendered by such companies from the date of the organization of the Fabulous Widgets Company, as well as all letters received by that company since its organization from all of its business partners." Can this subpoena be considered sufficiently particular?

individual who refuses to appear before the grand jury can be jailed until which point he or she agrees to appear. Note that the grand jury's contempt power is limited to compelling the presence of the witness, not his or her testimony. The witness who *does* appear can still invoke the Fifth Amendment privilege and not make a statement.

Challenging a Grand Jury Indictment

Restrictions on prosecutors' charging decisions were discussed earlier in this chapter. Restrictions are also placed on grand jury indictments. That is, it is possible to challenge a grand jury indictment on constitutional and similar grounds, including (1) lack of evidence; (2) misconduct by the prosecutor as the adviser of the grand jury; (3) unfair selection of grand jury members; and (4) use of different evidence at trial from that presented to the grand jury. When any of these circumstances exists, a grand jury indictment will be *quashed* or declared invalid.

There is considerable variation among the states as to what amount of evidence is necessary to secure a valid indictment. Some states hold to the probable cause standard. Others state that the grand jury can only issue an indictment when all the evidence before it would, if unexplained, warrant a conviction at trial. In Utah, an indictment can only be issued on clear and convincing evidence that a crime was committed and that the person charged committed it. In either case, a grand jury indictment can be quashed if the evidence relied on to obtain the indictment is insufficient. Also, if the evidence used to obtain an indictment is obtained in an unconstitutional fashion, the indictment can be quashed by essentially invoking the exclusionary rule.

Flagrant prosecutorial misconduct can also lead to an indictment being quashed. If, for instance, the prosecutor fails to supply the grand jury with exculpatory evidence, a subsequent indictment *may* be quashed but only if such misconduct violates existing law. There is, surprisingly, very little existing case law in this area. Indeed, the Supreme Court held in *United States v. Williams* (504 U.S. 36 [1992]) that federal courts cannot easily dismiss an indictment because of prosecutorial misconduct. "Because the grand jury is an institution separate from the courts, over whose functioning the courts do not preside, we think it clear that, as a general matter at least, no such 'supervisory' judicial authority exists" (p. 47).

While the courts have been hesitant to quash indictments based on insufficient evidence and prosecutorial misconduct, discrimination in the selection of grand jury members is taken very seriously. As indicated earlier in this chapter, the composition of the grand jury must comply with the due process and equal protection requirements. When it does not, subsequent indictments can be quashed. The Court noted in *United States v. Mechanik* (475 U.S. 66 [1986]) that "racial discrimination in the selection of grand jurors is so pernicious and other remedies so impractical, that the remedy of automatic reversal [may be] necessary as a prophylactic means of deterring grand jury discrimination in the future" (p. 70).

DECISION-MAKING EXERCISE 11.8

Deciding on Variance

A grand jury returned an indictment against two women, charging them both with conspiracy to commit murder. Typically, a criminal *conspiracy* exists when two or more persons agree to commit a crime and then commit some sort of overt act in furtherance of that agreement (e.g., *People v. Cockrell*, 63 Cal. 2d 779). The grand jury was presented with a recorded telephone call between the two women, in which they agreed to murder their husbands. The grand jury was *not* presented with evidence that the women bought handguns for themselves. That evidence was introduced by the prosecutor at trial, however. The women were convicted and are now appealing their convictions, claiming that there was a variance between their indictment and the prosecutor's case. Will they succeed?

Finally, if the prosecutor presents evidence at trial that departs significantly from that relied on by the grand jury for the purpose of issuing an indictment, sanctions will be imposed. If this **variance** between the trial evidence and the grand jury evidence is minimal, the indictment will probably not be quashed. Interpreted differently, if the evidence presented by the prosecutor to secure an indictment is "in no way essential to the offense on which the jury convicted," the indictment will probably not be quashed (see *United States v. Miller*, 471 U.S. 130 [1985]).

THE DEFENSE ATTORNEY

The Sixth Amendment to the U.S. Constitution provides "in all criminal prosecutions, the accused shall enjoy the right . . . to have the Assistance of Counsel for his defense." This right was applied to the states in the landmark decision of *Gideon v. Wainwright* (372 U.S. 335 [1963]). While on its face, this portion of the Sixth Amendment seems straightforward, it has actually given rise to two important questions: (1) What constitutes a *criminal prosecution*? and (2) What does *assistance of counsel* mean?

Gideon v. Wainwright (372 U.S. 335 [1963])

Answers to these two questions are provided in the subsections that follow. The right to counsel as applied at other stages of the criminal process and waiver of counsel and the right to counsel of one's own choice are also addressed.

The Right to Counsel in a Criminal Prosecution

DUE PROCESS ORIGINS   Prior to *Gideon*, the right to counsel did not exist for all individuals. Usually, counsel was provided only for defendants who could afford it. There were occasions prior to the 1960s, however, in which counsel was provided to criminal defendants who could *not* afford it. For example, the constitutional right of an indigent defendant to be represented by counsel was first announced in *Powell v. Alabama* (287 U.S. 45 [1932]). In that case, the Supreme Court reversed the convictions of several indigent defendants who were not represented by counsel at trial. Significantly, though, the Court based its decision on the Fifth Amendment's due process clause, not the Sixth Amendment. In the Court's words:

Powell v. Alabama (287 U.S. 45 [1932])

> The right to be heard would be, in many cases, of little avail if it did not comprehend the right to be heard by counsel. Even the intelligent and educated layman has small and sometimes no skill in the science of law. If charged with crimes, he is incapable, generally, of determining for himself whether the indictment is good or bad. He is unfamiliar with the rules of evidence. Left without aid of counsel he may be put on trial without a proper charge, and convicted upon incompetent evidence, or evidence irrelevant to

the issue or otherwise inadmissible. He lacks both the skill and knowledge adequately to prepare his defense, even though he may have a perfect one. He requires the guiding hand of counsel at every step in the proceedings against him. Without it, though he be not guilty, he faces the danger of conviction because he does not know how to establish his innocence. (pp. 68–69)

However, the right to counsel announced in *Powell* was not without limitations. It applied only to "capital case[s], where the defendant is unable to employ counsel, and is incapable adequately of making his own defense because of ignorance, feeble-mindedness, illiteracy, or the like" (p. 71).

Johnson v. Zerbst (304 U.S. 458 [1938])

THE CONTEMPORARY SIXTH AMENDMENT APPROACH   In *Johnson v. Zerbst* (304 U.S. 458 [1938]), the Court recognized the Sixth Amendment right to counsel in all federal prosecutions, stating that the Sixth Amendment "embodies a realistic recognition of the obvious truth that the average defendant does not have the professional legal skill to protect himself" (pp. 462–463).

But the Sixth Amendment's right to counsel was still not extended to the states. In *Johnson*, the Court refused to apply its decision to the states, and this holding was reaffirmed a few years later in the case of *Betts v. Brady* (316 U.S. 455 [1942]). There, the Court held that "[t]he Due Process Clause of the Fourteenth Amendment does not incorporate, as such, the specific guarantees found in the Sixth Amendment" (pp. 461–462). It would not be until the 1963 decision in *Gideon v. Wainwright* that the Sixth Amendment right to counsel became incorporated. In that case, the Court recognized that "lawyers in criminal courts are necessities, not luxuries" (p. 344).

Gideon dealt with a felony, which led the Supreme Court to conclude that the Sixth Amendment right to counsel applies only in felony proceedings. However, in *Argersinger v. Hamlin* (407 U.S. 25 [1972]), the Court held that the right to counsel applies in misdemeanor cases, also. According to the Court, "The requirement of counsel may well be necessary for a fair trial even in petty-offense prosecution. We are by no means convinced that legal and constitutional questions involved in a case that actually leads to imprisonment even for a brief period are any less complex than when a person can be sent off for six months or more" (p. 33).

This decision was then clarified in *Scott v. Illinois* (440 U.S. 367 [1979]), in which the Court held that the right to counsel does not apply where loss of liberty is merely a *possibility*. In short, when there is no possibility of confinement, the Sixth Amendment right to counsel does not apply. A twist on the *Scott* decision was recently handed down in *Alabama v. Shelton* (535 U.S. 654 [2002]), in which the Court held that "[a] suspended sentence that may 'end up in the actual deprivation of a person's liberty' may not be imposed unless the defendant was accorded 'the guiding hand of counsel' in the prosecution for the crime charged" (p. 654). *Shelton* differed from *Scott* because Shelton was placed on probation; Scott was not.

The Right to Counsel at Other Stages of the Criminal Process

Until the Supreme Court's 1963 decision in *Gideon*, its cases on the right to counsel had addressed this right primarily in the context of trials. After *Gideon*, however, the Court began to turn its attention to the right to counsel at other stages of the criminal process. This right can be tied to the Sixth Amendment, but the Court has also defended it (i.e., to the extent it exists) on grounds of self-incrimination, due process, and equal protection.

THE SIXTH AMENDMENT APPROACH   In order to determine whether the Sixth Amendment right to counsel applies outside the trial context, the Court once held that a *critical stage* analysis was necessary. In *United States v. Wade* (388 U.S. 218 [1967]), the Supreme Court announced a two-prong test for determining when counsel is required under the Sixth Amendment: (1) "whether potential substantial prejudice to the defendant's rights inheres in the particular confrontation;" and (2) whether counsel can "help avoid that prejudice" (p. 227). In support of its decision, the Court stated, "The trial which might determine the accused's fate may well not be that in the courtroom but that at the pretrial confrontation, with the State aligned against the accused, the witness the sole jury, and the accused unprotected against the overreaching, intentional or unintentional, [influence of the government]" (p. 235).

What, then, was considered a *critical stage*? The Court stated that the period from arraignment to trial was arguably the most critical period of the proceedings. Preliminary hearings and sentencing hearings were also considered critical stages in the criminal process (see *Mempa v. Rhay*, 389 U.S. 128 [1967]; *Coleman v. Alabama*, 399 U.S. 1 [1970]).

In the 1973 decision *United States v. Ash* (413 U.S. 300 [1973]), the Court abandoned the critical stage analysis and focused instead on whether "trial-like confrontations" necessitate counsel. The Court was unsatisfied with the open-endedness of the critical stage analysis. *Trial-like confrontations*, according to the Court, were proceedings that confronted the accused with the "intricacies of the law and the advocacy of the public prosecutor" (p. 309). Cases in which this definition was applied include but are not limited to *Gerstein v. Pugh* (420 U.S. 103 [1975]) and *Estelle v. Smith* (451 U.S. 454 [1981]). But since this definition is equally vague, the Court abandoned it for a third and final approach to the Sixth Amendment right to counsel outside trial.

In *Kirby v. Illinois* (406 U.S. 682 [1972]), the Court became even more specific and held, once and for all, that the right to counsel applies not only in criminal prosecutions but also at the "initiation of adversary proceedings." This means that the Sixth Amendment right to counsel applies not only after indictment, formal charging, and on through sentencing, but also as early on as the initial appearance (*Rothgery v. Gillespie County*, No. 07-440 [2008]).

Kirby v. Illinois
(406 U.S. 682 [1972])

THE FIFTH AMENDMENT APPROACH   As was already noted in Chapter 8, the right to counsel has also been applied through the Fifth Amendment. In *Miranda v. Arizona* (384 U.S. 436 [1966]), the Court held that the Fifth Amendment's privilege against self-incrimination grants suspects the right to counsel during custodial interrogations because of the "inherent coerciveness" of such activities. Furthermore, the right to counsel during custodial interrogations applies before or after commencement of formal adversary proceedings.

THE DUE PROCESS APPROACH   The right to counsel also stems from the due process clause of the Fourteenth Amendment, but only in certain circumstances. The Fourteenth Amendment has been used to justify the right to counsel primarily in criminal appeals and probation/parole revocation hearings. For example, in *Douglas v. California* (372 U.S. 353 [1963], the Court held that the right to counsel extends to convicted indigents for appeals of right (i.e., appeals to which the individual is legally entitled). And in *Gagnon v. Scarpelli* (411 U.S. 778 [1973]), the Court held that as a matter of due process, indigents are entitled to counsel at probation and parole revocation hearings but only on a case-by-case basis (e.g., whether the complexity of the issues at stake is significant).

In contrast, the right to counsel does not necessarily exist so that indigent convicts can prepare petitions for *discretionary* appeals (i.e., those that the reviewing court gets to decide it wants to hear) (see *Ross v. Moffitt*, 417 U.S. 600 [1974]). The Court noted that the government "does not automatically . . . act . . . unfairly by refusing to provide counsel to indigent defendants at every stage of the [appellate process]" (p. 611). Similarly, in *Pennsylvania v. Finley* (481 U.S. 551 [1987]), the Court announced that the right to counsel does not exist so that convicted criminals can prepare *habeas corpus* petitions. The reason offered by the Court is that "[post-]conviction relief is even further removed from the criminal trial than is discretionary direct review" (pp. 556–557).

Waiver of the Right to Counsel

Though the Sixth Amendment provides for the right to counsel, accused individuals sometimes prefer to represent themselves. Indeed, according to the Supreme Court, criminal defendants have a constitutional right to represent themselves at trial (*Faretta v. California*, 422 U.S. 806 [1975]). This is known as a ***pro se* defense**. In reaching this decision, the Court noted that the Sixth Amendment only guarantees the *assistance* of counsel, not necessarily *representation* by counsel:

> The language and spirit of the Sixth Amendment contemplate that counsel, like the other defense tools guaranteed by the Amendment, shall be an aid to a willing defendant—not an organ of State interposed between an unwilling defendant and his right to defend himself personally. . . . An unwanted counsel "represents" the defendant only through a tenuous and unacceptable legal fiction. Unless the accused has acquiesced in such representation, the defense presented is not the defense guaranteed him by the Constitution, for in a very real sense, it is not his defense. (pp. 820–821)

The Court also emphasized in *Faretta* that the framers viewed the "inestimable worth of free choice" as more important than the right to counsel. Also, "[t]o force a lawyer on a defendant can only lead [the defendant] to believe that the law contrives against him" (p. 834).

Johnson v. Zerbst
(304 U.S. 458 [1938])

Not every defendant who wishes to proceed without counsel is allowed to do so, however. In *Johnson v. Zerbst* (304 U.S. 458 [1938]), the Supreme Court stated that a defendant may only waive counsel if the waiver is "competent and intelligent." According to the Court in *Carnley v. Cochran* (369 U.S. 506 [1962]), "the record must show, or there must be an allegation and evidence must show, that an accused was offered counsel but intelligently and understandingly rejected the offer. Anything less is not a waiver" (p. 516). The Court elaborated further in *Von Moltke v. Gillies* (332 U.S. 708 [1948]):

> To be valid such waiver must be made with an apprehension of the nature of the charges, the statutory offenses included within them, the range of allowable punishments thereunder, possible defenses to the charges and circumstances in mitigation thereof, and all other facts essential to a broad understanding of the whole matter. A judge can make certain that an accused's professed waiver of counsel is understandingly and wisely made only from a penetrating and comprehensive examination of all the circumstances. (p. 724)

DECISION-MAKING EXERCISE 11.9
Right to Counsel in the Pretrial Phase

A man was arrested without a warrant when a police officer caught him robbing the First Street branch of American Bank. Four hours later, the man was brought before a judge for a probable cause hearing. The judge decided that the officer had probable cause to arrest. The man was convicted of the crime and sentenced to prison. He is now appealing his conviction, claiming that he should have been given access to counsel at the probable cause hearing. Is he right?

What constitutes a knowing and intelligent waiver is not always clear. However, in *Massey v. Moore* (348 U.S. 105 [1954]), the Court offered clarification by stating that "[o]ne might not be insane in the sense of being incapable of standing trial and yet lack the capacity to stand trial without benefit of counsel" (p. 108). But in *Godinez v. Moran* (509 U.S. 389 [1993]), a case decided some years later, the Court held that a person who is competent to stand trial is also competent to waive counsel at trial and for pleading purposes. This decision all but reversed an earlier decision in which the Court held that competence to stand trial could be interpreted as competence to waive counsel (see *Westbrook v. Arizona*, 384 U.S. 150 [1966]).

In certain circumstances, while permitting waiver of counsel, the court can require that *standby counsel* be available to the defendant—that is, an attorney who is standing by in order to assist the accused, if necessary. This was the decision reached in *McKaskle v. Wiggins* (465 U.S. 168 [1984]), in which the Court held that a judge can appoint standby counsel "to relieve the judge of the need to explain and enforce basic rules of courtroom protocol or to assist the defendant in overcoming routine obstacles that stand in the way of the defendant's achievement of his own clearly indicated goals" (p. 184). When waiver of counsel is knowing and intelligent, a judge's decision to appoint standby counsel will not be unconstitutional as long as (1) the defendant retains control over the case and (2) the jury understands that the defendant represents himself or herself.

In 2004, the Supreme Court decided that waiver of the right to counsel is one that the defendant takes, potentially, at his or her own peril. In *Iowa v. Tovar* (541 U.S. 77 [2004]), the Court decided that a trial court was not required to warn the accused that waiving the right to counsel at a plea hearing involves two risks: (1) the possibility that valid defenses will be overlooked and (2) the accused will be deprived of advice as to whether a guilty plea is warranted. At the same time, though, the Constitution does not prohibit a court from insisting on representation of counsel for criminal defendants who are competent to stand trial but who also suffer from serious mental illness that would compromise their ability to put on an effective defense (*Indiana v. Edwards*, 554 U.S. 164 [2008]).

Indigent versus Nonindigent Defendants' Right to Counsel of Their Choice

Clearly, the defendant who is not indigent can hire counsel of his or her choosing. What's more, the wealthier the defendant, the better counsel he or she can afford. Unfortunately, the indigent defendant does not have such a choice. The Sixth Amendment right to counsel does not guarantee the indigent defendant permission to *choose* counsel; rather, counsel will be *provided*. Usually, counsel will be a public defender. If, however, an indigent can show good cause that the attorney appointed to represent him or her is not doing so adequately, another attorney can be appointed. What constitutes *inadequate representation* is discussed in the next section.

Surprisingly, there are situations in which defendants, if they can afford representation, cannot hire counsel of their choice. If, for example, the defendant's choice of an attorney poses serious conflict-of-interest problems, the defendant may be forced to hire another attorney (e.g., *Wheat v. United States*, 486 U.S. 153 [1988]). Or if the defendant's attorney is not qualified to practice law, then another attorney may be required (e.g., cf. *Leis v. Flynt*, 439 U.S. 438 [1979]). And somewhat controversially, if a defendant's assets are frozen pursuant to a civil forfeiture statute and he or she cannot afford counsel of his or her choosing, then a less expensive attorney may be required or a public defender may be appointed (see *Caplin v. Drysdale v. United States*, 491 U.S. 617 [1989]).

On the other hand, if a defendant with means has his or her eye on a particular attorney who is qualified to practice law and does not have any conflicts of interest, the defendant must be able to hire the attorney. If a judge wrongfully prohibits the defendant from hiring the attorney of his or her choice, the defendant's ensuing conviction must be overturned (*United States v. Gonzalez-Lopez*, 548 U.S. 140 [2006]).

An issue related to counsel of one's choice is whether indigent defendants can retain expert witnesses of their own choosing. In *Ake v. Oklahoma* (470 U.S. 68 [1985]), the Supreme Court held that an indigent defendant enjoys a constitutional right to an expert witness when his or her sanity is at issue. However, the Court limited its holding to provide for only one expert and one who is state employed. States vary in their rules concerning expert witnesses for indigent defendants. Often there are price caps that limit how much an indigent defendant's expert can be paid. At a point, it becomes necessary to assume that the *state*'s experts (e.g., ballistics experts) present objective and accurate testimony that is not prejudicial to the accused.

Effective Assistance of Counsel

If the Sixth Amendment's right to counsel provision was extended to indigent defendants with a blind eye, then some defendants would be convicted and others acquitted because of varying levels of competence among attorneys. All attorneys are not the same. Some, while authorized to practice law, prove to be totally ineffective in their duties. As such, the courts have grappled with what constitutes **effective assistance of counsel**.

WHEN THE RIGHT APPLIES   The Sixth Amendment does not explicitly state that effective assistance of counsel is required, but the Supreme Court has interpreted it in this way. However, the right to *effective assistance* only applies when the right to *counsel* applies. For example, the Supreme Court has held that a defense attorney's failure to file a timely discretionary appeal is not ineffective because the right to counsel does not extend to such appeals (*Wainwright v. Torna*, 455 U.S. 586 [1982]). Only when counsel is required can an ineffective assistance claim be made out.

It is important to realize that claims of ineffective assistance can be filed against both retained and appointed counsel. For a time, the Supreme Court held that a nonindigent defendant who retained his or her own attorney was bound by that attorney's representation, for better or worse, because there was no state action responsible for the ineffective representation. However, in *Cuyler v. Sullivan* (446 U.S. 335 [1980]), the Court held that privately retained counsel can be ineffective in the same way a public defender can:

> The vital guarantee of the Sixth Amendment would stand for little if the often uninformed decision to retain a particular lawyer could reduce or forfeit the defendant's entitlement to constitutional protection. Since the State's conduct of a criminal trial itself implicates the State in the defendant's conviction, we see no basis for drawing a distinction between retained and appointed counsel that would deny equal justice to defendants who must choose their own lawyers. (p. 344)

THE MEANING OF *EFFECTIVE ASSISTANCE*   So, what constitutes effective assistance of counsel? The lower courts are somewhat divided in terms of how to answer this question, so it is necessary to focus on the Supreme Court's standard for deciding whether defense counsel's assistance is or is not effective. Before getting to the cases, however, Figure 11.6 reprints portions of the *Code of Conduct for Federal Public Defender Employees*, published by the Administrative Office of the U.S. Courts. Public defenders are defense attorneys for indigent individuals, but the Code is informative nevertheless.

In the first case, *McMann v. Richardson* (397 U.S. 759 [1970]), the Court held that counsel is effective when his or her legal advice is "within the range of competence

FIGURE 11.6

Code of Conduct for Federal Public Defender Employees

B. Code of Conduct for Federal Public Defender Employees

CANON 1: A FEDERAL PUBLIC DEFENDER EMPLOYEE SHOULD UPHOLD THE INTEGRITY AND INDEPENDENCE OF THE OFFICE

An independent and honorable defender system is indispensable to justice in our society. A defender employee should personally observe high standards of conduct so that the integrity and independence of the office are preserved and so that the defender office reflects a devotion to serving the public defender's clients and the principle of equal justice under law. Defender employees should require adherence to such standards by personnel subject to their direction and control. The provisions of this code should be construed and applied to further these objectives. The standards of this code shall not affect or preclude other more stringent standards required by law, by applicable codes of professional responsibility, by court order, or by the federal public defender.

CANON 2: A FEDERAL PUBLIC DEFENDER EMPLOYEE SHOULD AVOID IMPROPRIETY AND THE APPEARANCE OF IMPROPRIETY IN ALL ACTIVITIES

A defender employee should not engage in any activities that would put into question the propriety of the defender employee's conduct in carrying out the duties of the office. A defender employee should not use public office for private gain.

CANON 3: A FEDERAL PUBLIC DEFENDER EMPLOYEE SHOULD ADHERE TO APPROPRIATE STANDARDS IN PERFORMING THE DUTIES OF THE OFFICE

In performing the duties prescribed by law, by resolution of the Judicial Conference of the United States, by court order, or by the federal public defender, the following standards apply:

A. A defender employee should respect and comply with the law and these canons. A defender employee should report to the appropriate supervising authority any attempt to induce the defender employee to violate these canons.

> *Note:* A number of criminal statutes of general applicability govern defender employees' performance of official duties. These include:
>
> 18 U.S.C. § 201 (bribery of public officials and witnesses);
>
> 18 U.S.C. § 211 (acceptance or solicitation to obtain appointive public office);
>
> 18 U.S.C. § 285 (taking or using papers relating to government claims);
>
> 18 U.S.C. § 287 (false, fictitious, or fraudulent claims against the government);
>
> 18 U.S.C. § 508 (counterfeiting or forging transportation requests);
>
> 18 U.S.C. § 641 (embezzlement or conversion of government money, property, or records);
>
> 18 U.S.C. § 643 (failing to account for public money);
>
> 18 U.S.C. § 798 and 50 U.S.C. § 783 (disclosure of classified information);
>
> 18 U.S.C. § 1001 (fraud or false statements in a government matter);
>
> 18 U.S.C. § 1719 (misuse of franking privilege);

Figure 11.6 continued

18 U.S.C. § 2071 (concealing, removing, or mutilating a public record);

31 U.S.C. § 1344 (misuse of government vehicle);

31 U.S.C. § 3729 (false claims against the government).

This is not a comprehensive listing but sets forth some of the more significant provisions with which defender employees should be familiar.

B. A defender employee should be faithful to professional standards and maintain competence in the defender employee's profession.

C. A defender employee should be patient, dignified, respectful, and courteous to all persons with whom the defender employee deals in an official capacity, and should require similar conduct of personnel subject to the defender employee's direction and control. A defender employee should diligently discharge the responsibilities of the office in a nondiscriminatory fashion.

D. A defender employee should not solicit or accept a payment of money or anything of value from a client, except that a defender employee may accept an appropriate memento or token that is neither money nor of commercial value. A defender employee should never disclose any confidential communications from a client, or any other confidential information received in the course of official duties, except as authorized by law. A former defender employee should observe the same restrictions on disclosure of confidential information that apply to a current defender employee.

E. A defender employee should not engage in nepotism prohibited by law.

Note: See also 5 U.S.C. § 3110 (employment of relatives); 28 U.S.C. § 458 (employment of judges' relatives).

F. *Conflicts of Interest.*

(1) In providing legal representation to clients, a public defender should observe applicable rules of professional conduct governing the disclosure and avoidance of conflicts of interest. . . .

CANON 4: A FEDERAL PUBLIC DEFENDER EMPLOYEE MAY ENGAGE IN ACTIVITIES TO IMPROVE THE LAW, THE LEGAL SYSTEM, AND THE ADMINISTRATION OF JUSTICE

A defender employee, subject to the proper performance of official duties, may engage in the law-related activities enumerated below.

A. A defender employee may speak, write, lecture, teach, and participate in other activities concerning defender services, the legal system, and the administration of justice.

B. A defender employee may serve as a member, officer, or director of an organization or governmental agency devoted to the improvement of the law, the legal system, or the administration of justice. A defender employee may assist such an organization in raising funds and may participate in the management and investment of such funds. A defender employee may make recommendations to public and private fund-granting agencies on projects and programs concerning the law, the legal profession, and the administration of justice. A defender employee may solicit funds for law-related activities, subject to the following limitations:

(1) A defender employee should not use or permit the use of the prestige of the office in the solicitation of funds.

(2) A defender employee should not solicit subordinates to contribute funds to any such activity but may provide information to them about a general fund-raising campaign.

(3) A defender employee should not solicit or accept funds from lawyers, clients, or other persons likely to have official business with the federal public defender office, except as an incident to a general fund-raising activity.

C. A defender employee may promote the development of professional organizations and foster the interchange of information and experience with others in the profession. A defender employee may make himself or herself available to the public at large for speaking engagements and public appearances designed to enhance the public's knowledge of the operation of defender services and the criminal justice system.

CANON 5: A FEDERAL PUBLIC DEFENDER EMPLOYEE SHOULD REGULATE EXTRA-OFFICIAL ACTIVITIES TO MINIMIZE THE RISK OF CONFLICT WITH OFFICIAL DUTIES

A. *Avocational Activities.* A defender employee may write, lecture, teach, and speak on subjects unrelated to the profession, and may engage in the arts, sports, and other social and recreational activities, if such avocational activities do not detract from the dignity of the office, interfere with the performance of official duties, or adversely reflect on the public defender's role as an advocate. A defender employee may solicit funds for avocational activities, subject to the limitations set forth in canon 4B.

B. *Civic and Charitable Activities.* A defender employee may participate in civic and charitable activities that do not detract from the dignity of the office, interfere with the performance of official duties, or adversely reflect on the public defender's role as an advocate. A defender employee may serve as an officer, director, trustee or advisor of an educational, religious, charitable, fraternal, or civic organization, and may solicit funds for any such organization subject to the limitations set forth in canon 4B.

C. *Financial Activities.*

(1) A defender employee should refrain from financial and business dealings that tend to detract from the dignity of the office or interfere with the performance of official duties. . . .

CANON 6: A FEDERAL PUBLIC DEFENDER EMPLOYEE SHOULD REGULARLY FILE REPORTS OF COMPENSATION RECEIVED FOR ALL EXTRA-OFFICIAL ACTIVITIES

A defender employee may receive compensation and reimbursement of expenses for outside activities provided that receipt of such compensation or reimbursement is not prohibited or restricted by this code, the Ethics Reform Act, and other applicable law, and provided that the source or amount of such payments does not influence or give the appearance of influencing the defender employee in the performance of official duties or otherwise give the appearance of impropriety. Expense reimbursement should be limited to the actual cost of travel, food, and lodging reasonably incurred by a defender employee and, where appropriate to the occasion, by the defender employee's spouse or relative. Any payment in excess of such an amount is compensation. A defender employee should make and file reports of compensation and reimbursement for outside activities to the extent prescribed by the Ethics Reform Act, other applicable law, or the Judicial Conference of the United States.

Notwithstanding the above, a defender employee (other than a defender employee serving without compensation) should not receive any salary, or any supplementation of salary, as compensation for official government services from any source other than the United States.

Figure 11.6 continued

Note: See 5 U.S.C. App. §§ 101 to 111 (Ethics Reform Act financial disclosure provisions). See also 5 U.S.C. App. §§ 501 to 505 (outside earned income and employment).

CANON 7: A FEDERAL PUBLIC DEFENDER EMPLOYEE SHOULD REFRAIN FROM INAPPROPRIATE POLITICAL ACTIVITY

A. A defender employee should not be a candidate for or hold partisan elective office and should not solicit partisan political contributions. A defender employee should not engage in any political activity while on duty or in the defender employee's workplace and may not utilize any federal resources in any such activity. Political activity includes, but is not limited to, displaying campaign literature, badges, stickers, signs or other items of political advertising on behalf of any party, political committee, or candidate for political office and soliciting signatures for political candidacy or membership in a political party.

B. A defender employee may engage in political activity not otherwise prohibited, provided that such activity does not detract from the dignity of the office or interfere with the proper performance of official duties. A defender employee who participates in political activity should not use his or her position or title in connection with such activity.

Note: See also 18 U.S.C. Chapter 29 (elections and political activities).

Source: From *Code of Conduct for Federal Public Defender Employees.* Available Online: http://host4.us-courts.gov/guide/vol2/ch2b.html (accessed February 16, 2011).

Strickland v. Washington (466 U.S. 668 [1984])

demanded of attorneys in criminal cases" (p. 771). This is something of a vague standard, so the Court created a new test in *Strickland v. Washington* (466 U.S. 668 [1984]). There, the Court held that a two-prong test must be applied in order to determine whether counsel is ineffective:

> First, the defendant must show that counsel's performance was deficient. This requires showing that counsel made errors so serious that counsel was not functioning as the "counsel" guaranteed the defendant by the Sixth Amendment. Second, the defendant must show that the deficient performance prejudiced the defense. This requires showing that counsel's errors were so serious as to deprive the defendant of a fair trial, a trial whose result is unreliable. (p. 687)

The two prongs announced in this case are now known as the *performance* prong and the *prejudice* prong. With regard to the former, "The proper measure of attorney performance remains simply reasonableness under prevailing professional norms" (p. 688). Defense counsel's performance will be considered adequate if he or she avoids conflicts of interest, serves as an advocate for the defendant's case, and brings to bear "such skill and knowledge as will render the trial a reliable adversarial testing process" (p. 688). Furthermore, defense counsel "has a duty to make reasonable investigations or to make a reasonable decision that makes particular investigations unnecessary" (p. 691).

For example, in *Strickland*, the Court stated that "[a]ctual or constructive denial of the assistance of counsel" and "various kinds of state interference with counsel's assistance" are "legally presumed to result in prejudice" (p. 692). State interference of this sort can occur when the defendant is either denied counsel or provided with counsel too late. Also, if the state blocks counsel's performance to some degree or otherwise interferes with the attorney/client relationship, an ineffective assistance of counsel claim is likely to succeed.

With regard to conflict of interest, this form of ineffective assistance can be manifested in several ways. For example, ineffective assistance is likely if the attorney (1) tries to represent more than one defendant in the same trial; (2) has represented one of the prosecution's witnesses in a previous trial; (3) is being paid by a third party; or (4) is contracted with a publishing company to write the defendant's story. Numerous other conflict-of-interest scenarios are possible, as well. Recently, in *Mickens v. Taylor* (535 U.S. 162 [2002]), the Supreme Court considered the question of whether a defense attorney's conflict of interest violates the defendant's Sixth Amendment rights. The defendant in this case claimed his conviction should be overturned because the judge should have inquired about the conflict of interest at trial but did not. However, the Supreme Court held that the judge's failure to do so did not entitle the defendant to an automatic reversal. Instead, the Court held that the defendant had to establish that the potential conflict of interest adversely affected the trial attorney's performance.

In another case involving the ineffective assistance of counsel, *Bell v. Cone* (535 U.S. 685 [2002]), the Supreme Court held that defense counsel's failure to present any mitigating evidence or to make a closing statement at the defendant's capital sentencing hearing was not ineffective. Among the reasons for the Court's decision was that the mitigating evidence that was *not* presented during the sentencing hearing *was* presented at trial, so the jury did have an opportunity to review it. Likewise, if the defense attorney participates in a plea hearing by speakerphone, rather than in person, it does not mean he or she provides ineffective assistance (*Wright v. Van Patten*, No. 07-212 [2008]).

In *Rompilla v. Beard* (545 U.S. 374 [2005]), the Court declared that defense counsel is bound to make reasonable efforts to obtain and review material that it knows the prosecution will probably rely on as part of its case, something the defense attorney did not do. But, contrast *Beard* with the Court's decision in *Florida v. Nixon* (543 U.S. 175 [2004]). There, the defense attorney acknowledged—in open court—his client's guilt and instead focused his defense on reasons why the defendant's life should be spared. The evidence was so clearly indicative of the defendant's guilt, that the Supreme Court did not feel the defense attorney's strategy was ineffective.

Likewise, in *Schriro v. Landrigan* (No. 05-1575 [2007]), the Court held that a defense attorney was not ineffective when his client instructed him not to present mitigating evidence during the death penalty sentencing phase. And in *Harrington v. Richter* (No. 09-587 [2011]), the Court decided that defense counsel was not ineffective when it failed to utilize the testimony of its own blood evidence expert who could have testified to the defendant's account of the events. Blood evidence was not central to the case, and it was apparent that even the defense attorney questioned the defendant's account of the crime for which he was on trial. Finally, the Supreme Court held in *Premo v. Moore* (No. 09-658 [2010]) that defense counsel was not ineffective for failing to seek suppression of the defendant's unconstitutionally obtained confession.

Even without state interference or conflict of interest, there are countless other means by which counsel can be considered ineffective. Attorneys' errors can come in several varieties. Generally, though, the defendant must point to a specific error or set of errors, not the overall performance of his or her counsel. If defense counsel makes a specific error and can offer no explanation for the error, then the defendant will have a

DECISION-MAKING EXERCISE 11.10

Effective Assistance of Counsel

A woman has been convicted of check fraud. On appeal, she claims that she was denied access to effective counsel. She argues that her attorney, a young public defender, had never tried a jury case and did not have enough time to prepare an adequate defense. Will her appeal succeed?

good chance in succeeding with a claim of ineffective assistance of counsel. This chance hinges, however, on the second prong announced in *Strickland*: prejudice.

Proving defense counsel's ineffective assistance is not enough to ensure a conviction will be overturned. In addition, the defendant must prove that "there is a reasonable probability that, but for counsel's unprofessional errors, the result of the proceeding would have been different" (*Strickland*, p. 694). In other words, the burden falls on the defendant to show that the outcome of the case hinged on the ineffective assistance provided by his or her defense attorney. If defense counsel acted ineffectively but such actions did not influence the outcome of the case, then a *Strickland* claim cannot succeed. The Supreme Court has not elaborated extensively on these issues, but they have been touched on extensively in the lower courts.

THE COURTROOM WORK GROUP

It is fitting at this juncture to point out that prosecutors and defense attorneys do not always work independently of each other. In contrast, most prosecutors and defense attorneys see each other on a regular basis. Moreover, they often appear before the same judges. This leads to a great deal of familiarity among the three parties. Researchers have used the term **courtroom work group** to describe this relationship. Walker has described the process in this way:

> Working together every day, members of the courtroom work group reach a general consensus about how different kinds of cases should be handled. This involves shared understanding about how much cases are "worth." There are "heavy" cases (that is, serious violent crimes) and "garbage" cases (relatively minor theft). This valuation allows them to move cases along quickly. . . . Conflict between prosecution and defense is the exception rather than the rule. Although in theory we have an *adversarial* process, in which truth is to be determined through conflict between prosecution and defense, the reality is that an *administrative* system is in effect, with a high degree of consensus and cooperation. (*Federal Rules of Criminal Procedure*, Rule 6)

Thus, even though this chapter has treated the prosecution and defense as distinctly separate, in reality this is not the case. Indeed, the general perception is that criminal procedure in the United States is combative and adversarial. On the whole, this is not true, either. It is in the interest of prosecutors and defense attorneys, especially public defenders, to work together, and also with the judge, to speed up the administration of justice. A lengthy, drawn-out adversarial process would contribute to delay.

Summary

1. DESCRIBE THE PROSECUTOR'S ROLE, PROSECUTOR'S DISCRETION, AND THE ISSUES SURROUNDING PROSECUTORIAL MISCONDUCT.

A prosecutor's decision whether to charge is rarely challenged. Reasons for nonprosecution include a lack of evidence and too much court backlog. However, a prosecutor's decision not to press charges *can* be challenged. On rare occasions, a court can effectively overrule a prosecutor's decision not to charge someone. Also, a prosecutor's superior can demand that charges be brought.

Prosecutors' charging decisions are subject to certain constitutional restrictions. Unfair and selective prosecutions are inappropriate and violate the equal protection clause of the Fourteenth Amendment. Vindictive prosecutions violate due process. Prosecutors generally enjoy absolute immunity for their charging decisions. Methods of dealing with overzealous prosecutors range from reprimand to disbarment.

2. EXPLAIN THE CONCEPT OF JOINDER AND REASONS FOR IT.

Joinder refers either to (1) bringing several charges against the same individual in the same trial or to (2) bringing charges against multiple defendants in the same trial. Both methods of joinder are generally considered appropriate, but if the crimes (or defendants) in question are only tied together because they are similar, separate trials may be warranted. Assuming the court permits joinder, then for separate trials to be held, the defendant must prove that his or her interests will be prejudiced in some fashion by a joint trial.

3. EXPLAIN THE PURPOSE, FUNCTIONS, AND POWERS OF A GRAND JURY.

Approximately one-third of all states and the federal system require that prosecution in felony cases proceed by grand jury indictment. In the remaining states, prosecution can proceed by indictment or information. Grand juries are closely related to prosecutors in terms of their charging decisions. Frequently, the grand jury serves as a means of formalizing the prosecutor's decision to charge. A grand jury is useful when the case in question is of great public and/or political significance, when its extensive investigative powers are helpful, when time is of the essence, and when one or more witnesses is hesitant to speak in open court, preferring the secrecy that surrounds grand jury proceedings.

The size of a grand jury varies, depending on location. Typically, the smaller the grand jury, the higher the voting requirement. Grand jury selection pools must be representative in terms of race and gender. That is, a grand jury selection procedure that purposefully discriminates on the basis of race and/or gender will be unconstitutional. Indeed, if the selection procedure systematically excludes an identifiable segment of society, then it is inappropriate. The final grand jury itself does not need to be representative of the community.

Grand jury proceedings are typically held in secret. Thus, there are significant restrictions on what information from grand jury proceedings can be shared with the defense as well as other parties. There are several reasons for secrecy: (1) to prevent the escape of possible indictees, (2) to ensure freedom to the grand jury in its deliberations, (3) to prevent tampering with the witnesses who may testify, (4) to encourage persons who have information with respect to the commission of crimes to come forward, and (5) to protect the innocence of those who are ultimately exonerated by grand jury investigations.

An individual who is the target of a grand jury investigation does not have the right (1) to appear in front of the grand jury, (2) to have the assistance of counsel during the grand jury's investigation, (3) to be told he or she is the target of the investigation, or (4) to be reminded that he or she has the right to remain silent. In short, many of the constitutional rights that apply in the context of a criminal trial do not apply during the course of a grand jury investigation.

Grand juries possess extensive investigative powers. They can issue subpoenas *ad testificandum*, which require witnesses to appear and testify, and subpoenas *duces tecum*, which compel the production of evidence. Unlike subpoenas to elicit testimony, subpoenas to compel the production of tangible evidence must be sufficiently particular, relevant to the investigation, and not overly burdensome. As part of their investigative powers, grand juries can also grant immunity and hold people in contempt.

Just as there are constraints on prosecutors' charging decisions, there are restrictions on grand juries' indictment decisions; however, a grand jury indictment is rarely quashed. Only when there is evidence of serious prosecutorial tampering, discrimination in the composition of the grand jury pool, or variance between the evidence presented during the grand jury investigation and that presented at trial will a grand jury indictment possibly be quashed.

4. OUTLINE THE DEVELOPMENT OF THE RIGHT TO COUNSEL.

Criminal defendants enjoy the Sixth Amendment right to counsel once adversarial criminal proceedings have commenced; this usually means once charges have been filed. Otherwise, when there is no possibility of confinement, the right to counsel does not apply. Like many constitutional rights, the right to counsel can be waived, but the court can appoint standby counsel in certain circumstances. Finally, the Supreme Court has interpreted the right to counsel to mean the right to effective counsel. Counsel is ineffective when specific errors are made that are prejudicial to the defendant's case.

5. BE FAMILIAR WITH THE COURTROOM WORKGROUP AND ITS FUNCTIONS.

The courtroom workgroup consists of the prosecutor, defense attorney, and judge. Contrary to Hollywood's depictions, these professionals work closely together, as doing so promotes efficiency in the adjudication of cases.

Key Terms

contempt power	359	joinder	349	selective		subpoena *duces*	
courtroom work		pretextual		prosecution	345	*tecum*	359
group	372	prosecution	346	severance	349	true bill	354
effective assistance		prosecutorial		subpoena *ad*		variance	361
of counsel	366	discretion	340	*testificandum*	359	vindictive	
grand jury	350	*pro se* defense	364			prosecution	346

Key Cases

Prosecutor

- *Oyler v. Boles*, 368 U.S. 448 (1968)
- *Blackledge v. Perry*, 417 U.S. 21 (1974)
- *United States v. Lane*, 474 U.S. 438 (1986)

Grand Jury

- *Hurtado v. California*, 110 U.S. 516 (1884)
- *Taylor v. Louisiana*, 419 U.S. 522 (1975)
- *Rose v. Mitchell*, 443 U.S. 545 (1979)
- *Butterworth v. Smith*, 494 U.S. 624 (1990)

- *United States v. Mandujano*, 425 U.S. 564 (1976)
- *United States v. Calandra*, 414 U.S. 338 (1974)
- *Hale v. Henkel*, 201 U.S. 43 (1906)

Defense Attorney

- *Gideon v. Wainwright*, 372 U.S. 335 (1963)
- *Powell v. Alabama*, 287 U.S. 45 (1932)
- *Kirby v. Illinois*, 406 U.S. 682 (1972)
- *Johnson v. Zerbst*, 304 U.S. 458 (1938)
- *Strickland v. Washington*, 466 U.S. 668 (1984)

Review Questions

1. What is the role of the prosecutor?
2. What are some reasons for nonprosecution? What can be done to challenge a prosecutor's decision not to pursue charges?
3. What types of restrictions exist on the ability of the prosecutor to bring charges? Cite relevant cases.
4. How does qualified immunity and absolute immunity operate in the prosecution context?
5. What can be done with overzealous prosecutors?
6. What is joinder? Explain the differences between joinder of charges and joinder of defendants.
7. Referring to Figure 11.4, what is the size of the grand jury in your state? Investigate the voting requirements and selection methods of grand juries in your state.
8. Explain some significant Supreme Court decisions with regard to the secrecy of grand jury proceedings.
9. Explain the rights of witnesses testifying before grand juries.
10. Distinguish among three types of investigative powers that grand juries possess.
11. Can a grand jury indictment be challenged? If so, how? If not, why not?
12. What two constitutional provisions does the right to counsel in a criminal prosecution come from?
13. Explain how the right to counsel applies at other stages of the criminal process.
14. Can the Sixth Amendment right to counsel be waived? If so, what are the requirements for a valid waiver? Also, can a judge overrule a defendant's decision to waive counsel?
15. When might a defendant not be able to hire counsel of his or her choice?
16. Explain the meaning of *effective assistance of counsel.*
17. What must a defendant show in order to succeed with an ineffective assistance of counsel claim?

Web Links and Exercises

1. Prosecutors: Read more about prosecutors at the Web site of the National District Attorneys Association.
URL: http://www.ndaa.org (accessed February 16, 2011).

2. Grand juries: Read more about grand juries. How do federal grand juries differ from state grand juries?
URL: http://campus.udayton.edu/~grandjur (accessed February 16, 2011).

3. Defense attorneys: Read more about defense attorneys.
URL: http://www.nacdl.org (accessed February 16, 2011).

4. Public defenders: Read more about public defenders.
URL: http://www.nlada.org (accessed February 16, 2011).

When you complete this chapter, you should be able to:

▸ Define plea bargaining.

▸ Outline the history of plea bargaining and arguments for and against its use.

▸ Summarize the plea-bargaining process and the effects of plea bargaining.

▸ Outline the elements of a valid guilty plea.

▸ Summarize how a guilty plea may be contested.

Plea Bargaining and Guilty Pleas

INTRODUCTION

Methods of Avoiding Trial

Obtaining a guilty plea as the result of plea bargaining is the most common method of securing a conviction. The overwhelming majority—90 percent, by some estimates—of criminal convictions in the United States result from guilty pleas, rather than trials. Moreover, these pleas usually derive from some bargaining between the defense attorney and the prosecutor. Both parties stand to gain something from a guilty plea: The prosecutor obtains a conviction, and the defense attorney usually succeeds in getting lenient treatment for his or her client.

Plea bargaining is essential to the administration of justice. If every defendant demanded his or her right to a jury trial and succeeded in such a demand, the criminal justice system would literally collapse. In this vein, arguments against plea bargaining are really like thought exercises; nothing can be done to eliminate plea bargaining because there are just too many criminals and not enough prosecutors, courts, and prisons.

At the same time, though, critics' views should not be dismissed. Consistent with what Americans are all taught, many people believe that judges and juries should determine guilt and that prosecutors and defense attorneys should only play a secondary role in this process. Plea bargaining essentially permits attorneys to decide the outcome of a case without ever going to trial. And it is well known that when two defendants face the same charge, the one who plea bargains invariably receives a lesser sentence than the one who does not.

Understand, though, that plea bargaining is not the only way to arrive at a guilty plea. Many defendants plead guilty to the charges against them even when no bargaining takes place. The bulk of this chapter focuses on plea bargaining; however, the section "Elements of a Valid Guilty Plea" is especially important for both types of guilty pleas: those that follow bargaining and those that do not. A sample of the plea form that is submitted to the court is presented in Figure 12.1.

FIGURE 12.1

Sample Plea Form

PLEA FORM

		CAUSE NUMBER:
STATE OF TEXAS	§	**IN THE MUNICIPAL COURT**
VS.	§	**CITY OF** _____
_____	§	_____**COUNTY, TEXAS**

PLEA OF NOLO CONTENDERE

I, the undersigned, do hereby enter my appearance on the complaint of the offense, to wit: _____

_____

charged in Municipal Court Cause Number _____. I have been informed of my right to a jury trial and that my signature on this plea of *nolo contendere* (meaning "no contest") will have the same force and effect as a plea of guilty on the judgment of the Court. I do hereby plead *nolo contendere* to said offense as charged, waive my right to a jury trial or hearing by the Court, and agree to pay the fine and costs the judge assesses. I understand that my plea may result in a conviction appearing on either a criminal record or a driver's license record.

_____   _____

Date   Defendant's Signature

                                              _____

                                              Address

PLEA OF GUILTY

I, the undersigned, do hereby enter my appearance on the complaint of the offense, to wit: _____

_____

charged in Municipal Court Cause Number . I have been informed of my right to a jury trial and that my signature to this plea of guilty will have the same force and effect as a judgment of the Court. I do hereby plead guilty to the offense as charged, waive my right to a jury trial or hearing by the Court, and agree to pay the fine and costs the judge assesses. I understand that my plea may result in a conviction appearing on either a criminal record or a driver's license record.

_____   _____
Date   Defendant's Signature

                                         _____
                                         Address

PLEA OF NOT GUILTY

I, the undersigned, do hereby enter my appearance on the complaint of the offense, to wit:_____

_____

charged in Municipal Court Cause Number _____. I plead not guilty.

Initial One:

_____   I want a jury trial.

_____   I waive my right to a jury trial and request a trial before the Court.

_____   _____
Date   Defendant's Signature

                                         _____
                                         Address

PLEA BARGAINING

Definitions of *Plea Bargaining*

There is no agreed upon definition of **plea bargaining**, so the following subsections consider two definitions. The first is a specific definition found in *Black's Law Dictionary*, and the second is a more general definition.

A SPECIFIC DEFINITION   *Black's Law Dictionary* provides a specific definition of *plea bargaining*. Namely, it is "the process whereby the accused and the prosecutor in a criminal case work out a mutually satisfactory disposition of the case subject to court approval. It usually involves the defendant's pleading guilty to a lesser offense or to only some of the counts of a multicount indictment in return for a lighter sentence than the possible sentence for the graver charge."[1]

It is useful to distinguish between charge bargaining and sentence bargaining. *Charge bargaining* refers to the prosecutor's ability to negotiate with the defendant in terms of the charges that could be filed. *Sentence bargaining*, by contrast, is when the defendant agrees to plead guilty in exchange for a less serious sentence. Charge bargaining is largely carried out between the prosecution and the defense. Sentence bargaining requires getting the judge involved because he or she usually hands down the sentence. In fact, there is even such a thing as *count bargaining*, in which the defense negotiates to have the defendant charged with fewer counts of a certain offense.

Black's definition first states that a plea bargain results in "a mutually satisfactory disposition." It is true, as will be noted later, that a plea bargain must be intelligent and voluntary, but it is not always satisfactory to both parties. For example, the prosecutor may simply be *forced* to present a favorable offer to the defendant because of procedural

_____

[1] *Black's Law Dictionary*, 6th ed. (1990), p. 1152.

errors that would make it difficult to prove the state's case. Or the prosecutor may present the defendant with equally unfavorable choices. As one researcher observed, "[T]he right to reject the proposed plea bargain is largely chimerical. Fear of heavier sentence after trial and deference to advice of defense counsel might lead defendants to accept virtually all plea agreements."[2]

Black's definition of plea bargaining also states that each bargain must be "subject to court approval." While this is usually true, the plea-bargaining process is mostly carried on between the defense and the prosecution with little judicial oversight. For example, prosecutors can do a great deal to drop or alter charges against an individual prior to bringing any subsequent agreement to the attention of the trial judge.

Finally, the foregoing definition of plea bargaining states that it "usually involves the defendant's pleading guilty to a lesser offense . . . in return for a lighter sentence." While this statement is true, it also obscures the reality that many concessions (i.e., besides a lighter sentence) can be offered to the defendant in exchange for a guilty plea. For example, sentence-bargaining concessions may include, but are not limited to, (1) the judge agreeing to impose certain probation conditions; (2) the prosecutor recommending a certain sentence to the judge; (3) the prosecutor agreeing not to invoke certain sentencing provisions, say, for multiple offenders; and (4) an agreement that the defendant will serve his or her sentence in a certain institution.[3]

A GENERAL DEFINITION In light of some of the shortcomings of the *Black's Law Dictionary* definition of plea bargaining, at least one authority has offered a more general definition: *Plea bargaining* is "the defendant's agreement to plead guilty to a criminal charge with the reasonable expectation of receiving some consideration from the state."[4] This definition is far more inclusive in that it recognizes that several varieties of bargaining can actually take place. Several of these are considered throughout the remainder of this chapter.[5]

The History and Rise of Plea Bargaining

Plea bargaining supplants trial by jury. At what point in history did the practice of plea bargaining gain acceptance? This section looks at the history of plea bargaining, reasons for its rise, arguments for and against it, and attempts to restrict the practice. It also looks at the Supreme Court's view on plea bargaining.

HISTORICAL ORIGINS One of the earliest reported cases addressing plea bargaining was decided in the early 1800s. In that case, *Commonwealth v. Battis* (1 Mass. 95 [1804]), a court was hesitant to permit a guilty plea by a defendant charged with a capital crime. The court gave the defendant time to contemplate his plea and even "examined, under oath, the sheriff, the jailer and justice (before whom the examination of the prisoner was had [sic] previous to commitment), as to the sanity of the prisoner; and whether there had been tampering with him, either by promises, persuasions, or hopes of pardon if he would plead guilty" (p. 96).

Following *Battis*, other cases involving some degree of plea bargaining were reported. One court's opinion focused on a Michigan statute that set forth specific

---

[2] Anonymous Author, "Plea Bargaining and the Transformation of the Criminal Process," *Harvard Law Review* 90 (1977): 564–595, 579.

[3] See, for example, H. S. Miller, W. F. McDonald, and J. A. Cramer, *Plea Bargaining in the United States* (Ann Arbor, MI: Inter University Consortium for Political and Social Research, 1978), p. 17.

[4] Ibid., pp. 1–2.

[5] Much of the discussion that follows is based on D. D. Guidorizzi, "Should We Really 'Ban' Plea Bargaining? The Core Concerns of Plea Bargaining Critics," *Emory Law Journal* 47 (1998): 753–783.

requirements necessary for a valid guilty plea. The court expressed concern that some of what could be called *plea bargaining* was taking place without the approval of the courts (*Edwards v. People*, 39 Mich. 760 [1878]). The court observed that Michigan passed the statute "for the protection of prisoners and of the public" in response "to serious abuses caused by [prosecutors] procuring prisoners to plead guilty when a fair trial might show they were not guilty, or might show other facts important to be known" (p. 761). The court also found it "easy to see that the Legislature thought there was danger that prosecuting attorneys . . . would procure prisoners to plead guilty by assurances [that] they have no power to make[,] of influence in lowering the sentence, or by bringing some other unjust influence to bear on them" (p. 762). These claims suggest that plea bargaining was a somewhat common practice by the second half of the nineteenth century.

Plea bargaining became even more common in the early to mid-1900s. Many states had, by then, impaneled commissions to study the workings of their criminal justice systems. An example of one such commission was the New York State Crime Commission, which was impaneled in 1927. The studies published by these commissions reported an increase in the practice of plea bargaining. For example, the Georgia Department of Public Welfare reported that the rate of pleading guilty increased 70 percent from 1916 to 1921.[6] Similarly, statistics in New York revealed that between 1839 and 1920, the guilty plea rate rose to some 90 percent of all cases.[7]

REASONS FOR THE RISE   Why the apparent rise in plea bargaining? Historical accounts show that in the early days of English criminal justice, a jury would hear 12–20 felony cases in a single day.[8] Trials played out in a similar fashion in U.S. courts during the 1800s. One historian points out that many early trials in the United States were carried out without lawyers for the defendant and even, in some cases, for the government.[9] As the U.S. legal system began to mature and lawyers became regular participants, trials slowed down and guilty plea rates increased out of necessity. According to one source, "[P]lea bargaining should be viewed as a natural outgrowth of a progressively adversarial criminal justice system."[10]

Despite its apparent necessity, plea bargaining was criticized extensively by early commentators. Some called it an "incompetent, inefficient, and lazy method of administering justice."[11] Others suggested that plea bargaining was just a means of avoiding trials for individuals charged with committing criminal acts. The following section considers some of these criticisms in further depth.

Arguments in Support of Plea Bargaining

There are several arguments in support of plea bargaining. And given that plea bargaining is a widely accepted practice in the U.S. justice system, these arguments have clearly won out.

- Plea bargaining is widely accepted because, despite certain drawbacks (discussed later), it benefits all members of the courtroom work group: the judge, the prosecutor, and the defense attorney (not to mention the defendant). Thus, the arguments

---

[6] Georgia Department of Public Welfare, "Crime and the Georgia Courts," *Journal of the American Institute of Criminal Law and Criminology* 16 (1924): 16.

[7] R. Moley, "The Vanishing Jury," *Southern California Law Review* 2 (1928): 97–127, 107.

[8] J. H. Langbein, "The Criminal Trial before Lawyers," *University of Chicago Law Review* 45 (1978): 263–316, 277.

[9] L. M. Friedman, *Crime and Punishment in American History* (New York: Basic Books, 1993), p. 235.

[10] Guidorizzi, "Should We Really 'Ban' Plea Bargaining?" pp. 753, 760.

[11] A. W. Alschuler, "Plea Bargaining and Its History," *Law and Society Review* 13 (1979): 211–245, 211 (quoting the Chicago Tribune, April 27, 1928, p. 1).

in support of plea bargaining are really arguments concerning the *benefits* of reaching plea agreements. Each of these arguments needs to be viewed in context, however. In some situations, such as highly celebrated cases, the costs of plea bargaining may outweigh the benefits.

- Plea bargaining benefits the prosecutor because it provides him or her with a greater ability to dispose of a busy case load. District attorneys are often faced with limited resources and, as such, cannot prosecute every case that comes before them. Specifically, a district attorney may opt to pursue charges on cases that have a highly public element and/or are likely to result in guilty convictions. Cases that do not look promising may be prime candidates for plea bargaining. And according to one observer, plea bargaining may be favored by the prosecution simply because it allows the courtroom work group to further its "mutual interest in avoiding conflict, reducing uncertainty, and maintaining group cohesion."[12]

- Defense attorneys also benefit from plea bargaining. Public defenders, who are the most common type of counsel in criminal trials, face resource constraints similar to those of prosecutors. Thus, plea bargaining benefits public defenders by allowing quick disposition of cases. It also allows them to focus on cases that they perceive as being worthy of trial. Bargaining also benefits privately retained counsel because it speeds up the process, which translates into "more money for less work." This is not to suggest, however, that this is the prime motivation of defense attorneys. Many zealously guard the interests of their clients.

- Plea bargaining benefits the defendant perhaps more than the prosecutor or the defense attorney. The obvious reason for this is that the defendant generally receives a lesser sentence (or charge, which also affects the ultimate punishment) as a result of plea bargaining. On another level, as will be discussed later, the defendant loses his or her chance at an acquittal and, sometimes, important rights, including the right to a trial by jury. But the Supreme Court has said that these costs may be outweighed by the benefits of "avoiding the anxieties and uncertainties of trial" (*Blackledge v. Allison*, 431 U.S. 63 [1977], p. 71).

- The court also benefits from plea bargaining. The prompt disposition of cases saves judicial resources, as researching a plea bargain takes less time than holding a full-blown trial. In fact, to the chagrin of many, the victims of crime may even benefit from plea bargaining. A quickly reached plea bargain may give the victim the satisfaction of having the case closed sooner rather than later. Moreover, the victim may also not want to testify or risk the possibility that the prosecution will not succeed in obtaining a conviction.[13] Figure 12.2 summarizes the arguments for and against plea bargaining.

Criticisms of Plea Bargaining

Apart from the obvious concern with the prosecutor and defense attorney effectively deciding a defendant's guilt, there are other problems posed by plea bargaining.

- In an effort to secure a conviction, the prosecutor will start with the most serious charge and work down. That is, the prosecutor may *overcharge* as a first step in the bargaining process. This negotiation process is much like that of buying a used car at a dealership, in which the dealer usually starts with a ridiculously high price

---

[12] R. A. Weninger, "The Abolition of Plea Bargaining: A Case Study of El Paso County, Texas," *UCLA Law Review* 35 (1987): 265–313, 267, n. 5.
[13] C. E. Demarest, "Plea Bargaining Can Often Protect the Victim," *New York Times*, April 15, 1994, p. A30.

FIGURE 12.2

Arguments For and Against Plea Bargaining

Arguments for	Arguments Against
Contributes to cohesion in the courtroom work group	Behooves the prosecutor to choose the most serious charge from which to begin bargaining
Helps the prosecutor dispose of a busy case load	Contributes to inefficiency
Helps the public defender dispose of a busy case load	Wastes time; most defendants plead guilty anyway
Benefits the defendant by providing a reduction in charges and/or a favorable sentencing recommendation	Undermines the integrity of the justice system
Saves on judicial resources by avoiding the costs of going to trial	Decides the defendant's guilt without having a trial
May give the victim the satisfaction of having a prompt resolution of the case	Allows the criminal to get away with his or her crime
May benefit the victim who does not wish to testify at trial	An innocent individual may be coerced to plead guilty (i.e., legal versus factual guilt)

but is willing to negotiate. In the end, however, few buyers end up purchasing a car for its fair market value. The concern with plea bargaining, then, is that the defendant will be encouraged to plead guilty to an offense that is more serious than that for which he or she would be convicted at trial.

- Plea bargaining may contribute to *inefficiency*. As one researcher observed, "[D]efense attorneys commonly devise strategies whose only utility lies in the threat they pose to the court's and prosecutor's time."[14]
- Critics further contend that not only is plea bargaining inefficient, but it also wastes time. They claim that plea bargaining is not necessary to obtain guilty pleas and that most defendants plead guilty anyway, if they think it is highly likely that going to trial will result in a verdict of guilty.[15]
- Plea bargaining may undermine the integrity of the criminal justice system. Throughout this book, discussion has examined the complex rules of criminal procedure set forth by the U.S. Constitution and interpreted by the Supreme Court. Critics of plea bargaining claim that the practice circumvents these "rigorous standards of due process and proof imposed during trials."[16]
- Another reason that plea bargaining may undermine the criminal process is that it effectively decides the defendant's guilt without having a trial, an exhaustive investigation, or the presentation of evidence and witness testimony. As mentioned earlier in this section, the defendant's guilt is effectively decided by the prosecutor. One critic has argued that plea-bargaining decisions result from improper considerations:

> One mark of a just legal system is that it minimizes the effect of tactical choices upon the outcome of its processes. In criminal cases, the extent

---

[14] A. W. Alschuler, "The Prosecutor's Role in Plea Bargaining," *University of Chicago Law Review* 36 (1968): 50–112, 54.

[15] P. Arenella, "Rethinking the Functions of Criminal Procedure: The Warren and Burger Courts' Competing Ideologies," *Georgetown Law Journal* 72 (1983): 185–248, 216–219.

[16] A. P. Worden, "Policymaking by Prosecutors: The Uses of Discretion in Regulating Plea Bargaining," *Judicature* 73 (1990): 335–340, 336.

of an offender's punishment ought to turn primarily upon what he did and, perhaps, upon his personal characteristics rather than upon a postcrime, postarrest decision to exercise or not to exercise some procedural option.[17]

- Plea bargaining may also allow criminals to get away with their crimes—or at least to receive lenient sentences. Further, critics claim that providing reduced sentences may reduce the deterrent effect of harsh punishment. In both cases, plea bargaining may give the impression that defendants can negotiate their way out of being adequately punished for their crimes.
- Innocent individuals may be coerced to plead guilty. In such a situation, a plea bargain amounts to an admission of legal guilt, when, in fact, the defendant may not be factually guilty. An example of the pressure on innocent defendants to plead guilty is found in *North Carolina v. Alford* (400 U.S. 25 [1970]). In that case, the defendant, facing the death penalty if he was convicted, pled guilty to the crime, but did not admit to all elements of it. His plea (and other similar pleas) was promptly dubbed the *Alford* **plea**. Certain jurisdictions permit Alford pleas (also called "best-interests pleas"). A defendant who makes an *Alford* plea does not allocute, which means he or she does not—and indeed is not required to —explain the details of the offense for the judge (also see the Arraignment section in the previous chapter).

Attempts to Restrict Plea Bargaining

Concerns over plea bargaining have led some jurisdictions to abandon the practice. In fact, at one point, the whole criminal justice system of Alaska banned plea bargaining, which led researchers to conclude that "the efficient operation of Alaska's criminal justice system did not depend upon plea bargaining."[18]

Several other jurisdictions have experimented with restricting the practice of plea bargaining, and their experience is perhaps more illustrative than the Alaska experience. (Alaska is not representative of the overall U.S. crime problem.) Methods of restricting plea bargaining have ranged from outright bans to bans on bargaining in certain types of crimes.

One method by which some jurisdictions have restricted plea bargaining is to impose a cutoff date, which prohibits plea bargaining after a case has been in process for a certain amount of time. For example, the Brooklyn (New York) District Attorney has adopted a cutoff date of 74 days after indictment.[19] Plea bargaining is acceptable prior to the deadline. And if a case goes all the way to trial within the cutoff period, plea bargaining could conceivably take place all the way through jury deliberations.

Another method of restricting plea bargaining has been to ban the practice in some or all types of plea agreements. Alaska is, of course, the most notable example of a total ban. In 1975, the Alaska attorney general banned all forms of plea bargaining in an effort to increase convictions and restore public confidence in the justice system.[20] In a study on the ban, the Alaska Judicial Council concluded the following:

> Plea bargaining as an institution was clearly curtailed. The routine expectation of a negotiated settlement was removed; for most practitioners justifiable

---

[17] A. W. Alschuler, "The Changing Plea Bargaining Debate," *California Law Review* 69 (1981): 652–730, 652.
[18] M. L. Rubenstein and T. J. White, "Alaska's Ban on Plea Bargaining," *Law and Society Review* 13 (1979): 367–383, 367.
[19] C. Mirsky, "Plea Reform Is No Bargain," *New York Newsday*, March 4, 1994, p. 70.
[20] T. W. Carns and J. A. Kruse, "Alaska's Ban on Plea Bargaining Reevaluated," *Judicature* 75 (1992): 310–317, 317.

reliance on negotiation to settle criminal cases greatly diminished in importance. There is less face-to-face discussion between adversaries, and when meetings do occur, they are not usually as productive as they used to be.[21]

It is important to understand that Alaska banned plea bargaining but not the entering of guilty pleas. Defendants could still plead guilty to the crimes for which they were charged. In fact, the Judicial Council also found that the rate of guilty pleas remained essentially the same after the ban, suggesting that perhaps some degree of behind-the-scenes plea bargaining was still taking place. Also, in Alaska, the attorney general can hire and fire the district attorneys, which gives him or her substantial leverage to ban plea bargaining. (In most jurisdictions around the United States, district attorneys are elected officials and do not serve at the desire of the state attorney general.)

Some jurisdictions have also experimented with banning plea bargaining for certain offenses. For example, the Bronx County (New York) district attorney enacted a ban on plea bargaining whenever a grand jury returned a felony indictment. This move was seriously criticized, as are most attempts to restrict plea bargaining, but the district attorney stated that the ban "means that society has ceded control to those it has accused of violating its laws; and it means that our system is running us, instead of the other way around."[22] Critics challenged the Bronx County district attorney's ban on postfelony indictment plea bargaining for at least two reasons: (1) It did not eliminate plea bargaining, and (2) it encouraged plea bargaining prior to indictment.[23]

Another approach tried in Philadelphia was the *jury waiver*, which gives the defendant the opportunity to engage in plea negotiations in exchange for giving up his or her right to a jury trial. Actually, this approach is not plea bargaining in the traditional sense. Instead, the defendant gets his or her day in court, but to receive concessions from the state, he or she must not demand a jury trial. This process has come to be known as the *slow plea of guilty*, insofar as it does not result in the disposition of a case prior to trial. One researcher described the process in more detail:

> Slow pleas are informal and abbreviated, and consist largely of the defense's presentation of statements concerning the defendant's allegedly favorable personal characteristics. . . . The defense presentation is not concerned with guilt or innocence since it usually is implicitly assumed by all parties involved in the process that the defendant is guilty of at least some wrong-doing.[24]

Still other attempts to restrict or ban plea bargaining have occurred. California attempted to abandon plea bargaining by popular referendum in 1982. The voters passed the referendum and the resulting statute (Cal. Penal Code 1192.7) imposed the following restrictions: No plea bargaining in any case involving (1) a serious felony, (2) a felony in which a firearm was used, or (3) the offense of driving under the influence. Plea bargaining is permissible, however, if the prosecution's evidence is weak, witnesses are unavailable, or a plea agreement does not result in a significantly reduced sentence. Despite the statute, plea bargaining continues almost unabated in the state of California (*People v. Brown*, 223 Cal. Rptr. 66 [Ct. App. 1986], p. 72, n. 11).

---

[21] Guidorizzi, "Should We Really 'Ban' Plea Bargaining?" pp. 753, 775.
[22] Press release, statement from R. T. Johnson, District Attorney, Office of the District Attorney of Bronx County, New York, November 24, 1992.
[23] Guidorizzi, "Should We Really 'Ban' Plea Bargaining?" pp. 753, 778.
[24] M. A. Levin, *Urban Politics and the Criminal Courts* (Chicago, IL: University of Chicago Press, 1977), p. 80.

El Paso County, Texas, also experimented with plea-bargaining restrictions. In 1987, two state district judges adopted a policy of prohibiting all plea negotiations in their courts as a method of ensuring equal treatment for similarly situated defendants.[25] Maricopa County, Arizona, adopted a similar approach in 1995. Five Maricopa County Superior Court judges adopted a policy that prohibited plea agreements based on stipulated (i.e., agreed upon) sentences. In other words, the judges refused to accept any plea agreement that included a negotiated sentence, believing that sentencing should be a decision left to the trial courts (*Espinoza v. Martin*, 894 P.2d. 688 [Ariz. 1995]).

The Supreme Court's View on Plea Bargaining

Brady v. United States
(397 U.S. 742 [1970])

Notwithstanding the competing views on plea bargaining, the Supreme Court has essentially laid the debate to rest by upholding the validity of the practice. In *Brady v. United States* (397 U.S. 742 [1970]), for example, the Court stated, "Of course, that the prevalence of guilty pleas is explainable does not necessarily validate those pleas or the system which produces them. But we cannot hold that it is unconstitutional for the State to extend a benefit to a defendant who in turn extends a substantial benefit to the State" (pp. 752–753). Next, in the case of *Santobello v. New York* (404 U.S. 257 [1971]), the Court offered the following argument in support of plea bargaining: "The disposition of criminal charges by agreement between the prosecutor and the accused, sometimes loosely called 'plea bargaining,' is an essential component of the administration of justice. Properly administered, it is to be encouraged" (p. 260).

How, then, is plea bargaining to be properly administered? The following sections seek to answer this question. First, the plea-bargaining process is described, and then the effects of plea bargaining, the rules concerning plea bargaining, and situations in which guilty pleas can be challenged are all discussed. The reader will develop an understanding of the complex practice of plea bargaining as it has been interpreted through the courts—most notably, the U.S. Supreme Court.

THE PLEA-BARGAINING PROCESS

The prosecutor can make several different offers in order to secure a guilty plea. The most straightforward and common method is to reduce the charge or charges against the defendant. Other alternatives include dismissing other pending charges and promising to recommend a particular sentence.

Assuming that what is offered by the prosecution is acceptable to the defendant, then he or she can make one of two pleas: a simple plea of guilty or a plea of *nolo contendere*. The former is akin to saying, "I am guilty," and the latter is akin to saying, "I do not contest this." Both pleas are effectively the same. The only difference is that the *nolo* plea cannot be used as an admission of guilt in a subsequent civil case.

Constitutional Rights during Plea Bargaining

Plea bargaining is a method of circumventing criminal trial, so not surprisingly, the rights available to the defendant during bargaining are not the same as those available at trial. There are, however, important rights that the defendant still enjoys during the plea-bargaining process, including the rights to effective assistance of counsel and to be informed of exculpatory evidence. The defendant does not have the right to be present at important stages of the bargaining process, however.

---

[25] Weninger, "The Abolition of Plea Bargaining," p. 275.

The Sixth Amendment right to counsel applies during plea bargaining because charges have already been filed before bargaining commences. According to the Supreme Court in *Kirby v. Illinois* (406 U.S. 682 [1972]), the right to counsel attaches when, after charges have been filed, the "defendant finds himself faced with the prosecutorial forces of organized society, and immersed in the intricacies of substantive and procedural criminal law" (p. 689). This means that the prosecutor cannot bargain directly with the defendant unless counsel has been waived.

The Sixth Amendment also requires that defense counsel be effective during the plea-negotiation process. This means that the defense attorney must, at a minimum, investigate the case so as to make an informed decision with regard to what sentences and charges are offered by the prosecution. To be effective, counsel must also ensure that his or her client understands the consequences of the plea-bargaining process. This is not to suggest that the defendant can easily succeed in claiming ineffective assistance of counsel during negotiation, however. According to the Court in *Hill v. Lockhart* (474 U.S. 52 [1985]), the defendant must show "a reasonable probability that, but for counsel's errors, he would not have pleaded guilty and would have insisted on going to trial" (p. 58).

Next, the defendant enjoys the right to be informed of exculpatory evidence in possession of the prosecution. That is, if the prosecutor has evidence that casts doubt on the accused's guilt, he or she must inform the defense of that evidence. For evidence to be considered *exculpatory*, it must have a reasonable probability of affecting the outcome of the case. Evidence that is inconsequential to the question of guilt, which is clearly rare, need not be provided to the defense (*United States v. Bagley*, 473 U.S. 667 [1985]).

Finally, as will be considered in an upcoming chapter, the defendant enjoys the right to be present at his or her own trial. However, this right does not apply in the context of plea bargaining. That is to say, no court has required that a criminal defendant be provided a constitutional right to be present during plea bargaining. This could change, but for now, all that is required is that the defense effectively communicates to his or her client the nature of the sentence or charges offered by the prosecution.

Recently, in *United States v. Ruiz* (536 U.S. 622 [2002]), the Supreme Court decided that the defendant *does not* have the right to impeachment information relating to informants and other witnesses nor does he or she have the right to information supporting any affirmative defense that he or she might raise if the case went to trial. Thus, there are limitations to the defendant's rights during the plea-bargaining process.

Acceptable Inducements by the Prosecution

The Constitution places few restrictions on offers the prosecution may make during the bargaining process, which are known as **prosecutorial inducements**. Since *Brady v. United States* was the first Supreme Court case to condone plea bargaining, it is a fitting point of departure before considering the offers prosecutors can make. The defendant in *Brady* was charged with kidnapping under a statute that permitted (1) a jury to recommend the death penalty if it saw fit *or* (2) a judge to sentence the defendant to life in prison, if guilt was determined via a bench trial. The defendant opted for a jury trial but then changed his plea to guilty and was sentenced to 30 years. He then argued that the statute effectively compelled him to plead guilty because of fear of the death penalty. The Supreme Court rejected this claim.

The reasoning the Court offered for its decision is somewhat complicated but important. Justice White emphasized that the statute in *Brady caused* the guilty plea but did not *coerce* it. He then emphasized that coercion is possible only when physical force or mental pressure is applied. This means that if "Brady was so gripped by fear of the death penalty or hope of leniency that he did not or could not, with the help of counsel, rationally weigh the advantages of going to trial against the advantages of pleading guilty" (p. 750), then his argument would have succeeded. However, Justice White found that the statute at most *influenced* Brady and that the coercion argument was exaggerated. In further support of his opinion, Justice White quoted an appellate court decision dealing with plea bargaining, *Shelton v. United States* (246 F.2d 571 [5th Cir. 1957]):

> [A] plea of guilty entered by one fully aware of the direct consequences, including the actual value of any commitments made to him by the court, prosecutor, or his own counsel, must stand unless induced by threats (or promises to discontinue improper harassment), misrepresentation (including unfulfilled or unfulfillable promises), or perhaps by promises that are by their nature improper as having no proper relationship to the prosecutor's business (e.g., bribes). (p. 572)

In short, a guilty plea resulting from an inducement from the prosecution, like a confession obtained in a police interrogation room, should not be involuntary. A guilty plea will be considered involuntary when it results from prosecutorial coercion (e.g., physical force or strong psychological pressuring). If, by contrast, the prosecutor causes a guilty plea simply because the accused thinks that pleading as such is his or her best way of avoiding a long prison term, then the defendant cannot succeed by claiming such a plea is involuntary.

What, then, offers/inducements can the prosecution properly make? *Brady* answered this question only insofar as the Court held that the prosecutor cannot coerce a guilty plea. In *Bordenkircher v. Hayes* (434 U.S. 357 [1978]), the Court attempted to offer a clearer answer. In that case, the defendant was indicted by a grand jury for forging a check for $88.30. The range of punishment was 2–10 years in prison. The prosecutor offered to recommend a five-year sentence but threatened to seek an indictment under a habitual criminal statute if the defendant did not accept the offer. Since the defendant had two prior felony convictions, a conviction under the habitual criminal statute could have resulted in life in prison.

Bordenkircher v. Hayes (434 U.S. 357 [1978])

Somewhat controversially, in a 5 to 4 decision, the Supreme Court upheld the defendant's conviction under the habitual criminal statute on the theory that it resulted from a choice among known alternatives. Basically, the Court said that the defendant had the choice to accept five years in prison and neglected to take the opportunity. The defendant argued that his second conviction was vindictive, citing *North Carolina v. Pierce* (395 U.S. 711 [1969]; see Chapter 11). But the Court countered by stating that "the imposition of these difficult choices [is] an inevitable—'and permissible'—attribute of any legitimate system which tolerates and encourages the negotiation of pleas" (*Bordenkircher v. Hayes*, p. 364).

Reduced to its most fundamental elements, the Court's opinion in *Bordenkircher* thus implies that the prosecution has great latitude in terms of being able to persuade the defendant to accept a plea, as long as the higher charges are authorized by law and are openly presented to the defense. This suggests, as well, that the prosecution may offer a charge or sentencing concession in exchange for the defendant agreeing not to appeal or claim that some constitutional right has been violated. The Court stated further:

> There is no doubt that the breadth of discretion that our country's legal system vests in prosecuting attorneys carries with it the potential for both individual and institutional abuse. And broad though that discretion may be, there are undoubtedly constitutional limits upon its exercise. We hold

only that the course of conduct engaged in by the prosecutor in this case, which no more than openly presented the defendant with the unpleasant alternatives of forgoing trial or facing charges on which he was plainly subject to prosecution, did not violate the Due Process Clause of the Fourteenth Amendment. (p. 365)

In a related case, *United States v. Goodwin* (457 U.S. 368 [1982]), the Court reached a similar decision. In that case, the defendant was indicted on additional charges after plea negotiations broke down. The Court held that the prosecutor could file additional charges if an initial expectation that the defendant would plead guilty to a lesser charge proved unfounded. The Court refused to accept the defendant's argument that this prosecution was vindictive and, once again, gave broad authority to prosecutors in the plea-bargaining process.

United States v. Goodwin (457 U.S. 368 [1982])

Nonetheless, certain prosecutorial inducements are *not* permissible. For example, the Supreme Court has stated that "a prosecutor's offer during plea bargaining of adverse or lenient treatment for some person *other* than the accused . . . might pose a greater danger of inducing a false guilty plea by skewing the assessment of the risks a defendant must consider" (*Bordenkircher v. Hayes*, p. 365, n. 8). Also, if the prosecutor flagrantly deceives the accused or fabricates evidence and/or starts rumors concerning the accused's level of involvement in the offense, a resulting guilty plea will be deemed unconstitutional.

Questionable Inducements

Colquitt has recently used the term **ad hoc plea bargaining** to refer to some of the strange concessions that defendants agree to make as part of prosecutors' decisions to secure guilty pleas. He states:

Ad hoc bargains exist in at least five forms: (1) the court may impose an extraordinary condition of probation following a guilty plea, (2) the defendant may offer or be required to perform some act as a quid pro quo for a

---

DECISION-MAKING EXERCISE 12.1

What Constitutes Coercion?

The prosecutor approaches the defendant and his attorney and says, "I am prepared to charge you with petty larceny in lieu of grand larceny. If you plead guilty to the petty larceny charge, you will avoid being prosecuted under the state's 'three strikes' statute. If you don't plead guilty, I will charge you under the 'three strikes' law and I will make sure that you will go to prison for the rest of your natural life." The defendant accepts the plea agreement but later appeals it, claiming that it was coerced by the prosecution. How should the court rule?

DECISION-MAKING EXERCISE 12.2

Prosecutorial Deception

Assume that a prosecutor and a defendant are negotiating a plea agreement. In the negotiation, the prosecutor lies to the defendant, saying, "We have a videotape recording of you engaged in the crime. If you do not plead guilty, this evidence will be used against you at trial. No jury in its right mind would acquit you based on the recording. However, if you plead guilty to petty larceny, then you will be out of jail in no time flat." The defendant pleads guilty but later appeals his conviction, claiming that his plea was the result of prosecutorial deception. What should the court decide?

dismissal or more lenient sentence, (3) the court may impose an unauthorized form of punishment as a substitute for a statutorily established method
of punishment, (4) the State may offer some unauthorized benefit in return
for a plea of guilty, or (5) the defendant may be permitted to plead guilty to
an unauthorized offense, such as a 'hypothetical' or nonexistent charge, a
nonapplicable lesser-included offense, or a nonrelated charge.[26]

Colquitt also states that ad hoc plea bargaining "may involve neither a plea nor a
sentence. For example, if a defendant charged with public intoxication seeks to avoid a
statutorily mandated minimum sentence of 10 days in the county jail, the prosecutor
might agree to dismiss the charges if the defendant agrees to make a monetary contribution to a local driver's education program" (p. 711).

Judges can even get involved in ad hoc plea bargaining. Colquitt points to one
shocking example of this method of bargaining run amok. The case, *Ryan v. Comm'n on
Judicial Performance* (754 P.2d 724 [Cal. 1988]), involved a woman who was required to
participate in a drug treatment program as a result of several narcotics convictions. The
probation officer asked to have the woman removed from the program because she
supposedly failed to follow program guidelines. At a hearing to decide on the matter,
the woman, "who was wearing a low-cut sweater, bent over several times to remove
documents from her purse. Thereafter the judge dismissed all criminal charges against
her. When his clerk asked why the charges had been dropped, [the judge] replied, 'she
showed me her boobs' " (p. 734). The judge was subsequently removed from the bench.
Some less extreme examples of ad hoc plea concessions, as well as some relevant cases,
are described in Figure 12.3.

Statutory and Judicial Inducements

So far, the discussion has considered only what the prosecution can and cannot do as far
as inducing the defendant to plead guilty. There have also been some interesting cases
dealing with statutory and judicial inducements. **Statutory inducements** refer to laws
that provide lenient sentences in exchange for guilty pleas. **Judicial inducements**
include actions by judges that influence the bargaining process.

Corbitt v. New Jersey
(439 U.S. 212 [1978])

STATUTORY INDUCEMENTS   With regard to statutory inducements, an illustrative case
is *Corbitt v. New Jersey* (439 U.S. 212 [1978]). In that case, the defendant was convicted of
first-degree murder and sentenced to life in prison, as required by the state statute with
which he was charged. However, the statute provided that if he decided to plead guilty
to the crime, he could be sentenced either to life imprisonment or to a term of 30 years.
The defendant claimed that the statute violated due process, but the Supreme Court
upheld it in the spirit of consistency. That is, the Court stated that it could not permit
prosecutorial bargaining as in *Bordenkircher* "and yet hold that the legislature may not
openly provide for the possibility of leniency in return for a plea" (p. 221). Further, the
Court stated:

> It cannot be said that defendants found guilty by a jury are "penalized" for
> exercising the right to a jury trial any more than defendants who plead guilty
> are penalized because they give up the chance of acquittal at trial. In each
> instance, the defendant faces a multitude of possible outcomes and freely
> makes his choice. Equal protection does not free those who made a bad assess-
> ment of risks or a bad choice from the consequences of their decision. (p. 226)

---

[26] J. A. Colquitt, "Ad Hoc Plea Bargaining," *Tulane Law Review* 75 (2001): 695–776, 695.

FIGURE 12.3

Examples of Ad Hoc Plea-Bargaining Concessions

1. Charitable contributions in lieu of fines or jail terms: *State v. Stellato* (523 A.2d 1345 [Conn. App. Ct. 1987]); *Ratliff v. State* (596 N.E.2d 241 [Ind. Ct. App. 1992])
2. Relinquished property ownership: *United States v. Thao Dinh Lee* (173 F.3d 1258 [10th Cir. 1999])
3. Agreement to surrender a professional license or not work in a particular profession: *United States v. Hoffer* (129 F.3d 1196 [11th Cir. 1997])
4. Voluntary agreement to undergo sterilization: *State v. Pasicznyk* (1997 WL 79501 [Wash. Ct. App. Feb. 25, 1997])
5. Voluntary agreement to undergo surgical castration: *ACLU v. State* (5 S.W.2d 418 [Ark. 1999])
6. Agreement to enter the army on a four-year enlistment: *State v. Hamrick* (595 N.W.2d 492 [Iowa 1999])
7. Agreement not to appeal: *People v. Collier* (641 N.Y.S.2d 181 [App. Div. 1996])
8. Shaming punishments, such as bumper stickers for convicted DUI offenders: *Ballenger v. State* (436 S.E.2d 793 [Ga. Ct. App. 1993])
9. Agreement to seal the records of a case: *State v. Campbell* (21 Media L. Rep. 1895 [Wash. Super. Ct. 1993])
10. Ordering offenders to surrender profits, such as from books written about their crimes: *Rolling v. State ex rel. Butterworth* (741 So. 2d 627 [Fla. Dist. Ct. App. 1999])
11. Banishment to another location: *State v. Culp* (226 S.E.2d 841 [N.C. Ct. App. 1976]); *Phillips v. State* (512 S.E.2d 32 [Ga. Ct. App. 1999])
12. Pleading guilty to nonexistent crimes (i.e., crimes that are not prohibited by law): *Bassin v. Isreal* (335 N.E.2d 53 [Ill. App. Ct. 1975])

Source: Adapted from J. A. Colquitt, "Ad Hoc Plea Bargaining," *Tulane Law Review* 75 (2001): 69. See Colquitt's article for a *thorough* discussion of various, sometimes stranger concessions made as a result of *ad hoc* plea bargaining (i.e., note 26).

The Court also noted, though, that plea bargaining should be an *executive*, as opposed to *legislative*, function. That is, legislatures should not be permitted to decide "that the penalty for every criminal offense to which a defendant pleads guilty is to be one-half the penalty to be imposed upon a defendant convicted of the same offense after a not guilty plea" (p. 227).

JUDICIAL INDUCEMENTS   Traditionally, plea bargaining results from the prosecution and the defense reaching an agreement; the judge is usually not part of the negotia-

---

DECISION-MAKING EXERCISE 12.3

An Inducement of Banishment

Carl Moore was arrested for sodomy and other crimes. With the assistance of his counsel, Moore negotiated a guilty plea to three counts of sodomy, one count of violating the Controlled Substances Act, and one count of sexual exploitation of children. The trial judge accepted the guilty plea and followed the state's recommendation to impose (1) a 20-year sentence (i.e., 3 years to serve and 17 years on probation), (2) banishment from the state, and (3) a $10,000 fine. Is banishment an acceptable inducement by the prosecution?

DECISION-MAKING EXERCISE 12.4

Judicial Inducements

Judge Dubois has before her the prosecutor, defense attorney, and defendant in one of the cases slated to be heard in her court. The defense attorney and prosecutor tell the judge that they have reached a plea agreement and that Charles Down, the defendant, has agreed to plead guilty to manslaughter instead of first-degree murder. Judge Dubois then questions Down to ensure that the plea is voluntary, intelligent, and based in fact. During the questioning, Down begins to express reservations about the plea agreement and says, "On second thought, I don't want to plead guilty." Judge Dubois then looks at Down and says, "You should really plead guilty, because from the looks of things, you're going to get the chair if you don't." Down agrees to plead guilty but later appeals, arguing that his plea was not voluntary. How should the court rule?

tion process. Today, however, certain jurisdictions permit a degree of judicial involvement in the plea-bargaining process. For example, the American Bar Association standards regarding guilty pleas permit judicial participation when it is requested but only for the purpose of clarifying acceptable charges and sentences. The judge cannot at any point, "either directly or indirectly, [communicate] to the defendant or defense counsel that a plea agreement should be accepted or that a guilty plea should be entered."[27]

In order to summarize the plea-bargaining process, Figure 12.4 presents relevant portions of Rule 11 of the *Federal Rules of Criminal Procedure*. The procedures outlined are those by which the federal courts must abide.

FIGURE 12.4

Plea-Bargaining Procedure

(c) Plea Agreement Procedure.

(1) *In General.*

An attorney for the government and the defendant's attorney, or the defendant when proceeding pro se, may discuss and reach a plea agreement. The court must not participate in these discussions. If the defendant pleads guilty or nolo contendere to either a charged offense or a lesser or related offense, the plea agreement may specify that an attorney for the government will:

(A) not bring, or will move to dismiss, other charges;

(B) recommend, or agree not to oppose the defendant's request, that a particular sentence or sentencing range is appropriate or that a particular provision of the Sentencing Guidelines, or policy statement, or sentencing factor does or does not apply (such a recommendation or request does not bind the court); or

(C) agree that a specific sentence or sentencing range is the appropriate disposition of the case, or that a particular provision of the Sentencing Guidelines, or policy state-

---

[27] American Bar Association, Standard 14-3.3[d], from *Standards for Criminal Justice*, 2nd ed., supp., vol. 3 (Washington, DC: American Bar Association, 1986).

ment, or sentencing factor does or does not apply (such a recommendation or request binds the court once the court accepts the plea agreement).

(2) *Disclosing a Plea Agreement.*

The parties must disclose the plea agreement in open court when the plea is offered, unless the court for good cause allows the parties to disclose the plea agreement in camera.

(3) *Judicial Consideration of a Plea Agreement.*

(A) To the extent the plea agreement is of the type specified in Rule 11(c)(1)(A) or (C), the court may accept the agreement, reject it, or defer a decision until the court has reviewed the presentence report.

(B) To the extent the plea agreement is of the type specified in Rule 11(c)(1)(B), the court must advise the defendant that the defendant has no right to withdraw the plea if the court does not follow the recommendation or request.

(4) *Accepting a Plea Agreement.*

If the court accepts the plea agreement, it must inform the defendant that to the extent the plea agreement is of the type specified in Rule 11(c)(1)(A) or (C), the agreed disposition will be included in the judgment.

(5) *Rejecting a Plea Agreement.*

If the court rejects a plea agreement containing provisions of the type specified in Rule 11(c)(1)(A) or (C), the court must do the following on the record and in open court (or, for good cause, in camera):

(A) inform the parties that the court rejects the plea agreement;

(B) advise the defendant personally that the court is not required to follow the plea agreement and give the defendant an opportunity to withdraw the plea; and

(C) advise the defendant personally that if the plea is not withdrawn, the court may dispose of the case less favorably toward the defendant than the plea agreement contemplated.

(D) Withdrawing a Guilty or Nolo Contendere Plea.

A defendant may withdraw a plea of guilty or nolo contendere:

(1) before the court accepts the plea, for any reason or no reason; or

(2) after the court accepts the plea, but before it imposes sentence if:

(A) the court rejects a plea agreement under Rule 11(c)(5); or

(B) the defendant can show a fair and just reason for requesting the withdrawal.

(E) Finality of a Guilty or Nolo Contendere Plea.

After the court imposes sentence, the defendant may not withdraw a plea of guilty or nolo contendere, and the plea may be set aside only on direct appeal or collateral attack.

(F) Admissibility or Inadmissibility of a Plea, Plea Discussions, and Related Statements.

The admissibility or inadmissibility of a plea, a plea discussion, and any related statement is governed by Federal Rule of Evidence 410.

Source: Federal Rules of Criminal Procedure, Rule 11.

EFFECTS OF PLEA BARGAINING

A plea bargain ultimately affects four separate parties: (1) the court, (2) the prosecutor,(3) the defendant (the latter, most often through the defense attorney), and (4) the victim. How plea bargaining affects these individual parties is discussed in the subsections that follow.

Effects on the Court

The court is not directly bound by a plea agreement. In deciding whether to accept the bargain, the court weighs the sometimes competing interests of the agreement and the public interest. Thus, if accepting a plea agreement poses a significant risk to the public—say, because a dangerous criminal will be spared prison and placed on probation (an unlikely event)—then the court has the discretion to deny it.

An illustrative case is *United States v. Bean* (564 F.2d 700 [5th Cir. 1977]). The facts were as follow: Bean was charged on October 22, 1976, with theft of property (i.e., a car) and with burglary of a habitation, in violation of state law. At the initial arraignment, Bean pleaded not guilty to both counts. On November 30, another arraignment was held on Bean's request. At this time, the court was informed that a plea bargain had been reached between the government prosecutor and Bean and his counsel. Bean would plead guilty to the theft count and cooperate with the prosecutor in investigating others involved in the burglary. In return, the prosecutor would move for a dismissal of the burglary charge. Judge Spears rejected the plea because the offense of entering a home at night where people were sleeping was a much more serious offense than the theft of an automobile. The Fifth Circuit Court of Appeals upheld Judge Spears's decision, stating:

> Without deciding what unusual circumstances may result in the refusal of a plea bargain being an abuse of discretion, we find that Judge Spears' action in this case was well within the scope of his discretion. A decision that a plea bargain will result in the defendant's receiving too light a sentence under the circumstances of the case is a sound reason for a judge's refusing to accept the agreement. . . . In this case, Judge Spears was faced with a man who was charged with burglarizing at night a home on Fort Sam Houston in Texas, while Lieutenant Colonel Robert W. Oppenlander, his wife, two daughters and one son were asleep inside. In addition, the presentence report indicated that Bean had previously been committed to four years in the Texas Department of Corrections for state charges of burglary and theft of a business at nighttime. Bean had also served twenty days for unlawfully carrying a weapon in San Antonio. Given this information Judge Spears was reluctant to accept a plea bargain that would allow Bean to plead guilty to only the theft of an automobile. (p. 704)

Effects on the Prosecutor

The consequences of plea bargaining are of far greater magnitude for the prosecutor than for the court. Assuming the court accepts a plea bargain, whether it is a charge or sentence reduction, then the prosecutor must fulfill his or her part of the agreement. Note, however, that the prosecutor is not strictly obligated to fulfill his or her promises early in the plea-bargaining process. More specifically, the prosecutor is not bound by the plea bargain prior to the point at which it is accepted by the court.

PROSECUTORIAL OBLIGATIONS BEFORE THE COURT ACCEPTS THE BARGAIN   The prosecutor has a considerable amount of latitude with regard to fulfilling a plea bargain before it is accepted by the court. This should not be particularly surprising because before the court accepts (or rejects) the bargain, it is not formalized. When the court accepts the bargain, it becomes formalized, at which point the prosecutor must fulfill his or her promises.

A case dealing with the extent to which a prosecutor must uphold his or her end of the bargain prior to the point at which the court accepts it is *Mabry v. Johnson* (467 U.S. 504 [1984]). In that case, the defense attorney called the prosecutor to accept a plea offer, but the prosecutor told him that the offer was a mistake and withdrew it. The prosecutor then offered a harsher offer in its place, one that would have resulted in a longer prison term. The Supreme Court upheld this practice, arguing that the plea agreement was reached with full awareness on the part of the defendant and "was thus in no sense the product of governmental deception; it rested on no 'unfulfilled promise' and fully satisfied the test for voluntariness and intelligence" (p. 510). In an analogous decision, the prosecution agreed to a plea agreement, but then reneged when it became clear the defendant had aided a fellow inmate in another crime while awaiting sentencing. The Supreme Court sided with the prosecution (*Puckett v. United States*, No. 07-9712 [2009]).

Mabry v. Johnson
(467 U.S. 504 [1984])

PROSECUTORIAL OBLIGATIONS AFTER THE COURT ACCEPTS THE BARGAIN   In general, the prosecution is bound to its plea-bargaining promises after the court accepts the bargain. An illustrative case is *Santobello v. New York* (404 U.S. 257 [1971]). In that case, the defendant was indicted for two felonies. He first entered a plea of not guilty on each count. After subsequent negotiations, however, the prosecutor agreed to allow the defendant to plead guilty to a lesser offense. The defendant then withdrew his pleas of not guilty and agreed to plead guilty to the lesser offense. The court accepted the plea. At sentencing, however, a new prosecutor, who was unaware of what had transpired earlier, requested the maximum sentence. The defense objected on the grounds that the previous prosecutor promised not to make any particular sentencing recommendation. The judge then stated that he was not influenced by the second prosecutor's sentencing recommendation and imposed the maximum sentence.

Santobello v. New York
(404 U.S. 257 [1971])

In response to this turn of events, the Supreme Court declared that the sentence should be declared unconstitutional as a matter of due process. The Court stated that "when a plea rests in any significant degree on a promise or agreement of the prosecutor, so that it can be said to be part of the inducement or consideration, such promise must be fulfilled" (p. 262).

Unfortunately, though, the Court was not altogether clear in terms of what remedy is preferable when the prosecutor breaches his or her agreement. In *Santobello*, the Court voided the defendant's conviction, but the Justices seemed mixed on the appropriate remedy for future cases. Some agreed that if the prosecution breaches its promise after the court has accepted the bargain, then it must be forced to uphold the

DECISION-MAKING EXERCISE 12.5

Judicial Rejections

Roger Moss has been arrested for and charged with intentionally and with premeditation killing his wife. He reaches an agreement with Terry Stand, the local district attorney, to plead guilty to negligent manslaughter. Stand has a poor track record in the district attorney's office and has lost countless cases to shrewd defense attorneys. He figures entering into this plea agreement is his best shot at finally obtaining a guilty verdict. When Stand and Moss's defense attorney present the plea agreement to the judge, she rejects it on the ground that is unduly lenient. Can the judge reject the plea for this reason?

bargain or the defendant should be able to withdraw the guilty plea. Others felt that the trial court should decide what remedy is necessary. The issue remains unresolved.

Some years after *Santobello*, in the case of *United States v. Benchimol* (471 U.S. 453 [1985]), the Supreme Court seemed to change its opinion with regard to a prosecutor's breach of a plea agreement after the court has accepted it. In *Benchimol*, the prosecutor agreed to recommend a sentence of probation with restitution, but the presentence report mentioned nothing of the agreement. The defense attorney pointed out the error, and the prosecution agreed that an agreement had been reached. Even so, the court sentenced the defendant to six years. The defendant then sought to have his sentence vacated, and the court of appeals agreed. However, the Supreme Court reversed, holding that unless the prosecution supports a recommendation "enthusiastically" or sets forth its reasons for a lenient recommendation, the court is under no obligation to honor the agreement. According to the Supreme Court:

> It may well be that the Government in a particular case might commit itself to "enthusiastically" make a particular recommendation to the court, and it may be that the Government in a particular case might agree to explain to the court the reasons for the Government's making a particular recommendation. But respondent does not contend, nor did the Court of Appeals find, that the Government had in fact undertaken to do either of these things here. The Court of Appeals simply held that as a matter of law such an undertaking was to be implied from the Government's agreement to recommend a particular sentence. But our view of Rule 11(e) [of the *Federal Rules of Evidence*, which sets forth procedures for plea bargaining] is that it speaks in terms of what the parties in fact agree to, and does not suggest that such implied-in-law terms as were read into this agreement by the Court of Appeals have any place under the Rule. (p. 455)

Effects on the Defendant

The defendant who accepts an offer to plead guilty often faces consequences besides a reduced sentence or charge. Important rights are often waived, such as the right to appeal, the right to a jury trial, and privilege against self-incrimination. Also, if the defendant supplies inaccurate information during the course of plea negotiations, he or she may not benefit from lenient treatment. Furthermore, in exchange for pleading guilty, the prosecution may require that the defendant testify against a codefendant.

A significant Supreme Court case dealing with the latter consequence—that is, possible testimony against a codefendant—is *Ricketts v. Adamson* (483 U.S. 1 [1987]). In that case, the defendant testified against both of his codefendants in exchange for a reduction in the charge he was facing. He was then sentenced on the reduced charge. After that, the codefendants' convictions were overturned on appeal. The prosecution then retried the codefendants, but the original defendant refused to testify at the second trial, claiming that his duty had been fulfilled. The prosecution then filed on information charging him with first-degree murder. The Supreme Court did not bar the first-degree murder prosecution because the original agreement contained a clause to the effect that the agreement would be void if the defendant refused to testify against his codefendants. Justice Brennan did acknowledge, however, that the defendant could have construed the plea agreement only to require his testimony at the first trial. The Court noted that the proper procedure, if such a situation would arise in the future, would be to submit a disagreement over the plea to the court that accepted the plea. That way, the expense of a further trial and appeals could be avoided.

DECISION-MAKING EXERCISE 12.6

The Prosecutor's Duty to Fulfill the Bargain

Connor Leaves was charged with armed robbery and with possession of a firearm during the commission of a felony. A plea agreement was reached wherein Leaves would plead guilty to attempted armed robbery and to the possession charge. In exchange for this reduction in charges, Leaves would assist the police and prosecution in investigating an unrelated crime. Leaves proceeded to fulfill his end of the agreement and told authorities that his friend, Bill Wright, was the man they were looking for. The prosecutor then withdrew the plea offer, stating that it was contrary to his office's policy. Leaves moved to reinstate the negotiated plea agreement, and the motion was granted. The prosecution has now appealed this decision. How should the appellate court rule?

DECISION-MAKING EXERCISE 12.7

Two Prosecutors, One Bargain

A plea bargain was reached between Prosecutor 1 and the defendant, in which the defendant agreed to plead guilty to less serious charges. Three months later, at the defendant's sentencing hearing, a different prosecutor, Prosecutor 2, represented the state. The following exchange took place between the judge and Prosecutor 2:

PROSECUTOR 2: At this time, Your Honor, the government calls for sentencing the case of the *United States of America v. Defendant.*

JUDGE: Anything you wish to say, Mr. Prosecutor 2?

PROSECUTOR 2: Well, Your Honor, in light of the plea-bargaining agreement, the government, at this time, is recommending three years' incarceration. We also recommend that, if possible, the defendant be incarcerated at a minimum security prison.

JUDGE: Why?

PROSECUTOR 2: Well, Your Honor, that was part of the plea bargain.

JUDGE: Not because you believe in it?

PROSECUTOR 2: Well, Your Honor, I do have some problems with that, but this is the way I understand it.

JUDGE: Anything else?

PROSECUTOR 2: Nothing further.

The defendant was then sentenced to four years in prison at a different institution. He has appealed his sentence. How should the appellate court rule?

DECISION-MAKING EXERCISE 12.8

Waiving Rights as a Consequence of Plea Bargaining

Here are the facts from an actual case, *United States v. Black* (201 F.3d 1296 [10th Cir. 2000]):

On November 20, 1997, a grand jury charged Mr. Black with five federal firearms offenses. . . . On April 15, 1998, Mr. Black entered into a plea agreement with the government. . . . Under the agreement, Mr. Black agreed to plead guilty to count three of the indictment. . . . He also agreed to waive his right to appeal his sentence. . . . The agreement stated that "the defendant agrees to waive his right to appeal the sentence he receives as a result of this Plea Agreement." . . . The government agreed to dismiss the remaining counts of the indictment and to recommend that Mr. Black receive a three-level downward adjustment in his offense level for acceptance of responsibility. It also agreed that if it appealed the district court's sentencing decision, Mr. Black would be released from the waiver of his right to appeal. (p. 1298)

Should a defendant be required to give up his or her right to appeal pursuant to a plea agreement?

At the other extreme, the defendant can sometimes *preserve* certain rights following a plea agreement. These types of arrangements are known as *conditional guilty pleas*. For example, New York law provides that an order denying a motion to suppress evidence alleged to have been obtained as a result of unlawful search-and-seizure "may be reviewed on appeal from a judgment of conviction notwithstanding the fact that such judgment of conviction is predicated upon a plea of guilty" (N.Y. Crim. Proc. Law §§ 710.20 [1], 710.70 [2]). These types of agreements are rare, however. In *Tollett v. Henderson* (411 U.S. 258 [1973]), the Supreme Court stated that "[w]hen a criminal defendant has solemnly admitted in open court that he is in fact guilty of the offense with which he is charged, he may not thereafter raise independent claims relating to the deprivation of constitutional rights that occurred prior to the entry of the guilty plea" (p. 267).

Effects on the Victim

While plea bargaining mainly occurs between the prosecution and defense, it is important not to leave out the victim. Victims are affected by plea bargaining in at least two respects. First, a plea agreement may give the victim a measure of closure relatively quick. On the other hand, a plea agreement may be viewed by the victim as lenient. That is, he or she may feel the offender was not adequately "punished" for the offense in question. To address this problem, several states have laws that require victim involvement or input during the bargaining process.[28]

ELEMENTS OF A VALID GUILTY PLEA

Assuming the prosecutor offers an acceptable inducement to the defendant and assuming the defendant agrees to plead guilty in exchange for leniency, the judge still must determine that the defendant understands the plea. This is in addition to the need to determine that the plea conforms to statutory and other requirements, as discussed earlier. In *Boykin v. Alabama* (395 U.S. 238 [1969]), the Supreme Court held that it would be unconstitutional "for the trial judge to accept [a] guilty plea without an affirmative showing that it is intelligent and voluntary" (p. 242). In order to determine that the plea is voluntary, the judge usually questions the defendant. As the Court noted in *McCarthy v. United States* (394 U.S. 459 [1969]):

> By personally interrogating the defendant, not only will the judge be better able to ascertain the plea's voluntariness, but he also will develop a more complete record to support his determination in a subsequent post-conviction attack. . . . Both of these goals are undermined in proportion to the degree the district court judge resorts to "assumptions" not based upon recorded responses to his inquiries. (p. 468)

For a guilty plea to be valid, it must conform to three requirements: (1) it must be intelligent; (2) it must be voluntary, not coerced; and (3) it must be based in fact. That is, if the defendant pleads guilty to a crime he or she did not commit, then technically, the plea will be invalid. The following subsections consider the case law regarding these three important requirements.

---

[28] U.S. Department of Justice, *Victim Input into Plea Agreements* (Washington, DC: U.S. Department of Justice, 2002). Available online: http://www.ojp.usdoj.gov/ovc/publications/bulletins/legalseries/bulletin7/ncj189188.pdf (accessed November 7, 2008).

Once an arrestee is charged with a crime (now the defendant), he or she must enter a plea. If a guilty plea is entered, it must meet specific requirements, including voluntariness.

Intelligence

In general, for a plea to be *intelligent* (i.e., understood), it must conform to specific requirements. The defendant must understand (1) the nature of the charge or charges of which he or she is accused, (2) the possible sentence or sentences associated with the charges, and (3) the rights he or she may waive if a guilty plea is entered. A person whose mental capacity is called into question may be declared incompetent at a pretrial hearing and treated in order to restore his or her competency. (The issue of competency is discussed further in Chapter 14.)

UNDERSTANDING THE CHARGE   In *Henderson v. Morgan* (426 U.S. 637 [1976]), the defendant was charged with first-degree murder. However, he pleaded guilty to second-degree murder following an offer by the prosecution. Several years later, he sought to have his conviction voided on the grounds that at the time he entered his plea, he did not understand that one of the elements of second-degree murder was intent to cause death. The Supreme Court held that "since respondent did not receive adequate notice of the offense to which he pleaded guilty, his plea was involuntary and the judgment of conviction was entered without due process of law" (p. 647). The element of intent in second-degree murder (i.e., the *mens rea*) was viewed as critical, which meant it should have been explained to the defendant.

*Henderson v. Morgan
(426 U.S. 637 [1976])*

It is not clear based on *Henderson* whether the *judge* must explain the elements of the offense to the defendant or whether this is the job of *counsel*. The Court intimated that if defense counsel explains the offense to the accused, then little else is needed: "[I]t may be appropriate to presume that in most cases defense counsel routinely explain the nature of the offense in sufficient detail to give the accused notice of what he is being asked to admit" (p. 647). Nevertheless, the judge should at least inquire as to whether the defendant understands the charge.

UNDERSTANDING POSSIBLE SENTENCES   There are virtually no Supreme Court cases dealing with the defendant's understanding of the possible sentences that could result from a plea bargain. However, the *Federal Rules of Criminal Procedure* require that the

DECISION-MAKING EXERCISE 12.9

A Valid Guilty Plea?

Bill Dover, a federal prisoner, filed a *habeas corpus* petition (i.e., a method of challenging his confinement; see Chapter 15), claiming that his guilty plea was not knowing and intelligent because of ineffective assistance of counsel. Specifically, Dover claimed that his attorney mistakenly advised him that if he pleaded guilty, he would become eligible for parole after serving one-third of his prison sentence. In actuality, because Dover was a second-time offender, he was required under state law to serve one-half of his sentence before being eligible for parole. In other words, Dover claimed that he was not advised of the actual sentence that would result from his plea bargaining. Should he succeed with his petition?

defendant understand the consequences of the plea.[29] This includes an understanding of the minimum and maximum sentences as well as applicable sentencing guidelines that the judge might be required to abide by.

Whether other consequences attendant to plea bargaining and sentencing have to be explained depends on the situation. On the one hand, at least one lower court has held that the defendant does not need to be informed of the loss of the right to vote (e.g., *People v. Thomas*, 41 Ill.2d 122 [1968]). On the other hand, failure to tell the defendant that deportation is a possible consequence of a guilty plea may result in a decision that such a plea is invalid (see, e.g., *Padilla v. Kentucky*, No. 08-651 [2010]).

UNDERSTANDING OF RIGHTS WAIVED AS A RESULT OF PLEADING GUILTY   The rights *waived* as a result of plea bargaining are different than the rights *denied* as a result of plea bargaining. For example, loss of the right to vote is not a loss due to voluntary waiver; it is a consequence tied to being convicted (even if by guilty plea) of a serious crime. The rights *waived* are those the defendant would otherwise be granted by the Constitution but are essentially given up in exchange for lenient treatment.

The constitutional rights typically waived through plea bargaining are the right to trial by jury, the privilege against self-incrimination, and the right to confront adverse witnesses. By pleading guilty, the defendant forgoes having a trial, which is when these rights are frequently applicable. The privilege against self-incrimination, however, still applies outside the trial context, such as in pretrial custodial interrogations. Regardless, the defendant must be clearly informed of the constitutional rights that are waived as a result of plea bargaining. According to the Supreme Court in *Boykin v. Alabama* (395 U.S. 238 [1969]), there can be no presumption of "a waiver of these three important federal rights from a silent record" (p. 243).

Boykin v. Alabama
(395 U.S. 238 [1969])

Voluntariness

In addition to the requirement that a plea be understood, it also must be voluntary. Even though a plea may be understood, it may have resulted from coercion, threats, physical abuse, or the like. Thus, the *Federal Rules of Criminal Procedure* require that a plea be "voluntary and not the result of force or threats or of promises (other than promises in the agreement)."[30]

Factual Basis

For a plea bargain to be valid, the plea must result from conduct that has a basis in fact. In other words, a defendant cannot (i.e., according to the courts anyway) plead guilty to

---

[29] Ibid.
[30] *Federal Rules of Criminal Procedure*, Rule 11, Available online at http://www.law.cornell.edu/rules/frcrmp/.

DECISION-MAKING EXERCISE 12.10

Another Valid Guilty Plea?

Caroline Wynn pleaded guilty to federal drug charges and was sentenced to 247 months in prison by the U.S. District Court. At sentencing, the court neglected to inform Wynn of her right to appeal her sentence. Several months later, while Wynn was in prison, she filed a *habeas corpus* petition, alleging that the district court's failure to advise her of her right to appeal her sentence violated the express terms of Rule 32(a)(2) of the *Federal Rules of Criminal Procedure*, which provides that "[t]here shall be no duty on the court to advise the defendant of any right of appeal after sentence is imposed following a plea of guilty or *nolo contendere*, except that the court shall advise the defendant of any right to appeal the sentence." Wynn knew of her right to appeal at the time of sentencing but did not file an appeal. Now, she seeks postconviction relief. How should the court decide?

a crime he or she did not commit. This means that the court should inquire about the crime in question by, perhaps, having the accused describe the conduct giving rise to his or her guilty plea. This does not always occur, but according to the Supreme Court in *McCarthy v. United States* (394 U.S. 459 [1969]):

McCarthy v. United States
(394 U.S. 459 [1969])

> Requiring this examination of the relation between the law and the acts the defendant admits having committed is designed to "protect a defendant who is in the position of pleading voluntarily with an understanding of the nature of the charge but without realizing that his conduct does not actually fall within the charge." (p. 467)

Importantly, the Court in *McCarthy* did not state that a factual basis for the plea bargain is a *constitutional* requirement, only that there should be one.

The Court elaborated on this matter in a similar case, in which the defendant pleaded guilty but insisted on his innocence. The Court stated that "an express admission of guilt . . . is not a constitutional requisite to the imposition of a prison sentence even if he is unwilling or unable to admit his participation in the acts constituting the crime" (*North Carolina v. Alford*, 400 U.S. 25 [1970]). The Court upheld the man's plea but also pointed out the following:

> Because of the importance of protecting the innocent and of insuring that guilty pleas are a product of free and intelligent choice, various state and federal court decisions properly caution that pleas coupled with claims of innocence should not be accepted unless there is a factual basis for the plea . . . and until the judge taking the plea has inquired into and sought to resolve the conflict between the waiver of trial and the claim of innocence. (p. 38, n. 10)

Thus, while there appears to be no constitutional basis for requiring that a guilty plea be tied to specific criminal acts, the courts—including the Supreme Court—prefer to avoid guilty pleas accepted from otherwise innocent defendants. Unfortunately, it would be purely conjecture to estimate how many innocent criminal defendants plead guilty in order to "play the odds" and avoid potentially lengthy prison terms.

In summary, a valid guilty plea must consist of several elements: knowledge, intelligence, voluntariness, and factual basis. Figure 12.5 presents relevant portions of Rule 11 of the *Federal Rules of Criminal Procedure*, which succinctly summarizes the elements of a valid guilty plea from a perspective other than that of the Supreme Court.

FIGURE 12.5

Elements of a Valid Guilty Plea

(a) **Entering a Plea.**

(1) *In General.*
A defendant may plead not guilty, guilty, or (with the court's consent) nolo contendere.

(2) *Conditional Plea.*
With the consent of the court and the government, a defendant may enter a conditional plea of guilty or nolo contendere, reserving in writing the right to have an appellate court review an adverse determination of a specified pretrial motion. A defendant who prevails on appeal may then withdraw the plea.

(3) *Nolo Contendere Plea.*
Before accepting a plea of nolo contendere, the court must consider the parties' views and the public interest in the effective administration of justice.

(4) *Failure to Enter a Plea.*
If a defendant refuses to enter a plea or if a defendant organization fails to appear, the court must enter a plea of not guilty.

(b) **Considering and Accepting a Guilty or Nolo Contendere Plea.**

(1) *Advising and Questioning the Defendant.*
Before the court accepts a plea of guilty or nolo contendere, the defendant may be placed under oath, and the court must address the defendant personally in open court. During this address, the court must inform the defendant of, and determine that the defendant understands, the following:

(A) the government's right, in a prosecution for perjury or false statement, to use against the defendant any statement that the defendant gives under oath;

(B) the right to plead not guilty, or having already so pleaded, to persist in that plea;

(C) the right to a jury trial;

(D) the right to be represented by counsel – and if necessary have the court appoint counsel – at trial and at every other stage of the proceeding;

(E) the right at trial to confront and cross-examine adverse witnesses, to be protected from compelled self-incrimination, to testify and present evidence, and to compel the attendance of witnesses;

(F) the defendant's waiver of these trial rights if the court accepts a plea of guilty or nolo contendere;

(G) the nature of each charge to which the defendant is pleading;

(H) any maximum possible penalty, including imprisonment, fine, and term of supervised release;

(I) any mandatory minimum penalty;

(J) any applicable forfeiture;

(K) the court's authority to order restitution;

(L) the court's obligation to impose a special assessment;

(M) in determining a sentence, the court's obligation to apply and calculate the applicable sentencing-guideline range and to consider that range, possible departures under the Sentencing Guidelines, and other sentencing factors under 18 U.S.C. § 3553(a); and

(N) the terms of any plea-agreement provision waiving the right to appeal or to collaterally attack the sentence.

(2) *Ensuring That a Plea Is Voluntary.*

Before accepting a plea of guilty or nolo contendere, the court must address the defendant personally in open court and determine that the plea is voluntary and did not result from force, threats, or promises (other than promises in a plea agreement).

(3) *Determining the Factual Basis for a Plea.*

Before entering judgment on a guilty plea, the court must determine that there is a factual basis for the plea.

Source: Federal Rules of Criminal Procedure, Rule 11.

CONTESTING A GUILTY PLEA

The defendant may wish to contest the guilty plea he or she enters for several reasons, including the following: (1) if the plea was the product of coercion by the prosecution; (2) if the prosecution has failed to fulfill its end of the bargain; and (3) if other problems emerge, such as unconstitutional conduct on the part of law enforcement officials. A defendant who challenges his or her guilty plea does so in several ways, which include withdrawal of the plea and appeal.[31] Each mechanism is considered in a following subsection.

Withdrawing a Guilty Plea

Anytime the court refuses to accept a plea agreement reached by the prosecution and the defense, the defendant can usually withdraw the plea. Similarly, if the defendant pleads guilty even when there has been no plea bargaining, he or she can seek to withdraw his or her plea. However, if the prosecution disagrees with the court's decision to refuse the plea, then the defendant might *not* be able to withdraw his or her plea.

Once a plea has been accepted by the court, then it can only be withdrawn in limited circumstances. The *Federal Rules of Criminal Procedure* provide that a plea can be withdrawn prior to sentencing if the defendant shows a "fair and just" reason for overturning the plea.[32] Fair and just reasons are the same as those mentioned at the outset of this section: involuntary pleas, prosecutorial breaches, and lack of evidence or similar deficiency. Once a sentence has been entered, however, the only methods to challenge a plea are to appeal and, to a lesser extent, to have a *habeas corpus* review (see Chapter 15). Also, many jurisdictions place a time limit on plea withdrawals; usually, withdrawal is not permitted once a sentence has been imposed.

Readers may recall the case of Idaho Senator Larry Craig, who was arrested in the Minneapolis-St. Paul International Airport on suspicion of lewd conduct in a public restroom. Craig quickly pled guilty to criminal charges but later attempted to withdraw his guilty plea, claiming that it was not knowing and intelligent. A judge denied his motion. Craig served out his term as senator and did not run for re-election.

Appealing a Guilty Plea

If the defendant moves to withdraw his or her plea and is denied this request, then an appeal is appropriate. However, if the withdrawal period has passed, then the only

---

[31] *Habeas corpus* review is also possible. This is discussed further in Chapter 15.
[32] Federal Rules of Criminal Procedure, Rule 11.

other method of appealing a guilty plea is through *direct* appeal. This creates something of a difficult situation for the defense. Since an appeal is mostly considered based on the trial court record, then the defendant has limited resources with which to prepare an argument. Namely, there is no transcript of a trial because by entering a guilty plea, the defendant elected to forgo trial. Thus, the only record left may be that from the arraignment or a similar pretrial proceeding. In sum, it is *very difficult* to succeed with a direct appeal of a guilty plea.

Fortunately, some states and the federal government permit appeals based on specific pretrial motions, such as a motion to exclude evidence on constitutional grounds. This is the case in New York and in other jurisdictions that maintain conditional plea mechanisms, as mentioned earlier. These issues aside, there are few Supreme Court precedents addressing appeals of guilty pleas. In *McCarthy v. United States*, the Supreme Court held that the trial court's failure to abide by proper arraignment procedure required reversal of a guilty plea on appeal. This is because the arraignment procedure—especially when there is no trial—"is designed to assist the district judge in making the constitutionally required determination that a defendant's guilty plea is truly voluntary" (p. 465).

Note that the decision to appeal a court's denial of a motion to withdraw a guilty plea is not necessarily the same as an appeal of one's conviction. The former may go to the voluntariness of the plea. The latter may concern some other procedural matter, such as an improper search or seizure, and may be appealable, provided the defendant has not waived his or her right to appeal as a result of plea bargaining.

Finally, note that *plea bargaining* and *pleading guilty* are not the same. Plea bargaining often results in a guilty plea, but a defendant does not have to engage in bargaining to plead guilty. Regardless of how the guilty plea is arrived at, the defendant can still seek to withdraw the plea. By contrast, a guilty plea that is entered *without* plea bargaining is more appealable than one reached as a result of bargaining. In the latter instance, the accused often gives up important rights, such as the right to appeal.

Summary

1. DEFINE PLEA BARGAINING.

Plea bargaining occurs when the prosecution offers some concession to the defendant in exchange for a guilty plea. Two common forms of plea bargaining can be discerned. The first, charge bargaining, occurs when the prosecutor offers to charge the accused with a less serious offense in exchange for a guilty plea. The second, sentence bargaining, occurs when the prosecutor promises the defendant a favorable sentencing recommendation.

2. OUTLINE THE HISTORY OF PLEA BARGAINING AND ARGUMENTS FOR AND AGAINST ITS USE.

Plea bargaining is how most cases in the U.S. criminal justice system are disposed of. By some estimates, 90 percent of all criminal cases are plea bargained. Supporters of the practice claim that bargaining is necessary to ensure the orderly and prompt flow of criminal cases. Critics claim, among other things, that defendants are forced to give up important constitutional rights as a result of the plea-bargaining process. In response to criticism, some jurisdictions have experimented with banning or restricting plea bargaining. Despite these attempts, plea bargaining flourishes today. One of the reasons for this is that the Supreme Court condones the practice.

3. SUMMARIZE THE PLEA-BARGAINING PROCESS AND THE EFFECTS OF PLEA BARGAINING.

Despite the Supreme Court's support for plea bargaining, it still requires that certain procedures be followed. First, the defendant must be represented by counsel and that counsel must be effective. Second, the defendant has the right to be informed by the prosecution of exculpatory evidence in the state's possession. Third, the prosecution can offer a wide range of inducements to the defense in order to secure a guilty plea, but those inducements cannot be coercive in nature. Further, there is some question about the propriety of so-called ad hoc plea bargaining: the practice of offering inducements to the defendant other than charge reductions and sentencing recommendations. Finally, statutory and judicial inducements for the defendant to plead guilty should be kept to a minimum.

Plea bargaining affects four parties: (1) the court, (2) the prosecutor, (3) the defendant (most often through the defense attorney), and (4) the victim. It affects the court only insofar as the court has to decide whether to accept the plea. A plea agreement that is excessively lenient is likely to be rejected by the court. The prosecutor is affected by plea bargaining only after the agreement has been accepted by the court. That is, the prosecutor must honor the agreement after the judge has accepted it but is under no obligation to do so beforehand. The defendant is perhaps most affected by plea bargaining. He or she often gives up certain rights by pleading guilty but can preserve certain rights pursuant to conditional plea agreement statutes. Victims get closure but may also be put off by agreements that are perceived as "soft."

4. OUTLINE THE ELEMENTS OF A VALID GUILTY PLEA.

Not just any plea agreement suffices. All plea agreements must be valid; that is, they must be knowing and intelligent, voluntary, and based in fact. A knowing and intelligent waiver is one in which the defendant understands the charge, the possible sentences, and the rights waived as a result of bargaining. A voluntary plea is one that is not coerced by the state. Finally, a plea agreement should be based in fact—that is, premised on conduct that actually took place. In other words, the defendant should not plead guilty to a crime he or she did not commit, although this clearly happens from time to time.

5. SUMMARIZE HOW A GUILTY PLEA MAY BE CONTESTED.

A guilty plea can be contested in at least two ways. First, the defendant can seek to withdraw his or her guilty plea. Doing so is fairly difficult once the court has accepted the plea. The defendant must show, for example, that the plea was involuntary to have it withdrawn after the court accepts it. Next, if the defendant is denied a request to withdraw his or her guilty plea, he or she can appeal that decision. Also, the defendant can sometimes appeal his or her conviction (i.e., as opposed to a court's decision to reject a motion to withdraw a guilty plea). The latter is increasingly rare because the defendant often agrees to waive his or her right to appeal as a result of plea bargaining.

Key Terms

ad hoc plea bargaining	389	judicial inducements	390	prosecutorial inducements	387	statutory inducements	390
Alford plea	384	plea bargaining	379				

Key Cases

Supreme Court's View on Plea Bargaining

- *Brady v. United States*, 397 U.S. 742 (1970)

Plea-Bargaining Process

- *Bordenkircher v. Hayes*, 434 U.S. 357 (1978)
- *United States v. Goodwin*, 457 U.S. 368 (1982)
- *Corbitt v. New Jersey*, 439 U.S. 212 (1978)

Effects of Plea Bargaining

- *Mabry v. Johnson*, 467 U.S. 504 (1984)
- *Santobello v. New York*, 404 U.S. 257 (1971)
- *United States v. Benchimol*, 471 U.S. 453 (1985)
- *Ricketts v. Adamson*, 483 U.S. 1 (1987)

Valid Guilty Pleas

- *Henderson v. Morgan*, 426 U.S. 637 (1976)
- *Boykin v. Alabama*, 395 U.S. 238 (1969)
- *McCarthy v. United States*, 394 U.S. 459 (1969)

Review Questions

1. What is plea bargaining? Can a defendant plead guilty without plea bargaining?
2. Explain the historical origins of plea bargaining.
3. What are the reasons for the popularity of plea bargaining?
4. Summarize the arguments against plea bargaining.
5. What has been done in response to criticisms of plea bargaining?
6. Summarize the arguments in support of plea bargaining.
7. Explain the accused's constitutional rights during plea bargaining.
8. What are some examples of acceptable inducements by the prosecution?
9. Explain ad hoc plea bargaining. Cite some examples.
10. Explain how judges and statutes can induce guilty pleas.
11. Summarize the effects of plea bargaining on the court.
12. What are the prosecutor's duties before and after the court accepts a plea bargain?
13. In what ways does plea bargaining affect the defendant?
14. Explain the elements of a valid guilty plea.
15. How can a plea of guilty be contested, if at all?

Web Links and Exercises

1. Plea bargaining frequency: How common is plea bargaining?

Suggested URL: http://www.albany.edu/sourcebook/pdf/t5242007.pdf (accessed February 16, 2011).

2. The case against plea bargaining: Read more about arguments against plea bargaining.

Suggested URL: http://www.cato.org/pubs/regulation/regv26n3/v26n3-7.pdf (accessed February 16, 2011).

3. Victim input in plea bargaining: Read about the state of law as it concerns victim input into plea bargaining.

URL: http://www.ncjrs.gov/ovc_archives/bulletins/legalseries/bulletin7/2.html (accessed February 16, 2011).

Part 5

TRIAL, CONVICTION, AND BEYOND

LEARNING OBJECTIVES

When you complete this chapter, you should be able to:

▸ Summarize the right to a speedy trial.

▸ Explain the right to an impartial judge.

▸ Summarize the right to a jury trial.

▸ Outline the jury selection process.

Rights at Trial

INTRODUCTION

Ensuring an Expeditious and Fair Trial

At this point, the discussion turns to the defendant's rights at trial. Assuming a defendant does not plea-bargain, a trial will probably result. Thus, it is important to focus on constitutional rights during the trial stage. The three rights considered in this chapter are (1) the right to a speedy trial, (2) the right to an impartial judge, and (3) the right to an impartial jury. Additional rights afforded to the defendant at trial are covered in Chapter 14.

THE RIGHT TO A SPEEDY TRIAL

The Sixth Amendment provides, in part, "In all criminal prosecutions, the accused shall enjoy the right to a **speedy trial.**" The federal "Speedy Trial Act" (18 U.S.C. Sections

3161–3174) plus statutes in every state also set forth a right to speedy trial. But what constitutes a *speedy trial*? Unfortunately, there are no easy answers to this question.

Somewhat surprisingly, it was not until 1966 that the Supreme Court addressed the Sixth Amendment's speedy trial provision. In *United States v. Ewell* (383 U.S. 116 [1966]), the Court identified three advantages associated with having a speedy trial: (1) It prevents excessive incarceration; (2) it minimizes anxiety experienced by the accused as a result of a publicized accusation; and (3) it prevents damage to the defendant's case resulting from too much delay.

In *Barker v. Wingo* (407 U.S. 514 [1972]), the Court elaborated on these points:

> If an accused cannot make bail, he is generally confined, as was Barker [the defendant] for 10 months, in a local jail. This contributes to the overcrowding and generally deplorable state of those institutions. Lengthy exposure to these conditions "has a destructive effect on human character and makes the rehabilitation of the individual offender much more difficult." At times the result may even be violent rioting. Finally, lengthy pretrial detention is costly. The cost of maintaining a prisoner in jail varies from $3 to $9 per day, and this amounts to millions across the Nation. In addition, society loses wages which might have been earned, and it must often support families of incarcerated breadwinners. (pp. 520–521)

Not only does the defense benefit from a speedy trial, but so do the government and even society at large. First, having a speedy trial provides the opportunity for a guilty verdict to be secured quickly (assuming, of course, that the defendant is guilty). Also, having a speedy trial minimizes the opportunity for an individual out on bail to commit additional crimes while awaiting trial. However, if the accused is kept in detention prior to trial, too much delay can take a financial toll on the government.

For the reasons just set forth, having a speedy trial can prove advantageous. However, this can be a double-edged sword. Having a speedy trial may promote efficiency, but too much efficiency may damage the defense's case. That is, if the defense is not given adequate time to prepare, then an erroneous guilty verdict could result. In *Ewell*, the Court stated that "[t]he essential ingredient is orderly expedition and not mere speed" (p. 120).

When the Right to a Speedy Trial Applies

A fair amount of case law addresses when the right to a speedy trial applies. First, the right generally applies once a person has been *accused* of a crime. The timing of the accusation and the number of accusations can complicate matters, however. The accusation rule will be addressed next and then cases that have tested the limits of the rule. Note that this section focuses on *when* the right to a speedy trial applies, not *whether* the right has been violated. The violation issue is taken up later.

United States v. Marion (404 U.S. 307 [1971])

THE ACCUSATION RULE   In *United States v. Marion* (404 U.S. 307 [1971]), the defendants sought to dismiss the indictment against them by arguing that the government had known of their identities for three years prior to the indictment. More specifically, they argued that their Sixth Amendment right to a speedy trial had been violated because the government had known of them prior to the point at which they had been indicted. Their argument failed miserably; the Court held that the Sixth Amendment's guarantee to a speedy trial attaches only *after* the person (or persons) has been accused of a crime. The Court further stated that being accused of a crime did not necessarily mean that formal charges had to be filed. Namely, "[T]he actual restraints imposed by arrest and holding to answer on a criminal charge" (pp. 327–328) can be sufficient to amount to an accusation. This has since come to be known as the **accusation rule**.

CHARGED AND CHARGED AGAIN   What if a person is charged, has the charges against him or her dropped, and is then charged again at some point in the future? In *United States v. MacDonald* (456 U.S. 1 [1982]), the Court held that the right to a speedy trial does not apply until the second set of charges is filed. In *MacDonald*, there were four years of delay between the dismissal of charges against the accused and a re-indictment on the same charges. According to the Court, "Following dismissal of charges, any restraint on liberty, disruption of employment, strain on financial resources, and exposure to public obloquy, stress, and anxiety is no greater than it is upon anyone openly subject to a criminal investigation" (p. 9). The Court also observed that MacDonald had been "free to go about his affairs, to practice his profession, and to continue his life" (p. 10) in the period between the two sets of charges, so the right to a speedy trial did not apply until the second set of charges was filed.

An interesting twist on *MacDonald* was presented in *United States v. Loud Hawk* (474 U.S. 302 [1986]). In *Loud Hawk*, charges against the accused were dismissed but the prosecution appealed the dismissal. This action distinguished *Loud Hawk* from *MacDonald* because it suggested that the prosecution was not done accusing Loud Hawk. Even so, the Court still held that the defendant's right to a speedy trial was not implicated because he was granted unconditional release while the prosecution continued to mount its case. Thus, if an individual is accused but then released to go about his or her business *with no charges pending*, any attempt to claim a violation of the Sixth Amendment's speedy trial provision could prove difficult. However, if a person is released *while* charges are pending, a speedy trial argument could be successfully raised.

United States v. Loud Hawk (474 U.S. 302 [1986])

IGNORANCE OF CHARGES   In *Doggett v. United States* (505 U.S. 647 [1992]), the defendant did not know that he had been charged with a crime and was not restrained in any way. Doggett left the United States just prior to the government's attempt to arrest him and, still unaware of the charges against him, returned over two years later. Doggett was eventually found (although he never *evaded* authorities) and arrested over eight years after he was indicted.

Doggett v. United States (505 U.S. 647 [1992])

The Supreme Court held in *Doggett* that the speedy trial clause of the Sixth Amendment was implicated. This was a surprising decision because Doggett was never detained nor could he claim any anxiety associated with the charges being filed against him (since he failed to learn of them until some eight years later). Also, Doggett carried on a law-abiding life, so he was not a threat to society. The Court was then forced to fall back on the argument that the ability of the defendant to mount an effective defense was undermined by the delay. Despite the Court's somewhat controversial decision in this case, *Doggett* has probably had little influence on subsequent defendants' speedy trial claims. The simple reason is that most defendants *know* when they are charged.

VIOLATION OF DUE PROCESS   What if a person commits a crime and is not charged for some time thereafter? Usually, most jurisdictions do not have statutes of limitations for serious offenses (i.e., laws that place restrictions on when charges can be brought against someone). For not-so-serious offenses, however, failure to bring charges in a speedy fashion can amount to a due process violation. Indeed, even if the time period for bringing charges has lapsed, failure to bring charges quickly can rise to the level of a constitutional violation.

United States v. Lovasco (431 U.S. 783 [1977]) is an illustrative case. There, the Supreme Court held that even when the statute of limitations period has not expired, the due process clause is violated if the delay exceeds "the community's sense of fair

United States v. Lovasco (431 U.S. 783 [1977])

play and decency." In that case, two witnesses died during an 18-month delay between the crime and the indictment. The Court developed an *either/or* rule for determining whether this type of delay is unconstitutional: The delay must be for the purpose of gaining "a tactical advantage over the accused" or "in reckless disregard of circumstances . . . suggesting that there existed an appreciable risk that delay would impair the ability to mount an effective defense" (p. 796, n. 17).

Summary.   This section has focused on when the right to a speedy trial applies, not whether it is violated under various factual scenarios. The next section turns attention to *when* the right to speedy trial is violated. To this point, then, the right to a speedy trial applies when a person is accused of a crime. This usually occurs when charges have been filed but not always. If a person is charged, let go, and later recharged, the right to a speedy trial does not apply until the latter charge is made. Due process can also be violated if charges are not brought in a timely fashion. This is sometimes true even if charges are not brought against a person before the statute of limitations, if applicable, expires.

Violations of the Right to a Speedy Trial

So far, the right to a speedy trial has been shown to apply in two contexts: (1) when a person has been accused and (2) when too much time has elapsed between the criminal act and the point at which charges are made. The only remedy in either instance is to dismiss the charges. An important question has not yet been answered: Assuming the right to a speedy trial applies, when is the right violated?

Barker v. Wingo
(407 U.S. 514 [1972])

The Supreme Court sought to answer this question in *Barker v. Wingo* (407 U.S. 514 [1972]). In that case, the defendant did not assert his Sixth Amendment right until after the prosecution had sought 16 continuances, which lasted over five years. The Supreme Court announced a four-element test to assist in determining when the right to a speedy trial is violated: "(1) Length of delay; (2) the reason for the delay; (3) the defendant's assertion of his right; and (4) prejudice to the defendant" (p. 530). According to the Court, none of these four criteria is, by itself, determinative. Instead, the courts must balance one against the others in deciding whether a Sixth Amendment violation has taken place. Each of these four criteria will now be considered in depth.

WHEN TOO MUCH TIME HAS ELAPSED   In *Doggett v. United States*, introduced earlier, the Supreme Court suggested that a delay of one year could be "presumptively prejudicial"—that is, in violation of the Sixth Amendment. It also held that the lengthy period between the point at which charges were first filed and Doggett's trial violated the Sixth Amendment right to a speedy trial. However, in *Loud Hawk*, also discussed

---

DECISION-MAKING EXERCISE 13.1

Putting Charges on Hold

A prosecutor can sometimes use what is known as a *nolle prosequi* device, which involves charging a person with a crime but deciding, for the time being, not to prosecute the matter any further. The charges are not dismissed; rather, they are put on hold. The suspect can essentially be prosecuted thereafter at the whim of the prosecutor. Assume that a prosecutorial *nolle prosequi* is issued in Rick O'Shea's case. O'Shea has been charged with aggravated assault, but the primary witness against him is in a coma. Assume further that the witness does not come out of the coma for an entire year. O'Shea is then convicted and later appeals, claiming his Sixth Amendment right to a speedy trial was implicated once the *nolle prosequi* commenced. What should the court decide?

earlier, the delay was longer than seven years and the Court found no violation of the right to a speedy trial. In another case, *United States v. Eight Thousand Eight Hundred & Fifty Dollars* (461 U.S. 555 [1983]), the Court held that 18 months of delay prior to an asset forfeiture proceeding was "quite significant" but still not of constitutional magnitude.

These decisions seem controversial, but in light of the other three criteria announced in *Barker*, the delay was insufficient to cause any prejudice to the defendant. That is, a violation of one of the four criteria is not, in itself, determinative.

WHEN THE DELAY IS INTENTIONAL   *Barker* also suggested that the reason or reasons for the delay can be important:

> A deliberate attempt to delay the trial in order to hamper the defense should be weighted heavily against the government. A more neutral reason such as negligence or overcrowded courts should be weighted less heavily but nevertheless should be considered since the ultimate responsibility for such circumstances must rest with government rather than the defendant. [Finally,] a valid reason, such as a missing witness . . . should serve to justify appropriate delay. (p. 531)

A key element of this quote is that the delay should be deliberate. An accidental delay, or one that is beyond the control of the prosecution, would probably be constitutional. For example, if defense counsel is responsible for the delay, the speedy trial right will not be violated (see, e.g., *Vermont v. Brillon*, No. 08-88 [2009]). But even if the prosecution deliberately seeks to delay the case, it must be shown that the delay is prejudicial to the defense's case. A nonprejudicial delay is unlikely to violate the Sixth Amendment.

To clarify, consider what the Supreme Court stated in *United States v. Loud Hawk*, mentioned earlier. In that case, part of the reason for the delay was that the prosecution sought numerous appeals with regard to the trial court's decision. The Supreme Court then stated that courts should focus on "the strength of the Government's position on the appealed issue, the importance of the issue in the posture of the case, and—in some cases—the seriousness of the crime" (pp. 315–316). As to the seriousness of the crime, the Court also stated, "[T]he charged offense usually must be sufficiently serious to justify restraints that may be imposed on the defendant pending the outcome of the appeal" (p. 316). In other words, if the government delays a trial by appealing, for instance, a decision on a motion to suppress, its position must be persuasive and the case serious. Frivolous delays for the purpose of weakening the defense should be avoided.

When delay is a result of prosecutorial negligence (i.e., as opposed to unavailable witnesses, court backlog, etc.), the Supreme Court has been considerably more strict.

DECISION-MAKING EXERCISE 13.2
When the Defendant Is Responsible for the Delay

Charles Pitt escaped from jail while awaiting his trial on narcotics offenses. He was apprehended by the police nine months later. He was then tried, convicted, and sentenced to prison for 10 years. He has appealed his conviction, claiming that his Sixth Amendment right to a speedy trial was denied because of the nine-month delay. How should the appellate court rule?

Recall that in *Doggett*, six years elapsed between the defendant's return to the United States and his arrest. The Supreme Court pointed out that this delay occurred because the government failed to continue tracking Doggett once he left the country. In their words:

> Although negligence is obviously to be weighted more lightly than a deliberate intent to harm the accused's defense, it still falls on the wrong side of the divide between acceptable and unacceptable reasons for delaying a criminal prosecution once it has begun. And such is the nature of the prejudice presumed that the weight we assign to official negligence compounds over time as the presumption of evidentiary prejudice grows. Thus, our toleration of such negligence varies inversely with its protractedness, and its consequent threat to the fairness of the accused's trial. (p. 657)

WHEN THE DEFENDANT ASSERTS THE RIGHT   Obviously, if the defendant does not assert his or her right to a speedy trial, then the courts should view any subsequent appeals with skepticism. However, if the defendant does not *formally* assert his or her right, can the courts then infer a waiver? That is, just because a defendant does not expressly state that his or her right to a speedy trial has been violated, does this mean the defendant should not be able to claim the right was denied in a subsequent appeal?

Referring back to *Barker v. Wingo*, the Supreme Court stated that "failure to assert the [speedy trial] right will make it difficult for a defendant to prove that he was denied a speedy trial" (p. 532). The Court also stated that the "frequency and force of the [defense] objections [to delay]" need to be taken into account. This means that formally asserting the right to a speedy trial may not be enough; the defendant should be sincere in his or her claims that the right was violated.

Recall from the *Miranda* discussion in Chapter 8 that silence cannot be construed as a waiver of the right to remain silent. The same does not hold true, then, with regard to the right to a speedy trial. That is, total silence by the defense concerning the Sixth Amendment right to counsel means that, for all practical purposes, the defendant has waived the right.

WHEN THE DELAY IS PREJUDICIAL TO THE DEFENDANT   The fourth and final requirement for a defendant to succeed in raising a speedy trial claim is that the delay actually caused prejudice to him or her. In other words, an important question needs to be answered: Did the delay impair the ability of the defendant to mount an adequate defense? If the answer is yes and the three aforementioned requirements have been met, the Sixth Amendment right to a speedy trial may have been violated.

What exactly constitutes *prejudice* to the defendant? The Supreme Court *almost* answered this question in *Dickey v. Florida* (398 U.S. 30 [1970]), where it held that a

DECISION-MAKING EXERCISE 13.3
Court Backlog

Lorna Bath robbed the First Street branch of State Bank because she believed the bank did not care about its customers and needed to be "hit where it hurts." Unfortunately, she was caught and indicted for first-degree robbery. However, because the court had a significant case backlog, Bath was not tried until 15 months after the robbery. During that time, she never asserted her right to a speedy trial. She was tried, convicted, and later appealed. The appeal, which is before the court now, claims that Bath's Sixth Amendment right to a speedy trial was violated because of the 15-month delay. How should the court decide?

seven-year delay, during which time two defense witnesses died and another became unavailable, warranted dismissal of charges. And as noted in the *Doggett* case, a longer delay that resulted from government negligence was reason for dismissal. Thus, it would seem that an excessively lengthy delay can cause prejudice to the defense.

The Supreme Court *almost* answered the question as to what constitutes prejudice because its decision in *Barker* seems to suggest that a lengthy delay is not always prejudicial. In that case, the Court held that a delay of over five years was insufficient to be considered prejudicial. In that case, though, the question of prejudice hinged on the ability of a witness to remember certain events. The Court said that it would be difficult to show a memory lapse and, consequently, that such a memory lapse hurt the defense. More concrete reasons for prejudice—such as deceased defense witnesses, as in *Dickey*—would seem more acceptable.

In summary, then, the defense must show clear and substantial damage to its case for a prejudice claim to succeed. The mere possibility that prejudice occurred is not enough. Coupled with the three other requirements announced in *Barker*, this points to a clear message: Succeeding in a claim that one's constitutional right to a speedy trial has been violated is exceedingly difficult.

Consequences of Violating the Right to a Speedy Trial

Assuming prosecution is delayed to an unconstitutional degree, what is the appropriate remedy? This question was answered in *Strunk v. United States* (412 U.S. 434 [1973]). In that case, the defendant was found guilty of a crime in a federal district court after a 10-month delay between indictment and arraignment. The Seventh Circuit Court of Appeals held that the defendant was denied a speedy trial but only remanded the case for a reduction in the defendant's sentence. The U.S. Supreme Court reversed, holding that dismissal is the *only* remedy. Thus, any time a defendant's right to a speedy trial is denied, the charges against him or her will be dismissed altogether. This is in contrast to the plea-bargaining discussion in Chapter 12; in that context, if the prosecution fails to fulfill its end of a plea bargain, the accused does not necessarily go free.

*Strunk v. United States
(412 U.S. 434 [1973])*

THE RIGHT TO AN IMPARTIAL JUDGE

It is important to note that the Sixth Amendment speaks only of juries (in addition to other important provisions), not judges. But the Supreme Court has held that the due process clause of the Fourteenth Amendment guarantees a criminal defendant the right to trial by an **impartial judge**. This right applies in two situations: (1) a *bench trial*, in which the judge decides the defendant's fate instead of a jury; and (2) a *jury trial*, in which the judge acts solely as a trier of law (i.e., makes legal decisions, not factual ones). The discussion begins with the right to an impartial judge and then moves into the more complicated issue of the right to trial by an impartial jury.

DECISION-MAKING EXERCISE 13.4

Deceased Witnesses

To continue the case from Decision-Making Exercise 13.3, suppose that Lorna Bath is prepared to file another appeal. This time, she argues that during the 15-month time lapse, the lead defense witness—who was prepared to testify that Bath was nowhere near the scene of the crime on the day of the robbery—died of a massive heart attack. Bath argues this time that the delay was prejudicial to her case and that her conviction should be overturned. Will she succeed with this appeal?

Tumey v. Ohio
(273 U.S. 510 [1927])

The Supreme Court first decided on the matter of an impartial judge in *Tumey v. Ohio* (273 U.S. 510 [1927]). In that case, the judge of a municipal court was also the city mayor. In addition, he received the fines and fees that he levied against those convicted in his courtroom. The Supreme Court concluded that due process is violated when the judge "has a direct, personal, substantial pecuniary interest in reaching a conclusion against him in his case" (p. 523). This decision should sound somewhat familiar; recall from Chapter 4 that judges are not considered impartial when issuing warrants if they seek to gain financially from doing so.

Ward v. Monroeville
(409 U.S. 57 [1972])

Another impartial judge case was *Ward v. Monroeville* (409 U.S. 57 [1972]), in which the fees/fines collected by the judge did not go to the mayor/judge but instead to the town's budget. The amount of money collected was apparently substantial. The Court concluded, again, that due process was violated, this time stating that "the mayor's executive responsibilities for village finances may make him partisan to maintain the high level of contribution from the mayor's court" (p. 59). Contrast this decision with that of *Dugan v. Ohio* (277 U.S. 61 [1928]). There, the Supreme Court held that due process was *not* violated because the mayor/judge was one of several members of a city commission and, as such, did not have substantial control over the city's funding sources.

Methods of Removing a Judge Who Is Not Impartial

In most jurisdictions, either the defense or the prosecution can seek to have a judge removed *for cause*. That is, the individual seeking the judge's removal will argue that the judge is biased for or against a particular party to the case. Strangely, though, the only person who can remove such a judge is usually the judge himself or herself.

The second method of removing a biased judge is fairly rare. Some jurisdictions allow either party to a case to *peremptorily* remove a judge. This is akin to the jury selection process, which will be covered at length later in this chapter. Basically, the judge can be removed without any reason whatsoever. The number of peremptory removals, if permitted, is very small—usually one per case. If one judge has been removed, then the parties can only seek to remove the second judge with cause.

In most situations, the judge does not need to be removed at the request of another party. Responsible judges remove themselves when conflicts of interest exist. Indeed, most judicial codes of ethics require that a judge *recuse* (i.e., disqualify) himself or herself if, among other things, he or she has a personal bias or prejudice concerning a party, personal knowledge of disputed evidentiary facts concerning the proceeding, or some conflict of interest in the case (see, e.g., American Bar Association, Code of Judicial Conduct, Canon 3-C). Figure 13.1 presents relevant ethical canons from the Code of Judicial Conduct for United States Judges.

DECISION-MAKING EXERCISE 13.5

An Impartial Judge?

During Beau Archer's criminal trial for assault, Archer, who represented himself, engaged in disruptive conduct and made insulting and slanderous remarks to the judge, calling him a "dirty, tyrannical old dog," "stumbling dog," and "fool" and further charged him with running a "Spanish Inquisition" and telling him to "Keep your mouth shut." Archer was found guilty of assault by a jury. At a subsequent sentencing hearing, the trial judge also pronounced Archer guilty of criminal contempt arising from his conduct during the trial. The judge further sentenced Archer to an extra 11–22 years in prison on the contempt accounts. Archer appealed, claiming that he was denied an impartial judge. What should the court decide?

FIGURE 13.1

Code of Conduct for United States Judges

CANON 1

A JUDGE SHOULD UPHOLD THE INTEGRITY AND INDEPENDENCE OF THE JUDICIARY

CANON 2

A JUDGE SHOULD AVOID IMPROPRIETY AND THE APPEARANCE OF IMPROPRIETY IN ALL ACTIVITIES

CANON 3

A JUDGE SHOULD PERFORM THE DUTIES OF THE OFFICE IMPARTIALLY AND DILIGENTLY

CANON 4

A JUDGE MAY ENGAGE IN EXTRA-JUDICIAL ACTIVITIES TO IMPROVE THE LAW, THE LEGAL SYSTEM, AND THE ADMINISTRATION OF JUSTICE

CANON 5

A JUDGE SHOULD REGULATE EXTRA-JUDICIAL ACTIVITIES TO MINIMIZE THE RISK OF CONFLICT WITH JUDICIAL DUTIES

CANON 6

A JUDGE SHOULD REGULARLY FILE REPORTS OF COMPENSATION RECEIVED FOR LAW-RELATED AND EXTRA-JUDICIAL ACTIVITIES

CANON 7

A JUDGE SHOULD REFRAIN FROM POLITICAL ACTIVITY

Source: Administrative Office of the U.S. Courts. Available online: http://www.uscourts.gov/rulesandpolicies/CodesOfConduct.aspx (accessed February 16, 2011).

THE RIGHT TO AN IMPARTIAL JURY

As noted in the previous section, it is fairly easy to determine when a judge is impartial. After all, a judge is one person. Deciding on what constitutes an **impartial jury** is far more difficult and complex. For this reason, the remainder of this chapter focuses on the right to trial by an impartial jury.

Referring again to the previous section, it is important to note that the due process right to an impartial judge applies in *all* proceedings, whether petty or serious, pretrial or otherwise. By contrast, the right to a trial by jury is *qualified*; that is, it does not *always* apply, even though the Sixth Amendment seems to suggest otherwise. First, the process of plea bargaining can eliminate the need to have a trial altogether. But even if the defendant opts not to plea-bargain, the right to a jury trial may not exist. To begin, the discussion will focus on when the right to trial by an impartial jury applies.

When the Right to a Jury Trial Applies

The right to a jury trial has always been recognized in the federal courts, but this right was not extended to the states until 1968 in the case of *Duncan v. Louisiana* (391 U.S. 145 [1968]).

The Court noted in that case that the right to a jury trial is "an inestimable safeguard against the corrupt or overzealous prosecutor and against the compliant, biased, or eccentric judge" (p. 156). The right to a jury trial has therefore been incorporated, but subsequent decisions have restricted this right. The following subsections describe how.

THE NONCRIMINAL PROCEEDING RULE   First, there is no Sixth Amendment constitutional right to a jury trial in noncriminal proceedings. More specifically, there is no right to a jury trial in noncriminal proceedings that are nevertheless part of the "criminal" process. This excludes civil trials, which, of course, are by jury. This has come to be known as the **noncriminal proceeding rule**. The reason for this should be fairly obvious: The Sixth Amendment states, "In all *criminal prosecutions*, the accused shall enjoy the right to a . . . trial, by an impartial jury" (emphasis added).

McKeiver v.
Pennsylvania   *(403 U.S.*
528 [1971])

Unfortunately, it is not always clear what constitutes a noncriminal proceeding. An example is a juvenile delinquency hearing. In *McKeiver v. Pennsylvania* (403 U.S. 528 [1971]), the Court held that juveniles charged with delinquent acts do not enjoy a right to a jury trial. Also, civil commitment hearings do not need to be conducted before a jury (e.g., *Lynch v. Baxley*, 386 F. Supp. 378 [M.D. Ala. 1974]). Both juvenile delinquency hearings and civil commitment hearings are noncriminal for Sixth Amendment purposes, but they are still a part of the "criminal" process.

Note that the Seventh Amendment states, "In Suits at common law, where the value in controversy shall exceed twenty dollars, the right of trial by jury shall be preserved." Jury trials clearly take place in the realm of civil litigation. The noncriminal proceeding rule, however, is only concerned with criminal procedure. Civil procedure is another matter altogether.

Baldwin v. New York
(399 U.S. 66 [1970])

THE PETTY CRIME EXCEPTION   The Supreme Court has carved out a *petty crime exception* to the Sixth Amendment right to a jury trial. In *Duncan*, mentioned earlier, the Court expressly forbade jury trials for petty offenses, and in *Baldwin v. New York* (399 U.S. 66 [1970]), the Court announced its reasoning for this. It argued that the "disadvantages, onerous though they may be," of denying a jury trial for a petty crime are "outweighed by the benefits that result from speedy and inexpensive nonjury adjudication" (p. 73).

What exactly is a *petty crime*? Unfortunately, there are no easy answers to this question, either. *Duncan* failed to define a *petty* offense, but in *Baldwin*, the Court concluded that any crime that can bring punishment of more than six months is no longer a petty one. This has come to be known as the **six-month imprisonment rule**; thus, defendants do not enjoy a right to jury trial when the punishment they face is less than six months in jail or prison.

What if a person is charged with several crimes for which the combined term of imprisonment exceeds six months? Surprisingly, in *Lewis v. United States* (518 U.S. 322 [1996]), the Court announced that a defendant charged in a single proceeding with several petty crimes does not have a right to jury trial even if the maximum penalty for *all* offenses could exceed six months in prison.

Finally, what if a person is charged with a crime with a possible six-month imprisonment term and is sanctioned in some other manner, as well? This question was answered in *Blanton v. City of North Las Vegas* (489 U.S. 538 [1989]). The Court announced in that case that the right to a jury trial in such a situation applies "only if [the defendant] can demonstrate that any additional statutory penalties, viewed in conjunction with the maximum authorized period of incarceration, are so severe that they clearly reflect a legislative determination that the offense in question is a 'serious' one" (p. 543). The defendant was charged with drunk-driving, a crime that carried a penalty of, at most, six months as well as a 90-day suspension of his driver's license. The Court stated, "[W]e cannot say that a 90-day suspension is that significant as a Sixth

Amendment matter, particularly when a restricted license may be obtained after only 45 days" (p. 544, n. 9). In another case, *Muniz v. Hoffman* (422 U.S. 454 [1975]), the Court stated that a potential sentence of six months coupled with a *fine* does not require a jury trial.

In summary, the right to a jury trial applies in a criminal proceeding when the penalty for a single offense exceeds six months. In no other situation does the Sixth Amendment right to a jury trial apply, even if multiple charges for petty offenses could result in a lengthy prison term.

Jury Size and Voting Requirements

Many juries consist of 12 members, but the Supreme Court has stated that this is not a requirement. In *Williams v. Florida* (399 U.S. 78 [1970]), the Court stated that the 12-member jury was a "historical accident" and "unnecessary to effect the purposes of the jury system" (p. 102). The Court noted that a six-member jury would even provide "a fair possibility for obtaining a representative cross-section of the community, . . . [a]s long as arbitrary exclusions of a particular class from the jury rolls are forbidden" (p. 102).

However, in *Ballew v. Georgia* (435 U.S. 223 [1978]), the Court concluded that a five-member jury was unconstitutional and found it unlikely that such a small group could engage "in meaningful deliberation, . . . remember all the facts and arguments, and truly represent the common sense of the entire community" (p. 241). Thus, the appropriate size for a jury is anywhere between 6 and 12 members.

Jury size differs by state. See Figure 13.2 for a map of jury sizes by state, specifically for courts of general jurisdiction (i.e., those with jurisdiction to try several types of cases, including more serious criminal cases). There is more variability in misdemeanor jury sizes than felony, which is why the former is mapped (the vast majority of states require 12-member juries in felony cases).

As for voting requirements, a unanimous decision is not always required. In two companion cases, *Johnson v. Louisiana* (406 U.S. 356 [1972]) and *Apodaca v. Oregon* (406 U.S. 404 [1972]), the Court upheld a Louisiana statute that permitted 9 to 3 jury verdicts as well as an Oregon statute permitting 10 to 2 decisions. According to the Court:

Johnson v. Louisiana
(406 U.S. 356 [1972])

> In our view, disagreement of three jurors does not alone establish reasonable doubt, particularly when such a heavy majority of the jury, after having considered the dissenters' views, remained convinced of guilt. . . . That want of jury unanimity is not to be equated with the existence of reasonable doubt emerges even more clearly from the fact that when a jury in a federal court, which operates under the unanimity rule and is instructed to acquit a defendant if it has a reasonable doubt, . . . cannot agree unanimously upon a verdict, the defendant is not acquitted, but is merely given a new trial. (p. 363)

FIGURE 13.2

Jury Sizes by State for Misdemeanor Cases in Courts of General Jurisdiction

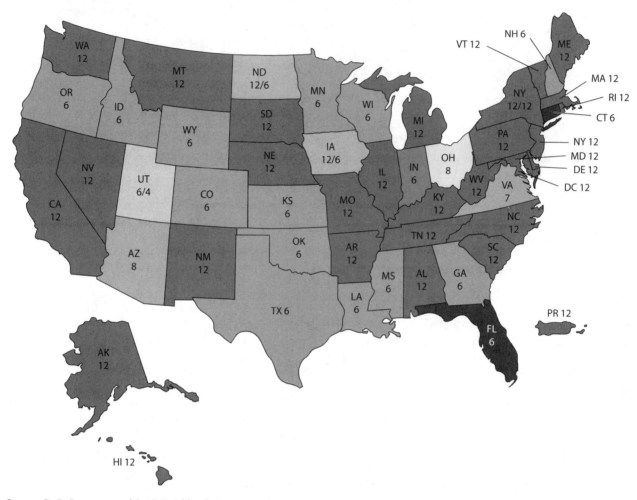

Source: D. B. Rottman and S. M. Strickland, *State Court Organization, 2004* (Washington, DC: Bureau of Justice Statistics, 2006).

In short, guilt can be determined by less than a unanimous jury in certain jurisdictions. This is somewhat controversial, however, because according to the dissent in *Johnson* and *Apodaca*, permitting a less than unanimous decision diminishes reliability. Namely, jurors may not debate as fully as they may if a unanimous decision is required; that is, people may succumb to group pressure. See Figure 13.3 for a list of jury voting requirements by state, again for courts of general jurisdiction.

Waiving the Right to a Jury Trial

Based on the discussion thus far, it appears that the Supreme Court has somewhat reduced the Sixth Amendment right to a jury trial. This may seem somewhat unfair to those concerned with the defendant's civil liberties. Nevertheless, there are occasions on which the defendant wishes to waive his or her right to a jury trial. If the case is particularly inflammatory or one with which the community is intimately familiar, then

FIGURE 13.3

Jury Voting Requirements by State for Courts of General Jurisdiction

State	Felony	Trial Type Misdemeanor	Civil
Alabama	U	U	U
Alaska	U	U	5/6
Arizona	U	U	3/4
Arkansas	U	U	3/4
California	U	U	3/4
Colorado	U	U	U
Connecticut	U	U	U
Delaware	U	U	U
Florida	U	U	U
Georgia	U	U	U
Hawaii	U	U	5/6
Idaho	U	U	3/4
Illinois	U	U	U
Indiana	U	U	U
Iowa	U	U	7/8 or U
Kansas	U	U	5/6 or U
Kentucky	U	U	3/4
Louisiana	10/12*	U	5/6
Maine	U	U	3/4
Maryland	U	U	U
Massachusetts	U	U	5/6
Michigan	U	U	5/6
Minnesota	U	U	5/6 or U
Mississippi	U	U	3/4
Missouri	U	U	3/4
Montana	U	U	2/3
Nebraska	U	U	5/6 or U
Nevada	U	U	3/4
New Hampshire	U	U	U
New Jersey	U	U	5/6
New Mexico	U	U	5/6
New York	U	U	5/6
North Carolina	U	U	U
North Dakota	U	U	U
Ohio	U	U	3/4
Oklahoma	U	U	U
Oregon	5/6**	5/6	3/4
Pennsylvania	U	U	5/6
Rhode Island	U	U	U
South Carolina	U	U	U
South Dakota	U	U	5/6
Tennessee	U	U	U

Figure 13.3 continued

Texas	U	U	5/6
Utah	U	U	3/4 or majority
Vermont	U	U	U
Virginia	U	U	U
Washington	U	U	5/6
West Virginia	U	U	U
Wisconsin	U	U	5/6
Wyoming	U	U	U

Key: U = Unanimous; 5/6 = 5 out of 6 jurors must agree (3/4, 7/8, etc., interpreted similarly)

*Some sentences.

**Not capital cases.

Note: There are exceptions to these size requirements in each state. Also, where two voting requirements are listed, the voting requirement differs depending on the crime or the nature of the case.

Source: D. B. Rottman and S. M. Strickland, *State Court Organization, 2004* (Washington, DC: Bureau of Justice Statistics, 2006).

obtaining a fair jury may be difficult. In such a situation, the defendant may opt for a *bench trial*, in which the judge decides the question of guilt.

The leading case dealing with waiver of the right to a jury trial is *Patton v. United States* (281 U.S. 276 [1930]). In that case, the defendants argued that their decision to waive the right to a jury trial was invalid because they lacked the authority to do so. The Supreme Court disagreed and stated that the right to a jury trial can be waived at the request of the defendant. The waiver must, however, be "express and intelligent." The waiver must also be voluntary, not a product of government coercion (see *United States v. Jackson*, 390 U.S. 570 [1968]).

It is important to note that waiver of the right to a jury trial can be vetoed. That is, the judge can *require* a jury trial, even if the defendant desires otherwise. Often, such a veto comes at the request of the prosecutor. In *Singer v. United States* (380 U.S. 24 [1965]), the Court upheld a federal statute permitting vetoes of this nature. According to the Court, refusal to grant the defendant a waiver merely subjects the defendant to "the very thing that the Constitution guarantees him" (p. 36)—namely, a jury trial. In describing some reasons for a veto, the Court stated further, "The Constitution recognizes an adversary system as the proper method of determining guilt, and the Government, as a litigant, has a legitimate interest in seeing that cases in which it believes a conviction is warranted are tried before the tribunal which the Constitution regards as most likely to produce a fair result" (p. 36). Thus, if the government feels that a jury trial is preferable, in the sense that it will produce a fairer result than a bench trial, then a veto of the defendant's waiver of a jury trial is constitutionally permissible.

DECISION-MAKING EXERCISE 13.7
Small-Jury Voting Requirements

A man was charged with the offense of obscenity and convicted in a state trial court before a six-person jury. A poll of the jury after the verdict indicated that the jury had voted 5 to 1 to convict. The man appealed his conviction, claiming that his right to trial by jury under the Sixth Amendment was violated when the state permitted a less than unanimous verdict by a six-member jury. How should the appellate court decide?

Selection of Potential Jurors

The process behind selecting an impartial jury is rather complicated. To begin, a list of potential, or prospective, jurors must be compiled. The creation of this list is critical, for without an impartial list, the final jury will not reflect a fair cross-section of the community. Once a list has been put together, then a panel of jurors is selected. This is when individuals are selected, usually randomly, for *jury duty*.

Thus, think of jury selection as a three-stage process: (1) a list of potential jurors is compiled; (2) potential jurors are selected from that list; and then (3) the jury itself is chosen. This section addresses the first and second stages; the third stage, *voir dire*, is addressed later.

The list of potential jury members can be called the *jury pool*, *master jury wheel*, or *jury list*. For simplicity, the term **jury list** will be used here. The jury list can be compiled from a number of sources. One of the most common methods is to draw from voter registration lists. The federal courts, the state of Washington, and several other states rely on this method. Another method of compiling the list is via driver's license registration lists. California currently uses this method. Some states even use telephone directory lists. Still other states rely on jury commissioners: individuals appointed by a judge who are responsible for compiling jury lists.

To be on the jury list, potential jurors usually have to possess important traits. For example, they must be of a certain age—usually, over 18. They must also be U.S. citizens and free of felony convictions. The requirements to serve on a jury vary considerably from one state to the next.

Once the jury list has been compiled, people are selected from the list for service. Individuals selected from the jury list are called a *panel* or *venire*. The term **jury panel** will be used here.

Anyone who has been called on for jury duty has, at one time, been part of a jury panel. And as most people know, there are several means by which one can be excused from a jury panel. Examples of people typically exempted from jury service are aliens, individuals unable to speak English, those under 18, those charged with a felony or who are serving a sentence, and those for whom jury service could cause severe hardship. People in law enforcement positions or who work in so-called critical occupations, such as the military and government, are typically exempted, as well.

Once the jury panel has been chosen, then *voir dire* commences. Before turning to *voir dire*, however, it is important to consider constitutional challenges to the jury selection process described thus far. Many defendants have appealed their convictions on the grounds that the jury list or panel was biased in some fashion. These challenges generally fall into two camps: (1) equal protection challenges and (2) fair cross-section challenges.

Both types of challenges can be made when the defendant examines the jury list for evidence of problems. Indeed, *Test v. United States* (420 U.S. 28 [1975]) grants federal defendants the right to inspect and copy jury lists in order to mount equal protection and/or fair cross-section challenges. Unfortunately, the jury list provides little more than individuals' names; sex and race must be inferred.

Note that an unbiased jury list or panel and an unbiased jury are *not* always the same. While the jury list or panel may be unbiased and highly representative of the community at large, the final jury may not be. Clearly, it is difficult to represent the community with 12 or fewer people. It is much easier to do so via the jury panel, however. Thus, the constitutional challenges discussed in the following sections apply to the selection of jury *lists* and *panels*, not to juries themselves. Jury selection is considered in the *voir dire* section.

EQUAL PROTECTION CHALLENGES   Before the Sixth Amendment was incorporated to the states, the only method of challenging the fairness of a jury pool or panel was based on the equal protection clause of the Fourteenth Amendment. In one case, *Strauder v. Virginia* (100 U.S. 303 [1879]), the Supreme Court declared unconstitutional a statute that explicitly excluded African Americans from jury service. The statute was a violation of equal protection, according to the Court.

Strauder was a fairly easy and predictable decision, given the nature of the statute involved. But what about exclusion of a particular group for other than statutory reasons? In *Whitus v. Georgia* (385 U.S. 545 [1967]), the Court held that an equal protection challenge will succeed when there is a significant disparity between, in that case, the proportion of African Americans on the jury panel and the proportion in the community. In another case, *Castaneda v. Partida* (430 U.S. 482 [1977]), the Supreme Court used the equal protection argument again. There, it held that systematic exclusion of people with Spanish surnames violated equal protection. In both cases, a *significant disparity* was deemed one that cannot be attributed to chance.

In summary, an equal protection challenge against the composition of a jury list or panel succeeded when (1) there was purposeful discrimination against certain individuals and (2) that discrimination was significant. The past tense is used here because the equal protection approach was abandoned in the 1975 case of *Taylor v. Louisiana* (419 U.S. 522 [1975]). That and some similar cases are considered next.

FAIR CROSS-SECTION CHALLENGES   Prior to 1975, the Supreme Court noted that the Sixth Amendment required that jury selection procedures be based on "the concept of the jury as a cross-section of the community" (*Glasser v. United States*, 315 U.S. 60 [1942], p. 86). That decision, however, only applied to the federal courts. It was not until 1975 and the case of *Taylor v. Louisiana* that the Supreme Court stated, "We accept the fair cross-section requirements as fundamental to the jury trial guaranteed by the Sixth Amendment." *Taylor* was therefore significant because (1) it abandoned the equal protection approach and (2) it applied the Sixth Amendment's fair cross-section requirement to the state courts through the due process clause of the Fourteenth Amendment.

Taylor was also significant because it abandoned the requirement of significant exclusion, replacing it with the lower standard of **systematic exclusion.** That is, in order to succeed with a fair cross-section challenge, the defendant need only show systematic exclusion of a distinctive group, not necessarily significant exclusion. *Taylor* also permitted fair cross-section challenges with regard to *any* distinctive group, not just racial and ethnic minorities, which were the only groups discussed in the equal protection cases from the previous section.

Duren v. Missouri
(439 U.S. 357 [1979])

In a later case, *Duren v. Missouri* (439 U.S. 357 [1979]), the Court clarified the *Taylor* language. Specifically, the Court required that the defendant prove three elements to succeed with a fair cross-section challenge:

> (1) that the group alleged to be excluded is a *"distinctive"* group in the community; (2) that the representation of this group in venires from which juries are selected is not fair and reasonable in relation to the number of such persons in the community; and (3) that this *underrepresentation* is due to *systematic exclusion* of the group in the jury-selection process. (p. 364, emphasis added)

The following paragraphs focus on these three elements: the distinctive group requirement, underrepresentation, and systematic exclusion.

First, what is a **distinctive group**? Generally, the group must be large and identifiable. The group must also meet with the spirit of the Sixth Amendment, which is to guarantee a fair cross-section of the community. In *Lockhart v. McCree* (476 U.S. 162 [1986]), the Court noted that the distinctive group requirement

> (1) "guards against the exercise of arbitrary power" and [ensures] that the "commonsense judgment of the community" will act as a "hedge against the overzealous or mistaken prosecutor;" (2) [preserves] "public confidence in the fairness of the criminal justice system;" and (3) [implements] our belief that "sharing in the administration of justice is a phase of civic responsibility." (pp. 174–175)

Examples of distinctive groups are, therefore, racial and ethnic minorities, including African Americans, Hispanic Americans, Native Americans, Jews, and others. Women are also considered a distinctive group. *Nondistinctive* groups include blue-collar workers (e.g., *Anaya v. Hansen*, 781 F.2d 1 [1st Cir. 1986]) and young adults (e.g., *Ford v. Seabold*, 841 F.2d 677 [6th Cir. 1988]). Basically, any group that has received protection via legislation and the equal protection clause (i.e., most notably, women and minorities) is considered distinctive for jury purposes.

Next, what is underrepresentation? This can be difficult to determine, but most Supreme Court cases to date have not dealt with difficult determinations. For example, in *Taylor*, the Court concluded that women were underrepresented in the jury panel because while they made by 53 percent of the population of people eligible for jury service, only 10 percent of the people in the jury panel were women. Similarly, in *Duren*, 54 percent of the adults in the county were women, but only 15 percent of the people on the jury panel were women.

It was easy for the Court to determine underrepresentation based on these startling percentages. When the discrepancies are not this apparent, however, determining underrepresentation can be quite difficult. It appears that a discrepancy of 10 percent or more between the jury panel and the distribution of a particular group in the community is unacceptable (*United States v. Rodriguez*, 776 F.2d 1509 [11th Cir. 1985]).

The last requirement for a fair cross-section challenge to succeed is whether the exclusion in question is a systematic exclusion or an accidental one. Some of the only guidance the Supreme Court has offered with regard to this matter was announced in *Duren v. Missouri*: "[I]n Sixth Amendment fair-cross-section cases, systematic disproportion itself demonstrates an infringement of the defendant's interest in a jury chosen from a fair cross-section" (p. 368). Proving systematic exclusion can be quite difficult, as was made clear in a recent case, *Berghuis v. Smith* (No. 08-1402 [2010]).

How does one obtain a copy of the jury list? It varies by jurisdiction. Some publish the list automatically. Others make the list available to the attorneys on request. The information revealed in the lists also varies. For example, in Virginia, the list is required to contain names, addresses, ages, occupations, and employers (Virginia Code, Section 8.01-353). Other jurisdictions require prospective jurors to complete "eligibility questionnaires" prior to their service. The results of these questionnaires are then made available on request. The intent is to assist defendants with challenging the jury list if it so desires.

The *Voir Dire* Process

Thus far, the focus has been on the composition of jury lists (i.e., consisting of all possible jurors) and jury panels (i.e., those called for jury duty). If either excludes a particular group of people to the extent that the defendant's equal protection rights are violated or

DECISION-MAKING EXERCISE 13.8

What Composes a Distinctive Group?

Tanya Oki, a resident of an elite suburban neighborhood, was charged with burglary. She was tried and convicted by a 12-member jury and later sentenced to five years in prison. While in prison, she acquired a copy of the jury list (which, incidentally, is now permitted following the Supreme Court's decision in *Test v. United States*, 420 U.S. 28 [1975]) and decided, based on the addresses in the list, that none of the jurors who convicted her were "yuppies." As such, she had her privately retained attorney draft an appeal, claiming that her Sixth Amendment right to an impartial jury was violated. In particular, she claimed that "yuppies" are a distinctive group and should be more adequately represented in the jury list. How should the appellate court decide?

the Sixth Amendment's fair cross-section requirement is violated, then any resulting conviction could be reversed. Next, the focus turns to **voir dire**, which is the process of selecting a jury from a jury panel.

It is important to understand that once *voir dire* commences, the concern is *not* to ensure that the jury represents a fair cross-section of the community. Instead, *voir dire* is concerned with the selection of jury members who can be *impartial*, as the Sixth Amendment requires. The term *voir dire* means "to see what is said." Thus, at this stage, the judge, prosecutor, and defense have an opportunity to review potential jurors for evidence of bias.

Voir dire can be simple or complicated. In some jurisdictions, the judge decides who will serve on the jury. The prosecution and defense merely suggest questions to the judge in these jurisdictions. Doing so speeds up the process and also helps ensure that jurors do not develop preconceived ideas about the case in question.

Usually, however, it is the attorneys who do the questioning. This process can take anything from a few hours to a few weeks. *Voir dire* at O. J. Simpson's criminal trial took several weeks. *Voir dire* can also take time because nothing precludes the attorneys from investigating jurors' backgrounds, interviewing their acquaintances, and even hiring social scientists who are experts in anticipating prospective jurors' probable decisions.

The main component of the juror selection process is *voir dire*. During *voir dire*, prospective jurors are asked questions relating to their potential to be impartial. Judges and especially prosecutors and defense attorneys ask the questions.

Most readers are familiar with the basic elements of the *voir dire* process. Each side, the defense and prosecution, has an unlimited number of so-called *challenges for cause.* A challenge for cause is when one or the other attorney argues that a particular person should be excluded from service on the jury because of bias or a similar reason. Each side is also given a certain number of *peremptory challenges,* which permit the attorney to exclude members of the jury panel without giving any reason. Before either challenge is used, however, the judge usually opens by asking questions of the jurors. Each of these three methods is considered in a following subsection. But before moving on, see Figure 13.4 for a summary of the *voir dire* process by state, including who conducts *voir dire* and the number of peremptory challenges allocated by specific crime type.

FIGURE 13.4

Voir Dire Processes by State for Courts of General Jurisdiction

State	Number of peremptory challenges					
	Criminal					
	Capital		Felony		Misdemeanor	
	State	Defense	State	Defense	State	Defense
Alabama	12	12	6	6	3	3
Alaska	N/A	N/A	10	10	3	3
Arizona	10	10	6	6	6	6
Arkansas	10	12	6	8	3	3
California	20	20	20/10	20/10	10/6	10/6
Colorado	10	10	5	5	3	3
Connecticut	25	25	15/6	15/6	3	3
Delaware	12	20	6	6	6	6
District of Columbia	N/A	N/A	10	10	3	3
Florida	10	10	10/6	10/6	3	3
Georgia	10	20	6	12	2	4
Hawaii	N/A	N/A	12/3	12/3	3	3
Idaho	10	10	10/6	10/6	4	4
Illinois	14	14	7	7	5	5
Indiana	20	20	10	10	5	5
Iowa	N/A	N/A	10/6	10/6	4	4
Kansas	12	12	12/8/6	12/8/6	3	3
Kentucky	8	8	8	8	3	3
Louisiana	12	12	12/6	12/6	6	6
Maine	N/A	N/A	10/8	10/8	4	4
Maryland	10	20	5	10	4	4
Massachusetts	N/A	N/A	12/4	12/4	4	4
Michigan	N/A	N/A	12/5	12/5	5	5
Minnesota	N/A	N/A	9/3	15/5	3	5

Figure 13.4 continued

Mississippi	12	12	6	6	6	6
Missouri	9	9	6	6	2	2
Montana	8	8	6/3	6/3	6/3	6/3
Nebraska	12	12	6	6	3	3
Nevada	8	8	4	4	4	4
New Hampshire	10	20	15/3	15/3	3	3
New Jersey	N/A	N/A	12	20	10	10
New Mexico	N/A	N/A	3	5	3	5
New York	N/A	N/A	20/15	20/15/10	10	10
North Carolina	14	14	6	6	6	6
North Dakota	N/A	N/A	6/4	6/4	6/4	6/4
Ohio	6	6	4	4	3	3
Oklahoma	9	9	5	5	3	3
Oregon	12	12	6	6	6/3	6/3
Pennsylvania	20	20	7	7	5	5
Puerto Rico	N/A	N/A	10/5	10/5	5	5
Rhode Island	N/A	N/A	6	6	3	3
South Carolina	5	10	5	10	5	5
South Dakota	20	20	20/10	20/10	3	3
Tennessee	15	15	8	8	3	3
Texas	15	15	10	10	5	5
Utah	10	10	4	4	3	3
Vermont	N/A	N/A	6	6	6	6
Virginia	4	4	4	4	3	3
Washington	12	12	6	6	3	3
West Virginia	N/A	N/A	2	6	4	4
Wisconsin	N/A	N/A	6/4	6/4	4	4
Wyoming	12	12	8	8	4	4

Note: The following states/territories do not have a death penalty statute or have abolished the death penalty: Alaska, District of Columbia, Hawaii, Iowa, Maine, Massachusetts, Michigan, Minnesota, New Jersey, New Mexico, New York, North Dakota, Puerto Rico, Rhode Island, Vermont, West Virginia, and Wisconsin.

Sources: D. B. Rottman and S. M. Strickland, *State Court Organization, 2004* (Washington, DC: Bureau of Justice Statistics, 2006); http://www.deathpenaltyinfo.org/states-and-without-death-penalty (accessed February 24, 2011).

QUESTIONING BY THE JUDGE *Voir dire* usually begins with the judge asking questions—for instance, dealing with potential jurors' familiarity with the case, attitudes toward one or the other party to the case, demographic information, and so on. In high-profile cases, prospective jurors are often asked to complete a questionnaire intended to divulge information that might lead to their disqualification or excusal. This is often done to guide the attorneys in their *voir dire* questioning. The Supreme Court has upheld this type of questioning, noting that it is perfectly acceptable for the judge to question jurors about their knowledge and opinions concerning the case (*Mu'Min v. Virginia*, 500 U.S. 415 [1991]).

Note that the reverse is also true: The judge is not required to ask any questions in certain types of cases. In an obscenity case, the Supreme Court noted that the judge is not required to ask questions as to "whether the jurors' educational, political, and religious beliefs might affect their views on the question of obscenity" (*Hamling v. United States*, 418 U.S. 87 [1974]).

However, the Supreme Court has required that in certain types of cases—notably, those dealing with racial prejudice and capital punishment—judges must ask certain types of questions. For instance, in *Ham v. South Carolina* (409 U.S. 524 [1973]), the Court noted that questions about racial prejudice must be asked if racial issues are closely tied to the criminal conduct at issue. *Ham* was a case in which an African American defendant was tried for marijuana possession. The defendant claimed that because he was a well-known civil rights activist, the police had framed him on the narcotics charge. The Supreme Court stated that the general introductory questions asked by the judge were insufficient and that special attention should have been given to the race issue.

In another case, *Ristaino v. Ross* (424 U.S. 589 [1976]), a black defendant was convicted of a violent crime committed against a white security guard. The trial judge denied the defendant's motion that specific questions about racial prejudice be asked of potential jurors. Instead, the judge just asked basic questions about *general* prejudice, not any directed at the facts of the case in question. Surprisingly, the Supreme Court upheld the trial judge's decision. This decision seems contradictory to *Ham*, but the Court noted that in this case, racial issues did not permeate. Instead, the fact that the defendant was black and the victim was white was secondary to the question of guilt.

The Supreme Court has also decided whether judges should ask detailed questions of potential jurors who serve on *death-qualified juries*—that is, juries that may recommend a death sentence.[1] The Court has actually been more emphatic with regard to death penalty cases than with those involving racial issues. It has stated that the judge *must*, at the request of either party and only in cases in which capital punishment is a possible outcome, ask specific questions of jurors so as to assess their attitudes toward capital punishment. This rule was announced in *Morgan v. Illinois* (504 U.S. 719 [1992]). There, the Court held that defendants in capital cases may require potential jurors to state whether they would automatically impose the death penalty on conviction.

More recently, the Court held that appellate courts "owe deference to the trial court, which is in a superior position to determine the demeanor and qualifications of a potential juror" (*Uttecht v. Brown*, 551 U.S. 1 [2007]). This means that trial judges are in the best position to determine whether certain potential jurors should be excused because of reservations concerning capital punishment.

In summary, there are few constitutional restrictions on judges' questioning of potential jurors. With the exceptions of capital cases and those in which racial and ethnic matters permeate the trial, judges are under no obligation to ask questions of potential jurors. By the same token, judges are given considerable latitude in terms of asking almost any questions they desire. Detailed questions, however, are mostly asked by the attorneys in the case.

CHALLENGES FOR CAUSE   The prosecution and defense are given unlimited opportunities to make **challenges for cause**. Convincing reasons can be found for the exclusion of potential jurors, some of which even have statutory origins. For example, if a member of the jury panel is related to the defendant, a challenge for cause will almost certainly

---

[1] A *death-qualified jury* is one in which each juror is at least open to the idea of sentencing someone to death. Death-qualified jurors are selected after being asked questions about whether they support the death penalty and would hand down a sentence of death, if the need arose.

succeed. Also, if the potential juror served on a past jury in a case dealing with a similar crime, a challenge for cause will probably succeed. If a potential juror stands to benefit financially from the outcome of the case, he or she will probably be excused based on a challenge for cause. While the list goes on, only two challenges have been dealt with by the Supreme Court: (1) those based on bias and (2) those based on attitudes toward capital punishment.

Challenges Based on Bias.   Generally, if a juror is unable or unwilling to hear the case fairly and impartially, he or she may be excluded in a challenge for cause. However, as Supreme Court precedent seems to attest, challenges for cause dealing with alleged bias rarely succeed. That is, in situations in which a person *appears* biased but does not state anything to this effect, it is difficult to succeed with a challenge for cause.

In fact, there is only one case in which the Supreme Court sanctioned exclusion of a potential juror because of alleged bias. In *Leonard v. United States* (378 U.S. 544 [1964]), the Court held that jury panel members who had heard the guilty verdict at the defendant's previous trial should have been excluded from serving on the jury in the present trial. The Court believed that the previous verdict may have influenced jurors in the second trial.

Leonard stands alone, though. In *Dennis v. United States* (339 U.S. 162 [1950]), the Court required a showing of *actual* bias, not *alleged* bias. In that case, the defendant claimed that his conviction on contempt charges for failure to appear before the Committee on Un-American Activities was tainted because the jury consisted mostly of federal employees, who were all subject to discharge if they were not loyal to the government. The Court disagreed with Dennis's argument, stating that "[p]reservation of the opportunity to prove actual bias is a guarantee of a defendant's right to an impartial jury" (pp. 171–172).

Smith v. Phillips
(455 U.S. 209 [1982])

In a more recent case, *Smith v. Phillips* (455 U.S. 209 [1982]), the Court held once again that actual bias must be shown for a challenge for cause to succeed. In that case, the Court did not infer bias from the fact that a potential juror had been seeking employment from the prosecutor's office. However, this decision and the one before it should not be construed to suggest that actual bias must *always* be shown over alleged bias. Alleged, or implied, bias may be sufficient in certain limited circumstances for exclusion of a potential juror based on a challenge for cause.

Challenges in Death Penalty Cases.   Defendants in capital trials have the right to exclude jurors who have certain preconceived ideas about the death penalty. In

Witherspoon v. Illinois
(391 U.S. 510 [1968])

Witherspoon v. Illinois (391 U.S. 510 [1968]), the Court decided on the constitutionality of a statute that provided for exclusion of all potential jurors who "expressed scruples" against the death penalty. The Court held that a death sentence returned from such a jury would be unconstitutional because the jury resulting from the statute would be "organized to return a verdict of death" (p. 521). Importantly, in Witherspoon, it was only the defendant's death sentence that was invalidated, not his conviction. Also, note that nothing prohibits a prosecutor from excluding a juror who would *never* return a verdict of death.

In short, challenges for cause in death penalty cases usually come in two varieties. If the defendant can show that a potential juror is predisposed to return a verdict of death, such a juror will probably be excluded. Similarly, if the prosecution can show that a potential juror is almost certain to oppose capital punishment, that juror will probably be excluded, as well.

PEREMPTORY CHALLENGES   The foregoing section showed that challenges for cause come in several varieties, but the only ones previously dealt with by the Supreme Court concerned bias as well as attitudes toward the death penalty. In either case, one of the parties to the case presented its argument to the judge as to why a potential juror should be excluded. **Peremptory challenges**, by contrast, call for removal of potential jurors *without* any type of argument.

Think of a peremptory challenge as a fallback measure. If, say, the defense fails with a challenge for cause to exclude a potential juror who it believes will be biased against the defendant, a peremptory challenge can be used. In fact, a peremptory challenge can be used to exclude a potential juror for any reason. As the Supreme Court stated in Swain *v. Alabama* (380 U.S. 202 [1965]), the peremptory challenge "is often exercised upon the 'sudden impressions and unaccountable prejudices we are apt to conceive upon the bare looks and gestures of another,' upon a juror's 'habits and associations,' or upon the felling that the 'bare questioning [of a juror's] indifference may sometimes provoke a resentment' " (pp. 242–243).

Because peremptory challenges need not be predicated on any type of argument, there are not many Supreme Court cases dealing with them. Of the few relevant cases, however, some deal with peremptory challenges by the prosecution. The rest deal with challenges by the defense.

Challenges by the Prosecution.   It is generally unacceptable for the prosecution (and the defense) to exclude a juror based on race or ethnicity. A *challenge for cause* arguing that a person's race or ethnicity will cause him or her to be biased will never succeed. But what if a *peremptory challenge* is used to exclude a juror based on race or ethnicity? This question was addressed in *Swain v. Alabama*, cited earlier. In that case, the defendant argued that the prosecutor excluded all minority jurors through peremptory challenges and, as such, violated the equal protection clause of the Fourteenth Amendment. The Court rejected this argument, as follows:

> [The peremptory challenge] is often exercised upon the "sudden impressions and unaccountable prejudices we are apt to conceive upon the bare looks and gestures of another," . . . upon a juror's "habits and associations," . . . or upon the feeling that "the bare questioning [a juror's] indifference may sometimes provoke a resentment." . . . It is no less frequently exercised on grounds normally thought irrelevant to legal proceedings or official action, namely, the race, religion, nationality, occupation or affiliations of people summoned for jury duty. For the question a prosecutor or defense counsel must decide is not whether a juror of a particular race or nationality is in fact partial, but whether one from a different group is less likely to be. (pp. 220–221)

DECISION-MAKING EXERCISE 13.9

Strong Opinions on the Death Penalty

Assume that during *voir dire*, the following exchange takes place between a defense attorney and a potential juror:

DEFENSE ATTORNEY: Do you have any reservations against the death penalty?

POTENTIAL JUROR: No, of course not. I firmly support capital punishment. I think we should execute all criminals.

DEFENSE ATTORNEY: Do you think you can set aside your personal convictions for the purposes of this trial and make an objective decision based on the evidence?

POTENTIAL JUROR: I suppose so. I think I could probably keep an open mind.

Now, assume that the defense attorney seeks to exercise one of her challenges for cause and asks the judge to exclude this juror. The judge denies the request. Assuming that the remaining jurors are not as opinionated, do you think the resulting jury will conform to the Sixth Amendment requirements discussed thus far?

The Court continued:

> Hence veniremen are not always judged solely as individuals for the purpose of exercising peremptory challenges. Rather they are challenged in light of the limited knowledge counsel has of them, which may include their group affiliations, in the context of the case to be tried. (p. 221)

Had the prosecutor in this case sought to exclude minorities from all juries and had this come to light, a successful equal protection challenge probably could have been mounted.

Batson v. Kentucky
(476 U.S. 79 [1986])

Several years after *Swain*, the Supreme Court revisited the issue of using peremptory challenges for excluding racial and ethnic minorities. In *Batson v. Kentucky* (476 U.S. 79 [1986]), the Court decided that prosecutors can be called on to explain their use of peremptory challenges to exclude minorities but only if the defense shows that the challenges were used for this purpose. This showing requires that the people excluded through the peremptory challenges constitute a distinct group, that these people were excluded by the prosecution through the use of peremptory challenges, and that "these facts and any other relevant circumstances raise an inference that the prosecutor used [peremptories] to exclude the veniremen from the petit jury on account of their race" (p. 124; see also *Johnson v. California*, 125 S.Ct. 2410 [2005], *Miller El v. Dretke*, 125 S.Ct. 2317 [2005], and *Snyder v. Louisiana*, 554 U.S. 472 [2008]).

If the defense makes the showing, then the prosecutor will be required to explain his or her reasons for excluding jurors based on race and ethnicity. However, this explanation does not need to be as convincing as one that would accompany a challenge for cause. It simply needs to be what the Court calls *race neutral*.

What is a race-neutral explanation? In *Hernandez v. New York* (500 U.S. 352 [1991]), the prosecutor sought to use peremptory challenges to exclude four potential jurors of Hispanic descent. They were the only three people on the panel with apparent Hispanic origins. The prosecutor argued that the jurors were excluded for two reasons: (1) that two of the panel members were involved in criminal activity and (2) that the other two "looked away" from him during questioning. The Court declared that this explanation was race neutral. Had the prosecution argued that the excluded jurors would likely decide a case in a certain way, given their Hispanic descent, the Court would have decided differently. Thus, a race-neutral argument is one that really has nothing to do with race or ethnicity.

In summary, peremptory challenges used to exclude racial and ethnic minorities are constitutionally valid only when (1) the prosecutor offers a race-neutral explanation for doing so and (2) the judge believes the reason is genuine. These two requirements only matter, however, if the defendant raises the argument that race or ethnicity was a motivating factor behind the prosecutor's use of peremptory challenges. In other words, the defense has the initial burden of showing racial or ethnic bias in the peremptory challenge stage. These guidelines apply not only to peremptory exclusion of racial and ethnic minorities (e.g., related cases include *Powers v. Ohio*, 499 U.S. 400 [1991]; *Holland v. Illinois*, 493 U.S. 474 [1990]) but also to gender-based exclusion (see *J.E.B. v. Alabama*, 511 U.S. 127 [1994]).

Challenges by the Defense. The defense also cannot exclude potential jurors through peremptory challenges based on race and ethnicity. For example, in *Georgia v. McCollum* (502 U.S. 1056 [1992]), the Court refused to sanction the exclusion of black panel members in the trial of white defendants charged with assaulting black individuals. At the same time, though, the defense cannot be forced to use a peremptory challenge to excuse a juror he or she argues should have been excused for cause. (See *United States v. Martinez-Salazar*, 528 U.S. 304 [2000], for a further explanation.)

DECISION-MAKING EXERCISE 13.10

Appropriate Use of the Peremptory Challenge

An African American defendant, who was charged in a state trial court with robbery, objected to the prosecutor's use of peremptory challenges to excuse two black men from the jury panel. The prosecutor explained that he excused the first juror because the juror had long unkempt hair, a mustache, and a beard. The prosecutor then said that he excluded the second juror because the juror had a mustache and a beard. The trial court overruled the defendant's objection, impaneled the jury, and convicted the defendant of robbery. How should the appellate court decide?

Remaining Supreme Court cases concerning peremptory challenges by the defense have revolved around the question of how many, if any, peremptory challenges should be constitutionally permissible. In response, the Court stated in *Gray v. Mississippi* (481 U.S. 648 [1987]) that peremptory challenges are not constitutionally guaranteed. And in *Stilson v. United States* (250 U.S. 583 [1919]), the Court held that in trials of codefendants, the number of peremptories should be reduced to the number each defendant would have if tried separately. Other cases suggest that the defense can be required to exercise its peremptory challenges before the government does (*Pointer v. United States*, 151 U.S. 396 [1894]) and that the defense can be required to exclude, through use of its peremptory challenges, jurors that the judge should have excused for cause (*Ross v. Oklahoma*, 487 U.S. 81 [1988]).

Gray v. Mississippi (481 U.S. 648 [1987])

What if the court mistakenly denies a defense counsel request to exercise a peremptory challenge? This issue came up in *Rivera v. Illinois* (No. 07-9995 [2009]). In that case, the Court held that the due process clause does not require automatic reversal of a conviction because the trial court erred in denying the defendant's right to exercise a peremptory challenge.

When Judges Preempt Juries

Recently, the Supreme Court gave some attention to what the jury must consider during its deliberations—and to what extent judges can preempt juries. In *Blakely v. Washington* (542 U.S. 296 [2004]), a man was convicted of kidnapping his estranged wife. After the jury returned its verdict, the judge decided that the man acted with "deliberate cruelty" and he handed down a harsher sentence than would have otherwise been authorized had he not identified such aggravating factors. The Supreme Court declared that the defendant's right to a jury trial was violated because the facts supporting the judge's finding of "deliberate cruelty" were not admitted by the accused *or* found by a jury. In other words, the judge could not preempt the jury's fact-finding role (see also *United States v. Booker*, 543 U.S. 220 [2005]).

Summary

1. SUMMARIZE THE RIGHT TO A SPEEDY TRIAL.

The defendant has three important rights at trial: (1) the right to a speedy trial, (2) the right to an impartial judge, and (3) the right to an impartial jury. The first and third rights have constitutional (i.e., Sixth Amendment) origins. However, the right to an impartial judge does not; it is a right created by the Supreme Court, in much the same way the exclusionary rule is a judicial creation.

The right to a speedy trial applies once a person has been accused of a crime. If the defendant is charged, let go, and then charged again, the right does not apply until the second set of charges has been filed. Even if the defendant does not know he or she has been accused of and/or charged with a crime, the right to speedy trial can apply. This right sometimes extends beyond the Sixth Amendment and, according to the Supreme Court, can have a due process component.

Four criteria are used to determine when the right to a speedy trial has been *violated*: (1) too much delay between accusation and trial, (2) intentional delay, (3) whether the defendant asserts the right to a speedy trial, and (4) whether the delay is prejudicial. No criterion by itself is necessarily enough for the right to be violated, however. If, for instance, the delay is too long, intentional, prejudicial, and accompanied by the defendant's demand for a speedy trial, the right will almost certainly be violated. The consequence of violating the right to a speedy trial is dismissal of charges. Finally, the federal Speedy Trial Act attempted to clarify important Supreme Court decisions regarding the Sixth Amendment right to a speedy trial.

2. EXPLAIN THE RIGHT TO AN IMPARTIAL JUDGE.

The defendant also enjoys the right to trial by an impartial judge. A judge cannot be considered impartial if he or she has a pecuniary interest in the outcome of a case. Usually, judges will remove themselves if they deem themselves less than impartial, but some jurisdictions permit the peremptory removal of judges. This allows counsel to remove one judge and request a second one. This method is extreme, however.

3. SUMMARIZE THE RIGHT TO A JURY TRIAL.

Finally, the defendant enjoys the right to trial by an impartial jury. However, the Supreme Court has held that this right applies only to criminal proceedings in which the possible punishment exceeds six months' detention. Jury size and voting requirements vary by jurisdiction, but as a general rule, the smaller the jury, the more unanimous the required verdict. Like many constitutional rights, the right to a jury trial can be waived, in which case the defendant opts for a so-called bench trial.

4. OUTLINE THE JURY SELECTION PROCESS.

Jury selection occurs in three stages. First, a list of potential jurors, known as the jury list, is compiled. From that list, potential jurors are selected for jury service. Those selected for jury service are part of a jury panel. From the jury panel, some people are selected and required to go to a courtroom, where *voir dire* commences. *Voir dire* begins with the judge asking questions, some of which he or she is required to ask. Next, the attorneys on both sides will exercise their peremptory challenges and challenges for cause. The former are almost unrestricted but limited in number. The latter must be argued before the judge and are not limited in number.

It is important to understand that the jury list and panel must be representative of the community at large but not the final jury. The only way for a defendant to succeed in arguing that the jury itself is not representative is if he or she can show that the prosecution used its peremptory challenges to exclude individuals from distinctive groups and engages in this practice during the *voir dire* process for *all* juries. If the prosecution uses its peremptory challenges to occasionally excuse a juror based on race or ethnicity, the Sixth Amendment will not be violated. Finally, judges cannot preempt the jury's role.

Key Terms

accusation rule	411	impartial jury	417	peremptory		speedy trial	409
challenges for		jury list	423	challenges	431	systematic	
cause	429	jury panel	423	six-month		exclusion	424
distinctive		noncriminal		imprisonment		*voir dire*	426
group	425	proceeding		rule	418		
impartial judge	415	rule	418				

Key Cases

Speedy Trial

- *United States v. Marion*, 404 U.S. 307 (1971)
- *United States v. Loud Hawk*, 474 U.S. 302 (1986)
- *Doggett v. United States*, 505 U.S. 647 (1992)
- *United States v. Lovasco*, 431 U.S. 783 (1977)
- *Barker v. Wingo*, 407 U.S. 514 (1972)
- *Strunk v. United States*, 412 U.S. 434 (1973)

Impartial Judge

- *Tumey v. Ohio*, 273 U.S. 510 (1927)
- *Ward v. Monroeville*, 409 U.S. 57 (1972)

Impartial Jury

- *McKeiver v. Pennsylvania*, 403 U.S. 528 (1971)
- *Baldwin v. New York*, 399 U.S. 66 (1970)

- *Johnson v. Louisiana*, 406 U.S. 356 (1972)
- *Duren v. Missouri*, 439 U.S. 357 (1979)
- *Smith v. Phillips*, 455 U.S. 209 (1982)
- *Witherspoon v. Illinois*, 391 U.S. 510 (1968)
- *Batson v. Kentucky*, 476 U.S. 79 (1986)
- *Gray v. Mississippi*, 481 U.S. 648 (1987)

Review Questions

1. Explain when the right to a speedy trial applies.
2. What criteria are used to determine when the right to a speedy trial has been violated?
3. Summarize the consequences of violating the accused's right to a speedy trial.
4. Briefly outline important provisions of the federal Speedy Trial Act, including the consequences of violating it.
5. Under what circumstances could a judge be considered *not* impartial (i.e., biased)? Cite relevant cases.
6. What methods are available for removing a judge who cannot be considered impartial?
7. When does the right to a jury trial apply?
8. Explain the jury size and voting requirements in your state.
9. Can the right to a jury trial be waived? If so, what are the requirements for doing so?
10. Identify the methods used for creating a jury list.
11. What are the three stages of jury selection?
12. What are the requirements for a successful fair cross-section challenge of a jury panel?
13. Summarize the *voir dire* process.
14. What questions has the Supreme Court required judges to ask during *voir dire*?
15. Under what circumstances has the Supreme Court imposed restrictions on the use of peremptory challenges?

Web Links and Exercises

1. Speedy Trial Act of 1974: What do the federal courts require with respect to the Sixth Amendment's speedy trial provision?
Suggested URL: http://www4.law.cornell.edu/uscode/uscode18/usc_sup_01_18_10_II_20_208.html (accessed February 16, 2011).
2. Code of Conduct for United States Judges: Read more about the canons introduced in Figure 13.1
URL: http://www.uscourts.gov/rulesandpolicies/CodesOfConduct.aspx (accessed February 16, 2011).
3. Origins of the American Jury: Why do we rely on trial by jury in this country, apart from what the Constitution requires?
Suggested URL: http://www.crfc.org/americanjury/origins.html (accessed February 16, 2011).

4. Mock *voir dire*: Create a mock jury.
Suggested URL: http://www.crfc.org/americanjury/voir_dire.html (accessed February 16, 2011).
5. Is there a "CSI Effect?" There is concern that jurors expect the same evidence presented in popular television programs like *CSI: Crime Scene Investigation*. Are such concerns merited?
URL: http://www.ncjrs.gov/pdffiles1/nij/221501.pdf (accessed February 16, 2011).
6. Jury Nullification: Read about the controversial practice of jury nullification.
Suggested URL: http://www.law.umkc.edu/faculty/projects/ftrials/zenger/nullification.html (accessed February 16, 2011).

LEARNING OBJECTIVES

When you complete this chapter, you should be able to:

▸ Summarize the right to a public trial.

▸ Summarize the right to confrontation.

▸ Summarize the right to compulsory process.

▸ Explain the concept of double jeopardy.

▸ Outline the classifications and origins of the entrapment defense.

More Rights at Trial

INTRODUCTION

More Protections for the Accused

In addition to guaranteeing the right to counsel, the Sixth Amendment provides that "[i]n all criminal prosecutions, the accused shall enjoy the right to . . . [a] public trial[,] to be confronted with the witnesses against him [and] to have compulsory process for obtaining witnesses in his favor." These rights are intended to assist the accused in mounting an effective defense. Without them, a criminal prosecution would be largely one sided; that is, it would favor the prosecution.

Besides the rights to a public trial, confrontation, and compulsory process, criminal defendants in the United States also enjoy other important rights at trial. One such right, known as protection from *double jeopardy*, is found in the Fifth Amendment: "[N]or shall any person be subject for the same offence to be twice put in jeopardy of life or limb." This means that an accused person cannot be convicted of or punished for the same offense twice. Finally, a defendant can assert the well-known *entrapment defense*. This defense is considered here, as well, even though it is not a constitutional guarantee, as the other rights are.

THE RIGHT TO A PUBLIC TRIAL

In re Oliver (333 U.S. 257 [1948])

In *In re Oliver* (333 U.S. 257 [1948]), the Supreme Court stated, "The knowledge that every criminal trial is subject to contemporaneous review in the forum of public opinion is an effective restraint on possible abuse of power. . . . Without publicity, all other checks are insufficient; in comparison of publicity, all other checks are of small account" (p. 271). Furthermore, "the presence of interested spectators may keep [the defendant's] triers keenly alive to a sense of their responsibility and to the importance of their functions" (p. 271, n. 25). This is what is meant by a **public trial**: It is one that is open to the public.

Waller v. Georgia 467 U.S. 39 [1984]

Oliver dealt expressly with criminal trials, but the Supreme Court has held that openness also applies to other hearings. For example, suppression hearings should be open to the public (*Waller v. Georgia*, 467 U.S. 39 [1984]), as should *voir dire* (*Presley v. Georgia*, No. 09-5270 [2010]). By extension, most other hearings—with the exception of grand jury proceedings, which are traditionally carried out in secret—should be considered public, as well.

When the Right May Not Apply

Most trials are open to the public but not all of them. Indeed, the defendant, whose interest is frequently served by openness, may want the trial closed to the public. This could be in an effort to minimize negative publicity, especially when the trial is for a heinous crime. In this way, the defendant's Sixth Amendment rights can be waived, just like many other constitutional rights can. The government can also seek to close a trial to the public. Each method of closure is touched on in a following subsection.

GOVERNMENT-SOUGHT CLOSURE In *Waller v. Georgia* (467 U.S. 39 [1984]), the Supreme Court created a test for determining when the government will succeed in closing a trial to the public. The government must show (1) that there is an overriding interest, such as protection of certain witnesses; (2) that the closure is no broader than absolutely necessary; and (3) that reasonable alternatives have been considered.

Waller dealt with the closure of a suppression hearing in which a video of people not yet indicted was played. The Court held that closure of the hearing was unconstitutional because the government did not identify "whose privacy interests might be infringed, how they would be infringed, what portions of the tape might infringe on them, and what portion of the evidence consisted of the tapes" (p. 48). At present, the threat of terrorism is being used as justification by the government for the closure of certain judicial hearings.

Sheppard v. Maxwell (384 U.S. 333 [1966])

DEFENSE-SOUGHT CLOSURE *Sheppard v. Maxwell* (384 U.S. 333 [1966]) illustrates the occasional conflict that can arise with the negative effects of trial publicity. In that case, the courtroom was packed with members of the public and media for all nine weeks of the trial. This made it difficult for people to hear one another. The press also handled and took pictures of evidentiary exhibits. The Supreme Court reversed the defendant's conviction, citing the "carnival atmosphere" of the trial in its decision.[1]

---

[1] While the defense in *Sheppard* did not directly seek closure of the trial, it did make requests for a continuance, a change of venue, and a mistrial.

In another case, *Estes v. Texas* (381 U.S. 532 [1965]), the Court also reversed the defendant's conviction, noting that the presence of television cameras distracted parties to the case in addition to the witnesses who gave testimony. This ruling does not provide a blanket prohibition of television cameras in courtrooms, however. In *Chandler v. Florida* (449 U.S. 560 [1981]), the Supreme Court upheld Florida's rule permitting the use of still photography and television cameras in court. Cameras are impermissible only if the defendant can show that "the media's coverage of his case—be it printed or broadcast—[compromises] the ability of the . . . jury . . . to adjudicate fairly" (p. 575).

The First Amendment and Public Trials

The First Amendment guarantees freedom of speech and of the press. Thus, any effort to close a trial or pretrial hearing to the public—be it by the government or the defense—may cause the press to rally in opposition. Supreme Court precedent suggests that unless the government or the defense can demonstrate that significant prejudice is likely to result from a public trial, closure of a trial is unlikely.

Gannett Co., Inc. v. DePasquale (443 U.S. 368 [1979]) is an illustrative case. There, the Supreme Court held that the trial judge may, at the defendant's request, close a pretrial suppression hearing in an effort to avoid the "reasonable probability of prejudice." The Supreme Court sanctioned closure of this nature because it was at the defendant's request and because the media did not oppose closure.

In *Richmond Newspapers, Inc. v. Virginia* (448 U.S. 555 [1980]), however, the Court indicated that closure will seldom be allowed if the media asserts an interest in having access to the hearing. The defendant in *Richmond Newspapers* sought closure of his trial because he had been through four previous mistrials, one of which stemmed from a juror telling other jurors about press reports of the case. The Court rejected the defendant's argument, noting that "the right to attend criminal trials is implicit in the guarantees of the First Amendment; without the freedom to attend such trials, which people have exercised for centuries, important aspects of freedom of speech and of the press could be eviscerated" (p. 580). And in another case, *Globe Newspaper Co. v. Superior Court* (457 U.S. 596 [1982]), the Court noted that the First Amendment serves "to ensure that the individual citizen can effectively participate in and contribute to our republican system of self-government" and "fosters an appearance of fairness, thereby heightening public respect for the judicial process" (p. 606).

In summary, with regard to the First Amendment and the defendant's interest in a fair trial, closure of a criminal trial is highly unlikely. None of the Supreme Court cases reviewed thus far has permitted outright closure. By contrast, closure of a pretrial hearing is more likely to be sanctioned. In either case, difficulty will only be encountered if the press raises a First Amendment objection to the proposed closure.

DEALING WITH MEDIA INFLUENCE   The media can seemingly influence the fairness of a criminal trial in two ways: (1) by its pretrial coverage and (2) by being present in the courtroom, as just discussed. However, if either form of coverage is prejudicial, this does not necessarily mean the media should be excluded and the hearing closed to the public.

In response to this problem, the Supreme Court has addressed several alternatives to the closure of pretrial hearings and/or the trial itself. Each is aimed at ensuring a fair trial for the accused. The alternatives are:

- *voir dire* with special attention to pretrial publicity,
- a change of venue,
- jury sequestration,

- a gag order on the media, and
- a gag order on other parties.

As explained in Chapter 13, *voir dire* is the process by which jury members are selected from a panel of potential jurors. The judge can ask several questions, and the attorneys can exclude jurors for cause and by use of peremptory challenges. When media coverage of a crime is extensive and presumed to have influenced members of the jury panel, *voir dire* can be used to detect that bias.

In *Marshall v. United States* (360 U.S. 310 [1959]), the Supreme Court held that potential jurors who have learned from news coverage of a defendant's prior record are presumed to be prejudiced. Similarly, in *Irvin v. Dowd* (366 U.S. 717 [1961]), the Court decided that pretrial publicity can be so influential that jurors' statements about being willing to make impartial decisions can be discounted. But in two later cases, *Murphy v. Florida* (421 U.S. 794 [1975]) and *Patton v. Yount* (467 U.S. 1025 [1984]), the Court indicated that unless a juror candidly admits bias due to pretrial publicity, a defendant's constitutional challenge to jury impartiality is unlikely to succeed. This point was echoed recently in *Skilling v. United States* (No. 08-1394 [2010]), a case involving a former Enron executive who claimed that most prospective jurors were biased because of press coverage of Enron's actions; the Court held that a change of venue was not constitutionally required.

As a second method of addressing bias induced by press coverage, a **change of venue** can be sought. In *Rideau v. Louisiana* (373 U.S. 723 [1963]), the Court overturned a defendant's death sentence because the trial court refused to grant the defendant's motion for a change of venue. In that case, Rideau's confession had been broadcast all over local television. The Court stated that "due process of law in this case required a trial before a jury drawn from a community of people who had not seen and heard Rideau's interview" (p. 727). Of course, a change of venue is not a realistic option when pretrial publicity has influenced potential jurors in multiple jurisdictions. A change of venue rarely succeeds, then, in the trial of someone whose crime is well known over a wide geographical area.

Rideau v. Louisiana (373 U.S. 723 [1963])

A third method of dealing with the influence of the press is **jury sequestration**. This method is mostly used to minimize the influence of press coverage *during* the trial. Sequestration is basically jury isolation. Members are usually put up in a hotel and denied access to television and print media coverage of the trial. Sequestration is an extreme method but necessary in certain cases. After all, judges' warnings to jury members to avoid media accounts while at home are probably naïve. The Supreme Court has recognized that jury sequestration is a valid option in certain extreme circumstances (see *Sheppard v. Maxwell*).

A **gag order** on the media can be used, as well. A gag order is a judge's order to keep the media quiet concerning a particular matter. In *Nebraska Press Ass'n v. Stuart* (427 U.S. 539 [1976]), the trial judge prohibited the media from reporting information regarding the defendant. While the Supreme Court disagreed, it did indicate that a gag order would be permissible given "(a) the nature and extent of pretrial coverage; (b) whether other measures [i.e., changes of venue, continuances, *voir dire*, sequestration, and/or instructions to jury to ignore press coverage] would be likely to mitigate the effects of unrestrained pretrial publicity; and (c) how effectively a restraining order would operate to prevent the threatened danger" (p. 562).

Nebraska Press Ass'n v. Stuart (427 U.S. 539 [1976])

Finally, the courts have experimented with gag orders on trial participants. This is an indirect method of reducing media coverage of a trial because it seeks to quiet the media's sources. This practice appears to have met with greater approval by the Supreme Court. In *Sheppard v. Maxwell*, for instance, the Court suggested that under certain circumstances, the judge has a constitutional obligation "to control the release of leads, information, and gossip to the press by police officers, witnesses and the counsel for both sides" (p. 333). For a gag order of this nature to succeed, it should be clear that the absence of a gag order presents a "clear and present danger" to the impartiality of the trial.

It is worth mentioning that with regard to attorneys, professional codes of ethics restrict them from making certain statements. For example, the *Annotated Model Rules of Professional Conduct* of the American Bar Association (ABA) prohibit lawyers from making "extrajudicial statements" that "will have a substantial likelihood of materially prejudicing an adjudicative proceeding." This includes statements as to "the character, credibility, reputation or criminal record of a party, suspect, . . . or witness, . . . the expected testimony of a party or witness, . . . [or the] . . . possibility of a plea of guilty, . . . the performance or results of any examination or test, [and] . . . any opinion as to . . . guilt or innocence."[2] The Supreme Court later held that state bars can reprimand attorneys for making statements that cause "a substantial likelihood of material prejudice" to the case, apparently expanding on the ABA's *Annotated Model Rules of Professional Conduct* (see *Gentile v. Nevada State Bar*, 501 U.S. 1030 [1991]).

DECISION-MAKING EXERCISE 14.1

The Right to a Public Trial

A nurse was charged with murdering 12 patients by administering massive doses of the heart drug Lidocaine. The judge granted her motion to exclude the public from her preliminary hearing under a state statute that requires such proceedings to be open unless "exclusion of the public is necessary in order to protect the defendant's right to a fair and impartial trial." Following the conclusion of the preliminary hearing, the judge refused a local newspaper's request to release the transcript of the proceedings. The matter went all the way to the state supreme court, which denied the newspaper's request, holding that there is no general First Amendment right of access to preliminary hearings and that under the state statute, if the defendant establishes a "reasonable likelihood of substantial prejudice," then the transcript does not need to be released. Assuming this case goes to the U.S. Supreme Court, how should it decide?

DECISION-MAKING EXERCISE 14.2

Gag Orders on the Media

Following are the facts from an actual case:

> After they had published articles identifying by name a 14-year-old youth who had been arrested for allegedly killing another youth, two newspapers which had learned the juvenile's identity through the use of routine reporting techniques—the monitoring of the police band radio frequency and the questioning of witnesses, the police, and an assistant prosecuting attorney at the scene of the killing—were indicted by a state grand jury in West Virginia for having violated a West Virginia law making it a crime for a newspaper to publish, without the written approval of a juvenile court, the name of any youth charged as a juvenile offender. . . . [T]he newspapers alleged that their indictment had been based on a statute violative of the First and Fourteenth Amendments to the United States Constitution. (1979 U.S. LEXIS 139 [1979])

The statute was not a gag order per se, but it acted as such. Does the statute violate the First Amendment?

---

[2] American Bar Association, *Annotated Model Rules of Professional Conduct* (Washington, DC: Center for Professional Responsibility, 2002), Rule 3.6[a][b].

THE RIGHT TO CONFRONTATION

Illinois v. Allen
(397 U.S. 337 [1970])

The Sixth Amendment's provision that an accused person enjoys the right to be "confronted with the witnesses against him" is manifested in three ways. The first method of **confrontation** is to allow the defendant to appear at his or her own trial. In fact, in *Illinois v. Allen* (397 U.S. 337 [1970]), the Supreme Court expressly stated that "[o]ne of the most basic of rights guaranteed by the Confrontation Clause is the accused's right to be present in the courtroom at every state of his trial" (p. 338). The other two methods of confrontation extended to the defendant are to require the live testimony of witnesses before the defendant and to permit him or her to challenge witnesses' statements in open court. Each of these methods of confrontation is considered in a following section.

The Defendant's Right to Be Present

The Supreme Court's opinion in *Illinois v. Allen* seems eminently sensible. Certainly, the defendant would be seriously hampered in his or her ability to confront adverse witnesses if he or she was not allowed to attend the trial. But allowing the defendant to be physically present in the courtroom may not be enough to satisfy the Sixth Amendment's confrontation clause. In particular, if the accused is not competent and is unable to understand what is taking place so as to be able to challenge the opposition, the Sixth Amendment may be violated. Given this, some Supreme Court cases have dealt with physical confrontation, and some have dealt with defendants' mental competence as it pertains to confrontation. Before considering these types of cases, however, refer to Figure 14.1, which presents Rule 43 of the *Federal Rules of Criminal Procedure.* It succinctly summarizes the discussion that follows.

FIGURE 14.1

Policy on Defendant's Presence

Rule 43. Defendant's Presence

(a) **When Required.**
   Unless this rule, Rule 5, or Rule 10 provides otherwise, the defendant must be present at:
   1. the initial appearance, the initial arraignment, and the plea;
   2. every trial stage, including jury impanelment and the return of the verdict; and
   3. sentencing.

(b) **When Not Required. A defendant need not be present under any of the following circumstances:**

   1. *Organizational Defendant.*
      The defendant is an organization represented by counsel who is present.

   2. *Misdemeanor Offense.*
      The offense is punishable by fine or by imprisonment for not more than one year, or both, and with the defendant's written consent, the court permits arraignment, plea, trial, and sentencing to occur in the defendant's absence.

   3. *Conference or Hearing on a Legal Question.*
      The proceeding involves only a conference or hearing on a question of law.

   4. *Sentence Correction.*
      The proceeding involves the correction or reduction of sentence under Rule 35 or 18 U.S.C. § 3582(c).

(c) Waiving Continued Presence.

1. *In General.*

A defendant who was initially present at trial, or who had pleaded guilty or nolo contendere, waives the right to be present under the following circumstances:

(A) when the defendant is voluntarily absent after the trial has begun, regardless of whether the court informed the defendant of an obligation to remain during trial;

(B) in a noncapital case, when the defendant is voluntarily absent during sentencing; or

(C) when the court warns the defendant that it will remove the defendant from the courtroom for disruptive behavior, but the defendant persists in conduct that justifies removal from the courtroom.

2. *Waiver's Effect.*

If the defendant waives the right to be present, the trial may proceed to completion, including the verdict's return and sentencing, during the defendant's absence.

Source: Federal Rules of Criminal Procedure, Rule 43.

PHYSICAL PRESENCE   Even though the Supreme Court's opinion in *Illinois v. Allen* suggests that the accused enjoys an unqualified right to **physical presence**, nothing could be further from the truth. In the cases decided after *Allen*, the Court placed significant restrictions on when the defendant is permitted to be physically present. By way of preview, the Court's decisions have indicated that the accused can only be present during critical proceedings. Also, the defendant's physical presence can be voluntarily waived or forfeited by failing to appear or by acting improperly.

First, even though *Allen* spoke of the right to be present "at every stage of [the] trial," the Court changed course in *United States v. Gagnon* (470 U.S. 522 [1985]) and *Kentucky v. Stincer* (479 U.S. 1028 [1987]). In the former case, the defendant was denied physical presence at a meeting between a judge and juror, while in the latter, the defendant was not allowed to attend a pretrial determination of a child witness's competence. The Court sanctioned the trial courts' actions in both cases. Generally, however, whether the defendant can be denied the right to be physically present at certain supposedly noncritical stages of the trial process depends on the nature of the communication in question and the hearing at issue.

Second, the defendant may not be physically present through waiver. That is, the defendant can waive his or her Sixth Amendment right to confrontation. Only the defendant can make this determination. In *Taylor v. Illinois* (484 U.S. 400 [1988]), the Court held that the defense attorney cannot waive the defendant's right to be physically present without his or her consent. The defendant can waive his or her right to be present through an express request (*Diaz v. United States*, 223 U.S. 442 [1912]) or by implying waiver. As an example of an implied waiver, in *Taylor v. United States* (414 U.S. 17 [1973]), the Court decided that the defendant's refusal to return to the courtroom after a lunch recess, even though it was not an intentional waiver, could have amounted to a violation of his Sixth Amendment right:

Taylor v. Illinois
(484 U.S. 400 [1988])

It is wholly incredible to suggest that [Taylor, the defendant,] . . . entertained any doubts about his right to be present at every stage of the trial. It seems equally incredible to us, as it did to the Court of appeals, "that a defendant who flees from a courtroom in the midst of a trial—where judge, jury, witnesses and lawyers are present and ready to continue—would not know that as a consequence the trial could continue in his absence." (p. 20)

Finally, the defendant may not be permitted to be physically present at his or her own trial for reasons related to conduct. In *Illinois v. Allen*, for instance, the defendant was removed from his trial following repeated warnings by the judge to cease his disruptive behavior. The Supreme Court sanctioned the trial court judge's decision, holding that the right to be physically present can be waived if, after several warnings, the defendant acts "in a manner so disorderly, disruptive, and disrespectful of the court that his trial cannot be carried on with him in the courtroom" (p. 343). The Court also noted, however, that the defendant can reappear in the courtroom when he is "willing to conduct himself consistently with the decorum and respect inherent in the concept of courts and judicial proceedings" (p. 343).

MENTAL COMPETENCE The Supreme Court has also held that the defendant must demonstrate **mental competence**. In other words, the conviction of an incompetent person is unconstitutional (*Pate v. Robinson*, 383 U.S. 375 [1966]). Specifically, due process—and by implication, the right to confrontation—is violated when the defendant cannot understand what is happening to him or her in a criminal trial.

Dusky v. United States
(362 U.S. 402 [1960])

The question of whether a defendant is mentally competent to stand trial was answered by a test announced by the Supreme Court in *Dusky v. United States* (362 U.S. 402 [1960]). The test assesses whether the defendant "has sufficient present ability to consult with his lawyer with a reasonable degree of rational understanding—and whether he has a rational as well as factual understanding of the proceedings against

The right to confrontation provides that an accused person can appear at his or her own trial, face the live testimony of witnesses, and challenge witness testimony.

him" (p. 402). The burden of proving *incompetence* falls on the defendant (*Medina v. California*, 505 U.S. 437 [1992]).

It is important to understand that this test for competency is different from the insanity defense often discussed in criminal law texts. *Competency to stand trial*—the type of competency considered here—deals with the defendant's ability to understand what is happening at trial (as well as at pretrial hearings, etc.). The *insanity defense* deals with the defendant's competence at the time he or she committed the crime. The competency to stand trial issue is narrowly concerned with the defendant's ability to understand what is happening and communicate with counsel.

The defendant's competency is usually considered in a separate pretrial hearing. This was the rule announced in *Pate v. Robinson* (383 U.S. 375 [1966]), a case dealing with an Illinois trial judge's decision not to hold a hearing on the question of the defendant's mental condition, even though he had a long history of mental problems. The Supreme Court held that a hearing was necessary, noting that "[the Illinois court's] reasoning offers no justification for ignoring the uncontradicted testimony of Robinson's [the defendant's] history of pronounced irrational behavior. While Robinson's demeanor at trial might be relevant to the ultimate decision as to his [present] sanity, it cannot be relied upon to dispense with a hearing on that very issue" (p. 385).

What happens to the defendant if he or she is declared incompetent to stand trial? Usually, the defendant will be hospitalized until his or her competency is restored, if it ever is. However, in *Jackson v. Indiana* (406 U.S. 715 [1972]), the Supreme Court held that there are constitutional limitations on how long a defendant can be hospitalized for the purpose of restoring competency. That case dealt with a 27-year-old deaf-mute individual with the mental level of a preschooler, who was being hospitalized until the staff determined him sane. The Court concluded that it was likely the defendant's condition would *never* improve. Thus, the Court said:

> We hold . . . that a person charged by a State with a criminal offense who is committed [to an institution] solely on account of his incapacity to proceed to trial cannot be held more than the reasonable period of time necessary to determine whether there is a substantial probability that he will attain that capacity in the foreseeable future. If it is determined that this is not the case, then the State must either institute the customary civil commitment proceeding that would be required to commit indefinitely any other citizen, or release the defendant. (p. 738)

DRAWBACKS OF BEING PRESENT Guaranteeing the defendant the right to be present at trial could be prejudicial—that is, it could be harmful. First, if the defendant is present but

---

DECISION-MAKING EXERCISE 14.3

Indigence and the Right to Be Present

Adam Fish was a soldier in the U.S. Army and stationed in Arizona. He was arrested and charged with the sale of marijuana, in violation of state law. Prior to his trial on this charge, Fish was discharged from the army and voluntarily left Arizona for New York. When the trial date was set, Fish's court-appointed attorney requested that he return to Arizona. However, because Fish lacked the funds necessary to travel from New York to Arizona, he did not appear in Arizona on the date set for trial. The trial proceeded without Fish's presence, and the jury returned a guilty verdict. After the verdict was rendered, Fish obtained the necessary travel funds and returned to Arizona in time for his sentencing. He was sentenced to not less than five or more than five-and-one-half years in prison. He is now appealing his conviction, claiming that his Sixth Amendment right to confrontation was violated. What should the court decide?

refuses to take the stand and testify (exercising a right guaranteed by the Fifth Amendment), the jury may conclude that he or she has something to hide. The Supreme Court has been so concerned with this possibility that it has prohibited the prosecution from calling attention to the defendant's refusal to testify (*Griffin v. California*, 380 U.S. 609 [1965]) and even required judges to advise jury members that no adverse inferences can be drawn from a defendant's refusal to testify (*Carter v. Kentucky*, 450 U.S. 288 [1981]).

The defendant's presence may also be prejudicial because by virtue of being in the courtroom, the defendant may remind jurors about the crime. It is often thought, in fact, that a defendant who is dressed in prison attire is not viewed the same, in the eyes of a jury, as someone dressed in a suit. An illustrative case concerning this matter is *Estelle v. Williams* (425 U.S. 501 [1976]). There, the Supreme Court held that a state may not compel the defendant to wear jail attire in the courtroom. The Court concluded that a "constant reminder of the accused's condition implicit in such distinctive, identifiable attire may affect a juror's judgment" (p. 504). This decision was extended to the sentencing phase in *Deck v. Missouri* (544 U.S. 622 [2005]), where the Court held that defendants cannot be forced to wear leg irons during their capital sentencing hearings.

The Defendant's Right to Live Testimony

Mattox v. United States (156 U.S. 237 [1895])

As mentioned earlier, the Sixth Amendment's mention of confrontation includes, according to the Supreme Court, the defendant's right to **live testimony**. That is, he or she enjoys the right to have witnesses physically appear in the courtroom to give their testimony. Even so, this right may be qualified for certain reasons. In fact, over 100 years ago, the Supreme Court stated in *Mattox v. United States* (156 U.S. 237 [1895]) that the defendant's right to live testimony is "subject to exceptions, recognized long before the adoption of the Constitution" (p. 243). The Court stated further:

> Such exceptions were obviously intended to be respected. A technical adherence to the letter of a constitutional provision may occasionally be carried farther than is necessary to the just protection of the accused, and farther than the safety of the public will warrant. For instance, there could be nothing more directly contrary to the letter of the provision in question than the admission of dying declarations. They are rarely made in the presence of the accused; they are made without any opportunity for examination or cross-examination; nor is the witness brought face to face with the jury; yet from time immemorial they have been treated as competent testimony, and no one would have the hardihood at this day to question their admissibility. They are admitted not in conformity with any general rule regarding the admission of testimony, but as an exception to such rules, simply from the necessities of the case, and to prevent a manifest failure of justice. (pp. 243–244)

The Supreme Court has considered several situations in which witness testimony can be admitted at trial without the physical appearance of the witness. First, if the witness, also known as the *declarant*, is unavailable because he or she is dead (as described in the previous paragraph), then an exception to the defendant's right to live testimony will be made. Similar exceptions are made when a witness is unavailable for other reasons, such as being in the hospital. Also, a witness may not be required to give live testimony if his or her statements fall under one of the established hearsay exceptions, permitting introduction of those statements by a third party. Each of these exceptions to the defendant's right to live testimony is considered in a following section.

DECEASED WITNESSES In *Mattox*, already mentioned, the Supreme Court upheld the admissibility of a witness's past testimony from the defendant's first trial in the defendant's second trial because the witness died between the two trials. According to the Court, "To say that a criminal, after having once been convicted by the testimony of a certain witness, should go scot free simply because death has closed the mouth of that witness, would be carrying his constitutional protection to an unwarrantable extent" (p. 243). The Court also stated, in relevant part:

> The primary object of the [confrontation clause of the Sixth Amendment] was to prevent depositions or ex parte affidavits, such as were sometimes admitted in civil cases, being used against the prisoner in lieu of a personal examination and cross-examination of the witness in which the accused has an opportunity, not only of testing the recollection and sifting the conscience of the witness, but of compelling him to stand and face the jury in order that they may look at him, and judge by his demeanor upon the stand and the manner in which he gives his testimony whether he is worthy of belief. (p. 259)

UNAVAILABLE WITNESSES The Supreme Court has held that an **unavailable witness**, for purposes of the confrontation clause, is one who permanently moves to another country (e.g., *Mancusi v. Stubbs*, 408 U.S. 204 [1972]), cannot be located after a careful search by the prosecution (e.g., *Ohio v. Roberts*, 448 U.S. 56 [1980]), or suffers from a lapse in memory (e.g., *California v. Green*, 399 U.S. 149 [1970]).

In *Motes v. United States* (178 U.S. 458 [1900]), the Court stated that it would violate the Sixth Amendment "to permit the deposition or statement of an absent witness . . . to be read at the final trial when it does not appear that the witness was absent by the suggestion, connivance, or procurement of the accused, but does appear that this absence was due to the negligence of the prosecution" (p. 474). In other words, if the prosecution fails to conduct a careful search for a certain witness and then claims that the witness is unavailable, then the defendant's right to live testimony will be violated.

Motes v. United States (178 U.S. 458 [1900])

In another case, *Barber v. Page* (390 U.S. 719 [1968]), the Court considered whether statements by a witness who was not physically present at a preliminary hearing conformed to constitutional requirements, even though the witness was later found to be available and could have given testimony at the hearing. The Court stated that "a witness is not 'unavailable' for purposes of the exception to the confrontation requirement unless the prosecutorial authorities have made a good-faith effort to obtain his presence at trial" (pp. 724–725).

The state of Washington recognized a privilege that barred one spouse from testifying against the other without the other's consent. As a result, a wife did not testify in court at her husband's domestic violence trial. Instead, a tape-recorded statement to the effect that she was stabbed by her husband was admitted in court. In *Crawford v. Washington* (541 U.S. 36 [2004]), the Supreme Court declared that the victim could not be considered unavailable. Consequently, it held that the accused's Sixth Amendment right to confrontation was violated. Some have argued that this case may deal a blow to the prosecution of domestic violence cases because it requires that victims must testify in person. In an analogous decision, the Supreme Court held that a state forensic analyst's laboratory report was testimonial and, as such, that the defendant should have been permitted to question its preparer (*Melendez-Diaz v. Massachusetts*, No. 07-591 [2009]). And in *Bullcoming v. New Mexico* (No. 09-10876 [2011]), the Court decided that confrontation was violated when prosecutors offered a crime lab report analyzing Bullcoming's blood sample and called the lab's supervisor rather than the technician who conducted the test. In other words, the lab report could not be admitted without also calling the analyst to the witness stand for cross examination.

Contrast *Crawford v. Washington* with the Court's more recent decision in *Davis v. Washington* (547 U.S. 813 [2006]). In that case, a recorded 911 call from a victim was introduced into evidence. Davis challenged the introduction of the recorded call,

DECISION-MAKING EXERCISE 14.4

An Unavailable Witness

In the space of six months, the prosecution sent five subpoenas to a person it wished to testify at four separate trials. All five subpoenas were sent to the witness's residence, but the witness never appeared at trial. Can the witness be considered unavailable for confrontation purposes?

arguing that not being able to confront the caller violated his Sixth Amendment right to confrontation. The Supreme Court disagreed with his argument, holding that the confrontation clause does not apply to such statements. It went on the explain that " . . . statements are nontestimonial when made in the course of police interrogation under circumstances objectively indicating that the primary purpose of interrogation is to enable police assistance to meet an ongoing emergency" (pp. 6–7). In other words, the Court held that 911 calls are not considered the same as testimonial statements.

Nor are inquiries of wounded victims considered testimonial if the intent is to assist police with locating a perpetrator (*Michigan v. Bryant*, No. 09-150 [2011]. In that case, a shooting victim informed police that Bryant had shot him. The victim died shortly thereafter, but the statement was introduced at trial (through the testimony of the officer who heard it) and used to establish his guilt. The Court observed that the victim's statements were "not testimonial . . . because they had a 'primary purpose . . . to enable police assistance to meet an ongoing emergence.'"

STATEMENTS UNDER HEARSAY EXCEPTIONS   The death or unavailability of a witness is considered an exception to the defendant's right to live testimony. In either situation, the witness's statements are introduced by a third party. This is known as *hearsay*. Hearsay is testimony about what a declarant who is not in court has previously said. It is often introduced by someone who *hears* and then *says* (hence, the term *hearsay*) what the declarant said.

Hearsay is generally not admissible in a criminal trial. It is regarded skeptically because if the declarant is not available to be confronted by the defense, then there is no opportunity to question the truthfulness of his or her statements. The possibility also exists that the person communicating the declarant's statements may have misunderstood his or her intentions or forgotten exactly what he or she said.

Even so, there are several **hearsay exceptions**, which permit out-of-court statements made by declarants to be admitted at trial. On the surface, these exceptions seem to violate the defendant's right to live testimony. But the Supreme Court, nevertheless, permits hearsay in limited circumstances. The reader is encouraged to consult an evidence textbook for a full review of specific exceptions to the hearsay rule. The following cases consider only two such exceptions.

White v. Illinois
(502 U.S. 346 [1992])

One pertinent case is *White v. Illinois* (502 U.S. 346 [1992]), which dealt with the admissibility of out-of-court statements made by a four-year-old girl. The prosecution argued that the statements should be admissible because of the "spontaneous declaration" and "seeking medical treatment" exceptions to the hearsay rule. The former admits statements made in the "heat of the moment," while the latter admits statements made while an individual is seeking medical treatment from a doctor. The Court held that the confrontation clause was not violated in this instance:

A statement that has been offered in a moment of excitement—without the opportunity to reflect on the consequences of one's exclamation—may justifiably carry more weight with a trier of fact than a similar statement made in the course of procuring medical services, where the declarant knows that a false statement may cause misdiagnosis or mistreatment, carries special guarantees of credibility that a trier of fact may not think replicated by courtroom testimony. (p. 356)

In another case, *United States v. Inadi* (475 U.S. 387 [1986]), the Court decided on the admissibility of out-of-court statements from a co-conspirator. The Court admitted the statements, claiming that they "derive much of their value from the fact that they are made in a context very different from trial, and therefore are usually irreplaceable as substantive evidence" (p. 406). Stated differently, the Court thought that the out-of-court statements made by one co-conspirator to another should be admitted at trial because it would be difficult to replicate the conversation in a courtroom.

As indicated in Figure 14.2, numerous other hearsay exceptions exist, as well. Indeed, even if a relevant exception does not exist, a court may still admit the hearsay. Generally, if other *indicia of reliability* exist such that the accuracy and truthfulness of a hearsay statement can be judged, then it may be admissible (see *Idaho v. Wright*, 497 U.S. 805 [1990]). These indicia must, according to the Court, be "particularized guarantees of trustworthiness" (p. 816).

The Defendant's Right to Challenge Witness Testimony

Part of the defendant's right to confrontation is the ability to challenge witnesses in the courtroom. This ability is manifested when each witness physically appears in court

---

FIGURE 14.2

Common Hearsay Exceptions

Present sense impression. A statement describing or explaining an event or condition made while the declarant was perceiving the event or condition, or immediately thereafter.

Excited utterance. A statement relating to a startling event or condition made while the declarant was under the stress of excitement caused by the event or condition.

Then existing mental, emotional, or physical condition. A statement of the declarant's then existing state of mind, emotion, sensation, or physical condition (such as intent, plan, motive, design, mental feeling, pain, and bodily health), but not including a statement of memory or belief to prove the fact remembered or believed unless it relates to the execution, revocation, identification, or terms of declarant's will.

Statements for purposes of medical diagnosis or treatment. Statements made for purposes of medical diagnosis or treatment and describing medical history, or past or present symptoms, pain, or sensations, or the inception or general character of the cause or external source thereof insofar as reasonably pertinent to diagnosis or treatment.

Recorded recollection. A memorandum or record concerning a matter about which a witness once had knowledge but now has insufficient recollection to enable the witness to testify fully and accurately, shown to have been made or adopted by the witness when the matter was fresh in the witness' memory and to reflect that knowledge correctly. If admitted, the memorandum or record may be read into evidence but may not itself be received as an exhibit unless offered by an adverse party.

Records of regularly conducted activity. A memorandum, report, record, or data compilation, in any form, of acts, events, conditions, opinions, or diagnoses, made at or

Figure 14.2 continued

near the time by, or from information transmitted by, a person with knowledge, if kept in the course of a regularly conducted business activity, and if it was the regular practice of that business activity to make the memorandum, report, record or data compilation, all as shown by the testimony of the custodian or other qualified witness, or by certification that complies with Rule 902(11), Rule 902(12), or a statute permitting certification, unless the source of information or the method or circumstances of preparation indicate lack of trustworthiness. The term "business" as used in this paragraph includes business, institution, association, profession, occupation, and calling of every kind, whether or not conducted for profit.

Public records and reports. Records, reports, statements, or data compilations, in any form, of public offices or agencies, setting forth (A) the activities of the office or agency, or (B) matters observed pursuant to duty imposed by law as to which matters there was a duty to report, excluding, however, in criminal cases matters observed by police officers and other law enforcement personnel, or (C) in civil actions and proceedings and against the Government in criminal cases, factual findings resulting from an investigation made pursuant to authority granted by law, unless the sources of information or other circumstances indicate lack of trustworthiness.

Records of vital statistics. Records or data compilations, in any form, of births, fetal deaths, deaths, or marriages, if the report thereof was made to a public office pursuant to requirements of law.

Former testimony. Testimony given as a witness at another hearing of the same or a different proceeding, or in a deposition taken in compliance with law in the course of the same or another proceeding, if the party against whom the testimony is now offered, or, in a civil action or proceeding, a predecessor in interest, had an opportunity and similar motive to develop the testimony by direct, cross, or redirect examination.

Statement under belief of impending death. In a prosecution for homicide or in a civil action or proceeding, a statement made by a declarant while believing that the declarant's death was imminent, concerning the cause or circumstances of what the declarant believed to be impending death.

Statement against interest. A statement which was at the time of its making so far contrary to the declarant's pecuniary or proprietary interest, or so far tended to subject the declarant to civil or criminal liability, or to render invalid a claim by the declarant against another, that a reasonable person in the declarant's position would not have made the statement unless believing it to be true. A statement tending to expose the declarant to criminal liability and offered to exculpate the accused is not admissible unless corroborating circumstances clearly indicate the trustworthiness of the statement.

Statement of personal or family history. (A) A statement concerning the declarant's own birth, adoption, marriage, divorce, legitimacy, relationship by blood, adoption, or marriage, ancestry, or other similar fact of personal or family history, even though declarant had no means of acquiring personal knowledge of the matter stated; or (B) a statement concerning the foregoing matters, and death also, of another person, if the declarant was related to the other by blood, adoption, or marriage or was so intimately associated with the other's family as to be likely to have accurate information concerning the matter declared.

Source: Federal Rules of Evidence, Rules 803 and 804.

before the defendant. This type of confrontation permits questioning by the defense and is intended to submit the witness's account to relevant scrutiny. Interestingly, though, the Supreme Court has identified at least one situation in which the defendant's right to challenge witness testimony is not compromised by the witness's absence.

Also, the Court has held that the defendant can be limited in terms of the nature of the confrontation, which is usually accomplished through questioning—specifically, *cross-examination.* Each of these limitations is discussed in a following subsection. First, the order of questioning in a typical criminal trial is considered. Then, the focus moves to when face-to-face contact is required and what Supreme Court case law addresses the defendant's right to cross-examine witnesses.

ORDER AND SCOPE OF QUESTIONS   Witness testimony proceeds in several stages. That testimony is examined at each stage by a particular party to the case: the state or the defendant in a criminal case and the plaintiff or the defendant in a civil case. And each examination is subject to limitations in terms of scope. In other words, the stages must occur sequentially, and only certain types of questions are permissible.

The four stages of witness examination, as first introduced in Chapter 9, are (1) direct; (2) cross; (3) redirect; and (4) recross. Every witness called to the stand in either a criminal or a civil case is questioned four separate times. However, because the focus here is on constitutional rights at trial, after the four types of questioning have been introduced, the focus will be mainly on the defendant's rights during cross- and recross-examination.

Direct Examination.   The first examination of a witness is called direct examination, and it is usually conducted by the party calling the witness. The scope of direct examination is broad. In general, questions are permitted about any consequential facts that may prove or disprove a certain point.

Cross-Examination.   The next step in examining a witness is cross-examination. It is conducted by a party other than the one who called the witness. For example, the state may call a witness in a criminal trial. Once the state's direct examination has concluded, the defense will have an opportunity to cross-examine the state's witness.

DECISION-MAKING EXERCISE 14.5

A Hearsay Exception?

Following are the actual facts from another Supreme Court case:

> Wright was charged under Idaho law with two counts of lewd conduct with a minor—specifically, her 5½- and 2½-year-old daughters. At the trial, it was agreed that the younger daughter was not "capable of communicating to the jury." However, the court admitted, under Idaho's residual hearsay exception, certain statements she had made to a pediatrician having extensive experience in child abuse cases. The doctor testified that the child had reluctantly answered questions about her own abuse but had spontaneously volunteered information about her sister's abuse. Wright was convicted on both counts

but appealed only the conviction involving the younger child. The state supreme court reversed, finding that the admission of the doctor's testimony under the residual hearsay exception violated Wright's rights under the confrontation clause. The court noted that the child's statements did not fall within the traditional hearsay exception and lacked "particularized guarantees of trustworthiness" because the doctor had conducted the interview without procedural safeguards: He failed to videotape the interview, asked leading questions, and had a preconceived idea of what the child should be disclosing. (*Idaho v. Wright*, 497 U.S. 805 [1990])

How should the Supreme Court decide?

Whereas the scope of questioning in a direct examination is broad, the scope of questioning on cross is restricted. In particular, cross-examination is limited to matters covered on direct examination. Inquiries into the credibility of the witness are also permissible. Together, these two restrictions constitute the *scope of direct rule*. This helps ensure that the opposing party (i.e., the party conducting the cross-examination) cannot use cross-examination of the witness to direct the jury's attention to other issues not raised by the party calling the witness. For example, assume that in a robbery trial, a defense witness testifies about the defendant's whereabouts on the day of the robbery. Assume further that on cross-examination, the prosecutor asks that witness whether the defendant expressed the desire to rob a bank on the day *before* the robbery. The prosecutor's question will not be permissible on cross-examination because it is beyond the scope of the original defense questioning (assuming, of course, that the defense did not ask its witness about the defendant's feelings the day before the robbery).

Redirect Examination. The party calling the witness conducts the redirect examination and does so *after* the cross-examination. Thus, the scope of questioning on redirect is limited to the scope of questioning on cross-examination. Again, new issues cannot be raised.

Consider another example: Suppose that on cross-examination, a burglary victim is asked about what persons have permission to enter his residence while he is away. Assume further that on redirect, the prosecutor asks the burglary victim about an incident that occurred several days prior to the burglary, in which he saw the defendant "casing" the neighborhood. The prosecutor's question is not permissible because it is beyond the scope of the cross-examination (assuming, again, that the prior incident did not come to light during the defense's cross-examination).

Recross-Examination. The last stage in witness questioning is known as recross-examination. This includes any subsequent examination of a witness by a party who has previously cross-examined him or her. Recross-examination is also limited in scope to the subject matter of the examination that preceded it. That is, the party engaged in recross-examination cannot probe issues not raised during redirect examination.

Assume that an eyewitness to an accident is testifying for the plaintiff and is asked on cross-examination if she was wearing her prescription glasses at the time of the accident. If, during redirect examination, it is determined that the witness could see fine *without* her glasses, then the defense cannot question her on recross-examination about her relation to the plaintiff.

Taken together, the four stages of witness examination follow a pattern of *progressive narrowing*. That is, each subsequent examination has an increasingly narrow focus, such that there is less and less to ask the witness. In other words, the four stages of examination should clarify, rather than confuse, the witness's testimony.

Coy v. Iowa (487 U.S. 1012 [1988])

FACE-TO-FACE CONTACT In *Coy v. Iowa* (487 U.S. 1012 [1988]), the Supreme Court considered the constitutionality of a state law that permitted the placement of a large opaque screen between the defendant and two young girls who testified that he had sexually assaulted them. The Court declared that the statute was unconstitutional because "the Confrontation Clause guarantees the defendant a face-to-face meeting with witnesses appearing before the trier of fact" (p. 1016).

Contrast *Coy* with *Maryland v. Craig* (497 U.S. 836 [1990]). In *Craig*, the Court considered whether a statute permitting a witness's testimony via closed-circuit television was constitutional. The statute provided for such a procedure in cases in which the judge determined that face-to-face testimony would "result in the child suffering serious emotional distress such that the child cannot reasonably communicate"

(p. 836). The Court upheld the statute, claiming that it did not violate the confrontation clause. It stated that a central concern of the confrontation clause "is to ensure the reliability of the evidence against a criminal defendant by subjecting it to rigorous testing in the context of an adversary proceeding before the trier of fact" (p. 845). Further, it held that the statute in question did "not impinge upon the truth-seeking or symbolic purposes of the Confrontation Clause" (p. 852).

CROSS-EXAMINING AND OBTAINING EVIDENCE   The Supreme Court has considered, more than once, the constitutionality of state- and court-imposed restrictions on the defendant's right to cross-examine (and by extension, to engage in recross-examination). For instance, in *Smith v. Illinois* (390 U.S. 129 [1968]), the Court considered whether the prosecution can conceal the identity of a witness who is a police informant. The Court held that the witness's identity must be revealed because such information "opens countless avenues of in-court examination and out-of-court investigation" (p. 131).

In another case, *Davis v. Alaska* (415 U.S. 308 [1974]), the Court considered whether the identity of a juvenile who testifies at a criminal trial can be disguised. There, the state's lead witness in the defendant's burglary trial was a juvenile. The Court held that the juvenile's identity should have been revealed and that "the right of confrontation is paramount to the State's policy of protecting a juvenile offender" (p. 319).

In still another case, *Chambers v. Mississippi* (410 U.S. 284 [1973]), the Court considered the constitutionality of a state statute that barred *any* cross-examination by the defense. In that case, the defendant sought to cross-examine a witness who, on three previous occasions, had confessed to the murder with which the defendant was charged. The state did not call the witness, so the defense was forced to. However, the judge prohibited cross-examination based on the *voucher rule*, which provides that the party calling the witness vouches for (i.e., attests to) his or her credibility. According to this rule, cross-examination would be pointless because that is not typically the job of the party calling the witness. But since this case placed something of a unique twist on the voucher rule, the Supreme Court unanimously reversed the defendant's conviction. According to the Court, "The availability of the right to confront and cross-examine those who give damaging testimony against the accused has never been held to depend on whether the witness was initially put on the stand by the accused or by the state" (pp. 297–298).

Chambers v. Mississippi (410 U.S. 284 [1973])

Finally, the Court has also considered whether the confrontation clause is violated when the prosecution withholds from the defense documentation of a witness's out-of-court statements. In *United States v. Bagley* (473 U.S. 667 [1985]), the Court held that the prosecution is not obligated to provide the defense with such information, unless it is exculpatory, in which case the due process clause requires disclosure. According to the Court, "[F]ailure [on the part of the prosecution] to assist the defense by disclosing information that might have been helpful in conducting . . . cross-examination . . . amounts to a constitutional violation . . . only if the evidence is material in the sense that its suppression undermines confidence in the outcome of the trial" (p. 678).

In summary, the defense is given wide latitude in terms of its authority to cross-examine. Courts, and states cannot conceal the identity of a witness testifying against the defendant, nor can they bar cross-examination simply because the defense is calling the witness it wishes to cross-examine. Finally, the defendant's right to cross-examine rarely is violated if the prosecution fails to produce documentation of witness's out-of-court statements when they are not at all exculpatory.

While the defense is given considerable latitude in terms of confrontation, there are still some restrictions in particular types of criminal cases. The *Maryland v. Craig* case mentioned in the previous section restricts confrontation in cases involving child witnesses. There are also restrictions in rape cases where so-called "rape shield" laws protect victims from over-reaching questioning by the defense. There are no Supreme

DECISION-MAKING EXERCISE 14.6

The Defendant's Right to Obtain Evidence

Vance Lester was charged with sexual offenses against his four-year-old daughter. The matter was referred to Children's Services, the state agency charged with investigating cases of suspected child abuse. During pretrial discovery, Lester served Children's Services with a subpoena, seeking access to its records related to his alleged crime as well as earlier records related to a previous investigation into another sexual offense against his daughter. Children's Services refused to supply the requested records, claiming that they were privileged under a statute that provides that the agency's records are confidential, subject to certain exceptions. One of the exceptions specified by the statute was that Children's Services may disclose reports to a "court of competent jurisdiction pursuant to a court order." At a hearing on the matter, Lester argued that he was entitled to the information because the file might contain the names of favorable witnesses and/or exculpatory evidence. Should his argument succeed?

Court cases dealing with rape shield laws, and the Court has been silent on child witnesses since *Craig*, but there are two Web exercises at the end of this chapter that cover child witness questioning procedures and rape shield laws in more detail. Readers are encouraged to access the respective links and learn more.

THE RIGHT TO COMPULSORY PROCESS

Washington v. Texas
(388 U.S. 14 [1967])

The compulsory process clause of the Sixth Amendment provides that the defendant can use subpoenas to obtain witnesses, documents, and other objects that are helpful to his or her defense. The right to **compulsory process** was incorporated to the states in *Washington v. Texas* (388 U.S. 14 [1967]), in which the Supreme Court stated that compulsory process protects "[t]he right to offer the testimony of witnesses, and to compel their attendance" (p. 19). Further, the Court stated:

> We hold that the petitioner in this case was denied his right to have compulsory process for obtaining witnesses in his favor because the State arbitrarily denied him the right to put on the stand a witness who was physically and mentally capable of testifying to events that he had personally observed, and whose testimony would have been relevant and material to the defense. The Framers of the Constitution did not intend to commit the futile act of giving to a defendant the right to secure the attendance of witnesses whose testimony he had no right to use. The judgment of conviction must be reversed. (p. 23)

Several state and federal statutes govern compulsory process, as do the *Federal Rules of Criminal Procedure*. Relevant portions of Rule 17 of the *Federal Rules* are reprinted in Figure 14.3. And Figure 14.4 is an example of a subpoena typically used in a criminal case.

Statutes and formal rules aside, at least two Supreme Court cases have considered aspects of the defendant's right to compulsory process. In particular, questions as to constitutional rights violations have been posed in instances in which the defense has been denied the right to subpoena a witness.

For example, in *Roviaro v. United States* (353 U.S. 53 [1957]), the prosecution refused to provide the defense with the identity of a police informant. The Court recognized that the government had a significant interest in concealing the identity of the informant, mainly to further its efforts in combating the trafficking of illicit drugs. But the Court also found that the defendant's right to confrontation was denied by the prosecution's refusal to release the witness's identity. The informant was the only

FIGURE 14.3

Policy on Subpoenas

Rule 17. Subpoena

(a) Content.

A subpoena must state the court's name and the title of the proceeding, include the seal of the court, and command the witness to attend and testify at the time and place the subpoena specifies. The clerk must issue a blank subpoena — signed and sealed — to the party requesting it, and that party must fill in the blanks before the subpoena is served.

(b) Defendant Unable to Pay.

Upon a defendant's ex parte application, the court must order that a subpoena be issued for a named witness if the defendant shows an inability to pay the witness's fees and the necessity of the witness's presence for an adequate defense. If the court orders a subpoena to be issued, the process costs and witness fees will be paid in the same manner as those paid for witnesses the government subpoenas.

(c) Producing Documents and Objects.

1. *In General.*

A subpoena may order the witness to produce any books, papers, documents, data, or other objects the subpoena designates. The court may direct the witness to produce the designated items in court before trial or before they are to be offered in evidence. When the items arrive, the court may permit the parties and their attorneys to inspect all or part of them.

2. *Quashing or Modifying the Subpoena.*

On motion made promptly, the court may quash or modify the subpoena if compliance would be unreasonable or oppressive.

(d) Service.

A marshal, a deputy marshal, or any nonparty who is at least 18 years old may serve a subpoena. The server must deliver a copy of the subpoena to the witness and must tender to the witness one day's witness-attendance fee and the legal mileage allowance. The server need not tender the attendance fee or mileage allowance when the United States, a federal officer, or a federal agency has requested the subpoena.

(e) Place of Service.

1. *In the United States.*

A subpoena requiring a witness to attend a hearing or trial may be served at any place within the United States.

2. *In a Foreign Country.*

If the witness is in a foreign country, 28 U.S.C. § 1783 governs the subpoena's service.

(f) Issuing a Deposition Subpoena.

1. *Issuance.*

A court order to take a deposition authorizes the clerk in the district where the deposition is to be taken to issue a subpoena for any witness named or described in the order.

Figure 14.3 continued

2. *Place.*

After considering the convenience of the witness and the parties, the court may order — and the subpoena may require — the witness to appear anywhere the court designates.

(g) Contempt.

The court (other than a magistrate judge) may hold in contempt a witness who, without adequate excuse, disobeys a subpoena issued by a federal court in that district. A magistrate judge may hold in contempt a witness who, without adequate excuse, disobeys a subpoena issued by that magistrate judge as provided in 28 U.S.C. § 636(e).

(h) Information Not Subject to a Subpoena.

No party may subpoena a statement of a witness or of a prospective witness under this rule. Rule 26.2 governs the production of the statement.

Source: Federal Rules of Criminal Procedure, Rule 17.

FIGURE 14.4

Subpoena in a Criminal Case

AO 89 (Rev. 01/09) Subpoena to Testify at a Hearing or Trail in a Criminal Case

UNITED STATES DISTRICT COURT

for the

United States of America	)	
v.	)	
	)	Case No.
_____	)	
Defendant	)	

SUBPOENA TO TESTIFY AT A HEARING OR TRAIL IN A CRIMINAL CASE

TO:

YOU ARE COMMANDED to appear in the United States district court at the time, date, and place shown below to testify in this criminal case. When you arrive, you must remain at the court until the judge or a court officer allows you to leave.

Place of Appearance:	Courtroom No.:
	Date and Time:

You must also bring with you the following documents, electronically stored information, or objects *(blank if not applicable)*:

Date: _____

CLERK OF COURT

_____

Signature of Clerk or Deputy Clerk

The name, address, e-mail, and telephone number of the attorney representing *(name of party)* _____ , who requests this subpoena, are:

Case No.

PROOF OF SERVICE

This subpoena for *(name of individual and title, if any)*
_____ was received by me on *(date)*
_____

❏ I personally served the subpoena on the individual at *(place)*
_____
_____on *(date)* _____

❏ I left the subpoena at the individual's residence or usual place of abode with *(name)*
_____
_____ , a person of suitable age and discretion who resides there, on *(date)*
_____ , and mailed a copy to the individual's last known address; or

❏ I served the subpoena on *(name of individual)*
_____ , who is designated
by law to accept service of process on behalf of *(name of organization)*
_____
_____ on *(date)* _____; or

❏ I returned the subpoena unexecuted because
_____; or

❏ Other *(specify)*

Unless the subpoena was issued on behalf of the United States, or one of its officers or agents, I have also tendered to the witness fees for one day's attendance, and the mileage allowed by law, in the amount of $_____.

My fees are $ _____ for travel and $ _____ for services, for a total of $_____0.00_____.

I declare under penalty of perjury that this information is true.

Date: _____   _____
                                                    Server's signature

                                    _____
                                                    Printed name and title

                                    _____
                                                    Server's address

Additional information regarding attempted service, etc:

Source: Administrative Office of the U.S. Courts. Available online: http://www.uscourts.gov/forms/ AO089.pdf (accessed February 16, 2011).

witness to the drug transaction for which the defendant was charged, so the defense clearly would have had a difficult time mounting an effective case without this witness.

Next, in *United States v. Valenzuela-Bernal* (458 U.S. 858 [1982]), the defendant was charged with transporting illegal narcotics. He was arrested along with three other individuals who were unlawfully in the United States. Immigration officials concluded that two of the three aliens were not needed for the prosecution, so it deported them. The defendant then argued that his right to compulsory process was violated by the deportation. Surprisingly, the Court held that the government's interest in deporting illegal aliens and minimizing overcrowding in detention facilities outweighed the defendant's interest in mounting an effective defense. The Court concluded that the defendant did not offer a valid reason why the two deported witnesses were necessary for his defense.

The Right to Present Evidence

The Sixth Amendment's compulsory process clause appears only to grant the defendant the right to subpoena and question witnesses. However, in *Washington v. Texas*, the Supreme Court modified the definition of compulsory process to include the right of the *defense* to present evidence. The Court stated that compulsory process also guarantees "the right to present the defendant's version of the facts as well as the prosecution's to the jury so that it may decide where the truth lies" (p. 19). Given this interpretation, the Court has more than once considered the constitutionality of restrictions placed on the defense's ability to present its case.

DECISIONS IN FAVOR OF THE DEFENSE   For example, in *Washington*, the Court decided on the constitutionality of a statute that prevented accomplices from testifying for each other. The statute was enacted out of fear that accomplices would give false testimony in order to benefit one another. The Court struck down the statute, stating that the defendant must be allowed to present the testimony of any witness who is capable of testifying.

In another case, *Chambers v. Mississippi*, the Court overturned the conviction of a defendant who was not allowed to put three witnesses on the stand. The defendant, Chambers, had attempted to prove that another person, MacDonald, committed the murder for which he was charged. The three people Chambers wanted to put on the stand were those to whom MacDonald had allegedly confessed. The Court felt the witnesses' testimony should have been admissible, even though it would have been considered hearsay, because MacDonald "spontaneously" confessed to each person, making it likely that these individuals' testimony would be truthful and accurate. The Court felt that "the exclusion of this critical evidence, coupled with the State's refusal to permit Chambers to cross-examine MacDonald, denied him a trial in accord with traditional and fundamental standards of due process" (p. 302).

Crane v. Kentucky
(476 U.S. 683 [1986])

In *Crane v. Kentucky* (476 U.S. 683 [1986]), another related case, the defendant sought to present evidence that his confession was unreliable because it had been obtained when he was young and uneducated and had been interrogated at great length. The trial court excluded this evidence and the defendant was convicted. The Supreme Court reversed that decision, however, declaring that a state may not exclude "competent, reliable evidence bearing on the credibility of a confession when such evidence is central to the defendant's claim of innocence" because "[w]hether rooted directly in the Due Process Clause . . . or in the Compulsory Process or Confrontation Clause . . . the Constitution guarantees criminal defendants a 'meaningful opportunity' to present a complete defense" (p. 690).

United States v. Scheffer
(523 U.S. 303 [1998])

DECISIONS AGAINST THE DEFENSE   On a few occasions, the Court *has* sanctioned exclusion of certain defense evidence. For example, in *United States v. Scheffer* (523 U.S. 303 [1998]), the Court upheld a trial court's decision to exclude polygraph evidence presented by the defense. The Court stated, "There is simply no consensus that polygraph evidence is reliable. To this day, the scientific community remains extremely polarized about the reliability of polygraph evidence" (p. 309). Thus, the defense's ability to present its case can be restricted if the evidence it seeks to present cannot be considered reliable (see also *United States v. Salerno*, 505 U.S. 317 [1992]).

Another important example of Court-sanctioned restrictions on the ability of the defense to present a case is *Michigan v. Lucas* (500 U.S. 145 [1991]). There, the Court held

DECISION-MAKING EXERCISE 14.7

Threatening a Witness

A man was convicted of burglary and sentenced to prison for 12 years. He appealed his conviction, claiming that the trial judge violated his Fifth Amendment constitutional right by harassing the only defense witness. Following is what the judge said to the witness in *Webb v. Texas* (409 U.S. 95 [1972]), the actual case on which this exercise is based:

> Now you have been called down as a witness in this case by the Defendant. It is the Court's duty to admonish you that you don't have to testify, that anything you say can and will be used against you. If you take the witness stand and lie under oath, the Court will personally see that your case goes to the grand jury and you will be indicted for perjury and the likelihood is that you would get convicted of perjury and that it would be stacked onto what you have already got, so

that is the matter you have got to make up your mind on. If you get on the witness stand and lie, it is probably going to mean several years and at least more time that you are going to have to serve. It will also be held against you in the penitentiary when you're up for parole and the Court wants you to thoroughly understand the chances you're taking by getting on that witness stand under oath. You may tell the truth and if you do, that is all right, but if you lie you can get into real trouble. The court wants you to know that. You don't owe anybody anything to testify and it must be done freely and voluntarily and with the thorough understanding that you know the hazard you are taking. (p. 96)

Did the judge violate the defendant's right to due process?

---

that the defendant can be prevented from presenting evidence because of his or her attorney's misconduct. In this case, the trial judge in the defendant's rape trial excluded evidence about the victim's sexual history because the defendant failed to give notice of this to the prosecution within 10 days of the trial, in violation of discovery rules. A similar decision was reached in *Taylor v. Illinois*, in which the Court sanctioned a lower court's decision to deny a defense witness's testimony because of providing short notice to the prosecution, again in violation of discovery rules.

THE RIGHT TO DOUBLE-JEOPARDY PROTECTION

The constitutionally guaranteed protection against **double jeopardy** is designed to ensure that a person who has been convicted or acquitted of a crime is not tried or punished for the same offense twice. Double jeopardy occurs when, for the same offense, a person is (1) reprosecuted after acquittal; (2) reprosecuted after conviction; or (3) subjected to separate punishments for the same offense. Double jeopardy does not apply, however, to prosecutions brought by separate sovereigns. The federal government, each state government, and each Native American tribe is considered a separate sovereign.

Early English common law contains the foundations of the modern-day protection against double jeopardy. The rule of *autrefois acquit* prohibited the retrial of a defendant who was found not guilty. The rule of *autrefois convict*, on the other hand, prohibited the retrial of a defendant who *was* found guilty. These rules were adopted by the American colonies.

Today, every state provides double-jeopardy protection because of the Supreme Court's decision in *Benton v. Maryland* (395 U.S. 784 [1969]), in which the Court declared that the Fifth Amendment's protection against double jeopardy is a fundamental right:

Benton v. Maryland
(395 U.S. 784 [1969])

> The fundamental nature of the guarantee against double jeopardy can hardly be doubted. Its origins can be traced to Greek and Roman times, and it became established in the common law of England long before this

Nation's independence. . . . As with many other elements of the common law, it was carried into the jurisprudence of this Country through the medium of Blackstone, who codified the doctrine in his Commentaries. "The plea of *autrefoits acquit*, or a former acquittal," he wrote, "is grounded on this universal maxim of the common law of England, that no man is to be brought into jeopardy of his life more than once for the same offence." . . . Today, every State incorporates some form of the prohibition in its constitution or common law. As this Court put it in *Green v. United States*, 355 U.S. 184, 187–188 (1957), "the underlying idea, one that is deeply ingrained in at least the Anglo-American system of jurisprudence, is that the State with all its resources and power should not be allowed to make repeated attempts to convict an individual for an alleged offense, thereby subjecting him to embarrassment, expense and ordeal and compelling him to live in a continuing state of anxiety and insecurity, as well as enhancing the possibility that even though innocent he may be found guilty." This underlying notion has from the very beginning been part of our constitutional tradition. Like the right to trial by jury, it is clearly "fundamental to the American scheme of justice." (pp. 795–796)

When Double-Jeopardy Protection Applies

The Fifth Amendment suggests that double jeopardy occurs when a person's "life or limb" is threatened. This language has been taken to mean that double jeopardy applies in all criminal proceedings. Determining whether a proceeding is criminal, however, is not always easy. Courts will often look to the legislature's intent in writing the statute that is the basis for prosecution. For example, in *Kansas v. Hendricks* (521 U.S. 346 [1997]), the Supreme Court found that a statute providing for a "sexual predator" proceeding, in addition to a criminal proceeding, did not place the defendant in double jeopardy because it provided for *civil* confinement. The Court stated:

Kansas v. Hendricks
(521 U.S. 346 [1997])

> Because we have determined that the Kansas Act is civil in nature, initiation of its commitment proceedings does not constitute a second prosecution. Cf. *Jones v. United States*, 463 U.S. 354, 77 L. Ed. 2d 694, 103 S. Ct. 3043 (1984) (permitting involuntary civil commitment after verdict of not guilty by reason of insanity). Moreover, as commitment under the Act is not tantamount to "punishment," Hendricks' involuntary detention does not violate the Double Jeopardy Clause, even though that confinement may follow a prison term. Indeed, in *Baxstrom v. Herold*, 383 U.S. 107, 15 L. Ed. 2d 620, 86 S. Ct. 760 (1966), we expressly recognized that civil commitment could follow the expiration of a prison term without offending double jeopardy principles. We reasoned that "there is no conceivable basis for distinguishing the commitment of a person who is nearing the end of a penal term from all other civil commitments." *Id.*, at 111–112. If an individual otherwise meets the requirements for involuntary civil commitment, the State is under no obligation to release that individual simply because the detention would follow a period of incarceration. (pp. 369–370)

The courts will also examine the punitiveness of the sanctions involved in determining whether a proceeding is criminal. In *Helvering v. Mitchell* (303 U.S. 391 [1938]), the Supreme Court upheld the constitutionality of a tax proceeding that was used to recover back taxes from a person *after* the person was acquitted on criminal charges. The Court declared that the proceeding was designed as a remedial sanction to reimburse the government. Because it was not considered punitive, double jeopardy did not apply. In the Court's words:

> The doctrine of double jeopardy is inapplicable because the 50% addition to tax provided by § 293 (b) is not primarily punitive but is a remedial sanction imposed as a safeguard for protection of the revenue and to reimburse the Government for expense and loss resulting from the taxpayer's fraud. As such it may be enforced by a civil procedure to which the accepted rules and constitutional guaranties governing the trial of criminal prosecutions do not apply. (p. 398)

THE *BLOCKBURGER* RULE   A rather complicated issue in double-jeopardy jurisprudence concerns the definition of **same offense**. In *Blockburger v. United States* (284 U.S. 299 [1932]), the Supreme Court developed a test that states that "[w]here the same act or transaction constitutes a violation of two distinct statutory provisions, the test to be applied to determine whether there are two offenses or only one, is whether each requires proof of an additional fact which the other does not" (p. 304). This test came to be known as the *Blockburger* rule.

Blockburger v. United States (284 U.S. 299 [1932])

According to the *Blockburger* rule, an offense is considered the same offense if two separate statutes that define the offense both contain elements A, B, and C. Moreover, if one crime contains elements A, B, and C and the other has elements A and B, both are considered the same offense because neither statute requires proof of a fact that the other does not. For example, assume that the offense of first-degree murder contains elements A (premeditated), B (deliberate), and C (killing) and that the offense of second-degree murder contains elements B (deliberate) and C (killing). Both offenses are considered the same for double-jeopardy purposes because second-degree murder does not require proof of another element that first-degree murder does not. If a person is convicted of first-degree murder, then, according to this example, he or she cannot be charged with second-degree murder.

Separate offenses can be identified when, for example, one crime contains elements A, B, and C and the other contains elements A, B, and D. Both crimes require proof of an additional element that the other does not. For example, assume the offense of joyriding contains elements A (unlawful taking), B (of an automobile), and C (the intent to *temporarily* deprive the owner of possession). Assume also that the offense of car theft contains elements A (unlawful taking), B (of an automobile), and D (the intent to *permanently* deprive the owner of possession). These are considered separate offenses because each offense requires proof of an element that the other does not. Thus, a person who is found guilty of joyriding can also be charged with the crime of car theft (see *Brown v. Ohio*, 432 U.S. 161 [1977]).

DECISION-MAKING EXERCISE 14.8

Case of Double Jeopardy?

In *United States v. Ursery* (518 U.S. 267 [1996]), an actual Supreme Court case, the issue was asset forfeiture. Police had found marijuana and growing equipment when they searched the defendant's house. He was prosecuted criminally, but the federal government also sought civil forfeiture of his house, pursuant to a federal law. The defendant filed a Section 1983 lawsuit against the government, claiming that the proposed forfeiture of his house would amount to double jeopardy, a violation of the Fifth Amendment. Does civil asset forfeiture in addition to criminal prosecution place a person in double jeopardy?

When Double-Jeopardy Protection Does Not Apply

There are four main exceptions to the *Blockburger* rule, which means that there are four situations in which double-jeopardy protection does not apply.

- Double jeopardy does not apply if the second prosecution is based on conduct committed after the first prosecution. This was the decision reached in *Diaz v. United States* (223 U.S. 442 [1912]). There, the defendant was convicted of assault and battery. When the victim later died, the defendant was charged with homicide. The Court stated, "The death of the injured person was the principal element of the homicide, but was no part of the assault and battery. At the time of the trial for the latter the death had not ensued, and not until it did ensue was the homicide committed. Then, and not before, was it possible to put the accused in jeopardy for that offense" (p. 449).
- If the defendant is responsible for the second prosecution, double jeopardy does not apply. In *Jeffers v. United States* (432 U.S. 137 [1977]), the defendant was indicted twice for two offenses. The state sought joinder on the charges, but the defendant successfully moved to have the charges tried separately. He was convicted in both trials but claimed that the latter conviction amounted to double jeopardy, in violation of the Fifth Amendment. The Court stated:

> In this case, trial together of the conspiracy and continuing-criminal-enterprise charges could have taken place without undue prejudice to petitioner's Sixth Amendment right to a fair trial. . . . If the two charges had been tried in one proceeding, it appears that petitioner would have been entitled to a lesser-included-offense instruction. . . . If such an instruction had been denied on the ground that § 846 was not a lesser included offense of § 848, petitioner could have preserved his point by proper objection. Nevertheless, petitioner did not adopt that course. Instead, he was solely responsible for the successive prosecutions for the conspiracy offense and the continuing-criminal-enterprise offense. Under the circumstances, we hold that his action deprived him of any right that he might have had against consecutive trials. It follows, therefore, that the Government was entitled to prosecute petitioner for the § 848 offense, and the only issue remaining is that of cumulative punishments upon such prosecution and conviction. (p. 153)

- Double jeopardy does not apply when the court hearing the first offense lacks jurisdiction to try the second offense. This exception came from the Supreme Court's decision in *Fugate v. New Mexico* (471 U.S. 1112 [1985]). There, the Court held that a defendant's conviction on drunk-driving charges in municipal court did not bar prosecution in a higher court for vehicular homicide tied to the same incident. The Court noted that the municipal court did not have jurisdiction to try a homicide case, so double-jeopardy protections did not apply.
- If the defense plea-bargains over the prosecution's objection, double-jeopardy protections do not apply. In *Ohio v. Johnson* (467 U.S. 493 [1984]), the defendant succeeded in convincing the judge to dismiss certain charges against him, over the prosecution's objection. The defendant was later tried on the dismissed charges, and the Court held that double-jeopardy protections did not apply. Had the prosecution acquiesced to the dismissal, the result would have been different. Indeed, it is unlikely the defendant would have been prosecuted on the dismissed charges if the prosecution had agreed with the judge's decision.

There are still other exceptions in which reprosecution for the same offense is permissible. First, if a defendant successfully appeals a criminal conviction or otherwise succeeds in overturning a conviction, he or she may be reprosecuted. In *United States v. Tateo* (377 U.S. 463 [1964]), the Court held:

> It would be a high price indeed for society to pay were every accused granted immunity from punishment because of any defect sufficient to constitute reversible error in the proceedings leading to conviction. From the standpoint of a defendant, it is at least doubtful that appellate courts would be as zealous as they now are in protecting against the effects of improprieties at the trial or pretrial stage if they knew that reversal of a conviction would put the accused irrevocably beyond the reach of further prosecution. In reality, therefore, the practice of retrial serves defendants' rights as well as society's interest. The underlying purpose of permitting retrial is as much furthered by application of the rule to this case as it has been in cases previously decided. (p. 466)

Second, if a case is dismissed by the judge but the defendant is not acquitted, he or she may be reprosecuted. In *United States v. Scott* (437 U.S. 82 [1978]), the Court held, in part, that "where a *defendant* successfully seeks to avoid his trial prior to its conclusion by a motion for a [dismissal], the Double Jeopardy Clause is not offended by a second prosecution. Such a motion by the defendant is deemed to be a deliberate election on his part to forgo his valued right to have his guilt or innocence determined by the first trier of fact" (p. 92).

Finally, reprosecution is permissible if a *mistrial* occurs over the defendant's objections and is a "manifest necessity." That is, reprosecution is permissible following a mistrial "when the defendant's interest in proceeding to verdict is outweighed by the competing and equally legitimate demand for public justice" (*Illinois v. Somerville*, 410 U.S. 458 [1973]; see also *Renico v. Lett*, No. 09-338 [2010]). Also, the defendant may be reprosecuted if the judge declares a mistrial with the defendant's consent or by the defendant's motion, provided that the prosecution does not agree to the defendant's consent or motion in bad faith (e.g., by intending to pursue a subsequent retrial for the purpose of subjecting the defendant to the harassment of multiple trials) (see, e.g., *Lee v. United States*, 432 U.S. 23 [1977]; *Oregon v. Kennedy*, 456 U.S. 667 [1982]).

Double Jeopardy and Sentencing

Double-jeopardy protection also extends to sentencing increases. First, the Supreme Court has considered whether double jeopardy is violated with the use of *consecutive punishments* (i.e., back-to-back punishments)—say, when the defendant is sentenced to a total of 10 years for convictions on two counts that each carry a 5-year sentence. The Court has held that this determination depends on legislative intent (see, e.g., *Albernaz v. United States*, 450 U.S. 333 [1981]). That is, provided the consecutive punishment is not for two of the same offenses, if the criminal law permits such punishment, double jeopardy is not violated.

Questions about double jeopardy have also been raised when a defendant is resentenced following some important development in the case. Increasing the sentence for the same charge (i.e., as opposed to increasing the sentence for separate charges, as in the case of cumulative punishments) after it has been imposed is permissible (1) when a conviction is reversed by an appeal (*North Carolina v. Pierce*, 395 U.S. 711 [1969]); (2) after the prosecution has appealed a sentence, provided there is legal authorization to do so (a rare occurrence, as Chapter 15 attests) (*United States v. DiFrancesco*,

DECISION-MAKING EXERCISE 14.9
Reprosecution after a Mistrial

In another actual Supreme Court case, *Lee v. United States* (432 U.S. 23 [1977]), the facts were as follow:

> After the prosecutor's opening statement in petitioner's bench trial for theft in violation of the Assimilative Crimes Act and the applicable Indiana statute, petitioner's counsel moved to dismiss the information on the ground that it did not allege specific intent as required by the Indiana statute. The court tentatively denied the motion subject to further study, whereupon petitioner's counsel outlined the defense and did not object to going forward with the trial. At the close of the evidence the court, though observing that petitioner's guilt had been proved beyond any reasonable doubt, granted petitioner's motion to dismiss. Thereafter, petitioner was indicted for the same crime and convicted.

The defendant in this case claimed that the double-jeopardy clause should have barred the second trial. Is he right?

449 U.S. 117 [1980]); and (3) after discovery of a legal defect in the first sentence (e.g., *In re Bradley*, 318 U.S. 50 [1943]).

In a recent—and controversial—case (*Sattazahn v. Pennsylvania*, 537 U.S. 101 [2003]), an individual was charged with capital murder, but the jury could not unanimously conclude that the death penalty was warranted. As required by a Pennsylvania statute, the judge then sentenced the offender to life in prison. The defendant was then retried and sentenced to death. He argued that the Fifth Amendment's double-jeopardy clause was violated, but the Supreme Court disagreed. The Court argued that the deadlocked jury did not amount to a "death penalty acquittal," so it saw no constitutional problems with retrying the offender.

THE RIGHT TO ASSERT AN ENTRAPMENT DEFENSE

A person tried for a crime can assert any of numerous defenses to criminal liability, including self-defense, insanity, involuntary intoxication, and others. Criminal law texts cover these in detail. One defense that straddles the line between criminal law and criminal procedure is the *entrapment defense*. It is a defense in the criminal law sense, but it is one of the only defenses that calls into question law enforcement's role in the instigation of a crime. Hence, it is almost always brought up in the realm of criminal procedure. The defendant can assert entrapment prior to trial, but for simplicity's sake, it will be discussed here. Entrapment is an affirmative defense, which means it can easily be raised at trial.

The heading of this section suggests that the defendant enjoys the *right* to assert an entrapment defense. It is important to note, however, that the Constitution does not provide this right. It is a right only in the sense that the Supreme Court has decided that an accused person can assert an entrapment defense.

The **entrapment defense** is based on the belief that someone should not be convicted of a crime that the government instigated. In its simplest form, the entrapment defense arises when government officials "plant the seeds" of criminal intent. That is, if a person commits a crime that he or she otherwise would not have committed but for the government's conduct, he or she will probably succeed with an entrapment defense.

Sorrells v. United States
(287 U.S. 435 [1932])

The first Supreme Court case recognizing the entrapment defense was *Sorrells v. United States* (287 U.S. 435 [1932]). In that case, Chief Justice Hughes stated, "We are unable to conclude that . . . [the] . . . processes of detection or enforcement should be abused by the instigation by government officials of an act on the part of persons otherwise innocent in order to lure them to its commission and to punish them" (p. 448). This reasoning underlies the treatment of the entrapment defense in U.S. courts to this day. The Court further stated:

> The appropriate object of this permitted activity, frequently essential to the enforcement of the law, is to reveal the criminal design; to expose the illicit traffic, the prohibited publication, the fraudulent use of the mails, the illegal conspiracy, or other offenses, and thus to disclose the would-be violators of the law. A different question is presented when the criminal design origi-nates with the officials of the Government, and they implant in the mind of an innocent person the disposition to commit the alleged offense and induce its commission in order that they may prosecute. (pp. 441–442)

Despite its apparent simplicity, the entrapment defense has been a contentious one. In particular, there has been some disagreement in the courts over the relevance of the offender's predisposition and how far the government can go in order to lure a person into criminal activity. When an entrapment decision is based on the offender's predisposition, this is known as a *subjective inquiry*. By contrast, a focus on the govern-ment conduct presumably responsible for someone's decision to commit a crime is known as an *objective inquiry*.

The American Law Institute's *Model Penal Code* takes an objective approach with regard to the entrapment defense: If the government "employ[ed] methods of persuasion or inducement which create a substantial risk that such an offense will be committed by persons other than those who are ready to commit it,"[3] then the defense is available regardless of the offender's initial willingness to offend. The Supreme Court, however, has opted to focus on the subjective predisposition of the offender instead of the government's role in instigating the crime in question (e.g., *Hampton v. United States*, 425 U.S. 484 [1976]).

In *Sorrells*, which was decided in 1932, the defendant was charged with violating the National Prohibition Act.[4] After two unsuccessful attempts, a law enforcement agent con-vinced the defendant to sell him whiskey. Chief Justice Hughes noted that "artifice and stratagem" are permissible methods of catching criminals, so entrapment did not occur. Instead, it was the defendant's predisposition to offend that was important.

Sherman v. United States
(356 U.S. 369 [1958])

In the next leading entrapment case, *Sherman v. United States* (356 U.S. 369 [1958]), the Supreme Court reached the opposite conclusion but still adhered to the predisposition test. In that case, a government informant met the defendant at a doctor's office, where both were being treated for narcotics addiction. After repeated requests by the informant, the defendant provided him with illegal narcotics. The Supreme Court reversed the defen-dant's conviction, noting that entrapment was "patently clear" as a matter of law. Even so, the Court also pointed out that it is difficult to judge the conduct of an informant without knowing how predisposed the offender was to act before the crime was committed.

United States v. Russell
(411 U.S. 423 [1973]),

In *United States v. Russell* (411 U.S. 423 [1973]), the Court continued to focus on the defendant's predisposition. In *Russell*, a narcotics agent posed as a narcotics manufacturer and offered the defendant a difficult-to-obtain ingredient used to manufacture a drug. The defendant accepted and was convicted. Justice Rehnquist, author of the majority opinion, observed that there was sufficient predisposition on the part of the defendant, so the entrapment defense did not apply.

---

[3] American Law Institute, *Model Penal Code* 2.13(1)(b)(1985).
[4] Recall that during the Prohibition era, from 1920 to 1933, it was illegal to produce and sell alcohol in the United States.

DECISION-MAKING EXERCISE 14.10

Outrageous Government Conduct

In an actual case, Drug Enforcement Agency (DEA) agents sought out a convicted felon, Kubica, and offered to reduce the severity of his sentence if he agreed to cooperate with them. At the request of the DEA, Kubica contacted another man, Neville, and suggested that they set up a lab to manufacture "speed." Neville agreed, and the government supplied Kubica with glassware and a difficult-to-obtain ingredient used in the manufacture of speed. The government also made arrangements for purchasing the chemicals and even supplied an isolated farmhouse to serve as the laboratory. The laboratory was set up at the farmhouse and operated for one week. The men produced approximately six pounds of methamphet-

amine hydrochloride (i.e., speed). Kubica was completely in charge of the entire laboratory. At the end of the first week of lab operations, Neville left the farmhouse with the drugs in a suitcase. Kubica notified the DEA agents, who arrested Neville driving down the road. A search of the car revealed, in addition to the suitcase containing six pounds of methamphetamine hydrochloride, a Lysol can containing cocaine and some more speed. Neville was arrested, charged, and convicted. He appealed his conviction not on entrapment grounds but by arguing that the government's outrageous conduct had violated the due process clause of the Fourteenth Amendment. What should the court decide?

Hampton v. United States (425 U.S. 484 [1976])

In *Hampton v. United States* (425 U.S. 484 [1976]), the Supreme Court once again focused on the defendant's predisposition. In that case, the defendant was convicted of distributing heroin supplied to the defendant by a government informant. The Court stated that "[i]f the police engage in illegal activity in concert with a defendant beyond the scope of their duties the remedy lies, not in freeing the equally culpable defendant, but in prosecuting the police under the applicable provisions of state or federal law" (p. 90). In other words, it is the defendant's predisposition that matters in the context of the entrapment defense, not the government's conduct.

To suggest that the Supreme Court has ignored the role of government conduct is not entirely true. In a concurring opinion cited in *Hampton*, Justices Powell and Blackmun argued that government behavior that "shocks the conscience" could conceivably violate due process. In their words, "[T]here is certainly a limit to allowing governmental involvement in crime. . . . It would be unthinkable . . . to permit government agents to instigate robberies and beatings merely to gather evidence to convict other members of a gang of hoodlums" (p. 493, n. 4).

The Supreme Court has yet to affirmatively recognize a due process-based defense to government entrapment, but some lower courts have. Generally, if government officials use violence, supply contraband that is wholly unobtainable, or engage in a criminal enterprise, then the defendant in such a case will often succeed with the entrapment defense based on a due process argument.

Summary

1. SUMMARIZE THE RIGHT TO A PUBLIC TRIAL.

This chapter concludes the focus on constitutional rights at trial. The first right is that of a public trial— one that is open to the public. This right has been expanded to cover several pretrial proceedings, such as suppression hearings. Sometimes, the right to a public trial does not apply. First, the government may seek closure, but to do so, it must show (1) that there is an overriding interest, such as the protection

of certain witnesses; (2) that the closure is no broader than absolutely necessary; and (3) that reasonable alternatives were considered. Second, the accused may seek closure of a trial but only if an open proceeding will compromise the ability of the jury to make a fair decision.

Attempts to close trials (and related proceedings) to the public often meet with resistance on First Amendment grounds. In response to this problem, the courts have recognized that there may be other ways to ensure an open trial that remains fair, despite media coverage. Some of these methods include (1) *voir dire* with special attention to pretrial publicity, (2) a change of venue, (3) jury sequestration, (4) gag orders on the media, and (5) gag orders on other parties.

2. SUMMARIZE THE RIGHT TO CONFRONTATION.

The right to confrontation refers to the ability of the defendant to face his or her accusers. This right is manifested in three ways: (1) by permitting the defendant to be present at trial, (2) by requiring live testimony, and (3) by allowing the defendant to challenge the government's witnesses through cross-examination.

The defendant enjoys the right not only to be physically present but also to be mentally competent. Deciding competence hinges on whether the defendant is able to consult with his or her lawyer with a reasonable degree of understanding. Physical presence can be damaging to the defense, however, in cases in which the defendant does not testify or his or her being in court reminds jurors of the crime.

The defendant's right to live testimony requires that witnesses appear in person. Recordings and the like are generally not permissible, but there are exceptions: (1) if the witness is unavailable because he or she is dead; (2) if the witness is unavailable for other reasons, such as by being hospitalized or confined to an institution; and (3) if the statement made by a witness who will not provide live testimony falls under one of the established hearsay exceptions, permitting introduction of those statements by a third party.

Finally, the defendant's third guarantee for confrontation concerns the right to challenge witness testimony. The defendant can challenge witness testimony by engaging in cross-examination and recross-examination. Both forms of examination follow prosecutorial questioning and are intended to cast doubt on the witness's testimony. The Supreme Court has restricted as well as enhanced the defendant's right to challenge witness testimony. It has restricted the right insofar as witnesses are not always required to testify before the defendant, and it has enhanced the right because the defense is given wide latitude in terms of its authority to cross-examine. Further, courts and states cannot conceal the identity of a witness testifying against the defense, nor can they bar cross-examination simply because the defense is calling the witness it wishes to cross-examine.

3. SUMMARIZE THE RIGHT TO COMPULSORY PROCESS.

Compulsory process is another right enjoyed by a criminal defendant in the United States. It means that the defendant is legally entitled to compel the production of witnesses. This can be accomplished via a subpoena, if the witness will not voluntarily come forward. Compulsory process also extends to the production of physical evidence. However, there are restrictions that stem from the rules of evidence.

4. EXPLAIN THE CONCEPT OF DOUBLE JEOPARDY.

The defendant further enjoys the right to double-jeopardy protection. In general, a defendant cannot, by the same sovereign, be reprosecuted after acquittal, reprosecuted after conviction, or subjected to separate punishments for the same offense. Several exceptions exist to the Fifth Amendment's double-jeopardy clause. First, double jeopardy does not apply if the second prosecution is based on conduct committed after the first prosecution. Second, double jeopardy does not apply if the defendant is responsible for the second prosecution. Third, double jeopardy does not apply when the court hearing the first offense lacks jurisdiction to try the second offense. Fourth, if the defense plea-bargains over the prosecution's objection, double-jeopardy protection does not apply. Fifth, if a defendant successfully appeals a criminal conviction or otherwise succeeds in overturning a conviction, he or she may be reprosecuted. Sixth, if a case is dismissed by the judge but the defendant is not acquitted, the defendant may be reprosecuted. Finally, reprosecution is permissible if the dismissal occurs over the defendant's objections and is a "manifest necessity."

5. OUTLINE THE CLASSIFICATIONS AND ORIGINS OF THE ENTRAPMENT DEFENSE.

The defendant also enjoys the right to assert an entrapment defense. While this is not a constitutional right, it has, nevertheless, been given a high degree of protection by the Supreme Court. This defense can be asserted prior to trial—say, in a probable cause hearing or a preliminary hearing—but entrapment is also a common-law defense that can be affirmatively asserted at trial. An entrapment defense will succeed if the defendant can show, in general, that government officials "planted the seeds" of criminal intent and induced him or her into committing the crime in question.

Key Terms

Blockburger rule	461	entrapment		jury sequestration	440	public trial	438
change of venue	440	defense	464	live testimony	446	same offense	461
compulsory		gag order	440	mental		unavailable	
process	454	hearsay		competence	444	witness	447
confrontation	442	exceptions	448	physical presence	443		
double jeopardy	459						

Key Cases

Public Trial

- *In re Oliver*, 333 U.S. 257 (1948)
- *Waller v. Georgia*, 467 U.S. 39 (1984)
- *Sheppard v. Maxwell*, 384 U.S. 333 (1966)
- *Rideau v. Louisiana*, 373 U.S. 723 (1963)
- *Nebraska Press Ass'n v. Stuart*, 427 U.S. 539 (1976)

Confrontation

- *Illinois v. Allen*, 397 U.S. 337 (1970)
- *Taylor v. Illinois*, 484 U.S. 400 (1988)
- *Dusky v. United States*, 362 U.S. 402 (1960)
- *Mattox v. United States*, 156 U.S. 237 (1895)
- *Motes v. United States*, 178 U.S. 458 (1900)
- *White v. Illinois*, 502 U.S. 346 (1992)
- *Coy v. Iowa*, 487 U.S. 1012 (1988)
- *Chambers v. Mississippi*, 410 U.S. 284 (1973)

Compulsory Process

- *Washington v. Texas*, 388 U.S. 14 (1967)
- *Crane v. Kentucky*, 476 US. 683 (1986)
- *United States v. Scheffer*, 523 U.S. 303 (1998)

Double Jeopardy

- *Benton v. Maryland*, 395 U.S. 784 (1969)
- *Kansas v. Hendricks*, 521 U.S. 346 (1997)
- *Blockburger v. United States*, 284 U.S. 299 (1932)

Entrapment

- *Sorrells v. United States*, 287 U.S. 435 (1932)
- *Sherman v. United States*, 356 U.S. 369 (1958)
- *United States v. Russell*, 411 U.S. 423 (1973)
- *Hampton v. United States*, 425 U.S. 484 (1976)

Review Questions

1. Explain the term *public trial*.
2. When may the right to a public trial not apply?
3. Why is the First Amendment relevant when discussing the right to a public trial?
4. What methods are available to deal with media influence on a criminal trial?
5. In what three ways is the defendant's right to confrontation manifested?
6. Explain both elements of the defendant's right to be present. Cite pertinent cases.
7. How might the defendant's right to be present do more harm than good?
8. Explain the exceptions to the defendant's right to live testimony.
9. Explain the order and scope of questions in a criminal trial.
10. Explain both elements of the right to compulsory process.
11. Summarize two Supreme Court decisions that address compulsory process: one in favor of the defense and another against the defense.
12. When does double-jeopardy protection apply?
13. What is the *same offense* for double-jeopardy purposes?
14. When can a defendant not assert double-jeopardy protection?
15. What is the entrapment defense? When can it succeed? Can entrapment rise to the level of a due process violation? If so, how?

Web Links and Exercises

1. Change of venue procedure: Read about the requirements for a change of venue in the state of California.

URL: http://www.courtinfo.ca.gov/reference/documents/factsheets/chgofven.pdf (accessed February 16, 2011).

2. Confrontation in the wake of *Crawford v. Washington*: What are the implications of the *Crawford* decision for domestic violence victims?

Suggested URL: http://www.law.cornell.edu/supct/html/02-9410.ZO.html (accessed February 16, 2011).

3. Questioning child witnesses: Read about Virginia's procedures relating to questioning of child witnesses via closed-circuit television.

URL: http://www.dcjs.virginia.gov/juvenile/cja/protocol.cfm (accessed February 16, 2011).

4. Rape victim questioning: Read about so-called "rape shield" laws.

URL: http://www.naesv.org/Resources/Articles/UnderstandingRapeShieldLaws.pdf (accessed February 16, 2011).

5. Double jeopardy in the war on terror: Read about Ehren Watada's double-jeopardy argument. He was the first commissioned U.S. soldier to refuse to go to Iraq.

URL: http://en.wikipedia.org/wiki/Ehren_Watada (accessed February 16, 2011).

6. Entrapment: Read more about entrapment.

Suggested URL: http://findarticles.com/p/articles/mi_m2194/is_n4_v62/ai_13859809 (accessed February 16, 2011).

LEARNING OBJECTIVES

When you complete this chapter, you should be able to:

▸ Describe various sentencing goals.

▸ Explain how an appropriate sentence is determined.

▸ Describe the various types of appeals.

▸ Outline the appeal process.

▸ Summarize the right to and restrictions on *habeas corpus*.

Sentencing, Appeals, and *Habeas Corpus*

INTRODUCTION

Closing the Door on the Criminal Process

The criminal process typically ends when the defendant is found *not guilty.* It does not end when the accused is found *guilty,* for three reasons. First, the accused must be sentenced, which is usually accomplished in a posttrial hearing. Second, the accused can appeal his or her conviction. Finally, if the accused's appeal fails to succeed, the U.S. Constitution provides the right to *habeas corpus,* a method of challenging the constitutionality of one's confinement.

SENTENCING

Once a person has been convicted at trial, he or she must be sentenced. Sentencing occurs at a separate, posttrial hearing but rarely for misdemeanor convictions. Individuals charged with misdemeanors are often tried and sentenced in the same hearing.

When sentencing is carried out in a separate hearing, however, it is usually preceded by the judge requesting a *presentence report.* This report provides the judge with information concerning the defendant's pretrial record, financial characteristics, family status, employment status, and other factors that can be relevant in deciding on the appropriate sentence. The time needed to complete this report is the main reason for the time lapse between trial and sentencing. The report is intended to assist the judge in reaching his or her decision and is usually completed by a probation officer retained by the court.

Several sentencing options are available to the judge. The judge may impose a sentence and then suspend it, pending good behavior on the part of the defendant. The judge may also require the defendant to pay a fine or, in more extreme cases, to serve a term in prison. Probation or another method of supervised release is a possibility, as well. In any case, the type of sentence can hinge on the judge's own goal of sentencing—that is, his or her view as to the most important purpose of sentencing. The following section considers leading goals of criminal sentencing.

Goals of Sentencing

Four broad goals of sentencing can be identified: (1) **rehabilitation**, or reformation; (2) **retribution**; (3) **incapacitation**; and (4) **deterrence**, either general or specific. **Specific deterrence** refers to what it takes to discourage the offender from committing additional crimes. **General deterrence** refers to what it takes to discourage all would-be offenders from committing crimes.

The differences among these four goals of punishment have been well described in a famous case heard by the Pennsylvania Supreme Court, *Commonwealth v. Ritter* 13 (Pa. D. & C. 285 [1930]):

- As far as the principle of reformation is concerned, however important it may be in the general run of cases, it obviously has little or no application to such a case as the present. Whichever be the penalty here inflicted, the defendant will not again be in contact with society, and since secular law is concerned with one's relation to the community and not primarily with his inward moral development, the spiritual regeneration of a defendant is not, in such a case as this, a dominant factor. In other words, it would not be a practical consideration weighing in favor of life imprisonment that thereby the defendant might be susceptible of moral reformation, whereas the opportunity for this would be denied to him if the death penalty were inflicted.
- The second theory, which has been urged as a basis for the imposition of penalties, is that of retribution. This may be regarded as the doctrine of legal revenge, or punishment merely for the sake of punishment. It is to pay back the wrongdoer for his wrongdoing, to make him suffer by way of retaliation even if no benefit results thereby to himself or to others. This theory of punishment looks to the past and not to the future and rests solely upon the foundation of vindictive justice. It is this idea of punishment that generally prevails, even though those who entertain it may not be fully aware of their so doing. Historically, it may be said that the origin of all legal punishments had its root in

the natural impulse of revenge. At first, this instinct was gratified by retaliatory measures on the part of the individual who suffered by the crime committed, or, in the case of murder, by his relatives. Later, the state took away the right of retaliation from individuals, and its own assumption of the function of revenge really constituted the beginning of criminal law. The entire course, however, of the refinement and humanizing of society has been in the direction of dispelling from penology any such theory. Indeed, even in classical times moralists and philosophers rejected the idea entirely. Plato puts into the mouth of Protagoras the words: "No one punishes those who have been guilty of injustice solely because they have committed injustice, unless indeed he punishes in a brutal and unreasonable manner. When any one makes use of his reason in inflicting punishment, he punishes, not on account of the fault that is past, for no one can bring it about that what has been done may not have been done, but on account of a fault to come, in order that the person punished may not again commit the fault and that his punishment may restrain from similar acts those persons who witness the punishment." . . .

- Rejecting, therefore, the theory of retribution as a proper basis upon which to impose the penalty of law, we come to the third principle which has been advocated, namely, the restraint of the wrongdoer in order to make it impossible for him to commit further crime. Here we arrive not only at a justifiable basis for action but at one which is vital to the protection of society. To permit a man of dangerous criminal tendencies to be in a position where he can give indulgence to such propensities would be a folly which no community should suffer itself to commit, any more than it should allow a wild animal to range at will in the city streets. If, therefore, there is danger that a defendant may again commit crime, society should restrain his liberty until such danger be past, and, in cases similar to the present, if reasonably necessary for that purpose, to terminate his life. Admittedly, restraint by imprisonment can never be as wholly effectual as execution, and there are, from time to time, cases where imprisonment may not be sufficient for the protection of society. It is on this ground that it is pertinent to take testimony in regard to the history of a defendant and of the circumstances attending his commission of crime. If his record shows that he is of a dangerous type, or that he habitually commits grave crimes, or that he has a homicidal tendency, or that he is hopelessly depraved, or that he has a savage nature, or that he has committed murder under circumstances of such atrocity and inhuman brutality as to make his continued existence one of likely danger to society, then, in my opinion, the sentence of death is both justifiable and advisable. The community may not be safe with such a man in existence even though he be serving a term of life imprisonment; he may again commit murder within the prison walls, or may escape and again make innocent victims his prey, or may even, by cunning simulation of repentance, obtain a pardon from governmental authorities. . . .

- This brings us to the final and what must be fairly regarded as one of the most important objectives of punishment, namely, the element of deterrence—the theory which regards the penalty as being not an end in itself but the means of attaining an end, namely, the frightening of others who might be tempted to imitate the criminal. From this angle, a penalty is a cautionary measure, aimed at the prevention of further crime in the community. There has been much controversy and an enormous amount of literature on the subject as to whether the death penalty does or does not act as a deterrent. With that controversy, we have nothing to do. As before stated, the law of Pennsylvania retains the death penalty as an optional alternative. The real question is not as to whether the death penalty is in general a deterrent, but as to the particular kinds of murder cases in which execution would or would not be most likely to effect deterrence. It becomes a problem of determining the basis upon which to make such classification. (pp. 15–21)

Types of Prison Sentences

At least four types of sentences can be identified, some of which are closely related to one another.

- **Indeterminate sentencing** gives the judge the authority to set the sentence. This form of sentencing empowers the judge to set the maximum sentence—that is, up to what the legislature will allow—or the minimum sentence for the offender to serve in prison. Under this system, a parole board usually ends up deciding the actual amount of time the offender will spend in prison.
- **Determinate sentencing.** The judge is permitted to hand down a fixed sentence that cannot later be altered by a parole board. Determinate sentencing has the effect of treating all offenders similarly. It also has the effect of ensuring that criminals will be incarcerated for longer periods of time than may be permissible under indeterminate sentencing.
- **Mandatory sentencing.** Mandatory sentencing is a form of determinate sentencing but differs insofar as it takes discretion away from the judge. "Three strikes" laws require mandatory sentencing. For example, under California's "three strikes" law, if a person who has two "strikeable" felonies on his or her record commits a third felony of any type, he or she will go to prison for life. The Supreme Court has decided that such laws do not constitute cruel and unusual punishment (*Lockyer v. Andrade*, 538 U.S. 63 [2003]; *Ewing v. Andrade*, 538 U.S. 11 [2003]).
- **Sentencing guidelines.** Sentencing guidelines can be used to determine the appropriate sentence. They constitute the middle ground between indeterminate and determinate methods of sentencing. As such, they serve to reduce disparities in sentencing by recommending a certain term of imprisonment for a certain type of offender. Sentencing guidelines can be voluntary or involuntary, depending on state or federal law. Sentencing guidelines that must be followed exactly are known as *presumptive guidelines.*

The U.S. Sentencing Commission was created in 1984 to deal with sentencing problems in the federal courts. It put together a *sentencing grid* that federal judges use to determine appropriate sentences (see Figure 15.1). Both criminal history (i.e., horizontal axis) and offense level (i.e., vertical axis) are taken into account, such that a judge can set the appropriate sentence in months. Readers are encouraged to visit the U.S. Sentencing Commission's Web site to learn more about these guidelines. It's link appears in the "Web Links and Exercises" section at the end of this chapter.

Determining the Appropriate Sentence

Determining the appropriate sentence almost always involves considering both the seriousness of the offense and the offender's prior record. Other factors that are considered include the defendant's possible threat to the community and his or her degree of remorse for committing the crime. Even age, family ties, employment status, and other demographic factors can come into play. Moreover, the defendant who pleads guilty may receive a different sentence than the defendant who is found guilty in a trial. A guilty plea suggests that the defendant is willing to admit what he or she did and, as such, should be treated more leniently.

FIGURE 15.1

Federal Sentencing Guidelines

SENTENCE TABLE (in months of imprisonment)

Criminal History Category (Criminal History Points)

	Offense Level	I (0 or 1)	II (2 or 3)	III (4, 5, 6)	IV (7, 8, 9)	V (10, 11, 12)	VI (13 or more)
Zone A	1	0–6	0–6	0–6	0–6	0–6	0–6
	2	0–6	0–6	0–6	0–6	0–6	1–7
	3	0–6	0–6	0–6	0–6	2–8	3–9
	4	0–6	0–6	0–6	2–8	4–10	6–12
	5	0–6	0–6	1–7	4–10	6–12	9–15
	6	0–6	1–7	2–8	6–12	9–15	12–18
	7	0–6	2–8	4–10	8–14	12–18	15–21
	8	0–6	4–10	6–12	10–16	15–21	18–24
Zone B	9	4–10	6–12	8–14	12–18	18–24	21–27
	10	6–12	8–14	10–16	15–21	21–27	24–30
Zone C	11	8–14	10–16	12–18	18–24	24–30	27–33
	12	10–16	12–18	15–21	21–27	27–33	30–37
	13	12–18	15–21	18–24	24–30	30–37	33–41
	14	15–21	18–24	21–27	27–33	33–41	37–46
	15	18–24	21–27	24–30	30–37	37–46	41–51
	16	21–27	24–30	27–33	33–41	41–51	46–57
	17	24–30	27–33	30–37	37–46	46–57	51–63
	18	27–33	30–37	33–41	41–51	51–63	57–71
	19	30–37	33–41	37–46	46–57	57–71	63–78
	20	33–41	37–46	41–51	51–63	63–78	70–87
	21	37–46	41–51	46–57	57–71	70–87	77–96
	22	41–51	46–57	51–63	63–78	77–96	84–105
	23	46–57	51–63	57–71	70–87	84–105	92–115
	24	51–63	57–71	63–78	77–96	92–115	100–125
	25	57–71	63–78	70–87	84–105	100–125	110–137
	26	63–78	70–87	78–97	92–115	110–137	120–150
Zone D	27	70–87	78–97	87–108	100–125	120–150	130–162
	28	78–97	87–108	97–121	110–137	130–162	140–175
	29	87–108	97–121	108–135	121–151	140–175	151–188
	30	97–121	108–135	121–151	135–168	151–188	168–210
	31	108–135	121–151	135–168	151–188	168–210	188–235
	32	121–151	135–168	151–188	168–210	188–235	210–262
	33	135–168	151–188	168–210	188–235	210–262	235–293
	34	151–188	168–210	188–235	210–262	235–293	262–327
	35	168–210	188–235	210–262	235–293	262–327	292–365
	36	188–235	210–262	235–293	262–327	292–365	324–405
	37	210–262	235–293	262–327	292–365	324–405	360–life
	38	235–293	262–327	292–365	324–405	360–life	360–life
	39	262–327	292–365	324–405	360–life	360–life	360–life
	40	292–365	324–405	360–life	360–life	360–life	360–life
	41	324–405	360–life	360–life	360–life	360–life	360–life
	42	360–life	360–life	360–life	360–life	360–life	360–life
	43	life	life	life	life	life	life

Source: U.S. Sentencing Commission, *Guidelines Manual* (Washington, DC: U.S. Sentencing Commission, 2010), p. 401. Available online: http://www.ussc.gov/Guidelines/2010_guidelines/Manual_PDF/Chapter_5.pdf (accessed February 16, 2011).

Sentencing can also be determined by the number of separate crimes growing out of a single criminal act. If, for instance, a defendant is convicted of killing another person with a handgun, he or she may be sentenced for the killing as well as for unlawful possession of a handgun, if the law permits the latter. In such a situation, the judge may sentence the defendant to consecutive or concurrent sentences. With a *concurrent sentence*, the defendant serves time for both crimes at once. *Consecutive sentences*, by contrast, are served separately, one after another. In the murder example, the defendant would serve time in prison for the killing, and then when that term was completed, he or she would begin serving the sentence for possession.

Roberts v. United States
(445 U.S. 552 [1980])

Indeed, sentencing can be influenced by the defendant's degree of cooperation with the police. In *Roberts v. United States* (445 U.S. 552 [1980]), the Court held that the sentencing judge was permitted to consider the defendant's refusal to cooperate with the police in investigating his crime. Still other factors, such as the offender's mental status, can be considered. In fact, it has been held that a mentally ill individual can be held in custody, such as in a mental institution, for a longer term than a traditional prison sentence for the crime charged (e.g., *Jones v. United States*, 103 S.Ct. 3043 [1983]). This often happens following an insanity plea.

Most jurisdictions have what is known as the "going rate" for a criminal offense.[1] Usually, this is an unwritten, informal agreement between members of a courtroom work group (i.e., a judge, defense attorney, and prosecutor) as to what sentence a typical case merits. Usually, if the seriousness of the offense and the offender's background characteristics are known, one can predict with a fair degree of accuracy what sentence will be imposed.

A judge's sentencing decisions can also be influenced by *victim impact statements*. For example, Proposition 8, adopted by California voters in 1982, provides that "the victim of any crime, or the next kin of the victim, . . . has the right to attend all sentencing proceedings . . . [and] to reasonably express his or her views concerning the crime, the person responsible, and the need for restitution."[2] The Supreme Court has decided that testimony in the form of a victim impact statement is admissible (*Payne v. Tennessee*, 501 U.S. 808 [1991]).

The judge is then required to take the victim's or next of kin's statement into account when deciding on a sentence for the offender.

DEATH PENALTY SENTENCING   The most serious punishment that can be imposed is *capital punishment*, or the death penalty. Prior to the 1970s, several executions were carried out each year. However, in 1972, the Supreme Court decided the landmark case *Furman v. Georgia* (408 U.S. 238 [1972]). In that case, the Court held that the death penalty was carried out in the United States in a way that amounted to cruel and unusual punishment, in violation of the Eighth Amendment. Then, in 1976, the Court reinstated the death penalty in *Gregg v. Georgia* (428 U.S. 153 [1976]), holding that death is an acceptable sentence, provided the sentencing process is reasonable.

Furman v. Georgia
(408 U.S. 238 [1972])

Determining whether death should be imposed is now frequently in the hands of a jury. Most state statutes call for, in essence, two trials. In legal parlance, this is called a **bifurcated trial**. In the first trial, the defendant's guilt or lack of involvement in the crime is determined. This is the traditional trial. Then, the jury sits for what is basically another trial to determine whether a death sentence should be handed down. The importance of such a procedure is that it allows a jury of the defendant's

---

[1] S. Walker, *Sense and Nonsense about Crime and Drugs*, 5th ed. (Belmont, CA: Wadsworth, 2001), p. 41.
[2] California Penal Code, Section 1191.1 (1996).

peers, not just a judge, to determine whether capital punishment is appropriate. Further, the jury must take into account aggravating and mitigating circumstances. As decided in *Roberts v. Louisiana* (428 U.S. 325 [1977]), failure to do so is unconstitutional. Importantly, though, if aggravating or mitigating circumstances presented to the jury are later found invalid, the Eighth Amendment will not necessarily be violated if a death sentence is imposed (*Brown v. Sanders*, 546 U.S. 212 [2006]).

Roberts v. Louisiana
(428 U.S. 325 [1977])

In *Stebbing v. Maryland* (469 U.S. 900 [1984]), Justice Marshall described one state's approach to death penalty sentencing that relies on a jury's decision:

> Like most death penalty statutes, the Maryland statute begins by requiring the sentencing authority—either a judge or a jury—first to consider whether the prosecutor has proved, beyond a reasonable doubt, the existence of any of 10 statutory aggravating circumstances. . . . If the sentencer does not find at least one aggravating factor, the sentence must be life imprisonment. . . . If the sentencer finds that one or more aggravating factors exist, it then must determine whether the defendant has proven, by a preponderance of the evidence, that any of eight statutory mitigating factors exist. . . . If no mitigating factors are found, the sentencer must impose death. If, instead, the sentencer has found at least one mitigating factor, it must determine, by a preponderance of the evidence, whether the proven mitigating factors outweigh the aggravating circumstances. If they do, the sentencer must impose a life sentence. If the mitigating factors do not outweigh aggravating factors, the jury must impose a death sentence. (p. 902)

Whereas a jury must take aggravating and mitigating factors into consideration when determining whether a death sentence is appropriate, it is not appropriate for a judge to do so. Such was the decision in *Ring v. Arizona* (122 S.Ct. 2428 [2002]). There, the Supreme Court held that allowing a sentencing judge, without a jury, to find aggravating circumstances necessary for imposition of the death penalty violated the Sixth Amendment's jury trial provision (incidentally, judges in some states can ignore jurors' sentencing recommendations in capital cases).

The death penalty is most commonly handed down for first-degree, premeditated murder. But whether death is the appropriate sentence for less serious offenses has raised some questions. The Supreme Court has answered these questions to some extent. For example, in *Coker v. Georgia* (433 U.S. 584 [1977]), the Court held that a sentence of death for the crime of rape against an adult woman was grossly disproportionate and in violation of the Eighth and Fourteenth Amendments to the U.S. Constitution.

DECISION-MAKING EXERCISE 15.1

Death Penalty Sentencing

Assume that a state law gives the trial judge authority to sentence to death a defendant convicted of a capital crime but also requires the judge to consider the jury's recommendation as to whether the death penalty should be imposed. Assume further that a man has been sentenced to death by the judge in his trial, even though the jury that convicted him recommended life in prison. The man appeals, claiming that the statute is unconstitutional because it does not specify the weight the judge must give to the jury's sentencing recommendation and thus permits the arbitrary imposition of the death penalty. He further claims that the judge should be forced to give "great weight" to the jury's recommendation. How should the appellate court rule?

OTHER IMPORTANT SENTENCING DECISIONS   Several other recent decisions have sought to clarify the circumstances in which death and/or other types of sentences can be imposed. A handful of the cases and their holdings are as follows:

- *Woodson v. North Carolina* (428 U.S. 280 [1976]). Decided on the same day as *Gregg*, the Court held that mandatory death penalty laws—that is, those that do not take aggravating and mitigating circumstances into account—are unconstitutional.
- *Enmund v. Florida* (458 U.S. 782 [1982]). It is unconstitutional to impose death on a person who participates in a felony that results in murder without considering the participant's level of intent.
- *Cabana v. Bullock* (474 U.S. 376 [1986]). The death penalty cannot be imposed on a mere accomplice, unless there is clear finding that the accomplice killed, attempted to kill, or intended to kill.
- *Ford v. Wainwright* (477 U.S. 399 [1986]). The execution of someone who is insane violates the Eighth Amendment.
- *Tison v. Arizona* (107 S.Ct. 1714 [1987]). The death penalty can be imposed in the absence of intent to kill if the defendant substantially participated in a felony likely to result in a loss of life.
- *Harmelin v. Michigan* (501 U.S. 957 [1991]). A life sentence without the possibility of parole for a first-time, nonviolent drug offender does not constitute cruel and unusual punishment.
- *Kansas v. Hendricks* (521 U.S. 346 [1997]). Civil commitment was upheld for convicted child molesters who have served their sentences under the state's Sexually Violent Predators Act.
- *Apprendi v. New Jersey* (530 U.S. 466 [2000]). Any fact, other than prior conviction, that increases the penalty for a crime beyond that allowed by statute must be submitted to a jury and proven beyond a reasonable doubt.
- *Atkins v. Virginia* (122 S. Ct. 2242 [2002]). The execution of a mentally retarded person violates the Eighth Amendment.
- *Kansas v. Crane* (534 U.S. 407 [2002]). Concerning the civil commitment of sexual offenders under Kansas's Sexually Violent Predators Act, such offenders cannot be civilly committed without having proof that they have serious difficulty in controlling their behavior.
- *Blakely v. Washington* (542 U.S. 296 [2004]). A fact, other than prior conviction, that increases a sentence to the maximum permitted by statute must be presented to a jury and proven beyond a reasonable doubt.
- *Roper v. Simmons* (543 U.S. 551 [2005]). The execution of offenders who committed their capital crime under the age of 18 violates the Eighth Amendment.
- *Deck v. Missouri* (544 U.S. 622 [2005]). The constitution forbids the use of visible shackles during a capital trial's penalty phase.
- *United States v. Booker* (543 U.S. 220 [2005]). Federal sentencing guidelines are advisory, not mandatory.
- *Oregon v. Guzek* (546 U.S. 517 [2006]). The Constitution does not permit defendants facing the death penalty to present new evidence during the sentencing phase.
- *Carey v. Musladin* (549 U.S. 70 [2006]). It was not unfairly prejudicial for trial spectators to wear buttons depicting the murder victim.
- *Rita v. United States* (551 U.S. 338 [2007]). Sentences that fall within the federal sentencing guidelines are presumptively reasonable.
- *Cunningham v. California* (549 U.S. 270 [2007]). State determinate sentencing laws violate the Sixth Amendment right to jury trial when they permit judges to impose enhanced sentences based on facts not found by a jury or admitted to by the defendant.

- *Kimbrough v. United States* (552 U.S. 85 [2007]). The federal cocaine sentencing guidelines, like other federal sentencing guidelines, are advisory.
- *Baze v. Rees* (553 U.S. 35 [2008]). A three-drug lethal-injection protocol does not violate the Eighth Amendment's prohibition of cruel and unusual punishment.
- *Graham v. Florida* (No. 08-7412 [2010]). Juvenile offenders cannot be sentenced to life in prison for nonhomicide offenses.
- *United States v. Comstock* (No. 08-1224 [2010]). It is constitutionally permissible for the federal government to use civil commitment to keep a sexually dangerous federal prisoners confined beyond the date of scheduled release.

Constitutional Rights during Sentencing

A convicted criminal enjoys several important constitutional rights during the sentencing process. First, the double-jeopardy provision of the Fifth Amendment, as discussed in the last chapter, applies. Further, the defendant is entitled to a reasonable punishment for his or her crime. Namely, the punishment should reflect the seriousness of the crime. For example, in *Solem v. Helm* (463 U.S. 277 [1983]), the Court held that a life sentence for the defendant's seventh nonviolent offense was unconstitutional. The Court prohibited the sentence, stating that the defendant "received the penultimate sentence for relatively minor criminal conduct" (p. 305).

The defendant also has the right to participate in the sentencing process. With the possible exception of misdemeanor sentencing, which may take place out of the presence of the defendant, the defendant has the right to be present during sentencing. Also, the defendant should be advised of his or her right to appeal. The defendant also has the right to have counsel present at the sentencing hearing to argue on his or her behalf. The Sixth Amendment right to counsel operates essentially the same way at sentencing as it does at trial.

The defendant also has the right to ask the sentencing judge to ignore past convictions that were obtained in violation of the right to counsel. For example, in *United States v. Tucker* (404 U.S. 443 [1972]), the Supreme Court invalidated an individual's 25-year sentence because the sentencing judge arrived at the sentence by considering the defendant's past convictions, for which he was not afforded counsel. The Court stated:

United States v. Tucker (404 U.S. 443 [1972])

> The government is . . . on solid ground in asserting that a sentence imposed by a federal district judge, if within statutory limits, is generally not subject to review. . . . But these general propositions do not decide the case before us. For we deal here not with a sentence imposed in the informed discretion of a trial judge, but with a sentence founded at least in part upon misinformation of constitutional magnitude. As in *Townsend v. Burke*, 334 U.S. 736 (1690), "this prisoner was sentenced on the basis of assumptions concerning his criminal record which were materially untrue." The record in the present case makes evident that the sentencing judge gave specific consideration to the respondent's previous convictions before imposing sentence upon him. Yet it is now clear that two of those convictions were wholly unconstitutional under *Gideon v. Wainwright*, 372 U.S. 335 (1963). (p. 446)

In summary, a defendant enjoys at least three important constitutional rights during the sentencing process: (1) the right not to be put twice in jeopardy; (2) the right to a sentence that conforms with the Eighth Amendment's proscription against cruel and unusual punishment; and (3) the right to counsel at sentencing-related hearings, regardless of his or her ability to afford representation.

APPEALS

An **appeal** occurs when an appellate court, such as one of the federal courts of appeal, examines a lower court's decision in order to determine whether the proper procedure was followed or the correct law was applied. In other words, when a defendant appeals, he or she is claiming that the court made an error. Thus, the appeal guarantees that a defendant who is found guilty can challenge his or her conviction. Further, the appeal guarantees that another judge or panel of judges, disconnected from the initial trial, will make the relevant decision.

Although appealing convictions is an important part of the criminal process, the Supreme Court has never held that doing so is constitutionally permissible. That is, nowhere does the U.S. Constitution specify that a certain number of appeals will be granted to each convicted criminal. In *McKane v. Durston* (153 U.S. 684 [1894]), the Supreme Court stated, "A review by an appellate court of the final judgment in a criminal case, however grave the offense of which the accused is convicted, was not at common law, and is not now, a necessary element of due process of law" (p. 687).

Most appeals are posttrial in nature and filed by the defense, which is why this topic is being discussed at the end of this book. However, in some situations, the defense appeals a court's decision, such as on a motion to suppress evidence, during the trial. And in some instances, the prosecution can even file an appeal. Thus, this chapter will consider three types of appeals: (1) appeals by the defense prior to adjudication; (2) appeals by the defense after adjudication; and (3) appeals by the prosecution. First, however, it is important to review the common types of appeals and their consequences and the important Supreme Court cases dealing with the appellate process (i.e., the procedures courts are required to follow).

Types and Effects of Appeals

Despite the Supreme Court's view that appealing one's conviction is not constitutionally guaranteed, every state and the federal government has rules providing a certain number of appeals to a convicted criminal. At both the state and federal levels, a convicted criminal is usually granted at least one **direct appeal** (also known as an appeal of right).

An appeal of right, or a direct appeal, is automatically granted to the defendant by law. That is, an appeal of right *must* be heard by an appellate court. It is not up to the appellate court to decide whether to hear such an appeal. By contrast, the appellate court can decide, at its own discretion, whether to hear a discretionary appeal. Also, appeals of right are limited, but discretionary appeals can be filed several times, provided they are not redundant.

When a defendant appeals a decision, there are a number of possible consequences. In the typical appeal, the defendant seeks to correct a decision by the lower court that he or she perceives to be in error. In such an instance, the appellate court will either affirm or reverse the lower court's decision. It may also remand (i.e., send back) the case for further proceedings, consistent with its opinion.

Another consequence of an appeal can be a trial *denovo*. When the defendant appeals for a trial *de novo*, he or she is essentially requesting a new, independent trial at the appellate level. Trials *de novo* are rare. Further, they are usually limited to appeals of decisions arising from misdemeanor courts of limited jurisdiction. Rarely, if ever, will a convicted felon succeed in obtaining a trial *de novo* in an appellate court. The primary reason for this is that an appellate court interprets the *law*, not the *facts*. It is the job of the trial court to determine guilt based on the facts.

Whether the defendant seeks a new trial or simply a review of the trial court's decision on some matter, he or she will not necessarily go free if a decision is returned in his or her favor. If, for example, the appellate court considers a lower court's decision not to exclude evidence and decides that the lower court's decision should be reversed, this means the evidence should have been excluded, not that the defendant should be acquitted. For example, in the famous *Miranda* case (*Miranda v. Arizona*, 384 U.S. 436 [1966]), the Supreme Court did not free Ernesto Miranda. Instead, it remanded his case for a new trial. He was subsequently found guilty and sentenced to more than 20 years in prison. It is, therefore, important when reading cases to understand precisely what the reviewing court is deciding. Rarely does an appellate court decide guilt; its job is to interpret the law and review the conduct of the trial court.

What happens to convicted defendants while they are appealing? In almost all cases, they serve out the conditions of their sentences. Assume, for example, that a defendant appeals his guilty conviction on the grounds that he was denied counsel at trial. Assume further that the defendant's appeal has merit. If he was sentenced to prison following trial, he will remain there until the appeal is heard, if it ever is. However, for a select few convicts, the judge will issue a *stay*, which means the convicted individual will not serve time before the appeal is heard. This is a rare situation and usually involves an individual who poses a low flight risk. The fact that most convicted criminals are considered flight risks further explains why stays of imprisonment are rarely granted.

The Appellate Process

Even though the Supreme Court has held that appealing one's conviction is not constitutionally required, it has held, on a number of occasions, that when an appeal is permissible, the government must follow certain procedures. Specifically, the government must ensure that the defendant has (1) access to trial transcripts; (2) the right to counsel; and (3) the right to be free from government retaliation for a successful appeal. Before these procedural issues can be considered, though, the defendant must file *notice of an appeal*. An example of such a notice, from the U.S. District Court for the Southern District of California, is presented in Figure 15.2.

The federal government and every state each has rules that provide a certain number of appeals to someone who has been convicted of a crime.

FIGURE 15.2

Example of a Notice of Appeal

Clear Form

NAME AND ADDRESS OF ATTORNEY

PHONE:

UNITED STATES DISTRICT COURT
SOUTHERN DISTRICT OF CALIFORNIA

TRIAL JUDGE   COURT REPORTER

)
)
)
)   CIVIL NO.
)
(Appellant/Appellee)   Plaintiff   )
)
            vs   )
)
)   NOTICE OF APPEAL   (Civil)
)
_____)
(Appellant/Appellee)   Defendant

        Notice if hereby given that

            Plaintiff   Defendant above named, hereby appeals to the United States

Court of Appeals for the: (check appropriate box)

            Ninth Circuit   Federal Circuit

from the: (check appropriate box)

            Final Judgment   Order (describe)

entered in this proceeding on the _____ day of   .20
Transcripts required   Yes   No.
Date civil complaint filed:

Date: _____
                                                            Signature

Source: U.S. District Court, Southern District of California. Available online: http://www.casd.uscourts. gov/uploads/Attorney%20Assistance/Filing%20Procedures/Forms/Civil/Post%20Judgement%20Forms/ cv_apl.pdf (accessed February 16, 2011).

ENSURING THAT THE DEFENDANT HAS ACCESS TO TRIAL TRANSCRIPTS In *Griffin v. Illinois* (351 U.S. 12 [1956]), the Supreme Court considered whether an Illinois appellate procedure that required the defendant to produce transcripts of the trial—even if he or she could not afford to do so—violated the Constitution. The Court struck down the procedure, claiming that the government cannot impose a restriction on the right to appeal "in a way that discriminates against some convicted defendants on account of their poverty" (p. 18). In a related case, *Entsminger v. Iowa* (386 U.S. 748 [1967]), decided some time later, the Court invalidated a state procedure that allowed defense counsel, rather than an indigent defendant, to decide whether an appeal could continue with an incomplete trial transcript. An actual trial transcript order form is presented in Figure 15.3.

Griffin v. Illinois
(351 U.S. 12 [1956])

ENSURING THE DEFENDANT'S RIGHT TO COUNSEL DURING APPEALS As has been discussed at some length in this text, criminal defendants enjoy the Sixth Amendment right to counsel under a number of circumstances. However, the Sixth Amendment expressly states that this right only applies in *criminal prosecutions*. Even so, the

FIGURE 15.3

Example of a Trial Transcript Order Form

TRANSCRIPT ORDER FORM

PART I - To be completed by appellant within ten days of filing the notice of appeal

Short Title: _____ District: _____

District Court Number: _____ Circuit Court Number: _____

Name of Attorney: _____

Name of Law Firm: _____

Address of Firm: _____

Telephone of Firm: _____ Attorneys for: _____

Name of Court Reporter: _____ Telephone of Reporter: _____

PART II - COMPLETE SECTION A OR SECTION B

SECTION A - I HAVE NOT ORDERED A TRANSCRIPT BECAUSE

[ ] A transcript is not necessary for this appeal, or

[ ] The necessary transcript is already on file in District Court

[ ] The necessary transcript was ordered previously in appeal

number _____

SECTION B - I HEREBY ORDER THE FOLLOWING TRANSCRIPT:

(Specify the date and proceeding in the space below)

Voir dire: _____; Opening Statements _____;

Trial proceedings: _____; Instruction Cnf: _____;

Jury Instructions: _____; Closing Arguments: _____;

Post Trial Motions: _____; Other Proceedings: _____.

Figure 15.3 continued

(Attach additional pages if necessary)

[ ] Appellant will pay the cost of the transcript.
My signature on this form is my agreement to pay for the transcript ordered on this form.

[ ] This case is proceeding under the Criminal Justice Act.

NOTE: Leave to proceed *in forma pauperis* does not entitle appellant to a free transcript. An order of the district court allowing payment for the transcript at government expense must be obtained. See 28 U.S.C. §753(f).

CERTIFICATE OF COMPLIANCE

I certify that I have read the instructions on the reverse of this form and that copies of this transcript order form have been served on the court reporter (if transcript ordered), the Clerk of U.S. District Court, all counsel of record or pro se parties, and the Clerk of the U.S. Court of Appeals for the Tenth Circuit. I further certify that satisfactory arrangements for payment for any transcript ordered have been made with the court reporter(s).

Signature of Attorney/Pro Se: _____   Date:_____

PART III - TO BE COMPLETED BY THE COURT REPORTER

Upon completion, please file one copy with the Clerk of the U.S. Court of Appeals and one copy with the Clerk of the U.S. District Court.

Date arrangements for payment completed: _____

Estimated completion date: _____

Estimated number of pages: _____

I certify that I have read the instructions on the reverse side and that adequate arrangements for payment have been made.

Signature of Court Reporter: _____ Date:_____

A-S Transcript Order Form 497

Source: U.S. District Court, District of Wyoming. Available online: http://www.wyd.uscourts.gov/pdfforms/tranord.pdf (accessed February 16, 2011).

Supreme Court has required that counsel be provided to indigent defendants *on appeal* as a matter of either equal protection or due process. Interestingly, though, the Court has also said that there is no right to self-representation at the appellate stage (see *Martinez v. Court of Appeal*, 528 U.S. 152 [2000]).

Douglas v. California
(372 U.S. 353 [1963])

The first case discussing the right to counsel during the appellate stage was *Douglas v. California* (372 U.S. 353 [1963]). There, the Court concluded that the government must provide an indigent defendant with counsel to assist in his or her appeals of right. The Court stated that "where the merits of the *one and only* appeal an indigent has as of right are decided without benefit of counsel . . . an unconstitutional line has been drawn between rich and poor" (p. 357). The Court has also held that the Constitution requires counsel—particularly, effective counsel—for a nonindigent defendant in his or her appeals of right (see *Evitts v. Lucey*, 469 U.S. 387 [1985]).

Both *Douglas* and *Evitts* dealt with the right to counsel in appeals of right. By contrast, the Supreme Court has held that counsel is not constitutionally guaranteed in *discretionary appeals*. Specifically, in *Ross v. Moffitt* (417 U.S. 600 [1974]), the Court held:

A defendant in respondent's circumstances is not denied meaningful access to the State Supreme Court simply because the State does not appoint counsel

DECISION-MAKING EXERCISE 15.2

Constitutional Rights during the Appeals Process

Judge Lawson has before him two convicted criminals who are giving notice of their intent to appeal their convictions for robbery. The two are indigent and thus pursuing their appeals without the assistance of counsel. They request access to the trial transcripts, but Judge Lawson rules against them, claiming that because, in his view, their appeals are frivolous, it would be a waste of taxpayer funds to supply them with the trial transcripts. Is this action constitutional?

to aid him in seeking review in that court, since at that stage, under North Carolina's multitiered appellate system, he will have, at the very least, a transcript or other record of the trial proceedings, a brief in the Court of Appeals setting forth his claims of error, and frequently an opinion by that court disposing of his case, materials which, when supplemented by any *pro se* submission that might be made, would provide the Supreme Court with an adequate basis for its decision to grant or deny review under its standards of whether the case has "significant public interest," involves "legal principles of major significance," or likely conflicts with a previous Supreme Court decision. (pp. 614–615)

GOVERNMENT RETALIATION FOR SUCCESSFUL DEFENSE APPEALS   Several times, the Supreme Court has dealt with retaliation by the prosecution for a successful defense appeal. The first noteworthy case in this regard was *North Carolina v. Pearce* (395 U.S. 711 [1969]). There, the defendant was reconvicted after a successful appeal and was actually punished more harshly the second time around (note that this is not a double-jeopardy violation—see Chapter 14 and *Green v. United States* [355 U.S. 184 (1957)]). The Court concluded that due process required that the "defendant be freed of apprehension of such a retaliatory motivation on the part of the sentencing judge" (p. 725).

North Carolina v. Pearce (395 U.S. 711 [1969])

In another case, *Blackledge v. Perry* (417 U.S. 21 [1974]), the Court decided against a prosecutor's decision to increase the charge against a defendant who was convicted but appealed to a higher court for a trial *de novo*. The Court held that "upping the ante" in this fashion, simply because the defendant had exercised his right to appeal, was unconstitutional.

By contrast, there have been a few cases in which the Supreme Court has held that vindictiveness cannot be inferred from the judge's or jury's decision to increase a defendant's *sentence* following appeal. For instance, in *Colten v. Kentucky* (407 U.S. 104 [1972]), the Court held that a judge did not act vindictively by increasing the defendant's sentence following his trial *de novo*. And in a similar case, *Chaffin v. Stynchcombe* (412 U.S. 17 [1973]), the Court held that a jury's decision to increase the defendant's sentence in his trial *de novo* was constitutional.

DECISION-MAKING EXERCISE 15.3

Effective Assistance of Counsel during the Appeals Process

June Gale was convicted in state court on several felony counts, and her convictions were affirmed by the intermediate appellate court. Gale then appealed to the state supreme court, but the court dismissed her application for a *writ of certiorari* because the application was not filed within the proper time frame as specified by state law. Gale then sought to have her appeal heard by the U.S. Supreme Court, claiming that she was denied effective assistance of counsel when her attorney missed the deadline for filing a discretionary appeal. Assuming the Supreme Court grants review, how should it decide?

In both *Colten* and *Chaffin*, the sentencing authority was disconnected from the first trial. That is, a different judge sentenced Colten the second time, and a second jury convicted the defendant in *Chaffin* following his trial *de novo*. What if, by contrast, the same judge who presided over the defendant's first trial then decided the defendant's sentence following an appeal? This question was answered in *Texas v. McCullough* (475 U.S. 134 [1986]), in which the Court held that the trial judge had no motivation to be vindictive. Importantly, the defendant's first sentence was decided by a jury. The judge only *presided* over the first trial. Had the judge actually handed down the defendant's sentences in both trials, the second, increased sentence probably would have been considered vindictive.

Summary. In order to make appealing meaningful for a criminal defendant, the Supreme Court has required that three important rights be observed during this process. First, the defendant must be given access to the trial transcripts, even if he or she cannot afford them, in order to make an appeal. Second, the defendant must be given counsel during the appellate process, regardless of whether he or she can afford representation. Finally, neither the judge nor the prosecutor can act in a retaliatory fashion when the defendant decides to appeal. It is not always easy to determine what constitutes retaliation, but it is safe to say that when the judge or prosecutor has an interest in the outcome of a defendant's appeal and, consequently, increases the charge or sentence following the appeal, that action will be considered unconstitutional.

Timing of Defense Appeals

The defense can file an appeal at one of two stages: (1) prior to the reading of the verdict—that is, prior to adjudication; or (2) following adjudication. The typical appeal is filed after adjudication, but there can be reasons to file an appeal prior to adjudication, as well. Both types of appeals are considered in the sections that follow. However, the bulk of the discussion will focus on appeals prior to adjudication because the Supreme Court has imposed far more restrictions on these.

APPEALS PRIOR TO ADJUDICATION An appeal filed prior to adjudication is known as an **interlocutory appeal.** This type of appeal is governed by a complex and confusing body of case law. In simple terms, though, an interlocutory appeal will only succeed if it is important and unrelated to the cause of action. That is, it must deal with a critical constitutional question and have nothing to do with determining the defendant's guilt. Otherwise, the defendant will face what is known as the **final judgment rule,** which generally limits appeals until the court hands down its final judgment as to the defendant's guilt.

DECISION-MAKING EXERCISE 15.4

Retaliation for a Successful Appeal

Here are the facts from an actual case, *Thigpen v. Roberts* (468 U.S. 27 [1984]), as reported by the Supreme Court:

> Following an accident in which he lost control of his car and collided with a pickup truck, killing a passenger in the truck, respondent was charged with four misdemeanors—reckless driving, driving while his license was revoked, driving on the wrong side of the road, and driving while intoxicated. Upon being convicted of these charges in a Mississippi Justice of the Peace Court, he appealed, and the case was transferred to the Circuit Court for a trial de novo. While the appeal was pending, he was indicted for manslaughter based on the same accident, and was convicted.

Note that the convictions were obtained by different prosecutors. Can the second prosecution be considered retaliatory?

Cohen v. Beneficial Industrial Loan Corp. (337 U.S. 541 [1949]) is perhaps the first noteworthy case in which the Supreme Court upheld certain interlocutory appeals: namely, "a small class [of preadjudication decisions] which finally determine claims of right separable from, and collateral to, rights asserted in the action, too important to be denied review and too independent of the cause itself to required that appellate consideration be deferred until the whole case is adjudicated" (p. 546). This quote does not lend itself to easy interpretation, unfortunately. But clarification can be provided by considering some examples of cases in which the Court applied its ruling in *Cohen*. The following two cases illustrate *successful* appeals prior to adjudication, while the subsequent cases focus on *unsuccessful* appeals.

Cohen v. Beneficial Industrial Loan Corp.
(337 U.S. 541 [1949])

In *Stack v. Boyle* (342 U.S. 1 [1951]), the Court held that the defendant could appeal a judge's decision rejecting his argument that bail was excessive, in apparent violation of the Eighth Amendment. The Court believed that the trial judge's decision on this matter was more or less independent of deciding the defendant's guilt. It also felt that delaying appeal until after adjudication would make it pointless; a bail determination after a guilty verdict would have virtually no bearing on anything.

In another case, *Abney v. United States* (431 U.S. 651 [1977]), the Court held that a defendant could appeal a preadjudication order denying dismissal of his indictment on double-jeopardy grounds. The reason for this decision should be fairly obvious: If the protection against double jeopardy is to have any meaning, then a defendant who claims double jeopardy must be able to appeal before the second conviction is handed down. Otherwise, the appellate court would have to consider whether a defendant's Fifth Amendment protection was denied in *hindsight*, which is not a preferable approach.

An example of a preadjudication appeal that did *not* succeed can be found in *Carroll v. United States* 354 U.S. 394 [1957]). There, the Court held that a defendant cannot appeal a decision on a preadjudication search-and-seizure motion until after final adjudication has taken place. In other words, the Court felt that an appeal of a decision addressing evidence critical to the defendant's case is not sufficiently independent of the trial.

Carroll v. United States
354 U.S. 394 [1957])

In another case, *DiBella v. United States* (369 U.S. 121 [1962]), the Court held that a judge's preadjudication decision not to suppress evidence following the defendant's assertion that his Fourth Amendment rights were violated was not appealable until after trial. The Court felt that "appellate intervention makes for truncated presentation of the issue of admissibility, because the legality of the search too often cannot truly be determined until the evidence at the trial has brought all circumstances to light" (p. 129).

Why does all this matter? Uninformed readers of Supreme Court cases often wonder why some cases are appealed after final adjudication and others before. Understanding the restrictions imposed by the Supreme Court on preadjudication appeals is important because it helps readers trace the progress of particular cases. But because preadjudication appeals can impose serious delays, they are usually the exception, rather than the rule.

Despite the obvious time- and resource-saving benefits of restricting preadjudication appeals, requiring that most appeals be filed after trial can have serious consequences for defendants. Many defendants who are found guilty on serious charges go to prison and are forced to pursue their appeals from there. Given that most appeals—especially those that raise constitutional questions and ultimately reach the Supreme Court—take several years, people who are wrongfully convicted can languish in prison. This is one of the weaknesses of the U.S. system of justice.

APPEALS AFTER ADJUDICATION Appeals filed after adjudication are subject to few restrictions. Indeed, there appears to be few Supreme Court cases addressing postadjudication appeals. Nonetheless, it is important to understand that postadjudication appeals are almost limitless in terms of their possible substance. Anything from the trial (i.e., as recorded in the transcripts) that the defense perceives to be in error can be appealed.

The constitutional rights violations that most commonly serve as the basis for an appeal (or appeals) involve convictions obtained by any of these means:

- A plea of guilty that was unlawfully induced or not made voluntarily with understanding of the nature of the charge and the consequences of the plea
- The use of a coerced confession
- The use of evidence gained pursuant to an unconstitutional search or seizure
- The use of evidence obtained pursuant to an unlawful arrest
- A violation of the privilege against self-incrimination
- The unconstitutional failure of the prosecution to disclose to the defendant evidence favorable to him or her
- A violation of the Fifth Amendment's double-jeopardy clause
- Action of a grand jury or petit jury that was unconstitutionally selected and impaneled
- The denial of effective assistance of counsel
- Denial of the rights to a speedy trial and appeal

Appeals by Parties Other than the Defense

Most commonly, an appeal is filed by the defense because the defendant arguably has the most to lose in a criminal trial (i.e., his or her liberty). However, in some limited circumstances, the prosecution or a third party can appeal a judge's decision. The following subsections briefly digress from the focus on the defendant and consider appeals by the prosecution and third parties.

PROSECUTION APPEALS As indicated in Chapter 14, the prosecution is usually barred from appealing a defendant's conviction because of the double-jeopardy clause of the Fifth Amendment. Trial court rulings besides those deciding the issue of guilt, however, can sometimes be appealed by the prosecution. As the Supreme Court stated in *Carroll v. United States* (354 U.S. 394 [1957]), "[A]ppeals by the government in criminal cases are something unusual, exceptional, not favored. The history shows resistance of the Court to the opening of an appellate route for the Government until it was plainly provided by the Congress, and after that a close restriction of its uses to those authorized by statute" (p. 400). In other words, appeals by the prosecution are possible in certain situations but only as authorized by state or federal law.

One statute that permits appeal by the prosecution can be found at the federal level. It is found in 18 U.S.C. Section 3731 and provides for interlocutory prosecution appeal of a district court's decision to suppress or exclude evidence from trial. This type of appeal is permissible because if the defendant is acquitted at trial, the prosecution

---

DECISION-MAKING EXERCISE 15.5

An Appeal Prior to Adjudication

Jennifer Couture sued the Albuquerque Public Schools system and several of its employees for repeatedly placing her emotionally disturbed kindergartener in "timeout" for acting up in class. The U.S. District Court for the District of New Mexico sided with Couture in its decision to deny qualified immunity to the school officials (qualified immunity was discussed in Chapter 2). The school officials are now seeking to appeal this decision. Can they? Note that there is no "final judgment" as yet.

will not likely appeal the defendant's conviction because of the double-jeopardy clause. The defendants cannot assert double-jeopardy protection at a preadjudication hearing, which is why it behooves the prosecution to appeal before the end of the trial. Indeed, many of the Supreme Court cases encountered in this book and elsewhere came before the Court because the prosecution disagreed with a trial judge's decision to exclude or suppress evidence.

Other prosecution appeals, besides those addressing decisions to exclude or suppress evidence, are severely restricted because of double jeopardy. These restrictions were discussed in the previous chapter. The most common type of prosecution appeal, however, is one addressing a judge's decision on whether to permit or exclude evidence that the prosecution wants to use against the accused. In criminal procedure, when a judge excludes or suppresses evidence, it is because the police acted in violation of some constitutional provision. Note, however, that evidence may not be admissible because it is irrelevant, incompetent, immaterial, or otherwise limited.

THIRD-PARTY APPEALS   Third parties—that is, individuals besides the prosecution and the defense—are sometimes permitted to appeal. For example, in *Cobbledick v. United States* (309 U.S. 323 [1940]), the Supreme Court held that a person can appeal a court order, such as a subpoena, but only if he or she has been found in contempt of court for failing to abide by that order. The Court said that a decision to the contrary "would forever preclude review of the witness' claim, for his alternatives are to abandon the claim or languish in jail" (p. 328).

Cobbledick v. United States   (309 U.S. 323 [1940])

Other varieties of third-party appeals are conceivable but rare. Only when a trial judge's decision impinges on another person's rights will a third-party appeal succeed. An appeal by the media to overturn a judge's gag order may be permissible on First Amendment grounds, but there appears to be no Supreme Court cases addressing this possibility. The number of third-party appeals pales in comparison to the number filed by defendants, either prior to or after adjudication.

When Appeals Do Not Succeed

As indicated already, an appeal may not succeed simply because the appellate court is unwilling to hear it, as is the case with many discretionary appeals. However, even when the appellate court agrees to hear an appeal and even when the court agrees with the defendant's position, it may decide that the defendant should remain in prison or otherwise receive the same sentence. In such an instance, the appellate court is saying that the trial court's decision is a **harmless error**, a mistake at the trial level that has little practical consequence in terms of deciding whether the defendant is guilty or innocent.

CONSTITUTIONAL VERSUS NONCONSTITUTIONAL ERRORS   Deciding what constitutes harmless error requires first determining what type of error is alleged. Two types of errors can be discerned: (1) constitutional and (2) nonconstitutional. *Constitutional errors*

DECISION-MAKING EXERCISE 15.6
A Prosecution Appeal

Martin Katt, who was indicted for federal drug charges, moved twice before trial and once during trial to dismiss the charges, claiming that the pre-indictment delay was unconstitutional. Once the government finished presenting its case, the court decided in Katt's favor and granted his motion for a dismissal. The government appealed the judge's decision to dismiss Katt's case. Should the prosecution's appeal be heard?

result from constitutional rights violations, such as denying the accused the right to confront adverse witnesses at trial. *Nonconstitutional errors* do not have constitutional implications. An example of a nonconstitutional error is a trial court's decision to admit hearsay evidence; there is no constitutional prohibition against hearsay evidence in the courtroom.

Kotteakos v. United States (328 U.S. 750 [1946])

Once a decision has been made as to the type of harmless error alleged, then the appropriate test for determining whether the error is harmless must be used. Two Supreme Court cases are helpful in this regard. The first, *Kotteakos v. United States* (328 U.S. 750 [1946]), set the test for deciding what constitutes a nonconstitutional error. The second case, *Chapman v. California* (386 U.S. 18 [1967]), set the test for constitutional error.

In *Kotteakos*, the Supreme Court held that a nonconstitutional harmless error occurs when it does not influence the jury but instead has a "very slight effect" on the outcome of the trial. In other words, "[I]f one cannot say, with fair assurance, after pondering all that happened without stripping the erroneous action from the whole, that the judgment was not substantially swayed by the error, it is impossible to conclude that substantial rights were not affected" (p. 765).

In *Chapman v. California*, discussed earlier, the Court concluded that the test for a constitutional harmless error requires the state to prove "beyond a reasonable doubt that the error complained of did not contribute to the verdict obtained" (p. 24). This test is reserved for what could be termed *modest* violations of constitutional rights. However, in situations in which a fundamental constitutional right has been violated, no harmless error test is required. Each scenario is considered in the next two subsections.

A REVIEW OF RELEVANT CASES   Since this book is geared toward constitutional criminal procedure, this section considers only cases in which the Supreme Court has applied the so-called *Chapman* test for determining constitutional harmless error. First, two cases are considered in which the Court held that the error *was not* harmless, and then one case is considered in which the Court held that the error *was* harmless.

In *Chapman v. California*, the Court considered whether a harmless error resulted when the prosecutor's closing argument repeatedly referred to the defendant's refusal to take the stand and testify. (As discussed earlier in this text, a jury cannot draw adverse inferences from a defendant's refusal to testify.) The Court reversed the defendant's conviction, reasoning that "though the case in which this occurred presented a reasonably strong 'circumstantial web of evidence' against petitioners, it was also a case in which, absent the constitutionally forbidden comments, honest fair-minded jurors might very well have brought in not-guilty verdicts" (pp. 25–26).

Similarly, in *Connecticut v. Johnson* (460 U.S. 73 [1983]), the Court refused to conclude that the judge's flawed instructions to the jury could be considered harmless. In that case, the judge instructed the jury that it could presume intent on the part of the defendant for a specific intent crime (i.e., a crime that requires the state to prove a specific type of intent). This error was considered so serious that, according to the Court, it "permitted the jury to convict respondent without ever examining the evidence concerning an element of the crime charged" (p. 88).

By contrast, an example of a harmless error can be seen in *Milton v. Wainwright* (407 U.S. 371 [1972]). There, the defendant claimed that his confession should not have been admissible because it was obtained following a conversation with an undercover police officer who was posing as the defendant's fellow prisoner. The prosecution was able to prove beyond a reasonable doubt that the confession did not constitute error because three other confessions made by the defendant were admissible. In other words, the Court concluded that the confession resulting from the prison conversation was a harmless error.

SERIOUS CONSTITUTIONAL ERROR   In some cases, the Supreme Court has concluded that an error was so serious as to require automatic reversal of the defendant's conviction. In such a case, the prosecution is not required to prove beyond a reasonable doubt that the error is harmless. Instead, the error is automatically presumed to be harmful because of its serious nature. In fact, in *Chapman v. California*, the Court concluded that some errors may involve "rights so basic to a fair trial that their infraction can never be treated as harmless error" (p. 23).

The Court has stated that serious constitutional errors—those that cannot be considered harmless—arise in the following specific circumstances:

- The defendant's confession was coerced (*Payne v. Arkansas*, 356 U.S. 560 [1958]).
- The right to counsel at trial was violated (*Gideon v. Wainwright*, 372 U.S. 335 [1963]).
- The right to an impartial judge was violated (*Tumey v. Ohio*, 273 U.S. 510 [1927]).
- The right to a speedy trial was violated (*Strunk v. United States*, 412 U.S. 434 [1973]).
- The defendant was put in double jeopardy (*Price v. Georgia*, 398 U.S. 323 [1970]).
- The right to a representative jury was violated (*Taylor v. Louisiana*, 419 U.S. 522 [1975]).

Retroactivity of Decisions from Appeals

A successful appeal clearly benefits the party who filed it. But what about third parties? In particular, should third parties who have been convicted be allowed to benefit from a successful appeal by another defendant? This question has been posed because at times, several defendants are filing similar appeals. The Supreme Court has been forced to decide to what extent its decision on one defendant's appeal should apply only to that person or have a more sweeping effect and benefit several defendants. This issue, **retroactivity,** is concerned with the extent to which a decision should be applied to each defendant in a similar predicament.

On one level, it seems fair to treat all defendants with similar appeals the same. However, the consequences of doing so could be enormous. Multiple reversals, for example, could require many new trials for several defendants, imposing a serious cost on the justice system. In light of this concern, the Court has handed down several important decisions. First, in *Linkletter v. Walker* (381 U.S. 618 [1965]), the Court held that whether a constitutional ruling on a defendant's appeal should be considered retroactive depends on the nature of the appeal. Next, in *United States v. Johnson* (457 U.S. 537 [1982]), the Court held that retroactivity depends on the *timing* of all appeals in question; in other words, all defendants who have appeals on file at the same time should benefit.

Third, in *Stovall v. Denno* (388 U.S. 293 [1967]), the Court handed down a specific test for determining whether a decision of constitutional magnitude should be retroactive. It requires determining "(a) the purpose to be served by the new standards, (b) the extent

---

DECISION-MAKING EXERCISE 15.7

A Harmless Error?

At Pat Warren's trial on charges of kidnapping and transporting women across state lines for immoral purposes, the victims testified that he repeatedly raped and sodomized them. The defense attorney argued that the women consented and that they had possibly misidentified Warren. Warren did not testify. During the prosecutor's closing argument, the defense attorney objected when the prosecutor began to comment on the fact that Warren never challenged the kidnapping, the interstate transportation of the victims, or the sexual acts. The defense then moved for a mistrial, claiming that Warren's Fifth Amendment protection against self-incrimination was violated when the prosecutor said what he did to the jury. How should the appellate court decide?

of the reliance by law enforcement authorities on the old standards, and (c) the effect on the administration of justice of a retroactive application of the new standards" (p. 297). This has come to be known as the *Linkletter-Stovall test*, and an example of it in application can be found in the *Stovall* case itself. There, the Court considered whether its decision in *United States v. Wade* (388 U.S. 218 [1967]), which required counsel at postindictment, pretrial lineups, should be retroactive to other defendants appealing violations of that decision. Surprisingly, the Court held that *Wade* should *not* be retroactive because even though such a decision would benefit certain defendants, it would mean that lineups could be challenged on due process grounds. In other words, according to the second element of the *Linkletter-Stovall* test, law enforcement was not heavily reliant on the *Wade* decision; lineups are governed by other constitutional provisions.

The Supreme Court also felt that making *Wade* retroactive would bog down the courts with many new trials, which corresponds to the third element of the *Linkletter-Stovall* test. Finally, the Court felt that the purpose of *Wade* was to ensure fairness at lineups, but it also felt that its decision was not *necessary* to ensure fairness; that is, a fair lineup can be held without the assistance of counsel. In short, the Court felt that its decision in *Wade* did not serve a purpose quite as lofty as, say, guaranteeing the right to counsel at trial, was not heavily relied on by the police, and would have a significant impact on the administration of justice if applied retroactively.

The Supreme Court has also refused to apply its decisions retroactively in other important cases already discussed in this text, including but not limited to *Mapp v. Ohio* (367 U.S. 643 [1961]), which requires that the exclusionary rule be recognized by the states, and *Katz v. United States* (389 U.S. 347 [1967]), which prohibits nonconsensual electronic eavesdropping without probable cause and a warrant. By contrast, the Court *has* held that the failure to provide counsel in misdemeanor trials (see *Berry v. Cincinnati*, 414 U.S. 29 [1973]) and also to require unanimous verdicts in six-member juries (see *Brown v. Louisiana*, 447 U.S. 323 [1980]), among other errors, *should* be retroactive.

In *Griffith v. Kentucky* (479 U.S. 314 [1987]), the Supreme Court finally clarified retroactivity in the appeals context. There, it held that any new rule it announces (i.e., one that does not involve applying precedent to a particular situation) should be retroactive to all other cases pending review at the time. The reasoning offered by the Court in this case was far more straightforward and sensible than that applied in *Linkletter, Johnson,* and *Stovall*: Failure to apply new constitutional decisions retroactively to other pending appeals would have the unfair consequence of benefiting the one individual whose appeal was selected for review by the Supreme Court. In other words, failure to retroactively apply new rules would be "unfair," because it would benefit only one individual, not others similarly situated.

It is important to note that *Griffith* applied to cases "pending review at that time." Contrast that with final judgments. Final judgments are those in which "a judgment of conviction has been rendered, the availability of appeal exhausted, and the time for a petition for *certiorari* elapsed or a petition for *certiorari* finally denied" (*Griffith*, p. 321). In contrast, pending review means that an appeal has not yet been heard. Why should retroactivity not apply to final judgments? There are two answers. One is that *habeas corpus* petitions can be filed (the topic of the next section). Another is that allowing new rules to be retroactive to final judgments opens the proverbial can of worms. Justice Harlan expressed this point eloquently in *Mackey v. United States* (401 U.S. 667 [1971], p. 690):

> It is, I believe, a matter of fundamental import that there be a visible end to the litigable aspect of the criminal process. Finality in the criminal law is an end which must always be kept in plain view.

HABEAS CORPUS

As already noted in this chapter, the most common method of challenging one's conviction is to appeal. However, filing an appeal or several appeals is not the only avenue of redress for a person who is wrongfully convicted. Another avenue is by means of a *habeas corpus* petition filed with the federal courts. This is known as a *collateral attack* and is a constitutional right.[3]

    Habeas corpus (Latin for "you have the body") plays out as follows: First, the accused individual petitions one of the federal district courts and asks the court to issue a *writ of habeas corpus*, which literally means "you have the body." Portions of an actual petition for *habeas corpus* form are reprinted in Figure 15.4. Then, if the court decides to issue the writ, the petitioner is brought before the court so the constitutionality of his or her confinement can be reviewed.

FIGURE 15.4

Example of a Petition for a Writ of *Habeas Corpus* Form

PETITION UNDER 28 U.S.C. § 2254 FOR WRIT OF
***HABEAS CORPUS* BY A PERSON IN STATE CUSTODY**

United States District Court	District:	
Name (under which you were convicted):		Docket or Case No.:
Place of Confinement:		Prisoner No.:
Petitioner (include the name under which you were convicted)	Respondent (authorized person having custody of petitioner) v.	
The Attorney General of the State of		

PETITION

1. **(a)** Name and location of court that entered the judgment of conviction you are challenging:

    (b) Criminal docket or case number (if you know):

2. **(a)** Date of the judgment of conviction (if you know):
    (b) Date of sentencing:

3. Length of sentence:

4. In this case, were you convicted on more than one count or of more than one crime? ❒ Yes ❒ No

Figure 15.4 continued

---

[3] U.S. Constitution, Article I, Section 9, Clause 2.

5. Identify all crimes of which you were convicted and sentenced in this case:

6.   **(a)** What was your plea? (Check one)

        ❑ (1) Not guilty   ❑ (3) Nolo contendere (no contest)

        ❑ (2) Guilty   ❑ (4) Insanity plea

   (b) If you entered a guilty plea to one count or charge and a not guilty plea to another count or charge, what did you plead guilty to and what did you plead not guilty to?

   (c) If you went to trial, what kind of trial did you have? (Check one)

      ❑ Jury   ❑ Judge only

7. Did you testify at a pretrial hearing, trial, or a post-trial hearing?

      ❑   Yes   ❑   No

8. Did you appeal from the judgment of conviction?

      ❑   Yes   ❑   No

9. If you did appeal, answer the following:

   (a) Name of court:

   (b) Docket or case number (if you know):

   (c) Result:

   (d) Date of result (if you know):

   (e) Citation to the case (if you know):

   (f) Grounds raised:

   (g) Did you seek further review by a higher state court?   ❑   Yes   ❑   No

      If yes, answer the following:

      (1) Name of court:

      (2) Docket or case number (if you know):

      (3) Result:

      (4) Date of result (if you know):

      (5) Citation to the case (if you know):

      (6) Grounds raised:

   (h) Did you file a petition for certiorari in the United States Supreme Court?   ❑   Yes   ❑   No

If yes, answer the following:

    (1) Docket or case number (if you know):

    (2) Result:

    (3) Date of result (if you know):

    (4) Citation to the case (if you know):

10. Other than the direct appeals listed above, have you previously filed any other petitions, applications, or motions concerning this judgment of conviction in any state court?   ❐   Yes ❐   No

11. If your answer to Question 10 was "Yes," give the following information:

  (a)   **(1)** Name of court:

      (2) Docket or case number (if you know):

      (3) Date of filing (if you know):

      (4) Nature of the proceeding:

      (5) Grounds raised:

      (6) Did you receive a hearing where evidence was given on your petition, application, or motion?
        ❐   Yes   ❐   No

      (7) Result:

      (8) Date of result (if you know):

  (b) If you filed any second petition, application, or motion, give the same information:

      (1) Name of court:

      (2) Docket or case number (if you know):

      (3) Date of filing (if you know):

      (4) Nature of the proceeding:

      (5) Grounds raised:

      (6) Did you receive a hearing where evidence was given on your petition, application, or motion?
        ❐   Yes   ❐   No

      (7) Result:

      (8) Date of result (if you know):

  (c) If you filed any third petition, application, or motion, give the same information:

      (1) Name of court:

      (2) Docket or case number (if you know):

      (3) Date of filing (if you know):

      (4) Nature of the proceeding:

      (5) Grounds raised:

      (6) Did you receive a hearing where evidence was given on your petition, application, or motion?
        ❐   Yes   ❐   No

Figure 15.4 continued

(7) Result:

(8) Date of result (if you know):

(d) Did you appeal to the highest state court having jurisdiction over the action taken on your petition, application, or motion?

(1) First petition: ❐ Yes ❐ No

(2) Second petition: ❐ Yes ❐ No

(3) Third petition: ❐ Yes ❐ No

(e) If you did not appeal to the highest state court having jurisdiction, explain why you did not:

12. For this petition, state every ground on which you claim that you are being held in violation of the Constitution, laws, or treaties of the United States. Attach additional pages if you have more than four grounds. State the facts supporting each ground.

CAUTION: To proceed in the federal court, you must ordinarily first exhaust (use up) your available state-court remedies on each ground on which you request action by the federal court. Also, if you fail to set forth all the grounds in this petition, you may be barred from presenting additional grounds at a later date.

Source: Administrative Office of the U.S. Courts. Available online: http://www.uscourts.gov/forms/ao241.pdf (accessed February 16, 2011).

Given that the Supreme Court hears a limited number of cases each term, it is unlikely that it will issue a writ. This leaves the defendant with the option of petitioning the federal district court. Also, it is important to remember that a *habeas corpus* petition must be limited to a constitutional claim. Finally, it is totally within the discretion of the court that is petitioned to decide whether the writ will be issued. The Constitution provides that the "privilege of the Writ of *Habeas Corpus* shall not be suspended," but this has been interpreted to mean that a defendant can *submit habeas petitions*, not that the defendant will necessarily get his or her day in court.

Sanders v. United States
(373 U.S. 1 [1963])

On several occasions, the Supreme Court has emphasized the importance of the writ. For example, in *Sanders v. United States* (373 U.S. 1 [1963]), the Court emphasized that "[c]onventional notions of finality of litigation have no place where life or liberty is at stake and infringement of constitutional rights is alleged" (p. 8). Similarly, in *Kaufman v. United States* (394 U.S. 217 [1969]), the Court held that the writ is necessary to provide "adequate protection of constitutional rights" (p. 226).

Stone v. Powell
(428 U.S. 465 [1976])

However, more recently, the Court has intimated that a *habeas corpus* review should be qualified. In particular, it has held that writs should not be liberally issued for claims arising from state courts. As the Court stated in *Stone v. Powell* (428 U.S. 465 [1976]), "Despite differences in institutional environment and the unsympathetic attitude to federal constitutional claims of some state judges in years past, we are unwilling to assume that there now exists a general lack of appropriate sensitivity to constitutional rights in the trial and appellate courts of the several States" (p. 494, n. 35).

These conflicting perspectives have influenced a number of important Supreme Court cases addressing the constitutional right to *habeas corpus*. Recently, the Court has placed limitations on the scope of the writ. Also, the Antiterrorism and Effective Death Penalty Act of 1996 has had important effects on *habeas corpus*. The following sections focus on some of these restrictions and modifications.

Restrictions on the Right to *Habeas Corpus*

The Supreme Court has restricted the right to *habeas corpus* in a number of ways. First, it has limited the types of claims that can succeed. Second, the Court has held that *habeas* review may not be granted if the petitioner fails to submit a claim within the time frame specified by state law. Third, it is generally necessary for a convicted individual to exhaust all state remedies before a federal *habeas* review will be granted. Finally, restrictions have been imposed in situations in which a prisoner filed multiple *habeas* petitions.

TYPES OF CLAIMS FOR WHICH WRITS WILL NOT BE ISSUED   Several types of *habeas corpus* petitions will not succeed, according to the Supreme Court. The first was announced in *Stone v. Powell*, discussed earlier. In that case, the Court held that "where the State has provided an opportunity for full and fair litigation of a Fourth Amendment claim," a federal court should not issue a writ of *habeas corpus*. Unfortunately, the Court has not been entirely clear as to how this first rule should be applied. For example, in *Jackson v. Virginia* (443 U.S. 307 [1979]), the Court granted *habeas* review of a claim alleging that the defendant's conviction was not based on proof beyond a reasonable doubt—mainly because it was not a Fourth Amendment claim. However, in *Kimmelman v. Morrison* (477 U.S. 365 [1986]), the Court did grant review of a Sixth Amendment claim of ineffective assistance of counsel.

Second, the Court held in *Teague v. Lane* (489 U.S. 288 [1989]) that unless a claim is dictated by precedent, it cannot be heard on *habeas* review. In other words, if *habeas* review would result in a new rule, then review is impermissible. Only claims based on existing case law should be granted review. The Court did announce two exceptions to this rule, however. If the claim questions the jurisdiction of the trial court or is central to the accused's guilt or innocence, then it can be granted review in federal court.

Teague v. Lane
(489 U.S. 288 [1989])

Next, *habeas* review will only be granted if it raises a federal constitutional question. In other words, review will only be granted to cases in much the same way the Supreme Court decides to hear a case: It must raise a constitutional question. This ruling was applied in *Herrera v. Collins* (506 U.S. 390 [1993]), in which the petitioner claimed that his death sentence should be vacated because new evidence pointed to his innocence. The Court held that the claim could not be heard on *habeas* review because it did not raise a constitutional question. The Court explained that "[i]n light of the historical availability of new trials . . . and the contemporary practice in the States, we cannot say that Texas' refusal to entertain petitioner's newly discovered evidence eight years after his convictions transgresses a principle of fundamental fairness" (p. 411).

Herrera v. Collins
(506 U.S. 390 [1993])

A *habeas corpus* review will sometimes be granted to a nonconstitutional claim but not if it fails to point to "an omission inconsistent with the rudimentary demands of fair procedure." That was the Court's decision in *Hill v. United States* (368 U.S. 424 [1962]). This is therefore the fourth limitation on *habeas* review; a nonconstitutional claim that does not allege that a fundamental defect took place at trial will not succeed. Admittedly, this ruling is something of a double negative, but it is stated in this fashion deliberately. That is, the ruling is intended to emphasize that nonconstitutional claims rarely succeed. The ones that *do* succeed must argue that a serious miscarriage of justice took place at trial.

Hill v. United States
(368 U.S. 424 [1962])

The fifth type of petition that will not be granted review is similar, in several respects, to the one just described. It is the *harmless error exception*—the same one encountered in the previous discussion of appeals. Recall that the appropriate test for determining whether a constitutional error is harmless is whether it is "harmless beyond a reasonable doubt" (*Chapman v. California*). By contrast, the test for nonconstitutional error is whether it has a "substantial and injurious effect or influence in determining the jury's verdict" (*Kotteakos v. United States*, 328 U.S. 750 [1946]). The Court has since held that the test announced in *Kotteakos* should be applied to *habeas corpus* petitions, as well. Such was the decision reached in *Brecht v. Abrahamson* (507 U.S. 619 [1993]) and recently reaffirmed in *Fry v. Pliler* (No. 06-5247 [2007]).

DECISION-MAKING EXERCISE 15.8

A Constitutional Question?

Ling Yu was convicted of first-degree murder and sentenced to death. The evidence against her consisted of the body of the victim, the murder weapon, and testimony from several witnesses that Yu spoke openly about wanting to kill the victim. Three years after her conviction, while she was awaiting execution on death row, new evidence was discovered, suggesting that Yu may not have committed the murder.

The new evidence came in the form of a witness who was prepared to testify that Yu was with her in a different city on the night of the murder. Assume that Yu exhausts all state-level appellate mechanisms, to no avail, and decides to petition a federal district court for a writ of *habeas corpus*. Will her petition be heard?

Finally, in the case of petitions from state prisoners, a federal court will not issue a writ of *habeas corpus* unless it first determines that the confinement violates federal law (*Wilson v. Corcoran*, No. 10-91 [2010]). In other words, *habeas corpus* is not the proper remedy for violations of state law.

RESTRICTIONS BASED ON THE TIMING OF A CLAIM A *habeas corpus* petition typically must be filed within a certain specified time period after the trial or sentencing hearing. When a defendant fails to appeal or file a *habeas* petition within that period, he or she is said to have *defaulted* or given up the right to appeal or to petition for *habeas* review. For a time, when the Supreme Court was trying to decide whether *habeas* review should be granted following default, it focused on the state rule or statute that imposed the time restriction (see, e.g., *Daniels v. Allen*, 344 U.S. 443 [1953]). If the statute was problematic, then review could be granted. Not satisfied with this approach, the Court then turned its attention to whether the defendant's default was intentional or accidental (*Fay v. Noia*, 372 U.S. 391 [1963]). Later cases required the defendant to demonstrate why a lack of *habeas* review, due to default, would be prejudicial to his or her case (e.g., *Davis v. United States*, 411 U.S. 233 [1973]).

Kuhlmann v. Wilson
(477 U.S. 436 [1986])

The current standard for determining whether *habeas* review should be granted is known as the *actual innocence standard*. It was first referenced in *Murray v. Carrier* (477 U.S. 478 [1986]) and then again in *Sawyer v. Whitley* (505 U.S. 333 [1992]). In *Kuhlmann v. Wilson* (477 U.S. 436 [1986]), the Court set a specific standard: "[T]he prisoner must show a fair probability that, in light of all the evidence, including that alleged to have been illegally admitted (but with due regard to any unreliability of it) and evidence tenably claimed to have been wrongly excluded or to have become available only after the trial, the trier of the facts would have entertained a reasonable doubt of his guilt" (p. 454, n. 17). In other words, when a prisoner has failed to file a *habeas* petition in a timely manner, he or she may still succeed in doing so provided that the petition sets forth sufficient facts as to his or her actual innocence.

Importantly, the appropriate standard of proof for granting review under this new rule is that there be a *fair probability* of the prisoner's innocence (see *Kuhlmann v. Wilson*). A different standard has been imposed in death penalty cases, however. Specifically, in *Schlup v. Delo* (513 U.S. 298 [1995]), the Court held that in order to be granted a *habeas* review, an individual convicted of a capital crime must show that "it is more likely than not that no reasonable juror would have convicted [the petitioner]" (p. 327). In *House v. Bell* (547 U.S. 518 [2006]), the Court found that a petitioner met this burden when, among other things, the petitioner provided that semen from a murder victim came from her husband, not the petitioner.

Summary. When a person is convicted of a crime, he or she is generally given a limited amount of time in which to file an appeal and/or a *habeas corpus* petition. Failure

DECISION-MAKING EXERCISE 15.9

Timing of a *Habeas Corpus* Petition

A man was convicted of the murder of a fellow prison inmate and sentenced to death. He claimed in a *habeas corpus* petition that a constitutional error had been committed at his trial and thus deprived the jury of critical evidence that would have established his innocence. In particular, he claimed that his defense attorney had acted ineffectively by failing to call witnesses who could testify to his innocence. The district court refused to consider the man's claim, holding that he could not satisfy the threshold showing of actual innocence. Was the district court correct in requiring this?

to do so in the required time period is known as *default*. In almost all cases, once a convicted individual has defaulted, he or she has no other means by which to challenge conviction. However, the Supreme Court has held that when a *habeas* petition goes to a prisoner's innocence and he or she can show a fair probability of innocence, review can be granted. (See the "Appeals" section for similar restrictions on appeals.) The higher standard of "more likely than not" is required for death penalty *habeas* petitions.

IMPORTANCE OF EXHAUSTING STATE REMEDIES   Before *habeas corpus* becomes an option, a convicted criminal typically must exhaust all available state-level appeals. As the Supreme Court stated in *Ex parte Hawk* (321 U.S. 114 [1944]), "[O]rdinarily an application for habeas corpus by one detained under a state court judgment of conviction will be entertained . . . only after all state remedies available, including all appellate remedies in the state courts and in this Court by appeal or writ of certiorari, have been exhausted" (pp. 116–117).

Most prisoners are denied *habeas* review until they have exhausted state-level remedies because imposing such a restriction ensures that the states can correct federal constitutional violations. However, if a federal court sees fit to grant a *habeas* petition before a prisoner has exhausted all available state-level appeals, that is its prerogative (see *Granberry v. Greer*, 481 U.S. 129 [1987]).

There is even a federal statute addressing *habeas corpus*. It states that *habeas corpus* is not available to state prisoners "unless it appears that the applicant has exhausted the remedies available in the courts of the State, or that there is either an absence of available State corrective process or the existence of circumstances rendering such process ineffective to protect the rights of the prisoner" (28 U.S.C. Section 2254[b]). Unfortunately, the meanings of some of the terms in this statute are not entirely clear. Thus, it is useful to consider the Supreme Court's response to some pertinent questions stemming from Section 2254(b).

First, what is the meaning of *available state corrective process*? The Court answered this question in *Fay v. Noia* (372 U.S. 391 [1963]), in which it held that prisoners must pursue appeals through all state-level appellate courts. Further, it held that prisoners do not necessarily have to appeal all the way to a state supreme court to satisfy the exhaustion requirement. In other words, a prisoner *can* be said to have exhausted state-level remedies even if he or she does not appeal all the way to the state supreme court. However, the Supreme Court has held that a prisoner must pursue direct as well as discretionary appeals (see previous discussion). The case from which this conclusion emerged was *O'Sullivan v. Boerckel* (526 U.S. 838 [1999]).

Fay v. Noia
(372 U.S. 391 [1963])

Section 2254(b) also mentions that state-level remedies must be pursued unless they are ineffective. What is an *ineffective* state-level remedy? In *Duckworth v. Serrano* (454 U.S. 1 [1981]), the Court held that exhaustion is not necessary if there is "no opportunity to obtain redress in state court or if the corrective process is so clearly deficient as to render futile any effort to obtain relief" (p. 3). What does this mean, precisely? For example, if a state prohibits all appeals of criminal cases (which is clearly unlikely), then that state's remedy can be considered ineffective because it is effectively absent.

RESTRICTIONS ON FILING MULTIPLE *HABEAS CORPUS* PETITIONS　Prisoners often file several *habeas corpus* petitions. (Some prisoners do not have much else to do while in custody.) Thus, the issue of filing multiple petitions has come before the Supreme Court more than once. In one of the more important cases, *Sanders v. United States*, the Court permitted successive petitions in which the same issues were raised. To do so, though, the petitioner must show that he or she was not given a "full or fair" hearing on the petition the first time around or that there has been "an intervening change in the law or some other justification for having failed to raise a crucial point or argument in the prior application" (p. 17). Later, in *Kuhlmann v. Wilson*, the Court held that successive petitions raising the same issues must be supplemented with a "colorable showing of factual innocence" (p. 436) (i.e., a fairly clear indication that the petitioner is possibly innocent). And in *Magwood v. Patterson* (No. 09-158 [2010]), the Court held that when a person is resentenced after receiving *habeas* relief, a subsequent *habeas* claim is not considered successive. The key restriction is that the second claim raise new issues.

The Supreme Court has also decided to seriously restrict successive petitions making *different* claims. For instance, if a prisoner accidentally fails to raise a claim the first time around, it will probably not be permitted the second time. Also, a successive petition that raises different issues from the previous one should be dismissed if "the applicant has . . . on the earlier application deliberately withheld the newly asserted ground *or* otherwise abused the writ" (*McCleskey v. Zant*, 499 U.S. 467 [1991], p. 486; see also *Slack v. McDaniel*, 529 U.S. 473 [2000]).

When a *Habeas Corpus* Proceeding Resembles a Trial

To reiterate, an appellate court cannot decide issues of fact. Instead, it is to focus on the extent to which proper rules and procedures were followed at the trial court level. If, as indicated earlier, an appellate court was permitted to be a fact finder, like a trial court, then its decisions would raise double-jeopardy problems. For example, if an appellate court acquitted a defendant because of an improperly obtained confession, then the prosecution's attempt to retry the defendant using other evidence (e.g., eyewitness testimony) would be tantamount to trying the defendant twice for the same crime. By contrast, an appellate court reviewing a *habeas corpus* petition *can* engage in fact-finding under certain limited circumstances. That is, a *habeas* court can effectively become a trial court when reviewing a prisoner's constitutional challenge to his or her confinement.

The leading case in this area is *Townsend v. Sain* (372 U.S. 293 [1963]). In that case, the Supreme Court identified six specific events that can permit a *habeas* court

---

DECISION-MAKING EXERCISE 15.10

Were All State Remedies Exhausted?

A man was convicted of murder in a trial court and appealed his conviction to the court of appeals, claiming that the trial judge's instructions to the jury were erroneous. The court of appeals affirmed the lower court's ruling. The man then appealed to the state supreme court. It, too, affirmed the man's conviction. He then petitioned the federal district court for a writ of *habeas corpus*, claiming that his constitutional right to due process was violated by the judge's erroneous instructions. He did not, however, raise the due process issue in any of the state-level appeals. Should his petition be heard?

to engage in independent fact-finding. The Court held that a fact-finding hearing should take place on *habeas* review only when

> (1) the merits of the factual dispute were not resolved in the state hearing; (2) the state factual determination is not fairly supported by the record as a whole; (3) the fact-finding procedure employed by the state court was not adequate to afford a full and fair hearing; (4) there is a substantial allegation of newly discovered evidence; (5) material facts were not adequately developed at the state court hearing; or (6) for any reason it appears that the state trier of fact did not afford the habeas applicant a full and fair hearing. (p. 314)

Importantly, a *habeas* court cannot engage in independent fact-finding if the petitioner deliberately bypasses state-level appellate mechanisms (*Keeney v. Tamayo-Reyes*, 504 U.S. 1 [1992]). In other words, the petitioner must exhaust state-level remedies before fact-finding can take place at a *habeas* proceeding. Taken together, *Townsend* and *Keeney* suggest that it is exceedingly difficult for a prisoner to succeed in having his or her guilt or innocence determined on *habeas* review.

The Right to Counsel in the *Habeas Corpus* Context

Earlier in this chapter, it was shown that the Supreme Court has guaranteed the right to counsel in direct appeals of right but not in discretionary appeals. Since *habeas corpus* is purely discretionary, the Supreme Court has held that no right to counsel exists, unless, of course, the prisoner can afford representation (see *Ross v. Moffitt*, 417 U.S. 600 [1974]). The Court has held, however, that federal prisoners have a "constitutional right of access to the courts" (*Bounds v. Smith*, 430 U.S. 817 [1977]).

The Supreme Court has also held that a state cannot prohibit prisoners from helping each other prepare and submit *habeas corpus* petitions (*Johnson v. Avery*, 393 U.S. 483 [1969]). Moreover, the Court has held that an indigent *habeas corpus* petitioner is entitled to a free transcript of his or her trial to assist in preparing the appropriate paperwork (see *Griffin v. Illinois*).

Retroactivity in the *Habeas Corpus* Context

Retroactivity in the *habeas corpus* context is different than it is in the appeals context. Specifically, *habeas corpus* decisions are less often made retroactive than appeals decisions. In *Teague v. Lane*, the Court decided that only those appellate decisions that are dictated by precedent should be retroactive; that is, new rules should not be retroactive, unless one of two exceptions is in place. Why such a strange rule? The Supreme Court has interpreted *habeas corpus* as deterring state courts from misapplying federal case law applying at the time. A new rule could have no deterrent effect because, by definition, it would not have been around long enough to serve a deterrent function.

Before getting to the exceptions, decisions that are *dictated by precedent* are those to which the reviewing court has applied a previous decision. Assume, for example, that a prisoner files a *habeas* petition claiming that he was denied counsel at trial (which is highly unlikely). Relief will almost certainly be granted because precedent (i.e., *Gideon*) requires having counsel at trial. When the reviewing court hands down a new constitutional rule, however, there is no precedent. An example of a new constitutional rule would be that the Sixth Amendment requires counsel to be present at all *pre*-indictment lineups; such a rule is not in place at present.

In *Teague*, the petitioner claimed that *Taylor v. Louisiana*'s (419 U.S. 522 [1975]) requirement that a jury list represent a cross-section of the community should be applied to the jury itself. In essence, the petitioner was asking the Court to hand down a new rule because the Court also held in *Taylor* that the final jury does not need to represent a fair cross-section of the community. The Court found that neither of the two exceptions applied to petitioner Teague's claim.

To backtrack, new rules are not retroactive on *habeas corpus* review unless one of two exceptions is in place. First, in *Teague*, the Court held that a new rule should not be retroactive unless it places certain types of private individual conduct "beyond the power of the criminal law-making authority to proscribe" (p. 307). Needless to say, this language is a little cryptic. An example of it in application can be found in *Bousley v. United States* (523 U.S. 614 [1998]). There, the petitioner claimed that his guilty plea was involuntary because it was based on a flawed interpretation of the statute he was charged with violating. Specifically, the petitioner pled guilty to a firearms offense because he was under the impression that the statute prohibited mere *possession* of a firearm when, in fact, it prohibited *active use* of the firearm. The Court held that the claim could be heard because the petitioner was essentially convicted (through a guilty plea) for an act the statute did not define as criminal. In other words, the act in question was one that was "beyond the power of the criminal law-making authority to proscribe" (*Teague*, p. 307).

Second, a "new rule" will not be retroactive to other cases pending review unless it is "implicit in the concept of ordered liberty" (p. 307). That is, only "watershed rules of criminal procedure (p. 311)," or those that are "central to an accurate determination of guilt" (p. 313) qualify as exceptions to the *Teague* rule.

To clarify this, the Court stated in *Sawyer v. Smith* (497 U.S. 227 [1990]) that a new rule is "implicit" to "ordered liberty" if it "alter[s] our understanding of the bedrock procedural elements essential to the fairness of a proceeding" (p. 242). The Court has yet to find a new rule that falls under this second exception. For example, in *Beard v. Banks* (542 U.S. 406 [2004]), the Court decided that its ruling in *Mills v. Maryland* (486 U.S. 367 [1988]), a case dealing with mitigating factors in capital sentencing, was a new one and therefore could not be applied retroactively. The *Mills* rule was one to the effect that the Constitution's Eighth Amendment forbids states from imposing a requirement that the jury *unanimously* identify mitigating factors before such factors could figure into their death penalty decisions. The Court further noted that *Mills* did not meet either of *Teague*'s exceptions, which would have been necessary for the decision to be applied retroactively (see also *Schriro v. Summerlin*, 542 U.S. 348 [2004]).

As another example, in the recent case of *Whorton v. Bockting* (549 U.S. 406 [2007]), the Court declined to classify its decision in *Crawford v. Washington* (541 U.S. 35 [2004]— limiting hearsay evidence in domestic violence cases) as a "watershed rule." Nothing, however, prohibits states from adopting broader retroactivity standards (*Danforth v. Minnesota*, No. 06-8273 [2008]).

The Antiterrorism and Effective Death Penalty Act (AEDPA) of 1996

To be sure, the *habeas corpus* process is fairly complex and difficult to understand. It has become even more clouded in light of the **Antiterrorism and Effective Death Penalty Act** of 1996, which was passed in the wake of the infamous Oklahoma City bombing.

The Oklahoma City bombing was arguably Americans' first real experience with terrorism. Even though it was *domestic* terrorism, as opposed to *international*, this event alerted policymakers to the fact that people can inflict catastrophic damage with relatively crude weaponry. The bombing led to numerous proposals in Congress for how to address terrorism. Early proposals called for drastic, controversial measures designed to curb the new terrorist threat. Several months after the bombing, however, the legislation agreed to by both the House and the Senate was significantly less forceful. It was signed into law by President Clinton in April 1996.

The AEDPA's supporters heralded it as a significant bipartisan achievement that would help root out terrorism. Critics of the new law claimed that it was so "watered down" that it had virtually nothing to do with combating terrorism. To an extent, the critics are correct. One of the most significant components of the AEDPA places restrictions on *habeas corpus* petitions for death row inmates. The reader can draw his or her own conclusion as to the relationship between *habeas corpus* and domestic terrorism. Even so, it is worth considering the AEDPA's effects at this point because it has altered the *habeas corpus* landscape in several unmistakable ways. The AEDPA also goes beyond restricting *habeas corpus*. Figure 15.5 offers some examples of how AEDPA does this.

FIGURE 15.5

Overview of the Antiterrorism and Effective Death Penalty Act (AEDPA) of 1996 (Unrelated to *Habeas Corpus*)

Mandatory Victim Restitution

The mandatory victim restitution provisions of the bill require a federal court to impose mandatory restitution, without consideration of the defendant's ability to pay. This applies in any case in which an identifiable victim or victims suffered physical or pecuniary loss from an offense that is a crime of violence, an offense against property (including any offense committed by fraud or deceit), or a crime related to tampering with consumer products. Last year, Judge Maryanne Trump Barry (D. N.J.), chair of the Judicial Conference Committee on Criminal Law, testified before Congress on the issue of mandatory restitution, pointing out that such legislation would replace a flexible system, based on common sense and judicial discretion, with an inflexible, mandatory system that would be extremely expensive to implement.

Closed Circuit Televised Proceedings for Victims of Crime

Another provision in the bill requires a federal trial court, in any criminal trial where the venue is changed from the state in which the case was originally brought and more than 350 miles from the location in which those proceedings originally would have taken place, to order closed circuit televising of the proceedings back to the original location. The televised coverage is to be provided for such persons the court determines have a compelling interest and who are otherwise—because of inconvenience or expense—unable to attend the trial.

The provision takes effect notwithstanding any contrary provision of the Federal Rules of Criminal Procedure, although there is a sunset mechanism. The Judicial Conference may promulgate and issue rules, or amend existing rules, to "effectuate the policy addressed by this section." Upon implementation of such rules, the closed circuit television provision ceases to be effective. The cost of such closed circuit proceedings will be paid for by appropriated funds and/or through donations.

Other Provisions

Among other provisions in the bill are those that:

- Create an Alien Terrorist Removal Court composed of five sitting U.S. district judges designated by the Chief Justice;
- Expand the definition of an aggravated felony under which aliens may be deported, and streamline the deportation of criminal aliens after they serve their sentences;

Figure 15.5 continued

- Create a five-member Commission on the Advancement of Federal Law Enforcement to study criminal law enforcement, the chair of which will be appointed by the Chief Justice;
- Authorize appropriations for the Judiciary of $41 million from the Crime Trust Fund from fiscal year 1997 to FY 2000 to help meet the increased demands for judicial branch activities resulting from enactment of the bill;
- Set compensation for court-appointed attorneys in capital cases at a rate of not more than $125 per hour for in-court and out-of-court time, but also authorize the Judicial Conference to increase the rate of compensation in the future under a "CPI escalator" mechanism;
- Cap fees and expenses paid for investigative and expert services in capital cases at $7,500, but provide for a waiver mechanism whereby such expenses can exceed that cap if the excess payment is certified by the court as necessary to provide fair compensation for services of an unusual character or duration and if the amount of the excess payment is approved by the chief judge of the circuit.

Source: "New Antiterrorism Law Contains Habeas Reform and Victim Restitution," *The Third Branch: The Newsletter of the Federal Courts* (Washington, DC: Administrative Office of the U.S. Courts, April 1996).

RESTRICTIONS ON *HABEAS CORPUS* PETITIONS RESULTING FROM THE AEDPA The first change to *habeas corpus* procedure resulting from the AEDPA is that review is permitted only when the state-level decision "(1) resulted in a decision that was contrary to, or involved an unreasonable application of, clearly established Federal law, as determined by the Supreme Court of the United States"; or (2) "resulted in a decision that was based on an unreasonable determination of the facts in light of the evidence presented in the State court proceeding" (28 U.S.C. Section 2254[d]). This is in contrast to *Stone v. Powell,* cited earlier, in which the Supreme Court held that *habeas* review should not be granted when "the State has provided an opportunity for full and fair litigation of a Fourth Amendment claim" (p. 465). The AEDPA limits this decision.

Second, the AEDPA alters *habeas* review in capital cases (i.e., in which the accused is on death row). The act provides that if a prisoner defaults and fails to submit a petition within a year, then review will only be granted when his or her failure to file a petition is "(1) the result of State action in violation of the Constitution or laws of the United States"; (2) "the result of the Supreme Court's recognition of a new Federal right that is made retroactively applicable"; or (3) "based on a factual predicate that could not have been discovered through the exercise of due diligence in time to present the claim for State or Federal post-conviction review" (28 U.S.C. Section 2264[a]). These new default rules are significantly more restrictive than those discussed earlier. In a recent decision, the Supreme Court stated that there is no extension to the one-year rule if a defendant has a petition for a writ of certiorari pending before the Supreme Court at the time (*Lawrence v. Florida,* No. 05-8820 [2007]; also see *Allen v. Siebert,* 552 U.S. 1 [2007]).

The AEDPA also places restrictions on filing successive *habeas corpus* petitions. It states that a "claim presented in a second or successive *habeas corpus* application shall be dismissed" (28 U.S.C. Section 2244[b][1]). Indeed, there has already been one challenge to this part of the legislation, but the Supreme Court held that the new restriction was well within constitutional guidelines (*Felker v. Turpin,* 518 U.S. 651 [1996]).

The AEDPA further restricts filing successive petitions that raise different claims. Specifically, the legislation restricts a prisoner's successive and different claim to one that (1) "relies on a new rule of constitutional law, made retroactive to cases on collateral review by the Supreme Court, that was previously unavailable" or one for which (2) "the factual predicate could not have been discovered previously through the exercise of due diligence" and which "would be sufficient to establish by clear and convincing evidence that, but for constitutional error no reasonable factfinder would have found the applicant guilty of the underlying offense" (28 U.S.C. Section 2244[b][2]). The Court interpreted some of this confusing language in *Tyler v. Cain* (533 U.S. 656 [2001]).

Next, the AEDPA imposes strict filing deadlines for *habeas corpus* petitions. Namely, most *habeas corpus* petitions must be filed within one year from the date of the final state-level appellate judgment. For a death penalty case, the legislation is even more restrictive. It requires that a death row petition be filed within six months from the "final state court affirmance of the conviction and sentence on direct review or the expiration of the time for seeking review" (28 U.S.C. Sections 2244[d][1][A] & 2263). Both restrictions are intended to reduce the opportunities prisoners have to challenge their confinement and, in the case of death row inmates, to speed up execution. A flurry of recent Supreme Court decisions (e.g., *Jimenez v. Quarterman*, No. 07-6984 [2009]; *Holland v. Florida*, No. 09-5327 [2010]) have addressed these timing rules, but a full discussion is beyond the scope of this text.

Another AEDPA restriction on *habeas corpus*, though certainly not the last, addresses the *habeas* court's ability to engage in independent fact-finding. The legislation prohibits a *habeas* court from holding hearings to determine questions of fact unless the petitioner can make a showing why it is necessary. The Supreme Court recently interpreted this requirement, making it even more restrictive (see *Williams v. Taylor*, 529 U.S. 420 [2000]).

The AEDPA imposes several other restrictions on *habeas* review that need not be addressed in depth here, although the Supreme Court is starting to address them on a fairly regular basis. For our purposes, it is just important to know that the AEDPA has altered *habeas corpus* procedure in a significant way.

To conclude the *habeas corpus* discussion, it is useful to consider the Supreme Court's opinion in *Sanders v. United States*. In that case, Justice Brennan announced the logic underlying *habeas corpus*: "Conventional notions of finality of litigation have no place where life or liberty is at stake and infringement of constitutional rights is alleged. If 'government [is] always [to] be accountable to the judiciary for a man's imprisonment, access to the courts on habeas must not be thus impeded' " (p. 8).

There is a tendency among many criminal justice critics to claim that criminals enjoy too many appeals. And while the AEDPA Act of 1996, not to mention a long line of Supreme Court cases, places significant restrictions on *habeas* review, the appellate and *habeas corpus* processes are still fundamental to the U.S. system of justice. Without them, the potential for mistakes would loom large.

Summary

1. DESCRIBE VARIOUS SENTENCING GOALS.

The criminal process concludes with sentencing, appeals, and *habeas corpus*. Every convicted criminal needs to be sentenced. A sentence can range from a modest fine or supervised probation to life in prison or even death. Once a defendant has been sentenced, if not before, he or she frequently appeals his or her conviction. Filing an appeal is often followed by filing a *habeas corpus* petition. If the defendant fails in his or her appeals and *habeas corpus* petitions, he or she will be forced to serve out his or her term.

Sentencing in the United States is carried out with one or more of four sentencing objectives in mind: deterrence, incapacitation, retribution, and rehabilitation. If a judge favors rehabilitation, he or she will probably be inclined to hand down a sentence of probation rather than imprisonment. Many judges and criminal justice commentators also believe rehabilitation is possible in a traditional prison environment. The aim of deterrence is to discourage others from committing crime by punishing the offender harshly. Finally, incapacitation and retribution simply remove the offender from society and give him or her what is deserved.

2. EXPLAIN HOW AN APPROPRIATE SENTENCE IS DETERMINED.

While a judge's goal or objective of punishment may guide his or her sentencing practices, other factors are considered, as well. Some of these factors include, but are not limited to, the crime in question, the defendant's prior record, his or her ties to the community and family, the defendant's employment history, whether he or she was convicted for several different crimes as opposed to one specific crime, the degree of the defendant's cooperation with authorities during the investigative stage, the defendant's mental status, his or her feelings of remorse, if any, and several other pertinent factors.

Death penalty sentencing must be carried out with special care. The preferred method is to have a jury, not a judge, decide whether death is appropriate and to take into account aggravating and mitigating circumstances (see *Ring v. Arizona*, 122 S.Ct. 2428 [2002]). The death penalty is unconstitutional for young offenders but *is* sometimes appropriate for offenses other than first-degree murder. The Supreme Court has also handed down other important restrictions concerning death penalty sentencing. Excessive punishments can violate the Eighth Amendment's cruel and unusual punishment clause.

3. DESCRIBE THE VARIOUS TYPES OF APPEALS.

Once a sentence has been handed down, the convicted person can appeal. An appeal can also be sought prior to sentencing. This type of appeal is known as an interlocutory appeal. Most jurisdictions favor appeals after final adjudication, but sometimes it is necessary to appeal prior to conviction. An appeal filed prior to adjudication must be unrelated to the cause of action. One filed after adjudication can be any of many varieties. Typically, the defendant is granted one appeal of right. Subsequent appeals are called discretionary appeals. They are discretionary because the appellate court decides if it wants to hear the appeal.

4. OUTLINE THE APPEAL PROCESS.

An appeal rarely results in the defendant going free. This point cannot be overemphasized. What happens, in most cases, is one of two things: (1) The appellate court agrees with the trial court, in which case it affirms the lower court's decision; or (2) the appellate court reverses the trial court's decision. A reversal typically results in a new trial for the defendant, or a remand.

Sometimes, a trial *de novo* is held at the appellate level, but usually only for a misdemeanor appeal.

The appellate process must be carried out such that the defendant's constitutional rights are respected. According to the Supreme Court, this means that the defendant (1) must have access to the trial transcripts; (2) must have access to counsel for appeals of right, though not necessarily for discretionary appeals; and (3) must not be retaliated against for exercising his or her right to appeal.

An appeal can also be filed by a party other than the defense, or a third party. For example, the prosecution can appeal the court's decision to exclude evidence. Another party, such as a witness, can appeal a subpoena requiring him or her to show up at court, but only if he or she is held in contempt for failing to appear.

Some appeals, though meritorious, may not succeed according to the harmless error doctrine. When a nonconstitutional harmless error occurs, it does not influence the jury but has a very slight effect on the outcome of the trial. By contrast, to show a constitutional error, the state must prove beyond a reasonable doubt that the error did not affect the verdict of the trial. However, in some cases, the Supreme Court has concluded that an error was so serious as to require automatic reversal of the defendant's conviction.

The last appeals issue considered in this chapter was that of retroactivity. To what extent should appellate court decisions benefit other defendants with similar appeals? The case law surrounding the issue of retroactivity is complex and confusing. But in sum, the retroactivity doctrine says that every new constitutional rule announced on direct review must be applied retroactively to other cases pending review that raise the same issue.

5. SUMMARIZE THE RIGHT TO AND RESTRICTIONS ON *HABEAS CORPUS*.

Habeas corpus is another method challenging one's conviction. It is also known as a collateral attack. The Supreme Court has restricted the right to *habeas* review in a number of ways. First, it has limited the types of claims that can succeed. Second, the Court has held that a *habeas corpus* review may not be granted if the petitioner fails to submit a claim within the time frame specified by state law. Third, it is generally necessary for a convicted individual to exhaust all state remedies before a federal *habeas* review will be granted. Finally, restrictions have been imposed in situations in which prisoners have filed multiple *habeas* petitions.

A *habeas corpus* proceeding can resemble a criminal trial in certain situations. In particular, a *habeas* court can engage in fact-finding (which is typically the province of the trial court). This is permissible when, for example, a factual dispute was not resolved at the state level or there is a substantial allegation of newly discovered evidence. Other such conditions have also been identified by the Supreme Court.

The Supreme Court has held that prisoners are not strictly entitled to counsel to assist in preparing their *habeas* petitions. They do, however, have constitutional access to the courts. In other words, the right to counsel is virtually nonexistent in the *habeas corpus* process, exists somewhat more so in the appellate process (i.e., mainly for direct appeals), and exists completely at trial.

Retroactivity is rare with regard to *habeas corpus* petitioners. Petitions that *do not* ask the reviewing court to hand down a new rule are retroactive. Those that *do* ask for a new rule are not retroactive unless (1) the new rule is one that involves individual conduct that cannot be prohibited by law or (2) the new rule is closely tied to the fairness of a criminal proceeding.

Finally, the Antiterrorism and Effective Death Penalty Act of 1996, passed in the wake of the Oklahoma City bombing, places significant restrictions on *habeas corpus*. The act does not completely supplant Supreme Court precedent pertaining to *habeas corpus* because the new restrictions imposed in the act rely heavily on past Supreme Court decisions.

Key Terms

Key Cases

Sentencing

- *Roberts v. United States*, 445 U.S. 552 (1980)
- *Furman v. Georgia*, 408 U.S. 238 (1972)
- *Gregg v. Georgia*, 428 U.S. 153 (1976)
- *Roberts v. Louisiana*, 428 U.S. 325 (1977)
- *United States v. Tucker*, 404 U.S. 443 (1972)

Appeals

- *Griffin v. Illinois*, 351 U.S. 12 (1956)
- *Douglas v. California*, 372 U.S. 353 (1963)
- *North Carolina v. Pearce*, 395 U.S. 711 (1969)
- *Cohen v. Beneficial Industrial Loan Corp.*, 337 U.S. 541 (1949)

- *Carroll v. United States*, 354 U.S. 394 (1957)
- *Cobbledick v. United States*, 309 U.S. 323 (1940)
- *Kotteakos v. United States*, 328 U.S. 750 (1946)
- *Chapman v. California*, 386 U.S. 18 (1967)

Habeas Corpus

- *Sanders v. United States*, 373 U.S. 1 (1963)
- *Stone v. Powell*, 428 U.S. 465 (1976)
- *Teague v. Lane*, 489 U.S. 288 (1989)
- *Herrera v. Collins*, 506 U.S. 390 (1993)
- *Hill v. United States*, 368 U.S. 424 (1962)
- *Kuhlmann v. Wilson*, 477 U.S. 436 (1986)
- *Fay v. Noia*, 372 U.S. 391 (1963)

Review Questions

1. Explain the goals of sentencing.
2. Identify several criteria used in determining the appropriate sentence.
3. What constitutional rights exist during sentencing?
4. What guidelines has the Supreme Court imposed on the appellate process?
5. Summarize the relevant rules governing an appeal before and after adjudication.
6. Who else besides the defendant can appeal? For what reasons?
7. Explain the harmless error doctrine.
8. Explain the differences between constitutional and non-constitutional errors.

9. What is retroactivity? How does it differ in the appeals process versus the *habeas corpus* process?
10. What is *habeas corpus*? From where does this right stem?
11. Summarize four restrictions on *habeas corpus* petitions.
12. When can a *habeas corpus* proceeding resemble a criminal trial?
13. Summarize the right to counsel as it applies (or does not apply) in the *habeas corpus* context.
14. Summarize the leading provisions of the Antiterrorism and Effective Death Penalty Act (AEDPA) of 1996.
15. How does the AEDPA place restrictions on *habeas corpus*?

Web Links and Exercises

1. U.S. Sentencing Commission: Read about federal sentencing guidelines, including recent changes.
URL: http://www.ussc.gov (accessed February 16, 2011).
2. Sentencing project: Read the latest in sentencing research. Is there racial disparity in sentencing? If so, what exactly is the disparity?
URL: http://www.sentencingproject.org (accessed February 16, 2011).
3. The appellate process: Read about the federal appeals process in detail, particularly on page 35 at the following URL: http://www.uscourts.gov/uscourts/Federal

Courts/Publications/English.pdf (accessed February 16, 2011).
4. History of *habeas corpus*: See the timeline for *habeas corpus* and significant milestones throughout history.
URL: http://www.aclu.org/national-security/habeas-corpus-timeline (accessed February 16, 2011).
5. AEDPA: Read the text of the Antiterrorism and Effective Death Penalty Act.
Suggested URL: http://thomas.loc.gov/cgi-bin/query/z?c104:S.735.ENR: (accessed February 16, 2011).

GLOSSARY

18 U.S.C. Section 242. A federal statute used to hold police officers (and other government actors) criminally liable for actions that cause violations of people's constitutional or other federally protected rights.

18 U.S.C. Section 3501. A federal statute enacted in the wake of the *Miranda* decision providing that any confession "shall be admissible in evidence if it is voluntarily given." The statute was deemed unconstitutional in *Dickerson v. United States* (530 U.S. 428 [2000]).

42 U.S.C. Section 1983. A federal statute that provides a remedy in federal court for the "deprivation of any rights . . . secured by the Constitution and laws" of the United States." Also called "Section 1983."

absolute immunity. A term referring to the fact that certain officials cannot ever be sued for their official decisions.

accrediting. It is the process by which the prosecution or defense attempts to support, bolster, or improve a witness's credibility.

accusation rule. The requirement that a person must first be accused (i.e., charged) for the Sixth Amendment's speedy trial provision to apply.

ad hoc plea bargaining. A term used to describe some of the strange concessions that defendants agree to make as part of prosecutors' decisions to secure guilty pleas.

administrative justification. A standard used to support certain regulatory and special needs searches. Created by the Supreme Court, it adopts a balancing approach, weighing the privacy interests of individuals with the interests of society in preserving public safety.

admission. When a person can simply admit to involvement in a crime without any police encouragement.

affirm. An appellate court verdict that expresses agreement with a lower court's decision.

Alford **plea.** A guilty plea in which the defendant admits to the crime, but not necessarily all elements of it. An *Alford* plea does not require the defendant to allocute.

allocution. When the defendant explains to the judge exactly what he or she did and why. The defendant is usually required to allocate when he or she pleads guilty.

Antiterrorism and Effective Death Penalty Act. Federal legislation enacted in the wake of the Oklahoma City bombing in 1996. The legislation places significant restrictions on *habeas corpus*.

apparent authority. A person has apparent authority if the police *reasonably believe* he or she has authority to grant consent.

appeal. The practice of asking an appellate court to examine a lower court's decision in order to determine whether the proper procedure was followed or the correct law was applied.

appellant. The party that appeals; both the prosecutor and the defendant can appeal, although defense appeals are more common than prosecution appeals.

appellee. Sometimes called the respondent, this is the party appealed against.

armspan rule. Part of the search incident to arrest exception to the Fourth Amendment's warrant requirement that allows officers to search not only the suspect incident to arrest, but also his or her "grabbing area."

arraignment. A hearing in which the defendant is formally notified of the charge lodged against him or her. The defendant also enters one of three pleas: (1) guilty, (2) not guilty, or (3) *nolo contendere.*

arrest warrant. An order issued by a judge directing a law enforcement officer to arrest an individual identified as one who has committed a specific criminal offense.

arrest. The act of taking an individual into custody for the purpose of charging the person with a criminal offense (or, in the case of a juvenile, a delinquent act).

articulable facts. Events that are witnessed and can be explained. Contrast articulable facts with hunches and guesses. Articulable facts are necessary for establishing probable cause.

automobile exception. An exception to the Fourth Amendment's warrant requirement that permits police to search a vehicle without a warrant, so long as they have probable cause to do so.

bail bond agent. A professional who posts the defendant's bail in exchange for a fee.

bail. A process by which a defendant pays a certain amount of money in order to be released from jail prior to his or her trial date. Defendants who appear for trial receive their money back. Those who fail to appear for trial forfeit the bail amount.

bifurcated trial. Holding two separate proceedings in the death penalty context, one for determining guilt and another for determining the appropriate sentence (e.g., death or life in prison).

Bivens **claim.** A Section 1983 lawsuit against a federal official.

Blockburger **rule.** A rule stemming from *Blockburger v. United States* (284 U.S. 299 [1932]) that helps courts determine what constitutes the "same offense" for double-jeopardy purposes: "[w]here the same act or transaction constitutes a violation of two distinct statutory provisions, the test to be applied to determine whether there are two offenses or only one, is whether each requires proof of an additional fact which the other does not" (p. 304).

booking. The process by which an arrest is officially documented and the arrestee is placed into custody. During booking, the arrestee's personal items will be inventoried and he or she will be fingerprinted and/or photographed.

bright-line decisions. A decision in which a court hands down a *specific rule*, one subject to very little interpretation.

case-by-case adjudication. The reality that some cases cannot result in bright-line rules. Courts often look to the "totality of circumstances" when taking a case-by-case approach.

chain of custody. A chronological documentation (or paper trail) showing how seized evidence has been preserved, transferred, analyzed, and disposed of. It is mainly a record of the individuals who have had physical possession of the evidence at any point during the criminal process.

challenge for cause. A means of excluding prospective jurors who cannot be impartial. Prosecutors and defense attorneys have an unlimited number of challenges for cause in criminal cases.

change of venue. A process by which a trial is heard in another jurisdiction, perhaps in another county in the state.

checkpoints. Brief detentions that do not require probable cause or a warrant. Their purpose should *not* be to detect evidence of criminal conduct, such as narcotics trafficking. Examples include border checkpoints, illegal immigrant checkpoints, sobriety checkpoints, license and safety checkpoints, crime investigation checkpoints, and airport checkpoints.

civil litigation. The same as a lawsuit.

civilian input. A method of citizen input into the complaint review process in which a civilian panel receives and investigates a complaint, leaving adjudication and discipline with the department itself.

civilian monitor. The weakest method of citizen input that leaves investigation, adjudication, and discipline inside the department. A civilian is allowed to review the adequacy and impartiality of the process.

civilian review. The strongest method of citizen input in which a civilian panel investigates, adjudicates, and recommends punishment to the police chief.

closely regulated business. A type of business subject to warrantless, suspicionless inspections. Examples include liquor stores and firearm dealerships.

color of law. One of two requirements for a successful Section 1983 lawsuit. An official acts under color of law when he or she acts in an official capacity.

common authority. "mutual use of the property by persons generally having joint access or control for most purposes" (*United States v. Matlock*, 415 U.S. 164 [1974], p. 172, n. 7).

competence. A term that refers to a witness's ability to remember events, communicate effectively, and understand the importance of telling the truth, as well as the consequences of not doing so.

compulsory process. The Sixth Amendment requirement that criminal defendants enjoy the right to compel the production of witnesses and evidence. This is often accomplished via subpoena.

concurring opinion. At the U.S. Supreme Court level, an opinion authored by a justice in the majority that supports the majority's decision but with different legal logic. Concurring opinions are sometimes authored in lower appellate court cases.

confession. When a person implicates himself or herself in criminal activity following police questioning and/or interrogation.

confrontation. The defendant's Sixth Amendment right to be present at his or her trial, hear live testimony of adverse witnesses, and challenge such witnesses' statements in open court.

consent search. A search based on voluntary consent. A valid consent search permits a police officer to dispense with the Fourth Amendment's warrant and probable cause requirements.

constitutional rights violation. One of two requirements for a successful Section 1983 lawsuit. Not every push or shove amounts to a constitutional rights violation.

contempt power. The grand jury's authority to hold people in contempt of court for failing to appear before it. Civil and criminal sanctions can be imposed.

courtroom work group. A three-member collective consisting of the judge, prosecutor, and defense attorney.

courts of general jurisdiction. The main trial courts at the state level. They are usually located at the county level and are often called "superior courts."

courts of limited jurisdiction. Courts that have jurisdiction over relatively minor offenses and infractions. An example of a limited jurisdiction court is a traffic court.

credibility. A term concerned with whether the witness's testimony should be believed.

crime control perspective. A perspective that emphasizes the importance of controlling crime, perhaps to the detriment of civil liberties.

criminal procedure. A vast set of rules and guidelines that describe how suspected and accused criminals are to be handled and processed by the justice system.

cross-examination. In-court questioning of a sworn witness by the opposing side's attorney.

culpability. In the Section 1983 context, the requirement that the plaintiff (i.e., the party suing) generally has to prove that the defendant officer intended for the violation to occur.

curtilage. The "area to which extends the intimate activity associated with the sanctity of a man's home and the privacies of life" (*Oliver v. United States*, 466 U.S. 170 [1984], p. 225).

custody. Typically an arrest. Custody is important in the *Miranda* context because *Miranda* warnings do not need to be read if a person is not in custody.

damage suit. A lawsuit in which one or more parties seek monetary compensation.

deadly force. Force that is likely to cause death or serious bodily harm.

defendant. The person charged with a crime.

deliberate elicitation. In the Sixth Amendment right to counsel context, deliberate elicitation occurs when police officers create a situation likely to induce a suspect into making an incriminating statement.

determinate sentencing. A sentencing strategy that permits the judge to set the sentence, and the sentence cannot later be altered by a parole board.

deterrence. A goal of sentencing that is concerned with punishing offenders such that they and others will be discouraged from committing crime.

direct appeal. An appeal that is authorized by law.

direct examination. In-court questioning of a sworn witness by the attorney who calls the witness.

discovery. The process by which each party to a case learns of the evidence that the opposition will present.

discrediting. When the prosecution or defense attempts to attack or challenge a witness's credibility.

discretionary appeal. An appeal that will be heard only if the reviewing court agrees to do so.

disparate impact. A method of acting that treats one group in a markedly different fashion than another.

dissent. At the U.S. Supreme Court level, an opinion written by a justice in the minority that expresses disagreement with the majority decision. Dissenting opinions are sometimes authored in lower appellate court cases.

distinctive group. Historically protected groups that should not be excluded from jury service, namely women and minorities.

distinguish. An appellate court's decision to treat a case before it as sufficiently distinct that it cannot be decided by looking to past rulings. In other words, the set of facts is unique and never before considered by an appellate court.

district courts. Federal trial courts. There are 94 federal district courts in the United States, including 89 district courts in the 50 states and 1 each in Puerto Rico, the Virgin Islands, the District of Columbia, Guam, and the Northern Mariana Islands.

double-blind lineup. A lineup procedure in which neither the witness nor the investigator staging the lineup knows who the suspect is.

double jeopardy. The Fifth Amendment requirement that a person cannot be reprosecuted after acquittal, reprosecuted after conviction, or subjected to separate punishments for the same offense.

drug and alcohol testing. A procedure of testing for drug or alcohol use, usually via urinalysis. Employees and school students can be subjected to warrantless, suspicionless drug and alcohol testing, but hospital patients cannot—if the evidence is turned over to law enforcement authorities.

drug courier profiling. A crime-detection process that makes use of what is known about the likely and observable characteristics of drug couriers. Drug courier profiling usually occurs in stop-and-frisk situations.

due process perspective. A general concern with people's rights and liberties. The due process perspective is closely aligned with a liberal political orientation.

due process voluntariness approach. The requirement that any confession be voluntary under the "totality of circumstances."

effective assistance of counsel. The requirement that a defense attorney must effectively represent his or her client. In *Strickland v. Washington* (466 U.S. 668 [1984]), the Supreme Court held that a two-prong test must be applied in order to determine whether counsel is ineffective: "First, the defendant must show that counsel's performance was deficient. This requires showing that counsel made errors so serious that counsel was not functioning as the 'counsel' guaranteed the defendant by the Sixth Amendment. Second, the defendant must show that the deficient performance prejudiced the defense" (p. 687).

Eighth Amendment. Part of the U.S. Constitution, which states: "Excessive bail shall not be required, nor excessive fines imposed, nor cruel and unusual punishments inflicted."

Electronic Communications Privacy Act. Federal legislation enacted in 1986 that amended Title III of the Omnibus Crime Control and Safe Streets Act to include "electronic communications."

entrapment defense. A criminal defense based on the belief that someone should not be convicted of a crime that the government instigated. It is a defense in the criminal law sense, but it is one of the only defenses that calls into question law enforcement's role in the instigation of a crime. This is why entrapment is important in criminal procedure.

evanescent evidence. Evidence that is likely to disappear. An example is alcohol in a person's bloodstream.

exceptions to the warrant requirement. Law enforcement actions that do not require a warrant. Examples include searches incident to arrest, searches based on exigent circumstances, automobile searches, plain view searches, arrests based on exigent circumstances, and arrests in public places.

exclusionary rule. The Supreme Court-created rule requiring that evidence obtained in violation of the Constitution cannot be used in a criminal trial to prove guilt.

exigent circumstances. Emergency circumstances, including hot pursuit, the possibility of escape, or evanescent evidence. When exigent circumstances are present, the police do not need to abide by the Fourth Amendment's warrant requirement.

extralegal remedies. Remedies conducted outside the legal process, such as a personal vendetta.

fair examination rule. The requirement that a witness, including the defendant, at either a trial or a grand jury hearing can be compelled to answer questions once he or she waives Fifth Amendment protection and begins to testify.

Federal Communications Act. One of the earliest federal statutes regulating electronic surveillance activities. It was enacted in 1934.

Federal Rules of Criminal Procedure. The rules that govern the conduct of all criminal proceedings brought in federal courts.

Fifth Amendment. Part of the U.S. Constitution, which states: "No person shall be held to answer for a capital, or otherwise infamous crime, unless on a presentment or indictment of a Grand Jury, except in cases arising in the land or naval forces, or in the Militia, when in actual service in time of War or public danger; nor shall any person be subject for the same offense to be twice put in jeopardy of life or limb; nor shall be compelled in any criminal case to be a witness against himself, nor be deprived of life, liberty, or property, without due process of law; nor shall private property be taken for public use, without just compensation."

final judgment rule. The requirement that interlocutory appeals dealing with questions of the defendant's guilt (rather than questions of a constitutional nature) cannot be heard until after final adjudication.

Foreign Intelligence Surveillance Act. Federal legislation enacted in 1978 that regulates electronic surveillance as it pertains to foreign intelligence gathering.

Foreign Intelligence Surveillance Court. A secretive court created by the Foreign Intelligence Surveillance Act. The court reviews applications for warrants related to surveillance in national security investigations.

formal criminal proceeding. In the Sixth Amendment right to counsel context, either a formal charge, a preliminary hearing, indictment, information, or arraignment.

Fourteenth Amendment. Part of the U.S. Constitution, which states: "All persons born or naturalized in the United States, and subject to the jurisdiction thereof, are citizens of the United States and of the State wherein they reside. No State shall make or enforce any law which shall abridge the privileges or immunities of citizens of the United States, nor shall any State deprive any person of life, liberty, or property, without due process of law; nor deny to any person within its jurisdiction the equal protection of the laws."

Fourth Amendment. Part of the U.S. Constitution, which states: "The right of the people to be secure in their persons, houses, papers, and effects, against unreasonable searches and seizures, shall not be violated, and no Warrants shall issue, but upon probable cause, supported by Oath or affirmation and particularly describing the place to be searched, and the persons or things to be seized."

frisk. A superficial examination by the officer of the person's body surface or clothing to discover weapons or items that could be used to cause harm.

"fruit of the poisonous tree" doctrine. An extension of the exclusionary rule. The poisonous tree is the initial unconstitutional search or seizure. Anything obtained from the tree is considered forbidden fruit and is not admissible at trial.

functional equivalent of a question. "[A]ny words or actions on the part of the police (other than those normally attendant to arrest and custody) that the police should know are reasonably likely to elicit an incriminating response from the suspect (*Rhode Island v. Innis*, 446 U.S. 291 [1980], p. 302, n. 8).

gag order. A judicial order limiting what the press and/or the parties to a particular case can divulge until the proceedings are completed.

general deterrence. When others besides the sentenced offender are discouraged from committing additional crimes due to sentencing practices.

"good faith" exception. An exception to the exclusionary rule providing that when an honest mistake is made during the course of a search or seizure, any subsequently obtained evidence will be considered admissible.

government action. Action on the part of paid government officials, usually police officers. Government action is one of two requirements (the other being infringement on one's reasonable expectation of privacy) that must be in place for a Fourth Amendment search to occur.

grand jury. A body of people selected to hear evidence against an accused person (or persons) and determine whether there is sufficient evidence to bring the case to trial.

guilty. A plea in which the defendant claims responsibility for the crime with which he or she has been charged.

habeas corpus. A means of challenging the constitutionality of one's confinement, best viewed as an alternative to appealing. *Habeas corpus* is a constitutional right (Article I, Section 9, Clause 2).

harmless error. A mistake at the trial level that has little practical consequence in terms of deciding whether the defendant is guilty or innocent.

hearsay exceptions. Exceptions to the rule that hearsay is not permissible in a criminal trial. Hearsay is something that is "heard, then said." It is considered unreliable because it is filtered through a second party. An example of hearsay would be this: A witness testifies that someone else told her the defendant committed the crime. Ideally, the "someone else" would appear in court. Generally, hearsay statements such as this are not admissible. There are, however, several established exceptions to the hearsay rule (see Figure 14.2).

hot pursuit. An exigent circumstance that permits dispensing with the Fourth Amendment's warrant requirement. Hot pursuit applies only when the police have probable cause to believe (1) that the person they are pursuing has committed a serious offense, (2) that the person will be found on the premises the police seek to enter, and (3) that the suspect will escape or harm someone or that evidence will be lost or destroyed. Also, the pursuit must originate from a lawful vantage point and the scope and timing of the search must be reasonable.

house. In Fourth Amendment terms, any structure that a person uses as a residence (and frequently a business) on either a temporary or long-term basis.

immediately apparent. One of the requirements for a proper plain view seizure. The police must have probable cause that the item is subject to seizure.

impartial judge. A judge who is capable of basing his or her decisions on the law and who has no conflict of interest or pecuniary stake in the outcome of the case. There is no constitutional right to an impartial judge. This right is a Supreme Court creation.

impartial jury. A jury that is capable of making a decision based solely on the facts of the case.

impeachment exception. An exception to the exclusionary rule providing that evidence considered inadmissible at one trial can be used in later trial to impeach (i.e., cast doubt on the credibility) the defendant.

impeachment. The formal term for attacking a witness's credibility (similar to discrediting).

incapacitation. A goal of sentencing that is concerned with removing criminals from society, usually through incarceration.

incorporation. The Supreme Court's practice of using the Fourteenth Amendment's due process clause, which holds that no state shall "deprive any person of life, liberty, or property, without due process of law," to make certain protections specified in the Bill of Rights applicable to the states.

in-court showup. A procedure in which a witness identifies the perpetrator in court. This sometimes occurs when a prosecutor asks a testifying witness to point to the perpetrator.

independent source. An exception to the fruit of the poisonous tree doctrine that permits the introduction of evidence if it has arrived via an independent source, such as a party disconnected from the case at hand.

indeterminate sentencing. A sentencing strategy that gives the judge the authority to set the sentence.

individual liability. In the Section 1983 context, the theory that the officer who allegedly committed the constitutional rights violation should be held liable.

inevitable discovery. An exception to the fruit of the poisonous tree doctrine that permits the introduction of evidence if it would have been discovered anyway.

initial appearance. The first appearance of an accused person before a judge. Trial may occur for misdemeanors.

injunctive relief. A court-ordered prohibition against a certain act or condition.

inspection. An exception to the Fourth Amendment's warrant requirement that permits certain authorities to inspect a closely regulated business.

interlocutory appeal. An appeal filed prior to adjudication.

intermediate appellate courts. At the state level, courts to which verdicts from courts of general jurisdiction are appealed.

internal review. A nonjudicial remedy in which the police investigate on their own complaints against officers.

interrogation. Express questioning (e.g., Where were you on the night of the crime?;) or the functional equivalent of a question (see definition). The definition of interrogation is important in the *Miranda* context because *Miranda* warnings do not need to be read if a person is not technically interrogated.

investigative detention. Also called a stationhouse detention, a less intrusive detention than an arrest but more intrusive than a *Terry* stop. Stationhouse detentions are used in many locations for such purposes as obtaining fingerprints and photographs, ordering lineups, administering polygraph examinations, and securing other types of evidence.

joinder. When the prosecutor either (1) brings multiple charges against the same individual in the same trial or (2) brings charges against multiple individuals in the same trial.

judicial activism. The opposite of judicial restraint. A judicially active judge is one who sees his or her role as more than interpreting the Constitution. A judicially active judge avoids precedent, preferring to hand down decisions with sweeping implications for the future.

judicial inducements. When a judge offers something to the defendant in exchange for a guilty plea. Most judicial inducements are prohibited.

judicial restraint. The philosophy of limiting decisions to the facts of each case, deciding only the issue or issues that need to be resolved in a particular situation.

jury list. The master list from which prospective jurors are subpoenaed. Examples include lists of those with drivers' licenses or voter registration lists.

jury panel. The list of individuals drawn from the jury list. The jury panel consists of those individual subpoenaed for jury service.

jury sequestration. The process of confining jurors during a trial. Sequestered jurors usually spend nights in the same hotel together and have little to no access to press coverage of the case on which they are serving as jurors.

justification. Also known as cause, justification is necessary for the police to engage in actions that trigger the Fourth Amendment. Examples of justification include probable cause and reasonable suspicion.

"knock and announce" requirement. The requirement that, before executing an arrest or search warrant, officers identify themselves and their intentions.

"knock and talk": A police tactic used to obtain consent to search, in which police officers approach a home, knock on the door, and request consent to search the premises.

lawful access. One of the requirements for a proper plain view seizure. The police must have lawful access to the item seized.

leading question. A question that suggests to the witness the answer that the examining party desires.

legal remedies. Remedies made available by the law, by a court decision, or by a police agency policy or procedure.

lineup. An identification procedure in which the suspect is placed alongside several other people who resemble him or her. The intent of the procedure is to ensure that a witness or victim picks the suspect out of the lineup.

live testimony. The confrontation requirement that adverse witnesses provide live testimony.

mandatory sentencing. A sentencing strategy that takes discretion away from judges. The law, not the judge, sets the sentence.

mediation. A method of alternative dispute resolution in which a neutral third party renders disciplinary decisions.

mental competence. One of two confrontation requirements. In order to be "present at his/her trial," the defendant must be not only physically present but also mentally competent. A defendant who is not mentally competent cannot adequately confront adverse witnesses.

military tribunals. A military court intended to try members of enemy forces, including suspected terrorists. Historically, military tribunals have not been bound by the rules of criminal procedure that apply to civilian courts.

Miranda **warnings.** While there are some variations, the *Miranda* warnings contain four elements: (1) You have the right to remain silent; (2) anything you say can be used against you in court; (3) you have the

right to talk to an attorney and to have the attorney with you during questioning; and (4) if you cannot afford an attorney, one will be provided for you.

municipal/county liability. In the Section 1983 context, the theory that a municipality or county should be held liable for the actions of one of its officers, such as for failure to train.

neutral and detached magistrate. One of the three elements of a valid warrant, any judge who does not have a conflict of interest or pecuniary interest in the outcome of a particular case or decision.

nolo contendere. A plea similar to guilty with a literal meaning of "I do not desire to contest the action." It resembles a guilty plea but is different in the sense that it may not be used against the defendant in any later civil litigation that arises from the acts that led to the criminal charge.

noncriminal proceeding rule. The rule that limits juries to criminal trials. The rule is a bit of a misnomer because civil trials are by jury. The noncriminal proceeding applies to steps of the criminal process that are not themselves considered "criminal." Examples are juvenile adjudicatory hearings and civil commitment hearings.

nondeadly force. Force that is unlikely to cause death or serious bodily harm.

nonreciprocal discovery. Discovery that benefits one side in a criminal case, but not the other. For example, the prosecution is required to share exculpatory evidence with the defendant, but there is no such requirement for the defense.

nonstop. A consensual encounter.

not guilty. A plea in which the defendant does not claim responsibility for the crime with which he or she has been charged. A not guilty plea is not the same as a plea of innocent. There is no plea of innocent.

objective reasonableness. When evaluating the actions of law enforcement officials, conduct that would be considered acceptable by a "reasonable person." A judge usually decides what a "reasonable person" would consider acceptable.

ombudsman. A term used to describe the neutral third party who conducts mediation.

open field. Any unoccupied or undeveloped real property falling outside the curtilage of a home (*Oliver v. United States*, 466 U.S. 170 [1984], p. 170).

opinion. The voice of the majority of judges in an appellate court decision. At the U.S. Supreme

Court level, the opinion is the voice of at least five justices.

papers and effects. In Fourth Amendment terms, nearly all personal items. Business records, letters, diaries, memos, and countless other forms of tangible evidence can be defined as *papers. Effects* is the catch-all category.

particularity. The Fourth Amendment requirement that an arrest warrant name the person to be arrested (or provide a sufficiently detailed description) and that a search warrant describe the place to be searched and the things to be seized.

Patriot Act. Controversial legislation passed in the wake of the September 11, 2001, terrorist attacks on the World Trade Center towers and the Pentagon.

peremptory challenge. A means of excluding prospective jurors with no reason offered. Peremptory challenges are limited depending on the case type and the jurisdiction. Peremptory challenges cannot be used to excuse prospective jurors based on race.

person inventory. A procedure used to take record of a person's personal possessions after he or she has been lawfully arrested. Person inventories do not invoke the Fourth Amendment and do not require probable cause—but they can only occur after an a lawful arrest (i.e., one satisfying Fourth Amendment requirements).

person. In Fourth Amendment terms, the individual as a whole, both internally and externally. The term "person" includes words communicated that are not used for identification purposes.

petitioner. The name given to a convicted criminal who challenges the constitutionality of his or her confinement via a *habeas corpus* petition.

photographic array. A procedure in which several photographs, including one of the suspect, are shown to a witness or victim, and he or she is asked to pick out the perpetrator.

physical evidence. The opposite of testimonial evidence. Physical evidence can include murder weapons, documents, and even the results from police lineups.

physical presence. One of two confrontation requirements. In order to be "present at his/her trial," the defendant must be physically present (as opposed, for example, to appearing via closed-circuit television).

"plain view" doctrine. An exception to the Fourth Amendment's warrant requirement that permits police to seize certain items in plain view.

plea bargaining. "The defendant's agreement to plead guilty to a criminal charge with the reasonable expectation of receiving some consideration from the state."[1]

police/probation partnerships. A practice of teaming probation officers with police officers to do crime control or prevention. Such partnerships are controversial because police officers can effectively skirt the Fourth Amendment's requirements when they team with probation officers who have more latitude to conduct searches of probationers.

precedent. A rule of case law (i.e., a decision by a court) that is binding on all lower courts and the court that issued it.

preliminary hearing. A hearing that serves as a check on the prosecutor's charging decision. The standard of proof is probable cause, and the main inquiry in the hearing is whether there is probable cause to take the case to trial. The preliminary hearing is to be distinguished from the initial appearance, the probable cause hearing, and the pretrial release hearing. It almost always takes place after one of these hearings as well as after the charging decision.

pretextual prosecution. When the prosecutor lacks the evidence to charge someone with a particular crime and so charges him or her with a lesser crime.

pretrial release. One of several methods to release a defendant prior to his or her trial date.

preventive detention. The act of denying bail to certain defendants who are either dangerous or pose a high flight risk.

pro se **defense.** When a defendant waives his or her Sixth Amendment right to counsel and defends himself or herself.

probable cause hearing. A hearing in which a judge decides whether there was probable cause to arrest. If the arrest was with a warrant, the probable cause hearing is not necessary. Also called a *Gerstein* hearing (for the Supreme Court's decision in *Gerstein v. Pugh*).

probable cause. More than bare suspicion; it exists when "the facts and circumstances within [the officers'] knowledge and of which they [have] reasonably trustworthy information [are] sufficient to warrant

---

[1] H. S. Miller, W. F. McDonald, and J. A. Cramer, *Plea Bargaining in the United States* (Ann Arbor, MI: Inter University Consortium for Political and Social Research, 1978), pp. 1–2.

a prudent man in believing that the [suspect] had committed or was committing an offense" (*Beck v. Ohio*, 379 U.S. 89 [1964], p. 91). In practical terms, more than 50 percent certainty. The comparable civil standard is preponderance of evidence.

procedural due process. Protection of significant life, liberty, or property interests, sometimes described as "procedural fairness."

prosecutor. The official representing the government in a criminal case.

prosecutorial discretion. A prosecutor's authority to decide whether to proceed with criminal charges against a particular suspect.

prosecutorial inducements. Offers made by the prosecution to the defendant.

Protect America Act. Controversial legislation enacted in August 2007 which revised the Foreign Intelligence Surveillance Act to permit *warrantless* interceptions of certain communications. It expired in February 2007.

protective sweep. A cursory visual inspection of those places in which a person might be hiding.

public duty defense. A defense that shields police officers from criminal liability when performing certain official functions, such as using deadly force.

public trial. A trial that is open to the public and/or complies with the Sixth Amendment's public trial provision. Courts can sometimes limit public access and the proceedings will still be considered public.

"purged taint" exception. An exception to the fruit of poisonous tree doctrine that permits the introduction of evidence if it has become attenuated to the extent that it dissipated the taint of the initial unconstitutional act.

qualified immunity. Immunity from suit that applies some of the time and in certain situations. Sometimes qualified immunity serves as an "affirmative defense," meaning that it is raised at trial—if the case goes that far. If a criminal justice official acts on a reasonably mistaken belief, as gauged from the standpoint of a reasonable officer, then qualified immunity can be granted.

racial profiling. The practice of stopping people based on race rather than legitimate criteria.

real world. A term used to describe the world in which criminal justice officials, including the police, operate on a daily basis.

reasonable expectation of privacy. An expectation of privacy that society (through the eyes of a judge) is prepared to accept as reasonable. For a search to occur, a reasonable expectation of privacy must be infringed upon by a government actor.

reasonable suspicion. Justification that falls below probable cause but above a hunch. Reasonable suspicion is Court-created justification; it is not mentioned in the Fourth Amendment. Reasonable suspicion is necessary for police to engage in stop-and-frisk activities.

reasonableness clause. The first part of the Fourth Amendment: "The right of the people to be secure in their persons, houses, papers, and effects, against unreasonable searches and seizures, shall not be violated . . . "

reasonableness. When evaluating questionable police action, it is first necessary to determine whether the Fourth Amendment applies. If it does, then we ask, Did the police act in line with Fourth Amendment requirements?; This question is concerned with the reasonableness of the action in question.

rehabilitation. A goal of sentencing that consists of a planned intervention intended to change behavior (e.g., drug treatment); the process of restoring a witness's credibility.

release on recognizance (ROR): The accused is released with the assumption that he or she will show up for scheduled court hearings.

remand. An appellate court verdict that sends a case back to the lower court for further action consistent with the appellate court's decision.

remedy. A method of rectifying wrongdoing.

retribution. A goal of sentencing that is concerned with punishing offenders based on the severity of their crimes (i.e., offenders "get what they deserve").

retroactivity. The extent to which appellate court decisions should apply only to the appellant or to other similarly situated individuals.

reverse. An appellate court verdict that is akin to nullifying or setting aside a lower court's verdict.

right to privacy. A judicially created right that is found nowhere in the Constitution.

rule of four. The requirement that four U.S. Supreme Court justices must agree to hear a case before it goes before the full Court.

same offense. For double-jeopardy purposes, the same offense is one that has the same elements as another offense. For example, first- and second-degree murders are considered the "same offense" for double-jeopardy purposes. First-degree murder is defined as the premeditated deliberate killing of another person. Second-degree murder is the same offense, less the premeditation requirement. A person cannot be convicted of both offenses, otherwise a double-jeopardy violation occurs.

school disciplinary "searches": Though they are not "searches" in the traditional Fourth Amendment sense, school officials can search (K–12) students' possessions without a warrant or probable cause for evidence of activity in violation of school policy.

search. For Fourth Amendment purposes, a government action that infringes on one's reasonable expectation of privacy.

search incident to arrest. An exception to the Fourth Amendment's warrant requirement that allows officers to search a suspect following his or her arrest.

search warrant. An order issued by a judge directing a law enforcement officer to search a particular location for evidence connected with a specific criminal offense.

seizure. One of two government actions (the other being searches) restricted by the Fourth Amendment. Seizures can be of persons or property.

seizure of a person. A seizure of a person occurs when a police officer—by means of physical force or show of authority—intentionally restrains an individual's liberty in such a manner that a reasonable person would believe that he or she is not free to leave (*Terry v. Ohio*, 392 U.S. 1 [1968]; *United States v. Mendenhall*, 446 U.S. 544 [1980]).

seizure of property. A seizure of property occurs when "there is some meaningful interference with an individual's possessory interest in that property" (*United States v. Jacobsen* (466 U.S. 109 [1984]).

selective prosecution. When an individual is targeted for prosecution merely because he or she falls into a certain group (e.g., a minority group).

sentencing guidelines. State and federal rules used to set sentences based on offense severity and the offender's prior record. Sentencing guidelines achieve a balance between determinate and indeterminate sentencing.

severance. The opposite of joinder. For example, severance occurs when separate trials are held for different charges against the same defendant.

showup. An identification procedure in which the suspect is brought before the witness (or victim) alone, so the witness can be asked whether that person is the perpetrator.

"silver platter" doctrine. A practice prior to *Elkins v. United States* (364 U.S. 206 [1960]) that permitted the use of evidence in *federal* court that had been obtained illegally by *state* officials.

six-month imprisonment rule. The rule that limits jury trials to cases where more than six-months' incarceration in jail or prison is possible.

Sixth Amendment. Part of the U.S. Constitution, which states: "In all criminal prosecutions, the accused shall enjoy the right to a speedy and public trial, by an impartial jury of the State and district wherein the crime shall have been committed, which district shall have been previously ascertained by law, and to be informed of the nature and cause of the accusation; to be confronted with the witnesses against him; to have compulsory process for obtaining witnesses in his favor, and to have the Assistance of Counsel for his defence."

specific deterrence. When a sentenced offender is discouraged from committing additional crimes due to his or her sentence.

specific question. A question that does not call for a narrative and can be answered with a simple yes or no. For example, "Were you the victim of a burglary on August 6 of this year?;"

Speedy Trial Act. Federal legislation aimed at ensuring speedy trials in federal courts.

speedy trial. A trial that meets with the Sixth Amendment's requirement for a speedy trial. A trial is no longer "speedy" when there is intentional delay that is prejudicial to the defendant's case.

standing. In Fourth Amendment terms, the requirement that a person cannot object to a wrongful search or seizure unless he or she is the victim of a Fourth Amendment violation.

stare decisis. A Latin term that means to abide by or to adhere to decided cases. Most courts adhere to the principle of *stare decisis*.

state supreme courts. The highest courts at the state level.

statutory inducements. Statutes that offer incentives for pleading guilty.

stop. Sometimes called an "investigative stop" or an "investigative detention," a brief nonconsensual encounter between a law enforcement officer and a citizen that does not rise to the level of an arrest; the detention of a person by a law enforcement officer for the purpose of investigation.

subjective reasonableness. When evaluating the actions of law enforcement officials, conduct that would be considered reasonable by the police officer engaged in the conduct.

subpoena *ad testifican dum*: A subpoena that compels a witness to appear before the grand jury.

subpoena *duces tecum*: A subpoena that compels the production of tangible evidence (e.g., a suspected murder weapon).

substantive due process. Protection from arbitrary and unreasonable action on the part of state officials.

suggestive lineup. A flawed lineup that almost ensures the victim or witness will identify the suspect. For example, if the suspect is male and the other lineup participants are female, this would be a suggestive lineup.

superior courts. The most common name for state-level courts of general jurisdiction.

supervisory liability. In the Section 1983 context, the theory that a supervisor (such as a sergeant or captain) should be held liable.

systematic exclusion. Exclusion of a distinctive group from jury service. Systematic exclusion is something more than just significant exclusion.

tainted identification. An identification that would not have taken place but for some earlier unconstitutional activity.

testimonial evidence. For Fifth Amendment purposes, "testimonial evidence" is loosely defined to include incriminating statements made at any point during the criminal justice process, whether or not the person making such statements is under oath.

theory of liability. The logic offered for who should be held accountable—and why.

theory world. A term used to illustrate the fact that some court decisions are divorced from reality and/or may not directly affect criminal justice officials.

Title III of the Omnibus Crime Control and Safe Streets Act. Federal legislation enacted in 1968 that set forth detailed guidelines on how authorities could intercept wire, oral, or electronic communications.

totality of circumstances. All the facts and circumstances surrounding the case. In case-by-case adjudication, these must be examined in order to determine whether a constitutional rights violation has taken place.

trespass doctrine. The practice of the U.S. Court prior to *Katz v. United States* that required a physical intrusion by authorities into a person's private property for the Fourth Amendment to be implicated.

trial *de novo*. A type of appeal in which with appellate court holds a new trial as if the prior trial never occurred.

true bill. The grand jury's endorsement that it found sufficient evidence to warrant a criminal charge.

U.S. courts of appeals. At the federal level, courts to which verdicts from the district courts are appealed.

U.S. Supreme Court. The highest court in the federal court system.

unavailable witness. For purposes of confrontation, an unavailable witness is one who permanently moves to another country, cannot be located after a careful search by the prosecution, or suffers from a lapse in memory.

vacate. An appellate court decision that is, for all practical purposes, the same as a reversal.

variance. When the prosecutor presents evidence at trial that departs significantly from that relied on by the grand jury for the purpose of issuing an indictment.

vehicle inventory. A procedure used to take record of a vehicle's contents after it has been lawfully impounded. Vehicle inventories do not invoke the Fourth Amendment and do not require probable cause.

vindictive prosecution. Prosecution based on revenge.

***voir dire*.** The process of selecting jurors for service. *Voir dire* proceeds through three stages: questioning by the judge, challenges for cause, and peremptory challenges.

warrant clause. The second part of the Fourth Amendment: " . . . and no Warrants shall issue, but upon probable cause, supported by Oath or affirmation, and particularly describing the place to be searched, and the persons or things to be seized."

Warren Court. The time from 1953 to 1969, during which Earl Warren was chief justice. The Warren Court handed down a number of decisions, particularly throughout the 1960s, that provided extensive constitutional protections for criminal defendants.

***writ of certiorari*.** An order by the court, requiring the lower court to send the case and a record of its proceedings to the U.S. Supreme Court for review.

CREDITS

Chapter 1: p. 2, Courtesy of Steve Petteway, Collection of the Supreme Court of the United States; p. 30, Ken Tannenbaum/Shutterstock.

Chapter 2: p. 40, Maksim Shmeljov / Shutterstock.com; p. 54, Phillip Kamrass/Agence France Presse/Getty Images.

Chapter 3: p. 72, © Dan Atkin / Alamy; p. 94, Mikael Karlsson/Arresting Images.

Chapter 4: p. 104, © Mikael Karlsson / Alamy; p. 143, Pres Panayotov/Shutterstock.com.

Chapter 5: p. 148, AP Image/The Californian/Richard D. Green; p. 161, Jeff Zelevansky\AP Wide World Photos.

Chapter 6: p. 182, Lisa F. Young \Shutterstock; p. 203, AP Image/Rick Maiman.

Chapter 7: p. 212, BRIAN KERSEY/UPI/Newscom; p. 234, A. Ramey\PhotoEdit Inc.

Chapter 8: p. 244, Digital Vision/Getty Images; p. 259, Spencer Grant\PhotoEdit Inc.

Chapter 9: p. 276, Peter Kim / Shutterstock.com; p. 292, Junial Enterprises/Shutterstock.

Chapter 10: p. 304, © Mikael Karlsson / Alamy; p. 311, © Aurora Photos / Alamy.

Chapter 11: p. 336, Comstock/Thinkstock ; p. 351, © Corbis Premium RF / Alamy.

Chapter 12: p. 376, © Konstantin Pukhov/Dreamstime.com; p. 399, Mark Richards\PhotoEdit Inc.

Chapter 13: p. 408, Stockbyte/Thinkstock; p. 426, Stockbyte/Thinkstock.

Chapter 14: p. 436, Joe Seer / Shutterstock.com; p. 444, Ludington Daily News, Andy Klevorn\AP Wide World Photos

Chapter 15: p. 470, Lou Oates/Shutterstock; p. 481, Carl J. Single\The Image Works.

CASE INDEX

Note: **Bold** entries indicate Key Cases.

A

Abney v. United States, 431 U.S. 651 (1977)
ACLU v. State, 5 S.W.2d 418 (Ark. 1999)
Adams v. Williams, 407 U.S. 143 (1972)
Adamson v. California and *Poe v. Ullman,* 367 U.S. 497 (1961)
Adamson v. California, 332 U.S. 46 (1947)
Adarand Constructors, Inc. v. Pena, 515 U.S. 200 (1995), 227
Agnello v. United States, 269 U.S. 20 (1925)
***Aguilar v. Texas,* 378 U.S. 108 (1964)**
Air Pollution Variance Bd. v. Western Alfalfa Corp., 416 U.S. 861 (1974)
Ake v. Oklahoma, 470 U.S. 68 (1985)
Alabama v. Shelton, 535 U.S. 654 (2002)
***Alabama v. White,* 496 U.S. 325 (1990)**
Albernaz v. United States, 450 U.S. 333 (1981)
Albright v. Oliver, 510 U.S. 266 (1994)
Alcorta v. Texas, 355 U.S. 28 (1957)
Alderman v. United States, 394 U.S. 165 (1969)
Allen v. Illinois, 478 U.S. 364 (1986)
Allen v. Siebert, 552 U.S. 1 (2007)
Almeida-Sanchez v. United States, 413 U.S. 266 (1973)
Anaya v. Hansen, 781 F.2d 1 (1st Cir. 1986)
Anderson v. Creighton, 483 U.S. 635 (1987)
***Andresen v. Maryland,* 427 U.S. 463 (1976)**
Apodaca v. Oregon, 406 U.S. 404 (1972)
Apprendi v. New Jersey, 530 U.S. 466 (2000)
Argersinger v. Hamlin, 407 U.S. 25 (1972)
Arizona v. Evans, 514 U.S. 1 (1995)
***Arizona v. Gant,* No. 07-542 (2009)**
***Arizona v. Hicks,* 480 U.S. 321 (1987)**
Arizona v. Johnson, No. 07-1122 (2009)
***Arizona v. Youngblood,* 488 U.S. 51 (1988)**
Arkansas v. Sanders, 442 U.S. 753 (1979)
Ashcraft v. Tennessee, 322 U.S. 143 (1944)
Ashcraft v. Tennessee and Mincey v. Arizona, 437 U.S. 385 (1978)
Atkins v. Virginia, 122 S. Ct. 2242 (2002)
Atwater v. City of Lago Vista, 533 U.S. 924 (2001)
***Atwater v. City of Lago Vista,* 532 U.S. 318 (2001)**

B

B.C. v. Plumas Unified School District, 192 F.3d 1260 (9th Cir. 1999)
***Baldwin v. New York,* 399 U.S. 66 (1970)**
Ballenger v. State, 436 S.E.2d 793 (Ga.Ct. App. 1993)
Ballew v. Georgia, 435 U.S. 223 (1978)
Barber v. Page, 390 U.S. 719 (1968)
***Barker v. Wingo,* 407 U.S. 514 (1972)**
Bassin v. Isreal, 335 N.E.2d 53 (Ill. App. Ct. 1975)
***Batson v. Kentucky,* 476 U.S. 79 (1986)**
Baxstrom v. Herold, 383 U.S. 107, 15L.Ed.2d 620, 86 S.Ct. 760 (1966)
Baze v. Rees, 553 U.S. 35 (2008)
Beard v. Banks, 542 U.S. 406 (2004)
***Beck v. Ohio,* 379 U.S. 89 (1964),** 91
Beck v. Washington, 369 U.S. 541 (1962)
Beckwith v. United States, 425 U.S. 341 (1976)
Beecher v. Alabama, 408 U.S. 234 (1972)
Bell v. Cone, 535 U.S. 685 (2002)
***Bell v. Wolfish,* 441 U.S. 520 (1979)**
***Benton v. Maryland,* 395 U.S. 784 (1969)**
Berger v. New York, 388 U.S. 41 (1967)
Berghuis v. Smith, No. 08-1402 (2010)
Berghuis v. Thompkins, No. 08-1470 (2010)
***Berkemer v. McCarty,* 468 U.S. 420 (1984),** 442
Berry v. Cincinnati, 414 U.S. 29 (1973)
Betts v. Brady, 316 U.S. 455 (1942)
***Bivens v. Six Unknown Named Agents,* 403 U.S. 388 (1971)**
Blackledge v. Allison, 431 U.S. 63 (1977), 71

***Blackledge v. Perry,* 417 U.S. 21 (1974)**
Blake v. Cich, 79 F.R.D. 398 (D. Minn. 1978), 403
Blakely v. Washington, 542 U.S. 296 (2004)
Blanton v. City of North Las Vegas, 489 U.S. 538 (1989)
***Blockburger v. United States,* 284 U.S. 299 (1932)**
Blum v. Yaretsky, 457 U.S. 991 (1982), 1004
Board of Commissioners of Bryan County v. Brown, 520 U.S. 397 (1997)
***Board of Education v. Earls,* 536 U.S. 822 (2002)**
Bond v. United States, 529 U.S. 334 (2000)
***Bordenkircher v. Hayes,* 434 U.S. 357 (1978),** 364, 365
Boumediene v. Bush (2008)
Bounds v. Smith, 430 U.S. 817 (1977)
Bousley v. United States, 523 U.S. 614 (1998)
Boyd v. United States, 116 U.S. 616 (1886)
***Boykin v. Alabama,* 395 U.S. 238 (1969)**
Bradley v. Fisher, 80 U.S. 335 (1871)
***Brady v. Maryland,* 373 U.S. 83 (1963)**
***Brady v. United States,* 397 U.S. 742 (1970)**
Brecht v. Abrahamson, 507 U.S. 619 (1993)
***Breithaupt v. Abram,* 352 U.S. 432 (1957)**
Brendlin v. California, 551 U.S. 249 (2007)
***Brewer v. Williams,* 430 U.S. 387 (1977)**
Brigham City v. Stuart, 547 U.S. 398 (2006)
***Brinegar v. United States,* 338 U.S. 160 (1949)**
Brogan v. United States, 522 U.S. 398 (1998)
Brooks v. Tennessee, 406 U.S. 605 (1972)
Brown v. Illinois, 422 U.S. 590 (1975)
Brown v. Louisiana, 447 U.S. 323 (1980)
***Brown v. Mississippi,* 297 U.S. 278 (1936)**
Brown v. Ohio, 432 U.S. 161 (1977)
Brown v. Sanders, 546 U.S. 212 (2006)
Brown v. Texas, 443 U.S. 47 (1979)
***Brown v. United States,* 356 U.S. 148 (1958)**
Bullcoming v. New Mexico, No. 09-10876 (2011)
Bumper v. North Carolina, 391 U.S. 543 (1968)
***Burdeau v. McDowell,* 256 U.S. 465 (1921)**
Burns v. Reed, 500 U.S. 478 (1991)
***Butterworth v. Smith,* 494 U.S. 624 (1990)**
Butz v. Economou, 438 U.S. 478 (1978)

C

Cabana v. Bullock, 474 U.S. 376 (1986)
Cady v. Dombrowski, 413 U.S. 433 (1973)
Calabretta v. Floyd, 189 F.3d 808 (9th Cir. 1999)
***California v. Beheler,* 463 U.S. 1121 (1983)**
***California v. Carney,* 471 U.S. 386 (1985)**
California v. Ciraolo, 476 U.S. 207 (1986)
California v. Green, 399 U.S. 149 (1970)
***California v. Greenwood,* 486 U.S. 35 (1988)**
***California v. Hodari D.,* 499 U.S. 621 (1991)**
***California v. Prysock,* 453 U.S. 355 (1981)**
California v. Trombetta, 467 U.S. 479 (1984)
***Camara v. Municipal Court,* 387 U.S. 523 (1967)**
Caplin v. Drysdale v. United States, 491 U.S. 617 (1989)
Cardwell v. Lewis, 417 U.S. 583 (1974)
Carey v. Musladin, 549 U.S. 70 (2006)
Carlson v. Green, 446 U.S. 14 (1980)
Carlson v. Landon, 342 U.S. 524 (1952)
Carnley v. Cochran, 369 U.S. 506 (1962)
***Carroll v. United States,* 267 U.S. 132 (1925)**
***Carroll v. United States,* 354 U.S. 394 (1957)**
Carter v. Kentucky, 450 U.S. 288 (1981)
Casteneda v. Partida, 430 U.S. 482 (1977)
Chaffin v. Stynchcombe, 412 U.S. 17 (1973)
Chambers v. Florida, 309 U.S. 227 (1940)
Chambers v. Maroney, 399 U.S. 42 (1970)
***Chambers v. Mississippi,* 410 U.S. 284 (1973)**
Chandler v. Florida, 449 U.S. 560 (1981)

SUBJECT INDEX